Ruling Britannia

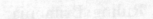

Glyn Williams and John Ramsden

Ruling Britannia
A political history
of Britain 1688–1988

Longman
London and New York

Longman Group UK Limited,
Longman House, Burnt Mill, Harlow,
Essex CM20 2JE, England
and Associated Companies throughout the world.

Published in the United States of America
by Longman Inc., New York

© Longman Group UK Limited 1990

First published 1990
Second impression 1992

British Library Cataloguing in Publication Data
Williams, Glyn
    Ruling Britannia: A political history of Britain 1688–1988
    1. Great Britain. Politics, history
    I. Title   II. Ramsden, John, 1947–
    320.941
    ISBN 0-582-48485-5 CSD
    ISBN 0-582-49073-1 PPR

Library of Congress Cataloging in Publication Data
Williams, Glyn.
    Ruling Britannia: a political history of Britain 1688–1988/Glyn Williams and
John Ramsden.
        p.   cm.
    Includes bibliographical references.
    ISBN 0-582-48485-5   — ISBN 0-582-49073-1 (pbk.)
    1. Great Britain—Politics and government—18th century.   2. Great
Britain—Politics and government—19th century.   3. Great Britain—
Politics and government—20th century.   4. Great Britain—Politics
and government—1689–1702.   I. Ramsden, John, 1947–   .   II. Title.
DA470.W55   1990   89-35959
941—dc20   CIP

Set in 10/12 pt Bembo
Produced by Longman Singapore Publishers (Pte) Ltd.
Printed in Singapore

Contents

List of maps

Preface

The origins of this book lie in the course of lectures in modern British history which we, together with colleagues, have given for some years in the history department at Queen Mary College. It is a course designed to meet the needs both of first-year history students and of students from other disciplines, and is supplemented by seminars which examine particular aspects of the period in more depth. We have tried here to bring together the approach both of the lectures and of the seminars, so that although a continuous narrative thread runs through the book, individual chapters contain analytical sections which often cross chronological boundaries. This is political history, with only as much of the economic and social dimensions as seem to us essential to an understanding of the politics of the period, and as space allows. We hope that we have taken enough account of recent scholarship to ensure that this is not simply 'high politics', that the unrepresented and the anonymous also find a place here. Certainly, we would not want readers to assume that we see the political history of Britain during the last three centuries as a smooth progression from a closed to an open system. If there is a main theme to this book, it is perhaps that expressed by Harley in Queen Anne's reign, when he wondered (in a narrow party context) 'how those who are the smaller part of the nation have made themselves formidable and terrible to the greater.'

This book has been from the beginning a collaborative project, with much interchange of ideas and comments between the two authors, but within this framework Glyn Williams is mainly responsible for the first half of the book and John Ramsden for the second. It was clear from an early stage that we should not make use of footnotes; the alternative in a work covering so long and so crowded a period seemed to be the baleful prospect of citations attached to almost every statement, and a loss of the narrative thread which was our chief objective. This decision has confronted us with problems, not least our inability to give precise acknowledgement to the work of other scholars. We have tried, in a general way, to indicate our debt in the bibliography, though even there much fine work has been omitted lest that section swell to monstrous proportions. Here, we must confine ourselves to thanking those individual scholars who have helped and reassured us by reading sections of the book in typescript, though they carry no responsibility for any errors which remain: David Brooks, Kathleen Burk, John Miller, Sarah Palmer, Michael Port, and Duncan Tanner.

G.W. and J.A.R.
Queen Mary and Westfield College
University of London

1 A revolution and its aftermath, 1688–1689

To contemporaries the 1680s encapsulated the strains and disorders which afflicted English political life in the seventeenth century. In the preceding decades civil war, military dictatorship, religious schism, plots and rebellions, political executions and crowd violence, had produced the impression of a country which was becoming ungovernable. Threats of royalist authoritarianism at one moment, of republican subversion the next, led to a neurotic uncertainty in which no settled form of government seemed possible. The restoration in 1660 of a system which had broken down twenty years earlier brought a nostalgic illusion of normality but no real solution to the problems caused by the shifting, often abrasive, relationships between monarch, ministers, Parliament and Church. Between the policies of Charles II, aiming at financial independence for the Crown backed by military power, and the concern of the aristocracy and gentry for their traditional share in government, both national and local, there seemed little possibility of lasting consensus. There was no agreement on the role and control of Parliament, whose hand still rested heavily on the purse-strings. The House of Commons remained difficult to manage, boisterously independent, and deeply suspicious of the executive. In religion, the continuing divide between Anglicans and Dissenters nullified claims that the Church of England was a truly national church, while the Catholics, small in number but often influential in position, made for further anxieties. Scotland and Ireland, though relatively subdued, remained lurking sources of worry after the disruption which events in those kingdoms had caused during the Civil War period.

Attempts by Charles II to strengthen his authority by measures which ranged from the long continuance of the Cavalier Parliament, elected in the first flush of royalist enthusiasm in 1661, to the negotiation of secret agreements with Louis XIV of France, had only limited success. In the end they resulted in a heightening of tension; and in the late 1670s the allegations of a Popish Plot in which the King was to be assassinated and replaced by his Catholic brother, James, Duke of York, plunged the country into the Exclusion crisis. The Cavalier Parliament was at last dissolved, and a political scene which had not been disturbed by a general election for eighteen years now experienced three in less than two years. Political differences polarised around a single issue – the attempt to exclude James from the succession. The struggle was a reminder that for many Englishmen Catholicism carried dark political implications. To folk memories of the fires of Smithfield, the Inquisition and Gunpowder Plot were added fears of a Popish Plot, international conspiracy, and French-style absolutism. New associations, arguably the first political parties, emerged in the constituencies and in Parliament to reflect the intensity of rival opinions. The pioneers of these novel forms of agitation and organisation were the Whigs, led by the Earl of Shaftesbury. They dominated the elections, and from a position of strength in the Commons mounted co-ordinated attacks on the court, the ministry, and above all the Duke of York.

The Whigs represented a formalisation of the 'Country' opposition of the previous years to the court and what was regarded as its pro-French, pro-Catholic attitudes. They included some of the leading territorial magnates, business men, and Dissenters. They stood for the ancient liberties of England, sometimes narrowly defined in terms of the protection of property, and against absolutist or arbitrary tendencies. In religion they were firm for Protestantism, and resistant to those forms of Anglican intolerance which they regarded as close to popery. The initial successes of the Whigs led to a predictable riposte in the forming of a rival party, the Tories, who saw their opponents as a culmination of the republican and dissenting trends of the century – 'the men of 1641 come again'. As a major political grouping they, too, represented the landed interest, but they were stronger among the squirearchy than were the Whigs; while their devotion to the Church of England ensured them firm support among the clergy. Both parties claimed to represent the national interest, and would happily have discarded the labels of abuse which their opponents had pinned on them; but Whig (in origin Scottish covenanting rebels) and Tory (Irish Catholic brigands) were to become part of the standard vocabulary of politics.

So strenuous were the political conflicts that at times civil war seemed likely; but Charles II through a combination of his own political expertise, French money, and Whig weakness in the Lords, had by 1681 won the day. He was helped by the reaction against what many saw as Whig extremism, and by the resurgent attachment to monarchy as the best counterweight to the whirling forces of radicalism and disorder. During the last four years of his reign Charles ruled without Parliament, and worked steadily to undermine Whig strength in their borough strongholds. This was made possible by the eccentricities of the electoral system, whose shape was still recognisably that of its founding years in the reign of Edward I. Most difficult for the crown to influence, at least directly, were the forty English counties where in the largest the electorate might total seven or eight thousand voters, for the old 40s. freehold franchise had enfranchised increasing numbers of voters over the years. But even with the twelve Welsh counties added, the counties returned only 92 MPs out of the 513 who sat in the Commons at this time. It was the 203 boroughs, ranging from London and the provincial towns to decaying villages, and mostly returning two MPs, where the opportunities for influence, whether by a private patron or the Crown, were greatest. The franchise ranged from the few open boroughs where all male inhabitants had the vote, to the 'scot and lot' constituencies, where the vote went to those liable to pay poor rates, the burgage boroughs, where the vote was attached to a particular property, and the freemen boroughs, where the electorate could be enlarged by the enrolling of new freemen. Crucial to Charles II's exercise of political manipulation were the corporation boroughs, where only the governing corporation had the vote, for by legal scrutiny of a borough's charter it was possible to change the membership and the political allegiance of the corporation. In borough after borough, some Whig controlled, some Tory, the enforced surrender of municipal charters brought in corporations more amenable to court direction and less subject to popular participation.

Further damage to the Whig cause occurred in 1683 with the death of Shaftesbury, followed by the Rye House Plot which led, on the basis of doubtful evidence and intimidated juries, to the trial and execution of several Whig leaders. These were years which saw a ruthless campaign of proscription against the Whigs – dismissed not only from government posts and the town corporations, but in the shires losing their positions as lord lieutenants, justices of the peace, and militia officers. The lord lieutenants were the most important link between the government and the localities. As custodians of law and order they controlled the militia, and beyond that the right to call in the army. They advised the Lord Chancellor on the appointment of justices of the peace, who bore the main weight of local government; for their multifarious duties varied from administering the Poor Law to fixing wages and prices, from keeping the roads in repair to setting the county rate. In a country where the parish, the municipality and the shire loomed larger in the life of most inhabitants than did Westminster or Whitehall, where the monarch governed through local magnates and the gentry, not through paid officials, the role of the lord lieutenants and justices was vital.

Confirmation of Whig weakness was shown in the general election which followed the accession of the Duke of York as James II in February 1685. Only about fifty Whigs were returned, and they suffered as heavily in the counties as in those boroughs which had seen existing charters and corporations swept away. With little hesitation Parliament voted James ordinary revenue for life, as the Cavalier Parliament had done for Charles II after his accession. It then passed further money bills to pay off debts from the previous reign, improve the state of the navy, and meet the cost of suppressing the rebellion in the West Country led by Charles II's illegitimate son, the Duke of Monmouth. This one serious challenge to James collapsed when Monmouth's ragamuffin forces were defeated by the royal army at Sedgemoor. Monmouth was executed, and his supporters treated with a legalised ferocity intended to terrify any remaining opponents of the new king. The aftermath of Sedgemoor helped to sow the seeds of James's downfall three years later. In November 1685 he announced that he intended to keep the army, doubled to about 20,000 because of the rebellion, at its enlarged size, and to continue in it the ninety or so Catholic officers, many Irish, appointed by use of the crown's dispensing power. The right of the monarch to use this power to alleviate the full rigour of the law in individual or exceptional cases was long-standing. Its wholesale use to bring Catholic officers into the army looked like a calculated defiance of the Test Act of 1673 which had required all office-holders to subscribe to a 'Test' denouncing the essential Catholic doctrine of transubstantiation.

The Test Act was the coping stone of a structure of legislation passed by the Cavalier Parliament to strengthen the position of the Church of England. Hopes that the Church would embrace the Presbyterians, wealthiest and most numerous of the Dissenters, vanished with the Act of Uniformity of 1662. This required acceptance of the 39 Articles in their entirety by all Anglican clergymen, and led to the secession of two thousand Presbyterian clerics. Further removed still from the idea of a national church were the separatist sects, the Independents, Baptists and Quakers. Religious conformity was seen essentially in political terms, for the upheavals of the 1640s had shown the disruptive effect of religious differences on the state. Although there was little attempt now to probe into private beliefs – as the future James II remarked in 1669, 'he was against all persecution merely for conscience sake' – the Restoration period saw a prolonged last-ditch attempt to force Dissenters to attend Church services. Alongside this went an effort to confine positions of political influence to Church members. The Corporation Act of 1661 limited membership of municipal corporations to Anglican communicants, and in 1678 the 'Test' was extended to members of both Houses of Parliament. The penal laws – many dating back to Tudor times – allowed for fines and other penalties on non-Anglicans, while the Licensing Act laid down that all printed material had to be approved by a bishop before publication. The effectiveness and direction of this battery of legislation varied according to time and circumstance. Catholics were suspect because their allegiance fell outside the country, and to a Pope seen to be in league with foreign powers. Dissenters were distrusted because of the part they had played during the interregnum, and because of their association with the opposition Whigs of the Exclusion period. Significantly, persecution was most consistently directed against the Quakers, for their refusal to take oaths was regarded as subversive of authority in Church and State alike.

As James prorogued Parliament in November 1685 after it dared to raise the question of the Catholic officers, so suspicion about his intentions grew. In a test case brought by James on his use of the dispensing power, the Lord Chief Justice declared in his favour with a resounding judgement: 'The Kings of England are absolute sovereigns; the laws of England are the King's laws; the King has power to dispense with any of his laws as he sees necessity for it.' The prorogation and eventual dissolution of a Parliament which was beginning to query James's actions was a reminder of the power of the Crown, evidence that the nerve-centre of politics was still the court, rather than the irregular and often brief meetings of Parliament – summoned, prorogued and dissolved at the King's pleasure. In another way the prorogation was an indication of the gulf beginning to open between the king and his natural supporters, the Tory loyalists, after less than a year of his reign. As James showed the extent to which he intended to use his dispensing power, and as from France reports arrived of the brutal treatment of Huguenot communities as Louis XIV with his revocation of the Edict of Nantes stripped away their last remnants of protection, so fears about standing armies, popery and absolutism revived. There is no evidence that James intended to model himself on the French king and his style of government. His use of prerogative powers was directed to the specific end of obtaining equal rights for his co-religionists, for with a convert's fervour he was convinced that once discrimination was removed Catholicism would make great strides among the population. His subjects could not be expected to understand or to follow this, for their identification of Catholicism and absolutism was rooted in past history as well as present observation of events in France. Tory MPs and Anglican clergy, so compliant in the first months of the reign, were confronted with an insufferable dilemma. They had supported James despite his religion, but few were willing to see Catholicism given equal status to the Church of England, or to accept Catholics in positions of power. Their dilemma was sharpened as it became clear that James intended to go beyond the use of his dispensing powers, and was determined on outright repeal of the Test Act and penal laws. This would involve Parliament, and one with a submissive majority willing to carry out the King's wishes.

It was to this end that James with the help of that agile political opportunist, the second Earl of Sunderland, introduced an extraordinary mix of policies, some intended to coerce, others to attract. In one direction James looked for support from those who at the time of the Exclusion crisis had been most bitterly opposed to his accession, for as the Declaration of Indulgence of April 1687 made clear, toleration was to be extended to Dissenters as well as to Catholics, as had already been done in Scotland where Presbyterians were offered positions of influence up to Privy Council level. But most ominous was the news from Ireland, where Protestants were being dismissed from army and administration alike in favour of Catholics. Further signs of James's general aims were glimpsed in America, where the bringing together in the Dominion of New England of the Atlantic seaboard colonies from New York northwards was accompanied by the suspension of their representative assemblies. In England itself, following the purge of intractable office-holders from central and local government, there were places available even for Whigs. James and his advisers were discarding the Tories who had fought for his right of succession only a few years earlier in favour of Whigs, Dissenters and political careerists. Town corporations were once again remodelled, while in the shires lord lieutenants, their deputies, and justices of the peace were dismissed and replaced either by Catholics or by non-Catholics willing to accept James's policies. Thirty-five boroughs were given new charters in 1688 alone, as part of what seemed an almost constant process of change since 1681. In the most portentous development of all, possible parliamentary candidates and their supporters were questioned about their willingness to support not only 'the King's Declaration for Liberty of Conscience' but also repeal of the Test Act and the penal laws. The canvass was inconclusive, but lists were drawn up of those favourably disposed. All this was accompanied, in what seemed an anticipation of trouble, by orders to the lord lieutenants to restrict musters of the militia, those amateur soldiers who were commanded by the gentry and represented the traditional means of keeping law and order. They may not have been very formidable as soldiers, but as an MP had told the Commons in Charles II's reign, they were 'our security . . . that will defend us and never conquer us.' A very different type of military presence was in evidence at Blackheath, where James's troops exercised only a few miles from the political heart of the capital. To some observers the obvious parallel was with those standing armies of the continent which symbolised absolutist rule; but an even more sensitive chord was struck by the recollection of Cromwell's use of the New Model Army to impose his rule on the country. If to the army in England were added the 7,500 troops in Ireland, the 2,000 in Scotland, and the 3,000 based in Holland as part of the Anglo-Dutch brigade, then James's regular forces fell not far short of Cromwell's in the last years of his military dictatorship.

James's plans for a general election in the autumn of 1688 were well advanced when a series of dramatic events deflected his aim. In April James's order that the republished Declaration of Indulgence should be read out in all churches met a defiant response from seven bishops, led by William Sancroft, the Archbishop of Canterbury. The words of their refusal made the political point clear: 'That Declaration is founded upon such a dispensing power, as hath often been declared illegal in Parliament.' The committal of the bishops to the Tower, accompanied by huge and sympathetic crowds, their trial on charges of seditious libel, the declaration of one of the judges that if the dispensing power were allowed 'there will need no parliament', and their acquittal, would have caused hesitation in someone less dedicated than James. Instead, he redoubled his efforts to ensure a satisfactory general election and a packed Parliament, and the atmosphere of looming crisis deepened with the birth of a son to the Queen in June. The attempts to discredit the birth by allegations that the supposed royal baby had been smuggled in by means of a warming-pan showed the importance of the event. No longer was it possible to argue that James's reign was an aberration, that on his death all would return to normal on the succession of one of his Protestant daughters, Mary, married to William of Orange, or Anne. Improbable though his prospects of success had once appeared, by mid-1688 James's policies seemed to have fallen into place. In his quest for equal rights for the small Catholic minority, he seemed to have confirmed that shift towards an English version of continental absolutism which had begun in the last years of his brother's reign. Remodelled corporations, docile lord lieutenants and justices, a half-intimidated Church, were the new realities of political life. Not far distant, it seemed, were a packed Parliament and a standing army purged of many of its Protestant officers. If the world had not yet been turned upside down again, it had by the fourth year of James's reign taken on a pronounced tilt.

In July a message was sent from England to William, Prince of

Orange, Stadtholder of the United Provinces and Captain General of the Dutch armed forces, who had led the resistance to Louis XIV since 1672. Married to Princess Mary, William as the grandson of Charles I also held a place in the line of succession in his own right. He had maintained an ostensible neutrality as far as James's policies were concerned, while keeping in close if sometimes misinformed touch with events in England. These he saw in the context of the developing crisis in Europe, where the aggressive moves of Louis XIV were seen as the prelude to a renewal of war. By early 1688 William feared an alteration in the succession which would keep Mary from the throne, and perhaps bring England into the expected European conflict on the side of France. By April he had decided on invasion later in the year, if continental events allowed, and if he received a request for help from England 'by some men of the best interest'. This he judged was contained in the July invitation from the 'Immortal Seven' of Whig historiography – the great magnate, Shrewsbury, four lesser Whig politicians, a superannuated Tory (Charles II's old minister, Danby), and a suspended Tory cleric, Bishop Compton of London. How far they represented anyone but themselves was not clear, and in any case their message was as much an appeal for help as a guarantee of support: 'we shall be every day in a worse condition than we are, and less able to defend ourselves'. It was a sign of weakness rather than of strength – evidence that, unlike the situation in the 1640s, the King could be overthrown only with aid from outside the British Isles. Sullen acquiescence, passive resistance, conspiratorial murmurings, rather than an instinctive turning to the sword, characterised the mood of 1688. Those who invited William saw in him the rescuer of English liberties and the Protestant religion, but for William the priority was to bring England into the forthcoming war against France. It was Louis XIV and his drive towards European aggrandisement rather than James II and his policies which loomed large in his line of vision.

James failed to recognise the danger of invasion until late September, when Louis XIV's invasion of the Palatinate removed the possibility of an imminent French attack on the Dutch republic. James's reaction was one of panic as he threw his policies into reverse, and dismissed Sunderland, but the concessions were too late and too blatant. They seemed intended, an opponent said, 'to still the people, like plums to children, by deceiving them for a while'. Meanwhile, William sought to gain support from as wide a range of English political opinion as possible with the issuing of a declaration condemning, not the King but those advisers who had 'overturned the religion, laws and liberties' of England and had submitted the country 'to arbitrary government'. Among their machinations, the declaration continued, was the invention of a fictitious pregnancy for the Queen, and a supposititious son. At this stage the enigmatic William made no claim for the crown himself. He insisted that his expedition 'is intended for no other design but to have a free and lawful Parliament assembled as soon as possible'; though it is clear that at the very least he was determined to secure the right of his wife to succeed James.

On 5 November William with an army of 14,000 men, about a quarter of them British, landed at Torbay, after risking autumnal gales and the possibility of interception by the English fleet. There was to be no great battle, no decisive engagement – instead a cat-and-mouse game in which James's nerve crumbled and his judgement vanished. To the political nation, waiting before it decided which way to move, William's slow march on London was neither quite a foreign invasion nor a rebellion. His public sentiments had been blazoned on the streamers flying at the mastheads of his ships – 'The Liberty of England and the Protestant Religion' – a promise rather than a threat to the majority of James II's subjects. Defections and confusion in the royal army were matched by reports of risings, often under Whig leadership, in the provinces, and of anti-Catholic riots. The trickle of pledges to William swelled to a stream, for as one observer put it, although there had been some hesitation to be among the first to declare for him, there was an even greater reluctance to be the last. In December James fled to France, after attempting the equivalent of a scorched-earth policy by destroying the writs for the parliamentary elections, throwing the Great Seal into the Thames, and disbanding but not disarming his troops. He left behind a country in a state of alarm, as roaming Irish soldiers from his army lent substance to wild stories of massacre and anarchy. The only hope of a restoration of authority was William, and as Christmas approached it was to him – not yet monarch, but the only ruler to hand – that the politicians turned.

For a few months in the winter of 1688–89 the bitterness of political and religious feuding which had scarred England since the Exclusion crisis faded, and was replaced by a grudging consensus that James II was no longer acceptable as king. The crudity of his assault on the political and religious beliefs of his subjects left most of them with no alternative but 'Dutch William'. James's flight to France settled the immediate issue; it also avoided civil war, and ensured that the Revolution (in England at least) was bloodless. But it was far from being simply a palace coup. It raised fundamental issues about the nature of kingship, introduced new and jarring concepts into politics and religion, brought a continental dimension to foreign policy, and led to a generation of party strife before the nation settled down to the relative calm of the Walpole era.

After the upheavals of November and December 1688, the first priority was to restore settled government. The dilemma of how Parliament could be summoned in the absence of the monarch was settled by an agreement to hold elections for a Convention, an assembly which did not need royal authorisation; and by late January 1689 this was in session. After much discussion – particularly agonising for the Tories – on the unprecedented issues involved, and some disagreement between Lords and Commons, resolutions were passed that James II had 'abdicated the government', and that since he had left the throne 'vacant' it should be tendered to William and Mary as joint sovereigns. In this way the awkward and emotive issue of 'deposition' was avoided, though there were Tories, particularly among the clergy, who refused to take the new oath of allegiance to 'their majesties King William and Queen Mary'. Other Tories took the oath reluctantly, 'out of pure necessity', as one put it; for with James gone, 'it became necessary that Government should be by somebody, to avoid confusion' and 'to prevent anarchy, and the rabble from spoiling and robbing the noble and the wealthy.' Accompanying and qualifying the offer of the throne was a Declaration of Rights, which listed James's misdeeds, and insisted that the consent of Parliament, meeting frequently and 'in freedom', was necessary for the raising of taxes, the suspending of statutes, and the maintenance of a standing army in peacetime. Even more radical clauses which were pressed by some Whigs demanding abolition of the royal veto, the ending of the King's right to make war and peace, and more frequent parliamentary elections, with voting by secret ballot, were defeated. With the Declaration of Rights accepted by the main parties involved, and with a bill passed declaring the Convention to be a Parliament the country by the end of February once more had a sovereign and a Parliament. Although William at no stage formally agreed to the Declaration of Rights, the reading to him before he became monarch of its limitations implied new conditions on kingship; 'he fancied he was like a king in a play', he grumbled at one point. The status of the Declaration of Rights, as with much else in these weeks, was ambiguous and imprecise – the best that could be obtained in difficult circumstances.

Likewise, the religious settlement was cast in the form of a series of negatives. The Bill of Rights excluded any Catholic from the throne, a novelty in a Europe where the religion of a state was normally that of the ruler, rather than the reverse; while the 'Toleration Act' of May 1689 is better understood under its full title, 'An Act for exempting their Majesties' Protestant subjects, dissenting from the Church of England, from the penalties of certain laws'. It allowed Dissenters, though not Catholics, Jews or Unitarians, the right of public worship in their own meeting places if these were licensed; but their political disabilities remained. William's proposal that the Test and Corporation Acts should be repealed was rejected, so Dissenters remained officially excluded from national and municipal offices, and from the universities. Toleration in the modern sense, with civil rights as well as freedom of worship for all, was advocated by only a handful. Instead, the bill's phrases dwelt, with a notable lack of enthusiasm, on the need for 'some ease to scrupulous consciences' in order to secure Protestant unity. As with the political settlement, the bill attempted to strike a balance between conflicting interests and attitudes – it was the maximum which could be wrung from an Anglican Parliament and the minimum which was acceptable to the Dissenters and their Whig allies.

Much remained to be settled, but more important than the specific legislation which followed were the past winter's events. Whatever glosses some might attempt to make, the clear fact was that the principles of hereditary, divine right kingship had been abandoned, and that Parliament had offered the crown to a foreign prince. As one pamphleteer put it, the Convention had held a crown in one hand, and terms in the other. The dominant role played by the peers in these weeks showed that the aristocracy was well on the way to recovering that grip on the reins of power which James II had managed to weaken. With its unassailable power-base in the House of Lords, it was strategically placed to take full advantage of Parliament's new importance, emphasised at the Coronation, when William and Mary promised to rule 'according to the statutes in Parliament agreed on'. By the end of the year, the provisions of the Declaration of Rights had, with a few strengthening amendments, been put into statutory form by the Bill of Rights. With many backward glances, to Charles II's reign as well as to James II's, the Bill declared illegal the suspending power of the Crown and restricted its dispensing power, prohibited a peacetime standing army except with parliamentary consent, and laid down that Parliament should meet often, and that parliamentary elections and debates should be free.

The slide towards absolutist forms of government which had characterised the 1680s had been halted; but strictures on past wrongs, and limitations on the royal prerogative, did little to indicate guidelines for the future. As significant as any of these constitutional adjustments was the financial settlement, finally agreed in 1690, but with its outlines visible the previous year. Instead of voting the King excise and customs duties for life, as was normal, Parliament voted only the excises (levied on home-produced commodities such as beer) for life. Customs duties (levied on imports) were limited to four years. Sharpening this restriction was a deliberate underestimation of the government's financial needs. The total yearly revenues of £1,200,000 voted by Parliament fell about £250,000 short of normal peacetime expenditure, and ignored a sum almost as large which was needed for annual debt charges. In the words of a contemporary, Parliament decided to keep the King 'at Board-wages'; and it was clear as early as the debates of January and February 1689 that this was a conscious policy intended to guarantee frequent parliaments. The fact that the King would in no sense be able to 'live of his own', and that he could not maintain a peacetime army without parliamentary consent were indications that Parliament expected to play a less subservient role than in the immediate past, and the outbreak of war with all its expense in May 1689 made the point more obvious still. Most would have put the matter more delicately than the MP who made a blustering speech in the Commons to the effect that 'if King William should destroy the laws, foundations and liberties, I doubt not but you will do with him as you did with King James'; but the general insistence that Parliament was now a regular feature of the political scene was the same. It was the power of the purse rather than the legal forms of the Revolution settlement which were to be decisive in shaping the political future; but how precisely Parliament's role was to be exercised, and how its new strength could be reconciled with effective government, were matters for conjecture.

Early in 1690 the publication of John Locke's *Two Treatises of Civil Government*, mainly written during the Exclusion crisis, seemed to provide theoretical justification for what had been done. Locke explained that government originated from a decision by men, 'by nature all free, equal and independent' to enter civil society 'for their comfortable, safe and peaceable living one amongst another, in a secure enjoyment of their properties.' Political power was shared, ideally, by a legislature and an executive; and was granted 'with trust, for the attaining an end, being limited by that end.' If the end were neglected or opposed, such as when 'a single person or prince sets up his own arbitrary will in place of the laws which are the will of the society', then the trust was forfeited. And on the crucial question, 'who shall be judge whether the prince or legislative act contrary to their trust', the answer seemed clear – 'the people shall be the judge'. Much of this was a refinement and elaboration of the traditional belief that the monarch should rule in the best interests of his subjects. The novelty lay in Locke's insistence on the right of resistance, and what could be taken to be an expression of the sovereignty of the people. The Commons, it seemed, was presenting a preview of Locke's publication when it insisted in January 1689 that James had broken 'the original contract between king and people'; but the fit between the events of the winter of 1688–89 and the arguments of the *Two Treatises* was a loose one. The members of the Convention were struggling with a dilemma whose essential element was not a rising of the people but the flight of a ruler, though whether this had been forced or not was one of the issues separating Whig and Tory. Although some radical Whigs contended that ultimate sovereignty lay in 'the people', mainstream Whigs were no more ready than the Tories to accept this. Whigs might reject, as Locke had done, many of the arguments set out in that handbook of divine-right monarchy, Filmer's *Patriarcha* (posthumously published in 1680); but they would not dispute Filmer's assertion that 'there is no tyranny to be compared to the tyranny of a multitude'. Locke was more read, or at least cited, in the Hanoverian period than in the years following the Revolution, and it was then that his elevation of 'the preservation of their properties' as the justification of civil society took on almost the status of a fortieth article of religion. The rule of law, the importance of the legislature, and a definition of liberty pointing back to the 1680s with its insistence that an individual should 'not be subject to the inconstant, uncertain, unknown, arbitrary will of another man', were all found to be compatible with the dominance of a land-owning oligarchy.

Some sense of the social and economic composition of England at the time of William's accession was given in the classification of families 'for the Year 1688' drawn up a few years later by Gregory King, secretary to the Commission of Public Accounts. This used official figures from the poll tax, hearth tax and excise returns, together with King's own local surveys, in an attempt to produce a breakdown of the population of England. In a non-statistical age, more than a hundred years before the first national census, King's survey forms a broad if slippery platform for those attempting to reconstruct the reality of pre-industrial England. It sketched the profile of a society in which land was the main source of income through rents, wages and profits; the largest single employer of labour; and the source of political influence. Much of industry and trade still depended on the land, which supplied the raw materials for the woollen and leather industries, brewing and baking. Whether viewed as a primary or secondary factor, land dominated the economy, and the critical feature of any year was the fullness or otherwise of the harvest. The town dweller, even allowing for London, was an exception. London with its population of about 575,000 was not only the largest city in Europe – just ahead of Paris – but its size was the more overwhelming because the population of England at about five million was only one quarter of that of France. The next largest city in England was Norwich, with a population of only 30,000, the same size as the largest city in Scotland, the capital Edinburgh. The importance of London extended well beyond its size, though its demands for food, fuel and services rippled out into distant regions. It housed the royal court and the government, parliament and the law courts; with its banks and trading companies it was the financial hub of the country; the arts, fashion and publishing were all centred there. But if one in eight of the population lived in London, three-quarters of the population was still rural, and most industry was tied to the soil and its products.

King's arrangement of families on either side of a line showing whether they increased or decreased the wealth of the nation exposed the extent of poverty in late seventeenth-century England. According to King, over half the population was unable to subsist on its income, and only the application of the Poor Law or private charity kept many of these alive. By the Act of Settlement in 1662 the parish of 'settlement' was the provider of relief for most of those shown beneath the subsidence line in King's classification. Some, the sick and the old, came into the category of the 'deserving poor'. Others, the able-bodied unemployed, unmarried mothers and the like, were regarded with a more jaundiced eye. Aghast at the rising cost of outdoor relief, local authorities tried a variety of expedients – workhouses, houses of correction, the 'privatisation' of relief through the use of contractors – but with only limited effect on the flood of demand or the strain on local resources. If famine had disappeared from the fields and streets of England (though not of Ireland and Scotland), misery and discontent had not. Although there was to be no revolution of the destitute to overthrow the 1688 revolution of the men of property, the defiance of the law and the amount of violence both in the rural areas and in London, kept the governing classes nervously aware of the level of resentment. Poaching, arson, riots, could all have political implications, and were treated accordingly.

Even for a ruler experienced in the constitutional intricacies of the United Provinces, William III's new inheritance presented daunting problems of government. Not the least of these was the fact that it consisted of three kingdoms, reluctant partners at the best of times, each with distinctive political, religious and social characteristics. The Civil War period had shown the impact which Scotland and Ireland could have on England; the Revolution was a further reminder of the interplay of events in the three kingdoms, and of the harder sectarian edge which Scottish and Irish affairs brought. In Scotland, the personal union of the crowns in 1603 had left intact a separate parliament, church and legal system, as well as a fierce sense of independence which could easily turn to one of grievance. In economic terms Scotland was still a backward country despite a growth in prosperity in the Lowlands, especially along the Clyde, and some improvement in agriculture. Many of the population of one and a quarter million remained wretchedly poor peasants, scraping a living from an infertile soil. It was a country where the nobility and, in the Highlands, the clan chiefs, still held sway, where religion was a violently divisive force, and where it was tempting to attribute all ills to domination from London. After the Restoration, Scotland was kept under close control by Charles II and James II, so much so that apprehensive observers in England saw the Scottish policies of the Stuart brothers as a rehearsal for methods which might later be tried in England. The single-chamber Parliament at Edinburgh was a body lacking in prestige and status, and it operated under the scrutiny of the Lords of the Articles, a committee of peers and royal officials which both initiated and supervised legislation. In ecclesiastical affairs, Episcopacy was restored after more than twenty years of Presbyterian dominance, though the bishops' new powers were subject to the King's right to remove bishops and clergy.

For most of Charles II's reign the effective ruler of Scotland was the King's intimate, the Duke of Lauderdale, who ruled by proclamation backed by force. On his accession James II pushed matters a stage further by ruling through a Privy Council to which he appointed Catholics and some Presbyterian collaborators in his new attempt to combine political autocracy with religious toleration. His flight in December 1688 threw political affairs in Scotland into the same confusion as those in England, but with very different results. The Convention in Edinburgh was dominated in tactics and organisation, if not in numbers, by Presbyterians, and James's intimidated supporters – 'Jacobites' as they were soon to be called – fled north. As civil war broke out, the Presbyterians, left in control of the new Parliament, drew up a programme of conditions for William significantly more restrictive than the Bill of Rights in England. It denounced previous violations of the law, declared that James had forfeited the crown – no diplomatic language of abdication and vacancies here – demanded the removal of the Lords of the Articles, the repeal of the Act of Supremacy, and the abolition of Episcopacy as 'a great and insupportable grievance and trouble to this Nation'. It was the programme of a minority, though one (in the words of one of William's Scottish advisers) 'more zealous and hotter' than the majority, but by 1690 William had agreed to its fundamental demands. He had little alternative but to accept this identification of the Presbyterian 'Whiggish' interest with the Revolution, for the Scottish bishops remained loyal to James, the clansmen of the Highlands were in arms, danger still threatened from Ireland, and above all there was war with France. The old tensions in the relationship between England and Scotland remained, and new ones had been added: the strength of Jacobitism in the north of Scotland, the bitterness caused by the ecclesiastical purge as the Presbyterians turned out more than six hundred Episcopalian clergy, and the economic crises of the mid and late 1690s.

In Ireland the situation was even more complex and perilous, despite the fact that on the face of it, English control was tight and effective. The Lord Lieutenant and his executive in Dublin were appointed from London; there was a sizeable standing army; most important posts in church and state were held by Englishmen; and the Irish Parliament operated under the cumbersome mechanism of Poynings' law of 1494 which provided for English supervision of Irish legislation. Yet there was no doubt that it would be in Ireland that James would make his first attempt at a reconquest of his lost kingdoms, for the Catholic community (about four-fifths of the population of something over two million) was separated from the Anglicans and Presbyterians both by religion and by an arbitrary and unequal division of the land. The approach of civil war in England fifty years earlier had split the English community in Ireland, where in 1641 the established Catholic 'Old English' had joined the Gaelic Irish in the Ulster rebellion, and so marked themselves off from the Protestant 'New English'. At the end of the decade Cromwell and his army had turned on the rebels with vindictive force, and had then set in train a shift in land ownership which saw the Catholic share fall from 60 per cent in 1640 to 22 per cent in 1660. It was this redistribution which strengthened the position of the Protestant Anglican minority, which co-existed uneasily with those other Protestants, mostly from Scotland, who had taken advantage of the interregnum to set up their own Presbyterian church system in Ulster.

Although Ireland was relatively quiet during the reign of Charles II, who managed to do without parliament there after 1666, old fears ran deep. The Popish Plot was accompanied by rumours of an Irish Catholic descent on England; a few years later at the time of the Rye House Plot it was a supposed rising by the Ulster Protestants which loomed large in the imagination of informants in London. The reign of James II saw the rise to prominence in Ireland of the Earl of Tyrconnel, an Irish Catholic soldier and an old associate of the king, who pushed ahead with policies which involved the restoration of Catholic lands, religious toleration, and a purging of the corporations, the civil administration, and – most sinister to Protestants – the army. Fear of Irish Catholic troops was an important factor in the turmoil of James's last months in England. The interval of Jacobite dominance in Ireland before William reasserted control saw much to alarm Protestants there, and in particular a land redistribution by the predominantly Catholic Parliament of these months which aimed to overturn the Cromwellian settlement. James's arrival from France in March 1689 was followed by a crumbling of Protestant resistance, though his forces failed to take Londonderry. In one of the most celebrated episodes in Anglo-Irish history the walled city held out for almost four months until relief arrived from the sea. By 1690 both sides were stronger in military terms. James's raw levies were stiffened with French regular troops, but William's army was larger, and was now under the personal command of the king. On 1 July 1690 the Battle of the Boyne was fought, a clash which was to have lasting repercussions. The impact of William's victory was felt immediately. James left Ireland as hurriedly as he had England eighteen months earlier, and although sporadic fighting continued, in 1691 the Treaty of Limerick brought peace – of a sort.

The events of these years were decisive. They confirmed the power of the Protestant minority, backed by English arms, and they deepened sectarian divisions. Protestants commemorated the siege of Londonderry and the Battle of the Boyne, while Catholics remembered Cromwell's sack of Drogheda, and nursed resentment at their dispossession of the land. The pattern of the future was soon discernible, as the victorious Anglicans in the Dublin Parliament ignored many of the terms of the Treaty of Limerick, and began a campaign of confiscation against Catholic landowners before moving into the first of a series of penal laws against those who were not members of the Church of Ireland, and against Roman Catholics in particular. It was these laws which, in Henry Grattan's words, formed 'the shell in which Protestant power was hatched'. Catholics were excluded from all positions of influence in Irish life: from Parliament, the army, government service, the law and the municipal corporations. Their right to hold, buy and bequeath land was severely restricted, and by the end of William's reign the Catholic majority in Ireland held only 14 per cent of the land. An Irish estate, title or pension became a standard reward for political services in England. The new landowners, whether by grant or purchase, greatly increased the proportion of absentee landlordism in Ireland, and swelled the volume of Irish revenues draining away to England.

The dominant Anglican minority – the Anglo-Irish Ascendancy of the eighteenth century – was loyalist but not subservient. It drank toasts to the 'glorious and immortal memory' of William III and the Boyne at the same time as it campaigned for a lifting of the irksome restrictions imposed by England on Irish trade and on the Irish Parliament. For most of the eighteenth century Irish nationalism was identified with the Ascendancy, a logical juxtaposition in an age when it was taken for granted that political power was conferred by the possession of land. But there was another, more foreboding dimension to the situation, expressed later by an Irish peer when he observed that the English settlers were 'hemmed in on every side by the old inhabitants of the island, brooding over their discontents in sullen indignation.'

2 Government and society, 1689–1702

The main aim of William's invasion of 1688, to bring England into the struggle against France, was achieved when James landed in Ireland in March 1689. The declaration of war on James's French ally in May was accordingly greeted with more enthusiasm in England than it might otherwise have been, though to put together a ministry able to wage that war proved a difficult business. William had hoped for a continuation of the national unity of 1688, to find a ministry of 'all the talents', Whig and Tory, who would engage in the great struggle against France without regard to petty party considerations. The hope was unrealistic. It ignored not only the personal hatreds which had marked the political scene in the 1680s – as the Whig Wharton complained to William of his tolerance of Tories, 'If you intend to govern like an honest man, what occasion can you have for knaves to serve you?' – but also the deep cleavages of opinion which had opened again after James's flight. Issues of principle, interest and personality continued to separate Whig and Tory, and the general election of 1690, which saw a record number of contested seats, and resulted in a strengthening of the Tory position, showed that the old antagonisms remained. So also did the perennial striving for place and power of the professional politicians, and that older schism between Court and Country which cut across acknowledged party divisions. To add to the problems of the government, the whole political system was placed under the strain of waging a war which became more expensive and less popular as each year passed.

William's first problem in forming a ministry was that although the Whigs had been his most enthusiastic supporters in 1688, and were committed to the war with France, they were after their recent harrowing experiences strong critics of the royal prerogative. Furthermore, after the purges of the 1680s they included few men with experience of government. The Tories were by nature more inclined to support the Crown, but they were still in disarray after the turmoil of 1688, and most were not in favour of a land war with France. From this unpromising material William put together an administration which not only had to function under his guidance, but also during his frequent absences abroad at the head of his army. The conduct of diplomacy and military matters William kept in his own hands wherever he was, though it was in his reign that the system under which foreign affairs were divided between two secretaries of state was formalised. The Southern Department, which usually attracted the more senior of the two ministers, oversaw relations with France, Spain, the Mediterranean and the colonies; the Northern Department was responsible for affairs in northern Europe, including Russia and the Baltic, Holland, and the German states. During William's stays in England he dominated all the great departments of state including the Treasury, and used his authority the more effectively by seeing departmental heads individually whenever possible. In the first years of his reign no single politician was allowed to have oversight of a wide range of issues; nor did William care much for the collective aspect of government as represented by the Cabinet Council. Although he met it weekly when he was in London, it developed less because of his presence than because of his absences; for then it was essential for Queen Mary to be given advice on those matters of state which could not be handled by William while on his campaigns. After Mary's death in 1694 it continued to meet, but throughout his reign, and that of Anne, its size and 'representative' nature made it an unwieldy, often disputatious body.

William was the last monarch to hold all the threads of power in this way; yet the system was a fragile thing. It was neither party government nor non-party government; while not royal government it was not cabinet government in any collective sense either. It contained a number of able men – Shrewsbury, Carmarthen (formerly Danby), Godolphin, Nottingham – but none had the full confidence of the King, whose closest advisers remained Dutch. If the ministry was predominantly Tory in character, this had come about less through Tory virtues than through Whig vices, 'for their principles, who set him up, would pull him down', one politician remarked of the relations between Whigs and monarch. William's insistent need for money for the war placed the administration increasingly at the mercy of Parliament, where party factions were growing in strength and virulence, but where distinguishing lines were far from clear. As opposition to the King's wartime government and its demands grew, the Commons formed a sounding-board for opposition to the heavy taxation being inflicted on the nation. As one MP complained, with a touch of dramatic licence, 'the courtiers hug themselves in furs, and the humble country gentleman is half-starved.' The paradox was that although the war forced the Crown to turn increasingly to Parliament, the growth of the army and navy, the diplomatic service, and the revenue-collecting departments, led to a strengthening of the executive, and an increase of the patronage at the Crown's disposal. If the shift towards absolutism had been arrested, the trend towards centralisation quickened in pace. It was a continuation of the process evident under Charles II and James II, when administrative efficiency was increasing, and permanent officials held immense if sometimes ill-defined power as they operated the essential machinery of state regardless of the noise and tumult of political life. Permanent civil servants, as they would be termed later – men like William Blathwayt and Josiah Burchett – built up a fund of knowledge and experience which governments used whatever their political complexion.

As the work of government became more complex, so the need for professional services increased. The period saw an expansion of the professions well beyond the traditional categories of 'Divinity, Law and Physic', though in these too there was growth and change. The years of war from 1689 to 1713 brought a tenfold increase in the number of army officers, and the introduction of a half-pay system in both the army and navy opened the way to lifetime careers. In the revenue departments also, more staff were needed, and although by later standards the numbers seem derisory, complaints were voiced early in George I's reign about the 'army' of twelve thousand government employees. Surveyors, estate stewards, schoolmasters, all swelled the numbers of those in the professions, which by 1730 stood at between 55,000 and 60,000. They represented a more mobile part of society than the landed interest, although many came from landed families; for if the expansion of the professions showed the growing need for services, it also represented the demands of the gentry for career openings. A new sense of identity and mutual self-preservation was created between the government of the day and the most influential sections of the population; and this became an important stabilising element in post-Revolution England. Amid the intricate political manoeuvres and disputes an implicit consensus held among the propertied classes that any renewal of civil disturbance would inflict serious, perhaps fatal, damage on their position. This consensus was reinforced by the steadying influence of successive monarchs, William III and Anne, who in their different ways were insistent on the need to protect the national interest. Despite the heats of party conflict, the fear of the return of civil war and revolution imposed its own limitations on political partisanship. Opposing forces were grouping in Parliament, not on the battlefield; voters rather than regiments were being raised in the localities; and in the political vortex of the nation, differences were being settled, not by the sword, but by debate and vote.

The war brought pressures and strains, not least in the House of Commons, politically divided, suspicious of the looming growth of the executive, and appalled by the cost of William's continental strategy. Those who had seen the Revolution of 1688 as a declaration of the independence of Parliament regarded the growth of the executive as betrayal. In this atmosphere of resentment and faction, with William's 'balanced' ministry proving unequal to its task, a redeployment of political forces took place. A new sense of identity emerged between many of the Whig and Tory backbenchers, the Country interests who found their leader in Robert Harley. At the same time the aristocratic Whigs abandoned all pretence of sympathy with either Country or radical forces, and in the shape of the 'Junto' of Somers, Wharton, Montagu and Russell, emerged as a coherent governing force whose power lay in the Lords rather than in the Commons. The last fling of the old, anti-monarchical Whiggery came with the Triennial Bill of 1694. In the City of London, too, the Whig leaders had moved away from their populist proposals of 1689–90 intended to enhance the role of the annually elected Common Council at the expense of the oligarchic Court of Aldermen. Instead, by the middle of the decade they were preparing a new wealth test for entry to the livery companies, which would eliminate the lesser tradesmen from elections for Common Council. Here, as nationally, most Whigs were as ideologically conservative as their Tory counterparts in their belief that political rights should be confined to men of property.

The years 1694 to 1698 saw a Junto government engaged in vigorous pursuit of the war, closely allied with the Court and the moneyed interests. While it justified its existence to the King by assisting in the foundation of the Bank of England and raising the level of taxation, the Harley-led opposition agitated for bills aimed against 'placemen' in the Commons which if passed would have snapped the links between executive and legislature, and would have restored much of the older character of the House as the natural habitat of the squirearchy. To the traditional tenets of Toryism – allegiance to hereditary kingship and the established Church – were added more negative sentiments: suspicion of the continental war and of foreigners generally; dislike of Dissenters, financiers and placemen; concern about increased taxes, particularly on land. It was a Country programme, the demands of an opposition party whose strength lay on the back benches. To many Tories, unity was not an unqualified virtue, and their standard criticism of the Junto Whigs was that they 'always kept together in close and undivided phalanx, impenetrable either by shame or honour, voting always the same way.'

The Triennial Act of 1694 was passed despite the lack of enthusiasm for it among the Whig leaders who were at this time finding their way into office. With Parliament limited to a maximum of three years (and between 1695 and 1715 there were to be no fewer than ten general elections), the intensity of party conflict increased despite the Act's hopeful observation that 'frequent and new Parliaments tend very much to the happy union and good agreement of the King and people . . .' Faced with the growth of political passions, William was forced to recognise that government based on party was his best guarantee of stability and effectiveness, and it was a Whig-dominated administration which carried the country through the final years of war with France and to the Treaty of Ryswick in 1697. Sunderland, whose talents gained him office under William despite his activities in the previous reign, sensed the truth of the matter: 'Whenever the government has leaned to the Whigs it has been strong, whenever the other has prevailed it has been despised.' He was one of a new breed, the 'Managers', astute non-party or moderate politicians such as Shrewsbury, Godolphin, and for a time in the next reign Harley. They interposed themselves between the Crown and the warring factions in the Commons, stressed the national interest, and built support for the government through a careful distribution of the increasing amount of Crown patronage available through contracts, places and pensions.

At the same time, Tories who had always regarded themselves as by nature Court or ministerialist were learning the necessity, if not yet all the arts, of opposition – not a role they found easy to adopt. When Nottingham, now out of office, but unswervingly loyal to William as monarch, felt able to attack the Junto government, then the way seemed clear for both government and opposition to operate on more narrowly party lines than before. There was, however, an inbuilt, almost instinctive, arrangement of checks and balances which resisted such a process. Just as political exigencies might create coherent groups out of a mass of 'floating' MPs, so the reverse could easily happen. The Whigs in office, clustered around the Junto, began to behave as if they had a monopoly of government, an attitude which was bound to arouse the King's old suspicion of the Whigs. Outside court and administration circles the Junto's arrogance generated a backwash of resentment, in which Whigs excluded from office mingled with Tories and disgruntled independents. These 'Old Whigs' shifted their criticism from the abuses of Crown prerogative which had loomed large in the previous reigns to the growing exercise of ministerial patronage and influence. It was a line of attack which was to continue throughout the eighteenth century, and it secured one of its first successes in the Triennial Act. Fundamental to the difficulty of government was the fact that among the gentry, Whig and Tory, there was an intuitive distrust of 'government', whether it was the authoritarian regime of James II or the aristocratic war administration of the Junto; and this distrust could always be exploited by politicians in opposition.

These years also witnessed the beginnings of a 'financial revolution', brought about by the overriding demands of war. The tax system was reorganised to bring in revenue from three main sources, and was to remain unchanged in outline for more than a hundred years. During William's reign, customs brought in £13,200,000, excise £13,600,000, and the greatly increased land taxes £19,200,000. An Act of 1692 which granted an aid of four shillings in the £ for carrying on the war against France was the foundation of the land tax of the eighteenth century which became one of the mainstays of the public revenue. By its very nature it fell heavily on the landowners, but since it was assessed locally with marked variations, and the valuation did not increase with the rise in actual values, the land tax was in the long run regarded as more tolerable than such centralised and frightening alternatives as an income tax. For the government, an adjustment of the rate between one and four shillings in the £ brought in annual amounts ranging between £500,000 and £2 million; and for this, and the relative ease of collection, it turned a blind eye to the anomalies which lay buried deep in the system. But heavy though these taxes seemed to contemporaries, they did not meet the total cost of the war, and the government had to borrow almost £12 million. Such a sum would have been impossible to raise in any earlier reign, and William's government was able to succeed only by associating Parliament with a series of new, long-term loans which were underwritten (or 'funded') by Parliament's allocation of revenue from specific taxes to pay the interest.

It was this use of taxation to service government debts which lay at the heart of the new system. The first of these measures was nursed through Parliament in the winter of 1692–93, and raised £1 million in long-term loans secured on excise duties. The moderate Tory Godolphin at the Treasury was in charge of national finances, but in seeing this bill through he was dependent on the Junto Whigs, Montagu and Somers. In 1694 the Bank of England was founded to raise £1,200,000 for William's continental campaign of that year, and since parliamentary approval was essential for any loan made by the Bank its stock had all the safety of gilt-edged securities. Other joint-stock companies were also founded in this period, and older ones such as the East India Company much enlarged, until by the mid-1690s it was estimated that a tenth of the personal wealth of the country was invested in them. The number of people holding stock was a tacit guarantee of the stability, not only of the governments of William III and Anne, but also of the Hanoverians, when attention to the size and funding of the National Debt became one of the primary concerns of the Treasury. In the war with France the system of public credit gave England an inestimable advantage, even though the new long-term loans of William's government amounted to less than £7 million out of a total government expenditure of more than £72 million. The very figures, when compared with what was regarded as normal government expenditure of about £1,500,000 a year at the beginning of the reign, show the impact of war on the political and financial system, and form an ironic comment on earlier complaints about Stuart profligacy. In William's reign the financial basis was established for the increasingly expensive wars of the eighteenth century, which were to turn England into a major world power at the cost of becoming one of the most heavily-taxed nations in Europe.

There was a reverse side to this process, and it also had political implications. The new land tax stood at the top level of four shillings in the £ throughout the war years – bringing in £46 million up to 1713, compared with a little over £3 million taken from landowners in direct taxation in the twenty years before William's accession – and this at a time when rents were static, the price of land falling, harvests mostly poor, and mortgages hard to obtain. By contrast, the great financiers seemed able to double and redouble their money without effort or risk. They were courted by King and government, and each year saw new, incomprehensible devices emerging as part of a financial system spreading, one Tory critic wrote, 'like a canker, which will eat up the gentleman's estates in land, and beggar the trading part of the nation, and bring all the subjects in England to be the monied men's vassals.' To the landed gentry, backbone of the Tory interest in the Commons, these developments were anathema. Their hostility to the growth of the moneyed classes, and to the increasing power of the executive, was shown in the partisan operations of the Commission of Public Accounts after 1691. In origin a concession by the King to soothe the sting of war taxation, the Commission soon took on a political rather than administrative role in the face of government attempts to stop its enquiries digging too deep. With Harley becoming increasingly influential on the Commission its activities helped to unite Country MPs, both Whig and Tory, as it probed with vigour if not with much permanent effect into the expenditure and suspected extravagance of government departments.

Adding to Tory resentments was the overdue but unpopular recoinage operation pushed through by the Junto in 1696. The whole of the country's defective silver currency was withdrawn and replaced, but with inevitable hardship to many individuals, already suffering from the succession of poor harvests and high food prices. The gentry saw themselves as being ruthlessly taxed to support a war they only half believed in, at the same time as the moneyed interest, many of them Dissenters, or Dutch or Huguenot in origin, were making fortunes out of the same war. The financial system was seen as a subterranean channel through which sinister forms of political influence were introduced, and the situation was regarded as the more intolerable since to the plain country gentleman it was self-evident that land, not stocks, represented real wealth. As a later Tory put it, 'the landed men are the true owners of our political vessel, the moneyed men as such are no more than passengers in it.' To an extent the invective obscured the fact that no rigid division existed between land and money. There are many individual examples of a fusion between the two, but there was enough truth in the complaints to forge a sharp political weapon. The association between thej Whigs and high finance which had done much to entrench them in William's governments in the middle years of the reign, seemed to be demonstrated in 1696 by the failure of the Tory-sponsored Land Bank to make any headway. It represented the wish of the country gentry for an institution which would be in many ways the antithesis of the Bank of England – based in the provinces rather than in London, providing low-cost mortgages for landowners, allied with the agrarian rather than the commercial interests of the country. Not surprisingly, its failure was attributed by Harley and others to sabotage by the Bank of England and its Whig allies.

It was at this time of frustration and resentment that Gregory King produced in 1695–6 his 'Scheme of the Income and Expense of the several Families of England . . . for the Year 1688.' Even within the limits of King's assumptions and information, his tabular classification portrayed a society different in some respects from other European countries of the period. The landed class was fragmented rather than monolithic. At the top was an élite of fewer than two hundred peers which, when joined by an even smaller number of non-noble landowners with estates of 10,000 acres or more, owned one-fifth of the cultivated land of England and Wales. Although the main income of the territorial magnates came from rents, their association with government also brought rewards from office, sinecure and pension. Next came the gentry, a more amorphous group, 15,000 in number according to King's estimate, living mainly off rents, supplemented by income from investments, office or profession. They were followed by 150,000 lesser freeholders, whose income and life-style were often matched by the 180,000 'farmers', that is those who rented land. The dominance of the land was muted by the interposition of merchants and shopkeepers, artisans and professional men, to a greater extent than King recognised. It was a society more mixed than any of its continental neighbours, except perhaps Holland, but there was no serious clash between agriculture on one side and commerce and industry on the other. The lines of demarcation between these interests were not tightly drawn, and just as merchants and professional men sought to acquire land, so many employed in trade and industry were the younger sons of landed families. It was a hierarchy, but one of 'ranks', 'orders' and 'connexions' rather than of rigid castes. A seepage of individuals across the joins of this hierarchical structure gave it some flexibility, though it is possible to exaggerate the 'openness' of society in this period. It was as difficult to escape from the misery of the lowest layers as it was at the top to gain entry to the peerage. Social climbing was a tricky business, and although there were well-publicised exceptions, many more aspirants remained on the lower slopes than ever reached the top.

In his efforts to influence the fiscal policies of the government, King was, in effect, recreating the society which had existed before the war. His was a traditionalist's concept of how the world had been, and ought again to be once the deplorable innovations of the 1690s had sunk from sight. Instinctively, and by casting back to the pre-war period, King had produced a society tinged with anachronism. He underestimated the gross national income, and understated the importance of the commercial, industrial and 'monied' classes – probably even in terms of the 1680s, and clearly so by the 1690s. Outside his terms of reference was the way in which foreign trade was increasing both the supply of raw materials and the market outlets available to manufacturers. Traditionally, the cloth industry had dominated England's foreign trade, with woollen cloth accounting for between 80 and 90 per cent of all exports in the early seventeenth century. Since then there had been a significant diversification in England's foreign trade, both with Europe, where the Mediterranean became of increasing importance, and with the new colonies across the Atlantic. The expansion of seaborne trade, supported in its colonial context by the protective legislation of the Acts of Trade and Navigation since the 1660s, was reflected in the steady increase in merchant shipping. More than a third of mercantile tonnage was prosaically employed in the coal trade, but by the later decades of the century profitable trades had developed in commodities barely known in 1600: sugar and tobacco from the American and West Indian plantations, and calicoes from Asia. In the last forty years of the century imports increased by a third, and exports (including re-exports) by more than a half. Halifax remarked in the

1680s, 'We are a very little spot in the map of the world and make a great figure only by trade'; and the protection and expansion of that trade was becoming a prime concern of government.

If a society was developing which in some respects was more 'modern' than King cared to admit in 1695, in political terms the events of the previous ten years had confirmed a shift of power into the hands of the aristocratic landowners. The peerage, consisting mainly of Stuart creations, was kept small by primogeniture and by a limited granting of new titles. When William came to the throne there were 160 temporal peers, together with 26 lords spiritual (two archbishops and twenty-four bishops), and this number was not to increase much over the next hundred years. The peers were more than a group of courtiers, though in their proximity and access to the monarch lay the root of their influence. In political terms they formed a working aristocracy which held most of the senior ministerial offices, and exercised patronage over a host of lesser posts. Moreover, as their own House lost power in the eighteenth century so their influence as great landowners increased over elections to the Commons – from total dominance of some of the smaller parliamentary boroughs to a considerable voice in many of the larger boroughs and in the counties. In the shires it was the peers who mostly filled the office of lord lieutenant, and the purges of the 1680s among the lord lieutenants and the lesser cogs of local government had shown their importance as well as their vulnerability. Crucial to the working of government, at both local and central level, were the gentry or squirearchy. As justices of the peace they were the driving wheels of local government; at Westminster they formed the majority of MPs, though not necessarily the most active or ambitious ones. James II's actions had confirmed their suspicion of strong, centralised government and this was renewed by William III's policies, which seemed designed to burden them with ever-increasing tax burdens to fight a war whose purpose was yearly becoming more obscure. By the end of the reign they were mostly Tory, and their number and attitude were significant problems for the government of the day.

The period after the Treaty of Ryswick in 1697 brought a variety of resentments to a head. It was an unexciting settlement which put an end to a grim-fought war in which allied victories had been few and far between. To the hard-pressed, the overtaxed, the malcontents, it was greeted as an opportunity for relaxation and change. All the more disconcerting, therefore, was the realisation that William seemed to regard the Ryswick settlement as little more than a truce. While deeply involved with the French monarch in partition negotiations to try to resolve the intricate question of the Spanish succession, he was nevertheless determined to keep a large (by English standards) peacetime army – something which the Bill of Rights had prohibited except with parliamentary consent. In a period of continuing international uncertainty the King was insistent on the need to have trained soldiers at the ready. By contrast, country politicians worried about the cost and possible political threat of these same troops, many of them foreign, which made up an army of 60,000 men – three times the size of James II's. Even if the direct threat to political liberty which a standing army was felt to pose did not, in the end, carry complete conviction, its growth was for many symbolic of the changes which had taken place in the previous few years.

With the ministry under increasing fire, Sunderland in retirement, and a general election due, the political ground began to crumble under William's feet. Whigs as well as Tories voted against the government on the standing army, and the election of 1698 in which taxes and placemen were prominent issues saw losses among ministerial supporters, the 'court or army' party, to quote one contemporary. While some 'Old Whigs' looked back to the republican ideology of an earlier age for inspiration, the main voting strength and practical leadership of the opposition was Tory. It was Harley who emerged as acknowledged leader of the 'New Country' party, critical of the Junto and of much of the king's policy. One by one ministers were picked off during what William described in April 1700 as 'the most dismal session I have ever had.' By now Tories were being taken into the government, despite the King's doubts on 'running from one extreme to another', and in 1701 Harley was elected as Speaker of the Commons (a key post, the election to which at this time signified the balance of political forces in the House). Under his prompting an elaborate Act of Settlement was passed which went far beyond decisions about the succession – a task made necessary by the death the previous year of the last surviving child of Princess Anne, heiress to the throne.

Apart from its avowed purpose of vesting the succession after Anne's death on the Electress Sophia of Hanover (the Protestant grand-daughter of James I), the Act of Settlement was a hostile retrospective scrutiny of William's reign. It contained a long list of Country restrictions on the Crown's rights, some of them narrowly xenophobic in purpose (such as the prohibition of any war waged on behalf of foreign countries unless with the express approval of Parliament). Among the Act's clauses was one which secured judges in office during their good behaviour, an important guarantee though a superfluous one as far as William was concerned. Another clause represented the climax of a whole series of efforts to remove placemen from the House, for it stipulated that after Anne's death no office-holder was to be an MP. Had this measure been put into practice it would have changed the whole balance and nature of government by separating the executive and legislature, and weakening any doctrine of ministerial responsibility. (The clause was repealed in 1705 before it took effect, and its only remnant was the insistence that an MP appointed to any ministerial office which existed before that date had to submit to re-election, not normally a very onerous undertaking). If the country was to be ruled by another foreigner in the future, then the Tories were determined to clamp restrictions on him or her much firmer than those of 1688–89. The formal title of the 'Act of Settlement' revealed much – 'An Act for the further limitation of the Crown and better securing the Rights and Liberties of the Subject'. From being the party of prerogative, the Tories were being pushed by events, prejudices and instinct onto a course which seemed designed to make effective government impossible.

In line with these political developments was the pressure on William in ecclesiastical matters to recall Convocation, the clerical equivalent of Parliament which had last met in 1689 when it had adopted a hard-line attitude towards the proposed religious settlement. The Revolution had brought an even more acute crisis in the Anglican Church than in the Tory party, and when in 1689 the new oaths had to be sworn to William and Mary by all office-holders and clergy, a significant minority of the latter refused. Among the non-jurors, as they were called, were Archbishop Sancroft, five bishops and four hundred clergy. They were a reminder of old traditions and beliefs, a continuing reproach to the conforming Anglican Tories. The uneasiness of many of these was increased during William's reign when under the terms of the Toleration Act of 1689 hundreds of new Dissenting meeting-houses were established (2,356 by 1710). There were, it was clear, many more Dissenters than the 108,000 listed in the religious census of 1676. Local clergy were faced with a challenge in their own parishes from Dissenting ministers, holding services with the full authorisation of the law; and their resentment and discomfort increased as they saw William appointing bishops of Whiggish Low Church rather than Tory persuasion in his efforts to build a body of dependable ministerial supporters in the House of Lords. Anglicans in the capital found Dissenting meeting-houses being built of a size and splendour to rival their own churches; two-fifths of the directors of the Bank of England were either Dissenters or came from a Dissenting background. Just as alarming to many Anglicans was the suspicion that the concessions of 1689 had allowed many people to avoid public worship altogether. Fears of the rise of a secularised society were sharpened by the number of sceptical pamphlets which appeared after the lapsing in 1695 of the Licensing Act – though hardly enough to justify Francis Atterbury's outburst that 'Deism and atheism overrun us like a deluge'.

The cry of 'The Church in danger' was to prove an alarming one, with overtones of blind prejudice and mob violence, but it was stimulated by a genuine revulsion against the heterodox opinions which were becoming fashionable, and was accompanied by a new concern for the unprivileged and distressed. Thomas Tenison, Archbishop of Canterbury from 1695 to 1715, had set an example when Vicar of St Martin's-in-the-Fields with relief work among the poor of his parish. As Archbishop he encouraged the formation of voluntary societies in which clerics and laymen worked together to set up parochial schools for the children of the poor, and organised missionary endeavours overseas. The Society for the Promotion of Christian Knowledge (1698), and the Society for the Propagation of the Gospel in Foreign Parts (1701), were as much hallmarks of the restless Anglicanism of William's reign as the polemic tracts. Politically, however, the main thrust of High Church activity was the demand, supported by Tory groups in Parliament, that Convocation should be summoned. This William finally had to concede in 1701. The sessions were noisy and tumultuous; and Convocation was finally prorogued as a gulf opened between the bishops in the upper house and the lesser clergy in the lower house. As dangerous a split existed within the ecclesiastical order of England as within the political, for not only did the Church feel itself threatened by nonconformity and deism; it was bitterly, perhaps irretrievably, divided into High Church and Low Church parties.

The final years of the reign provided ample evidence of the continuing differences between Whig and Tory which the 'balanced' ministries of the earlier years had helped to blur. With four general elections held between 1698 and 1702 political and religious passions rode high. To William these partisan clashes were always subordinate to the main objective of containing the France of Louis XIV. After the equivocations and ambiguities of later Stuart foreign policy, William's accession to the English throne was a decisive event in the history of late seventeenth-century Europe. Since the Restoration, England had played an undistinguished part in continental affairs, receiving subsidy payments from Louis XIV to ensure acquiescence in French policies in the same way as minor states in Germany and elsewhere. The alliance of the Emperor, the United Provinces and England in 1689 marked the end of that submissive posture, and introduced a diplomatic and military combination which was to survive until the mid-eighteenth century. William was determined to use his new kingdom's resources to the full in order to preserve Europe from the dominance of Louis XIV, but how precisely this was to be done was a matter of dispute. The Tories were unenthusiastic about land campaigns on the continent, and advocated a maritime strategy based on the use of the navy. This had none of the alarming political overtones of a standing army; it protected the British Isles against invasion; it might even bring a profit from attacks on France's seaborne commerce and colonies. To William, on the other hand, as to Marlborough later, a maritime strategy was at best a diversionary one: France would be defeated only when its main land forces were broken.

If the strategy of the war was a matter of contention, there can be no doubt about the general determination of the governing classes in England to stop the French advance in Europe – and this remained true although war weariness set in long before 1697. Louis XIV threw a menacing shadow across the island kingdom in a way no foreign ruler had done since Philip II. France threatened the Low Countries and England's interests there; seemed poised to take over Spain's vast empire; embodied intolerant, persecuting Catholicism; and provided a refuge and a recruiting base for the Stuart Pretenders. As an English diplomat later observed, it was 'a truth inculcated into John Bull with his mother's milk . . . that France is our national enemy.' These feelings William channelled in his dogged leadership of the allied armies, even though the popular acclaim which greeted the declaration of war in May 1689 soon faded. Apart from the naval victory over the French fleet at La Hogue in 1692 which dashed French plans for an invasion of England in concert with a Jacobite rising, and the recapture of Namur in 1694, the continental war provided no clear-cut victories to gladden the hearts of English taxpayers. Instead, they saw large sums of money disappearing overseas to support allies whose appetite for subsidies was matched, it seemed, only by their unreliability. It was not easy for Englishmen to understand the complex diplomatic and military alliances of continental warfare, nor for them to recognise the truth of Daniel Defoe's comment that it was 'not the longest sword, but the longest purse that conquers'. They rather saw that purse being drained by French privateering activities against England's seaborne trade. Four thousand merchantmen were lost to enemy action during the nine years of war, and although this represented only a small fraction of England's growing seaborne trade William Blathwayt had to acknowledge the 'great scandal' of such losses 'while we are so much superior at sea'.

William himself was engaged in a war of attrition, mainly in Flanders, in which each year from 1691 onwards saw him grappling with generally superior French forces. As the struggle wore on in bloody but undecisive campaigns, with disease usually killing more men than the enemy, and with English participation increasing from a token contribution to tens of thousands of men, so the French armies came to a standstill, their best commanders gone, their supplies exhausted. It was William's greatest achievement, and with grim relentlessness he was in the field even as the peace negotiations of 1697 were nearing completion for, as he warned, 'the only way of treating with France is with our swords in our hands.' The Treaty of Ryswick signalled the failure of Louis XIV's attempts to accomplish the dominance of the Low Countries and the subordination of England. Among its terms was the French recognition on the throne of England of William and his successors. Unknown to most of those who greeted the treaty with relief and joy, it was the prelude to a greater struggle, for the childless Charles II of Spain lay dying with the future of his vast empire in Europe and America undecided.

William's attitude to the Spanish problem showed that he was not anti-French in a simplistic national sense. He had opposed the France of Louis XIV since 1672 because its policies threatened the independence of his homeland and the general stability of Europe. Between 1698 and 1700 he worked with his recent enemy to devise a solution to the Spanish Succession crisis which would safeguard that stability; and he prepared for war again only when he saw Louis apparently ready to abandon all undertakings in pursuit of new and even more grandiose ambitions. Since his accession, William had been his own foreign minister, helped chiefly by his unpopular Dutch advisers, especially Bentinck (naturalised and given a peerage as the Earl of Portland). Ministers and Parliament alike were kept in the dark about William's diplomacy, conducted for the most part during his months at the Hague through the Dutch diplomatic corps; and three luckless Whig ministers were impeached for negotiations in which they had played virtually no part. For much of his reign William was able to exploit the conventional secrecy which surrounded foreign policy to keep its conduct away from parliamentary scrutiny. The fact that from March to October each year the King was on the continent, negotiating and campaigning, added a practical difficulty to parliamentary involvement in an area traditionally reserved for the royal prerogative. Only in November, when the armies went into winter quarters, and William returned at the beginning of the parliamentary session to present the military and naval estimates, was there regular opportunity for debate and criticism.

Problems after the Treaty of Ryswick showed the disadvantages of this attitude of aloofness and condescension. Not only had William negotiated a peace settlement without consulting Parliament about its terms, but there was uncertainty in and out of Parliament about the implications of the secret partition treaties which followed. Clear though it may have been to the King that until Louis's words of reason were matched by action the country should be kept on at least a semi-war footing, many of his subjects thought otherwise. The impeachment proceedings against the Whig ministers, the disbanding of most of the wartime army, and the humiliating restraints of the Act of Settlement, all showed the weakness of William's position once the dangers of war and invasion lessened. In 1701 William could sway a largely Tory House of Commons to contemplate the possibility of renewed hostilities against France only by prolonged persuasion and exhortation, a process to which the pro-war petitions organised in the constituencies by Whig interests gave a colouring of popular support. The importance of Parliament was acknowledged in the King's speech at the beginning of the 1701 session: 'The eyes of all Europe are upon this parliament; all matters are at a stand till your resolutions are known.' The concession once made, there could be no going back, and in Anne's reign foreign affairs and the conduct of the war became a staple diet of parliamentary debate.

Inconclusive though the Revolution settlement had been in many ways, the following dozen years had seen a tilting of the balance between Crown and Parliament – and this despite the formidable personality of the King. Much of the royal prerogative remained intact: the right to appoint ministers, dissolve Parliament, create peers, choose bishops. But William's reluctance to put the full resources of the Crown behind the party politicians was an inhibiting factor for much of his reign. With the Commons prepared to vote supplies for the army and navy only on an annual basis, the government's financial needs led for the first time to Parliament meeting each year as a matter of course. Nor was the Commons content merely to approve supplies; through the Commission of Public Accounts it attempted, in the end without much effect, to control the expending of the vast sums voted. The Triennial Act and the bills against placemen, the 'tacking' of redress of grievances onto money bills, the reduction of the standing army, the intervention in foreign policy, were all signs of the growing ambition of the Commons, however obscured this might be by the partisan confusion of its proceedings.

The last months of the reign were dominated by William's concern to rebuild the alliance against France, and as in 1689 Louis XIV proved to be his best ally in this task. His repudiation of the second partition treaty, and his acceptance instead of the will of Charles II of Spain which bequeathed his whole empire to a grandson of the French monarch was only the prelude to a series of threatening moves. Louis

XIV's recognition of the 'Old Pretender' as James III after the death of the ex-king James II in September 1701, his threat to English trading interests both in Spain and in the Americas, and his menacing troop movements in the Low Countries, brought the weight of responsible opinion in England behind the Grand Alliance with the Emperor and the Dutch. As the opposing forces moved slowly towards war, in March 1702 William died after a riding accident, and was succeeded by the last of the Protestant Stuarts, James II's daughter, Anne.

3 The rage of parties, 1702–1714

On the accession of Anne, exuberant Tories hoped that at last they had come into their own, that they might reach the promised land of power, security and respectability. Although her views could never be ignored, the difference in personality and experience between the new Queen and her predecessor made more impact on the political scene than any number of constitutional enactments. William had been head of the executive in every sense, working it is true within the limitations imposed on him by Parliament, and dependent on his ministers to get his business done, but always a dominant, forceful figure, one of the great men of his age. Anne, by contrast, though conscientious and stubborn, was of modest abilities and indifferent health, a woman ruler whose reign was dominated by the masculine theme of war. Devoted to the Church of England, she dismayed many Whigs with the sentiments she expressed in the speech from the throne with which she dissolved Parliament in the summer of 1702: 'My own principles must always keep me entirely firm to the interests and religion of the Church of England, and will incline me to countenance those who have the truest zeal to support it.'

Even if the Queen was by temperament inclined towards the High Tories, she soon showed herself to be as opposed to ecclesiastical faction and to party dissensions as her predecessor. Her first ministry, with the austere figure of Nottingham as Secretary of State, was Tory-dominated, but the non-partisan Godolphin was Lord Treasurer; Marlborough, Tory by inclination but aware of Whig support for the war, was Captain General of the Armed Forces; and his wife Sarah, Duchess of Marlborough, was still the Queen's closest confidante. In contrast to the centralist position of the ministry was the situation in the Commons, where even before the general election of August 1702 Tory groups were on the rampage, attacking the employment of foreigners in the army and elsewhere, hardly waiting for the outbreak of war in May to denounce any thought of continental campaigning, and demanding a purge of

Whigs from office. It was the ominous opening to a reign which saw – if not the sophistication of a modern party system – the undoubted grappling for power of two great political combinations, separated by differences of principle, unperturbed by those doubts of identity which some historians have discerned in them. There was a social cohesiveness about the political groups, and they were united in an instinctive determination not to share power with the rest of the population. But in politics and religion they were so divided that Addison could write in 1711 that it was as though Whigs and Tories were 'born with a secret antipathy to one another, and engage when they meet as naturally as the Elephant and the Rhinoceros'.

Tory strength in the House increased after the election by perhaps fifty MPs to give a majority of about 150, and so did feelings of partisanship and political venom. The session saw the first of several attempts to pass an Occasional Conformity Bill, a measure which again illustrated the combustible interaction between politics and religion. Occasional Conformity was a by-product of the legislation of Charles II's reign which barred a man from holding office, at either national or local level, unless he took Anglican communion. To observe the letter of the law, many Dissenters received communion once a year, a practice which smacked of blasphemy to devout Anglicans, and infuriated Tories who saw Dissenting Whigs dominating some of the town corporations, and from there the parliamentary constituencies. That the Commons remained overwhelmingly Anglican in composition, with no more than thirty MPs who were Dissenters throughout Anne's reign, did nothing to calm Tory resentments. High Church feeling was characterised in its noisiest form by Dr Henry Sacheverell at Oxford, whose thundering sermons proclaimed that 'these shuffling, treacherous Latitudinarians ought to be stigmatised, and treated equally as dangerous enemies to the government as well as Church.' The Occasional Conformity issue led to a deepening estrangement between the High Tories and the Queen, while Godolphin wrote in despair that 'A discreet clergyman is almost as rare as a black swan'. In December 1703 the Queen's Speech commended 'perfect peace and union' to her subjects in place of the existing 'heats and divisions', but 1704 saw the Tories manoeuvring to 'tack' an Occasional Conformity Bill onto the essential Land Tax Bill after two previous attempts had been blocked in the Lords.

To play party and church politics at a time when the struggle against France was reaching its peak seemed the height of irresponsibility to the Queen, and to the moderates in general. The Solicitor-General complained that 'Universal madness reigns', and Marlborough referred to 'the detested names of Whig and Tory'. The two most important High Tories, Nottingham and Seymour, left office amid the furore and were replaced, not by Whigs, but by moderate Tories – the Speaker Robert Harley who became Secretary of State for the Northern Department, and the younger Tory, Henry St John, as Secretary at War, a junior post but a key one in the waging of the great continental campaigns. For the next four or five years the close relationship between these two men in the Commons was to be an essential link in the working of the political machinery, for Godolphin was in the Lords, and Marlborough usually abroad. Different in age, attitude and temperament, they made a formidable political combination. St John was volatile, dynamic, fertile in ideas; Harley more calculating, sensitive to the political pulse, and adept in using the still considerable powers of the Crown to further the cause of moderate Toryism. The reconstruction of the ministry under the triumvirate of Godolphin, Marlborough and Harley was a sign of the gap between the extreme Tories, apparently indifferent to the fate of Europe when lured by the more exciting pursuit of Whigs and Dissenters, and those Tories who were weary of the obsessive concern with Occasional Conformity. The task of Godolphin's ministry in rallying support for the war was helped by Marlborough's startling and distant victory over the French at Blenheim on the Danube. It was the first major defeat in the field for Louis XIV's armies, as shattering a blow to French prestige as it was an unexpected achievement by a general from a nation which not many years earlier had been regarded as insignificant in military terms.

At the general election of 1705 the government coalition emerged with a marginal increase of support, and many of the Tory 'tackers' lost their seats. Whatever the personal predilections of the Queen, the most logical support for the government lay in the Whig Junto (reinforced by Marlborough's son-in-law, the third Earl of Sunderland) since it commanded the largest organised group of MPs, and was committed to the continental war. The Queen saw the dangers rather than the benefits of bringing in the hard men from the Junto, and wrote to Godolphin that as far as Whigs and Tories were concerned 'if I should be unfortunate as to fall into the hands of either, I shall not imagine myself, though I have the name of Queen, to be in reality but their slave.' Anne was over-dramatising the situation, but her strong views added to the intricacy of parliamentary politics between 1705 and 1708, with Godolphin engaged in a balancing act by which he succeeded in attracting the support of the Junto without conceding more than a minimum of government office in return.

For Godolphin, in the end all was subordinate to the immense and costly business of waging war, now costing an unprecedented £4 million a year as it spread from the traditional battlegrounds of Flanders to the Rhine and the Danube, into the Iberian peninsula, and overseas to North America and the Caribbean. This extension of the war was in one way a sign of England's strength, in another it was a dissipation of strength – a compromise between Marlborough's insistence on striking at the main enemy armies, and the preference of many Tories for peripheral operations which made use of the country's naval power. The most draining of these operations took place in Spain, as early triumphs drew British arms into a blind alley where success, honour and profit proved more difficult to find than the amateur strategists had predicted. This costly diversion reached its nadir at the battle of Almanza in 1707 which gave French forces control of most of the country. Despite this setback, the middle years of the decade were marked by the remorseless application of pressure on France by the partnership of Godolphin and Marlborough. Essential to Godolphin's position at home were the continued successes abroad by Marlborough, who broke with conventional notions of warfare, and in particular with the Dutch preference for steady siege warfare rather than the astonishing forced marches and decisive battles which had become his hallmark. Blenheim had been his first triumph, and it was followed in 1706 by the victory at Ramillies which drove French forces out of the Spanish Netherlands. Godolphin was also helped at this critical stage of the war by a series of gratuitous blunders by the High Tories who made themselves as obnoxious to the Queen as the Junto leaders had done with their proposal that the heiress-presumptive to the throne, the Electress Sophia, should be invited to England. Tory reasoning was that if the government accepted the suggestion it would antagonise the Queen, understandably touchy at the idea of having her successor at hand waiting for her demise; if it rejected the proposal, then the ministry could be accused of jeopardising the Protestant succession. Godolphin steered around this pit dug in his path, and with the help of the Junto passed a Regency Act in 1706 setting up practical and sensible machinery to ensure the succession after Anne's death.

The Junto leaders also played a prominent part in an even more significant piece of legislation – the Union with Scotland. Attempts in the seventeenth century to turn the personal union of crowns of 1603 into something more binding and comprehensive had all failed, and after the Revolution William III was confronted with a situation in which the Crown had lost much of its influence over the Scottish Parliament at a time when new tensions overlay relations between the two countries. Dissatisfaction in the Highlands at the replacement of a Catholic monarch by a Protestant led to risings of the clansmen, and although by the winter of 1691–92 these were largely subdued, the brutal and unnecessary massacre of the MacDonalds at Glencoe in February 1692 brought both the King and his ministers into disrepute.

Also disturbing was the evidence of Scottish determination to pursue an independent economic policy, already apparent in the retaliatory measures taken by each country against the trade of the other. In 1695 the Company of Scotland for Trading to Africa and the Indies was established, and its attempt to found a colony in fever-stricken Darien threatened, with its infringement of Spanish territory in central America, to jeopardise William's foreign policy. The failure of the Darien scheme, at a cost of two thousand lives and perhaps a quarter of Scotland's capital resources, was blamed by the Scots on English opposition rather than on their own foolhardiness. Glencoe and Darien became bloody symbols of English arrogance and indifference, shown in a more general way by the damage suffered by the Scottish economy during the war with France. Poor harvests, and famine, between 1695 and 1698, added to the sense of vulnerability and crisis.

Yet within five years of Anne's accession, union was accomplished – a development which bewildered many contemporaries. Renewed English insistence on some sort of union is less difficult to explain than Scottish acquiescence. In the same way that Ireland had posed a threat to England's security in the recent past, so measures passed by the Edinburgh Parliament in the first years of Anne's reign demonstrated the alarming possibility of a Scotland with an independent foreign policy moving into alliance with France. The chances of this happening were remote as long as the French court sheltered the Pretender, but the uncomfortable fact remained that in 1703–04 the Scottish Parliament passed two Acts, one of 'Security and Succession', and the other concerning 'Peace and War', which showed that England's external policies were no longer binding on the Scots. The weakness of a personal union of the crowns of the two countries which left their separate parliaments intact, and apparently drifting in different directions, was clearly shown. The 1701 Act of Settlement which had vested the succession in the House of Hanover did not apply to Scotland, and it appeared that the union of crowns would end with Anne's death.

The reaction of the Westminster Parliament to these dangers was the Alien Act of 1705, a measure calculated to force the Scots into negotiating Union under the threat of economic boycott. Its terms were a sharp reminder to the Scots of their economic vulnerability, for their exports to Europe had been in decline for decades, and the prospect of exclusion from the English market was a dismaying one. Commercial weakness on the Scottish side, and defence worries on the English, provided strong motives for some kind of union of convenience. Other Scottish anxieties centred on the deep political and religious differences between the Jacobite or Cavalier party and the Presbyterian Whigs. Even more surely than in England the accession of a Catholic monarch to the throne of Scotland would result in civil war, quite apart from the certain English invasion that would result.

There was, then, a reasonably strong pro-Union lobby in Scotland, whose arguments revolved – both in debates within Parliament and in the pamphlet warfare outside – around trade and internal peace, and were deployed to try to calm the Anglophobia still apparent in many areas. The usual methods of political jobbery, influence and patronage were also used to smooth the path towards Union, although the precise extent and effect of these is difficult to evaluate. Equally difficult is any assessment of popular feeling in Scotland about the negotiations – petitions of protest certainly came in from some of the boroughs and shires, but not in overwhelming numbers. Potential sources of opposition were placated by careful concessions: the independence of the Presbyterian Church of Scotland was guaranteed, the Scottish legal system was retained, subscribers to the unfortunate Darien venture were to get their money back, and other minor amendments were made to the draft treaty of Union as it was considered by the Scottish Parliament at the end of 1706. A particularly important concession to Scottish interests was the article which opened the trade and navigation of Britain and its overseas empire to all British subjects, though the imposition of a common customs and excise system which this entailed introduced a new stringency to commercial regulations at the Scottish ports.

The Treaty of Union came into force in May 1707. It established a new political and economic entity, 'Great Britain', which was to have a single Parliament. The Scots were to send forty-five MPs to the House of Commons (one more than Cornwall), and sixteen 'representative' peers to sit in the House of Lords. This was a proportion (in a Parliament which now numbered 558 MPs and about 200 peers) which reflected the English insistence that representation should reflect the lowly economic status of Scotland rather than the Scottish hope for representation in proportion to population (about a quarter of England's at this time). In general, and despite the concessions made, the Act represented absorption rather than partnership. Nor was it likely that Scottish representation at Westminster would form a powerful force working for local interests, for in the next reign it became clear that the forty-five MPs, elected on a very narrow franchise (the voters in the burghs and counties totalled only about three thousand) tended to form a servile bloc of government supporters. With no legitimate means left of opposition to the government in London, and with much of the country remaining desperately poor, many in Scotland continued to look to Jacobitism as a way of expressing national sentiments.

The help given by the Junto in the negotiations over both the Union and the Regency Act was recognised by the appointment of Sunderland as Secretary of State for the Northern Department in December 1706. Slowly, the administration was changing its political colour, though the process was an uneven and blotchy one. For Godolphin and Marlborough tensions were increased, not only by the political differences between Harley and St John on the one side, and the Junto on the other, but by court personalities. The clangorous replacement at the Queen's side of the Duchess of Marlborough by Abigail Masham (a distant relative of Harley) was the most striking example of this, and helped to nerve Godolphin and Marlborough to demand the resignation of Harley. A damaging scandal over discrepancies in the muster-roll of English troops at Almanza (Parliament had voted supply for thirty thousand but for reasons which were not at all clear at the time less than nine thousand were actually present) was the occasion used to discredit Harley. The period of the triumvirate was over, and Harley and St John were replaced by Whigs, not from the Junto it is true, but Whigs nevertheless, who included the young and able Robert Walpole as the new Secretary at War. In the general election of 1708 which returned for the first time Scottish MPs to Westminster (mostly Presbyterian and anti-Tory), and at which the Tories were damaged by an invasion attempt by the Pretender on the Scottish coast, the Whigs gained about thirty seats. The pressure on Godolphin to admit further Whigs grew, and before the end of the year those Junto stalwarts Somers and Wharton had joined Sunderland in the ministry. The course of events and their own inclinations had confirmed the Whigs as the war party, committed to a strong executive working in partnership with the great financial and trading interests.

Although the 1708 election was one of the quietest of the reign, party feelings ran high throughout this period. The unsettling effect of the Triennial Act spread far beyond the confines of election time and the hustings, for as Defoe explained, with elections every three years, 'Parties are ever struggling; they contend on every occasion, choosing their parish officers, their Recorders, their magistrates, and everything that has the least face of public concern; all runs by parties.' The electorate itself was growing fast, especially in the expanding towns, where the number of voters was rising steeply. The most recent estimates put the size of the electorate in England and Wales at more than 300,000, but this figure on its own is not a reliable guide to actual voting or to political participation. If the turnover of electors through changes in circumstance and location is taken into account, the number who had voted in at least one parliamentary election could be as much as twice the number eligible to vote at any particular time – and if this was so it does much to explain the intensity of electoral politics in this period. The general elections showed a clear division on party lines in the electorate, with a floating vote of varying size, and sixty or so pivotal constituencies whose returns were often decisive. Although to modern eyes the number of contested elections was remarkably small, in both the counties and the 'narrow' boroughs there were many more than in the less turbulent Hanoverian period. Unlike later elections, those of Anne's reign saw not only the usual local power struggles in the constituencies but also differences on national issues – war (or peace) with France, the Church, the Succession.

In the constituencies, as in Parliament, it was Whig versus Tory. The shires felt the impact of party politics, with a jostling for place and office which ranged from lord lieutenants at the top to militia officers and justices of the peace lower down the scale. Commissions in the enlarged army and navy depended to a large extend on political connection, and until about 1710 Marlborough's influence was immense. In the world of finance, attempts were made to infiltrate Tories into the directorates of the Bank of England and the East India Company, and the South Sea Company of 1711 was Harley's Tory riposte to these Whig financial giants. The struggle was a party one, and it grew steadily more ruthless and uncompromising, as the threat of impeachment succeeded verbal criticism, and fear of 'the mob' added to the tension. In London at least, and among the politically articulate, party seemed to dominate daily life. Whatever 'settlement' had been reached twenty years before, there now seemed little acceptance or definition of it. Not since the Civil War had the ruling class been so sharply split. In the bitterness of party conflict social contacts between Whigs and Tories became rare. They had their own clubs, coffee houses, theatres, and perhaps most influential of all their own newspapers.

The lapsing of the Licensing Act in 1695 had given rise to a new generation of newspapers, many of them politically committed. To the official *London Gazette*, the only newspaper regularly published before 1695, was 'sprung that inundation of *Postmen, Postboys, Evening Posts, Supplements, Daily Courants*, and *Protestant Post Boys*, amounting to twenty-one every week', a contemporary writer noted. In addition, an array of literary talent found outlet in the new periodicals of the period – Swift's *Examiner*, Defoe's *Review*, Steele's *Tatler*. The *Review*, which began publication in 1704, and was soon published three times a week, was the outlet Harley had sought since in 1702 he had pointed out to Godolphin the advantage of having 'some discreet writer on the government's side.' Its studied assumption of impartiality hid the fact that it was a propaganda device in the service of the government of the day. Until the last years of the reign the Whigs were slower to respond, but even so the amount of political material published at this time was impressive in quantity if not always in quality. Circulation figures are hard to obtain, and readership figures a matter of guesswork; but a tradition of vigorous, iconoclastic journalism was established which survived recurrent bouts of government displeasure, and although hindered was not emasculated by the prohibition on reporting parliamentary debates. Outside London the first provincial newspapers appeared. In Norwich, Bristol, Worcester, Shrewsbury, Nottingham, Liverpool, Stamford, Newcastle, there was a growing swell of newsprint which would give fifty or so towns their own papers by mid-century. The provincial newspapers took their political and foreign news from the London press, whose views were thus duplicated in the major towns. In contrast to earlier periods, when provincial knowledge of national events was out-of-date and inadequate, an informed public opinion began to emerge on a countrywide basis.

Attempts to exercise some control over the press were made on several occasions, but the measure finally agreed, the Stamp Act of 1712, was less repressive than the censorship urged by some ministers. This tax on newspapers and pamphlets, which was to remain in one form or another until the mid-nineteenth century, led to the disappearance of some publications, including Defoe's pro-government *Review*. In general, the flow of newspapers, pamphlets and periodicals exaggerated the differences between the parties, smeared the respectable majority of both sides with the wilder eccentricities of a minority, and through its invective helped to sustain that savage quality which marked the politics of Anne's reign. Journalists, despite their frequent denigration as Grub Street hacks, became figures to be reckoned with – a fact which explains attempts by the politicians to intimidate or buy some of the most prominent.

The sources provide ample evidence of the degree of popular interest in the party struggles of the period. Yet radical demands were notably lacking, and the disputes, inside and outside Parliament, were between men of property. There was no equivalent of the levellers of the Commonwealth period nor of the reformers of George III's reign. The reasons for this lack of radical political activity are not easily established, though the growth of a populist Toryism, driven by a distaste for foreigners and Dissenters, 'Fanaticks' and high taxes, may be among them. The ready availability of cheap spirits which dulled the mind, lengthy hours of work, and lack of education, all probably played some part. The relative stability of grain prices, wages, and the population level, blunted the sharper edges of the economic system except at times of bad harvests, such as those of 1708–10. The operation of the Poor Law relieved some of the worst distress, reduced vagrancy, and kept the rural areas quiet.

There was also the forbidding unanimity of both parties on the continuance of a hierarchical society. So Defoe, when he wrote in defence of an Englishman's political rights, stressed that he did 'not place this right upon the inhabitants, but upon the *Freeholders* . . . the other inhabitants are but sojourners, like lodgers in a house.' The Whigs might be more prepared than the Tories to recognise the new forms of property created by the financial and commercial developments of the period, but this enlargement of the governing classes was a limited exercise. With a record number of voters involved in the electoral process, there were no calls for parliamentary reform in the sense of extending the franchise or redistributing seats. What criticism there was from discontented or radical Whigs focused on the power of the executive, and the political influence thought to stem from its financial resources. While the sums disbursed on military and naval purposes were so huge that effective parliamentary scrutiny of them was impossible, the relatively small amounts available to the government through the Crown's Civil List (the sum voted by Parliament for the monarch's own use) were constant targets for inquiry and attack. The neurotic reaction aroused by the very term, 'prime minister', was further proof of the distrust of anything which smacked of strong, centralised government. In this sense at least Parliament was 'eternally vigilant' in the cause of liberty, but the latter was a quality viewed narrowly in both ideological and practical terms.

Since the beginning of the reign, Godolphin and Marlborough had formed the core of the government with the support of the court and administration MPs, but during the six years since Anne's accession the vital buttressing groups 'of party MPs were increasingly Whig rather than Tory.' Ironically, in the period from 1708 to 1710 the party most committed to war was in office at a time when the most challenging task was to negotiate peace with a defeated and humbled France. Marlborough's third successive victory at Oudenarde had helped the Junto to gain power, but the government showed itself insensitive both to feeling at home, where war weariness had set in, and to the difficulties of negotiating with Louis XIV. In the summer of 1709 he was willing to agree to all allied demands except the one which expected him to use French troops to force his grandson Philip out of Spain. As Marlborough remarked, 'If I were in the place of the King of France I should venture the loss of my country much sooner

than be obliged to join my troops for the forcing of my grandson.'
Widespread feeling that the war was being protracted beyond reason
was increased in September 1709 with the 'very murdering battle' of
Malplaquet, another victory for Marlborough, but one in which allied
losses (mostly Dutch) were heavier than the French. Tories denounced
'the butcher's bill', attacked Marlborough and his Whig associates as
militarists, and pressed for peace and lower taxes. Although great
landowners with money to spare could invest in government funds,
and so compensate for any fall in land values and rents, many of
the gentry were experiencing hard times. In 1709 and 1710 harvests
were poor, tenants' rents fell into arrears, and any money received
continued to be subject to the land tax of four shillings in the pound,
a galling burden to men who saw tax-free fortunes being made on
the money markets. It was this general resentment which lay behind
Tory attitudes in and after 1710, and which found its barbed voice in
Henry St John.

Faced with a rising storm of grievances, the government stumbled
from mishap to crisis. Its bill of 1709 to naturalise foreign Protestant
refugees (a measure which revealed the enlightened side of Whiggism)
roused the xenophobic fury of High Tories and many others; but the
din on this issue was low-pitched compared with the clamour of the
Sacheverell trial. On 5 November 1709 Henry Sacheverell preached
at St Paul's a sermon in which he moved from routine attacks on
Dissenters to the more dangerous topic of 'the utter illegality of
resistance upon any pretence whatsoever'. The sermon, printed as
a pamphlet entitled *The Perils of False Brethren, both in Church and State*,
was an attack on the Whig government of the day and, by inference,
on the 1688 Revolution and the Protestant Succession. The episode is
a reminder of the continuing importance of the pulpit as a channel
of political propaganda. With most of the clergy Tory in sympathy,
parish churches reverberated with political sermons at election time,
as effective a method of reaching the electorate as the newspaper and
pamphlet polemics of the day. The printed version of the 5 November
sermon probably ran to a hundred thousand copies, and the fearsome
paper war which followed drew in some six hundred titles within the year.
Moving onto the offensive, the government determined to impeach
Sacheverell, 'the inconsiderable tool of a party', as a salutary lesson
to the High Tories. The impeachment proceedings at Westminster
Hall testified once more to the endemic violence which lurked behind
religious and political differences. In contrast to the legal dignity and
fashionable attendance in evidence at the trial were scenes of terrifying
disorder in parts of the capital, with Dissenting chapels being burnt
in the most serious disturbances in London in the early eighteenth
century. A verdict of guilty was reached by a narrow majority, and

accompanied by a penalty – abstention from preaching for three years – which may have been a heavier cross for Sacheverell to bear than most, but was still derisory.

More important than the wild scenes of rejoicing at the 'acquittal' were the political calculations of Harley. Sensing the discomfiture of the ministry as the addresses coming in from the counties and boroughs showed how opinion had turned against it, he continued to build up a strong opposition – High Tories, disenchanted Scottish Whigs, Shrewsbury (the respected moderate who had worked with him on the Triennial Bill in 1694) – and to negotiate with the Queen. Piece by piece during 1710 the administration was dismantled, ministers being quietly eased out of office until the final stroke came with Godolphin's dismissal and Harley's appointment as Chancellor of the Exchequer. All this was accompanied despite a Whig majority in the Commons, a sign that royal favour or disfavour was still of crucial importance. The general election of October, which saw a landslide Tory victory, was perhaps the most bitterly fought of the reign. It followed rather than preceded the shaping of the ministry, though its outcome was not unexpected given, as one Whig had noted months before, the way 'the common people are now set.' The unpopularity of the long war and the threat to the Church which the Sacheverell impeachment seemed to portend, all helped to give Harley what appeared to be a solid majority. As he commented, 'What a difference there is between the true strength of this nation, and the fictitious one of the Whigs.'

Although the palace revolution engineered by Harley was supported by the results of the election, the size of the Tory victory increased rather than lessened Harley's problems. Walpole noted, 'The changing hands in England always ends in the changing of measures', but what the new measures might be was far from clear. The defeat of another British army in Spain in 1710 at the battle of Brihuega, and the failure of an amphibious assault on Quebec in 1711, knocked away two of the supports from the favoured Tory strategy of a maritime war. The dismal news of these disasters compared poorly with Marlborough's final achievement, the forcing of the defensive lines which guarded northern France. Harley's administration was still a coalition of different interests, though it was far removed from the 'balanced' ministries attempted earlier in the reign. Party feeling between Whigs and Tories was at its highest pitch, with 'Monarchy and the Church' pitted against 'The Revolution Settlement and the Protestant Succession'. In general attitude Harley was far removed from the 'hot Tories' who flocked to Westminster after their election triumph – 'naturally selfish, peevish, narrow-spirited, ill-natured, conceited of themselves, envious of any ability in others', he had once described them. They represented the feelings of the landed gentry, but these amounted to a series of grievances rather than a positive policy: hostility to a continental war and continental allies, to corruption in high places (this last given a sharper edge by Marlborough's demand to be made Captain General for life), to Dissenters and moneyed men. It was a *pot-pourri*, with Jacobitism one of its ingredients, the sentiments of an opposition party as aired at the meetings of the new backbench October Club. Its main triumph came with the passing of an Act in 1711 insisting on a qualification in landed property for MPs. Candidates were to possess real estate worth £600 a year for county seats, £300 a year for borough seats. The provisions of the Act were easily evaded by men of substance, but its symbolic importance was shown by the fact that more than a century later its abolition was one of the Six Points of the Chartist programme. The strength of the Tory conviction that only those with a genuine stake in the country through the possession of land – rather than in stocks and shares, cash or goods – should participate in its governance was shown by the passing through the Commons (though it was defeated in the Lords) of a bill imposing similar qualifications on potential JPs.

In one direction at least the mood of the Country Tories reflected that of the nation at large – the insistent demand for peace. Since 1709, perhaps indeed since 1706 and Ramillies, it was hard to see why the war continued. Suspicions increased that it was being prolonged to protect vested financial interests at home and the grasping Dutch abroad. For Harley the opening of peace negotiations had both national and political advantages. Peace would cut taxes and help the landed classes, distinguish his administration from its Junto-dominated predecessor, keep the fissiparous Tory groups under control, and guarantee popular acclaim. Yet the thing was easier sketched in theory than done in practice. A dash for peace might wreck the Grand Alliance, and undermine the system of credit and investment on which the war economy was based. There was a wide gulf between the responsibilities of government and the demands of headstrong Tory backbenchers, and Harley's own personality had to be taken into account. In personal and financial matters he displayed a puritan probity; in politics a predilection for the devious and subtle. So it was by way of a baffling 'double policy' of secret negotiations and public pronouncements, oblique manoeuvres and ambiguous dealings, that Harley moved slowly towards a negotiated settlement. To reassure the Queen (anxious for peace, but not at any price), the financial interest, the Dutch and Austrian allies, Tories in and out of Parliament, was a task calling for the most delicate political touch.

Harley's position was more precarious than it seemed at first sight, with the government opposed in the Commons not only by the Whigs but by many of its own backbenchers. St John had come into the ministry in 1710 as Secretary of State for the Northern Department, but because of his anti-Dutch views and his reputation for indiscretion was kept in the dark about the full extent of the peace negotiations until the spring of 1711. Nor did Harley help matters by accepting the title of Earl of Oxford and the ancient office of Lord High Treasurer at this time, for although his new finance agency, the South Sea Company, was successfully launched and took over £9,500,000 of floating or unfunded government debt, his departure from the Commons loosened his grip on political developments. The ministry, as Swift put it, stood 'like an isthmus between the Whigs on the one side and the violent Tories on the other', but he feared that the tempest would be too great for Harley to succeed. Both Swift, through his authorship of two powerful pamphlets in support of the government's negotiating stance, *The Conduct of the Allies* (published ten days before the Commons was due to debate the issue) and *Some Remarks on the Barrier Treaty*, and Defoe, by way of the *Review* as well as a number of pamphlets, were used to effect by Harley at this crucial time. These two famed writers, a contemporary noted, had become 'fellow labourers' in the Lord Treasurer's service.

If on the issue of the peace, Harley was despite all difficulties and distractions in a stronger position than the Whigs, on the other looming question, the succession, danger lay ahead. On this matter – 'the circumstance that sits heaviest upon the hearts of all thinking and serious men', one observer wrote in 1712 – the Whigs were rock-solid for Hanover, while the Tories were racked by indecision. The comparative unanimity with which they had accepted the Act of Settlement in 1701 had long since disappeared. For many Tories, the choice between a distant German prince (for Sophia was almost eighty, and her son George was likely to be Britain's next monarch), unknown but by all accounts unprepossessing, and the Stuart claimant, was not an easy one. Some were for Hanover, some for the Pretender, many undecided, pulled one way by reason and calculation, another by emotion and tradition. Nor could the two issues be kept separate. Harley's secret diplomacy, his use of Jacobite sympathisers in the negotiations and his need for Jacobite votes in the Commons to push through the peace terms, alienated not only the Dutch but also Hanover, and at home the great non-party magnates such as Shrewsbury. To some, the government's readiness to accept a Bourbon on the Spanish throne, the rumour of the 'restraining orders' which limited British troops to strictly defensive operations (orders communicated to the French but not to the allies), and the obvious indifference to Austrian and Dutch interests, signified a new understanding with France, and possibly an acceptance of the Pretender.

Danger also threatened Harley from another quarter, in the unlikely shape of an alliance between the Whig Junto and Nottingham, whose loss of office and anger at Harley's peace negotiations had made him, so one associate reported, as 'fiercely wild as a creature of the desert'. The agreement was based on the discreditable concession by the Junto that it would support an Occasional Conformity bill on condition that its sponsor Nottingham would oppose the peace terms laid before Parliament. The bill was passed – though its practical effects were to be slight – but the menace to the government's position in the Lords, where Nottingham's motion of 'No Peace without Spain' had been approved, dissolved when Harley in an unexpected move persuaded the Queen in January 1712 to create twelve new Tory peers. This stroke threw the Whigs into confusion, but the aftermath emphasised the now irreconcilable differences between Harley and St John. In later life St John explained his aims at this time: 'To have the government of the state in our hands . . . to break the body of the Whigs, to render their supports useless to them, and to fill the employments of the House, down to the meanest, with Tories.' The main targets were Marlborough and Walpole. The former was dismissed from all his posts, while Walpole who had already resigned as Secretary at War was found guilty of corruption, expelled from the Commons, and sent to the Tower. From there he wrote darkly, 'I heartily despise what *I shall one day revenge.*'

To take the assault further, to strike at the Whigs in the localities, took time; and this was denied to St John. Like Harley the year before, he accepted a peerage (as Viscount Bolingbroke), and so removed himself to the Lords at a critical moment in the fast-developing political situation. The events of these years illustrated the continued prestige and role of the House of Lords. At a time when Whigs were outnumbered by Tories in the Commons by two to one, the upper house remained a bastion of Whig strength with its ranks of Whig peers and bishops. The Junto had dominated government from the Lords earlier in the reign, and to contemporaries it seemed natural that leading ministers should be in the Lords, leaving direct contact with the Commons to more junior politicians. Harley, it is true, had refused to leave the Commons in 1710, and St John's demand of a peerage in 1712 seems to have been dictated by reasons of personal pride rather than political calculation. Whether in the Lords or Commons, he was faced with a situation which combined exciting opportunities with formidable difficulties. Harley above all, though declining in health and sobriety, stood in his way – a shambling figure, but still one to be reckoned with. In addition to the differences of temperament between the two men a fundamental divergence of political purpose was now evident. St John, though hoping to the end that the Pretender might give a signal from St Germain of his conversion to Protestantism, had accepted for all practical purposes a Hanoverian succession, and his concern was to confront the new monarch with the inevitability of single-party government. His efforts to root out the Whigs from both national and local office, and replace them with Tories, would ensure that whoever succeeded Anne would have to deal with a solid front of office-holders with himself at their head. Harley, in contrast, was nearer the now-antiquated tradition of the impartial 'managers' who had played so important a role in government since 1688. Like St John, he also kept in touch with the Pretender (as did Marlborough and many others), but as an insurance policy rather than in any active, purposeful way.

Although the government with the help of Jacobite MPs got the terms of the Treaty of Utrecht through Parliament in April 1713, and the Tories went on to win the general election in the late summer with a massive total of more than 360 seats, the struggle between Harley and St John (Oxford and Bolingbroke as they now were), and the conflict of principles and emotions in many Tory hearts, were taking an ominous toll. As one of Oxford's associates pointed out to him, the pamphleteers were no longer concerned with the fight between Whigs and Tories – the distinction they were making was 'between the Tories themselves, as Hanover Tory and Pretender Tory, English Tory and French Tory, for trade and against it.' When Parliament assembled it contained a few more Jacobites, making a total of perhaps fifty or sixty in all, but this minority was divided even on the issue which seemed to bind them together. Some were ready for armed intervention by the Pretender; others hoped that their pressure would smooth the way for a peaceful accession by James. Although there was a group of committed Hanoverian Tories, the majority were Tory doubtfuls, swinging first one way and then another, but in the end never likely to overturn the Hanoverian succession in favour of a Catholic Stuart. With Anne's health declining fast, the divisions within the Tory party over the succession were a recipe for disaster; for as always the Whigs 'were intire', as one put it, on the dynastic question.

The Tory peace, with well-publicised gains in Spanish American trade, was a popular one, and it was not Oxford's fault that the Treaty of Utrecht gave little to the allies that they could not have gained in 1708. Although the crowns of France and Spain were to be kept separate, Louis XIV's grandson was recognised as Philip V of Spain, albeit without the Spanish Netherlands and the Italian territories which went to the Emperor. France kept some of the gains of Louis's earlier years, but the Dutch right to garrison a line of 'barrier fortresses' in the new Austrian Netherlands promised to check future French designs in that sensitive area. Apart from confirming British possession of Gibraltar and Minorca, bases which strengthened the nation's new position as a Mediterranean power, the Treaty settled some long-standing wrangles in marginal but nevertheless valuable areas of the Atlantic empires. Britain gained Acadia (Nova Scotia) from France, together with recognition of its sovereignty over Hudson Bay and Newfoundland, and was granted full possession of the Caribbean island of St Kitts. Finally, Spain granted the *asiento*, (the right to supply its American possessions with slaves) for a period of thirty years to the South Sea Company – a clause which led to much excitement, but in the end produced more trouble than profit for the new corporation. In general the peace settlement indicated the arrival of Britain as a formidable new power on the international scene. The retention of naval and commercial bases showed a determination, spurred by increasingly influential merchants and financiers, to secure and expand the nation's trade overseas – if necessary by force.

That their continental allies were less than enthusiastic about the terms of the treaty, and the way in which they had been negotiated, was of little concern to most Englishmen; and in any case diplomatic niceties, even diplomatic realities, were soon overshadowed by the Queen's worsening health. The very mention of the succession was now enough to throw the Tory ranks into disarray. No pledge arrived from the Pretender, and none ever would, but many Tories still clung to the unlikely prospect of a Protestant James III. In an effort to attract more Tory support, Bolingbroke pushed through the Schism Act, intended to weaken nonconformity by abolishing Dissenting schools and academies. It was never to be properly enforced, and its immediate result was to deepen the split with Oxford, and to heighten still further the alarm of Whigs and Dissenters about what might happen after Anne's death. Nor, in a more general way, did the measure help Bolingbroke's reputation, already tainted by his dubious private life and his deism; for, like Oxford, he had been educated at a Dissenting academy.

The events of the summer of 1714 have a lurid air of drama, as the weakening Queen inched towards the decision to dismiss Oxford. The deed was finally done on 27 July, but Bolingbroke was to enjoy his hard-won triumph for only two days. He was not called upon to form a new ministry, and if he had been, ranged against him were Whigs and Dissenters, Hanover Tories and the moneyed interest, the formidable figure of Marlborough, and the Elector of Hanover – still distant in person, but present in the thoughts and calculations of the politicians. As Anne lay dying her last conscious act of state, on 30 July, was to make Shrewsbury, one of the men of 1688, Lord

Treasurer. On 1 August the Queen died and Bolingbroke could only lament, 'the Earl of Oxford was removed on Tuesday, the Queen died on Sunday. What a world is this! And how fortune banters us.' With Anne's death, the careful procedure set out in the Regency Act of 1706 was put into effect, and a Regency Council ruled England until George I arrived from Hanover in September.

4 The triumph of the Whigs, 1714–1742

As George I slowly made his way towards his new kingdom it was by no means a foregone conclusion that he would turn exclusively to the Whigs for his first ministry. The Council of Regency included some Tories, and it seemed possible that, like William III on his arrival in England, the new monarch would look for a 'balanced' administration. Although repelled by Tory dabblings with the cause of the Pretender, and angered by the tactics of Tory ministers in the peace negotiations, and by their abrupt ending of subsidies to Hanover, the King had, according to one observer, a 'desire at first to employ those of both denominations whom he had heard a good account of.' No ruler could ignore the fact that the political nation as represented by the electorate in Anne's reign had shown itself to be largely Tory, but in 1714 the Tories paid the penalty for their indecision on the succession, and for their hostility to the continental war. As George I and his German advisers reconstructed the ministry, Bolingbroke's vision of single-party government came close to reality, but not in the sense he had intended. One or two Tories remained, but the new ministry was overwhelmingly Whig. Halifax, Orford, Wharton, Stanhope, Townshend, Sunderland, Walpole, Pulteney, made an impressive combination of veterans and younger men. The general election of early 1715 swung the Whigs' way after an intensive campaign by the Whig press to identify Toryism with Jacobitism, and the new House contained 372 Whigs and 186 Tories – a reversal of the party balance after the Tory landslide victory two years before. Although the Tories were by no means crushed, and their support in the counties and open boroughs probably displayed as much popular strength as the Whigs, in parliamentary terms the election was decisive.

The election and its aftermath took their toll both of Tory numbers and Tory nerve. Bolingbroke fled to the continent and into the Pretender's service, so lending credence to Whig assertions about his Jacobitism, while Oxford was impeached and sent to the

Tower. The Tories were further racked by the dilemma presented by Jacobite risings in Scotland and Northumberland in the autumn of 1715, followed by the landing of the Pretender at the end of the year. Without the support either of troops from France (where Louis XIV had just died) or of High Tory groups, these were forlorn ventures and in February 1716 a disconsolate Pretender returned to France. He had always maintained that a successful coup could not be attempted simply on the basis of a Scottish rising, and that it was essential to gain support at the heart of England's political and military establishment. Faced with the actual presence of the Pretender on British soil most Tories rallied, with whatever reservations, to the Protestant succession, as they had done in 1688 and 1701. The reaction of King and ministers to the Fifteen was, by the standards of the time, lenient, and took due regard of class differences – sequestration for the propertied, transportation for the poor – but the risings were a reminder both of the deep-rooted discontent in much of Scotland, and of the vulnerability of the Hanoverian succession. As long as a rival claimant existed there was the threat that with external help he might turn from a wanderer in foreign courts to the leader of an invading army. From 1714 onwards British foreign policy, intricate enough since the Revolution because of its continental and overseas dimensions, was further complicated by the new problem of security for Hanover, and by the necessity of preventing an alliance between foreign powers and the Pretender.

More immediately, the rebellion, which had been preceded by serious disturbances in London and other parts of the country, some of them Jacobite in sympathy, served to justify the Whig pursuit of hapless Tory opponents. Leading the hunt was Robert Walpole, appointed First Lord of the Treasury and Chancellor of the Exchequer after the death of Halifax. His search for Tories extended down to the small fry of the bureaucracy, while in the shires the earlier Tory purge of Whig JPs was reversed. A belated sense of realism among the Tories, and the demonstration that the party was still a force at election-time, could not halt the Whig march to power, and it soon became clear that ambitious Tories who wanted political office would have to turn Whig. Bolingbroke had written even before George I reached England, 'the grief of my soul is this, I see plainly that the Tory party is gone', and if he was thinking of the Tories as a party of government he was right. Although Toryism in opposition was far from being a negligible force, for years to come attention turned to the manoeuvres of the Whig leadership. The party struggle of Anne's reign was over. The issues which had divided the political nation had disappeared or were subsiding. Peace had been made with France, and the events of 1714–15 had shown a general acceptance of the Hanoverian succession. Moreover, the final prorogation of Convocation in 1717, and the repeal in the winter of 1718–19 of the Occasional Conformity and Schism Acts of the last years of Anne's reign, brought a lessening of tension in religious affairs. The Church's attempt to reassert its independent authority had failed, and it became ever more dependent on the government of the day. Suddenly, the world of Sacheverell and the non-jurors seemed far distant, and a theologian pondered the different atmosphere when he wrote 'how the world's changed, since the time when a word against the clergy passed for rank atheism, and now to speak tolerably of them passes for superstition.' Pamphlets and periodicals reflected the trend away from religious controversy; the paper wars of the future would be fought not on the issue of the Church in danger, but over such secular matters as the South Sea Bubble and the Excise Bill.

Evidence of the changed circumstances came in 1716 with the repeal of the Triennial Act and its replacement by a Septennial Act. It was an alteration in the rules of the political game by a party in office, and determined to stay in power. Under the old legislation there would have been general elections in 1718 and 1721, years of maximum discomfort for the Whig leadership, split on the first occasion, and reeling from the shock of the 'Bubble' crisis on the second. The Septennial Act was of a piece with the legislation of 1711 introducing property qualifications for MPs, the Stamp Act of 1712, and the Riot Act of 1715 which made the continuation of unlawful assembly by twelve or more persons a felony, carrying the death penalty. The Septennial Act strengthened the executive, reduced political activity, and lessened popular participation in the constituencies. Ostensibly designed to put an end to expensive and unnecessary elections which it claimed had caused 'more violent and lasting heats and animosities among the subjects of this realm, than were ever known before', the Act laid the foundations for the solid platform of Walpole's future government. Coinciding with the fading of party passions in the parliamentary arena, it brought an unfamiliar calm to the constituencies which had for so long reverberated to the din of Whig and Tory campaigning.

The Whig administration was no happy band of brothers. Men as powerful and ambitious as Sunderland, Walpole, Townshend and Stanhope could not be expected to co-operate in easy harmony, and the restraints imposed on them by the experienced veterans of the Junto were removed with the deaths in 1715 of Halifax, Wharton and Somers. The political scene was in any case subject to new tensions and problems. The 'reversionary interest', that is the presence of the heir to the throne, the Prince of Wales, made its appearance at this time. It was to be a disturbing factor for most of the reigns of George I and

George II, for the eldest sons of both monarchs formed a focal point of opposition around which discontented politicians could gather without incurring charges of disloyalty to the Hanoverian dynasty. In domestic politics the King's accompanying Hanoverian advisers, mistresses and friends, the unpopular 'German junta', had to be taken into account. On the continent, the King's possessions brought a new and troubling dimension to British diplomacy, embroiling it in the difficult affairs of northern Europe, where Britain's commercial interests in the Baltic often seemed at odds with Hanover's German concerns.

The difficulties associated with the new connection proved particularly acute over the issue of whether the traditional ally, Austria, or the rising military power of Prussia – neighbour and rival of Hanover – should become Britain's partner against France. The problem was muffled for most of George I's reign by the coming together of Britain and France in formal alliance in late 1716, an unexpected but logical development. For Britain the alliance neutralised the Jacobite threat, for the Pretender was forced to leave French territory, and turned to the less formidable powers of Spain and Sweden for support. It also removed the danger of one powerful enemy from Hanover's exposed borders. For France the alliance promised some strengthening of her international position in the fraught years following the accession of a minor. In more general terms, the understanding between the two most powerful enemies of the war years brought some guarantee of permanence to the Utrecht settlement, already under threat from revived Spanish ambitions. When the Dutch joined the alliance in 1717, James Stanhope, Secretary of State for the Northern Department, had the satisfaction of bringing together in alliance with Britain a traditional ally and a traditional enemy. In this he was helped by the advice and European contacts of the King. To most of his new subjects a dull man with few redeeming features, able at first to speak only rudimentary English, George I was one of the builders of the new system of alliances which was to keep the peace of Europe for a generation.

By 1717 rifts within the Whig ruling front had turned into a power struggle between Stanhope and Sunderland on the one hand, and on the other Walpole and his brother-in-law Townshend. Townshend's opposition to moves against Sweden which he saw as being Hanoverian rather than British in origin and interest led to his dismissal in April 1717, and the next day Walpole followed him out of office. The first open schism in the Whig ranks had been revealed, and one result was that the continued existence of the Tory party was assured. The next two years of manoeuvring and wrangling between the main Whig groups had much significance for the shape of politics to come. Both factions were committed to the Hanoverian dynasty, and any political difference between them was of emphasis rather than principle. Since by the terms of the Septennial Act no election was due until 1722 – and ministries in any case were not turned out by election results – the only way back into office for Walpole and Townshend was by hindering the government from carrying out its essential business. This they might do by a variety of methods; appeals to the national interest, links with other dissident Whigs and the heir to the throne, alliances of convenience with the Tories. All these were likely to involve them in postures inconsistent with their earlier declarations and actions. So Walpole and Townshend denounced the Septennial Act, which they had helped to push through while in office, complained of the corruption of the ministry, and opposed the repeal of the Schism and Occasional Conformity Acts.

Although the government was concerned by the campaign of dissident groups which Walpole organised, it was not seriously shaken until it introduced in 1719 the ill-conceived Peerage Bill, a measure which would have permitted the creation of only a further six peerages (except those replacing extinct titles). This attempt by Stanhope and Sunderland to make the House of Lords virtually a closed corporation was accompanied by vague but ominous talk about repealing the Septennial Act so that the existing House of Commons could run on indefinitely. In December 1719, after much lobbying behind the scenes, Walpole spoke against the Peerage Bill in one of the great set-piece triumphs of parliamentary history, and it was defeated in the Commons by almost a hundred votes. Walpole had made his point, and in the spring of 1720 he and Townshend were readmitted to the ministry. Though for the moment Walpole held the junior position of Paymaster General, there is evidence that he was in fact already back in control of the Treasury. Walpole's tactics formed a prototype for later politicians out of office, though rarely did they apply the same skill to their predicament, nor did they often find the same opening offered by the government of the day.

The timing of these events was crucial, for Walpole and Townshend returned to office just as excitement was mounting over the spiralling profits being made through buying and selling South Sea Company stock. The episode of the South Sea 'Bubble' demonstrated not only evidence of the credulity of English investors, but also the close links between financial confidence and political stability. Harley's South Sea Company of 1711 was essentially a finance company designed to take over part of the National Debt, although it had as its ostensible commercial base the trading rights in Spanish America which it was hoped would be wrested from Spain at the peace settlement. After the Treaty of Utrecht formalised various concessions in Spanish America, the Company rapidly developed into a powerful rival to the Bank of England. Between 1717 and 1720 it negotiated with the Stanhope–Sunderland ministry to take over £31 million of the National Debt. The bait used by company directors to persuade holders of high-interest annuities to convert them into Company stock was the considerable capital now at the Company's disposal (for it was authorised to create £1 of new stock for every £1 of Debt it took over), and the lucrative trade expected after the Utrecht concessions. The unusual, arguably fraudulent, element was the omission of any agreed ratio of stock to be given in exchange for the annuities; as Company shares rose in market value, the Company offered fewer and fewer to bond-holders anxious to join in the scramble, and so created a surplus stock which was all profit. The higher the price of the shares the more profit accrued to the directors and their associates, and by June 1720 their own actions and the lemming-like rush of the investing public to buy at almost any price, had pushed up the price of £100 of Company stock to the staggering figure of £1050. The inevitable crash, and the ruin of many companies and individuals, not only tore at the financial fabric of the nation, but seemed likely to damage the whole political system.

In an atmosphere of hysteria, recrimination and panic, Walpole exuded a massive calming influence. He resisted the temptation to seek easy popularity by attacking corrupt and inefficient ministers, and instead took expert advice to patch together a rescue operation, which impressed on the financial institutions the fact that Treasury affairs were being handled with a sureness of touch not seen since Godolphin. In effect, Walpole placed himself between the ministry and its vengeful opponents, so earning himself the first of his several opprobious titles – 'the Screenmaster General'. As always, he acted with calculation. To lash the Stanhope–Sunderland ministry for its mishandling of the crisis might topple his immediate political rivals, but it would wreck his reputation with the King, and the ensuing chaos might bring a Tory, even a Jacobite, revival. To calculation was added fortune. Stanhope died early in 1721 while defending his reputation in the Lords. Sunderland, suspected of complicity in the manipulation of stock, had to give up the Treasury, though he retained the confidence of the King and remained a dangerous political opponent.

Walpole had made himself indispensable on political and financial grounds, and his reward came in April 1721 when he regained his old posts of First Lord of the Treasury and Chancellor of the Exchequer, with Townshend as Secretary of State for the Northern Department. This new position of strength was confirmed by the election of 1722, which saw a series of Whig gains. It was a sign of the importance of Crown influence and of the weakening of the Tory party that even after the scandals and mishaps of the previous two years the Whigs met little effective resistance. Sunderland's death during the election meant that in little more than a half-dozen years death or disgrace had removed most of the leading Whigs who had formed George I's first ministry. It was Walpole, the great survivor, who profited most from this casualty list, but skill as well as luck explains his rise to power. His political acumen and lack of scruple were revealed by his exploitation of a feeble Jacobite plot of 1721–22 associated with Francis Atterbury, the High Tory Bishop of Rochester who had been tireless in opposition to the Whigs. Flimsy evidence was inflated to threatening proportions by Walpole, who succeeded in convincing King and Parliament that a serious Jacobite danger existed. The imprisonment and subsequent banishment of Atterbury was the final demonstration for many Tories that acceptance of and by the Hanoverian regime was their only path to political office. Astride this path, however, now stood the heavy figure of Robert Walpole, whose hold on power for the unprecedented span of twenty years, was to stamp a deep imprint on English politics.

After the political changes and turmoil which at times seemed designed to make effective government impossible, the nation was entering under Walpole a period of stability. His long – to his opponents endless – period of office makes it easy to overlook the fact that Walpole had already been an MP for twenty years. He first entered Parliament in 1701, had cut his political teeth on the party rivalries of Anne's reign, had seen the effect of the long wars on England's manhood and money, and had come to political maturity during the first uncertain years of the new dynasty. He was more often in than out of post, a Whig but a Court Whig, tenacious of office for both the power and the perquisites which it brought. His reinstatement to senior office in 1721 opened the way to his personal dominance, the 'Robinocracy'. Since the Revolution, with Parliament meeting in regular session for mainly financial reasons, the head of the Treasury was the crucial link between the executive and the legislature. Godolphin and Harley had both held the position, and, significantly, had been known as 'prime minister', but unlike Walpole they were in the Lords for all or part of the time, held office for shorter periods, and were confronted and at times overwhelmed by the problems of war finance. Walpole's combination of the First Lordship of the Treasury with the Chancellorship of the Exchequer gave him a stronger base both in Parliament and within the government. Much ink has been spilt on Walpole's reasons for remaining in the Commons; it seems to have been less a specific decision than a gradual realisation of the advantages of staying put, and perhaps as much a matter of personal predilection as political calculation.

In the Lords were arrayed Walpole's principal rivals and associates, from Carteret to Townshend; in the Commons, with neither supporters nor enemies of comparable stature in sight, Walpole was a dominant figure who engrossed all aspects of government business and established a rapport with many backbench MPs. He was, his opponent Chesterfield admitted, 'the best parliamentarian, and the ablest manager of parliament, that I believe ever lived.'

In both Houses, Walpole exploited to the full the patronage of the Crown in building a supportive Court party. In the Lords he took care with the aid of Bishop Gibson of London to maintain the Whiggish character of the twenty-six bishops, to nurture the sixteen representative and generally acquiescent Scottish peers, and to hold out hopes of posts or honours to other peers (it was Walpole who revived the Order of the Bath). In the Commons, Walpole brought an unsurpassed dedication to the art of putting together a larger Court party than had ever existed before. Personally unsentimental but politically discriminating in his distribution of place, promotion, pension and contract, Walpole subordinated all other considerations to the single criterion of loyalty to his administration. The Septennial Act helped him in this process; for after 1722 Walpole had to face only three further elections in the next nineteen years. Towards the end of his tenure of office it was estimated that about a third of MPs were placemen. In the absence of party cohesion and party discipline, they formed the essential core of government support – but to the opposition they were stigmatised as 'a packed jury, a corrupt majority of his creatures [with] those posts and places which ought never to be given to any but for the good of the public.'

As necessary as parliamentary votes was the continuing support of the monarch. The return to office of Walpole and Townshend despite their association with the Prince of Wales had shown that George I's reaction to his ministers depended less on personal than on political considerations. The vulnerability of Walpole, or of any other minister of this period, was shown by the general expectation when George I died in 1727 that the new King would remove Walpole from office in favour of Spencer Compton, who had been treasurer of his household. Fortunately for Walpole, the change could not be made at once, and he had not only the Queen on his side but also the confessed ineptitude of his supposed successor. Walpole was able to demonstrate his usefulness, if not indispensability, by securing for George II the most generous civil list ever provided by Parliament, and meanwhile – as that shrewd if not always reliable observer Lord Hervey put it – the King had time to cool, the Queen to think, and Walpole to work.

Whig dominance was accompanied by Tory proscription as

Walpole continued to eliminate his old political opponents from both central and local government. Arguments have recently been advanced that most Tories by now had abandoned Jacobitism, that they formed an identifiable party loyal to the Hanoverian dynasty, commanding considerable public support, and eager to share office. Of these assertions only that relating to the Tories' continuing electoral support would find complete acceptance. On the key issue of Jacobite sentiments conclusive evidence is hard to find; what is beyond doubt, and politically decisive, is that Walpole managed to brand the Toryism of his day with the imprint of the Pretender, and with the support of the monarch acted accordingly. Place and pension, contract and court sinecure, were denied to the Tories. There would be no creation of Tory peerages to counterbalance Whig dominance in the Commons. In the localities the Tories found that lord lieutenantships eluded them at one level, commissions of the peace at another. High Anglican clerics did not obtain bishoprics; the younger sons of Tory families could no longer look for a career in the armed forces. There was no purge as drastic as in 1715–16, no more wholesale dismissals, simply a care that the Tories should never hold more than a minority position. The whole system of official appointments and influence gradually closed against those who from the evidence of the number of Tory MPs returned by the more open constituencies may well still have formed a majority of the politically articulate part of the nation. As one of them lamented, 'We are kept out of all public employments of power and profit, and live like aliens and pilgrims in the land of our nativity . . . no quality, no fortune, no eloquence, no learning, no wisdom, no probing is of any use to any man of our unfortunate denomination.'

Careful distribution of patronage, manipulation of political machinery, effective parliamentary oratory, and those financial and administrative abilities which led a contemporary to describe him as 'the best figureman in the kingdom', explain only in part Walpole's political longevity. In as far as it is possible to discern a general tide of opinion in the country, then Walpole – until 1733 at least – swam with it rather than against it. Public weariness with war and high taxes, with religious fervour and political strife, struck a sympathetic chord in the new first minister. There would be no repetition of the Tory attempts of 1710–14 to introduce radical changes in the political and ecclesiastical structure. Working within a consensus, using existing political methods to the full, he increased his personal powers at the same time as he brought stability to the nation. For Walpole the two achievements were indistinguishable, and there is no doubting the strength of his conviction that he alone could bring the nation what it most needed: peace, low taxation, and a calming of political and religious fervour. Beyond that, he saw the needs of the country mainly in economic terms, and here he was helped by a recovery in trade after the long years of war, and by the falling grain prices which followed the good harvests of the 1730s. A series of Acts between 1721 and 1724 demonstrated the approach of an administration intent on reform and efficiency – up to a point. In an attempt to cut down smuggling, increase revenue and encourage re-exports, the government established a bonded warehouse system for tea, cocoa and chocolate; export duties were removed from more than a hundred manufactured articles; bounties were given to selected industries; and a simplified Book of Rates was introduced. The Sinking Fund established in 1717 to help reduce the National Debt by an accumulation of regular instalments set aside for that purpose was kept in being by Walpole, though after 1733 he did not hesitate to raid the Fund to help meet current expenditure. In Walpole's book a country lightly taxed would be one politically content, unlikely to welcome Jacobite claimants who might, among other horrors, repudiate the National Debt. In this context the cutting of the land tax from the three to two shillings in the £ in 1725 had for Walpole significant political implications.

One of the most difficult crises to confront Walpole in his early years of power occurred in Ireland, where a furious controversy blew up over the affair of Wood's Halfpence. It was a crisis Walpole inherited rather than created, but his handling of it showed more concern for political advantage in England than for the roots of the grievance in Ireland. The dominance of Protestant landowners, the operation of Poynings' Law, and the appointing of the Irish executive in London, seemed to ensure comfortable control of the island's affairs; and since the accession of George I Irish affairs had slipped low in the priorities of Whig ministers in London. The 1715 election had returned a Whig majority to the Irish House of Commons, and since neither the Triennial Act nor its successor, the Septennial Act, applied to Ireland, there need be no further election for the rest of the reign. Irish indignation had already been roused by the passing at Westminster in 1719 of a Declaratory Act which gave Parliament the right to hear legal appeals from Ireland and to pass laws 'of sufficient force and validity to bind the kingdom and people of Ireland'; and this reached new and passionate heights over the patent obtained by an Englishman, William Wood, in 1722 to mint copper coins for Ireland. At first sight an unlikely issue to provoke such uproar, the affair aroused Irish fears about interference with their coinage, and strengthened feelings of resentment about English patronage and exploitation. Walpole's solution to a situation which he found both irritating and preposterous was to send to

Dublin a new Lord Lieutenant in the person of Carteret, Secretary of State for the Southern Department since 1721, and a politician of independent opinion working too closely with the King for Walpole's peace of mind. That Carteret succeeded in controlling the situation, and persuaded the London government to withdraw Wood's patent, did nothing to endear him to Walpole. His order of priorities was revealed when he obtained Carteret's dismissal in 1730, and replaced him by a mediocre politician with no experience of Irish affairs, the Duke of Dorset. In Scotland, too, outbreaks of rioting – most serious in Glasgow over the malt tax of 1725 – led to a hasty reappraisal of the situation, the dismissal of a Secretary of State, and the reliance on the Campbell faction in the person of the second Duke of Argyll to control the country and manage the Scottish MPs and peers at Westminster.

It was also domestic political considerations which dominated Walpole's approach to questions of international diplomacy. Although he had once remarked, 'I do not love to give long opinions nor reasonings upon foreign politicks', Walpole needed no telling that war, or even the threat of war, would bring expense, excitement, and a revival of Jacobite hopes. Nor did he need reminding that the conduct of foreign policy was seen as the most important function of government, and one in which the literate public and newspapers of the day showed unending interest. Alarmed by the bellicose reaction of Townshend, the dominant Secretary of State after Carteret's departure to Dublin, to the unexpected alliance of Spain and the Emperor by the Treaty of Vienna in 1725, Walpole cautioned against being 'quite carried away by heroism, unless it was as easy really to conquer and reduce kingdoms as to magnify our own power in writing.' The Treaty presented a double danger to Britain. It threatened the balance of the Utrecht settlement with its concessions by the Emperor to Spain's territorial ambitions in Italy – thwarted as recently as 1719 when British naval power destroyed the Spanish fleet off Cape Passaro – while in compensation Spain granted trading rights to the Emperor's new overseas trading venture, the Ostend Company. Townshend's response was to bring together Britain, France and Prussia in the Treaty of Hanover. The confrontation of the two alliance systems produced tensions from the Baltic to the Caribbean, and took Europe perilously near to general war. The crisis was followed by lengthy and inconclusive negotiations until in 1729 Spain signed the Treaty of Seville with the Hanover allies. Ominously, it left unresolved some of the major commercial disputes between Britain and Spain. At a more parochial level, it marked the parting of the ways for Walpole and Townshend, who resigned in 1730. Free of Townshend's presence, Walpole now thrust on towards the second Treaty of Vienna in 1731 with the Emperor, which Spain soon signed. Agreement was reached over Italy, and the Ostend Company was suppressed in deference to British trading interests. The resultant isolation of France, which since 1716 had been a stabilising force in British diplomacy, was a cloud on the horizon, but in Walpole's view a small and distant one.

Walpole's position now seemed unassailable. The land tax, which had climbed to four shillings in the £ in 1727 at the high-point of international tension, was down to one shilling by 1732, the lowest level since its introduction forty years earlier. Both Townshend and Carteret, the only two men in the government who could approach Walpole in ability and experience, had gone. The strength of George II's support was shown when he set aside his Hanoverian claims against the Emperor as an inducement to the latter's agreement to the Treaty of Vienna. There was opposition to Walpole, in and out of Parliament, but it seemed to have faint chance of success. In the Commons Pulteney, a respected politician, headed the independent Whigs, in loose alliance with the Hanover Tories led by Wyndham. Outside Parliament, Bolingbroke, back from exile but forbidden to take his seat in the Lords, hit at Walpole in the pages of *The Craftsman*. This was one example of the growing use of the press by opposition groups to circumvent Walpole's formidable parliamentary position. Anti-ministerial newspapers printed attacks on the ministry, explanations of the Country programme, constituency 'instructions', and sometimes division lists. A new dimension was added by the appearance of monthly periodicals, the *Gentleman's Magazine* (founded in 1731) and the *London Magazine* (founded in 1732), which used their extra space to print summary versions of parliamentary debates. As in earlier periods the small size of print runs – rarely more than a few thousand – gives little indication of the number of readers. The influence of the press is impossible to measure, but it became a consistent factor in the politics of the period, spreading both news and opinion. It is some recognition of its importance that Walpole, the political arch-realist, showed the same concern with the mailing and distribution through government agencies of printed material as Harley had twenty years earlier.

Despite its showing in the press the opposition was a hybrid affair, an awkward mix of Tories trying to free themselves from Jacobite connections, and of dissident Whigs, critical of Walpole but often seeking to inherit rather than overthrow his system of government. On religious affairs, in particular, there was no unity of outlook between the High Church Tories and the Whigs. In this unpromising situation, Bolingbroke tried to devise a broad enough platform to accommodate the various opposition groups. He railed against a Hanoverian-dominated foreign policy, and the expense and danger of a standing army. He sympathised with the middling gentry who saw themselves set against the great landed families and the moneyed interest, and with those traders opposed to the monopolistic companies. Above all, he stressed the threat to the constitution posed by a corrupt ministry which influenced elections, bought votes and packed Parliament. 'Modern Whiggism', he wrote in *The Craftsman*, 'is only the practice of the worst Principles that were ever imputed to Tories.' Some of these points found responsive hearers, but in general the campaign orchestrated by Bolingbroke was more likely to irritate than endanger the government. Bolingbroke's own dubious past, the suspicion that lofty principles expressed in opposition might be quietly dropped if office were gained, and the wide gulf between opposition groups, all left the unmistakable impression of a losing cause.

It was, then, from a position of strength that Walpole launched the project which was to lead to one of the sharpest rebuffs experienced by any eighteenth-century government. In a further attempt to cut down smuggling and fraud Walpole decided to extend to tobacco the bonded warehouse system he had introduced in 1723. Under this arrangement no duty was liable if imported goods were re-exported; if they were intended for home consumption a duty, or excise, was paid when they were taken out of bond. A simple, efficient system, it was enforced by excise men who had the right to enter premises containing excisable goods. It was intended by Walpole to mark a major shift in taxation from direct to indirect, perhaps leading to an eventual elimination of the land tax. To Walpole both the fiscal and political benefits of the measure were considerable; what he did not anticipate was the political storm it provoked. The opposition conjured up melodramatic charges about the threat to liberty which the new excise represented, with an army of excise officials searching homes at one moment, obediently voting for ministerial candidates at elections the next. 'Excise, Wooden Shoes, and no Jury' summed up the connection seen by many, while in the City the great commercial interests of tobacco and wine felt threatened. In a sense Walpole was a victim of his own success, his apparent invulnerability, his growing complacency and arrogance. After ten years the stability which he had brought to the country was beginning to look like permanent one-man rule, and nothing he said could remove the suspicion that the bill was a step towards a general excise on all commodities – 'food and raiment and all the necessaries of life', as the opposition put it. A massive outburst of public hostility, expressed through instructions to MPs (from fifty-four constituencies) and petitions, shook the ministry. Its majority slumped to seventeen on a critical petition from the City, with normally firm supporters of the ministry, including office-holders, voting against the government.

As a furious Walpole withdrew the excise bill he revenged himself on errant ministerial supporters by dismissing them from office and place. It was an early example of what later became an accepted convention – that all who held office must be prepared to vote as the first minister indicated. Satisfying though this act of retribution may have been to Walpole, it strengthened the jubilant opposition groups rather than the ministry. In the general election of 1734 the government majority slumped from 272 after the previous election to 102, and this it owed mainly to the returns from the narrow constituencies. In the larger constituencies where opinion had some effect the opposition groups made some significant gains. The lesson of 1733 was that Walpole was not omnipotent; given an issue on which national emotions were raised, his parliamentary majority might melt away. Time in a sense was now against him. Some of those hopefuls for office who had not been given posts were disillusioned; the men of stature and ability had gone; and although Walpole's personal dominance of the political scene remained, both the debating strength and the confidence of the opposition had increased. The months of the excise crisis coincided, in awkward fashion for Walpole, with the outbreak of war on the continent between France and the Emperor over the Polish succession. Caught between George II's eagerness to intervene and the knowledge that involvement in a war fought over so distant an issue would be political suicide, Walpole managed to slide away from his treaty obligations of 1731 by offering the Emperor not armed help but mediation. Walpole's instincts probably served the country well on this occasion, when his insistence that 'other nations must be supposed to have honour as well as we' overcame the King's warlike reaction that 'it was with his sword alone that he desired to keep the balance of Europe'.

There was little in the Polish issue to enable the opposition to embarrass the government, but gradually Walpole's difficulties mounted. As relations between the King and Frederick, Prince of Wales, degenerated in time-honoured Hanoverian fashion, so the opposition grouped itself around the heir to the throne. Walpole quarrelled with Gibson, leader of the Whig bishops whose votes were so valuable in the House of Lords. The Porteous riots in Edinburgh, now the second city of the United Kingdom, lost Walpole popularity in Scotland, and the support of Scottish members in both houses became less reliable. A further blow, by this time probably of more personal than political significance, was the death in 1737 of Queen Caroline, his main ally at court. Most serious of all, long-standing disputes with Spain over the terms of the Treaty of Utrecht began to attract the same kind of emotional response as had the excise proposals. The concessions which the South Sea Company had gained in 1713 – the *asiento*, and the right to send a yearly ship to the trade fairs of the Spanish Main – had been obstructed by the Spanish authorities, resentful at the amount of illegal trading carried on by the British in the Caribbean, and still lamenting the loss of Gibraltar. Both sides had justifiable grievances. The British government was more lax than other European governments in controlling its subjects; on the other hand it refused to accept Spanish claims to intercept foreign vessels on mere suspicion. Not only was the inference that the Caribbean was a Spanish lake objectionable in principle, but the Spanish authorities were entrusting the enforcement of the rules to private coastguard vessels, the notorious *guardacostas*. Ships were seized on dubious evidence, cargoes confiscated, and crews beaten and imprisoned.

Walpole was insistent, as always, on the virtues of a negotiated settlement; but the opposition had no intention of allowing the laborious investigations and negotiations to run their course. Petitions demanding forceful action came in from the trading cities – often from those who had taken the lead in the excise crisis. The events of these months showed that the oligarchy was not in undisputed control. Led by London, the commercial middle classes launched a campaign of petitions and instructions which with the help of the press became nationwide in character, and gave an impression of determination not matched by the uncertain movements of the parliamentary opposition. The political importance of London was again shown, though the reasons for distrusting a Whig government had shifted since the days of the Sacheverell riots. Within the City the spearhead of opposition was the largely Tory Court of Common Council, representing the 'middling men', the smaller merchants and tradesmen, together with the Court of Common Hall, which was open to all freemen members of the livery companies. Although the Court of Aldermen with its great merchants and financiers had close links with the government, the City in the wider sense was opposed to Walpole. It reflected suspicion of the growing power of the executive, resentment at the political dominance of the landed aristocracy, and dismay at the government's lack of enthusiasm for the rich pickings expected from a seaborne war with Spain.

Outside the City limits were other focal points of agitation – in particular Westminster, whose electorate of about nine thousand made it the most 'popular' parliamentary borough in the country. The size and wealth of London, its vigorous political life and lively press, its proximity to court and government, and the spectre of its unpredictable 'mob' gave political agitation in the capital a unique importance. There is evidence that this campaign, like that over the excise bill, was something more than the extra-parliamentary manoeuvres of the opposition – that it took its impetus from the genuine popular hostility which Walpole now aroused. One pamphleteer claimed of the City that 'the sense of the Whole Nation breathed through all her Remonstrances, and animated all her Resolutions'. Even so, the agitation had few radical implications, and opposition Whigs were not likely to advocate greater participation which might bring about a pro-Stuart, populist electorate. Instructions and petitions, attacks in the press, desertions in the Commons, the defeat of government candidates at election time, may have had deeper roots in popular disquiet than the government realised, but they were weapons used in a conventional way against the ministry.

Negotiations between Britain and Spain finally broke down when a complicated settlement of the various disputes was held up by the obstructiveness of the South Sea Company, and the Spanish government in retaliation suspended the *asiento*. Fleets put to sea from both countries in the summer of 1739, and in October hostilities were formally declared. Substantial sections of the nation seem to have been spoiling for war. Their motives were mainly discreditable, springing from greed, boredom and hopes of political gain; but beneath the unedifying froth of the agitation for war lay serious considerations. William Pitt had given expression to these earlier in the year: 'Our trade is at stake, it is our last entrenchment; we must defend it, or perish.' As a leading commercial power Britain had interests in the New World which had to be protected, and they were being threatened not only by archaic Spanish pretensions, but by the more menacing activities of French traders and producers overseas. The wider significance of the war was that it was the first major conflict fought because of overseas disputes. The assumption that colonial issues should not be allowed to complicate serious diplomacy was disappearing fast. Colonies were regarded as integral parts of the national economy, and overseas trade of sufficient importance to justify war, though this was still regarded as a last resort.

The war signed Walpole's political death warrant as surely as it was to bring actual death to thousands of sailors and marines in the Caribbean, but his withdrawal from . the scene which he had dominated for so long was slow and grudging. He had lost both dignity and effectiveness as a result of the events of 1739, and his best chance of survival lay in a short, successful war. It was precisely this which the remoteness of the main theatre of war, the disorderly state of Britain's armed forces, and the lack of firm strategic direction, made unlikely. Even Vernon's early and delusory victories along the Spanish Main did the government as much harm as good, since the admiral was also an MP and one of Walpole's most persistent critics. The vulnerability of Hanover in the hostilities sweeping across Germany as more general war broke out on the death of the Emperor Charles VI in October 1740, led George II as Elector of Hanover to negotiate a convention of neutrality with the French in 1741 – a move which gave the parliamentary opposition the chance to accuse the ministry of subordinating British to Hanoverian interests. To attack Walpole was one thing; to lever him out of office another, and he might have continued indefinitely were it not for the timing of the next election. If 1734, hard on the heels of the excise crisis, had been an unwelcome date for the last election, 1741 was still less propitious. Although the ministry suffered no spectacular losses, there was a marginal erosion of its voting strength, with losses both in the larger constituencies and in the close boroughs. Given the government's unpopularity at this time, the results showed the difficulty of reflecting any sort of national sentiment in electoral or parliamentary terms; even so, the shift in voting terms within the Commons was to be enough. As Parliament met for the first time at the end of the year and settled to its customary task of determining disputed elections, the balance gradually tilted against Walpole. After a few narrow victories, a handful of MPs changed sides until the government suffered seven successive defeats on election petitions, the last in February 1742 by sixteen votes. They were the equivalent of votes of confidence, in Walpole as distinct from the ministry; and before the seventh and final division he had decided to go.

It was the first occasion on which a minister who possessed the full confidence of the Crown, as well as a safe majority in the Lords, was forced to resign; for the constitutional theory of the period still maintained that ministers held their offices from the monarch and were responsible to him. Walpole's fall showed that political practice determined that the king's choice must be able to carry his measures through the Commons. Another step had been taken along the road from royal to parliamentary government, although its significance was to be more evident later than it was at the time. The dramatic, to some almost unbelievable, fact was that after twenty years the colossus had fallen, and Walpole's retirement to the Lords as the Earl of Orford showed that he accepted the finality of that decision.

Walpole's long period of political dominance raises many questions both about the nature of that dominance, and its effect upon the politics and public life of his time. At one level there was little dispute. Walpole was an accomplished parliamentarian, an effective debater, and a hard-working administrator – a professional politician of the first rank. He realised, sooner and clearer than most, that there were two essential and related sources of power – the King and the Commons. Walpole not only held the confidence of both, he was the link between them, and as a commoner he was able to occupy a pivotal position at the centre of the political machine. To call him prime minister – as the opposition often did as a reproach since 'according to our constitution we can have no sole and prime minister' – brings to mind inappropriate modern analogies. It is true that Walpole dominated government business through the inner cabinet, that effective body of about five ministers which dealt with important matters, but his dependence on the Crown, as shown in the hiatus of 1727, and the lack of any notion of collective cabinet responsibility and support, were weaknesses. It is significant that on his resignation most of his ministerial colleagues remained in office. The challenge had been to Walpole, not to the Whig oligarchy, even though some of the agitation had been couched in traditional Country terms, with demands for repeal of the Septennial Act, removal of placemen from the Commons, and the like. It was evidence of the personal nature of Walpole's predominance, that no immediate attempt was made to reconstruct the bases of his political power.

Historians are generally agreed as to the sources and limitations of Walpole's power; there is less concurrence on the wider effects of his period of office. The lessening of religious animosities was accomplished at a cost – the widening of the gulf between higher and lower clergy, and the subsequent relapse of religious observation into a somnolent formalism in many parishes. Foreign visitors such as Voltaire looked with admiration on a land free from tyranny and bigotry, where, it seemed, Montesquieu's balanced constitution could be seen in operation. As Walpole claimed, 'the perfection of our constitution consists of this, that the monarchical, aristocratical and democratical forms of government are mixt and interwoven'. Yet the same period saw vehement attacks on the corruption and malevolence of Walpole's system, expressed most memorably by Bolingbroke and his literary associates – Swift, Pope and Gay. Behind the satires and polemics lay the suspicion that the growth of bureaucracy, taxation and patronage was undermining the liberties of Englishmen, that Walpole's 'mixt and interwoven' constitution was a device to perpetuate the power and wealth of the ruling oligarchy. This criticism was no longer the preserve of Tories and Jacobites, for independent or dissident Whigs added their voices to it, both in Parliament and from their local power bases in London and some of the provincial towns. A case can be made out that the number of independent and Tory MPs returned for the more open constituencies, and the anti-ministerial bias of most newspapers, shows a majority of the political nation set against the Whig establishment.

The resignation of Walpole, the Jacobite scare of 1745, and the growing expense of contested elections, halted the shaping of any new political alliance. Other considerations hindered the infusion of any genuine popular element into this anti-ministerialism; for however opposed some men of substance might be to the 'Venetian oligarchy' it would be difficult and unwise for them to forget that it had helped to organise society in their favour. Peers, MPs, justices of the peace, law officers, even jurymen, were men of property. Eighteenth-century law was calculated to protect that property rather than to defend liberty in any abstract sense. A feature of the legislation of the early Hanoverian period was the number of laws extending property rights – whether concerned with enclosures or turnpikes – and the startling increase in the number of capital offences against property. Given the lack of a professional police, and the gentry's instinctive aversion towards the introduction of such forces, associated as they were with England's continental neighbours or with Cromwellian days, the imposing structure of legal retribution existed to frighten and deter. It was an effort by a ruling class nervously aware of the dangers of Jacobitism and sedition, of urban and rural disorder, to keep control. The operation of the new statutes was selective and to some extent unpredictable, and a paradoxical situation resulted in that as the list of capital offences lengthened so the number of actual executions fell, and most of those who went to the gallows did so for 'traditional' offences such as burglary and highway robbery. This gap between the full severity of the law and its application in practice may have diluted but did not remove the general intimidatory intention of the new legislation; and transportation – the usual substitute for hanging – was in its own way a fearful punishment.

Though the period was marked by riots and disorders, there was no discernible radical motivation to them. They sometimes frightened governments, occasionally caused ministries to change course, but in no sense did they represent an alternative system. Those which were political echoed the slogans of the parliamentary groupings of the day, from the Sacheverell disturbances to the excise riots. However eager politicans were to regain office they were disinclined to enlist the support of the lower orders if that meant undermining and challenging the existing system. Walpole in 1734 spoke for the whole ruling class when he warned that 'In all the regulations we make with respect to the constitution, we are to guard against running too much into that form of government which is properly called democraticall.' Further evidence of the direction of legislation was to be found in the shift from direct taxation, which most affected landowners, to indirect taxation, which in the form of excises and other duties affected all – and in the nature of things bore most heavily on those who could least afford them. In political life the definition of property steadily widened to include office, sinecure, contract and vote. Ties of sentiment and friendship, common ideals and principles, might help – but the only firm cement of political strength was material gain. And office, once achieved, became a distribution centre for further benefits. Compared with the autocracies of the continent, Walpole's England was a haven of free speech, a hotbed of political activity. And however incensed political feelings became on occasion, there was no revival of those murderous clashes of arms which had marked the previous century. The balance between the advantages which Walpole's long period of office brought in terms of trade, finance and peace, and the murkier aspects of his rule, is a difficult one to strike. It is easy to accept that the political quiescence of the Walpole era did more for the country than a Jacobite restoration, a Bolingbroke coup, or street rule would have done; but this careful range of alternatives was Walpole's. There were others compatible with the Hanoverian dynasty, the Protestant religion, and constitutional government – though events after 1742 were to show how difficult it was to translate them into terms of practical government.

5 Oligarchy and war, 1742–1763

The period between the general elections of 1741 and 1761 formed the high plateau of Whig oligarchical rule. Polled seats at election time were few and declining still – 62 in 1754, a mere 53 (out of 558) in 1761. A failure to go to the poll was not necessarily proof of political torpor, for it sometimes masked a spirited struggle behind the scene; but this was likely to be fought within a narrow circle. By mid-century, almost two-thirds of the English borough seats were subject to patronage, for the most part of the great landowners; the number of seats under direct government control was comparatively small, about thirty at this time. The aristocracy itself was at its most exclusive, and the total of 172 temporal peers at the end of George II's reign showed that under the first two Hanoverians new peerage creations had only just kept pace with extinctions. One of the paradoxes of the eighteenth-century political scene was that at a time when the House of Lords itself was diminishing in activity and importance, the power of the peerage had never seemed greater.

At one level aristocratic ministers filled most of the great offices of state. Too much can be read into the fact that the most effective prime ministers of the century were commoners – Walpole, Pelham, North, and the Younger Pitt. All save Walpole were sons of peers, and in office they were surrounded by aristocratic colleagues; not until the second half of the nineteenth century did peers lose their majority in the cabinet. At another level, the aristocracy had its hand firmly planted on the levers of political power in the Commons. As the cost of parliamentary seats and electoral struggles soared, so the number of seats controlled in whole or in part by peers increased – from 105 in 1715, to 167 in 1747, and reaching a peak of 236 at the 1807 election. Within the House, there was a sharp rise in the number of MPs who were sons of peers, to a total of 120 (or about a fifth of the total) before the end of the century. If baronets and sons of baronets are taken into account, then these lesser ranks of the aristocracy made up another fifth of MPs by the time of the Younger Pitt. Aristocratic power was not only felt at Whitehall and Westminster, for in the shires peers continued to dominate local government through their hold on the office of lord lieutenant.

Some of this consolidation of power, particularly in the area of parliamentary seats and influence, had occurred at the expense of the gentry, but by and large the latter were partners, if junior ones, rather than challengers. Their ranks continued to supply the majority of MPs and almost all the JPs. If they had consistent political views, these tended to be conservative, even reactionary, with a suspicion of strong government prominent among them. Whatever the degree of their grumbling disaffection with some government novelty or other, it was not likely to turn into a bid for leadership or a rallying-point for the more permanently alienated sections of society. Nor was there the clash between aristocratic interests and a centralising bureaucracy that was taking place in many continental states. The Whitehall bureaucracy, such as it was, was slim. In 1745 there was a total of 23 staff at the Treasury; 26 in the offices of the two Secretaries of State; and 31 scattered between the War Office, the Board of Trade, and the Admiralty. Since the political heads of these offices were often peers, there was neither motive nor means for any assault by 'government' on the aristocracy, for the identification between the two, if not complete, was close.

The role of the confident, exclusive élite which made up the peerage was far removed from that of a passive upper class relying on legal and fiscal privileges. Of the latter it had few; its dominance was rather guaranteed by its involvement in government at all levels. It represented an aristocratic leadership in which self-interest, class interest, and the national interest were hard to disentangle. It was a governing class later to be idealised by Burke, as one composed of men of birth, land and patriotism which would never 'work with low instruments for low ends'. A more detached assessment might conclude that this élite took good care to govern in its own interests. It dominated the affairs of the nation at a time when the weight of taxation shifted from the land to consumption; when the game and property laws increased in number and severity; and when the perquisites of office grew in terms of an all-embracing patronage. Political power was buttressed by economic buoyancy, for both the area and profitability of cultivated land under aristocratic ownership increased, and obstacles in the way of exploitation of the land were removed with the help of private legislation. The main business of the government of the day was the conduct of foreign affairs and the securing of finance bills. Otherwise, the legislation carried through in the relatively short parliamentary sessions (from November to May or June) tended to be local and piecemeal – dealing with enclosures, turnpike trusts and corporation business. Earlier worries that the moneyed men and great financial institutions would steal political influence from the landed interest had subsided. Landowners invested in government funds, while the financial interest worked in collaboration with the Treasury. Commercial and manufacturing interests had limited political representation; though by 1761 about 50 or 60 MPs were merchants, a similar number held commissions in the army or navy, and a rather smaller number were lawyers.

Looming over the mid-century political scene is the sense that many of the issues which preoccupied politicians were petty and personal, the manoeuvring for place and power which ruffled feelings but never shook the fundamental assumptions of Whig dominance. After the final alarm of the Forty-Five the Jacobite threat dwindled to a forlorn hope, and a dozen years later the allurement of a seaborne war tempted even Tories to support the administration. The political partisanship of Walpole's last years faded, and despite the growing wealth and literacy of the population there seemed little disposition to seek fundamental changes in the system. The only serious challenge to the Whig consensus, more intriguing in retrospect than noticed at the time, was a form of Tory populism. It represented a protest at continued exclusion from office, but with its complaints about the manipulation of the electoral system, and its agitation for the repeal of partisan legislation, it anticipated some of the main radical demands of the later decades of the century.

Politics of the 1720s and 1730s had centred on a single dominant politician. A study of Walpole, and of the relation to him of other actors on the political stage, provides a key to unlock the secrets of that era. No such device exists for the following decades, when clusters of politicians form, separate, and regroup in kaleidoscopic fashion. Even the periods of settled administration, such as Henry Pelham's between 1746 and 1754, do not carry the assurance of permanence which was a hallmark of the 'Robinocracy'. Difficulties of comprehension increase in that the intractable issues of war, foreign policy, and colonial affairs, became more dominant. In this unquiet atmosphere the search for stability and continuity was a dominant motif, just as the presence of Walpole had been earlier. Considerable reconstruction of the ministry was necessary in 1742, both to fill the huge gap left by Walpole's resignation, and to bring into government some of the opposition politicians. The job was done by turning to the groups led by Pulteney and Lord Carteret. Pulteney went to the Lords as the Earl of Bath, Carteret became Secretary of State alongside Walpole's old subordinate, the Duke of Newcastle, and the Treasury went for a brief spell to the Earl of Wilmington (fifteen years after he had failed, as Spencer Compton, to wrest that position from Walpole).

It was a sign of the continued awareness of Whig and Tory separateness that once Walpole had gone, the dissident Whigs who had formed an alliance in opposition with the Tories deserted them for office with the ministerial Whigs. The most interesting appointment was that of Carteret, out of office since 1730, and intent on displaying his skills in the tangled maze of foreign affairs, where differences with Britain's allies, the vulnerability of Hanover in the growing swell of continental warfare, and the failure of the Caribbean campaigns mounted under Walpole, all called for urgent action. On his abilities the fate of the remodelled administration might depend, for it was incompetence and failure in those areas which had sapped confidence in Walpole.

The omens were not good. All the leading ministers were in the Lords except for Henry Pelham – Newcastle's quiet, efficient brother who became First Lord of the Treasury in 1743 on Wilmington's death. His task was not eased by the growing bill for the war (£5,000,000 in 1742, more than twice the peacetime average budget), and by the widespread belief that the country's diplomacy in the hands of George II and Carteret was directed towards Hanoverian rather than British interests. Those groups in the City and elsewhere who had pressed for the removal of Walpole were dismayed to find that his departure had led only to a reshuffling of ministers, not a change of policies. They were outraged by the taking of sixteen thousand Hanoverian troops onto the British payroll, a decision which led to the celebrated outburst in the Commons by William Pitt that 'this great, this powerful, this formidable kingdom, is considered only as a province to a despicable electorate', an accusation long remembered, not least by the King. In constructing an alliance system against France, with which formal hostilities began in 1744 after years of phoney war, Carteret showed considerable diplomatic skills, but they were not accompanied by much concern for his political footing at home. Without support from other ministers, and with little obvious benefit to show for his elaborate negotiations, the diplomatic expertise possessed by Carteret ran to waste, and by the end of 1744 he had gone. Less than three years after the fall of Walpole the King had lost the services of another leading minister, and Carteret's boast that 'give any man the Crown on his side and he can defy everything' had revealed only his lack of political realism.

The new ministry, the Broad Bottom administration, included some of the Whig outsiders – though not Pitt – and even some moderate Tories. It lasted little more than a year, and its unhappy experiences showed the King's ability to obstruct a ministry that was not to his taste. Resentful at losing Carteret (by now Earl

Granville) George II continued to consult him 'behind the curtain'. An unsatisfactory situation turned into something altogether more serious in 1745, when the Young Pretender, Charles Edward, landed on the west coast of Scotland. He had come at an awkward moment and in an awkward place as far as the government was concerned. The government's own Highland companies had been sent to fight in Germany, the Disarming Acts had left the Whig clans rather than the disaffected ones weaponless, and there was no co-ordination of authority in either Edinburgh or London. The military roads constructed at great expense in Walpole's period to help control future Scottish disaffection now had their usefulness proved – by the Jacobite forces which rallied to the Stuart cause. With the King away in Hanover on one of those regular visits which irritated many of his English subjects, Newcastle and the other ministers cut unimpressive and nervous figures. The Jacobite army, only a few thousand strong, took Edinburgh, defeated government troops in a confused scuffle at Prestonpans, and in November marched into England. By December it was at Derby, and although panic affected sections of London society, the southward trek revealed the weakness rather than the strength of the Jacobite cause. Charles Edward invaded England on the assumption that the English Jacobites would rally to him. Few did, and the lack of response showed the reality behind the toasts and sentiments which still overtook some Tories at moments of high emotion or particular disgruntlement with their Whiggish government. The Pretender's weary forces turned back to Scotland, pursued by troops brought from the continent under the command of the King's son, the Duke of Cumberland. In April 1746 the Jacobite army was defeated at Culloden, and its remnants hunted down in an operation which earned Cumberland his nickname of 'the Butcher'.

Except as a useful term of abuse for political opponents and an excuse for romanticising about 'Bonnie Prince Charlie', Jacobitism was dead; and the failed uprising was followed by punitive legislation by the government aimed at destroying the remaining vigour and symbolism of the Scottish clan system. The lack of support for the Pretender in England showed that the perennial outbreaks of discontent with monarch, ministry or Hanover, fell short of offering practical support to a French-based Catholic prince. On the other hand, the Forty-Five was a posthumous vindication of Walpole's obsession with Jacobitism, for the thrust deep into England by a small Jacobite army demonstrated the vulnerability of the Hanoverian system to an armed threat. If the government seemed to act more decisively in the later stages of the rising this owed something to the securing of its domestic base, for after a brief resignation by the Pelhams over the question of a ministerial appointment for Pitt showed George II their indispensability, they returned to office guaranteed 'that degree of authority, confidence, and credit from His Majesty, which the ministers of the Crown have usually enjoyed in this country'. Pitt at last came into the government, though as Paymaster General rather than as Secretary at War as first proposed, and some of Granville's remaining supporters were dismissed.

The affair had demonstrated once more the limitations of the King's prerogative, but its more practical effect was the evolution of a grudging marriage of convenience into a harmonious working relationship. It was this, together with the careful management by the Pelhams of their parliamentary support, which once more brought a sense of stability to the political scene until the death of Henry Pelham in 1754. Developments both planned and unplanned helped this process. The election of 1747, held a year early to frustrate the plans of the opposition which was grouping in time-honoured fashion around Frederick, Prince of Wales, as usual went the government's way. The Prince himself died in 1751, and with him went not only the threat of the reversionary interest but the hopes of the Tories allied to him that an end to their ostracism was in sight. Without even such a feeble prop as Frederick represented, not all the combined efforts of Tory electoral strength in many of the open constituencies, and the Tory propaganda of the newspapers and coffee houses, could prise open a way into government.

The main preoccupation of the ministry restored to office in February 1746 was the war, or rather a way out of it. Britain's main objectives were traditional ones; the protection of Austria, and in particular the Austrian Netherlands; security of the Hanoverian succession and of the Electorate; some mark of success in the overseas war which had begun as long ago as 1739. Appalled by the heavy cost of the war, Pelham was eager for a conclusion to the negotiations. The King and Newcastle by contrast were hopeful that further campaigns would check the run of French military successes and bring a more favourable settlement. In what was to become a familiar pattern, British naval successes balanced French land victories, and with a stalemate recognised by most belligerents, the Treaty of Aix-la-Chapelle was signed in October 1748. For Britain there were no territorial gains, for its only overseas conquest, the great stone fortress of Louisbourg on Cape Breton Island, was restored to France, which gave up its gains in the Austrian Netherlands, as well as Madras in India. No decision was reached over spheres of influence in North America; while in the Caribbean an agreement to treat Dominica, St Lucia, St Vincent and Tobago as 'neutral islands' – occupied by neither Britain nor France

– was an ingenious but temporary solution. For few participants did the adjustments seem to justify the expenditure of men and money, and the common suspicion among the powers that somehow they were losers rather than gainers boded ill for the future.

With the end of the war, Pelham's first task was to restore the country's finances. The army and navy were swiftly cut down to their peacetime establishment. In a complicated series of moves Pelham converted the unfunded debt, which as a result of the war stood at what was thought to be an alarming level, to lower interest-rate stock, and consolidated individual stocks into 3 per cent holdings, the celebrated 'Consols'. He resisted on the one hand the attempts by Newcastle to continue doling out subsidies on the continent, and on the other the temptation to restore the land tax to peacetime levels. Not until 1752 was it down to the rate considered acceptable by the landed interest of two shillings in the £. To Pelham sound management of the national finances was a guarantee of national stability; all proposals were scrutinised with an eye to their cost. In this he inherited Walpole's mantle, though George II thought him a better financier than Walpole. In other areas, the Pelham ministry carried out some worthwhile reforms, not all of which fit the picture of an oligarchy interested only in the continuance of its own power. The calendar was changed by eleven days to bring it into line with the continent's – amid considerable protest at the disruption this brought to rents, wages and legal agreements. A Gin Act did something to restrict the consumption of cheap spirits. Most controversial of all, the Pelhams supported a private measure, the Jew Naturalisation Bill, which allowed for naturalisation by special Act of Parliament. This sensible if limited measure was passed without difficulty in a thin Parliament, but a storm of anti-Semitic feeling persuaded the government to repeal it. A general election was due, and there were too many echoes of the uproar of the excise crisis of 1733 for ministers to take risks. The 1754 election provided the government with a slight increase in numbers which gave some compensation for the loss of Pelham, who died shortly before the election, and was replaced as First Lord of the Treasury by his brother the Duke of Newcastle. With almost forty years' experience of office Newcastle brought a close knowledge to the endless work of persuading, exhorting and bribing Whig supporters to return MPs loyal to the ministry, and to the equally important task of keeping those MPs, once returned, in faithful attendance to their parliamentary duties. It was an intricate business, for the appeal varied from person to person. Moralising on the national interest might be sufficient for one; the promise or half-promise of a place for another. The hint of a threat or the reminder of a favour owed might be used, for of places, contracts and the like there were never enough. As Pelham had complained, 'the House of Commons is a great unwieldy body, which requires great Art and some Cordials to keep it loyal; we have not many of the latter in our power.' It was Walpole's system, with the same attention to detail, but operated with a more delicate touch.

Despite his move to the Treasury, Newcastle was not the man to surmount the problem of leading an administration from the Lords. Reluctance to share his new-gained authority with a strong leader in the Commons meant that William Pitt and Henry Fox, powerful and ambitious men, were both kept from high office. It was Fox who was first admitted to the cabinet, and then in 1755 was appointed Secretary of State and Leader of the House of Commons. Regardless of his position as Paymaster of the Forces, Pitt attacked the government's policy of subsidy agreements and its concern for the safety of Hanover as the international situation became more threatening by the day. Hanover should be left to its fate, over-run if need be, for it could always be recovered at some future peace conference. Only the interests of 'the long injured, long neglected, long forgotten people of America' could justify war; and supported by two other ministers, Legge and Grenville, Pitt voted against the government. In November 1755 all three were dismissed.

The international storm clouds which had produced this parliamentary squall had been gathering for some time over both Europe and North America. Fearful of renewed warfare on the continent, where Austria and Prussia remained at odds, the Newcastle government had to look to the security of Hanover – hence the subsidy agreements with Russia and Hesse-Cassel to which Pitt objected and which, Fox gloomily noted, were becoming 'as unpopular as the Excise'. The agreements set off a chain reaction of diplomatic negotiations and treaties which within the year were to bring about a complete reversal of the alliance system which had existed since the beginning of the century. Frederick II of Prussia, alarmed by the Anglo-Russian agreement, made haste to negotiate a defensive alliance with Britain by way of the Convention of Westminster in January 1756. For different reasons both Austria and Russia were mortified by this: the former by Britain's negotiating of a treaty with Austria's deadliest enemy, the latter by the nullifying of plans to attack Prussia with the aid of the recently-promised British subsidy. Austria's response was to sign the Treaty of Versailles with France, indignant at Prussia's agreement with Britain, with which a state of unofficial hostilities existed overseas. The result of this whirlwind of diplomatic activity was that once the dust had settled the line-up of antagonists which entered the war which broke out in 1756 was very different from that at any previous time in the century. The forces of Austria,

France and Russia were marshalled against those of Prussia and Britain, with the United Provinces remaining neutral. The reversal of alliances reflected the changing circumstances of the mid-century, in which old threats receded and new ones appeared. The degree of foresight in this overturn of the old alliance system is debatable, though well before the end of the War of the Austrian Succession there were those in England, including Pitt, who saw the importance of Prussia as a potential ally. Although it was Newcastle's anxious search for security for Hanover which set the whole process in motion, that alone would not have led to so drastic a diplomatic shake-up were it not for a general realisation that traditional alliances no longer met the dangers of the changing international situation.

Alongside its concern for the Electorate the Newcastle government was exercised by the growing seriousness of overseas rivalry with France. In India a policy of territorial expansion by the French under Dupleix menaced the trading settlements of the East India Company; in the Caribbean the French showed no inclination to evacuate the 'neutral islands' as agreed in 1748; and in North America frontier friction threatened to turn into open warfare. It was there, above all, that developments made it most difficult for the British and French governments to remain detached from the actions of their subjects. Since the early eighteenth century the population of Britain's North American colonies had risen from four hundred thousand to about one and a half million. Although the colonies were still largely rural, along the settled coastal strip sophisticated urban communities had developed – in Philadelphia, Boston, New York and Charleston. Above all it was a restless society, and the most marked feature of the colonial scene in the first half of the century was the westward movement across the barrier of the Appalachians. This was an expansionist surge in which private enterprise was more prominent than state planning, where the London government followed rather than led, and which was bound to bring the British colonists into conflict with the French. Although their progress was less striking on the map than that of the French explorers and traders on the Great Lakes and in the Mississippi valley, there was a solidity about it which their rivals could not match. They were militarily inefficient compared to the French; but behind them lay the Royal Navy, a powerful weapon if unleashed since in any conflict both sides would be dependent on supplies, munitions and reinforcements from Europe.

The peace settlement of 1748 sharpened rather than solved the problem of Anglo-French relations. The fertile lands of the Ohio valley had long attracted the attention of Virginians, and after the peace freed the colonists from the irksome necessity of occupying defensive positions along their frontiers, land companies were formed to settle the region. Largest of these was the Ohio Company, founded in 1748, which was given a grant by the Crown of half a million acres. The French response was to send troops into the region, who expelled the British traders and began building forts. These advances by the French into territory granted to the Ohio Company by the British Crown turned a local dispute into an international confrontation. Hostilities escalated from skirmishes between small groups of Virginians and French soldiers to an action in 1755 near Fort Duquesne where a small army of British regulars – the first to serve in America – and colonial militia under the command of Major-General Braddock suffered a thousand casualties. News of the disaster and of its effect on the Indian nations of the western interior brought despondency to the frontier settlements, and made even more disturbing the failure of a British naval squadron under Admiral Boscawen to stop French reinforcements reaching America. Overseas warfare between Britain and France was official in all but name, and an MP of forty years' standing told the Commons that the breakdown of relations with France was 'the most momentous event that ever happened in the course of my observation . . . decisive of the empire in America no doubt'.

It was fighting nearer home which finally brought the declaration of war between Britain and France in May 1756 (three months before hostilities became European in scale following Prussia's invasion of Saxony). An inconclusive fleet action in the Mediterranean which led to the fall of Minorca to the French brought not only the declaration of war but dire political consequences for the Newcastle government. Calls for the court-martial of John Byng, the British admiral concerned, widened to include attacks on the administration. With French advances continuing in America, and with the threatening figure of Pitt waiting for the new parliamentary session to renew his attacks, the ministry began to fall apart. In October Fox resigned, and in November Newcastle went, complaining that it was not 'numbers' he lacked in the Commons, but 'hands and tongues'. Two days later Pitt took office as Secretary of State and effective head of the administration, though the Treasury went to the Duke of Devonshire. The new ministry, which lasted only four months, was a false start for Pitt. Some members of the administration, and the 'Old Corps' Whigs, still owed loyalty to Newcastle; while the King had lost none of his suspicion of Pitt, despite the latter's acceptance of the need to defend Hanover. Although Pitt tackled the problems of war with vigour, no quick victories were likely; and his attempts to save Byng from execution cost him popularity. In these circumstances, and with Newcastle standing by, the King thought it safe in April 1757 to dismiss Pitt, and with him went Legge and a few close colleagues.

Public unease at Pitt's dismissal was shown by demonstrations of which the most striking, and best-orchestrated, was the conferring of the freedom of the City of London on Pitt (and Legge), an honour followed by a dozen other corporations through the country. The 'rain' of golden boxes containing the ceremonial documents was never quite as heavy as Pittite propaganda implied, and some of the decisions to bestow civic freedom on him owed much to the sort of political manipulation which Pitt affected to despise. The City, consistently hostile at its middle and lower levels to the Hanoverian court and ministry, saw in Pitt a true 'Patriot'. It was this belief which gave Pitt a broader base of support than any other politician of his time. The loudness of the outcry in his favour, combined with the alarming war situation, produced apprehension among his opponents and confidence among his supporters. To his admirers Pitt was the old Country creed personified. He was the politician who spoke out fearlessly for the national rather than factional interest (his enemies would argue that he simply identified the two as one); who lashed incompetence, greed and corruption; who represented those excluded from office by a tight-knit oligarchy. Office and time were to tarnish this image, but in 1757 it was a potent force; and in June Pitt returned to office as Secretary of State for the Southern Department, this time in an administration altogether more stable, for after much swallowing of pride on all sides Newcastle was also back as First Lord of the Treasury. The dominant personality of Pitt and the crucial situation of the war meant that for Newcastle the Treasury was not the path to supreme power as it had been for Walpole and Pelham. His job was to service the war effort, Pitt's to direct it. Pitt might consider the coalition a 'bitter, but necessary cup', words which no doubt reflected the feelings of the King and Newcastle as well; but in practical terms the new administration was assured of the political support and the financial resources necessary to fight the war.

By general acknowledgement 1757 was an even more depressing year than the previous one. The projects begun by Pitt during his short-lived first administration show the partial outline of a strategy which was to reach maturity in 1759; but they met with little success even when Pitt returned to office. Across the Atlantic the planned assault on Louisbourg was abandoned for the year, and an amphibious attack on the French naval base at Rochefort was a fiasco. More damaging still was the threatened collapse of the government's continental strategy. A British-paid 'Army of Observation' of Hanoverian, Hessian and Prussian troops had been formed under the command of the Duke of Cumberland with the aim of protecting both Hanover and Prussia's western frontier against the French. In September 1757 Cumberland, hard-pressed by superior

French forces, agreed to the humiliating Convention of Klosterzeven by which his army was neutralised and partly disarmed. Finally, Frederick II of Prussia, the new ally for whom subsidy agreements were being voted, went down to heavy defeat in Bohemia, though he recovered with victories in the last months of the year. News of a rare triumph for British arms came from India where Clive routed the forces of the Nawab of Bengal at Plassey after recapturing the important centre of East Indian Company trade and administration at Calcutta. This recovery of the British position in Bengal owed little to government support, but Pitt made the most of Clive's successes when he paid tribute in the Commons to 'that heaven-born general'.

The fiasco of Klosterzeven, and the whole thrust of government policy in central Europe, laid Pitt, the arch-critic of continental entanglements, open to charges of inconsistency. In 1757 Pitt could rightly argue that circumstances had changed since the days when he criticised the obsession with Hanover. Defence of the electorate could now be regarded as part of an overall plan to weaken and distract the French military effort, particularly given the agreement with Prussia – altogether a more formidable fighting partner than the minor German states of earlier subsidy agreements. So Pitt turned the alliance with Prussia, so fortuitous an affair it had seemed in early 1756, into a main plank of the war effort. He poured money and, from 1758 onwards, men into what he admitted was an 'ocean of fire' in Germany, a change of heart watched with growing disapproval by the heir to the throne, the young Prince of Wales, and his adviser the Earl of Bute. More coherent in retrospect than at the time, Pitt's strategy slowly began to emerge in diplomatic negotiations and in operational planning. The nature of Pitt's role in the ultimate triumphs of the Seven Years War is still a matter of debate. Older assessments which tended to grant him sole credit have been abandoned, as have those interpretations which saw his success based on a revolution in Britain's wartime administration. There were no major alterations to administrative practice by Pitt, who operated the machinery which had served in the previous war, though with a greater sense of urgency – as Newcastle later said, 'With all his faults . . . there is no one so able to push an expedition as he.'

What Pitt brought to the war effort was an absolute determination to defeat and humble France, regardless of cost, domestic political considerations, or accusations of inconsistency. As Secretary of State, not prime minister, Pitt operated within a collective relationship, and although ultimate responsibility rested with him the conduct of the war was by no means a single-handed affair. With Cumberland in disgrace, the able veteran Ligonier became Commander-in-Chief, and in his selection of commanders for the difficult overseas operations, age and seniority were no longer decisive. By army standards Howe (at 28), Wolfe (31), even Amherst (40), were young men. At the Admiralty the experienced Anson was back as First Lord, despite Minorca, and was able to reap the benefits of the preparations he had made since becoming First Lord in 1751. With 239 ships in commission (about a hundred of them ships of the line), and many others building, the navy was far larger than that of France. Ships were one thing, crews another, and although by the end of the war 82,000 men were serving with the fleet there were never enough to go round. Of capable officers there seemed no shortage, and at sea Anson had officers of the calibre of Hawke, Saunders and Rodney. The Admiralty's policy of a tight blockade of the French coasts, costly though it was in terms of wear and tear on ships and men, was the essential prerequisite to Pitt's aggressive overseas operations.

Within the government Pitt left all matters other than the direction of the war to Newcastle. The 'Minister for Money', as his biographer terms Newcastle at this stage of his career, ensured Pitt a parliamentary majority – not a difficult matter with Whigs and Tories, court politicians and independents in general support – and also found the wherewithal to pay for a war effort which grew in size and cost each month. If Pitt and his supporters were often dismissive of the Duke's role, this can be explained by the fact that underneath the war effort old rivalries still ran deep. The huge sums voted for the war never came near meeting the total bill despite the inevitable raising of the land tax to four shillings in the £, the increasing of taxes on malt, beer, newspapers, coal, houses and windows, and the raiding of the Sinking Fund. By such resorts the normal peacetime income was doubled from about £2 million a year to £4 million. By the closing years of the war this amounted to only a quarter of government expenditure, and the balance had to be raised by loans of unprecedented size – £8 million in 1760, £12 million in 1761 and £12 million again in 1762. As previously, the increased taxes served as security for the interest payable on these loans, and so the two aspects of the Treasury's policy were interdependent. Newcastle, despite much hand-wringing and prophecies of imminent doom, carried out this massive job of financing the war in businesslike fashion. He was helped by Legge at the Exchequer, by the experienced John West, Secretary to the Treasury, and not least by the great City financiers who acted as intermediaries and underwriters for the huge loans. Despite the size of the loans raised, interest rates went up only from 3.4 per cent in 1756 to 4.8 per cent for the vast 1762 issue of £12 million.

With war finances taken care of, Pitt was able to put considerable forces into the field, though not without meeting acute manpower difficulties. In the first years of the war disappointments abroad were compounded by serious problems at home. 1756 and 1757 saw outbreaks of rioting in many parts of the country. Common to the disturbances were grievances about high food prices following hard winters and wet summers, and to these in 1757 was added opposition to the new Militia Act. The main intention of the measure was to provide more soldiers for home defence, but it roused suspicions that it was a device for sending men abroad, and there was particular resentment at the way in which exemptions could be purchased. Defiance of the Act was accompanied by widespread rioting. In 1757 more than fifty towns were involved, and in all 50,000 troops were called out at one time or another – a particular awkwardness in wartime. Meanwhile, expedients conventional and unconventional were tried by the government in its efforts to enlarge the small peacetime army. Some noblemen raised troops on their own account; while Highlanders from clans which only a dozen years earlier had been in rebellion were formed into regiments – though not for home service. By 1759 170,000 troops were on the payroll (70,000 of them German); by the next year the number was over 200,000. What these forces still lacked in numbers when compared to the huge armies of the continental powers they made up in seaborne mobility. The assault on Quebec was made by a fleet of 200 warships and transports carrying 8,500 soldiers. An amphibious 'raid' on the French coast might involve 13,000 troops and 130 ships; the expedition which took Martinique in 1762 included 14,000 troops. It was not only leadership, both in London and in the field, which counted, but the sheer weight of men, ships and munitions. The equipping and dispatch of a whole series of expeditions, some of them travelling thousands of miles to their destinations, was a tribute to the administrative departments concerned.

While on the continent British money and 'His Britannic Majesty's Army in Germany', commanded by Prince Ferdinand of Brunswick, played their part in keeping Frederick II in the field, the most spectacular triumphs of the Pitt–Newcastle ministry were overseas. Mortified by 'the late inactive and unhappy campaign', Pitt planned a three-pronged assault on New France for 1758. With the Royal Navy blockading French ports to stop reinforcements reaching North America, one British army was to clear the Ohio valley, while another was to strike north by way of Lake Champlain at the heart of Canada. The most ambitious assault of all was to be directed at Louisbourg, as a prelude to a thrust at Quebec, capital of New France. Although the central prong was badly blunted by a repulse at Ticonderoga, elsewhere all went according to plan, and 1759 saw a renewal of the offensive. Quebec fell in September 1759, after Wolfe's nerve-racked operations there hung perilously near failure; and the following year New France capitulated to the overwhelming force of British and colonial fighting power. As the balance on the North American continent tipped in Britain's favour, Pitt turned his attention to the Caribbean. Expeditions against the French West Indies made good sense from both a commercial and strategic point of view. Capture of the rich sugar islands would strike a blow at France more damaging in the short term than any achievement of British arms in North America, and would stop the islands being used as bases for privateers, which were taking hundreds of British prizes each year. As a preliminary to these attacks, expeditions in 1758 captured French slaving and trading stations on the West African coast. After this ominous prelude the French islands fell one by one to strong British forces. Guadeloupe, taken in 1759, and Martinique, finally captured in 1762, were the richest of the islands; but Grenada and the 'neutral islands' of Dominica, St Lucia and St Vincent also fell into British hands. With these conquests came trade, prizes and booty, to the applause of Pitt's merchant supporters. Even Newcastle agreed in 1760 that there was 'now happily a great deal of money in the kingdom'. The French government had done little to help its beleaguered possessions, for British naval victories in 1759 off Lagos and in Quiberon Bay had crippled the French navy. The latter battle, dramatic and chaotic among the shallows, set the seal on the policy of tight blockade. In India, too, the French were in disarray as a combination of British naval forces under Admiral Pocock and Company land armies commanded by Clive and his old mentor Stringer Lawrence drove the French from the Deccan as well as from Bengal. Defeated at Wandiwash in January 1760, dispirited French forces gave up one place after another on the Coromandel coast until in January 1761 their final base at Pondicherry fell.

The unprecedented sequence of triumphs had left the political nation exhilarated, but also satiated and with growing signs of division. To outward appearance Britain's main objectives in the war had been achieved, but Pitt – flying 'into a violent passion', Newcastle complained, if the word peace was mentioned – planned further operations in Europe and overseas. The Duke's conviction that the costly war should be brought to a close ran counter to Pitt's insistence that yet more conquests were necessary to strengthen Britain's hand at the peace negotiations. It was at this time of growing differences between leading ministers that in October 1760 George II died and was succeeded by his grandson. The accession of George III was to have profound consequences for British politics, but they were scarcely felt in the first months of the new reign. With a war still to be fought, and a general election to be held, there was no question of any shift as drastic as removing the Pitt–Newcastle ministry. Some changes there were: Bute was now the channel of communication between the new King and his ministers, and in a reshuffle in March 1761 became Secretary of State for the Northern Department. Furthermore, it had long been clear that George did not share his grandfather's attachment to Hanover, nor his views on the importance of the German theatre of war. The King's unenthusiastic reference in the speech from the throne to a 'bloody and expensive' war (later altered at Pitt's angry insistence to an 'expensive but just and necessary war') was the more worrying because it reflected a growing mood in the country. This feeling was given expression in Israel Mauduit's clever pamphlet of November 1760, *Considerations on the Present German War*, which went through five editions and gave critics of the government's continental policy much ammunition. As Pitt wryly observed in the December debate on the Prussian subsidies, 'A certain little book that was found somewhere or other, has made a great many orators in this House.'

If peace negotiations with France were hindered by Pitt's unbending attitude, the situation was further complicated by the worsening relations with Spain. One of the first actions of Charles III, who had come to the throne in 1759, had been to warn Britain that Spain would not stand by and watch the overturning of the equilibrium established by the Utrecht settlement; and in August 1761 the Bourbon rulers of France and Spain signed a secret family compact. Pitt's reaction to rumours of this was to demand a pre-emptive strike at the Spanish treasure fleets. When this was resisted by other ministers in a series of vehement discussions in which the Secretary of State was accused of seeking 'eternal war', Pitt resigned in October 1761. He found justification after the event when war with Spain was declared in January 1762, and when in May Newcastle also resigned, over the question of Prussian subsidies. Bute now became First Lord of the Treasury with the responsibility of concluding the war with a peace settlement that would be found generally acceptable. Meanwhile the war went on, and news of continued successes hindered rather than eased Bute's search for peace. Spain's entry into the war simply provided further targets for British forces. Havana, that great citadel of the Indies, fell in August 1762, with an enormous amount of booty, and in September on the other side of the world the Philippines surrendered to a British assault force. By now peace negotiations were almost concluded, though the definitive Treaty of Paris between Britain, France and Spain was not signed until February 1763.

The settlement was a complex and controversial one. To Pitt it 'obscured all the glories of war, surrendered the dearest interests of the nation, and sacrificed the public faith by an abandonment of our allies.' Much of the uproar stemmed not so much from the terms of the treaty itself as from Bute's role in its negotiation. As Chesterfield said, 'The nation universally condemned it, not upon knowledge, but because it was made by a Favourite and a Scotchman.' Pitt's criticism that Britain had abandoned her allies referred to the government's refusal to continue the payment of subsidies to Frederick II after the coalition against him collapsed with the unexpected withdrawal of Russia from the war. This might not be the bad faith which Pitt alleged, but it was bad diplomacy by a government which was soon to find itself isolated in Europe. Also pertinent was Pitt's accusation that important conquests had been surrendered without adequate compensation. France received back Guadeloupe and Martinique, the smaller but strategically important St Lucia, Gorée in West Africa, her trading factories in India (though they were no longer to be fortified), and Belle Isle. She also kept vital fishing rights off Newfoundland, that famous if over-rated 'nursery of seamen', while both Havana and Manila were returned to Spain. Even so, Britain's gains were unprecedented. In North America the cession of Canada and Louisiana by France, and of Florida by Spain, gave Britain possession of the whole continent east of the Mississippi. Elsewhere, Grenada, the long-disputed 'neutral islands' of St Vincent, Dominica and Tobago, and Senegal, were ceded to Britain, while Minorca was restored. Bute and Pitt considered the negotiations from opposing viewpoints. The minister and some of his colleagues were alarmed at the prospect of an over-mighty Britain, an imperial colossus that would draw the hostility of a fearful and united Europe. They preferred to show moderation at the peace conference, and to work for a future in which the friendship of France and Spain would be assured. Pitt's attitude was sterner and less hopeful. He foresaw the war as the prelude to new dangers. To Pitt the Family Compact, not British power, was the greatest menace to the peace of Europe, and he would have conducted the negotiations on the sombre assumption that the Bourbon powers were planning a war of revenge.

Whatever its defects, the Treaty of Paris marked a further stage in Britain's growth as the dominant imperial power in Europe. The Utrecht settlement half a century earlier had pointed the way, but the achievement of the Seven Years War was greater, both in terms of victories won and of territories gained. Also much in evidence had been the necessary qualities of luck and daring, both for Frederick as he kept the continental war in being by surviving one desperate situation after another, and for Britain's own forces. That *annus mirabilis*, 1759, would have looked very different if Wolfe's men had stumbled below Quebec on the night of 12 September, or if Hawke's headlong chase into Quiberon Bay on 20 November had run his ships onto the shoals of a lee shore. It was only a short time since the early disasters of the war had been taken to be proof of the national decline forecast by many. 'We have had our day', one prophet of doom had written in 1752, 'it ended with Queen Anne'. As late as August 1757 Pitt had complained that the benefits of the Treaty of Utrecht, 'the indelible reproach of the last generation, are become the almost unattainable wish of the present.' Britain had profited from the French commitment to a war on two fronts, and from the belated entry of Spain into the fighting. These alone go far towards explaining the difference between British fortunes in this war and those in earlier and later conflicts.

Although the foundations had been laid, and some of the superstructure built, for the greatest overseas empire Europe had known, there is little evidence that this was done in conformity with any long-term government planning. There was a general acknowledgement that war was a method of promoting colonial and commercial growth, but it is difficult to see even in the considerable gains of the 1763 settlement a positive commitment to expansion once Pitt had gone. The annexation of Canada was looked on as a defensive measure to protect the American colonies and trade, and the other acquisitions were largely the result of the successes of the war machine set in motion by Pitt. If power, wealth and willpower all seemed to be present, especially among the mercantile sections of the nations, yet the dangers were as great as the opportunities. The Bourbon powers had been defeated, not crushed. One phase of the contest for empire had ended in Britain's favour, but a new one was beginning which would test the country's political and military resources to the utmost.

6 Challenges to authority, 1763–1775

The end of the Seven Years War saw a shift in the emphasis of political activity as the pressure of global events died away. Politicians were able to turn to the more familiar and reassuring matters of place and power, though it was clear that much had changed since the last years of peace. The Whig–Tory–Jacobite divisions had blurred almost to the point of disappearance. The 'Old Corps' of Whigs was in a state of feud and disintegration – now only, as one observer pointed out, 'an alliance of different clans . . . professing the same principles but influenced and guided by their different chieftains.' The Tories generally had supported the Pitt–Newcastle war ministry, and after its fall although some reverted to their traditional backbench stance, others settled down on the court side or became absorbed into the various groups seeking office. Jacobitism was an indulgence in nostalgia, no longer a political threat. With the accession in 1760 of the youngest monarch for two hundred years, the fall-back position of opposition groups in search of respectability and future influence had also vanished; for it would be many years before a reversionary interest could again excite the political scene. With a monarch who made a point, indeed a merit, of proclaiming indifference to his ancestral domains on the continent, not even Hanover was available as a focal point for complaint and a means of gaining easy popularity. Politicians were forced to head across a country from which leading landmarks had been removed, and with guides whose advice was shaky and conflicting.

It is tempting to see the first decade of George III's reign as a period in which political faction rather than political principle loomed larger than ever. The actions of politicians seemed to centre on competition for the favour of the King and with it the support of the permanent body of court and ministerial supporters in the Commons. Horace Walpole was able to write of 'the extinction of parties' at this time, and the period has long been seen as the heyday of personal linkages, the so-called 'clientage groups', rather than formed political parties. A sign of the dying away of political conflict came in the low-key general election of 1761, with the smallest number of contested seats since the Revolution. And on the throne was a King whose view was that when forming a government he had 'the right to the services of all his subjects', a consideration which seemed to override the conflicting views of politicians. Yet it is possible to push this atomistic interpretation too far, for an overview of the political manoeuvres of the decade shows that the followers of Bute, Bedford and Grenville were usually linked with the court party, and were in office; while the remnants of the Newcastle Whigs, together with the followers of Pitt and of the youngish Whig magnate Rockingham, tended to be in opposition. In a more fundamental sense, the political game – to all appearances still played within the confines of court, Parliament, and the great houses – was influenced by stirrings, both in the country and on the other side of the Atlantic. To the discontented parliamentarians' criticism of what they were beginning to persuade themselves was the improper influence of the crown were added more strident voices from the streets, the corporations and the radical associations, attacking crown and aristocracy alike.

Even the placid waters of the Church of England were being rippled by the breezes of Methodism. The fervent field preaching during the 1740s of John Wesley, George Whitefield and a handful of other itinerants in those areas out of sight and mind of the established Church was hardening into something altogether more formidable. Though ostensibly remaining within the Church, 'Pope John' soon set up an autonomous organisation, whose cellular structure was later reflected in many working-class societies and unions. There were a few full-time Methodist ministers, moving from circuit to circuit every three years, and meeting in annual Conference; but the pivotal role was played by laymen (and women), acting as class leaders and preachers. Methodist services, with their spirited hymns and histrionic sermons, differed from the stately, often perfunctory form of the Anglican ritual, and so did Methodist congregations. At Halifax, in 1748, Wesley wrote that he preached to 'an immense number of people, roaring like the waves of the sea.' Like missionaries braving the perils of unknown regions, Wesley and his colleagues rode and walked across England, in search of the unenlightened, the neglected, the deprived. If Methodism was a protest movement, its force was directed less against Anglican doctrine than against the Church's neglect of its spiritual and pastoral role. Even though there was no formal separation of the Methodist movement from the Church until after Wesley's death, his actions were bound to be seen as a provocation and a challenge. And if Wesley in political terms was a High Tory, many of his followers were not. 'Their doctrines are most repulsive, and strongly tinctured with impertinence, and disrespect towards their superiors', was an early, and characteristic, complaint; and in many areas the appearance of Methodist revivalism added to the sense of unease of parson and squire alike.

However, the first constitutional lesson of the new reign was a traditional one in its stress on the continuing importance of royal influence as Bute – a man without political experience, evident ability, or even a seat in Parliament (though he had once sat in the Lords as one of the Scottish representative peers) – became Secretary of State within six months of the King's accession. A year later he was First Lord of the Treasury and head of the administration. Although Bute became a more substantial political figure when he took over leadership of the Scottish parliamentary interest after the death of the third Duke of Argyll in 1761, he owed his rise to the insistence of George III that he could not face the task ahead without the help of his former tutor. For more than one reason the new monarch and his mentor were unlikely to be satisfied simply with a smooth takeover of the existing system. Viewing both the policies and the ministers of the Pitt–Newcastle administration with distaste, brought up on textbook constitutional maxims, George with the help of Bute had shaped a series of principles ready to be put into operation when he became King. They rested on the conviction that George II had been a 'King in chains', at the mercy of an unscrupulous Whig oligarchy, which used office and patronage to cement its position at home, while abroad it manipulated policy in favour of Hanover. 'I will not permit ministers to trample on me', the King told Bute after his accession; the guiding stars of the Whig grandees, he concluded were 'ingratitude, avarice and ambition'. At a time when the war ministry attracted support from an unusually wide span of the political nation, George and Bute seemed almost to be playing the role of an opposition party. Like other oppositions of other times, experience of office led to disillusionment. For Bute it brought the awkwardness of working with politicians in an atmosphere of mutual disdain; for the King it showed the difficulty of putting ideals into practice.

In April 1763 Bute retired, at least from public office, buffeted by resentments near at hand, and subjected to abuse on the streets. George III, his dreams of a partnership of virtue with his 'dearest friend' vanished, turned to the job of finding an acceptable first minister – a quest which became a recurrent theme during the next half-dozen years. The procession of first ministers, potential and actual, wending its way across the political stage, affords evidence of the delicate balancing act needed to find a politician acceptable both to the King and to a majority in the Commons. Grenville, Rockingham, Pitt, Grafton, all moved centre-stage at brief intervals to kiss hands with the King, watched from the wings by figures at court whose importance was inflated by rumour and suspicion – Cumberland (until his death in October 1765), Bute (until his final slide from influence in 1766), and George's mother, the Princess Dowager. Whatever their various talents, none of the first ministers can be judged a success. The hectoring Grenville made himself so obnoxious to the King that some of George's most crucial decisions of the next few years can be explained only by fear of finding Grenville close at hand again. Rockingham, silent and ineffective despite his following of a hundred Whig MPs, had neither a wide enough political base, nor enough of the King's trust, to remain first minister for more than a year. Some of his problems can be explained by the maverick role being played by Pitt, refusing office on any but his own terms, yet still a figure to be courted and feared. In July 1766 what appeared to be a logical resolution of this problem was reached when Pitt became head of the ministry – though moving to the Lords as Earl of Chatham and declining any executive responsibility. Whether the ministry would ever have operated effectively is doubtful, but it was not put to the test because Chatham's long illness from 1767 left him a recluse. The death of Charles Townshend, the wayward and unpredictable Chancellor of the Exchequer, later in the year brought the Duke of Grafton to the fore – if only by default. Under him the ministry was reconstructed, with Lord North filling Townshend's positions as Chancellor of the Exchequer and leading government spokesman in the Commons. When Grafton, struggling with problems real and imagined, resigned in early 1770 North became First Lord of the Treasury. There was no inkling that he was to remain at the head of affairs for twelve years, a term of office matched only by Walpole among his predecessors.

The shufflings of administrations, none showing much confidence in its own longevity, made the problems of the 1760s the more perplexing. As North was to complain in 1769, the 'chopping and changing' of ministries had produced 'a terrible effect upon public measures.' At times, particularly in the most chaotic months of Chatham's administration, ministers were arguing and voting against each other in Parliament. At home the affair of John Wilkes, so insignificant a matter in origin, had by the end of the decade swollen into a challenge to the political establishment of the day. In America resentment at the new thrust of British policies had begun to push the relationship between Britain and its mainland colonies close to breakdown. Such a rupture carried more dangers because of Britain's uneasy relationship with former foes and allies alike in Europe, where the repercussions of the Seven Years War were slow to die away. Not the least worrying feature of the period was the rising tide of economic distress and social disorder. A cider tax imposed by the Bute ministry in 1763 brought out hostile crowds in the western counties; other disturbances were less the result of specific government policies than of poor harvests, fluctuating food prices, and falling employment. During the rural riots of the late summer of 1766, troops were used more than eighty times, and so stretched were the army's resources that the autumn reviews were cancelled. In 1768 there were riots in London arising from disputes involving silk-weavers, coalheavers, seamen and Thames watermen – and these were the more ominous because they coincided with the renewed Wilkite disturbances which had begun to excite and alarm London that spring.

The Wilkes affair, however personal and trivial it seemed to be at times, introduced a new dimension to politics. A Pittite MP of no great mark, Wilkes had in the last months of the war founded the *North Briton*, a journalistic counterblast to the pro-Bute *Briton*. Early in 1763 Wilkes and the *North Briton* crossed the boundaries of accepted journalistic licence, first with innuendos about a sexual relationship between Bute and the Princess Dowager, and then in issue No. 45 with an attack on the King's Speech and its support of the Treaty of Paris. The Grenville government responded by issuing a general warrrant for the arrest of all those connected with the publication of No. 45. In doing so, it raised a whole series of legal issues, and though Wilkes himself failed to return from France to face trial for seditious libel, the matter dragged through the courts in 1764 and 1765. Before his disappearance across the Channel Wilkes had shown what was to become a hall-mark of his technique as he turned his personal predicament into one of universal dimensions. What was at stake, he claimed, was the liberty of 'all peers and gentlemen' and 'what touches me more sensibly, that of all the middling and inferior set of people'. The decision of the courts was that Wilkes's alleged offence was covered by the protection of parliamentary privilege; that general warrants issued against unnamed persons were illegal; and that ministers could not issue warrants, general or specific, save in cases of suspected treason. Wilkes was expelled from the Commons, but an attempt by his supporters to declare all general warrants illegal failed by only fourteen votes. If the Commons had little time for Wilkes and his posturings, there was clear recognition of the importance of the issues raised, and in particular their relation to the conduct of the government.

Wilkes had been supported by powerful friends from within the political world, and by noisy demonstrations on the streets of London; but his move abroad and the slow battle of the law courts removed some of the interest in his cause. After four years of self-imposed exile, hard-pressed by creditors, Wilkes returned to

England to contest the 1768 election, despite the sentence of outlawry passed upon him. As he told friends, 'What the devil have I to do with prudence? I must raise a dust or starve in a gaol.' Finishing bottom of the poll in the City of London, Wilkes stood in Middlesex, an increasingly urbanised county whose 40s freeholders saw in him an attractive candidate. Helped by radicals such as Sergeant Glynn and Parson John Horne, Wilkes planned his campaign, not simply by demagogic appeal, but by methodical organisation of voters and helpers; and he won comfortably. Wilkes's election victory marked only another twist in the story of his fortunes. Drama and violence were never far away from Wilkes, and to the strikes and food riots already sweeping the capital were now added Wilkite demonstrations. One of these in St George's Fields near the King's Bench prison where Wilkes was confined produced the first Wilkite martyrs when the Scots Guards opened fire and killed a half-dozen demonstrators and bystanders. To the government, now headed by Grafton, the sight of striking coal-heavers wearing Wilkite badges displaying 'No. 45' was a portent and a threat.

With the political temperature rising as Wilkes accused the government of planning 'the horrid massacre' of St George's Fields, proceedings began in the Commons to expel Wilkes. An extraordinary sequence of events followed, in which Wilkes was expelled from the Commons, only to be twice re-elected before finally a candidate, Colonel Luttrell, was found to oppose him. At the final by-election in this sequence, Luttrell was declared the victor even though he polled only a quarter of Wilkes's votes. The Leader of the House, North, put the matter bluntly: 'The freeholders who polled for Mr Wilkes, in my opinion, threw away their votes.' The episode gave Wilkes a cause comprehensible to all, not hedged around by pedantic legal arguments. The government's handling of a special case was taken by Wilkes as proof of general, sinister intentions: 'If ministers can once usurp the power of declaring who *shall not* be your representative, the next step is very easy . . . It is that of telling you whom you *shall* send to Parliament, and then the boasted Constitution of England will be entirely torn up by the roots.'

Wilkes had turned his personal problems and ambitions into a populist challenge to the oligarchical politics of his day. It was this challenge, not the supposedly authoritarian tendencies of George III's ministers, which was novel. They could cite precedent for their actions – whether on the issue of general warrants, the move to expel Wilkes, or the continuing ban on the publication of parliamentary debates – whereas the radicals and their aristocratic supporters were often treading new ground with their insistence that the restrictions were unacceptable if not illegal. In London, traditionally hostile to

Hanoverian government, tense with economic distress in some areas, Wilkes found receptive audiences. His supporters were more than silent listeners – they were participators, encouraged by pamphlets, ballads, the wearing of cockades, colours and badges, to play an active, truculent role, to take their lead from Wilkes himself. It was the first political experience for many, the first time that the feelings of resentment, distress and dissent had found so sharp a focus. 'Wilkes and Liberty' was a political slogan, however crude, and it had a potent appeal for the wage-earners and small artisans who made up a large part of the crowds who turned out to march, to demonstrate, and sometimes to riot. The defiance of authority was taken into the courts of law where defendants, helped by Wilkite lawyers, challenged laws which they regarded as 'engines of oppression', and rulings which they condemned as political.

With forty or fifty provincial newspapers to report his activities, and with improved roads and postal services to bring the news, Wilkes had become a national figure. Wilkite clubs sprang up in London and the provinces, some as much convivial as political. In London radical merchants, lawyers and other professional men, formed in 1769 the Society for the Supporters of the Bill of Rights, but it was at this point that difficulties began. The more explicit Wilkes's radical colleagues were about their programme, the less likely were they to hold the support of MPs whose main interest was harassment of the government. Inheritance of the system rather than its overthrow was their aim; and they looked with a cold eye on proposals for shorter parliaments, abolition of the rotten boroughs, and vote by secret ballot. The tentative alliance between radicals out of Parliament, and the Rockingham and Grenville groups within, held together only as long as the Middlesex election was the main point of attention. Even then, the petitioning campaign of 1769–70, which took the Middlesex election as the basis of a request to the king to dissolve a corrupt Parliament, attracted support from less than half the English counties and only a dozen of the larger boroughs.

Rockingham had doubts about the whole petitioning exercise, while his junior colleague, Edmund Burke, showed in his *Thoughts on the Causes of the Present Discontents*, published in 1770, the gulf between the Rockinghams' position and that of the Bill of Rights Society. Burke insisted that a secret, inner court cabal determined both policy and distribution of patronage; that 'the power of the Crown, almost dead and rotten as Prerogative, has grown up anew under the new name of Influence.' His remedy for this situation was not sweeping political reform but the legitimisation of 'party'. Given the fragmentation of group and party at this time, the insistence of the Rockinghams that government should be conducted by politicians sharing agreed principles and policies, was as premature as the programme of the metropolitan radicals; but it became important in defining the position of the Whigs in the 1770s. Opposition politicians on their way to the City to dine with the Lord Mayor, William Beckford, noted with disapproval that the crowds wore tickets in their hats demanding 'Annual Parliaments, Equal Representation, Place and Pension Bill'; but Beckford himself showed how radical proposals were emerging, even in unlikely quarters. At the general election of 1761 he had reflected the customary anti-Court stance of the City when he supported the 'middling classes of England' against 'Your Nobility [who] receive more from the Public than they pay to it.' By the year of his death in 1770 he had moved to an attack on rotten boroughs, electoral corruption, placemen and pensioners, and to a demand for 'a more equal representation of the people'. Here, in the Wilkite period but owing little in formulation to the great opportunist, was the outline of a radical programme. It was ill-defined, driven by property rights and individual eccentricity rather than by any concept of popular sovereignty, but it was enough to attract reformers and disconcert conservative interests for the next twenty years.

Although the Wilkes issue dominated parliamentary and public attention for long periods, an even more insistent theme in the politics of the 1760s was the relationship with the American colonies – never before a subject of major political concern. For the first time, political developments on both sides of the Atlantic were linked, as attacks in Britain on the behaviour of ministers and the role of the crown fuelled suspicions in America about the intentions of the imperial government. Wilkes's warning cry that liberty was at risk sharpened the determination of the colonists to safeguard their constitutional rights. The efforts of British administrations to inject an element of financial realism into the relationship between mother country and colonies were seen as part of a planned assault by the King and corrupt ministers on the traditional rights of English subjects living in the colonies.

To outward appearance Britain's American empire at the beginning of George III's reign set the rest of Europe an object lesson in economic progress, political sophistication, and cultural achievement. The colonies ranged in character from the productive farming lands of Pennsylvania to the busy and cosmopolitan 'middle colonies' of New York and New Jersey, from the slave-based plantation economies of Barbados and Virginia to the seaboard mercantile communities of New England. They accepted immigrants from many countries; the birth-rate was rising; living standards generally were higher than in Europe. The colonies possessed printing presses, newspapers and libraries – and politically articulate leaders. They were based on a more solid foundation of genuine settlement and local enterprise than those of any other nation. Yet the growth of the American colonies had brought problems, best appreciated at first hand; but just as no Hanoverian monarch had visited Scotland, Wales or Ireland, so no leading politician had crossed the Atlantic. If one had made the journey he would have found societies developing which differed in many respects from Britain. Some of the colonies were a century or more old. Most of their inhabitants had never seen England, and many were not of English stock. Better communications had brought increasing contacts between the colonies, and although parochialism was still strong a conviction was emerging among some colonists that they were 'American' as well as British. On the frontiers were vigorous, self-reliant men who had little time for the rules and regulations of a remote imperial government. In the towns and ports merchants chafed at the paternalistic system of economic regulation imposed on colonial trade and industry, and evasion had been honed to a fine art. Though there was as yet no thought of independence, self-confidence had been strengthened by the conquest of New France. The threat which had hung over the colonies for the best part of a century had been removed, and with it one pressing reason for loyalty to Britain.

During the critical years of the struggle against France in North America the Pitt–Newcastle government had been careful to avoid colonial disputes, but from 1759 onwards it showed itself less sensitive about colonial susceptibilities. Although colonial militia and colonial taxes contributed more to the campaigns than metropolitan critics would allow, ministers saw the triumphs of the war as those of British regular forces backed by British financial resources. The trend was the more serious because the acquisition of what was almost a new empire in 1763 involved complex problems of administration, finance and defence. The latter was the most urgent. Well before the end of the war the colonists had lost interest in costly defence schemes. Yet there were still Frenchmen, defeated but not subdued, to the north, Spaniards to the south, and thousands of hostile Indians along the frontiers. The need for keeping a regular army in America was brutally emphasised by the 'Conspiracy of Pontiac', an attempt by a confederacy of Indian tribes to drive British settlers into the sea. The weight of the fighting was borne by British regulars; and although the decision to keep an army of about eight thousand men in America had been taken before the uprising, the Indian campaigns of 1763 and 1764 strengthened the government's determination to maintain this force. This in turn led to financial problems, which had been anticipated, and political ones, which had not. One result of the Pontiac rising was the hastening by the Grenville ministry of its Proclamation of 1763, intended to reassure the Indians that white settlement west of the Alleghenies would be strictly controlled, a measure which aroused predictable resentment in the colonies. For the next dozen years successive British administrations pondered the problem of priorities in the vast hinterland. The interests of Indians, settlers, traders, questions of cost and defence – all had to be taken into account. For the moment, the moving frontier of American history had been halted, and metropolitan policy appeared to be in direct conflict with the natural ambitions of the colonists.

Meanwhile, the government was faced with a narrower but no less pressing problem, the cost of the peacetime army in America. The Seven Years War was the costliest Britain had ever fought. The land tax had risen to four shillings in the £, the National Debt had doubled, and at its end the government was introducing new and unpopular taxes such as that on cider. It seemed reasonable that the colonies, still lightly taxed in comparison, should help to meet the cost of British garrisons in America, stationed there for the colonists' own defence. Reasonable the suggestion might be, but such proposals had long been regarded as politically explosive. Various colonial governors had suggested the need for regular colonial contributions to defence costs for more than fifty years, but British governments had always resisted the temptation. Now, Grenville put one foot over a line which no British minister had previously crossed. On the face of it the Plantation Act of 1764 (known as the Sugar Act) was a conventional enough measure, but one clause raised an issue of principle: a 3*d.* per gallon duty on imports of foreign molasses into the colonies. The Act's preamble revealed that this was something more than the type of trade regulation measure which the colonies had accepted, if at times irritably, for a century, for it was also intended to raise revenue. On these grounds three colonies challenged it, for Englishmen, they argued, could be taxed only with the consent of their elected representatives, in this case the colonial assemblies. With appeals to Magna Carta, the Bill of Rights, and John Locke, 'No representation, No taxation' was advanced as one of the inalienable rights of a free Englishman. As on later occasions, it is difficult to distinguish between principle and pocket – some at least of the indignation seems to have stemmed from the suspicion that the measure had been pushed through in the interests of the West India lobby. The colonial case was stated, with some extravagance, by the Massachusetts Assembly. 'If our trade may be taxed, why not our lands, and everything we possess, or make use of? If taxes are laid upon us in any shape without ever having a legal representation where they are laid, are we not reduced from the character of free subjects to the miserable state of tributary slaves?'

Colonial fears were soon heightened, for in 1765 the Grenville government, having discovered that the molasses duty was covering only a fraction of the cost of the American garrisons, introduced the Stamp Act. This tax on legal and commercial transactions had been in force in England since 1694, and its extension to the colonies had been suggested more than once. The money raised was to be kept in a separate fund, and used for the defence of the colonies. Like the Sugar Act, the measure passed through the Commons with little debate, and less than fifty members voted against it. The colonial petitions of protest were ignored, Grenville loftily remarking that the government was aware that no man liked to be taxed. Ministers also had to hand a ready argument with which to refute the colonial complaint that they were being taxed by a body on which they were not represented. The colonies were 'virtually represented', as Soames Jenyns proceeded to explain in his *Objections to the taxation of our American Colonies*. 'Every *Englishman* is taxed, and not one in twenty represented . . . Manchester, Birmingham and many more of our richest trading Towns send no Members to Parliament.' Long after American independence the repercussions of this argument rang through English radical politics, for unrepresented cities were to form part of the indictment of a political system under attack.

Across the Atlantic the colonists were quick to grasp the implications of the Stamp Act. A tax was being laid upon Americans which affected their everyday transactions, which was in no sense a trade regulation measure, and which they could not avoid. It revealed the sham of virtual representation – 'a mere cobweb, spread to catch the unwary and intangle the weak', a colonial lawyer argued. This tax on business dealings, on newspapers and periodicals, united some of the most vocal and influential elements in the colonies; merchants, printers and lawyers. It allied the southern plantation colonies (little affected by the molasses duty) with the northern colonies; and in 1766 delegates from nine of the thirteen mainland colonies met at New York to co-ordinate opposition – in itself an unusual step. This 'Stamp Act Congress' passed a motion agreeing to parliamentary legislation but not to parliamentary taxation, and its stand was supported throughout the colonies by violent demonstrations. Rioting broke out in several cities, stamp distributors were forced to flee for their lives, and for the first time the 'Sons of Liberty' appeared on the streets to lead the agitation. More telling as far as the British government was concerned was agreement among the merchants not to import British goods; if continued, this boycott would strike at the heart of the colonial system.

In England Grenville had been replaced by Rockingham. Grenville's policies had reflected the feeling in ministerial circles that the time had come to put an end to the policy of drift which had characterised most governments of the Hanoverian period as far as colonial affairs were concerned. There was widespread agreement, and not only on the government side, that more incisive policies were needed to collect American revenue, to eliminate smuggling and violations of the trade laws, and in general to bring into line colonies which were straying dangerously outside the bounds of metropolitan control. Several members of the new Rockingham administration had opposed the Stamp Act, yet they could not appear to be giving way to intimidation and mob violence on what the King declared was 'the most serious matter that ever came before Parliament'. Helped by hints that the colonists objected only to internal taxation (such as the Stamp Act), and not to every kind of parliamentary tax and duty, the government hit on a compromise solution. With some difficulty it put together a package of measures: repeal of the Stamp Act, reduction of the molasses duty from 3*d.* to 1*d.* a gallon, and the passing of a Declaratory Act reiterating Parliament's legal right to tax the colonies as it thought fit. This last was to be criticised as an ungracious and provocative measure, but even with the promise of the Declaratory Act it was difficult to get an uneasy George III, and some other senior political figures, to accept repeal. As it was, the King refused to take action against those fifty or so placemen who voted against repeal, a betrayal, as the Rockinghams saw it, which in the long term hardened the group's determination to limit royal power.

Rockingham's brief ministry was followed by the ill-fated Chatham administration, with Charles Townshend as Chancellor of the Exchequer. Ministries came and went, but the financial problem remained. The new Chancellor, with the Commons insisting that the land tax be cut from four to three shillings, looked once more to the colonies. Revenue was to be raised by new import duties of paper, glass, paint and tea. These were external taxes, and if the colonists followed the line of argument put forward only the year before they would find it difficult to oppose them. If they did, then they were challenging the right of Parliament to levy any kind of tax or duty, and were well on the way to denying the sovereignty of Parliament. Townshend died soon after the new duties were passed, and never realised the extent of his miscalculation. The colonists had made clear their objection to revenue-raising measures levied without their consent, and hostile reaction to the new duties was soon forthcoming. John Dickinson's 'Letters from a Farmer in Pennsylvania' denied Parliament's right to impose any taxes, while in Massachusetts the 'Circular Letter' drawn up by Sam Adams urged the colonial assemblies to combine in upholding the principle of no taxation without representation.

How to preserve British sovereignty without running into violent conflict with the colonists was a dilemma which seemed to have no ending, and was made more intractable by the insistence of opponents of the government at home and in America that they were joined in a common struggle to protect 'liberty'. In America new non-importation agreements were made, in some cases reluctantly and under pressure. Once more, popular leaders stepped forward to lead resistance to the duties, and at the same time to challenge the powers of established and generally conservative leaders of colonial society. They accused the British government of undermining accepted colonial rights; for money from the Townshend duties was to be used to pay colonial governors, and so assemblies would be deprived of the powerful weapon of withholding salaries from royal officials. They pointed to New York as a sign of things to come. There the Assembly had been suspended for non-fulfilment of an earlier act. Other measures added to the tension. The enforcement of trade regulations was tightened with the establishment in America of boards of customs commissioners and vice-admiralty courts (sitting without juries) which soon ended the relaxed colonial convention of acquitting local smugglers. In Massachusetts the situation became so tense that British regulars were sent into Boston, where in March 1770 five inhabitants were killed in a street clash which colonial propagandists soon turned to good effect as the 'Boston Massacre'. It was the equivalent, radicals on both sides of the Atlantic were quick to point out, of the St George's Fields killings in London two years earlier. The withdrawal of troops from the streets of Boston, and the news that Parliament had repealed three of the Townshend duties (coincidentally, on the day of the 'massacre') calmed feelings in America, while in Britain the attention of the new government under North was diverted to the looming crisis with Spain.

If ministerial instability in the first decade of George III's reign explains some of the difficulties with the American colonies, it also had an unsettling effect on the conduct of British diplomacy during these years. Six changes of first minister, nine changes of Secretary of State for the Northern Department, seven changes of Secretary of State for the Southern Department, made continuity in policy almost impossible. In the years after the Treaty of Paris attempts by British ministers to repair relations with Prussia or negotiate an alliance with Russia failed. Nor was there any repetition of the reconciliation of fifty years earlier with the wartime enemy, for not only the menacing figure of Chatham but a succession of mediocre

Secretaries of State still thought in rigidly anti-Bourbon terms, while in France the dominant Duc de Choiseul pondered the chances of a war of revenge. Unexpectedly, it was from the junior partner in the Family Compact, Spain, that the challenge came. Under Charles III, as the reforms to put her American empire on a better military and economic footing took effect, ministers adopted an uncompromising attitude towards Britain. It was against a background of contention and bickering that in 1770 a crisis flared over the windswept group of barren islands in the south Atlantic known to the British as the Falklands and to the Spaniards as the Malvinas. Interest in the strategic possibilities of the islands had been growing with the new ambitions of European nations in the Pacific, and at the end of the Seven Years War British and French expeditions set up small bases in the group. Negotiations between Madrid and Paris led to the transfer of the French settlement to Spain in 1767, but the British refused to budge, and hinted that Spain ought to recognise British sovereignty over the whole group. Spain's answer came in 1770 when it launched from Buenos Aires an attack on the British post at Port Egmont, and forced the garrison to abandon it.

In Britain this exploit produced an uproar which was exploited by the opposition in a way reminiscent of 1739, while in Spain Charles III accepted that this was the *casus belli* which he and Choiseul had been awaiting. But of the three governments involved, only the Spanish was committed to war. In Britain the new North administration was uneasily aware of the low state of the navy after peacetime retrenchment, and its reservations were supported by those who failed to see the importance of the Falklands, 'a morsel of rock that lies somewhere at the bottom of America', as Horace Walpole wrote. The decisive developments were in France, where Louis XV, with memories of the disasters and expense of the Seven Years War still fresh, dismissed Choiseul, and forced Charles III to the negotiating table. The British base was restored, with a secret pledge by North for future evacuation. In 1774 the government put the whole affair in perspective by withdrawing the garrison on grounds of expense, leaving only a flag and an inscription to uphold British claims. For the time being the Family Compact had been deprived of its force, although the underlying motives which had brought France and Spain together before 1770 remained unchanged. British expansion still posed a threat to both nations, and as the dispute between Britain and her American colonies worsened so the danger grew of French and Spanish intervention.

North had shown coolness in dealing with the crisis, and the same quality was evident in his early dealings with the American colonies. His reputation has fluctuated over the years – at one time condemned as a tyrant, at another as a royal puppet – until he has now found a respectable if unexciting resting-place in historical scholarship. He emerges as a minister of ability, charm and shrewdness, whose chief strength was displayed in financial matters, but who in the end could not cope with the triple burden of being First Lord of the Treasury, Chancellor of the Exchequer, and Leader of the Commons in a crisis-ridden period. On America North's attitude was orthodox and unimaginative. His judgement was clouded by a lack of knowledge about a fast-changing situation, and by an inability to sense when toughness might or might not be appropriate. When he became prime minister in February 1770 he was confronted by an absurd and dangerous situation in America, in which the few thousand pounds trickling in from the Townshend duties were dwarfed by the merchants' losses (estimated at £700,000 a year) resulting from the American boycott. North decided to put into effect the policy agreed by the previous government to drop the controversial duties, except that on tea. This was to be kept, he explained, not so much because of its fiscal importance, but 'as a mark of the supremacy of Parliament'. The tactics of the Declaratory Act had been repeated, and the retention of the tea duty made it clear that the government did not admit to any shift of principle. It was a compromise designed to attract moderate support in both Britain and America, which would leave the opposition isolated. It was to be seen as a concession, not as a collapse of will in the face of intimidation.

In America the non-importation agreements were abandoned and with a boom in trade came a reaction in some colonies against the populist politicians who had come to the fore in the previous decade. To many conservatives their zeal for colonial liberties looked suspiciously like a device for gaining power; and it is true that to the radical leaders the lull, disturbed though it was by occasional acts of violence and by continuing disputes in several colonies between governor and assembly, was unwelcome. At the end of 1773 the 'Boston Tea Party' brought a crisis atmosphere once more. A decision by the North government to encourage the East India Company to become the main direct exporter of tea to the colonies, free of British duties though still carrying the Townshend levy of 3*d.* a pound, alarmed American merchants (and smugglers) and aroused the suspicions of radical groups. It was a worrying sign of the difference in perspective between London and the colonies that a measure which to the North government was primarily a device to help the ailing East India Company was seen by Americans as a plot against their constitutional rights. A campaign of intimidation was directed against the masters of ships bringing tea into American ports, and in December the cargo of one of these ships lying in

Boston harbour was thrown overboard. To the injury of this attack on property was added the insult of a calculated defiance of imperial legislation. In March and April 1774 North introduced into Parliament a series of coercive measures: among them the closing of the port of Boston until compensation had been paid, and modification of the Massachusetts charter to cut the powers of the Assembly. The measures passed with only slight opposition in Parliament, and in the general election of that autumn American affairs played little part. With opposition morale low the government's majority remained a comfortable one – 321 supporters in a House of 558 MPs was North's calculation.

Coincidental with the coercive acts was the passing in May 1774 of the Quebec Act, which after many delays provided a form of government for Canada. It allowed Canada to be governed in a way more familiar to most of its French-speaking inhabitants than the normal pattern of the British seaboard colonies, though whether this was a statesmanlike or reactionary move depended on one's own prejudices. There was to be no elected Assembly but a legislative council appointed by the Crown and including Roman Catholics. French law was to be observed in civil cases, and Catholic priests would still receive tithes. The Act appalled many Americans. It seemed to re-establish a despotic, popish colony to their north, and strengthened the fears roused by other British policies. Furthermore, the great southwestern extension of Canada's borders to the Ohio blocked the expansion of the middle colonies. In its own right a generous measure for a defeated people, the Quebec Act was unfortunately timed as far as the American crisis was concerned, though defenders of North would later point out that it helped to keep Canada quiet during the turbulence of the revolutionary war.

Coercive measures had been introduced, but not the means to enforce them if resistance spread outside Boston, as it soon did. Help was sent to Massachusetts from other colonies, and the new British governor, General Gage, found himself bottled up in Boston with his regiments, unable to move outside the town for fear of precipitating hostilities. A policy intended to isolate Massachusetts had produced the opposite effect. North's measures threatened the colonies with a military solution to the crisis, without providing the necessary force. Instead, British policy halted awkwardly between coercion and compromise. The initiative passed away from the British government as colonial delegates met at Philadelphia in September 1774 to consider the situation. The Continental Congress – a significant name, and one difficult to associate with colonial status – saw the triumph of the popular leaders over their conservative opponents, and the transfer of policy-making from the individual colonies to a central body. In

October a Declaration of Rights was drawn up which accepted that Parliament could regulate colonial commerce in imperial interests, but denounced revenue-raising Acts, demanded the repeal of thirteen Acts (including the Coercive Acts and the Quebec Act), and severed commercial relations with Britain. As the colonists collected arms, so the North government set its face against negotiation despite Gage's warning that he needed another twenty thousand men if he was to be effective. The King's comment to Gage on the colonists summed up the attitude of the government and of the majority of MPs, the press and the political public: 'We must either master them or totally leave them to themselves and treat them as aliens.'

In February 1775 North, moved by the awful realisation of possible war, made an attempt at conciliation. Like earlier responses, it dealt with the last colonial grievance but one, assuming that the American position was static whereas all the evidence of the previous ten years showed it to be dynamic and advancing. It made concessions on taxation, as long as the Assemblies provided the required amounts of money, but none on that issue of Parliament's legislative authority over the colonies which the Continental Congress had recently challenged. In any event by the time the offer reached America the situation had deteriorated almost beyond recall. In April British and colonial forces were involved in a running skirmish at Lexington, and lost four hundred men between them. In June an even more serious clash at Bunker Hill outside Boston represented an attempt by Gage to apply military sanctions to a situation fast drifting out of control. As the two sides moved towards war so the conviction grew among the colonial leaders (patriots to one side, rebels to the other) that independence must be their objective. Men could not be expected to suffer and die for so flaccid a slogan as improved rights within the imperial system. The decision was not an easy one. At the Second Continental Congress in May 1775 only a minority favoured independence, and in July Congress sent the 'Olive Branch Petition' appealing for an end to the bloodshed, and for reconciliation, after repeal of those Acts of Parliament which the colonies found impossible to accept. The petition was seen in London as a divisive attempt, and was summarily rejected, while the growing bitterness of the fighting in America led to a hardening of attitude on each side. While Dr Johnson in his *Taxation No Tyranny* insisted that 'in sovereignty there can be no gradations', for the colonists Tom Paine in *Common Sense* trod new ground with his attack on the King and the whole institution of hereditary monarchy. In July 1776 came the Declaration of Independence, a moving call to arms even if some of its assertions were of doubtful historical validity. Certainly its attempt to hold George III responsible for British actions is untenable: the King was interested and active, but not dominant in the formulation of policy. The Declaration sent many waverers into the ranks of the loyalists, but for the rest it committed them to separation and independence.

Behind the interplay of British measures and colonial reaction lay the fact that the old colonial system was no longer appropriate to the American colonies. In many ways they were as politically conscious and economically ambitious as the mother country. They had come of age at a time when the expulsion of French power from Canada had lessened their need for British protection. Even if the crisis points of the 1760s and 1770s – internal taxation, salaries, troop requisitions – had been successfully negotiated, others were looming which called for a new framework of political relations if there was not to be a continuous state of tension and confrontation. Some members of the opposition groups pleaded for a fundamental rethinking of the colonial relationship. Burke's speech of March 1775 on conciliation with America showed his perception of the importance of the growth in population and wealth of the colonies, and of the spirit and character of their inhabitants. Taken together, Burke argued, these developments showed the futility of using force. His own suggested policy would have turned the clock back to 1763 and the convention that the colonies were taxed only through their assemblies. Chatham in one respect would have gone further than Burke by accepting the distinction between internal and external taxation despite the limitation on parliamentary sovereignty this involved, in an effort to 'restore America to your bosom'. Such rhetoric is appealing, but it took for granted an instinctive American loyalty to the Crown which no longer existed in large areas of the colonies. The problems Burke and Chatham tackled were those of the mid-1760s rather than the mid-1770s. Burke's appeal to the 'ties which, though light as air, are as links of iron', was as unlikely to sway the organisers of the Boston Tea Party as it was to move those in Britain who demanded that those involved must be caught and punished.

To hear orators on both sides of the Atlantic appealing to the Glorious Revolution or to Blackstone's *Commentaries on the Laws of England* as justification for their different stances was to appreciate the limitations rather than the links of a shared constitutional heritage. Even more damaging were mutual misunderstandings. In the colonies many were convinced that British policies were the work of George III, North and a cabal unrepresentative of the British nation as a whole; the mirror image of this illusion led British ministers to the conclusion that American opposition was confined to small groups of plotters, and that the explosions of popular support were the familiar excesses of the 'mob'. The fog of war hung over relations between Britain and the colonies long before the actual outbreak of hostilities. Ministers had no deep plans to subvert colonial liberties, but to the complex problems posed by colonial expansion they could offer only the tightening of a system already being called into question. In and out of Parliament the more conciliatory propositions of opposition members found little backing, and although the City of London – where Wilkes was Lord Mayor in 1775 – showed support for the American cause through petitions and remonstrances, this faded once the fighting began. North's statement of 1770, 'I am for retaining our right of taxing America, but of giving it every relief that may be consistent with the welfare of the mother country', probably represented the mass of opinion. After it was all over, North remarked with some justice of the American war that 'it was the war of the people'. In a period of tense international rivalry, disobedience by the colonies was seen as an intolerable affront to British prestige, and a threat to national security.

7 Years of crisis, 1775–1784

The war which began with the clash of arms at Lexington in April 1775 presented a series of worrying military and diplomatic problems to the British government. In essence the military problem could be simply stated: the British regular army was small, the potential area of rebellion vast. By European standards communications in America were poor, and there was no national capital whose capture might fatally wound the patriot cause. Difficulties of finance and equipment would keep the colonial forces commanded by George Washington small in size; but to counterbalance this, British forces would have to receive supplies and reinforcements from a home base three thousand miles distant. With the probability emerging of small armies harassed by supply problems, and moving cautiously across a terrain much of which was wilderness, the key to the war was the attitude of the civilian population. If, as George III and the North government suspected, defiance was confined to a hard core of dissidents, then one or two sharp blows at Washington's little army would knock the heart out of the rebel cause. But if patriot sympathisers were either more numerous or more active than the loyalists, then British forces would be committed to that most demoralising form of hostilities, guerrilla warfare. Beyond these immediate uncertainties and difficulties loomed an even more worrying problem – the possibility of French and Spanish intervention. Unless swift and decisive victory could be achieved in America, this possibility might become a calamitous reality; yet it was that type of victory which American conditions made most difficult to obtain.

In Britain the war was fought by a government secure in office, at least during the early years, but uninspired in leadership. Able politician though he was, North was no war supremo. As First Lord of the Treasury and Chancellor of the Exchequer he saw his main duty as financing the war. This he did with considerable skill, using a variety of inducements, including the sale of lottery tickets, to keep interest rates on his war loans within bounds, and showing ingenuity in devising new taxes – ranging from one on servants to an entertainment duty – to fund those loans. Only in 1781 and 1782 did the situation threaten to slide out of control, but in general North was as capable a war financier as any of his predecessors. His failure was not one of financial competence but of political leadership. Given to bouts of introspection and lethargy, favouring government by departments under the general oversight of the cabinet, North neither provided overall management of the war effort nor saw it as his duty to do so. The main burden of the war rested on two controversial politicians, Lord George Germain and the Earl of Sandwich. Secretary of State for the American Colonies (as he became in 1775), Germain was an impatient, forceful man whose career lay under the shadow of allegations of cowardice during the Seven Years War. The personal life of the First Lord of the Admiralty Sandwich left something to be desired in the eyes of many of his contemporaries, but the charges levelled against him of the mismanagement of naval affairs were unjustified. No First Lord in the eighteenth century was faced with the mounting anxieties which weighed on Sandwich, and he emerged from the ordeal with considerable credit. The performance of individual ministers did not alter the fact that there was no decisive voice in the cabinet, for Germain, virtual Minister of War, lacked the political strength and personal authority of Pitt twenty years earlier. Nor were there commanders of first rank in the army and navy. Washington was confronted with generals of mediocre ability; and the navy was split with quarrels in which political partisanship played a heavy part.

British strategy for the first full year of the war in 1776 was to isolate the centre of revolt in New England by seizing New York and the Hudson valley. This would link the British forces in Canada with those along the Atlantic seaboard, and cut the rebel territory in two. Under its new commander, Howe, the British army was strengthened by the arrival of reinforcements from home, and Brunswick and Hessian troops from Germany. This last was a conventional enough military transaction, but it outraged American opinion. With loyalist support it was hoped that Howe would extinguish the rebellion in New England, but his overall strategy was disrupted by an unexpected American push into Canada. Furthermore, Washington's pressure in the early spring caused Howe to evacuate his uncomfortable berth in Boston. Despite these setbacks the British summer campaign gathered momentum as New York, Rhode Island and New Jersey were all taken. New York became the centre of British strategy for the rest of the war. It had a good harbour, commanded the entrance of the overland route to Canada, and forced rebel forces to make a huge detour around it whenever they moved in a north–south direction. It was soon clear that Washington's continentals were no match in warfare for Howe's regular troops, and the American commander avoided full-scale engagements whenever possible. When Howe's army lumbered back into winter quarters Washington struck late in the season, and retook most of New Jersey. This was the only gleam of light in a depressing year for the Americans, but the fact remained that Washington's army was still in existence. During the winter months it dwindled to three thousand men, but it would grow again in the spring, and with French arms arriving from Europe would be better equipped than in 1776.

The year 1777, then, was likely to be crucial, and British strategy changed, with Howe moving south. Philadelphia was the target, for the capture of the largest colonial city and the seat of Congress was expected to demoralise the rebels and leave only the malcontents in New England. After long delay Howe took Philadelphia, but the victory had none of the impact that had been predicted. Washington's army, though hard pressed, remained intact; and meanwhile to the north the British army under Burgoyne coming down from Canada to strike at New England met disaster. By mid-October Burgoyne was surrounded at Saratoga, able neither to advance nor retreat, and he had no alternative but to surrender. Saratoga had an effect out of all proportion to the number of men involved. It was for the Americans the first real victory in a grinding war fought mainly on the retreat. The news helped to keep Washington's men going through a hard winter at Valley Forge near Philadelphia; the British army in comfortable winter quarters not twenty miles off, the tattered continentals existing on meagre fare in their flimsy tents and log-huts. Saratoga threw into doubt the entire British strategy in America, with its confident assumption that British regulars could brush aside any continentals or militia who tried to obstruct their work of bringing areas back to allegiance to the Crown. An indication of the sagging in morale which followed Saratoga was shown in the peace proposals which North laid before Parliament in February 1778 – as the opposition pointed out, they were in essence those suggested by Burke three years earlier. The same month saw a development which made North's peace feelers irrelevant even before they crossed the Atlantic. In France Choiseul's successor, the Comte de Vergennes, had hesitated to intervene in the struggle until he was certain that the American rebellion would not collapse and leave France isolated against Britain. Saratoga was the assurance he needed, and in February treaties of alliance and commerce were signed between France and the Americans. France agreed not to make peace until American independence was assured, gave up all claims to North America east of the Mississippi, and was left a free hand in the Caribbean.

The entry of France into the war changed the nature of the struggle. European waters, the West Indies, India – all now became theatres of war. When in June 1779 Spain followed France into the war with the avowed intention of regaining Gibralter and Minorca, the North government was faced with a swelling resistance in America which pinned down most of its troops and many of its ships, and a union of the two Bourbons without continental distractions. Pitt's forebodings had become reality, for unlike the situation in January 1762 the French and Spanish navies were both intact. Sandwich warned: 'England till this time was never engaged in sea war with the House of Bourbon thoroughly united, their naval force unbroken, and having no other war or object to draw off their attention and resources. We have no one friend or ally to assist us.' That home forces could not be weakened to meet the multitude of threats overseas was shown by an invasion attempt in 1779. Though it was unsuccessful, for a few days French and Spanish fleets controlled the Channel with the British fleet far away to the west. The British government was caught in an agonising predicament. Abandonment of the American war would involve giving up all that Britain was supposedly fighting for. Concentration on America would leave Britain's possessions elsewhere exposed to attack and capture. The only answer was to stretch all available forces to the limit, and pray that they would be in the right place at the right time. Reinforcements were doled out in dribs and drabs; in America Philadelphia was evacuated to cut British commitments; nowhere did resources appear to be adequate for the tasks in hand.

Saratoga was a turning point in more ways than one. In Parliament the ministry's majority began to fall away with, as North complained, MPs becoming 'very indifferent to the cause of government.' More alarming still, the American war led to a crisis in Ireland at the very moment when hostilities became European in dimension. Despite the outward trappings of independent sovereignty, Ireland's practical status remained that of a colony. It had its own monarch, but he was George III; it possessed its own Parliament, but its legislative powers were constrained by the ancient but still effective Poynings' Law, by the Declaratory Act of 1719, and by the usual tools of political management. The main effect of this subordination was felt in the economic sphere, for Irish trade and industry were constrained within a straitjacket designed to protect British mercantile interests. Membership of the Irish House of Commons with its 300 MPs was limited to the 10 per cent of the population who were Anglican. Excluded altogether from the political process was the Roman Catholic majority, who had no vote, could not acquire land on a long-term basis, and were denied membership of the Dublin Parliament, the corporations, the bar, and commissions in the army and navy. The role of the other main religious community, the Presbyterians, though not as constricted as the Catholics', was much diminished by the operation of the Test and Corporation Acts. The Lord Lieutenant or Viceroy spent more time in England than in Ireland, and during his absence political affairs were managed by two or three Irish magnates, the 'undertakers', in return for a share of patronage. General elections took place only on the death of the monarch (so there had not been one between 1727 and 1760), and Parliament was summoned only every other year.

It was a political system narrow and corrupt even by the standards of the day, and by the time of George III's accession its blatant management in English interests was causing anger and frustration. The main demand for change came not from the Catholic majority but from Protestant politicians, the patriots as they were soon to be known, such as Henry Flood and Henry Grattan, who in the 1760s advanced a series of demands: commercial equality with Britain, regular elections, a Habeas Corpus Act, and security of tenure for judges during good behaviour. The patriot demands were the more awkward to resist because they represented, in the main, existing practice in the sister kingdom; and because they coincided with the developing American crisis. At times government difficulty in the one area had a direct impact on policy in the other. It was in part the failure to raise money from the American colonies for imperial garrisons which led the new and vigorous Lord Lieutenant of Ireland, Viscount Townshend, to dispense with the 'undertakers' in 1767, and to put before the Irish Parliament a package which offered reforms in exchange for additional troops. In the event, hesitation on both sides of the Irish Sea meant that only one measure was adopted – the Octennial Act, which resulted in a general election in 1769.

When Townshend stepped down in 1772 he left behind a scene of confusion and irritation, and a patriot opposition strengthened by the discarded political operators of the previous decade. The replacement of indirect control of the Irish Parliament by a resident Lord Lieutenant might be a logical development, but it made British authority in Ireland more visible at the very time when the colonists were seeking to diminish it in America. After 1775 constitutional issues in Ireland were sharpened by economic distress as war in America closed important channels of Irish emigration and trade, while the spread of hostilities led to the loss of some of Ireland's most important European markets. Attempts by the North government in 1778 to remove some of the restrictions on Irish trade were blocked in the Commons by MPs responding to the protectionist pressure of British merchants; and the concessions made the next year were not only slight in themselves but compared unfavourably with those which had been offered to America in the abortive peace moves of 1778. The lesson was not lost in Ireland, where the Protestant Volunteer organisations set up in case of French invasion mustered about eight thousand uniformed and armed members by 1779. Non-importation agreements were made on the American model, while the Irish House of Commons passed a motion demanding free trade, and voted financial supply for only six months instead of the customary two years. With British merchant opposition muffled by the threat of the Irish trade boycott, North was able to take action before the end of 1779. He resisted demands for constitutional change, but removed some of the more vexing restraints on Irish commerce. For the moment the government had bought peace in Ireland, but the political turbulence of the preceding years was not to be calmed by a few trading concessions.

Coincidental with tension in Ireland was a surge of opposition to the government in England, where dismay over the course of the war, irritation at high taxes, and suspicions about ministerial corruption, came to a head in 1779. The issue of America had drawn an unusually sharp dividing line across the floor of the Commons since the 1774 election, but not until the end of the decade did the opposition groups pose a serious threat. Even then, the highest number of MPs voting against the government was 170, and more worrying to ministers was the resignation of several disillusioned office-holders during 1779, and the growing swell of extra-parliamentary agitation. There had been a few earlier glimpses of this. In 1776 Major John Cartwright, at the beginning of a radical career lasting fifty years, first came to public attention with the publication of his spirited reform tract, *Take Your Choice*. The same year had also seen a final radical outburst by Wilkes, who argued unavailingly for disfranchisement of corrupt and decayed boroughs, and for an extension of the franchise. If Wilkes was a spent force, the gathering reform movement was more purposeful than years earlier, and its supporters were more substantial than the 'Wilkes and Liberty' demonstrators. The lead came, not from London, but from Yorkshire, where the Rev. Christopher Wyvill, a considerable landowner, after some skilful preliminary work persuaded a meeting of 600 gentry at the end of the year to pass a petition protesting against the government's waste of public money. The protest was as much political as financial, for Wyvill saw it as a wedge which would split open the closed political system. As he told Yorkshire MPs, 'if once the fund of corruption were reduced, it would be an easy matter to carry the other regulations, annual parliaments, more county members, etc., which are thought necessary to restore the freedom of Parliament.' With Wyvill directing a committee of correspondence from Yorkshire, twenty-six counties and a dozen boroughs submitted identical petitions in the early months of 1780 demanding a programme of 'economical reform' designed to save public money and reduce the influence of the Crown.

London soon followed the example of Yorkshire with committees of association established in the counties of Middlesex and Surrey, and in several of the boroughs. The MP for Westminster, Charles James Fox, became chairman of the committee of correspondence, and supported by Wilkites pushed his demands far beyond Wyvill's careful programme. If the Commons refused to respond to the petitions, he asserted, then it would be for 'the people to assume that trust which their delegates had thrown off', and there can be no doubt that Fox's definition of 'the people' was altogether wider than Wyvill's assumption of them as the property-owning classes. The metropolitan radicals, working through new organisations such as Cartwright's Society for Constitutional Information, and the Westminster Association, demanded an extension of the franchise, annual parliaments, and abolition of the rotten boroughs. The opposition groups in Parliament, especially those gathered around Rockingham and Shelburne (the latter had on Chatham's death in 1778 assumed leadership of his followers), snatched at the lead given by Wyvill, though they did not share his enthusiasm for a network of local associations bringing pressure to bear on Parliament. The petitions supported the complaint the opposition had been making for a decade – that it was royal influence and ministerial corruption which kept the government in office.

In the Commons the Rockinghams attempted to give Wyvill's demands legislative shape with the introduction of a series of economical reform bills aimed at reducing government influence by abolishing various offices and departments of state, disfranchising officials, and debarring those holding government contracts from sitting in the Commons. The dual objective of Wyvill's Yorkshire movement was still present. As the MP John Dunning explained, 'The saving of money is but a secondary object. The reduction of the influence of the Crown is the first.' At one level the campaign aimed to correct that imbalance in the constitution which opponents of the ministry claimed to detect; at another it strove to introduce new standards of probity and efficiency to central government. It was the type of reform, precise and controllable, which Rockingham supported rather than what he termed 'the many visionary schemes and expedients' which were being aired at this time. It was doubtful whether the latter had much solid support. The radical leaders, for the most part men of some substance, showed no inclination to share power with the labouring classes. The wistful glances back to the supposed purity of an earlier age, and the repeated proposals to extend the number of county MPs (and so, indirectly, the influence of the landed interest), offered little challenge to the hierarchical society of the day. Even those radicals, and they were a minority within a minority, who argued for universal suffrage did so without any real hope that it would come in their lifetime.

Helped by his proposal to set up an independent commission of enquiry to report on the public accounts, North succeeded in fending off the various economical reform bills, sometimes by very narrow majorities. He did, however, have the mortification of seeing Dunning's well-phrased motion that 'the influence of the Crown has increased, is increasing, and ought to be diminished', passed by 233 votes to 215. In terms of definable forms of influence such as seats, places and money the motion was inaccurate, and its political impact – if not its role in myth-making – was shortlived. Faced with the rejection of its economical reform programme the loose alliance of parliamentary groups, county associations and metropolitan societies began to disintegrate. The government's position was helped by some good news from America, where in May 1780 Cornwallis captured Charleston, and indirectly by the Gordon Riots which devastated parts of central London early in June in the most frightening outburst of crowd violence of the century.

It is now clear that the Gordon Riots resulted from an attempt to bring pressure to bear on Parliament (to repeal the Catholic Relief Act of 1778, in itself a very limited measure) which veered out of control. To many contemporaries the riots were a sombre warning of the danger of summoning popular support through the organising of petitions, marches and demonstrations. After an attempt to intimidate the Commons in early June by a march led by Lord George Gordon and his Protestant Association, numbering some tens of thousands of supporters, parts of the crowd and some criminal hangers-on began attacking Catholic premises. This was the beginning of several days and nights of rioting which resulted in at least three hundred deaths, mostly caused by the military, and considerable destruction of property. Not only Catholic property was attacked; the rioters soon turned their attention to the houses of those they suspected of being Catholic sympathisers, and to the prisons and the Bank of England. Anti-popery was joined by an instinct to strike at the rich, and to destroy symbols of authority and repression. With the City magistracy ineffective if not downright supine, the riots died down only with the arrival of troop reinforcements in the capital with orders to open fire without reference to the formalities of the Riot Act. The later days of the disturbances, with Wilkes shooting rioters, and Gordon trying to stop looters, showed the sense of shock which united the propertied classes regardless of their political inclinations.

If in one way the Gordon Riots were a reminder of the fragility of the social order, in political terms the disturbances rallied support to the beleaguered administration. There was a closing of ranks behind King and ministers, and an understandable reluctance by opponents of the government to push differences too far. North was too shrewd a hand at the political game to miss the opportunity; in September Parliament was dissolved a year early, and the October general election brought little change in the political composition of the Commons.

By good luck and some good management North had survived the alarms of 1780; but the future of his administration depended on the outcome of the war. The election result had obscured but not eliminated public concern about its conduct, and within Parliament the polarisation of parties over America was more marked than ever. The capture of Charleston showed that Britain had not entirely fallen back on the defensive, but the initiative could not be long sustained. War with Holland at the end of 1780 after disputes over the Dutch supply of naval stores to France and Spain added to the government's difficulties. There was another enemy fleet to shadow, and another area of operations – the North Sea and the Baltic – to police. In the same year the formation of the Armed Neutrality of Russia, Sweden, Prussia, Denmark and Portugal reflected the resentment of non-belligerents at Britain's brusque attitude towards neutral trading rights. On the other side the financial strain of the war was telling on France, in the frustrating position of being theoretically superior to her old adversary, yet unable to strike a decisive blow. In 1781 the main French fleet under de Grasse sailed into American waters, a move urged by Washington for three years. It was ill luck for the British that the same summer Cornwallis followed up his success at Charleston by pushing north into Virginia, where he hoped the loyalists would rally to him. Once there, he made for the coast at Yorktown to await orders from Clinton in New York, only to learn that de Grasse and his fleet lay offshore. Superior in numbers, the French were able to hold off the British fleet which tried to force a passage through to Cornwallis, whose six thousand men were outnumbered two or three to one by the surrounding American and French forces. De Grasse's fleet had not only prevented relief by sea; it had landed French troops and artillery to support Washington. After enduring a week of bombardment Cornwallis surrendered on 17 October 1781, four years to the day after Burgoyne's surrender at Saratoga.

Although more than 25,000 British troops remained in America, to all intents the fighting there was over after Yorktown. The British commanders had been burdened throughout by problems of supply, had been hampered by the restraints imposed on them in the early stages of the war, and were always fearfully aware of the portentous consequences of defeat. The loyalists (estimated to be a third or more of the population) had never made their mark as allies: intimidation, lack of organisation, and doubts about their reliability, all made their contribution a minor one. Washington, too, was subjected to harassing strains. The militia were a cause of despair to him as they came and went without explanation, though at Saratoga they had played a crucial part when they flocked to the scene of action to support the hard core of continentals. After the war Washington paid tribute to his continentals when he wrote that for eight years British armies had been resisted by 'numbers infinitely less, composed of men sometimes half starved, always in rags, without pay, and experiencing every species of distress which human nature is capable of undergoing.' The words revealed as much of Washington as of his men. Measured against the American commander-in-chief, the British generals, for all their knowledge of the formal arts of war, lacked stamina, a sense of political realities, and the devotion of their men.

In a wider context the catastrophe at Yorktown came at the end of a depressing year in which Britain suffered setbacks in India, the Caribbean and the Mediterranean, experienced another invasion threat, and in which discontent at the cost and course of the war mounted at home. Yorktown demonstrated to the world at large what Sandwich had long known, that Britain's naval resources were not equal to the country's commitments. For an empire based on seapower the implications were ominous. At best it meant that Britain would be unable to follow Pitt's old policy of switching forces from one theatre of operations to another, using command of the sea to obtain supremacy in one area at a time. At worse the Bourbons might adopt this strategy, and there were signs that this was happening as de Grasse sailed south to the nerve-centre of Britain's trading interests in the Caribbean. In the face of this threat the Admiralty cut to the bone the squadrons protecting the coasts of Britain and the homeward bound convoys, in order to send Rodney across the Atlantic with reinforcements. In April 1782 Rodney defeated de Grasse just north of Dominica at the Battle of the Saints, when instead of fighting in formal line ahead British ships broke through the enemy line in several places to give the French a foretaste of the annihilating battles of the Nelson era.

The victory came too late to aid the North government, which had not long survived the news of Yorktown. In the clashes with the opposition in the early months of 1782 North had taken one blow after another. In January he was forced to dismiss Germain; in February the

Commons carried a motion demanding an end to 'offensive war' in America; in March came news of the loss of Minorca. The struggle was less one between North and his opponents – for both agreed that his position had become untenable – than between minister and monarch, the latter so distraught at the prospect of the opposition leaders taking office that he drew up a draft message of abdication. North had to put the situation to the King in simple and dignified terms – 'The Parliament have altered their sentiments, and as their sentiments whether just or erroneous must ultimately prevail' – before he was finally allowed to resign. His departure on 20 March marked the beginning of two years of turmoil and crisis in British politics in which at times the very future of the monarchy appeared to be in doubt. The immediate message of North's resignation was a more limited one. It showed, as Walpole's fall forty years earlier had done, that the inclination and capacity of the gentry in the Commons to support the King's minister had limits, though they were distant limits, approached only in times of national crisis.

The North administration was replaced by a coalition of the opposition groups led by Rockingham and Shelburne which had led the attacks on the ministry. Unlike the aftermath of Walpole's resignation the changes were comprehensive rather than piecemeal, only the Lord Chancellor, Thurlow, remaining of the old cabinet. Under the pressure of events and the frustrations of opposition, Rockingham and his colleagues had moved far since the limited manoeuvres and shuffles of office in the 1760s. Although Rockingham at the Treasury was nominal leader of the ministry, the dominant personalities were Shelburne and Fox, both in charge of new departments of state – Shelburne at the Home Office, and Fox at the Foreign Office. The coalition carried through bills for economical reform along the lines of those introduced two years earlier: to eliminate a number of sinecures, disfranchise revenue officers, and prevent government contractors from becoming MPs. On the more difficult question of parliamentary reform it was far from united. As Wyvill had suspected the year before, Rockingham's main intention was 'to effect a change of ministers, without any engagement, or security obtained for the people.'

In any case, other problems were looming, especially in Ireland, where North's concessions had bought only a short period of grace. In April 1782 the Irish Commons demanded sweeping changes in the relationship with Britain. The new government was more sympathetic to the Irish cause than its predecessor, and also weighing with it was the knowledge that the Volunteers were now thought to number 40,000 men. A helter-skelter of changes was rushed through in the next twelve months. The Declaratory Act was repealed, and in a Renunciation Act British legislative authority over Ireland was abandoned. Poynings' Law was modified to remove the Privy Council's control over the powers of initiation and legislation of the Irish Parliament. Irish judges were given tenure during good behaviour. A Catholic Relief Act removed some civil disabilities. Much had been conceded – Grattan exulted, 'Ireland is now a nation' – but with the Lord Lieutenant remaining head of the Irish executive with considerable powers of patronage and a place in the British cabinet, it was unrealistic to talk of sister kingdoms with equal status. Even so, the Irish Parliament had gained power at the expense of government in both London and Dublin, and some vexing irritants had disappeared.

Although peace was the priority of the new government, Fox and Shelburne differed as to how the negotiations should be handled. The problems were such that Fox had already decided to throw in his hand when, on 1 July 1782, Rockingham died. His ministry had lasted only three months, but both in the way it had gained office, and in the determined legislation it had introduced on Ireland and economical reform, it had broken new political ground. Rockingham's death showed the King a way out of a humiliating situation. He offered the Treasury to Shelburne, who brought in the young William Pitt as Chancellor of the Exchequer, and replaced Fox with a career diplomat. In a speech to the Lords shortly after his appointment Shelburne showed that in attitude he was the heir of Chatham, who accepted the king's right to choose his ministers, and 'had always declared that this country ought not to be governed by any party or faction'. With Parliament going into recess until the late autumn the constitutional clash receded into the background, and Shelburne was able to turn his attention to the peace negotiations. In 1762 difficult decisions had to be made about which captured territories should be handed back; twenty years later the decisions were on the much more painful subject of which British possessions must be conceded. The American mainland empire of the Thirteen Colonies had gone, and Bourbon ambitions threatened the other British empire of tropical dependencies in the Caribbean, Africa and Asia. Shelburne, for all his gifts, was never a trusted or very adept politician, but his achievements in the difficult negotiations of 1782–83 deserve more understanding than they received at the time.

The process of peace-making was complicated by any criterion. To begin with, there were two distinct sets of negotiations: the Anglo-American discussions to settle the terms of American independence; and the negotiations between Britain and the partners in the continental coalition which had fought against her. On all sides the financial strain of the war introduced an element of urgency into the negotiations, but in both Britain and France the principal negotiators had to contend with bellicose groups who were convinced that perseverance in the fighting would bring triumph. Shelburne never wavered in his conviction that there should be a generous settlement with America which would encourage the maintenance of close commercial relations, and might even one day lead to political reunion. As far as Britain's European enemies were concerned he advocated concessions which would remove some of the sting of the 1763 treaty, and yet would preserve intact Britain's essential interests overseas. In pursuing this policy he was helped by some late British successes in the war: Rodney's victory at the Saints, the repulse of the Spanish assault on Gibraltar, and the vigorous defence of British possessions in India by Warren Hastings.

By November 1782 the preliminaries of the settlement between Britain and her former colonies were concluded. Since Yorktown there had been no question about independence; what was at stake was the extent of territory which was to accompany it. Shelburne accepted the claims of the American negotiators that the fertile tract of land between the Ohio and the Great Lakes should go to the United States, not to Canada (as in 1774). Shelburne would have no truck with French and Spanish moves to restrict the United States to the Atlantic seaboard, and insisted that the new nation should extend to the Mississippi. Influenced by the arguments of the new economic thinkers led by Adam Smith, Shelburne argued that the Americans must be free to open up the West; the more territory they settled, the greater would be the opportunities for the import of British manufactures. To the orthodox mercantilist of the day Shelburne's policy was inexplicable, but his contention that commercial expansion need not be accompanied by a weight of administrative and defensive responsibilities was in line with British imperial trends in other parts of the globe. His revolutionary plan for a commercial union between Britain and the United States did not survive his fall from office, but the close economic ties between the two countries in the nineteenth century showed that the idea was not as preposterous as it appeared to many at the time.

The Treaty of Versailles which concluded peace with France and Spain was far from being the total overthrow of the 1763 settlement that the French and Spanish governments had envisaged after Yorktown. Britain's military recovery, the withdrawal of America from the war, and the lack of co-ordination among the continental allies, led to less drastic terms than seemed at one time probable. Of its conquests in the West Indies France kept only Tobago. New French fishing rights on the west coast of Newfoundland were less valuable than they appeared to be on paper. In India French hopes of gaining extensive new spheres of influence dwindled in the peace treaty to the acquisition of a small strip of territory around Pondicherry. In West Africa the situation was as it had been before 1763; France regained the Senegal River area, and Britain kept the Gambia. Elsewhere, Spain recovered Minorca and Florida, but was unable to press her other claims. At home the complexities and concessions of the settlement were used by Shelburne's political opponents, Fox on one side, North on the other, to defeat his ministry. The war had proved that Britain could not at one and the same time subdue her rebellious colonists and defeat a coalition of the leading powers of Europe. But victories in the last year of the war had shown that under normal circumstances Britain might still be more than a match for France and Spain overseas. In no theatre of operations had the Bourbons taken full advantage of the British predicament. They had gained some possessions in 1783, but these were little enough to compensate for the cost of the war (which in France was to be a decisive factor in the financial difficulties which led to the crisis of 1789). The United States had won independence with Bourbon help, but had not become a client state of France or Spain. The loss of the American empire was a mortifying blow to British prestige, but the main foundations of the nation's strength and prosperity remained intact.

The loss of the American empire was followed in domestic politics by the most serious constitutional confrontation since the 1688 Revolution. The King refused to accept the political logic of the situation which followed Shelburne's resignation in late February 1783, and did not summon the victorious majority to take office until early April. Once again he busied himself drafting a doleful statement of abdication, which insisted that rather than 'submitting to be a cipher in the trammels of any self-created band', he would retire to Hanover. The size of the gulf between the King's understanding of what was constitutional and that of the Rockingham group (now under the leadership of Portland) was shown in Fox's declaration at the same time – 'I have always acknowledged myself to be a party man . . . a systematic opposition to a dangerous government is, in my opinion, a noble employment for the brightest faculties. Opposition is natural in such a political system as ours.'

Fox was for personal and political reasons the least acceptable of the opposition leaders as far as George III was concerned. His erratic private life, his supposed influence over the young Prince of Wales, his lacerating attacks on ministers during the war, and now his repugnant political doctrines, caused the King to regard him with unwavering distrust. The King's forebodings in the spring of 1783 were increased by the new claim put forward by Portland when he named the seven leading ministers (including Fox) of his proposed administration for George to take or leave as a whole, and also insisted on a free hand in the selection of junior ministers. These demands struck at the heart of the royal prerogative, for the King's right to choose his first minister, and to have a voice in the other appointments, was a regular part of the political system. In the 1760s, as in earlier periods, this had led to difficulties when the King's choice was regarded with less than total enthusiasm by the Commons; but at no time had his right to make that choice been denied. The change had come about largely because of the American war, and the opposition's interpretation of its cause, summed up by Fox when he insisted that 'to the influence of the Crown we must attribute the loss of the thirteen provinces of America.'

For the King the situation was the more galling because the new group pressing for admission to office represented an alliance between Fox and North – 'the most unprincipled coalition the annals of this or any nation can equal', George thought. The coalition was the result of personal preference and arithmetical calculation. Most politically committed MPs belonged to one of three largish groups led by Shelburne (140), North (120) and Fox (90). The fall, first of North and then Shelburne, had shown the difficulty of a single group retaining office; and there seemed to both Fox and North good reason for choosing the other rather than Shelburne, whose unrivalled capacity for inspiring suspicion had been confirmed during his brief spell in office. Another element in the situation was the blank refusal of Shelburne's young lieutenant, William Pitt, to contemplate a link with North. The King's anguish was sharpened by what he regarded as the desertion of North; but his general view of the new alliance was shared by many. Although most eighteenth-century governments were coalitions of one sort or another, the attacks on North by the opposition during the American war had been too persistent and deadly for the sight of the former antagonists in office together to be easily accepted. North and his colleagues, as Fox had put it in one bruising outburst, 'in every public and private transaction, as ministers, had shewn themselves void of every principle of honour and honesty'; and although he later withdrew some of this it was the accusation, not the half-apology, which was remembered.

When, in early April, the King finally admitted the new political allies to office, he wrote that they would not have 'either my favour or confidence'. Without this essential, the ministry was weakened from the beginning. There were many across a wide political spectrum uneasy at a ministry thus forcing itself upon the monarch, while those who looked for place and favour noted the King's refusal to co-operate with the government on, for example, the creation of peerages. Among those dismayed by the return to office of North were Wyvill and his associates, who had looked to the Shelburne–Pitt administration to support a motion, backed by petitions from the counties, urging parliamentary reform. When Pitt introduced the motion in May 1783 he was out of office, and despite his declaration against 'visionary and impracticable ideas' such as universal suffrage, his proposals for the addition of a hundred MPs to the counties and London were defeated by 293 to 149 votes. Pitt's abortive programme was curiously old-fashioned, for its proposed increase in the counties threw into even sharper relief the lack of representation for many of the industrial and commercial areas of the country.

There now seems little doubt that the King was hoping to dismiss the Fox–North ministry at the earliest moment, and to replace it with one led by Pitt. The occasion of the dismissal was provided by Fox's India Bill, yet another attempt to resolve the problem of government in British India, where the triumphs of the Seven Years War had been followed in 1765 by the transfer from the Mogul Emperor to the East India Company of the *diwani* or right of revenue collection in Bengal. Not only did the collection of rents and taxes become the Company's most profitable activity in India, but the implications of the change were far-reaching, since authority in Mogul India was traditionally associated with the collection of revenue. The Company was not equipped to handle this enlargement of its role, and its military superiority in Bengal removed all restraints from its servants, who energetically operated a system of 'small salaries and immense perquisites'. Robert Clive and then Warren Hastings attempted to end the consequent misrule, but the Company which now exercised power over a state more populous than France remained in structure and outlook a private trading organisation. North's Regulating Act of 1773 was the first government attempt to control Indian administration, with a Governor-General and Council established in Bengal with some powers over the other presidencies of Madras and Bombay, but reports of abuses and scandals continued to reach England. Fox's bill set up a board of seven commissioners in London to run Indian affairs and to control appointments. All seven commissioners, who were named in the bill, and were appointed for four years, were supporters of the coalition; and to Fox's opponents the bill smelt of a massive patronage job. Even so, the bill's second reading at the beginning of December 1783 saw a comfortable two to one government majority, but before it reached the Lords the King struck a fierce and unexpected blow at the ministry when he sent a message by way of Pitt's cousin, Lord Temple, that those peers who voted for the measure 'were not only not his friends but he should consider them as his enemies'. Recent research has confirmed some contemporary suspicions that Pitt himself was involved, at a safe distance and by means of an intermediary, in this formidable intervention. On 17 December the government was defeated a second time in the Lords on the India Bill, and was dismissed. The next day Pitt was appointed First Lord of the Treasury at the age of twenty-four.

The extraordinary crisis had another three months to run. Pitt was in office, but without a parliamentary majority. It was, for some, the 'mince-pie administration', not expected to last out Christmas. Other ministries of the Hanoverian period had taken office without a certain majority – none had faced the overwhelming majority of an outraged opposition. In a situation without precedent the government endured, and ignored, a series of defeats. To outward appearance the situation was deadlocked, with a government which could not get its measures through the Commons, but which refused to resign. The political reality was different, for as frustration gripped the opposition so its majority fell, from more than a hundred to single figures. Equally demoralising to Fox, and heartening to Pitt, were the addresses pouring in from the country attacking the one and supporting the other – over two hundred in all, many more than the elder Pitt had attracted in his wartime glory almost thirty years before. On 8 March Fox's majority was down to one, and Pitt could reflect that 'our present situation [is] a triumph, at least compared with what it was'. Before the end of the month the King took another weapon from the armoury of the royal prerogative, more thinly stocked now than formerly, but still with enough resources to cripple if not kill an opponent, and dissolved Parliament – three years before its appointed course had run, but three months later than Fox and North had assumed after their dismissal.

The election which followed has attracted much scholarly attention, focused on the issue of whether it was decided – uniquely in the Hanoverian period – by public opinion rather than 'managed' in the usual way. Undoubtedly, and despite the rather surprising fact that there were fewer contested seats than in the record year of 1774, there was more countrywide excitement than usual. This was reflected (to take one narrow but measurable example) in the number of political cartoons, most directed against the coalition. This antipathy helped to give the government a larger majority than it might otherwise have had, but the decisive reason for Pitt's success lay – as in other elections of the period – in the fact that it was called by the government, and at a moment convenient for the government. As a contemporary explained it, 'the influence of the Crown, being now combined with the inclination and independent interest of the country at the general election, the effect produced was prodigious.' Pitt made about seventy net gains; the losses were equally divided between the Fox and North groups. The most striking feature of the results was that Pitt won the day not only through routine government victories in many of the narrow boroughs, but also through an unusually large number of successes in the counties and open boroughs. These results always caught public attention, for it was in these seats that electoral opinion rather than political management was assumed to play an influential role. Both the quality and the quantity of the government's triumph seemed to denote a decisive mood of political opinion in the country – for Pitt and against the coalition.

The coalition had been out-thought and out-fought. In practical terms royal hostility counted for more than public disapproval; but the latter had an unsettling effect on the morale of opposition MPs and their supporters. Pitt, opposing himself to Fox as a politician of unshakable integrity, benefited from his commitment to reform, and from the public's refusal to believe ill of the son of Chatham. With more confidence than calculation, Fox and his associates underestimated the resourcefulness of George III and Pitt, and the uneasiness caused by their actions over the previous twelve months. There was some substance in North's complaint after the December dismissal that 'we carried on our advances regularly, and above ground, in view of the foe, not by mining in the dark, and before the garrison knew there was an intention to attack it' – but in its own way it was a damning confession of political naivety.

8 National recovery and political reaction, 1784–1799

Victory in the 1784 election and the firm support of the King gave Pitt some guarantee of six or seven years of power. What could not have been foreseen was the length of office which stretched ahead, and the growth during the latter part of problems such as no eighteenth-century minister had faced. The issues confronting Pitt in his first years were daunting enough. The American colonies were gone, with results to Britain's prosperity and prestige yet to be calculated. Within Europe Britain was isolated, while the Indian issues which had brought down the Fox–North coalition remained to be settled. Most worrying in the short run was the frightening legacy of the war in financial terms, with the National Debt almost doubled in ten years, and more than half the government revenue soaked up in debt charges.

It was in finance that Pitt made his first moves with measures which, though for the most part not novel, in combination represented a coherent attempt to put the national finances on a sounder footing, while at the same time encouraging the flow of production and trade on which they ultimately depended. Duties on tea, wine and spirits were reduced (on tea from 119 per cent to 12½ per cent), a move which did much to eliminate smuggling, and with it that shortfall in anticipated income which was one of the bugbears of the eighteenth-century Treasury. The value of the East India Company's tea imports trebled after the reduction in duty, and the tea trade to China spearheaded an expansion of British activity in the eastern seas which did something to compensate for the loss of empire in America. In part to compensate for the resulting loss of revenue, Pitt devised a wide range of taxes of varying ingenuity, acceptability and permanence. More debatable, in an attempt to reduce the alarming size of the National Debt, he introduced in 1786 a more rigid Sinking Fund, regulated by statutory commissioners. Its main importance was political, even psychological, rather than fiscal. It became a symbol of the determination of the government to stop the upward spiralling of the Debt and its interest charges which threatened before long to consume the whole national revenue.

The way in which the operation was organised so as to prevent the raiding of the Sinking Fund (as happened in Walpole's time) for short-term political gain, was evidence of the financial rectitude which Pitt was at pains to cultivate. One of his first acts on taking office was to submit government contracts to genuine tender, and to continue North's practice of insisting on sealed tenders to encourage competition among financiers for the raising of government loans. He did much to stop the practice of ministers and officials holding surpluses in their personal accounts; and stamped out many minor abuses. Much of this work had begun under the guise of economical reform by the Rockinghams; and others among Pitt's measures stemmed from the commission set up by North in 1780 to examine the public accounts at a time when the burdens of war were placing intolerable strains on the old, incoherent system of collecting, disbursing and auditing government funds. This part of Pitt's work reached fulfilment in 1787 with the establishment of the consolidated fund which for the first time made some sort of national accounting possible. Nothing better demonstrated the detailed grasp and patient exposition of complex matters which were among Pitt's outstanding political strengths. Until this time eleven loan stocks were supplied from no fewer than 103 separate accounts, with the result explained by Burke a few years earlier when he complained that 'neither the present, nor any other First Lord of the Treasury, has ever been able to take a survey, or to make even a tolerable guess, of the expenses of the government for any one year.'

A priority for the new administration was to find a more acceptable settlement for the affairs of the East India Company than Fox had proposed in his ill-fated India Bill of 1783. Pitt's India Act of 1784 established a legal foundation for the relations between company and state which was to last until 1858. It clamped a close control over the company, which was left in charge only of trading affairs and Indian patronage. Final authority for all political, military and revenue matters was transferred to a Board of Control in London under a President who was a government minister. Until the fall of the Pitt government in 1801 the Board was dominated by Henry Dundas, who in 1793 became its President – effectively Secretary of State for India. There was no declaration of sovereignty, but the Act made clear Parliament's ultimate responsibility for the government of those regions in India under British sway. The short-lived period of rule by a trading company over millions of Indians was at an end, and the impeachment of Warren Hastings, Governor-General from 1773 to 1785, on charges of corruption and cruelty was a warning that the activities of British subjects in India were subject to scrutiny. Hastings was innocent of the more serious charges brought against him by his political enemies, and the early excitement and later tedium of his eight-year trial obscured the real damage being done in India as the supremacy of British traders and financiers brought hardship, and sometimes ruin, to many of their Indian counterparts.

Nearer at home, Pitt's external policies aimed to end Britain's diplomatic isolation and to increase the nation's commerce. This last he accomplished by a combination of protectionist and free trade measures. So, a traditional-looking Navigation Act in 1786 made certain that British rather than American shipbuilders would profit from the demand for merchantmen which followed the loss of the colonies and colonial-built shipping. On the other hand, the same year saw a commercial treaty with France which promised not only the lowering of tariffs between the two countries, but also the possibility of better political relations. In 1788 the negotiating of the Triple Alliance with Prussia and the Dutch brought Britain a further measure of international security, and allowed Pitt to cut still further expenditure on the country's armed forces. Much of the recovery, and expansion, of industry and trade owed little to specific government policies, and in 1790 the Inspector-General of Imports and Exports wrote to Pitt, 'The vast increase of the trade of this country since the termination of the last war must be a matter of astonishment even to those who are the best acquainted with the flourishing state of our manufactures and our internal industry.'

What was a mystery to Pitt's official in 1790 would become familiar to later generations as a first manifestation of the industrial revolution – stark, dramatic and portentous in historical hindsight, little noticed as a general phenomenon at the time of its making. Although historians agree that Britain became the first industrialised nation in Europe, they find difficulty in determining the causes and timing of this development. If the search for a 'primary cause' has been abandoned, a long list of possible explanatory factors amounts to a virtual summation of British history from the late seventeenth century to the early nineteenth. It includes the greater internal demand generated by an increased population; a favourable physical environment which brought mineral resources and communications close together; a diffusion of scientific knowledge and technical ingenuity into improved production methods; a benevolent if non-interventionist government; a caste-free social system able to subsume the forces of industry, commerce and land; an accumulation, often through war, of new territories and trade overseas; and political stability which encouraged long-term investment.

Although it was in the later eighteenth century that a quickening and coalescing of economic developments became evident, they occurred in the context of a general, if not interrupted, growth in population and production in the hundred years *before* 1780. Stretched across the length of the eighteenth century industrial output increased almost fourfold, home consumption trebled, and exports increased more than sixfold. During this time the population of England grew from just over 5,000,000 in 1700 to more than 8,500,000 at the time of the first census in 1801 – close on 11,000,000 when the populations of Wales at 560,000 and Scotland at 1,625,000 are added. The rise was the steepest in Europe except for Ireland, where numbers doubled from 2,500,000 in 1700 to more than 5,000,000 in 1800. Clearly, no analysis of the economy can ignore this growth; but until the census of 1801 contemporaries seem to have had little awareness of it. Malthus, for example, in the first edition of his *Essay on Population* in 1798, put the population of Britain at only 7,000,000. One reason for this failure to recognise the rise in population was that the normal warning signals were absent. Until now, the general rule was that when population grew, prices rose and standards of living declined. It was one of the distinctive features of the period usually seen as marking the beginning of the industrial revolution that this link snapped.

By the outbreak of war in 1793 many of the developments and technical innovations associated with the new industrialism were already in place. In the early 1700s had come Darby's breakthrough when he developed the smelting of iron with coke; in the middle decades of the century Watt's steam pumping-engines; and in the 1780s Cort's puddling and rolling process which made possible the large-scale production of bar iron. In textile manufacture there had been a whole rush of labour-saving machines, and it was the factory-based cotton industry of the north which seemed to typify the new era, for there mass production processes were developed in factories reliant on steam power. The year 1785 saw the first steam-engine used to power a spinning mill, followed by a rapid sequence of innovations and improvements which reached a climax with the spread of the power loom in the next century. In little more than a generation cotton production had moved from a low-grade commodity based on domestic labour to the first of the new manufacturing processes turning out high-quality goods at a price which swept away competition at home and abroad.

The developments in the iron industry in the late eighteenth century were even more critical to the spread of industrialisation, for machinery lay at the heart of the new processes. Already the industry had shifted northwards from the Sussex weald and other traditional woodland locations; and by the 1760s the beginnings of capitalist industry were evident in the forges, furnaces, blade and slitting mills of Birmingham, Wolverhampton, Sheffield, Newcastle and Falkirk. The use of coal (now falling in price as more steam-pumping engines were brought into the mines) instead of charcoal, and of steampower for the new blast furnaces, released the industry from its old constraints. Britain not only possessed the raw materials of industrialisation – coal and iron ore – but they were close to good water communications, coastal or river. If the seventeenth century saw the improvement of river navigation, the latter part of the eighteenth century was the canal age. Of the two thousand miles of usable waterways in 1800, about one-third consisted of canals which had been built in the previous forty years, prompted by the consideration that the price of a bulk commodity such as coal moved by land doubled within five miles of the point of output. The 'trunk' canals of the 1770s released traffic from the straitjacket of the river systems by joining up river routes across country. They revolutionised the carriage of general merchandise, met the spiralling demand for coal supplies, and in the peak years of their construction until the end of the century gave a sustained boost to employment.

Factories, steampower and canals symbolise the early industrial revolution, but in 1780 cotton and iron accounted for only 3 per cent of national income. Although expansion was so rapid that by 1800 the share of the cotton industry was 5 per cent of the national income, and within another ten years it had overtaken the woollen industry in value terms, it was unique in this rate of growth. In 1800 steam supplied only one-tenth of the motive power for industry, and even in the cotton industry the new mass-production methods applied only to the spinning side, for weaving was not mechanised until the 1830s. A machine was still more likely to be found in a cottage than in a factory, coal mining was still unmechanised apart from the use of pumping engines, and the prototype inventions of the eighteenth century often had their main impact only with the development of improved versions in the nineteenth century. Geographically, the early industrial revolution was centred on south Lancashire (by 1800 the most densely-populated part of the country outside London), the West Riding, and parts of the Midlands and Scottish Lowlands. Urbanisation and industrialisation were not always linked like Siamese twins. Away from the factory and mining areas, there was a general increase in the size of provincial towns as rural and craft industries, commerce and services, all expanded. Workers in the new industries were far outnumbered by traditional craftsmen, small artisans, farm labourers and domestic servants. The industrial pacesetters were not a microcosm of the economy, for they operated within a variegated system in which domestic textile manufacture, brewing, milling, distilling, leather processing and other established industries still made a massive contribution to the economy. In them a range of new processes led to better quality and higher productivity, though in the last respect they could not match the dramatic leaps in cotton, iron and coal output. What had emerged was a dual economy, with the smaller, modern sector showing after 1780 a growth rate perhaps three times that of the traditional sector.

Emphasis on the new technology should not obscure the fact that agriculture, the most traditional form of economic activity, also showed substantial gains in production. The proportion of the labour force in agriculture fell from about 55 per cent of the employed population of England and Wales in 1700, working on about 29,000,000 acres of land, to around 48 per cent in 1758 and 42 per cent in 1801. By this last date the number employed on the land had risen to 1,700,000 (though this crude census category included forestry and fishing as well as agriculture), and the extent of land under usage had increased to almost 32,000,000 acres. Both these increases were slight compared to the growth of population and of agriculture output, for there was a 44 per cent increase in the productivity of the land during the course of the century. One man employed in farming in 1700 produced enough to feed 1.7 persons; by 1800 this had increased to 2.5 persons. Even though agriculture was in 1800 still by far the largest employer of labour, the numbers on the land had in no sense kept pace with the increase in population. Such statistics seem to point to a startling success story – an enviable example of population growth matched by the output of foodstuffs, a confounding of Malthusian predictions that an increased population would be caught in the inexorable jaws of a poverty trap, that more meant poorer.

The term 'agricultural revolution' should not suggest that there was during the eighteenth century a great leap forward from an obsolete system based on the open field and small-scale cultivation to a system of capitalist farming and wage labourers. In terms of the structure of agriculture and cultivation methods the process of improvement was a gradual one, uneven both in terms of chronology and region. About half of the country's arable land had been enclosed by 1700, and by then most of the new methods of cultivation associated with the growth in agricultural output were known, if not yet widely used. By the mid-eighteenth century enclosure by agreement was almost exhausted, and was overtaken by the more contentious method of enclosure by Act of Parliament. The number of such Acts increased in the 1760s and 1770s as grain prices rose, and reached a record level in the war years after 1793. There can be no doubt that enclosures, however established, quickened the pace of agricultural improvement, and the rise in rents for enclosed acreages was a recognition of their enhanced productivity. The main innovations on the land came not so much from mechanical improvements – though new types of ploughs such as the Rotherham triangular plough, Jethro Tull's seed drill, and better hand implements all brought benefits – as from a more imaginative and supportive rotation of crops. With the characteristic mix of arable and livestock farming which the new rotations encouraged, farmers gained something in security as well as productivity – because the wet summers which meant poor grain harvests produced favourable conditions for livestock. Specialisation according to region increased, for as the former sheep pastures with their light soils came under the plough, so some of the arable land on the clay soils was converted to pasture. Despite contemporary complaints, the enclosures of the period did not have the depopulating effect of the Tudor movement which turned land used for subsistence crops into pasture. Their most disruptive effect on village life came with the shutting off of stretches of common land where customary grazing rights helped the domestic self-sufficiency of rural households. They quickened the trend towards the demoralisation and eventual pauperisation of the farm labourer. On balance the new enclosures, with their fencing and building activities, land reclamation and intensive methods of husbandry, needed more labour, not less. Despite the occasional threshing machine which clanked into view in the last years of the century, mechanisation had not yet come to English farming.

From the 1760s England was for the first time importing rather than exporting wheat in most years, but it experienced none of the cataclysmic subsistence crises which afflicted France and other continental countries. Although the number on the land rose, the increase was less than the growth in rural population. The important question as to whether the surplus labour remained in the country areas, an increasing burden on the Poor Law, or was ready and fit for factory employment, is not one which can be answered in general terms. In parts of the Midlands, the North and the Scottish Lowlands there was a drift from the land to the new industrial villages; but there was no neat nationwide equation whereby the surplus working population from the land was transferred to the factories. Yet the contribution of agriculture in this period was substantial and varied. It sustained a fast-growing population, with only a minimal recourse to food imports. Its success provided both a margin of purchasing power for the products of British industry, and through its profits investment opportunities in industry and commerce for landowners and large farmers.

One of the most spectacular growth areas was foreign trade, where a boom which began in mid-century lasted until the War of American Independence. This brought more than usual disruption to trade, but exports were back to pre-war levels by 1784, though re-exports had to wait until 1794, and another war, before recovering to the levels of the early 1770s. Extra-European trade had become more important in terms both of markets and products. The range of exotic products imported into England, and then often re-exported, increased to include cotton, dye-woods, rice, tea and coffee, as sugar, tobacco and Indian textiles lost their old predominance. By the early 1770s there was for the first time a roughly equal division of exports between Europe and the overseas markets in America, Africa and Asia, with the American colonies growing fast in population and forming a captive market, with an insatiable demand for iron goods in particular. A captive market of a more sinister kind was the shipping of slaves across the Atlantic, an activity not yet under concerted attack. It formed part of a complex trading interchange between England, Africa and America which involved plantation products and manufactured goods, and employed large numbers of ships and seamen. If not as profitable as once thought, the slave trade and its offshoots loomed large in the eys of ministers and merchants, 'an inexhaustible fund of wealth and naval power', as one pamphleteer insisted.

As far as trade with Europe was concerned, woollen cloth still accounted for 40 per cent of English exports by value as late as the early 1770s, but it had long since lost its quasi-monopoly position. There was now less trade with France, Germany and the Low Countries, and more with the Baltic and the Mediterranean, suppliers of essential supplies such as naval stores (timber, hemp, flax), oil and dyestuffs. The shift in the geographical distribution of England's foreign trade had its effect on port development, with a rise in the fortune of the western ports, Bristol, Liverpool and Glasgow in particular, associated with the Atlantic trades. On the east coast Hull and Newcastle benefited from the growth of the Baltic trade. Even so, London, with its experienced merchants, finance houses, port facilities and good inland communications, still handled almost three-quarters of the nation's foreign trade at the height of the boom before the American war. During the century generally the proportion of industrial output which was exported rose from about a fifth to a third. Expressed in the most general terms, the ratio of exports to national production doubled (to about 15 per cent) between the beginning and end of the century, with the fastest-growing areas of trade the colonial ones. By the time Pitt took office the American colonies had broken free from the imperial system, but early industrialisation had given British manufactures a competitive advantage which lessened their dependence on the constraints and compulsions of legislation. Although attempts by

Shelburne to forge a commercial union with the newly-independent United States failed, much of the trade between the two nations continued to flow in traditional channels until well into the nineteenth century.

Among those variables which affected growth in this period, one of the most important and yet elusive was the role of the landed élite. The great landowners increased their share of the land during the century from a fifth to a quarter of the cultivated area – mainly at the expense of the smaller freeholders. Along with this increase came a steady rise in land values and rents, probably a doubling during the course of the century. With agriculture still the most important source of national income, the largest employer of labour, and the basis of political power, its interests were well protected. This was not, however, accomplished at the expense of trade and industry, whose contribution to the national well-being was acknowledged in and out of Parliament. In political terms the influence of the landed oligarchy, most noticeable in the imposition of a series of corn laws to protect English agriculture from the 1770s onwards, was significant if sometimes blurred. Parliamentary legislation eased the work of enclosure, permitted town improvement schemes, regulated the turnpike trusts, and encouraged the boom in canal construction. This is not to say that the increased productivity of the period owed much to direct government stimulus. There was no equivalent of the state decrees aimed at promoting industry which were familiar in countries such as France and Prussia. Adam Smith in *Wealth of Nations*, that work lauded by Pitt in 1792 as furnishing 'the best solution of every question connected with the history of commerce and with the system of political economy', had argued strenuously for the ending of government interference and the acceptance of a self-regulating market economy. Yet in a number of ways, government policies helped to shape the environment in which the economy operated. Trade had long benefited from commercial treaties, ranging from the Methuen Treaty of 1703 with Portugal to the path-breaking agreement with France in 1786. The erection of tariff barriers and the outright prohibition of some foreign imports protected and encouraged industry and agriculture alike.

Although government expenditure grew steadily during the century (in real terms the tax burden increased 18-fold between 1660 and 1815), a tax system which depended heavily on excises made the most of economic growth, and left capital, profits and high incomes relatively untouched until the 1790s and the wartime innovations. For landowners, financiers, industrialists and merchants, the first requirement of government was to provide security, and in this Hanoverian governments were successful for most of the century. There were no civil wars, no revolutions, and after 1745 no invasions. Riots and strikes might give a surface impression of turbulence, but the country's main agricultural and manufacturing activities were little affected. And if the rich grew richer, the evidence also suggests that in the second half of the eighteenth century there were fewer poor families, and that the increased national prosperity was spreading downwards, however slowly and unevenly.

Although Pitt's encouragement of trade and industry by a mixture of commercial treaties, fiscal reforms and cheap government proved effective in the years of peace after 1783, he experienced failures on the political front. His final attempt in 1785 to introduce parliamentary reform, which envisaged buying out the voters in 36 narrow boroughs, and a limited extension of the county franchise, was defeated by 248 votes to 174. Unlike earlier efforts, there seemed little support in London or among the county associations for the proposals. They were, as North taunted Pitt, greeted with 'horrid silence'. William Paley in his *Principles of Moral and Political Philosophy*, published in the same year as the failure of Pitt's bill, argued that despite some vagaries in the electoral system, in terms of balance, outlook and independence the Commons represented the true national interest. The rejection of so limited a measure raised anew the whole question of how and when any significant change in parliamentary representation could be made, and indeed whether the pressure existed for such a change. Recent scholarship has altered the traditional picture of a deferential electorate manipulated by corruption and intimidation. An alternative interpretation, while allowing that more than two-thirds of borough seats were under some sort of patronage in this period, has stressed the mutual dependence of landlords and voters. The latter were moved by persuasion rather than by bullying, and then often only to the extent of casting one of their two votes in the direction indicated by their patron. Many 'uncontested' seats were the scene of intense electioneering activity and a thorough canvass, so that only the final, polling stage of an election struggle was missing. The size of the electorate did not lag far behind the growth of population, and between 1780 and the 1832 Reform Act it probably increased by over half – an increase most marked among the craftsmen, retailers and artisans of the 141 boroughs (returning half of the House of Commons before the 1800 Act of Union) which had freemen, householder or 'scot and lot' franchises. If abstentions, intermittent voting and property changes are taken into account, then the pool of electors under the unreformed system amounted by the early nineteenth century to more than a million individuals, or about 30 per cent of the male population of England and Wales. In time, this increased representation of the 'middling classes' would sharpen the resentment of the labouring masses who remained outside the political nation; but in the late eighteenth century it made support for parliamentary reform a minority occupation. Most seemed content with trimming the edges of the system with economical reform scissors, an activity which left in operation much of the heavy machinery of aristocratic control.

For his part Pitt recognised the political reality of the situation, and attempted no further measures of parliamentary reform. Especially damaging had been the King's refusal to allow the proposals to be put forward as a government measure. Between George III and Pitt there was little of the warmth between monarch and minister which had marked the North years. After the traumas of 1782–84 both needed the other, if only as protection against Fox. Pitt's appetite for business enabled the King to begin that withdrawal from detailed interest in the government's affairs which characterised the second half of his reign, but George's hold over any ministry through his powers of appointment and patronage (though the amount of the latter was declining), and the convention that on major policy matters King and government should agree, meant that there was no significant diminution of the royal prerogative. The events of 1783–84 had shown how powerful this still could be, and Pitt was to discover in 1801 the risk of policies which ran counter to the King's principles and prejudices.

Pitt's main setback in this period came in his failure to persuade opinion in either England or Ireland of the wisdom of his proposals for an Anglo-Irish commercial treaty. In the hope of encouraging a growth of mutual trade, Pitt suggested extensive commercial concessions to Ireland in return for an agreement to contribute to imperial defence. To find a unifying rather than a divisive issue in Anglo-Irish relations seemed too good to be true, and so it proved. On one side of the Irish Sea there was opposition from British manufacturing interests worried about Irish competition; on the other there were those in Ireland who saw the proposals for defence contributions and a linked commercial policy as a step backwards from the position of partial independence achieved earlier in the decade.

Prominent in the wrecking operation was the opposition at Westminster, where Fox made little attempt to assess the proposals on their merits. The constitutional crisis which had brought Pitt to power had resulted in a formalising of the opposition, for the political claims which had been pressed by Rockingham, Fox and Portland gave the post-1784 Whig party a distinctive if narrow set of principles, hardened by the memory of what it saw as the duplicity of the King and Pitt which had denied it the right to office. The sapping of its parliamentary majority in early 1784, and the loss of the general election, had shown the necessity of better organisation, in and out of Parliament. So, tentative steps were taken to improve the state of party funds, to gain the support of more London and provincial newspapers, and to introduce some sort of 'whipping' system in both Houses. A Whig Club grew out of the electoral machine in Fox's Westminster constituency, and William Adam emerged as the nearest equivalent to a national party agent that the eighteenth century was to see. Differences between leading members of the opposition, as well as the disinclination of eighteenth-century politicians to accept any rigorous form of discipline, set limits to the amount of organisation among the 140 or so MPs who now made up the regular opposition. Even so, the 'party' nature of that opposition stood in contrast to Pitt's support. An estimate in 1788 suggested that he could look to 180 MPs of the court and administration group, who formed the bulky mass of support for any government, together with those from the hundred or so 'independent' MPs likely to be attracted by his insistence that he governed in the national interest, not for sectional advantage. His own following numbered only about fifty. It was this balance of forces, which in general terms would have been familiar to an observer from the days of Walpole and Pelham, which made Fox's task so difficult. The more Fox raged against the unconstitutional influence of the Crown, the deceits of 1783–84, and the renegade who was now in office, the more he seemed to be fighting ancient battles.

Each year in office seemed to confirm Pitt's ascendancy. His competence and his mastery of the business of government attracted to him the practical men of politics: William Eden (largely responsible for the detailed negotiation of the trade treaty with France), Charles Jenkinson (from 1786 President of the Board of Trade, revived after its abolition by the Rockingham ministry), and the formidable Henry Dundas, dominant on the Indian Board of Control, and as political manager for Scotland as important to the Pitt ministry as the Argylls had been to George II's ministries. There is an air of desperation about Fox in these years. With no election due until 1790 or 1791, with a monarch as firm in the support of Pitt as he was set against Fox, it was difficult to see what turn of the political wheel could bring better fortune to the opposition. When that turn came with the onset of the Regency crisis, so unexpected was the sudden weakening of Pitt's position that Fox overplayed his hand in a way which harmed his reputation for years to come.

The crisis broke in the autumn of 1788 when the King, who had been in indifferent health for some months, became to all appearances insane. The suggested modern diagnosis that the King's illness was porphyria, a metabolic disorder which can produce severe mental effects, does something to explain the nature of the intermittent symptoms which so baffled contemporaries. Personal concern for the King became submerged by political calculation. If he were permanently insane, a Regent must be appointed, and that could only be the Prince of Wales, by convention and temperament enemy of his father and of his father's ministers. A change of government would be bound to follow. But whether the King's breakdown was lasting, and if not how long it would take him to recover, and what the constitutional position was in the meantime, were matters as obscure as they were crucial. In a miscalculation of the situation and of public anxieties Fox insisted on an immediate, unconditional regency for the Prince of Wales. With this single speech, in which the headlines if not the fine print seemed to be written in High Tory terms, Fox as in 1783 left himself open to the charge that factional gain was more important to him than the national interest. Pitt's Regency Bill, which provided for a Regent with limited powers for twelve months, was accepted as being a sensible measure in a fraught and murky situation; but by February 1789 the crisis was over as the King recovered. The damage done to Fox had a significance which lasted beyond the winter of 1788–89, for it weakened confidence in his judgement when the greater crisis of the French Revolution overshadowed country and party.

Initial reaction to the startling news from France in 1789 gave little indication of how divisive an issue the French Revolution and the war which followed were to become in British politics. Many saw the events in Paris as a rather over-dramatised, Gallic version of the 1688 Revolution, a belated effort to introduce some form of constitutional monarchy. Some, including Pitt, viewed the turn of events in France with comparative detachment, and assumed that the obvious confusion there could only benefit Europe. To others, including some of the opposition Whigs, and radical groups outside Parliament, the Revolution carried a more positive message. The attack on the monarchy, priesthood and aristocracy in France encouraged them to continue the task of reform which had been shouldered again in the late 1780s – the several attempts to repeal the Test and Corporation Acts, the founding of the first anti-slave trade association, and renewed interest in parliamentary reform by Cartwright's Society for Constitutional Information, now slowly coming to life again. A well-publicised address by Richard Price claimed to 'see the ardour for liberty catching and spreading' from France, and urged further movement towards political and religious equality in Britain. The infection was seen more clearly outside than inside Parliament, where a proposal in 1790 for parliamentary reform was turned down without a division. Wyvill's attempt to resurrect the old county associations also failed, and the general election of 1790 saw little change in the respective strength of the parliamentary groupings.

In the country more significant reform forces were mobilising through societies which attracted both middle-class recruits and artisans, small shopkeepers and the like. In organisation they were often based on the journeymen's clubs of the period, though a more potent example of what could be accomplished by committed men was provided by the achievement of the Committee for the Abolition of the Slave Trade in educating public opinion and bringing pressure to bear on Parliament. Best known of the new associations was the London Corresponding Society, whose founder and first secretary was the master shoemaker Thomas Hardy, and which numbered tailors, shoemakers and weavers among its activists, alongside smaller numbers of lawyers, doctors, booksellers and printers. It was accompanied, and in some cases predated, by provincial societies, whose names form a roll-call of radical activity in this period. The movement was strong in Scotland, where in December 1792 delegates from eighty radical associations met in convention in Edinburgh. In geographical and ideological terms, radicalism had broken away from the metropolis on the one hand, and from the gentrified county associations on the other. For the first time, the fast-growing cities and towns of the midlands and north were involved, both among the middling orders and the artisans.

In the new societies self-education was as prominent as political agitation. They supplied their members with cheap literature, established their own newspapers, met regularly to debate political issues, and aimed at a mass membership. The foundation meeting of the London Corresponding Society was attended by nine men, but its rules held that 'the number of our members be unlimited', and within months they were being counted in hundreds, and then thousands. To cope with these numbers, the example of the Sheffield Constitutional Society was followed, with members organised into small 'divisions' or classes. Many exchanged messages of goodwill with societies in France until it were 'as if the Strait between Calais and Dover were no more'; but a sharper stimulant came from resentment at local forms of political, economic and religious discrimination. The Manchester Constitutional Society was formed in 1790 largely as a reaction by leading Dissenters to the establishment by the local Anglican community of a 'Church and King' society to celebrate the retention of the Test and Corporation Acts. Most of the founder members of the Norwich Revolution Society were also Dissenters, but they saw their mission as encouraging working-class members to take a more active part in the political process. The Sheffield Constitutional Society was more radical in outlook and more working-class in membership than either the Manchester or the Norwich societies, and economic grievances and class bitterness played an important part in the growth of membership to about two thousand within a year of its foundation in 1791. In Scotland the remarkable number of societies owed something to the outburst of intellectual activity associated with the Scottish Enlightenment of the second half of the century, and also much to local grievances which fuelled continuing resentment at the political and economic domination of England.

The radicalism of the decade showed an extent of support across the country and between classes missing in earlier periods, but the variety of motives which gave it energy hindered attempts to turn this new manifestation of popular protest into a co-ordinated movement. The London Corresponding Society, with its self-appointed role of advising other societies, and its charismatic itinerant lecturer, John Thelwall, was the most important link in the radical chain; but there was no single unifying force or agreed programme. Most of the societies stood for manhood suffrage, accompanied, as one put it, by 'annually elected Parliaments, unbiased and unbought Elections, and an equal Representation of the Whole Body of the People'. Unlike the gradualist schemes put forward by Pitt and the moderate reformers associated with Wyvill, the proposals of the new societies would have led to a radical redistribution of political power in the country. However shortlived the formal structure of these organisations proved to be when subjected to legal prosecution and government intimidation, they marked an important stage in the development of political aims among the working classes. They represented a more serious and purposeful agitation than the sporadic outbursts of protest which had characterised popular opposition earlier in the century. This is not to say that they were mass movements in later Chartist terms, or that they brought into active political participation the rural or urban labouring poor. With a few exceptions, they were the preserve of the skilled artisans and small tradesmen. The London Corresponding Society, largest of the associations, claimed about five thousand members at its maximum, and only a minority of these seem to have been regular attenders at meetings, or to have paid the modest weekly subscription.

The link between the societies and the opposition in Parliament was provided by the Friends of the People, a title which reveals the distinction which most Whigs made between sympathy with a cause and identification with its supporters among 'the lower sort of people'. It included twenty or thirty MPs in favour of parliamentary reform, though not Fox, whose most important contribution in this period came with his Libel Act of 1792, which made juries competent to judge the libel instead of merely the fact of its publication. The defeat by 282 votes to 41 of a reform motion put forward in the Commons by Charles Grey in 1793 showed the size of the task. While Grey argued for reform on the very Whiggish ground that 'the constitution was beautiful in theory but corrupt in practice', Pitt expressed the government's conviction that 'this is not a time to make hazardous experiments'. That less than a third of the Whig opposition voted for the motion was one of several signs that under the pressure of events in France, where revolution seemed to have turned to terror, the Whig party was becoming confused and divided. In particular many found it difficult to agree with Fox that tyranny was a worse evil than anarchy, and that 'the danger to this country chiefly consists in the growth of Tory principles'. A different view had been argued with great vehemence by Burke, concerned as few others in Britain had been in 1789 by the implication of events in France. In the autumn of 1790 appeared Burke's defence of existing institutions and of the rights of property, *Reflections on the Revolution in France*. He denied that the French Revolution was based on popular support – like the radical agitation in England it was the conspiracy of the few, 'the little, shrivelled, meagre, hopping though loud and troublesome, insects of the hour'. In his *Appeal from the New to the Old Whigs* of 1791 he went further, denying the rights of the majority as 'one of the most violent fictions of positive law'. The state he saw as a partnership in virtue, 'a partnership not only between those who are living, but between those who are living, those who are dead, and those who are to be born'. Sudden changes and experiments were ruled out, and he warned the Foxite Whigs that their role was akin to that of those Frenchmen whose criticism of the defects of the old order had brought the whole edifice of society crashing about their ears.

While Fox struggled on the floor of the House to counter Burke's arguments, and to prevent his secession from the Whig party, the news from France seemed month by month to confirm the apocalyptic interpretation of the Revolution advanced in the *Reflections*. As late as February 1792 Pitt had incautiously told the Commons that 'There never was a time in the history of this country when, from the situation of Europe, we might more reasonably expect fifteen years of peace.' Within two months war had broken out on the continent, and within the year was to draw in Britain. Hostilities, and the instinctive emotions of patriotism and Francophobia they produced, moved domestic political disputes onto a different plane.

Fox's insistence that Pitt was a greater menace to English liberties than the armies of revolutionary France had a hollow ring for most of his listeners. Slowly and painfully the Whig party of the Rockingham era broke up under these strains as most of its members, with much hesitation and many backward glances, began to move towards the government benches. Led by Portland, most of the Whig peers and about fifty MPs decided to support the government which became in 1794 a wartime coalition, with Portland and four other Whigs in the cabinet. Fox, supported by the younger reformers Grey and Sheridan, could count on the loyalty of a few peers and about sixty MPs.

In party terms the outline of the two great parties of the nineteenth century can be dimly discerned once these movements across the floor of the House subsided. But of wider importance was the impact of revolution and war on extra-parliamentary politics. Burke's statement of conservative beliefs had encountered a fierce response in Tom Paine's *Rights of Man*, published in two parts in 1791 and 1792. Paine attacked hereditary monarchy, as he did Burke's appeal to tradition and precedent – a 'presumption of governing beyond the grave'. The constitution of England which Burke revered Paine saw as a 'sepulchre of precedents'. His only precedent was the French Revolution, which showed how a new political structure could be erected from first principles, from a doctrine of natural rights which obliterated 'the meagre, stale, forbidding ways of custom, law and statute'. For Paine there was no appeal, as with many other radicals, to the Bill of Rights, Magna Carta, the Anglo-Saxon *witan*, no attempt to return to an idealised constitution of an earlier era. Paine's rhetoric was more inconoclastic, more explosive, in expression and implication. In its cheap edition *Rights of Man* became as familiar a book in humbler homes, one government minister was told, as *Robinson Crusoe* or *Pilgrim's Progress*. The resolutions of many of the radical societies now took on Painite characteristics with their references to natural rights, their support for a National Convention on the French model, and their declarations of no confidence in existing political institutions and parties.

The influence of Paine widened the divisions already opening on the reform side under the pressure of war, public disapproval and government uneasiness. In May 1791 Pitt saw 'no cause for immediate alarm' in the flood of publications issued 'with a view to extol the French revolution'; a year later a Royal Proclamation forbade seditious writings and meetings. Fox, shocked by the first part of *The Rights of Man*, had no stomach even to approach the second, and the Whig MP who chaired the Friends of the People complained of 'the indefinite language of delusion'. Wyvill, worried by the drift of moderates away from the reform cause, regretted that Paine 'had formed a party for the Republic among the lower classes of the people, by holding out to them the prospect of plundering the rich.' Other reformers preferred to cling to the respectability which their search for historical precedents was thought to give them, and still insisted that they were demanding the restoration of lost rights rather than the granting of new ones. The Sheffield radical periodical, *The Patriot*, saw parliamentary reform as a necessary middle way to 'preserve the English constitution from the sap of Royal influence and from the storm of tumultuous democracy'.

If on the reform side there were divisions and doubts, behind Pitt there was a closing of ranks of which the adhesion of the Portland Whigs was only one symbol. Scholarly fascination with the new reform manifestations of the 1790s can lead to an understatement of the continuing strength of conservative opinion at all levels of society. In parliamentary terms this had been shown earlier in the reign by the support of stern policies towards the American colonies. After the American war it could be seen in the revulsion against the constitutional doctrines preached by the Foxite Whigs, the opposition to Pitt's modest proposals on parliamentary reform, the refusal to take Irish reform further, and the blocking of attempts to repeal the Test and Corporation Acts. With the outbreak of the French Revolution the conservative reaction became more explicit and strident. It found articulation not only in Burke's writings, but in those of a host of literary and political camp-followers. 'Church and King' crowds appeared again, most uncontrollably in Birmingham where with the connivance of magistrates they destroyed the houses and chapels of Dissenters in three days of looting and burning.

In the winter of 1792–93 as fear of French spies, perhaps even French invasion, increased, there was a mushroom growth of the Loyal Associations or Reeves Societies. More than a thousand associations appeared within a few months, until one excited observer reported that 'the whole country is forming itself into an association'. Although for the most part lasting only two or three years, these associations, supported by the local governing classes both through their pockets and in their roles as magistrates, mayors, aldermen and rectors, represented a groundswell of local opinion against what was regarded as the subversive, unpatriotic activity of the reform societies. These experienced increasing difficulty in finding premises in which to meet, and such meetings as were held were often broken up by loyalist bully-boys. Intimidation and ostracism were accompanied by a general decline in support. Many from the middling or professional classes, who had regarded themselves as sympathetic to reform, began to dissociate themselves from the working-class radicals with their demands for political education of the masses, national conventions, and manhood suffrage. To some radicals the Convention was an alternative Parliament, a challenge by the delegates of the people to the unrepresentative assembly at Westminster; others saw its importance in more practical terms as a means of bringing together the reform societies and uniting them behind a common programme. To a government haunted by the spectre of French revolutionary crowds and massacres neither proposition was acceptable. 'The very name of British Convention carries sedition along with it', one minister declared. The Convention threatened the end of Parliament, universal suffrage was tantamount to subversion, and parliamentary reformers were Jacobins – or so it appeared to a government which seemed to follow rather than lead public expressions of uneasiness and fear.

The holding of a Convention at Edinburgh in November 1793 which was attended by some delegates from England, and plans to hold a nationwide 'British Convention' the following spring, swung the government towards a decision to suspend Habeas Corpus for a limited period, and to prosecute the radical leaders for high treason. The state trials of 1793 and 1794 led to convictions and savage sentences in Scotland, acquittals in England by juries which refused to be browbeaten; but the overall result of this frightening exercise of the legal process was the same. Despite the triumphant scenes in London which marked the acquittal of Hardy, Thelwall and Horne Tooke, the withdrawal or flight of the radical leaders had begun. The public mood in London in these years is difficult to gauge. In 1794 and 1795 there were further demonstrations against the government, but they seemed to have less to do with the ideological split which had polarised political opinion in the country than with specific grievances arising from an unsuccessful war, recruitment abuses, and high food prices following the bad harvest of 1794.

The seriousness of the economic situation was shown by the gradual introduction in many rural areas of a system by which the amount of parish relief given to a labourer and his family was linked to the price of bread in order to bring wages up to a bare subsistence level – the 'Speenhamland System', so called from the decision of Berkshire magistrates at Speenhamland in 1795. The mood of despair and anger was shown in outbursts of rioting in several parts of the country, and reached a dramatic highpoint in October 1795 when the ceremonial opening of Parliament was marked by violent demonstrations against Pitt, the King, and the war. To the ministry the most sinister aspect of this outbreak was that it followed hard on the heels of a mass meeting organised by the London Corresponding Society where Thelwall had told his listeners that 'if you obtain annual parliaments and universal suffrage it will be no longer in the power of a worthless set of beings to crimp, starve and murder you.' Economic grievances of a familiar kind had combined with novel political demands to present the government with what it considered to be a full-blooded challenge to its authority in the middle of a war effort as unsuccessful as it was expensive. Just as the earlier Conventions had given the government justification for the treason trials, so the events of October 1795 prompted ministers to introduce the 'Gagging Acts'. These prohibited unauthorised meetings of more than fifty persons, and extended the definition of treason to include the inciting of hatred for the King, constitution and government. Despite this alarming extension, few prosecutions for treason followed, but there were about two hundred successful prosecutions of radicals on the lesser charge of seditious libel, together with another hundred men held in prison without trial – and even those put on trial and found innocent endured months of imprisonment, and loss of income and jobs.

In the face of continual harassment, and already demoralised by internal rifts, financial troubles, and above all the inability after years of struggle to make any impact on the political structure of the country, the radical societies crumbled and disappeared. The frightening naval mutinies of 1797 at Spithead and the Nore, a fiscal crisis which led the Bank of England to suspend cash payments, and growing discontent in Ireland, brought a crisis situation which rallied support to the government rather than to its opponents. That the government exaggerated the danger from the reformers and misunderstood their aims is now clear. Only a handful were planning a violent overthrow of the established order. The touching faith of many radicals in the efficacy of parliamentary reform showed in their desire to renovate the existing system rather than replace it. A wider participation by working men in the political process would put an end to the inequalities of economic and social conditions, eliminate corruption at home and stop aggressive war abroad. A few, such as Thomas Spence, went further and advocated nationalisation of land as a way forward to 'a beautiful and powerful New Republic'. Such hopes may have been visionary; in normal times they were not treasonable. But the government, alerted and alarmed by its network of spies and informers, saw Jacobins everywhere, shadowy figures behind any expression of discontent, the 'enemy within our bosoms' according to one minister. As Fox had feared, the war had become an ideological one, and men as unbalanced as during the wars of religion. Pitt insisted that behind their 'mask of attachment to the state and country' the reform societies were committed to conspiracy and insurrection, and in this he seems to have been supported by the weight of opinion in the country. John

Wesley had died in 1791, but his authoritarian political views were reflected in the statutes drawn up at the Methodist Conference in the next year: 'None of us shall either in writing or in conversation speak lightly or irreverently of the government.' Not all Methodists shared this view, as the secession of Alexander Kilham's 'New Connexion' – the 'Tom Paine Methodists' – showed in 1797; but the general reaction of churchmen of all denominations was revulsion at the anticlerical excesses of revolutionary France.

Ironically, the measures taken by the government produced the situation it had most feared. The reformers' failure to make progress by open, constitutional means, and the scrutiny of their activities by spies and law officers, drove some underground into a murky world of clandestine activity. Particularly unnerving to ministers was the evidence of contact between individual radicals and the United Irish movement. The United Irishmen had been founded in 1791, with branches in both Belfast and Dublin, pledged to a programme of parliamentary reform and equal rights for men of all religious persuasions. In 1792 and 1793 the Irish government, under pressure from Pitt, introduced a series of Catholic relief measures. Restrictions on the right of Catholics to own property, serve on juries, carry arms, enter university, and hold legal and judicial positions, were lifted. Most important, they were given the franchise on the same terms as Protestants, though they were still excluded from the Irish Parliament. This sudden swirl of change was less the result of United Irish campaigning than routine English concern about the situation in Ireland in wartime. Pitt was no more prepared to concede parliamentary reform to the United Irishmen than to English radicals, and his abrupt recall of the new Viceroy, Earl Fitzwilliam, who had proposed full political rights for Catholics so as to make 'the people of Ireland *one* People', further disillusioned those who advocated change through constitutional means. The United Irishmen formed a separatist movement which in turn evolved into a secret, insurrectionary organisation aiming at independence with French help. One of the most charismatic of the United Irish leaders, Wolfe Tone, persuaded the French government to mount an invasion of Ireland, and although storms dispersed the French fleet as it neared the Irish coast in December 1796, smaller French expeditions landed in Ireland in the summer of 1798 to link up with disaffected Irish groups. It was a case of too little and too late. Ulster with its equipment and expertise left over from the days of the Protestant Volunteer movement had been disarmed the previous year, and in the Catholic south the flickers of rebellion were stamped out with a ruthless brutality last seen in Cumberland's ravages in Scotland after the Forty-Five. Parts of Ireland were subjected to a counter-revolutionary terror, both official and unofficial, which English protesters had feared but never experienced.

It was into this maelstrom of conspiracy and rebellion that some English radicals were drawn. After the suppression of the Irish rebellion the British government uncovered evidence of communication between the United Irishmen, the United Englishmen (modelled on the Irish organisation, with an illegal oath and a commitment to armed rebellion), and some militant remnants of the London Corresponding Society. Ministers were already alarmed by the naval mutinies which threatened to dissolve the nation's main line of defence against the French, and in particular by the suspicion that English Jacobins and United Irishmen among the seamen recently forced into the fleet were responsible for turning grievances about pay and conditions into a challenge to the government. Triangular contacts between England, Ireland and France in wartime posed a threat of unknown but worrying dimensions to the security of the state, so in 1798 Habeas Corpus was again suspended, this time for three years, and in 1799 the few remaining radical societies – some of them now only shells – were dissolved by parliamentary legislation. At the same time a miscellany of existing legislation prohibiting combinations of workers in particular trades was brought together in the Combination Acts, which declared all associations of workmen illegal, and provided for offenders to be dealt with by summary jurisdiction without the right of trial by jury.

These measures went through Parliament with little debate, for the formal opposition led by Fox had ceased to attend. From 1794 onwards Fox and his remaining Whig associates had protested with vigour against what they saw as the progressive erosion of English liberties by the government, though with his conventional ideas of a balanced constitution and the primacy within it of the House of Commons, Fox stood poles apart from the new radicalism of the period. As the war dragged on, the opposition Whigs increased in unity and even in numbers from the low point of 1794. Grey's standard motion for parliamentary reform attracted 91 votes in 1797 compared with 41 in 1793. It was this defeat, however, coupled with a sense of futility and helplessness, which drove the opposition into a secession from Parliament which lasted from 1797 to 1800. The secession, informal rather than official, and never fully observed, had several dimensions. It was a confession of failure, a protest against the government's manipulation of the political process, and a refusal to legitimise that manipulation by according it the formalities of parliamentary opposition and vote. Given the predictable result of the 1796 election with its return of well over 400 ministerialist MPs, and the apparent immovability of Pitt, Fox decided on the only protest left to him.

Although within Parliament the Foxite opposition had ceased to attend, and outside Parliament the radical societies had been suppressed, the government continued to be disturbed by reports of mass meetings, petitions, oath-taking, strikes and riots. Some of this activity had a political dimension, but it was in the main a protest against economic distress, and in particular the high food prices which followed the poor harvests of 1799 and 1800. A Jacobin underground of some sort existed. Glimpses of it can be seen in the reports of government spies, and in the Despard plot of 1802 to seize key points in London with the aid of disaffected soldiers, but it had no realistic chance of success without a French invasion. As difficult to assess as these conspiratorial activities was the wider legacy of the participation in the radicalism of the 1790s of working men who had never before seen themselves in a political role. Some had been cowed, others had retracted, but as John Thelwall wrote in 1796, 'hence every large workshop and manufactory is a sort of political society, which no act of parliament can silence, and no magistrate disperse.' If on the one hand the identification by ministers and loyalist opinion of the radical societies with revolution and treason had stifled the prospects of even limited political reform for years to come, the emergence of plebeian radicalism in these years was to give a new breadth to the demand for reform after the French wars.

9 The struggle against France, 1793–1815

The outbreak of war between Britain and France in February 1793 was greeted by Pitt with a warning to the Commons that the nation now confronted 'a system, the principles of which, if not opposed, threaten the most fatal consequences to the tranquillity of this country, the security of its allies, the good order of every European Government, and the happiness of the whole of the human race.' Despite his apocalyptic tone, Pitt assumed that France's financial difficulties would make the war a short one; and his strategy for fighting it was conventional enough. In many respects it resembled his father's in the Seven Years War – financial help to European allies, a minimal British troop presence on the continent, and offensive operations against France's overseas trade and colonies. As far as the main purpose of the war was concerned there was a clear divide between ideologues such as Burke who considered it to be one of 'social order' against 'Barbarity', and those moved by a more traditional concern, brought to life when French forces overran the Austrian Netherlands in 1792 and opened the Scheldt in defiance of previous treaty engagements. Fox put his finger on the problem when he told the Commons that 'of all wars he dreaded that the most which had no definite object, because of such a war it is impossible to see the end.' In sombre mood the *Morning Chronicle* warned that if the war was indeed to be fought over 'principles', then 'we must go on killing as long as there are any Frenchmen left to kill' – a very different concept of war from the limited hostilities fought by professional forces which had been the norm during the century.

As British diplomacy and money helped to bring together the First Coalition of Austria, Russia, Prussia and Spain, so uncertainties developed about British strategy, awkwardly divided in planning and execution between Grenville at the Foreign Office and Dundas, first holder of the new office of Secretary of State for War. Desirable objectives were as endless as British forces were limited: French colonies in the Caribbean, where the rich sugar island of Saint Domingue was in a state of anarchy following a slave uprising; military operations alongside the Austrians in the Low Countries; naval and military aid to counter-revolutionary forces within France, perhaps at Toulon, or at Nantes, or in the Vendée. With Grenville's diplomatic priorities often running counter to the military considerations of Dundas, British policy was reduced to a doling out of forces to cover most areas of opportunity and danger – with predictable consequences. Co-operation with loyalists at Toulon in 1793 and on the Quiberon peninsula in 1795 ended in defeat and withdrawal. British forces under the command of the Duke of York were involved in the general shambles of the Austrian retreat from the Netherlands. Only the navy maintained its reputation, with the Channel fleet under Howe defeating the French fleet from Brest on 'The Glorious First of June' 1794, but even that victory could not prevent a large French grain convoy from America slipping into port. The main weight of the war effort was directed at the French West Indies in an effort, as Pitt put it, to 'destroy the sinews of their commerce'. To Dundas, also thinking in terms of earlier wars, it was plain that 'by success in the West Indies alone you can be enabled to dictate the terms of peace'. That proposition was not be put to the test, for after some initial successes British forces in the Caribbean were bled white. If discharges and desertions are added to its 45,000 deaths, the army suffered a 70 per cent casualty rate in the most demoralising overseas campaign Britain had ever fought.

With a population still only half the size of France's, Britain was forced into new devices to find manpower for the war. As the size of the navy increased from 16,000 men to 135,000 not even the most ruthless forays of the impress service could keep up with demand, nor could the mercantile marine sustain continued depredations on its manpower. In 1795 the Quota Act laid the whole country under assessment to provide men for the navy: 10,000 from the inland counties, and 20,000 from the seaports – and with further contributions to follow. The arrival of large numbers of reluctant landmen on the king's ships produced acute training problems, and played a part in the resentment at low pay (unchanged for seamen since Cromwell's day) and poor conditions which led to the naval mutinies of 1797. Recruitment for the army was equally difficult, and there was no equivalent of the mercantile marine to provide trained manpower. Britain, one minister warned, was not like those continental powers which had large reserves of men 'having little else to do than to come forth for war when wanted . . . we have no second army to produce if we waste the first'. The militia was confined to home defence, though in an attempt to overcome this restriction cash bounties were offered to militiamen willing to serve abroad. The appointment of the King's second son, the Duke of York, as Commander-in-Chief in 1795 brought much-needed reforms in army training, weaponry, and promotion procedures; but the improvements were bound to take time to become effective.

As dismaying as these problems was the break-up of the First Coalition in the face of the massed armies of the French revolutionary regime. The outbreak of war with Spain and Holland threatened Britain's position in the Mediterranean and on the distant Asian sea-routes, while in 1797 Britain's last ally of any consequence, Austria, made peace with France. The war had somehow changed from an overwhelming assault from all quarters on a beleaguered France to a conflict in which the enemy had secured its own frontiers, seized large areas of the Low Countries and Italy, was negotiating with the rebel Irish, and by the autumn of 1797 had grouped an ominously named Army of England under the brilliant young General Bonaparte on the Channel coast. Bad harvests, high taxes and disruption of trade increased the unpopularity of the war, and led to abortive attempts by the government to negotiate peace. Not all was discontent and riot: Britain's isolation, and the threat of invasion, seemed to make the war a more clear-cut struggle, free from the machinations of devious and expensive allies. The upsurge of patriotic feeling was reflected in the numbers joining the Volunteer associations. And there were naval victories to keep up morale. In early 1797 the Spanish fleet was defeated off Cape St Vincent by Jervis and Nelson, and despite its mutiny in the summer the North Sea fleet of the Nore defeated the Dutch fleet at Camperdown later that year.

With little hope of controlling the Channel, Bonaparte gave up his invasion plans in 1798, and instead led a huge expeditionary force into the Mediterranean. There it seized Malta before heading for Egypt, and possibly India. However menacing this was in terms of Britain's global interests, Bonaparte's new thrust did not have the frightening proximity of his invasion force camped across the Channel, and it exposed him to the weight of British naval power. After several near misses, Nelson destroyed the French fleet at the Nile, and trapped Bonaparte and his army in Egypt. In India a new Governor-General, Richard Wellesley, reacted vigorously to the possibility, however remote, of a French descent. Indian princes with suspected French sympathies, or with French advisers, were hammered into submission: Tipu Sultan of Mysore, the Nizam of the Deccan, the Nawab of the Carnatic. Other areas, such as the important buffer-state of Oudh, north-west of Bengal, were subdued on grounds of their misrule. Finally, in the first years of the new century, Arthur Wellesley (younger brother of the Governor-General, and the future Duke of Wellington) led Company forces in a series of campaigns which broke the power of the great Maratha confederacy, and put Delhi and the Mogul emperor under British control. Although in the awful stress of war with France these exploits seemed almost irrelevant, they opened the way for future British control of all India. As Arthur Wellesley wrote to his brother: 'You have not only saved but enlarged and secured the valuable empire entrusted to your government at a time when everything else was a wreck and the existence even of Great Britain problematical.'

Having survived the crisis year of 1797, and crushed the Irish rebellion the next, Pitt and Grenville embarked on patient nego-tiations to construct a Second Coalition, a task made the more urgent when in 1799 Bonaparte returned from Egypt and seized power as First Consul. The problem of how to pay for the colossal expenses of the war – its military operations, subsidies to continental allies, and in years of bad harvests the purchase of grain abroad – remained. The balance of payments crisis became so serious in 1797 that the government was forced to release the Bank of England from the obligation to honour its paper currency with gold. Pitt had exhausted all conventional expedients: he had raised loans (one of them, the 'Loyalty Loan' of 1796, by direct appeal to the public), introduced new taxes, and trebled existing assessed taxes. His struggles over a five-year period to finance the war represented the climax of attempts throughout the eighteenth century to avoid the necessity for some form of income tax, but 1798 saw a flurry of activity designed to tap new sources of income. The land tax was declared permanent at a rate of four shillings in the £, but landowners were allowed to cancel their annual payment by making over a capital sum. This cleared the way for Pitt's main innovation – the introduction in 1799 of an income tax, self-assessed, and with a maximum rate of 10 per cent. Deficient though the new measure proved to be in actual operation, it marked a radical shift from taxing expenditure to taxing income. There was some uneasiness both about the financial burden of the new tax, and the intrusion into private affairs which it represented. Most, however, accepted it as a wartime measure, and would probably have agreed with the MP who said that he would give up one-tenth of his income forever, 'if the remainder of his property was secured from the inroad of French pikes and French principles'.

It was this guarantee which proved difficult to implement, for the first year of the new coalition in 1799 failed to live up to expectations. Once again the long-suffering Duke of York took a British army to the Low Countries; and once again the failure of continental allies to play the role allotted them by their British paymaster led to its failure and withdrawal. The events of the year seemed to bring nearer Pitt's fear of 'a remote and perhaps lingering war, supported for a longer period and without decisive issue, at our expense'. They led to a reappraisal of the war situation in London, but the triumvirate of Pitt, Grenville and Dundas was divided by differences of temperament and outlook. Dundas pressed for a reversion to limited warfare – on the 'narrowest line', as he put it – with the defeat of the French army in Egypt high on his agenda. Grenville, by contrast, was insistent that Jacobinism must 'be attacked and subdued in its citadel at Paris', and busied himself with fresh plans for the encirclement of France. His calculations respecting the allies rested on a mixture of optimism and speculation. To the dismay of Dundas he skimmed lightly over those problems related to British forces which concerned the War Ministry: their numbers and training, and above all the logistics of the complicated operations sketched out for them and the allies. These ranged from the Alps to the North Sea, from the Mediterranean to the Channel, and were directed against an enemy commanded by an aggressive, unconventional general who combined military and political authority in his own person. Bonaparte's defeat of the Austrian army at Marengo in June 1800 foreshadowed both the break-up of the Second Coalition, and the collapse of Grenville's grandiose but fragile strategy.

To add to the stresses on Pitt, 1800 saw serious food riots as the price of wheat rose to 150s. a quarter (compared to the previous wartime peak of 96s. in 1796). There was grumbling from the King at the conduct of the war, increased bickering among the cabinet, and above all a looming crisis over Irish policy. The sequence of rebellion, invasion and repression in Ireland brought home to British ministers that they were dependent there on a group of politicians who were opposed, for political or religious reasons, by most of the population. The bizarre possibility that a French invasion might be supported by Ulster Protestants as well as by Catholics in the south was clear indication that fundamental changes were needed. After the 1798 rebellion had been put down at the cost of twelve thousand Irish lives, Pitt turned to the task of bringing together the Catholic majority and Protestant minority under the protection of direct rule from Westminster. Pitt had mulled over the advantages of a union of the two kingdoms several times in the past. Now, caught between fear of further French-supported risings in Ireland and alarm at what a bigoted ruling class might do, Pitt saw incorporation in a single kingdom as the only safe way forward. If union was to be acceptable to the majority in Ireland then it must, argued Pitt, be accompanied by Catholic emancipation, with an oath of allegiance replacing the sacramental test, and a reform of the hated tithe system. After the application of much persuasion and patronage in Dublin, where many members of the Irish House of Commons were disinclined to vote for their own extinction, the Act of Union was passed by both parliaments in 1800, to take effect on 1 January 1801. It brought to Westminster 100 Irish MPs (a considerable under-representation in terms of population) and 28 representative Irish peers together with an archbishop and three bishops. The two countries were also joined in a commercial union, to the long-term detriment of Irish manufactures, left unprotected against the more competitive English industrial products.

A union of institutions, finance and churches was one thing; a union of societies so different in tradition and culture another. The Act of 1800 built a structure subject from the beginning to corrosion, but its most immediate defect was the failure to include any measure of Catholic emancipation. Leading Catholics thought they had received an assurance from Pitt that under the new arrangement Catholics would be able to sit at Westminster, but this message was never clearly or publicly transmitted. In London, as realisation of the second stage of Pitt's policy became known, about half the cabinet seems to have been opposed, and this was a weakness in Pitt's position when George III, finally and fatally, got wind of the proposal. In words which echoed his warnings of December 1783 the King told Dundas in public that he would regard every supporter of Catholic emancipation 'as my personal enemy'. As the immovability of the King on one side, and the rifts within the cabinet on the other, became clear, Pitt resigned in February 1801, together with most of his leading ministers. He was replaced by Henry Addington, the respected if uninspiring Speaker of the Commons. Much ink has been spilt on this episode: on the constitutional implications of the King's stand; on Pitt's failure to prepare the ground better; on the reasons why Pitt simply did not drop the measure and remain in office; and on the relation between this issue and the range of other problems confronting the government. This last was perhaps crucial. Although the Irish question was the occasion of Pitt's departure, his resignation has to be seen in the wider circumstances of his physical health and mental resilience after eight years of war. 'He felt himself', one of his colleagues wrote, 'incapable either of carrying on the war, or of making peace.'

It was this last task which the new government turned to, buttressed by a naval victory at Copenhagen and a military triumph in Egypt. The preliminaries of peace with France were concluded by October 1801, and the definitive Treaty of Amiens was signed in March 1802. Britain agreed to return most of its colonial conquests in the interests of a wider peace in Europe. This the government believed would come from combining the Amiens settlement with the previous year's

Treaty of Lunéville negotiated between France and Austria, which gave France the left bank of the Rhine, and appeared to guarantee the independence of the new republics in Holland, Switzerland and Italy. The Amiens treaty was attacked, particularly by some ex-ministers, on the grounds both of the giving up of territory and of reliance on the good faith of Bonaparte. For most, however, it was the coming of peace, rather than its precise terms, which was important. As festivities and illuminations were held throughout the country, the King summed up most informed opinion when he commented that it was an 'experimental' but 'unavoidable' peace.

None of Britain's war aims had been accomplished. France had neither been held in Europe nor plundered overseas. It was altogether a more formidable power than it had been during the *ancien régime*, standing as it did at last on the banks of the Rhine, and holding a dominant position in the Low Countries, northern Italy, Spain and Portugal. Pitt, though he appeared in the public mind as the symbol of defiance to France, 'the Atlas of our reeling globe', as a colleague expressed it, had not shown the capacity for sustained leadership which so strenuous and complex a war demanded. 'All modern wars are a contention of the purse', Dundas assured him in 1794, and in this respect Pitt had been successful; but ignorant, as he admitted, of 'military subjects', he never dominated the direction of the war as he had done the process of reconstruction in his first decade in office. Plans were adopted, modified, dropped; the Foreign Office marched in one direction, the War Ministry in another; urgent Cabinet meetings were called, only to end with no decisions taken. The determination to wage war, and to demand from the nation unprecedented sacrifices in men and money, were never in question under Pitt; but the main shape of the war effort remained nebulous, and its direction unclear.

The Amiens peace lasted little more than a year. During that time drastic cuts were made in the army, more modest ones in the navy. Addington's first budget repealed income tax on the grounds that 'it should be reserved for the more important occasions'; and the return of released servicemen together with a drop in war orders gave a glimpse of the problems which were to loom large after 1815. The fact that the army despite reductions remained at the unprecedented peacetime figure of 132,000 men was a sign of those mutual suspicions which eroded the Amiens settlement before it had a chance to take hold, and in May 1803 war broke out again. It might, Addington prophesied in a moment of gloom, last twelve years. By 1804 Pitt was back in office, but not before Addington in his war budget of 1803 had introduced a more effective form of income tax, thinly disguised under the term 'property tax'. Different forms of income were classified under different schedules, and most tax paid was deducted at source – innovations as important as Pitt's original measure of 1799.

When Pitt returned to office he did so not as head of a national coalition, as many had anticipated, for the King's continued veto on Fox also shut out Grenville who refused to join the ministry at a time of national crisis unless it included the leading politicians 'without any exception'. Instead, in what a few years earlier would have seemed an unlikely turn of events, Grenville moved close to Fox. The only minister apart from Pitt of seniority and repute was Dundas (now Lord Melville), and it was a serious blow to the ministry when he was forced to resign after a scandal over misuse of public funds. The episode added to a growing sense of unease, both inside and outside Parliament, about what appeared to be the cynical manoeuvres of politicians since Pitt's resignation in 1801 had fragmented his former colleagues into a half-dozen different groups. Accompanying this was a suspicion that at a time of hardship and suffering for many there were others who were doing well out of the war. The old reformers, Wyvill and Cartwright among them, dusted off their battle-standards, public protest meetings were held, and petitions sent to Parliament 'to save from rapacity, from peculation, and fraud, a people who contribute cheerfully to the real wants of the state'. A new and effective journalistic recruit to the reformers' ranks was the former Tory, William Cobbett, whose *Political Register* specialised in exposing government mismanagement and corruption.

Pitt's few remaining months in office were ones of acute national danger as Napoleon concentrated his forces for invasion. The government began to build elaborate coastal fortifications, including 73 Martello towers along the vulnerable coasts of Kent and Sussex, but the system was not complete until late 1806. Before that, the government's strategy in case the invading army managed to slip through British naval cover, was to confront it with masses of armed men. The old distrust of a standing army, and the new suspicion of anything resembling French practices ruled out universal conscription, but measures passed by both the Addington and Pitt ministries produced by ballot, bounty or patriotic appeal what were by British standards enormous numbers of men. Often lacking arms and proper training, they were organised in a variety of categories – Volunteers, Militia, Supplementary Militia, Sea Fencibles, and the Army of Reserve. These amateur soldiers may have been in the unflattering words of one minister, 'painted cherries which none but simple birds would take for real fruit', but as an expression of national defiance the mobilisation was impressive as it brought 800,000 men, or one in five of the adult male population, under arms. It was part of a tide of patriotic fervour which swept the country in these crisis months, with Gillray's cartoon portrayals of 'Boney' symbolising the mixture of fear and hatred with which the demonic Emperor of the French was regarded in Britain.

In the event, the country's part-time soldiers were not put to the test. To gain temporary control of the Channel, Napoleon drew up an intricate plan of decoy and bluff by which the combined fleets of France and Spain would attack, or pretend to attack, in the Caribbean and in the Mediterranean, while at Boulogne the invasion flotilla with room for 165,000 men lay poised to strike. This triple threat was intended to confront the Royal Navy with an insoluble dilemma about where to deploy its ships, but it was the Franco-Spanish fleet which proved unequal to its task. On 21 October 1805 it was shattered at Trafalgar in yet another exhibition of the power and ferocity of British naval might under Nelson, but two months before the famous victory the threat of invasion had already been lifted. The entry of Austria into the war in August as a partner in the Third Coalition, and the continued inability of the French admirals to guarantee a crossing of the Channel, had emptied the invasion camps around Boulogne as Napoleon turned east to meet the armies of Austria and Russia, and to defeat them at Ulm and Austerlitz. Nelson's final great victory saved Britain from any immediate renewal of the invasion threat, gave her control of the Mediterranean, and exposed her enemies' colonies to attack throughout the world. Even before Trafalgar the West Indian territories of St Lucia, Tobago and Dutch Guiana had been taken once again by British forces; and after 1805 the tempo of conquest quickened. Year after year the expeditions sailed, and the list of captures grew: the Cape of Good Hope in 1806; Curaçao and the Danish West Indies in 1807; some of the Moluccas in 1808; Martinique and Senegal in 1809; Guadeloupe, Mauritius, Amboina and Banda in 1810; Java in 1811. Sometimes there was fighting, often there was not. Local resistance was feeble, and help from Europe unlikely. There were few dramatic feats of arms, but quietly the overseas empires of France and Holland disappeared into Britain's grasp.

At the strategic level the conflict between Britain and France followed the traditional pattern of Anglo-French hostilities. A power supreme on land was the enemy of one invincible at sea; and neither could strike a decisive blow at the other, though Britain attempted to do so by proxy as it increased its continental subsidies (to £7 million in 1806 alone). After Trafalgar the French fleet was rebuilt; but like his Bourbon predecessors Napoleon was not prepared to give priority to the maritime effort despite his assertion of 1805 (ironically on the day of Trafalgar) that 'I want peace on the continent. What I long for is ships, colonies and commerce.' On the other hand Britain's navy, now being stretched beyond the limits of safety by the tasks demanded of it, was in terms of grand strategy a defensive force. It was a destroyer of enemy shipping, a protector of the country's seaborne trade, a carrier of armies – but it was not a war-winning weapon in its own right.

The dilemma of how to break this deadlock was tackled, in the end with some success, by governments lacking outstanding individual leadership. Pitt died in January 1806, and Fox in September 1806 after a few months as Foreign Secretary in Grenville's ill-starred Ministry of all the Talents – that coming together in office of the old Foxite opposition with the Grenville group which was to be the only collective experience of government for the Whigs between 1784 and 1830. Working in harness with ministers such as Grenville and Addington (now Lord Sidmouth), the Foxites had neither the opportunity nor, perhaps, the inclination to introduce the reform measures long expected by radicals outside Parliament. A bill to abolish the slave trade passed in the summer of 1806 was by any measure a great stride forward, but in the end it was done without much fuss and bother, and not as a party measure. The decline in importance of the West Indian sugar interest as industrialisation produced new sources of wealth may have played some part in abolition; but it also represented that union of humanitarian and evangelical sentiment in this period which led to the formation of several new missionary societies – the Baptist in 1792, the London in 1795, and the Church in 1799. An attempt by Fox to initiate peace negotiations with Napoleon failed, and soon after his death the ministry foundered on 'a rock above water' – Wilberforce's phrase to describe George III's continued obduracy over Catholic relief, this time with regard to senior appointments in the army. The Talents were replaced by a government composed mainly of Pittites, under the leadership of the aged Duke of Portland, and it was confirmed in office by the election of 1807.

The new administration was characterised by one contemporary as 'a compound of vanity and incapacity', but it contained men who were to dominate the politics of the second decade of the century: Canning, eloquent and combative, the self-proclaimed heir of Pitt; Castlereagh, less flamboyant and more reserved; and the solid, pragmatic Hawkesbury (later Earl of Liverpool). The ministry was committed to a maximum war effort, but just where Britain's forces should be directed remained a matter of dispute, and elsewhere there were serious differences between ministers. On Catholic emancipation a deep divide separated Canning and Castlereagh, generally in favour, from the evangelical Spencer Perceval, who succeeded Portland as First Lord of the Treasury in 1809, and other 'red-hot Protestants' in the cabinet. To differences of principle between some ministers were added personal rivalries between others – displayed when Canning and Castlereagh fought a duel in 1809 which for a time removed both from the government. Even this fracas paled before the resignation of the Duke of York as Commander-in-Chief following a parliamentary enquiry into accusations by his discarded mistress about the sale of commissions and promotions in the army. The affair brought huge crowds onto the streets of London, but then so did the jubilee celebrations for George III, whose popularity grew as his health and well-being declined. An alarming aspect of the political situation to dispassionate observers was the way in which scandals in government overshadowed the mundane necessities of war against Napoleon. As one said, 'the progress of the French, the ruin of Spain, and the disasters and disgraces of our arms are banished from the memory' – a condemnation provoked by the disorganised failure of another attempt to intervene in the Low Countries in the shape of the Walcheren expedition of 1809, originally intended to strike up the Scheldt at Antwerp.

There was little sign that the opposition was in any position to benefit from the disarray of the government. On the war, it remained defeatist – 'The next French battle will be fought in Ireland, or perhaps in Kent', one Whig pronounced in 1809. The bonds between the Foxite Whigs and Grenville were firm only on the Catholic issue, and 1807 had shown that this was unlikely to endear them to King or electorate. Parliamentary reform, likewise, was more divisive than unifying. Although the patrician brewer, Samuel Whitbread, led a group of radical Whigs, the 'Mountain', who were in favour, Grenville was strongly opposed, and Grey hesitant. Economical reform was fashionable again as public uneasiness grew about government extravagance and corruption, but the failure of the Whigs to take action when in office in 1806–07 made it difficult for them to mount a convincing campaign. The loss of Fox was a severe blow, for whatever his defects he was not only a politician of national stature but within the Whig party a great conciliator, a leader who commanded loyalty across a wide spectrum of political opinion.

Neither government nor opposition could live long on memories of dead leaders. Perceval reminded ministers that 'We are no longer the sole representatives of Mr. Pitt. The magic of that name is in a great degree dissolved, and the principle upon which we must rely to keep us together is the public sentiment of loyalty and attachment to the king.' Cast in wider terms, this was to characterise the Toryism of the postwar years, though its reverential references to Pitt ignored the awkward fact that he had never seen himself as a Tory but rather as a Whig in the tradition of the Glorious Revolution. His governments had rested on the support of the court and administration group (now shrinking in size), independents and some personal followers rather than on an organised party grouping, and it was a sign of his passing from the scene that in the 1807 election the terms Whig and Tory were heard once more. The logic of the political situation meant that the first moves towards a sharper party identification would come from the Whigs. To some radicals, disillusioned with the brief reign of the Talents, the opposition was indistinguishable from the government, but there were issues which separated the two main parliamentary groupings – the royal prerogative, Ireland and the Catholic question, and in time parliamentary reform. Some of the new generation of Whigs such as Brougham, Romilly and Whitbread came from a different background, and held different views on the necessity of change, from the ranks of aristocratic Whiggery. For a time between 1810 and 1812 as George III fell ill again – this time without recovery – and as Fox's old friend the Prince of Wales became Regent, it seemed as if past associations would help the Whigs, but the Prince was a more cautious man than he had been in 1788. His insistence on a broad-based government was partly met when Perceval brought in Sidmouth and Castlereagh, and despite the continued absence of Canning and Grenville it was a ministry broadly within the Pittite tradition which Liverpool inherited after Perceval's death in 1812. The awkward issue of Catholic emancipation was pushed to one side for the time being as an 'open question' on which the government was not committed one way or the other – an understandable wartime exercise in political fence-sitting which was to continue long into peacetime.

Liverpool took over a war effort which was faltering, possibly on the edge of disaster, after almost twenty years of fighting. The failure of Fox's peace efforts in 1806 had been followed by an intensification of hostilities which included commitment by both France and Britain to forms of economic warfare unknown to previous generations. Frustrated by his inability to strike a direct blow at Britain, Napoleon decided to turn his remaining adversary's strength into weakness by closing the markets of Europe to British traders. The Berlin decrees of 1806 and the Milan decrees of 1807 established the Continental System which prohibited British goods from entering French-controlled ports, and stopped neutral trade with Britain by seizing all vessels so engaged. 'I mean to conquer the sea by the land', Napoleon declared. The British response came with the Orders in Council of 1807 which blockaded all ports attempting to exclude British vessels and goods, and prohibited trade between French-controlled regions and overseas countries, including the

United States. Once more the struggle was between Napoleon's control on land and Britain's command of the sea, with the ports and coastal approaches forming the battleground, and customs officials, police and black-market operators the combatants in this new form of warfare.

Partly as a result of this escalation of the war peripheral areas of Anglo-French tension such as the Baltic and Portugal moved centre-stage. In the summer of 1807 the Treaty of Tilsit between France and Russia threatened Britain's position in the Baltic – the main gateway into northern Europe for British manufactures and colonial products, and the source of essential naval stores. In a ruthless exercise of seapower a British fleet bombarded Copenhagen, killing several thousand civilians, and seized the Danish navy rather than run the risk of it combining with the French fleet. Convoys grew larger and more heavily-guarded: one of 1809 numbered a thousand vessels and included the *Victory* among its escorts. At the same time as the Treaty of Tilsit attempted to shut off the Baltic, so Napoleon's armies invaded Spain and Portugal as another part of the process of closing the coasts of Europe to British trade. This move brought a new theatre of operations into existence which, almost by chance, gave Britain an opportunity of grappling with France in a more favourable region than the traditional killing grounds of Flanders. The Iberian peninsula lay within the reach of British seapower, and its peoples were fiercely hostile to the French invader. Arms, money, and finally men, were sent, and although British forces were defeated in 1808 during the only campaign in which Napoleon took personal charge of the French forces, the commitment to the peninsula remained. In 1809 Arthur Wellesley (enobled as Viscount Wellington the same year) was made Commander-in-Chief of British forces there, and this proved an inspired appointment. With military experience in India, and political in Ireland where he had been Chief Secretary, Wellington was to spend five years fighting in the peninsula in campaigns which were to test to the full his abilities as soldier, administrator and diplomat. Despite having to cope with deficiencies in supplies, unpredictable allies, and an antiquated command structure, Wellington turned his army – still small by continental standards – into an effective fighting force.

The original intervention of 1808 had been prompted by naval and colonial rather than continental considerations – by the threat that Napoleon would seize the fleets of Spain and Portugal, and possibly their great American empires. Within this maritime context, the British army was seen at first as an auxiliary force, whose main function was to help keep Portuguese and Spanish forces in the field. As Wellington and his French foes danced a deadly pavan of advance and retreat across the peninsula – in the winter of 1810–11 as far back as Lisbon where Wellington took refuge behind the prepared lines of Torres Vedras – the question was whether his army, the only British one in the field, should continue to be put at risk. The decision was taken that it should remain, for as a minister explained in 1811 in a statement which reflected the change in role, it was 'the cheapest and easiest mode of defending our own country'.

Wellington's operations in the peninsula brought no immediate relief to the Perceval government. From Walcheren to Torres Vedras the war effort seemed to be marked by retreat and disappointment. There was criticism not only of the ministry but of the whole political system, which divided the country, one radical put it, between 'those who fatten upon corruption and those who are a prey to corruption'. Military incompetence, bureaucratic scandal, interference with trade, and the alarming growth of the National Debt – all came under attack. Wyvill continued to call, as he had done for thirty years, for a reduction in the power of the executive; Cobbett's *Political Register* denounced the growth of government patronage through war; the philosopher and legal reformer Jeremy Bentham argued that a more representative electoral system was essential if much-needed changes were to be made to the penal system, the Poor Law, and the status of Catholics and Dissenters. The protests were more impressive in variety than in coherence, for the critics were separated by generation and political outlook. In practical terms they were weakened by their distance from the parliamentary Whigs, regarded by some of them (in the words of Henry Hunt, now making his mark in popular radicalism) as 'a despicable, a hypocritical, and a tyrannical faction'. Even so, it was a Whig motion in 1810 for the setting up of a committee to consider parliamentary reform on the grounds that some measure of reform was supported by the 'sensible and reflecting part of the nation', which attracted 115 votes in the Commons. New political societies appeared in London – the Hampden Club in 1811–12 and the Union for Parliamentary Reform in 1812 – while Cartwright, active at different times in both, attempted to rouse the provinces with meetings and petitions in favour of annual Parliaments and a householder franchise. But the new societies were small and exclusive, and the support the veteran reformer found outside London was too narrowly linked to the economic discontents of the war to guarantee a stable radical platform for the future.

By the end of 1810 the tightening by Napoleon of his Continental System, together with two poor harvests, had run the country full tilt into severe economic problems. Accompanying the general depression was a financial crisis in which several dozen banks collapsed, and it seemed for a time as if the entire credit system of the country might disintegrate. Demands for cash from

Wellington in the peninsula and from the commanders of Britain's far-flung garrisons and fleets, together with the necessity of once more importing grain after the harvest failures, had resulted in a shortage of specie, and a depreciation of the paper currency issued by the banks in increasing quantities since 1797. By now the guinea (face value 21s.) was fetching 27s. in banknotes. The intricate business of the relation between bullion and paper currency was examined by a Commons committee in 1810–11 which decided in favour of a gradual resumption of cash payments by the Bank of England. The threat which this triumph of the bullionists posed to the financing of the war effort was staved off when the House decided that such a resumption should be postponed until the coming of peace. In broader terms the economic situation remained gloomy. The inability of merchants to re-export goods brought in from the Caribbean and South America, and the passing of non-intercourse legislation by the United States as retaliation for the Orders in Council, hit both trade and industry. Despite the grouping of increasing numbers of ships into convoys, losses of merchant shipping to enemy privateers in 1810 reached record dimensions.

Among the chief sufferers was the textile industry, and its plight prompted a stream of petitions from the manufacturing areas – against the war, corruption, and the Orders in Council. There was, however, another dimension to the agitation; for the textile areas of Nottingham, Yorkshire and Lancashire saw outbreaks of rioting, intimidation and machine-breaking by the Luddites. The economic grievances behind Luddism were plain enough, though they varied in emphasis from region to region: the problems of the hosiery industry faced with changes in fashion and technique, opposition in south Lancashire to the new power-looms and in the West Riding to the new shearing-frames. What remains in doubt is the degree of co-ordination between the various outbreaks of protest and violence, and the extent of their political motivation. Some historians have argued that the insurrectionary sentiments of the late 1790s, driven underground but not eliminated, surfaced in 1811–12 under the direction of 'General Ludd' with illegal oaths, arming, and drilling. Certainly there was a sense of control and organisation behind the Luddite violence lacking in the spasmodic food riots and other popular disturbances of the earlier years of the war. Others see the machine-breaking episodes as a form of industrial sabotage to extract concessions from employers, and stress that the violence occurred only after conventional petitions had failed to bring results. What now appears clear is that in the distressed areas the economic hardships and starvation wages were leading to demands for changes in the political system and an end to the war.

Something of the divided mood of the country was shown in the reactions to Perceval's assassination by a deranged individual in May 1812. In Parliament all shades of opinion were united in 'an agony of tears', but in parts of the country there were celebrations at the news. After some weeks of uncertainty Liverpool became prime minister, and one of his first decisions was to recognise that the pressure for repeal of the Orders in Council had become irresistible. The campaign against them in the industrial areas of the north had been orchestrated by a new, maverick force on the Whig benches, Henry Brougham, who compared their effect on British trade and industry with the Great Plague. On 23 June they were withdrawn, but too late to prevent a declaration of war by the United States, pushed beyond endurance by the strict British interpretation of neutral rights, and by the raids of Royal Navy press-gangs on American merchantmen. A combination of the Continental System and war with the United States would have inflicted more damage on British trade than anything it had experienced so far, but the same summer saw the collapse of Napoleon's economic strategy as he invaded Russia. This move was in part brought about by the strain placed on relations between France and Russia over Napoleon's insistence on controlling the Baltic. Not the least part played by Britain in the ultimate defeat of Napoleon was in causing much of his over-commitment, from the Iberian peninsula to the Russian frontier, which stemmed from his attempts to close the ports of Europe to British trade. The war with the United States saw invasion and counter-invasion along the Canadian frontier, clashes between naval units, and raids along the American coastline which reached as far as Washington and New Orleans. Despite individual triumphs, mostly on the American side, neither protagonist looked like gaining a war-winning position; and the harm done to the trade of both countries by capture, blockade and boycott proved a powerful incentive for the settlement of differences that was reached in 1814.

For Britain the American war was a distraction in the closing stages of the struggle against Napoleon. As French forces were weakened by the demands of the Russian campaign so in the peninsula Wellington was at last able to mount a sustained offensive. His army of British, Spanish and Portuguese troops won their first major victory of the war at Salamanca in 1812, then the next year defeated the French at Vitoria near the border, and invaded France itself. After Vitoria even Whig critics of the peninsular strategy had to admit that the British commitment there was more than a minor diversion. For the first time a Wellington battle had European repercussions, and although Vitoria was a skirmish compared with the giant battles taking place farther east, it helped to bring about the creation of the fourth, and last, coalition against France. As Napoleon's depleted forces fell back in the campaigns of 1813, and as his vassal states rose in revolt, so differences opened between Russia, Austria and Prussia, busy quarrelling about the spoils of peace before the war was won. As important as British subsidies in the military and diplomatic manoevrings of this period was the skill of Castlereagh, who acted as a mediator with adroitness and a sense of Europe's long-term interests. With a subsidy of £5 million being paid to the three continental allies in 1814, with a promise of an army of 150,000 men, and with Wellington advancing steadily into south-west France, there could be no doubt, as Castlereagh put it, 'as to the claim we have to an opinion on Continental matters'.

The spring of 1814 saw a swift succession of events: the final crumbling of the French armies, the entry into Paris of the Russian army, a Bourbon restoration, and the retirement of Napoleon – if only as far as Elba. In May 1814 the Treaty of Paris brought peace with France, but the wider question of what should happen to the territories of Napoleon's empire was referred to negotiations between the powers at Vienna. By February 1815 agreement was in sight, but before it could be embodied in formal terms Napoleon landed in France, and Louis XVIII fled. Once more Britain took the lead, and increased its subsidy to £9 million with the aim of putting allied armies of a million men into the field. In the event, the campaign was over before these huge forces could be brought together, for in June a hastily improvised allied army under Wellington put an end to Napoleon's hopes at Waterloo. Incredible though it seemed to contemporaries, the resurgent power of Napoleon had been destroyed in a single day, and by an army led by a British commander. It seemed altogether appropriate that it was to the commander of a British naval vessel that Napoleon surrendered, and that his fate was left to the decision of the British government. By the end of the year the jigsaw of the diplomatic settlement of Europe was complete. A second Treaty of Paris pushed France back to her 1790 frontiers, and imposed an army of occupation and an indemnity. The Congress of Vienna accepted the general territorial arrangements agreed by Austria, Russia, Prussia and Britain earlier in the year, and the Quadruple Alliance came into being to ensure that the terms of the treaty were observed.

The balance of British interests was shown in the peace negotiations. At first sight, Castlereagh had followed the line suggested by Pitt in 1805 and had returned most of Britain's overseas conquests in order to secure a stable settlement in Europe. Apart from Tobago (which had been French only since the War of American Independence) and part of Dutch Guiana, no captured territories were kept for commercial reasons; and this despite protests from British merchants and planters who had invested capital in the occupied territories. As Castlereagh declared in reply to demands for the retention of territory in the Dutch East Indies, 'I am sure our reputation on the Continent as a feature of strength, power and confidence is of more real moment.' Nevertheless, there were 'certain exceptions', and although these appeared modest in comparison with what was handed back, they were acquisitions which Britain had aimed at for many years. Malta became British to give added control in the Mediterranean. In the Caribbean St Lucia, with its fine harbour, was retained. Most important of all, the Cape and Mauritius were kept to give Britain command of the long sea-route to the East, where Ceylon had already been gained at the Amiens settlement. The pattern of 1713 and 1763 had been repeated: with comparatively modest ambitions on the continent Britain had used war and treaty-making to damage rival empires and enlarge her own. If the Ionian Islands, Ascension and other small territories are included, the number of British colonies had increased from 26 to 43 since 1793. The empire of 1815 differed from that of 1763 in that it was truly worldwide. The dramatic expansion in India, the beginnings of settlement in Australia following the shipping of convicts to New South Wales in 1788, the increase of trade with China and in the Eastern seas, and finally the wartime acquisitions, had shaped an empire which was better balanced and more strongly guarded.

Britain's role in the peace-making reflected the scale of the nation's war effort. Alone of the allies she had fought France with dogged consistency, year in, year out. Her military contributions never matched in manpower Marlborough's a hundred years before, but the naval effort and the financial cost were incomparably greater. In all, Britain expended about £66 million in subsidies, almost half in the last five years of hostilities. In 1815 no fewer than thirty European powers, from Russia to Sicily, received payments from Britain. The rivulet of aid which had begun to flow with Pitt's subsidy treaty with Prussia in 1794 had turned to a mighty torrent twenty years later. Even so, the subsidies amounted to only a fraction of the total Britain spent on her own army, navy and ordnance in the same period. Total war expenditure between 1793 and 1815 was £1,658 million (compared with £49 million in William III's wars). Taxation increased to an unprecedented one-fifth of national income, and by 1814 the ratio of government spending to national income had reached 29 per cent (as against an average of 3.5 per cent in the last years of peace). Agriculture, trade and industry all entered a period of turbulence and sharp fluctuation once hostilities began in 1793. The continuing rise in population, fears that imports of foodstuffs might be blocked, and disastrous harvests between 1795 and 1800, and again between 1808 and 1812, led to huge swings in grain prices and a rush to cultivate land previously regarded as unsuitable. Despite the problems of bringing in foodstuffs from abroad in wartime, grain was imported in record quantities, though except in the very worst years these were still marginal when set against total consumption.

Not all war expenditure was loss of course. Heavy industry received a powerful stimulus. Iron doubled its output between 1796 and 1806, by which time more than two hundred blast furnaces were in operation (compared with seventeen in 1760). Some of the money which appeared to drain out of the country in foreign subsidies was spent on British manufactures, especially munitions and uniforms. The war years saw an increase of more than a half in shipping tonnage as foreign vessels disappeared from many trade routes; and a surge of dock-building in London resulted in the vast complexes of the West India, East India, London, and Surrey Docks. New overseas markets opened up as enemy territories and enemy trade fell into British hands, though there were disappointments as well as gains. The collapse in 1809 of the new South American market from which so much had been expected sent shock waves through trading and manufacturing circles which were already trembling on the edge of depression. Throughout the war years the erosion of private incomes by taxation reduced the amount available for consumption, and apart from the hardship caused to families whose meagre budgets were dominated by the price of bread, the leap in grain prices shifted income away from both capital-owners and labourers, and into the pockets of landowners. The incessant demands of the government for capital had a 'crowding-out' effect on its supply, and if the Treasury was greedy for money, then the armed forces had an equal appetite for manpower. The number of men in the army and navy rose from a peacetime figure of less than 100,000 to more than half a million in 1812 (with the casualty figures to be added). Blockade, the shutting of many European markets to British goods between 1806 and 1812, sinkings of merchantmen, higher insurance and freight rates, and war with the United States, all affected trade and industry.

By the last years of the war the consensus between government and governed was under strain. The unprecedented number of men in uniform, the introduction of income tax, the passing of legislation such as the Combination Acts, all represented a large increase in the intrusive power of the state. The traditional fabric of government was stretched to breaking point at both national and local level, and if ministers were able to present a stern face to the Luddites, they were vulnerable to agitation among the natural supporters of law and order. The repeal in 1812 of the Orders in Council after a concerted campaign by manufacturing and commercial interests, and the passing of the Corn Law of 1815 as landowners fought to protect their privileged position, were surrenders to sectional pressures. As hostilities came to an end, an administration struggling with the burdens of war was to be confronted with the no less pressing problems of peace and depression.

10 Problems of peace, 1815–1828

The dominant role Britain played in the final stages of the long struggle against Napoleon was a notable achievement, but the war had its malevolent, distorting effect long after the guns had fallen silent. Peace brought predictable problems in commerce, agriculture and industry – 'such a stagnation of internal trade, such a consequential check to circulation and credit, such an interruption to all adventures, either in buildings, or lands, in raw produce or manufactured goods', lamented one minister. The depression was felt throughout the economy in terms of overproduction, excessive capitalisation, and falling prices; and mingled with the cries of distress – not least from the third of a million men released by the army and navy – were demands that the government take action. One problem was that efforts made to placate one section of the community might well antagonise another; as shown by the controversy over the Corn Law of 1815, passed in the weeks of phoney peace before the return of Napoleon from Elba, and greeted with protests, petitions and riots in many parts of the country. The Bill was passed, the London radical Francis Place wrote, 'behind immensely strong double barricades of timber which blocked up the street and other avenues to the House under the cannon of the artillery, the swords of the cavalry, and the bayonets of the infantry.'

To its critics the Corn Law was a monument marking the spot where a Tory government surrendered to the landed interest at the expense of the manufacturing community and the labouring masses. Ministers, weighed down by the knowledge that the war effort in its final years had been borne only by huge increases in taxation and in the National Debt, and by a depreciated currency, saw matters in a different light. With wartime inflation and blockade, agriculture had prospered as prices remained high, and more land came under the plough. But in the last years of the war the bumper harvest of 1813 glutted the market, while by contrast so poor was the harvest of 1814 that foreign corn had to be imported. The average price of wheat almost halved from 118*s*. a quarter in January 1813 to 60*s*. in January 1815 – an alarming drop when set against the findings of a select committee of 1814 that 80*s*. a quarter was the minimum price to give the domestic producer adequate remuneration. The Corn Law, passed by comfortable majorities in both Houses, prohibited the import of foreign grain until that level was reached. It was a blunt instrument, for unlike earlier legislation which introduced varying rates of duty at different price levels, it allowed no compromise between unrestricted entry on one side of the 80*s*. mark and total prohibition on the other. The agricultural interest saw the Act as a guarantee of prices; ministers rather regarded it as protection for a staple commodity during the transition from the high taxes, rents and costs of wartime to what they hoped would become the more settled conditions of peacetime. Their main worry, prompted by the rise in population revealed by the censuses of 1801 and 1811, was of a shortage of wheat leading to uncontrollable social turmoil, perhaps even famine.

The price of wheat was only one issue for a government suddenly confronted with the perplexities of peace. 'Economy is more the order of the day than war ever was', wrote Castlereagh in March 1816. As Leader of the House of Commons (as well as Foreign Secretary) he had to cope with the political repercussions of the widespread anticipation of a return to dimly remembered peacetime levels of taxation and government expenditure. This feeling was represented and channelled with enthusiasm by the Whig opposition, at last released from the fear of being branded unpatriotic if it criticised the government. To attack unpopular taxes and swollen government expenditure followed the best Whig traditions of economical reform, ran no dangers of splitting the party, and attracted the votes of independent MPs. The government, handicapped by the lack of effective spokesmen in the Commons to support Castlereagh, endured detailed scrutiny, and in some cases reductions, of its estimates. Vansittart, the Chancellor of the Exchequer, was a lame and halting speaker at the best of times. His explanations that armies and fleets could not be made to disappear with the stroke of a pen, and that in any case pension and half-pay commitments remained, as did the interest on the enormous war debt, were listened to with ill-concealed impatience. More enticing was the Whig proposal for 'a careful revisal of our establishments, civil and military, with a view to such an immediate reduction of the same as may be required by the principles of a rigid economy, and by a due regard of the Liberties of the Subject.'

Encouraged by 400 petitions and the backing of many newspapers, the opposition gained enough votes from MPs who normally supported the government to inflict a major defeat on the ministry when the House rejected the proposal to continue the property or income tax (at a halved rate) for another two years. In fiscal terms the abolition lightened the tax load on those classes, the commercial and industrial, which were to be most buoyant in the coming decades, and forced the government to rely on loans and indirect taxes to close the gap between income and expenditure. Since taxes on consumption bore most heavily on the poorer classes a popular victory in the Commons had results other than those intended, and removed an important element of equity from the tax system. Castlereagh, not normally seen as an advocate of social justice, developed this point when explaining that the government had decided to drop the malt tax also, rather than 'force this tax upon the agriculturists and upon the poor, when the rich had deliver'd themselves from the property tax'. The loss of revenues further postponed the difficult decision to resume cash payments – supposed by the decision of 1811 to come into effect six months after the signing of peace – and encouraged Vansittart to continue short-term policies of raising money in the City, juggling with the Sinking Fund, and increasing the 'floating' or unfunded debt.

However embarrassed the government might be on questions of supply, its vulnerability had limits. MPs not normally associated with the opposition might vote with it on occasion, but their demand for cheap government did not extend to a wish for Whig government. Away from matters of taxes and estimates their votes were safe enough, especially when opposition attention in the last months of 1816 switched from alleged government profligacy to alleged government repression. A bad harvest after the wettest summer in living memory added to existing problems of depression and unemployment, and by the New Year the price of wheat stood at over 100s. a quarter. Liverpool, more lugubrious than ever, warned that 'if our commercial situation does not improve, emigration or premature deaths, are the only remedies'. The government had neither the means nor the inclination to swim with any vigour against what it considered to be the relentless tides of economic dogma, and although it passed some palliative measures in the summer of 1817 its main concern was to deal with the violence which the widespread distress brought in its train. Different regions produced different upsurges of protest according to their economic and social configuration. Lancashire, whose landscapes and communities were being transformed by the cotton-mills and by Irish immigration, continued to be a particular area of radical anger and disaffection long after the decline of Luddism. There was, however, no national movement calling for reform. Given the legislation of the 1790s still on the statute book it was difficult to see how such a movement could be organised, and in the period before the railways and cheap postal services the practical obstacles were as daunting as the legal ones.

Nor were the leading radical personalities of the day inclined to submerge their ambitions in deference to a common cause. As the radical MP for Westminster, Sir Francis Burdett, complained, they squabbled with the rancour of hostile religious sects. Cartwright's wartime speaking tours had provided a link, but only a momentary one, between different areas of the country, and not until 1817 did the local Hampden Clubs (more working men's associations than the exclusive London organisation from which they took their name) attempt a meeting of delegates. This set on foot a national petitioning campaign under Cartwright's guidance which produced more than 700 petitions, but their rejection by Parliament, and the hurt uncertainty about what to do next, revealed the weakness of this tactic. It was now that Cartwright reverted to the Convention or 'anti-parliament' suggestions of the late eighteenth century, with his plan for the larger unrepresented towns to elect 'legislatorial attorneys' at election-time to put their case to Parliament. A different kind of effort at providing a common forum of discussion, albeit on his own terms, came from William Cobbett. In 1816 he began publishing a cheap broadsheet edition of his *Political Register* which was not subject to stamp duty and sold for 2*d*. Aimed at a working-class readership, its attacks on 'Old Corruption' and its support for parliamentary reform soon achieved nationwide circulation.

London radicalism, restless, personalised, occasionally conspiratorial, seemed incapable of providing sustained leadership, and the capital was in any case distant from the worst areas of distress. The 'March of the Blanketeers' from Lancashire to London with a petition for the Prince Regent was an attempt to bring the problems of the periphery to the attention of the centre, but intervention by the magistrates stopped most of the marchers before they had got clear of Stockport. It was in the capital, though, that the giant meetings at Spa Fields addressed by 'Orator' Hunt in 1816–17 caused particular alarm, for the government saw such meetings, and the distribution of radical tracts which accompanied them, as attempts to copy the French Revolution – never far from the official memory. There had been no equivalent of Hunt's meetings in London since 1795; they represented a return to the mass platform, to the 'members unlimited' policy of the London Corresponding Society, and to demands for manhood suffrage. In a prefiguration of later Chartist arguments, Hunt insisted that economic distress was directly related to the political system – 'the cause of our misery was not to be traced in a transition from war to peace; but in supporting the establishments and the expenditure of war during a peace.' Hunt stood at a considerable remove from those pragmatic radicals such as Burdett, who explained that he 'was not one of those captious reformers that would take nothing, if they could not get everything they wished for.' The division was of aims, tactics, and – not least – of class. As Hunt declared during his election campaign of 1818 in Westminster, he was opposed to the 'petty shop-keepers, and little tradesmen, who . . . set themselves up as a sort of privileged class, above the operative manufacturer, the artisan, the mechanic and the labourer.' The limitation of this appeal was shown in the derisory number of votes (84 against Burdett's 5,239) which Hunt obtained in the largest borough electorate in the country. From the other side of the political fence Robert Southey warned that the struggle was no longer between different parliamentary groupings, but 'between those who have something to lose, and those who have everything to gain, by a dissolution of society.'

As the agitation continued, the government professed to regard the most innocuous petitions as cover for conspiratorial plots. Few Tories needed reminding that they owed much of their identity as a party to their fierce opposition to the doctrines of revolutionary France; and that even the term Tory which had at last replaced Pittite had regained its respectability during that struggle. Though there was no longer the nightmare prospect of a French army landing to support the disaffected, ministers conjured up memories and fears of the war years. When Parliament met in February 1817 each House set up a secret committee to examine the evidence of sedition produced by Sidmouth at the Home Office from the reports of magistrates and spies. As Cobbett wrote to Hunt, 'They sigh for a PLOT. Oh, how they sigh.' The committees agreed that there was a London-based 'traitorous conspiracy' for a 'general insurrection', and that this was supported in many of the manufacturing areas. After hearing this, Parliament suspended Habeas Corpus and passed a series of Acts to strengthen the hand of the government. In the event the new laws were more intimidating on paper than in practice, but the suspension of Habeas Corpus was enough to imprison some reformers and to prompt Cobbett to sail for America. The emphasis on law and order, and the hapless rising of June 1817 at Pentrich in Nottingham, helped the government to brush off Whig suggestions that further retrenchment as 'the first step to relieve the distresses, and redress the grievances of which the people so justly complain', would be more to the point than punitive legislation. On this the Whigs were in any case divided. At no time did they vote their full strength against Sidmouth's new laws, but the flirting of some Whigs with the popular cause was enough to bring about the long-expected break with Grenville and his small group of followers. Generally, the Whigs exuded more uneasiness than confidence as to how they would meet the situation. The advantage of being in opposition, as Grey was to remark, was that it relieved them of 'all responsibility for the measures which the times require'.

Despite the individual brilliance of Brougham and the doggedness of Tierney, there was no consistent leadership among the Whigs. As the old issues of Crown influence and economical reform were replaced by more portentous questions as to how the landed classes could sustain their dominance in an era of change and challenge, so Whig uncertainty about the correct answers grew. The need for some movement on parliamentary reform was widely recognised, but most Whigs were repelled by the mass popular agitation of the period and the accompanying demands for manhood suffrage. Grey pronounced that the aim of these demands was 'not Reform but Revolution', and that he had 'now no hope of seeing a moderate and useful reform effected during my life.' The Whigs pinned their hopes on the campaign for the disqualification of corrupt boroughs and the transfer of the franchise to the new areas of population and importance; but the limitations of this piecemeal approach were shown in the time and energy expended in the prolonged struggle over the fate of Grampound, one of several corrupt boroughs which were under threat. Given this general malaise in the Whig ranks, it was a sign of the dissatisfaction with the government of the day that in the general election of 1818 the Whigs gained some seats. The ministry which had won the war had certainly not won the peace. Lack of decisiveness and oratorical ability in the leadership – 'how we want Billie Pitt now', lamented one Tory backbencher – spread doubts about the capability of the government from Parliament into the country at large. Routine references to the problems inherent in a transition from a state of war no longer carried much conviction three years after Waterloo. 'The feeling is strong in the country that we have not done enough', Huskisson told Liverpool.

In the new Parliament the pattern of the old was repeated. The government, which now included the Duke of Wellington in a minor cabinet position, had a comfortable majority on Tierney's motion for a Committee on the State of the Nation (in effect a vote of confidence); but this was followed by a series of defeats and narrow escapes for the ministry on specific measures. By May 1819 Liverpool was convinced that 'a strong and decisive effort can alone redeem our character and credit', and this effort was to be made in the area of financial policy, where the government had never regained full credibility since its defeat on taxation in 1816. In a change of course the government abandoned the passive policies of the immediate postwar years and adopted measures intended to reduce the Debt (and, hopefully, inflation) by imposing new taxes, raiding the Sinking Fund, and aiming at a genuine surplus of £5 million for debt redemption. With this resolved, it was at last possible to resume cash payments, a process to be carried out by a step-by-step reduction from market to mint price as the Bank of England redeemed its notes in gold. The decision to return to gold was greeted with mingled enthusiasm and relief in which patriotic and moral fervour outweighed technical considerations. As Liverpool wrote the next year, 'the country appears, for the time being, to be settling itself into a state of peace'.

If the government was satisfied with the ease with which this policy of deflation and dear money passed through Parliament, its mood was not reflected in the country. The effect of the 1819 Act on the economy, already moving into recession, was compared by one critic to the depredations of Attila the Hun, and distress in both the manufacturing and agricultural areas led to a predictable revival of radical agitation. With petitioning discredited after the fiasco of 1817, radical societies turned to displays of massed support at open-air meetings and rallies. If the aim was to frighten rather than persuade, then the organisers succeeded too well, for on 16 August 1819 eleven people were killed and several hundred injured at St Peter's Fields, Manchester, as ill-disciplined yeomanry broke up a meeting addressed by Hunt. Sidmouth, nervously aware of the government's dependence on the magistrates in such situations, congratulated those in Manchester on their prompt action. In private, Liverpool doubted whether the magistrates' action was 'in all its parts prudent', but 'being satisfied that they were substantially right, there remained no alternative but to support them.' His reaction illustrates the dilemma of a government faced with discontent on a national scale, and with possible insurrectionary activity in some areas, at a time when there was still no effective police force, when the number of regular troops was limited, and in any case their use regarded with suspicion. Although troops had been called in after the Manchester deaths, Liverpool was opposed to any large increase in the numbers or deployment of the regular army. Its main internal function was to protect the national institutions of government, justice and finance in London; for the most part 'the property of the country must be taught to protect itself.' Among the witnesses to the cutting-down of women and children, as well as men, on 16 August, were reporters from national and provincial newspapers; and as the protest meetings swelled, and the emotive, ironical term 'Peterloo' found its way into the language, the Whig opposition made the radical cause – for the moment at least – its own. Among the county meetings held to demand an enquiry, that in Yorkshire was called by the Lord Lieutenant of the West Riding, Earl Fitzwilliam, one of the most respected of the Whig peers, who was dismissed for his action.

The government response to the increasing number of huge open-air meetings, and to the spread of what it regarded as seditious sentiments, was cast in the shape of the 'Six Acts'. The most drastic limited the right of public meeting; others strengthened the hand of the magistrates, prohibited private drilling, taxed pamphlets, and increased the penalties for seditious libel. They represented the choice, Sidmouth maintained, 'between Laws suited to the Danger, a Military Government, or Anarchy'; and under them many of the radical leaders were imprisoned, including Hunt. The radical cause suffered a further blow with the Cato Street conspiracy of early 1820 – a madcap scheme to assassinate the entire cabinet – which was perhaps the last flash of the insurrectionary Jacobinism of the war years. A sign of the future, rather than of the past, was an attempt in Glasgow and the surrounding region to organise a general strike in April 1820, so that the workers could attend 'to the recovery of their rights'. The Six Acts represented a political rather than an economic response to the distress and disorder of the recession. This ministers regarded as a cyclical phenomenon – 'one of those fluctuations in commerce, which every five or six years usually occur', as the financier Alexander Baring put it. It might well last longer if ministers introduced short-term relief measures, for such incautious tampering might delay the recovery of the private sector. As Castlereagh retorted to a parliamentary demand for relief, 'When the honourable member said, "give the people food and employment", did he think that it was possible for the legislature to do that?' Liverpool acknowledged the hardship and disruption caused by the increase in population, market fluctuations, and the use of labour-saving machinery. 'Yet all these circumstances would not have accounted for the present state of the public mind in certain parts of the country if the events of the French Revolution . . . had not shaken all respect for established authority and ancient institutions.'

It was this same fear which provided an important element in the crisis of the 'Queen's affair' which broke in January 1820 with the death of the old King, hidden and forgotten at Windsor, and the accession of George IV. Wider issues were at stake than the status of Queen Caroline – as the new King's discarded wife considered herself – or indeed the future of the Liverpool ministry, trying to cope with an angry monarch intent on a divorce, a roused public opinion, and a tangle of intricate legal questions. A central consideration through the months of crisis was whether the scabrous revelations about the personal lives of the royal pair would not do permanent damage to the monarchical constitution of the country. Peterloo and the trial of Queen Caroline were too close in time for those who feared for the stability of the existing order. It was difficult for the ruling establishment, ministers and royalty alike, to retain dignity and respect in the midst of popular demonstrations in favour of Caroline larger than any since the days of Wilkes, continuous newspaper comment, and ribald gossip. As Castlereagh put it, issues were being raised 'that shake not only the Administration, but the throne itself to its foundations'. One peer warned that the cause of the Queen was also that of 'all those who are desolate and oppressed'. It was in these months that William Hone's radical lampoon, *The Political House that Jack Built,* sold in its tens of thousands. In verse and picture it showed the depredations of aristocracy, clergy, lawyers, and an army of officials and tax collectors on 'The People, all tattered and torn, who curse the day wherein they were born.' In the end a financial allowance was made to Caroline, but her demands for recognition as Queen Consort were rejected. Meanwhile Canning had resigned in protest at her treatment, and as damaging to the government was the clear evidence that despite the Six Acts it could not control vociferous outbursts of popular resentment, in 1820 directed against an unpopular King and his unpopular ministers.

The death of Caroline in August 1821 put an end to a saga which had strained relations between King and government almost to breaking point. The residual importance of the monarch even in the shape of so seedy a representative as George IV was shown by Liverpool's continual anxiety that he was about to be replaced as prime minister, and in a more specific way by the king's refusal to reinstate Canning. Liverpool's position was safer than he realised, given the lack of support for alternative candidates, and the King's distaste for the Whigs over Catholic emancipation, parliamentary reform, and their support for Caroline. George IV had neither the stubbornness nor the popularity of his father, but the decline in royal influence was more than personal, for among the casualties of economical reform was the amount of patronage at the disposal of the Crown. In response to a critical motion by Brougham, Castlereagh claimed that of 2,000 offices which had disappeared since the first assaults of the Rockingham ministry in 1782, 1,800 had gone since 1810, and of the 80 or so placemen who could be identified in the Commons, two-thirds were so only in the sense that they held ministerial or 'efficient' office. Radical opponents retorted that 'Old Corruption' consisted of more than offices and sinecures; it involved the growing links with the government of a whole range of business and professional activities, all operating within the context of an unreformed parliamentary system. In the Commons Joseph Hume proved a terrier-like critic of the administration as he nosed out extravagances buried in the details of the military and civil estimates. And, as Cobbett pointed out, although the number of sinecures and pensions might be fewer than hitherto, they remained 'the grease and tar . . . without them the waggon can't stir'. For the Liverpool administration the amount of lubrication was never enough, and one of its difficulties was that it operated at a stage in the development of parliamentary tactics when the old days of a large court grouping had gone, and the era of disciplined party voting had not yet arrived. Adding to its difficulties was the awkwardness that attempts to carry out the programme of retrenchment demanded by the opposition helped to produce the conditions of deflation and distress which those same MPs insisted it was the government's job to cure. On such issues a working alliance between the Whigs and a group of thirty or forty radical MPs was clearly visible by the early 1820s, though differences in ideology and personality make it difficult to see the anti-ministerial groups as a united opposition party.

In the long term a more important result of the disillusionment with the government which began with the passing of the Corn Law, and was fuelled by the ministry's handling of the economic and social problems of the period, was the growth in influence of the Benthamites. The anti-aristocratic thrust of two of the key works published at this time, David Ricardo's *Principles of Political Economy* (1817) and James Mill's reprinted *Essay on Government* (1820) fitted well with the mood of frustration and apprehension felt by many. Ricardo argued that the landed interest was parasitic, living at the expense of both the manufacturing and labouring classes; Mill denounced the selfishness and narrowness inherent in an aristocratic ruling élite. It was Mill rather than Jeremy Bentham (now in his seventies) who became the leader of that group recently categorised as 'intellectuals in politics'. They applied Bentham's general principles on human behaviour and motivation to the operation of political institutions. These they saw as 'an aristocratical engine' which served the interests of a narrow cluster of privileged groups – the great landed families, the Church, the legal profession, and the universities. Educated, proselytising, optimistic, they regarded their programme as a more fundamental affair altogether than the simple, often incoherent, demands of the popular agitators. They stressed that their recommendations for an end to corruption, for a wider suffrage and a secret ballot, were preliminaries to a reconstruction of government on rational principles. Prolific writers and untiring polemicists, they found their own exclusive outlet with the establishment by Bentham in 1824 of the *Westminster Review*. Operating awkwardly alongside the Whigs, these Benthamites, Utilitarians, philosophic radicals – to give them their varying designations – remained a distinctive and uncompromising force on the political scene until well into Victoria's reign.

As the ministry cleared away the debris surrounding the Queen's affair, it was clear that some strengthening was essential. On too many occasions, from the failure over income tax in 1816 to this most recent débâcle, the government had lacked authority and conviction. With the prime minister in the Lords, there was no one in the Commons with what one Tory called 'the gift of the gab' to support Castlereagh. The changes began with the replacement at the end of 1821 of Sidmouth at the Home Office by Robert Peel, one of the most promising of the younger politicians, who had made his reputation in the unrewarding office of Chief Secretary for Ireland, and in 1819 had taken charge of the complex Currency Act. The most dramatic change came in August 1822, when Castlereagh, operating under the tension of political worries and personal problems, committed suicide. Hatred followed him in death as it had in life, with the London crowds jeering at his funeral cortège, for above all other ministers he stood in the popular mind as the symbol of reaction and repression. He was replaced both as Foreign Secretary and Leader of the Commons by the very different personality of Canning, and this change was followed early the next year by the replacement of Vansittart by the more articulate Robinson as Chancellor of the Exchequer, and by the appointment of Huskisson as President of the Board of Trade. The most significant of these shifts was the securing by Canning of that central position in the ministry which had long been his aim, and which the King now conceded. Although his foreign policy differed little in substance from the lines laid down by Castlereagh in his state paper of May 1820, it was justified with a rhetoric which his predecessor would have abhorred. Within the cabinet, Canning was a restless, divisive force. His popularity in the country, his undisguised ambition, and above all his capacity for intrigue – he could not, it was said, 'take tea without a stratagem' – made him a dominant and awkward colleague. Although in one sense Canning's appointment represented an accession of strength to the ministry, which had by now also gained the formal support of the Grenvilles, much of Liverpool's remaining energy was devoted to preventing a split in his cabinet between the supporters and opponents of Canning.

Two of the problems which were to dominate the political scene in the years ahead were brought to the surface in 1822, when Lord John Russell's motion in favour of substantial parliamentary reform attracted 164 votes, and Canning's bill to allow Catholic peers to sit in the Lords passed the Commons, only to be defeated in the Upper House. The support for Russell reflected several different factors:

continued Whig revulsion at what had happened at Peterloo and after; a practical recognition that moderate reform would increase the number of Whig MPs; a growth of interest in parliamentary reform in some of the counties hit by the agricultural depression; and not least the dying down of the popular agitation for universal suffrage which had embarrassed the Whigs. The long exclusion from office had not shaken the confidence of the Whigs that by virtue of their wealth, breeding and outlook, they remained the most reliable defenders of the constitution against despotic abuses on one side and radical excesses on the other. Even so, the stereotype of the great landed Whig aristocrats, conservative and complacent, no longer fitted that small but increasing number who expressed disquiet at government policies which seemed, by accident or design, to increase friction between classes. Among them was Russell, whose speech introducing the motion for parliamentary reform had made the point that 'the ministers of the Crown possess the confidence of the House of Commons, but the House of Commons does not possess the esteem and reverence of the people.'

The support for Canning's bill, and for other measures aimed at relieving Catholic disabilities, was evidence that opinion in the Commons, though probably not in the country at large, was shifting on the Irish question. As Liverpool conceded, emancipation was only a matter of time. This was an issue of major political concern in a way that parliamentary reform was not in this period, for it had already brought down two governments in 1801 and 1807, and its status as an 'open question' within the cabinet was recognition of its potential explosiveness rather than evidence of official indifference. The compromise of 1812, forced on the ministry by the way in which the Catholic question cut across established political groupings, was increasingly difficult to sustain as Canning became a dominant force in the government, and pressure mounted in the Commons. Even more alarming to the ministry, developments in Ireland began to push the situation there towards a crisis point as the Catholic Association under the leadership of a prominent Irish lawyer, Daniel O'Connell, drew together opposition not only to Catholic disabilities but to a whole range of English discriminatory legislation. What started in 1823 as a small, middle-class organisation attracted increasing support from priesthood and peasantry, and with the financial help of the 'Catholic Rent' of a penny a month, the Association had the makings of a formidable mass movement, nationalist and democratic. Catholicism and nationalism had joined in confrontation to the British government in a way which was to shape the future course of Irish history.

This array of problems was to be dealt with by a government

which has been seen as 'liberal Tory' in its new incarnation. The differences were of personality and style as much as of measures, for the foundations of several of the policies pursued after 1822 had been laid earlier. There was a more vigorous exposition of government policies from the new team of Canning, Peel, Robinson and Huskisson in an attempt to win over or at least deflect that increased pressure from public opinion which, Peel had noted, was 'growing too large for the channels that it has been accustomed to run through'. Public opinion might be, as Peel complained, a 'great compound of folly, weakness, prejudice, wrong feeling, right feeling, obstinacy, and newspaper paragraphs', but the important point was that it was, as he admitted, 'more liberal than the policy of the Government'.

The sharpest break in continuity came in the Home Office. Pressures on the obdurate Sidmouth had been growing for years as successive committees of the House of Commons examined and criticised the operation of the penal system. Bills to reduce the number of capital offences were passed in the Commons, only to be rejected in the Lords. There was mounting concern about the deficiencies of a system which, ferocious as it appeared on paper, in practice was capricious and, from the evidence of an increase in recorded crime, ineffective. Prompted by the penal reformer Sir James Mackintosh, the Commons brushed aside the objections of Sidmouth and the Lord Chancellor, Eldon, and set up a committee to scrutinise the list of 200 existing capital offences. When Peel became Home Secretary he introduced bills in 1823 and 1824 reducing the number of capital offences, and reforming the prison system, in line with the recommendations of the Mackintosh committee. With the minister committed to reform, rather than resistant as Sidmouth had been, the measures went through the Lords without much difficulty. They were followed by further Acts which did much to codify, consolidate and simplify the tangled mass of criminal law. In four years no fewer than 278 Acts were repealed, and those clauses which remained were brought together in eight statutes. Though Peel did not move as far and as fast as penal reformers such as Bentham wished, the legislative achievement revealed the technical mastery and political willpower that were to stamp Peel's later career. What remained a cause for concern to Peel was failure of his tentative attempts to improve the policing of London, and the continuing upward trend of recorded crime. The period 1818 to 1825 saw a doubling of convictions compared with the previous eight years, particularly worrying since the improvement in the economic situation seemed to have little impact on the crime figures. Despite the reduction in the number of capital offences, the number of death sentences increased; and there was no significant drop in actual executions until after Lord John Russell became Home Secretary in 1835. On his return to the Home Office in 1828 as a member of the Wellington administration, Peel completed much unfinished business despite the mounting political pressures of that period. Further consolidated bills relating to criminal law were passed; while the Metropolitan Police Improvement Act of 1829 at last gave the sprawling, densely populated mass of the capital a single, regular police force. Greeted at first with some suspicion, which lingered longest in the poorest districts, the uniformed 'Peeler' or 'Bobby' on his beat soon met with general approval, and provincial equivalents of the London police force began to develop.

In the area most closely associated with the tenets of 'liberal Toryism', that of economic policy, ministers were turning – in terms of disposition if not action – towards free trade well before 1822. When a (pre-arranged) petition to the prime minister from the City in 1820 argued that 'freedom from restraint is calculated to give the utmost extension to foreign trade, and the best direction to the capital and industry of the country', Liverpool confirmed what was already clear from his comments as far back as 1812, that 'there was not a principle, not a sentiment, in which he did not entirely and most cordially concur.' The move towards free trade, however, would be made not in any sweeping or doctrinaire way, but a step at a time, trying to keep in step with the mainstream of contemporary opinion. One of the leaders of that opinion, the inheritor of Adam Smith's intellectual mantle, David Ricardo, insisted that the national interest would be best served by transferring resources from agriculture to industry, and allowing the shortfall in foodstuffs to be made good by cheap imports. While in manufacturing capacity Britain held all the advantages, her agriculture, he argued, was subject to the law of diminishing returns in that the extra grain needed for the rising population could only be obtained from marginal land, at high cost. Liverpool's more emollient views were set out in an important speech of May 1820 (later published as a pamphlet) in which he insisted that what many saw as the competing interests of agriculture, industry and trade were links in the same chain. At the same time he argued that British supremacy had developed despite rather than because of the protectionist system, and he foresaw a steady move towards free trade even at the expense of the agriculturists.

Ministers had few powers to lift the economic activity of the country out of the post-war depression, and there were difficulties in the way of removing the restrictions which economists of the Adam Smith persuasion insisted were inhibiting factors. As Robinson pointed out, whereas all men seemed in favour of the principle of freer trade, 'he never could get the individual to allow that the general principle ought to be applied in his case'. Most vociferous of the special interest groups were the farmers, hard hit by the agricultural depression of the early 1820s when at one point the price of wheat tumbled below 40s. a quarter. In 1822 the government met the pressure of the agriculturist lobby by replacing the 1815 clause which allowed unrestricted entry at 80s. a quarter by a sliding scale of duties starting at that price (rarely reached in this period). Liverpool answered more general demands for tax cuts by pointing out that the government had already given up a quarter of its tax revenues since 1815, and that the low food prices of which the landowners complained would in time increase the demand for agricultural produce. The bitterness of feeling in the rural areas was shown in a series of county meetings, the most notable of which was a meeting of 7,000 Norfolk freeholders called by the large Whig landowners of that county in January 1823. This stunned its convenors by following Cobbett's advice to pass resolutions urging the sale of crown and church lands, the abolition of sinecures, a reduction in the army, and the repeal of many taxes on consumption.

The government was already moving towards the last of these proposals in a change of fiscal policy shown in Vansittart's last budget in 1822. 'Prosperity' Robinson was to sharpen the emphasis with his budgets, of which that of 1823 reduced most assessed taxes by a half. Those of 1824 and 1825 cut duties rather than taxes in an effort to bring down costs for industry (coal duties were reduced, for example), and to encourage consumption (so there was a reduction of duties on wine, spirits and tobacco). The erosion of the protectionist system had begun under Wallace, Vice-President of the Board of Trade, who in 1821 cut duties on timber from the Baltic to remove the virtual monopoly enjoyed by Canadian timber. Although Wallace resigned in 1823 the policy he had begun was continued and extended by Huskisson, who turned the Board of Trade into one of the key departments of state. He further reduced and simplified duties, and negotiated a series of reciprocity treaties which allowed for a mutual reduction of duties between Britain and individual foreign countries. This work was carried out in close collaboration with Robinson, who announced the Treasury's determination – in terms unusually flamboyant for that department – 'to cut the cords which tie down commerce to the earth, that she may spring aloft, unconfined and unrestricted, and shower her blessings over every part of the world.' Although the logical end of these changes might seem to be abolition of the protectionist system, their short-term effect was simply to rationalise the edifice. Little more could be done until new forms of taxation could be found to compensate for the revenue lost from decreasing tariffs, while the reliance of a Tory government on the political support of the landed interest warned against any full-blooded assault along Ricardian lines on protection for agriculture. Huskisson typified the government's approach, piecemeal and pragmatic, when he warned in 1825 that ministers had 'to watch the issue of each experiment, and not attempt too much at once, until we felt our way, and until the public were prepared to accompany us in our further progress.'

The years of economic buoyancy brought a dulling to political conflict. As the Whig Lansdowne commented, 'the prosperity of the country has driven reform almost out of the heads of the reformers.' The flow of petitions to the Commons on parliamentary reform slowed to a trickle, and then dried up entirely; not one was presented between 1824 and 1829. Liverpool's policy of encouraging administrative and economic reforms while avoiding fundamental constitutional changes seemed set steady. The repeal at the instigation of Francis Place and Joseph Hume, supported by Huskisson, of the Combination Acts in 1824 symbolised the more relaxed approach, in which free collective bargaining would replace outmoded restrictive legislation. The expansion in industrial production, overseas trade and stock-exchange activity were all expected to continue, with a consequent fall in unemployment, distress and discontent. The young John Stuart Mill summed up the mood of the time when he wrote on the occasion of the Ricardo Memorial Lectures in 1824, attended by an array of dignitaries, including Liverpool, that 'If there is a sign of the times upon which more than any other we should be justified in resting our hopes of the future progression of the human race [it is] the demand which is now manifesting itself on the part of the public for instruction in the science of Political Economy.'

Only Ireland cast its long shadow over the scene. At the same time as the Catholic Association was suppressed as a mass organisation, the Commons in early 1825 passed a comprehensive Catholic relief bill, introduced by Burdett, which was then rejected in the Lords. A prolonged cabinet crisis developed, during which for a time Liverpool thought he could not continue as prime minister, while the 'Protestant' Peel threatened resignation at one moment, and the 'Catholic' Canning at another. As the ministry emerged from this episode, shaken but intact, it was confronted with a sudden change in the economic climate as a financial plunge in the winter of 1825–26 spun out of control and brought the collapse of a hundred banks and other financial institutions, and the ruin of many investors. The business depression which followed was made more acute since it coincided with a grain shortage after a poor harvest in 1825. A sign of second thoughts by the government had already been glimpsed with the passing of a new Combination Act, which allowed the legal existence of trade unions, but restricted the right to strike and picket. In the changed atmosphere of bewilderment and alarm, Huskisson and his policies came under attack both from erstwhile supporters and from those who had never ceased to regard them with suspicion.

By 1826 the government was faced with high food prices, panic in some financial circles, depression in manufacturing areas, and waves of protest and disorder. Critics such as Sir James Graham, a Whig landowner, linked the crisis to the government's decision in 1819 to return to the gold standard. Now, he wrote, 'amidst the ruin of the farmer and the manufacturer, the distress of the landlords, and the insurrection of a populace without bread and without employment, one class flourished and was triumphant; the annuitant and the taxeater.' In ways other than those implied by Graham it was a return to 1819, but the government's reaction was more measured and less alarmist. In part this arose from the presence of Peel at the Home Office, for although he sent troops to Lancashire to support the magistrates, he was more sympathetic than his immediate predecessors to the root of the trouble. In a reversal of their interpretation he declared that 'the great cause of apprehension is not in the disaffection but in the real distress of the manufacturing districts'. Though like Liverpool he was opposed to the 'quackery' of government hand-outs to industry in the form of direct subsidies, he supported cash payments to relieve distress in some of the worst-affected areas. Liverpool and other ministers also played their part. A Banking Act curtailed the circulation of bank notes, and controlled the activities of the country banks.

More controversially, and against some angry Tory opposition, the Corn Laws were relaxed for the time being to allow the import of foreign corn in the emergency. This was the harbinger of an attempt by the government to rethink the structure and operation of the Corn Laws – a sign that the agricultural interest was beginning to lose its power to hold the country to ransom, though it was another twenty years before its bluff was finally called. As Secretary at War Palmerston put it, in a situation where the government was becoming increasingly dependent on Whig votes, the real opposition was 'the stupid old Tory party, who bawl out the memory and praises of Pitt while they are opposing all the measures and principles which he held most important.' The new corn bill was to be put to the Commons when it reassembled in February 1827, at the same time as it was known that Burdett intended to introduce a fresh motion on the Catholic question which was likely to open fresh rifts in the cabinet. What was bound to be a difficult passage for the government, which would need all the prime minister's experience and skills as a mediator to negotiate, changed dimension to a crisis situation when

Liverpool suffered a disabling stroke within a few days of Parliament convening, and died the next year.

The removal of Liverpool from the political scene was the collapse of the dam which had held at bay the swirling issues of the period – the Catholic question, the Corn Laws, and parliamentary reform. Undoubted though Liverpool's tactical skills were, he had postponed, not in any sense resolved, those problems. They were left, with varying degrees of urgency, for his successor to face; although the identity of this successor was a difficult question in its own right, for after fifteen years the political nation had not thought far beyond the steadying presence of Liverpool as prime minister. The appointment of Canning, after some weeks of indecision, and much agonising by the King, brought the crisis to a head when half of Liverpool's cabinet, including Wellington and Peel, refused to serve in the new government. Among the new ministers were Tierney, Lansdowne and Carlisle – the first taste of high office for the Whigs for twenty years – but other leading Whigs held aloof from a ministry whose leader opposed parliamentary reform. The coalition of Canningites such as Huskisson, Robinson (now Lord Goderich) and Palmerston, with Whigs and moderates, had little time to prove itself, for in August Canning himself died. The intervening months had been ones of suspense and stalemate. Burdett's motion on Catholic emancipation had been lost by four votes in a packed house. Huskisson's new corn bill, with its sliding scale, had been postponed after a misunderstanding in the Lords. The faint figure of Goderich became prime minister, but for a few months only, for he never met Parliament, and resigned in January 1828. With a more decisive swing of the political pendulum the Duke of Wellington became prime minister, and with Peel formed an administration whose actions were to have a cataclysmic impact on British politics.

11 The constitutional revolution, 1828–1835

The tumultuous sequence of events which followed the resignation of Liverpool was to transform the political scene, but it failed to produce any universally acceptable settlement. The changes of the next few years were so bitterly contested that when politicians stopped for breath in the mid-thirties, the most they felt had been achieved was an unsteady equilibrium. Some of the difficulties which lay ahead were glimpsed in May 1828 when, within months of Wellington and Peel taking office, Huskisson and several of his associates resigned from the government over the details of the disfranchisement of the parliamentary boroughs of Penryn and East Retford. The corruption of these boroughs was acknowledged; the dispute was whether their franchises should be transferred within the locality, or used to give representation to the fast-growing conurbations of Manchester and Leeds. It illustrated once more the limitations of the gradualist approach, when the redistribution of even a single seat was fought every inch of the way.

The departure of the Canningites left a ministry more narrowly Tory than any since the war, much to Peel's dismay. How, he asked, could government business be carried on by 'the mere Tory party'? Although Wellington was one of the most respected figures in public life he had little political flair, and none of Liverpool's instinctive touch for bridge-building between one political group and another. His sense of duty to king and country was paramount, and it was this which led him to a course of action which was to leave the High or Ultra Tories, who had been jubilant at his accession to power, in a state of shock and confusion. In the previous years both Wellington and Peel had edged away from the Ultras' hard-line position on Catholic emancipation, and two developments in 1828 hinted that Wellington was not the unyielding opponent of change which both his political enemies and supporters tended to assume. Under the guidance of Peel and Huskisson (before his resignation) a new corn law reached the statute book, which significantly amended the Acts of 1815 and 1822 by allowing in foreign wheat free of duty once the domestic price had reached 73s. a quarter, and below that level introduced a new sliding scale of duties. If this was a blow from one direction at the landed interest, another was the repeal, at Russell's instigation but in the end with government acquiescence, of those clauses of the Test and Corporation Acts which excluded Dissenters from office. Such clauses had long since been only a nominal obstacle, but one argument against their removal had always been that this would encourage agitation against the more serious discrimination which affected Catholics. The repeal, one Whig said, 'explodes the real Tory doctrine that Church and State are indivisible'.

It was with this stimulus that yet another bill for Catholic relief in Burdett's name passed the Commons by six votes, to be rejected once more by the Lords. This stop-go process was a familiar one, but events in Ireland made the sequel very different. O'Connell decided to stand as candidate at a by-election in County Clare, and with the support of the 40s. freeholders (the 'pauper freeholders' as they were known) mustered by a revived Catholic Association, won by more than two to one despite the fact that as a Catholic he would be unable to take his seat. The prospect of a similar sequence of events in scores of county constituencies at a general election was a horrendous one for the government, for, as the Lord Lieutenant warned from Dublin, O'Connell could lead his supporters 'to open rebellion at a moment's notice'. Both Wellington and Peel now accepted that Catholic emancipation must be conceded; as Peel said, Clare was 'the turning point'. Despite the King's opposition an emancipation bill was passed in the spring of 1829 by large majorities in both Houses. In his speech introducing the measure Peel made it clear that he could see no alternative, and that he was 'unwilling to push his resistance to a point which might endanger the Establishments that I wish to defend.' Coercion had been tried and failed, and there was not in any case a majority in Parliament for further repressive legislation. The Act opened, with a few exceptions, all offices of state to Catholics; but as a double riposte to the mass agitation O'Connell had organised, the voting qualification in the counties was raised from a 40s. freehold to £10, and the Catholic Association was suppressed.

Despite the government's plea of overwhelming necessity, Ultra feelings ran high. Wellington, described by one Tory as more dangerous than Cromwell, was challenged to a duel, and Peel was defeated in a by-election in his Oxford University constituency. The Wellington administration, having lost the support of Huskisson and some of his colleagues one year, forfeited the allegiance of the High Tories the next, when 202 MPs and 118 peers, almost all Tories, voted against the Bill. The coalition of Tory groups which Liverpool had held together for so long had disappeared amid rancour and bitterness. The reaction of the Ultras consisted of more than outrage at what they saw as betrayal on a single issue. They sensed the encouragement which this concession, made under pressure, would give reform groups throughout the country. With so huge a breach made in the constitution, the demands of the parliamentary reformers would be difficult to resist. Some Tories thought that a system which could allow through the Bill of 1829 against the clear feeling of the country was no longer worth defending. As one asked, how can 'you talk of preserving the tree of the constitution, when you have laid your axe to the root?'

Other, more fortuitous developments seemed calculated to demoralise the Ultras and encourage the reformers in the following months, as the economic depression of 1829 lingered and deepened. The death of George IV, with all his prejudices (against the Whigs in general, and against Grey specifically), and the news from France of the deposition of the Bourbon monarch by the bloodless July Revolution, came in quick succession in the summer of 1830. Although the general election after the King's death was a quiet one, it was an ominous portent that Brougham was returned as a county member for Yorkshire, pledged to introduce a motion in favour of parliamentary reform as soon as Parliament met. Ominous in a different way were the reports coming in from the southern counties, where the Swing riots of the farm labourers were spreading panic and destruction in some of the most placid areas of the country. With his usual sense of timing Cobbett began in July to produce a new cheap monthly paper, issued under the derisive title his opponents had invented for his broadsheet of 1816, *Two-Penny Trash*.

Only Wellington, accustomed perhaps to noisier intimations of coming battle, seemed impervious to the growing expectancy of some great clash of principles. As Parliament assembled at the beginning of November he made a fateful response in the Lords to Grey when he announced, with an eye on the Ultras, that he saw no need for change 'in the state of representation'. Within a fortnight his government had gone, defeated on what was recognised on all sides to be a vote of confidence. The government lost by 29 votes, about the same number as that of the Ultras who voted against Wellington. As worrying for the Tories as this small-scale if crucial defection was that the government's main support came from MPs from the narrow boroughs – the chief targets of the reformers' zeal. The ministry resigned at once, rather than await the outcome of the debate and vote the next day on Brougham's motion for parliamentary reform. It was that issue which was to dominate the next two years in one of the most dramatic periods in British political history.

Despite the importance which 1830 has assumed as a political watershed, distress rather than reform dominated most of the year. Grey was convinced that distress was both 'general' and 'intense', and the Wellington cabinet's insensitivity on the issue reminded him of the fatal blindness of the French aristocracy just before the 1789 revolution. On the surface the situation in 1830 resembled that of those other crisis years such as 1819 in which demands for reform had swelled, only to subside as the economic situation improved and the government stood firm. Once again, motions on reform were put to the Commons, and were defeated by greater or lesser majorities according to how sweeping their proposals were. The attempts revealed those differences on reform between radical demands based on a theory of natural rights and timid Whig efforts to eliminate the worst abuses of the existing system – which had long played into the hands of the defenders of the status quo.

If disunity of aim was a familiar sight among those pressing for reform, it was matched this time by uncertainty among those opposing it. After the shock of 1829 the defenders of the old system were no longer united; and distress on the one hand and disenchantment on the other produced a new political situation. Tory unity and Tory self-confidence had been shaken. The veteran Lord Eldon complained that Catholic emancipation had been a precedent 'so encouraging to the present attempts at revolution under the name of reform that he must be a bold fool who does not tremble at what seems to be fast approaching.' O'Connell's example was cited by several of the new associations which now sprang up. The short-lived London Radical Reform Association adopted a 'radical rent' of a penny a meeting similar to his 'Catholic rent'. Thomas Attwood, as he organised his more effective Birmingham Political Union, hoped for 'an array no less formidable' than O'Connell's. Slowly emerging in opposition to the unreformed system was a community of antagonism: radicals aiming to sweep it away root and branch; Ultras disillusioned by the betrayal of 1829; Whigs frustrated by the long years out of office, and by the difficulty in getting even a modest measure of reform accepted. Currency reformers such as Attwood, ascribing distress to 'the gross mismanagement of public affairs', those advocating repeal of the corn laws or factory reform or abolition of slavery – all considered some change in the old system as essential to the success of their particular cause. A coalition stretching from radicals who saw parliamentary reform as the first step in the dismantling of the existing system to those who viewed it as a device to preserve the fundamentals of the same system, was likely to be precarious; but for a period in the early thirties it was a potent political force. Whereas for decades the coherence of the Tory establishment, and the differences among its opponents, had prevented movement on the reform question, for the time being the situation was reversed.

The Grey government which took office in November 1830 included Canningites and one Ultra, but it was predominantly Whig both in ministerial appointment and parliamentary support. The fact that nine out of a cabinet of thirteen were peers (with one of the four 'commoners', the Foreign Secretary Palmerston, an Irish peer who sat in the Lower House), testified to the continuing aristocratic nature of the Whig party in its upper echelons. The replacement of Wellington by the patrician Grey, for forty years a reformer, if sometimes a reticent one, was at once symbolic and of deep practical significance. In setting out the priorities of his administration, Grey promised the introduction of a measure to reform 'the representation', but declared that relief of distress would be his 'first and most anxious object'.

Parliament met amid growing concern about recession, disorder and riot. The rural disturbances in Kent and other southern counties as far west as Dorset were unprecedented in their wholesale destruction of machinery and ricks. The Swing riots were an explosion of frustration and misery among the agricultural labourers of southern England, fast becoming a pauperised population under the operation of market forces, machine farming, and the Speenhamland subsidies. Cobbett was later to give much prominence to rural disorder (along with his own exhortations) as a decisive factor in the coming of reform – 'I sowed the thoughts; but it was the operations of poor Swing that made those thoughts spring up into action.' In Birmingham, Attwood drew much the same conclusion, 'Distress was the cause – Reform the effect.' But however urgent an issue Grey considered distress to be, the continuing rural violence and the attacks on property instinctively turned his government towards repression rather than relief. The Home Secretary, Melbourne, established special commissions to try the rioters, and their sentences of death and transportation were as harsh as any carried out in the years of Sidmouth and Eldon. With order restored, the Swing disturbances faded into the background as Grey turned to the question of political reform.

The prime minister entrusted a committee of four – Lord John Russell and Lord Durham (radical Whigs as far as parliamentary reform was concerned) together with Sir James Graham and Lord Duncannon – with the task of drafting a measure. Their instructions, Graham later recalled, were to propose a bill 'large enough to satisfy public opinion and to afford sure ground of resistance to further innovation', while ensuring the retention of property qualifications, existing franchises and territorial divisions. Grey was confident that the measure would pass through both Houses in a relatively short time; instead, it was to take fifteen months of growing difficulty and crisis during which at times the country seemed to be near revolution. The story of those months has the drama of a theatrical performance, as scenes shifted from the deliberations of the committee of four to the cabinet, and then to the packed arenas of the Commons and Lords, with an anxious William IV from one wing and 'the people' from another intervening at critical moments in a way which changed their role from spectators to participants.

The draft measure submitted by the committee of four to the cabinet contained most of the main features of the Act as finally passed. There was to be widespread disfranchisement of the smaller boroughs, which were to lose 168 seats, without compensation (unlike Pitt's abortive measure of 1785, or the Irish disfranchisements of 1800). Roughly half the new seats were to go to London and the unrepresented larger towns (the choice among them to represent interests as well as population), and half to the counties. The chaotic medley of borough franchises was to be replaced by a uniform householder qualification to enfranchise the male owner or tenant of a home worth £20 a year who paid his own rates. The high level of this qualification was counterbalanced by the introduction of that favourite feature of radical reformers, vote by secret ballot. The length of Parliament was to be reduced from seven to five years. The measure would, the committee told Grey in words which echoed his original instructions, be a 'permanent settlement', standing against 'that restless spirit of innovation', and removing 'all rational grounds of complaint'. To these draft proposals the cabinet, prompted by the King, made some important changes. The secret ballot was dropped, and was not to reappear for forty years, but the borough franchise was halved to £10. The length of Parliament was to remain at seven years. Other changes of detail were made to the disfranchisement lists – both to List A, of boroughs which were to lose both seats, and list B, those which were to lose one – the first of many such revisions.

The Reform Bill as such applied to England and Wales; Scotland and Ireland had their own measures. That for Scotland brought the most far-reaching changes, for the system there since 1707 had rested on a number of close burghs and counties with tiny electorates, only about 4,500 voters in the whole of Scotland. The burghs themselves were in an advanced stage of institutional decay – 'omnipotent, corrupt, impenetrable' was the description applied to the town council of Edinburgh. A broadening of the electorate increased the number of voters to about 65,000, and at the same time eight new burgh seats were created. In Ireland, by contrast, the changes were limited, and 1832 saw less significant revisions than 1800 (when 84 parliamentary boroughs disappeared) or 1829 (when the county voting qualification was raised). There was some enlargement of the Irish county electorate, but in the boroughs where property values were generally much lower than in England the £10 householder franchise of the new measure was a high and exclusive qualification.

It was the Bill in this shape which was introduced by Russell on 1 March 1831 to an astonished House of Commons. There had been no anticipation of a measure which, among much else, removed a quarter of the existing seats in the Commons. Politicians, whether reformers or anti-reformers, had been accustomed to the snail's pace progress of the previous decade over Grampound, East Retford and Penryn. The Bill, said one Whig after listening with a mixture of approval and incredulity to Russell's steady listing of its clauses, 'made his hair stand on end'. Another thought that 'having for so long refused to do anything, we are now driven to do too much.' For nine days it was debated, and the arguments and counter-arguments heard which were to become familiar during the next fifteen months. On the Whig side it was claimed that the Bill rationalised rather than revolutionised the representative system, which remained based on property, but brought in men of wealth, social standing and education from the middle classes. No small-scale measure could meet the urgency of the situation after decades of Tory immovability on the issue. From the Tory benches Peel led the assault on the bill: defective in detail, wrong in principle and intent, and a bribe which could only be an instalment, not a final measure.

The debate in the Commons was set against a background of intense public excitement which produced about three thousand petitions, most of them in favour of the Bill. Some of these came from the new political unions which were being formed in cities, towns and even villages throughout the country. There were those which followed the moderate programme of the Birmingham Political Union; others took their lead from Hunt's Metropolitan Political Union which demanded manhood suffrage and vote by ballot. The cause of most of the excitement lay in the fact that it was the government of the day, not a splinter group of radical MPs, which had introduced this comprehensive measure. On 22 March, in one of the most dramatic scenes in parliamentary history, the Bill was carried by one vote – 302 to 301. A majority of English MPs voted against, a majority of Irish MPs for – an unforeseen consequence of Pitt's Act of Union. The momentum of the victory could not be sustained at committee stage, and as the ministry experienced defeat on what it regarded as issues of principle the King agreed, with some reluctance, to Grey's request for a dissolution.

The election was a triumph for the government, which made extensive gains in the counties and larger boroughs, and a disaster for the Tories, who were driven back on the smaller boroughs – most of them due to lose their Parliamentary seats if the Bill went through. As a single-issue election, almost a referendum, the election was unique. Wellington took to reading Clarendon's *History of the Great Rebellion* and 'is much alarmed', a colleague wrote, 'by the resemblance between the commencement of the Civil War and the present times'. The extent of the government's election gains was seen when the Bill passed its second reading by 367 votes to 231. But if Tory forces in the Commons were depleted, they remained formidable in the Lords, where almost all the new peerages since Pitt's time had been Tory. The Bill's rejection in the Lords by 41 votes in October resulted in a stalemate which, it seemed, could be broken only if sufficient peers were created to force through the measure; but this the King, increasingly disturbed by the trend of events, refused to do. Such a creation, opponents of the Bill argued, would remove the last barrier against the pell-mell rush of democracy and would make the House of Lords 'a dead letter in the Constitution'. Tension at Westminster was reflected outside. There were serious riots in Nottingham, Derby and Bristol – the last leaving several hundred dead and injured in the most frightening outbreak of crowd violence since the Gordon Riots. With the forces of law and order stretched to breaking point, appeals were heard in newspapers and elsewhere for the establishment of local vigilante groups. To the government the prospect of private armies was almost as alarming as the danger of rampaging mobs, and it hastily issued a proclamation against such organisations. But the threat of violence hung heavy over the political scene. There were perhaps a hundred political unions by now, but like Falstaff's assailants in buckram suits they multiplied with every report until Grey was told they existed 'in every county and almost every parish in England'.

In the late spring of 1832 the ministry, unable to extract a commitment from the King on the creation of peers, resigned. The final crisis of 'the days of May' was now played out as Wellington's attempts to form an administration faltered and failed against a background of public uproar, 'the whole country in a state little short of insurrection', one MP wrote. Once more the petitions flooded in, one from the Common Council of the City of London urging the Commons to refuse supply until the Whig government was restored to office. Francis Place and his National Political Union called for a run on the banks with the slogan, 'To stop the Duke, go for gold'. In Birmingham 500 professional men and merchants declared their intention of joining the Political Union, until now composed mainly of shopkeepers and artisans. In the shops notices appeared – 'No Taxes Paid here Until the Reform Bill Is Passed'. The propertied classes, or a significant section of them, were threatening at the very least a campaign of civil disobedience. Confronted with a situation as novel as it was threatening William IV gave way, and agreed to a full-scale creation of peers – fifty if necessary – if the Bill was again blocked in the Lords. With this guarantee known, the reinstated Grey government got the Bill through the Upper House without further difficulty, and it was given the royal assent (*in absentia*) on 7 June 1832. Grey's short, sharp measure had taken fifteen months to become law, and had done so only after a prolonged crisis during which at times the whole political system of the country seemed near collapse.

The Bill as finally approved differed in detail from that introduced by Russell in March 1831, but the three major struts of the original measure were still in place – the abolition of the narrow boroughs, the redistribution of seats among the unrepresented towns and the counties, and the uniform £10 franchise. As the Bill proceeded, various anomalies were spotted and corrected, others which were not there in the first place crept in as the result of some hasty improvisation or tactical compromise. There were no precedents for the Reform Bill, no blueprints in government departments to which ministers could refer. Apart from the visionary schemes of generations of individual reformers and theorists, the whole exercise was carried out without the benefit of previous experience or much agreement on the effect of specific changes. In retrospect, it is clear that the critical decisions were taken early on: Grey's commitment on becoming prime minister to the introduction of a reform measure, his choice (rather casual if Durham's recollection was correct) of the members of the drafting committee, and the approval by the cabinet of the main lines of their proposals. Once Russell introduced the Bill in March 1831, although the way forward was unpredictable there was a compelling momentum about the process. Whatever crises were encountered before the Bill became law they were less alarming than the situation would be were it to be rejected, given the balance of political forces in the Commons and the mood of public feeling.

How close the country was to revolution, and in particular what would have happened in May 1832 if the King had refused to guarantee a creation of peers, are questions impossible to answer in any definitive way. There is no doubt that many responsible politicians believed that violent upheaval was a real possibility; by comparison the constitutional crisis of 1782–84 was a genteel affair, a series of palace coups. Memories of revolution elsewhere, usually an argument against reform in England, now came into play as a reason for acting before it was too late. The young Whig MP Thomas Macaulay was not born when the French Revolution shattered the complacency of old Europe, but he was quick to point out that 'the great cause of revolutions is this, that while nations move onwards, constitutions stand still.' There is no doubt that the threat of revolution was used as a tactical device, by middle-class radicals in particular, but also by some ministers, as a way of bringing pressure to bear on Parliament and the King. And at this level it is impossible to tell what was real and what was not. The wording of James Mill's statement of October 1831 hints at a process of bluff and counter-bluff rather than bloody revolution when he advised that the people 'should appear to be ready and impatient to break out into action, without actually breaking out.'

Equally difficult is the disentanglement of government motives, for just as the Whig party in the past had been divided on reform, so there was little unanimity of view at this time. Contradictions, tactical interventions, calculated diversions abound in the speeches, letters and publications of these months. Depending on his audience, a minister might at one time stress the conservative nature of the Bill, its preservation of the influence of the landed classes, the 'finality' of the whole thing. At another, he might hold it forth as a prerequisite for shaking the country out of the lethargy and mismanagement of the Tory decades, proof that the Whigs recognised what Grey described as 'the wonderful advances both in property and intelligence' made by the middle classes. It is of course possible to reconcile many of these arguments. If the Bill was intended as a defensive measure, the minimum necessary to fend off radical demands for fundamental changes, then to associate more of the middle classes with the landed interest was a sensible strategy. In discussions with William IV shortly after the Bristol riots the Lord Chancellor, Brougham, insisted that the middle classes must be kept on the side of the government, and he was careful to distinguish between respectable reformers and the 'mere rabble' led by Hunt and his kind.

The determination of the landed interest to maintain its dominant position was reflected in several ways. First, and most significant, was the rejection of the notion of a secret ballot. Second, although in the redistribution of seats it was the new constituencies which caught the eye – Manchester, Birmingham and the others – roughly half the new seats went to the counties. And these were less susceptible to urban influence after 1832 because whereas under the unreformed system property owners in towns which had no parliamentary representation could vote in their county if they met the 40s freehold qualification, they could now do so only if they failed to meet the borough qualification. Furthermore, the landed interest was strengthened by the extension of the county franchise to £50 tenants-at-will, usually thought to be vulnerable to pressure from their landlords. Despite Tory complaints that northern areas were set to gain more than a hundred MPs at the expense of the agricultural south, the latter was still over-represented. Many features of the unreformed system remained: electoral corruption and violence, unrepresented towns, vast differences in size between the constituencies. One of the most important long-term effects of the Act was neither planned nor foreseen. The enlargement and opening of the Scottish system, added to the Irish reform of 1829, brought over the horizon a possible alliance of Scottish and Irish MPs with those from the large English boroughs. Such an alliance would affect the disposition of party forces, and pose a worrying problem for governments (and in particular Tory governments) seeking the support of acquiescent MPs in the Commons, some equivalent of the 'court and administration' grouping of earlier days.

The most important category of new voter was the £10 householder, though uniformity on paper did not mean uniformity in practice because of different house values in different parts of the country. In cities such as London and Bristol some artisans would qualify; in other towns where property values were lower some householders who regarded themselves as middle-class might well fall under the £10 level and so not receive the vote. The exact number of new voters after 1832 is impossible to establish: estimates vary from an increase of about 50 per cent to one of about 80 per cent. The latter assumes a pre-1832 electorate in England and Wales of 366,000, set against a registered electorate of 653,000 in 1833 – but this is not comparing like with like, and there is a real problem on both sides of the 1832 divide in determining the ratio between eligible and actual voters. The enlargement of the urban franchise, together with the grant of parliamentary seats to many towns previously without representation, were sufficient to ensure solid middle-class backing for the Bill. In party terms the changes were expected to benefit the Whigs, for although they had held a share of the close boroughs which had just been swept away, it was thought that the Tories controlled three times as many – a proportion borne out by the results of the 1831 and 1832 elections.

The working classes gained little in visible terms from the measure. Despite the increase in the electorate, still only one Englishman in five had the right to vote (and fewer than this among males in Scotland and Ireland). The small numbers of working men enfranchised under the £10 householder clause were counterbalanced by those in towns such as Preston whose qualification under one of the eccentricities of the old system was abolished in 1832. The working classes and their leaders were caught in a dilemma, and their response to the Bill differed according to region, time, and political attitude. To begin with, working-class political activity in these years was not confined to the issue of parliamentary reform. Trade union activity was growing, particularly in the cotton industry, where John Doherty established a spinners' union in 1829, and the next year began to build up a general union, the National Association for the Protection of Labour. Others were active in factory reform, and in the spreading ideas of the co-operative movement. In three cities which were obvious candidates for parliamentary representation, the attitude of the working classes differed considerably. In Birmingham, a city of small workshops rather than factories, there was collaboration between middle and working classes; but in Manchester strenuous class antagonism between factory owners and workers ruled out joint action, and there as in Leeds working-class activists ignored the political unions in favour of Huntite associations campaigning for universal suffrage and for factory reform. Hunt refused to support a Bill which offered nothing to the working classes; while Place thought that the desperate handloom weavers of Manchester looked to revolution rather than reform, 'a revolution in which they might gain, but could not lose'. On the other hand Doherty, after initial doubts, saw the Bill as 'one grand step towards the point we aim at – the universal establishment of political liberty.'

The Commons returned on the new register in the election of December 1832 was far from the 'democraticall assembly of the worst description' feared by Wellington, but emphasis on the continuity of social and economic background among MPs (nearly half of them in the House for the first time) hides a massive shift in political balance. The Tories numbered no more than 150, trailing far behind the ministerialist Whigs at 320. In Ireland, O'Connell's group of 39 MPs was now the single largest party, just ahead of the Whigs (36 seats) and the Tories (29 seats). When Parliament met it did so in a state of excited anticipation of further reform, for on all sides it was hoped, feared, or simply expected that the Reform Act was the prelude to a whole series of changes. It was the aftermath of 1832, stretching over a period of years, rather than the struggle over the Reform Bill itself, which saw the shaping of the two great parties of Victorian Britain, though this process was obscured for some time by misguided speculation and wishful thinking. To some, the political struggles of the future would be between moderate Whigs and radical Whigs, with the Tories slipping into obscurity. More sober political observers were aware of the difficulties which lay ahead for the government, not least from the entrenched Tory majority in the Lords, whose failure to block the Reform Bill had made it the more determined to prevent further reform legislation reaching the statute book.

The Whigs, for all their numerical superiority, were divided and uncertain. Among the ministry's supporters in the Commons were those who saw the Reform Act as the precursor to a comprehensive updating of the institutions of the old regime; others had more limited targets; some none at all. Differences over Ireland and the Church brought about the resignation of four ministers in 1834, two of whom, Stanley and Graham, were eventually to become important assets to the Tories. This split was followed by the resignation of Grey himself – the whole affair yet another instance in which governments tottered and fell over Ireland. The King's wish for a coalition government under Melbourne came to nothing; and in a final flourish of the royal prerogative William IV let his dislike of Russell (and particularly of his views on Irish Church reform) persuade him to dismiss the Whigs and install a Tory government under Peel. The new ministry proved to be only a Hundred Days wonder, for there was no longer a large enough court and administration group in the Commons to sustain a manoeuvre reminiscent of George III's stratagem of December 1783. Although in the January 1835 election the Tories almost doubled their following in the Commons (to about 290), this spectacular increase was not enough to keep Peel in power, and by April Melbourne was back in office.

Melbourne's position, damaged by losses in the January election, was retrieved by the Lichfield House Compact of April 1835, a tactical alliance between Whigs, radicals and O'Connell's Irish group. In return for a promise of political and ecclesiastical reform in Ireland O'Connell dropped his campaign for repeal of the Union, and agreed to support the Whigs. As he had said after the Whig split of 1834, 'We are on the way from a half Whig, half Tory government to one half Radical, half Whig.' There was a large element of wishful thinking about this, as there had been about the assumptions of the philosophic radicals who came into Parliament in 1833 – Grote, Roebuck, Buller, Molesworth – that together with the old hands James Mill and Joseph Hume, they would exercise a decisive influence on political developments. They saw, or thought they saw, a new spirit at large – as Roebuck put it, 'a spirit of questioning every institution . . . of bringing back society to its first principles'. The fact that estimates of the number of radical MPs varied from 50 to 120 was a warning sign of the lack of identity and unity among them. They ranged from Cobbett to Attwood, from vaguely liberal Whigs to doctrinaire Benthamites, a 'jarring miscellany of irreconcilable theorists', as one of their number complained. Within this wide range of political attitude and behaviour the philosophic radicals formed a compact if not always harmonious group, but their expectation of fundamental reform was unrealistic. If the Whigs, as James Mill insisted, were 'only reformers by compulsion', then the philosophic radicals possessed neither the persuasive force nor the political firepower to turn Roebuck's claim into reality. Both Grey and then Melbourne were more intent on attracting moderate support than on allowing the radicals their head. As Melbourne appealed during the delicate negotiations of the winter of 1834–35, 'For God's sake get our people, if you can, not to pledge themselves about Ballot and the duration of parliaments.'

The Lichfield House Compact, and Peel's increasing ascendancy on the Tory side, marked a shifting of political forces towards the centre. While in the 1835 election some of the more conservative Whigs were defeated, in 1837 prominent radicals lost their seats. Another mark of this shift was the growth of party organisations. Conservative and Constitutional Associations burgeoned after the stimulus of the Hundred Days, and found a headquarters at the Carlton Club; the Whigs in turn set up constituency associations, and used the Reform Club as their meeting place and party centre. Each side, too, had its election organiser – Francis Bonham for the Tories, Joseph Parkes for the Whigs. The clause in the Reform Act which laid down that all voters had to be registered was only one incentive for better organisation in the constituencies. In the Commons, party whipping became more efficient. Another factor in the growth of party activity was the succession of regular borough elections which followed the Municipal Corporations Act of 1835. After a long campaign the reduction of the newspaper tax in 1836 from 4*d*. to 1*d*. led to an increase in the number of newspapers, and before long most towns of any size boasted a Liberal and a Conservative paper. The process tended to squeeze out the smaller groups, the fringe elements, and the independents, and although it is possible to exaggerate the solidity of the main parties, which began to be known by their new labels of Liberal and Conservative, the transformation was a real one. The enlarged electorate, the excitement of four general elections in eight years, the bustle of the legislative scene, all led to a hardening of political attitudes and loyalties.

In party mythology the 1835 election was marked by Peel's address as Prime Minister to his constituents, published in the national press as the *Tamworth Manifesto*, the best known of a series of pronouncements by Peel which attempted to chart the future course of the Tory or Conservative party. Even before the passing of the Reform Act, Peel had insisted that 'we look beyond the Bill', though it was left to lesser figures to plan the survival and reorganisation of the party during what might be a long period in opposition. The *Tamworth Manifesto* repeated Peel's advice to party die-hards that the Reform Act had conclusively settled 'a great constitutional question'; as far as other institutions were concerned, a balance had to be struck between redressing abuses and preserving existing rights. Public addresses in 1837 and 1838 gave Peel further opportunities of explaining the nature of modern Toryism – which he saw not only as defending the great institutions of the country, the Crown, the House of Lords, the Church, but as 'widening the foundations' on which that defence stood. His appeal to 'that great and intelligent class of society which is much less interested in the contentions of party, than in the maintenance of order and the cause of good government' he took with him to the opposition benches. There, he adopted a quasi-ministerial attitude of constructive criticism which not only suited his own temperament but brought important political advantages. It enabled him to trawl support from moderates of all groups, and to dull memories of Ultra extremism by focusing on radical excesses.

There was no equivalent of the *Tamworth Manifesto* on the Whig side. The party in power could instead point to a mass of legislation, though it is difficult to organise the Whig measures of this period into any kind of 'programme'. Among its first measures in 1833 was a tough Coercion Act for Ireland, which seemed to embody conventional Tory ideas of dealing with agrarian unrest and violence. But the same year saw the passing of a bill to abolish slavery throughout the British empire – a gesture to the old Whiggism of Fox and his abolition of the slave trade a quarter of a century earlier – and a bill on factory reform. Although there had been factory acts introduced in 1802 and 1819 as private measures, the 1833 Act represented a more official interest. It was a response to an alliance between humanitarians, working–class groups in the textile areas and parliamentary radicals, and a few evangelical Tories of independent views such as Michael Sadler, Richard Oastler and Lord Ashley (later seventh Earl of Shaftesbury). Efforts to get a Ten Hours Bill through the Commons faltered in the face of a series of distractions – the Reform Bill agitation, the loss by Sadler of his seat at Leeds in the 1832 election, and the enquiries into the subject first of a Select Committee and then of a Royal Commission. The latter brought a Benthamite rather than a humanitarian approach to the problem, and was prepared to recommend limits only on the hours worked by children – on the grounds that because they were not free agents they needed protection in a way that adults did not. An innovation was the appearance of an inspectorate to regulate and enforce the complicated regulations of the Act, for lack of this had reduced the earlier measures of 1802 and 1819 to virtual dead letters. Only four inspectors were appointed to cover the whole country and they did not always have the support of the local magistracy which the Act assumed, but the precedent was an important one. Despite its limitations the 1833 Act was a recognition that control of working hours and conditions were legitimate objects of concern for the state.

None of the legislative measures of the Whigs after 1832 did much to reassure the working classes; but one, the 'New Poor Law' of 1834, seemed to strike directly at their interests. Even before the passing of the Reform Bill the Grey government had set up a Royal Commission to report on the operation of the Poor Law, the latest in a series of such investigations. It was the Swing riots which pointed to the hopeless inadequacy of the administration of poor relief, for the fact that the disturbances were widespread in those areas which had adopted the Speenhamland system revealed that it was as unsatisfactory to its recipient as it was expensive to the ratepayer. The Royal Commission was well manned with members of Ricardian, Malthusian and Benthamite views, and included Edwin Chadwick, 'the grey eminence' of the period. Its report made a firm distinction between the helpless and the able-bodied poor. The latter were to be made to seek employment by ensuring that their lot under the new system would be 'less eligible' than that of the poorest labourer in work. By eliminating outdoor relief, and introducing the disciplined regime of the workhouse, the Commission intended the labourer to regard the parish as 'his last and not his first resort'. A Board of Commissioners with Chadwick as its Secretary was set up to administer the new system on a countrywide basis, and though there were to be separate Poor Law Unions in the localities, the parish would lose its responsibility. The appearance of a centralised bureaucracy implementing social policy on a national basis was a striking precursor of things to come. There was uneasiness among both Tories and radicals about some aspects of the new provisions, but in general there was little opposition to a measure which promised to save money and to replace a system whose original structure was hardly visible beneath the accretions of generations of additions and alterations.

By the end of 1834 the modestly entitled Poor Law Amendment Act was law, and in 1835 and 1836 assistant commissioners set up the new Poor Law Unions throughout the southern counties and in East Anglia. Recent memories of the repression of the Swing riots limited the protests to sporadic demonstrations and riots; but as the commissioners, 'travelling legalised Shylocks' in the words of a radical newspaper, moved north in 1837 and 1838 a different situation developed. The assumptions of the 1834 Act, and particularly that which regarded most unemployment as voluntary, were largely based on rural experience, and were shown to be untenable as the growing economic recession hit the manufacturing districts. Tens of thousands were losing their jobs, and not even the threat of the workhouse, the neighbourhood 'bastille', could turn them to non-existent employment. Some of the contemporary criticism of workhouses was exaggerated, and took as commonplace what was exceptional; but even in the better-run ones severe discipline and family separation were normal. Opposition to the commissioners became more vociferous, and troops were called out on several occasions. Outdoor relief had to be allowed in many cases, the attempt to apply a uniform policy nationwide was tacitly abandoned, and ten years after the passing of the New Poor Law four out of five of those who received relief still did so outside the workhouse.

The reform measure which best represented the central thrust of Whiggism at this time, uniting moderates and radicals alike, was the Municipal Corporations Act of 1835. Preceded by measures of the previous year which provided for elected town councils in Scotland where the £10 householder obtained the vote, the measure as it applied to England and Wales was a logical sequel to the Reform Act. That had struck at the influence of the narrow corporations over parliamentary elections, but a larger question was the role of such bodies in local government, where small, self-perpetuating corporations dominated most boroughs. Their archaic nature was thrown into sharp relief by the Reform Act, for many of those now able to vote in parliamentary elections still had no vote in borough elections. In July 1833 a Royal Commission – rapidly becoming the favourite weapon of this government – was set up with radicals as chairman and secretary, and in the next sixteen months carried out investigations of the situation in almost three hundred towns. After enquiries (often partisan in nature), the commissioners reported that the corporations were at best 'inadequate', at worst areas of privilege, self-seeking and neglect. The report of the Royal Commission was quickly followed by a government bill which abolished more than two hundred closed corporations, and established 178 municipal boroughs with a standardised system of government in which the new councils were elected every three years by all ratepayers. With Peel accepting the inevitability of the measure, the Bill passed through the Commons without much difficulty, but underwent such extensive amendments in the Lords that once more a constitutional crisis threatened.

It was just one of several measures which were drastically amended, or abandoned, because of the opposition of the Lords; and angry radical MPs urged the reform or even abolition of the Upper House. With neither side quite as committed as in the struggle of 1831–2, a compromise was reached on this particular Bill by which property qualifications were introduced for councillors, and a new and senior category of 'aldermen', elected by their fellow councillors and serving for six years, appeared. At first sight, the Act was a more 'democratic' measure than the Reform Act. There was, for example, no restriction of the vote to £10 householders; but some of the advance was illusory. Many working-class householders did not pay rates in their own names, and so were ineligible to vote. Some of the largest of the new conurbations such as Manchester, Sheffield and Birmingham fell outside the terms of the Act because they had not previously been incorporated, and so had to apply for incorporation under a separate procedure. London was not included. The new councils tended to consist of shopkeepers, tradesmen, and some professional men, for the most part devoted to economical administration and low rates. All too often they viewed the growing responsibilities of town government in a narrow, penny-pinching way. What was beyond question was that when taken together with the Reform Act the Municipal Corporations Act confirmed the new position of influence obtained by the middle classes.

The difficulties encountered in trying to introduce a similar measure to the Irish corporations was evidence of a more general problem – how to bring any reform to Ireland without seeming to strike at the roots of the Protestant Ascendancy and to threaten the Union itself. As the diarist Charles Greville wrote on a later occasion, there was a gulf between 'what the people of England could be brought to consent, and what the people of Ireland would be content to receive.' Eventually a bill went through in 1840, but so eroded had it been by amendments in the Lords that its general effect in many areas was of municipal disfranchisement. Even more contentious were bills touching on religious matters. The repeal of the Test and Corporation Acts, Catholic emancipation and the passing of the Reform Act gave a new impetus to attempts to reform the Church of England. Alarm and despondency were felt among churchmen and in the Tory ranks, for the Church was a target for radicals, nonconformists, and those simply moved by anti-clerical sentiments. It held a privileged position marked by the payment of Church rates, the exclusiveness of the ancient universities, and the compulsory Anglican marriage service. Furthermore, its regional structure no more corresponded to the reality of England in the early nineteenth century than had the unreformed electoral system, for the growth of population in the new industrial areas had not been followed by the creation of new sees, and the division of parishes under the Church Building Act of 1818 had failed to meet the needs of the day.

Some progress was made by the Whig government on both fronts. Marriages were allowed in nonconformist chapels, the new University of London provided for non-sectarian higher education, sees were established at Manchester and Ripon, tithes were commuted for corn-rent, and the Ecclesiastical Commission of

1836 was established to regulate both the income and the territorial boundaries of the dioceses. But there were obstacles to going further than this, as was shown by the government's failure in 1837 to press through a Church Rates Bill which would have shifted responsibility for the upkeep of Anglican churches from local ratepayers to the Church itself. Few Whigs were prepared to follow the logic of those radicals and nonconformists who wished to mark the fact that despite the Anglican resurgence of the 1830s the Church of England no longer represented the majority of the population, by pressing for its disestablishment. As it was, Melbourne was nervously aware of the problems of steering an acceptable course through the passions aroused. He told the House of Lords in 1837: 'On one side we have been accused of acting with the recklessness of a Wat Tyler or a Jack Straw; while, on the other side, we have been accused of acting with a timidity and a hesitation that is perfectly contemptible.'

If church reform proved a prickly issue in England, it was still more contentious in Ireland – yet the mounting agitation there, and the government's dependence after February 1835 on the votes of the O'Connell group in the Commons, kept its nose to the Irish grindstone. One of the most urgent problems was the swelling campaign for abolition of the tithe, backed by an alarming increase in rural disorder. The issue combined in the most awkward fashion for the government the two main Irish grievances of religion and land tenure. Payment of the tithe was a continual reminder to 6,500,000 Catholic Irish that they were forced to contribute to the upkeep of a church representing less than 10 per cent of the population, but which enjoyed an annual income of almost a million pounds, and supported a superstructure of four archbishops, eighteen bishops and two thousand clergymen. It was a church, in Macaulay's phrase, which produced 'twice as many riots as conversions'. And to the religious anomaly of the tithe was added the economic grievance of payment from people some of whom were often near starvation. A lessening of the burden, and a cutting down of the top-heavy ecclesiastical structure of the Church of Ireland, became priorities for the government, not least because of its fear that refusal to pay tithe one day might lead to refusal to pay rent the next.

The King's Speech of December 1831 had looked forward to legislation which would 'afford the necessary protection to the Established Church, and at the same time remove the present cause of discontent.' It was this balance, so simple to express, so difficult to attain, which dominated parliamentary politics in the months after the Reform Act. As the shape of the Church Bill emerged, difficulties grew, and what had been a secondary issue in the tithe debate began to assume mountainous proportions – the question of the 'appropriation' of surplus revenue from the tithe for secular purposes. Threats of resignation came from the Irish Secretary Stanley at one moment, from Russell at another – and in the end Stanley went, accompanied by Graham, before Grey himself resigned. What appeared to be a triumph for the more liberal elements in the government had little impact on the hard rock of the political fact that Peel, Wellington and the Conservative majority in the Lords were implacably opposed to lay appropriation. With first Grey and then Melbourne reluctant to risk a clash with the Lords so soon after the crisis of 1831–32, appropriation even for 'religious and charitable purposes' disappeared from the proposals. Not until 1838 did a Tithe Act reach the statute book. By reducing the amount to be paid, exempting the poorest tenants, and making landlords responsible for collecting tithe payments in the rent, the Church of Ireland was for the time being removed from the direct line of fire. But a sharper cutting edge was added to the bitter struggle between tenants and landlords which was beginning to dominate the Irish scene.

The attempts by governments of this period to find legislative answers to the multitude of problems which arose from the changing economic and social conditions have attracted much attention. Some historians have stressed the influence of Benthamism, in particular among a small group of men highly placed in public life; others the general influence of humanitarian sentiments; yet others the overwhelming pressure for change generated by the revelation of countless cases of individual misery amid a growing national prosperity. Those who regard the measures as adding up to 'a revolution in government' are countered by others who emphasise the limitations of the new approach. In a confused mêlée of interpretation and counter-interpretation, terms such as state collectivism, *laissez-faire*, individualism, interventionism, and social engineering, meet and clash. There is in the midst of this much common ground. All would acknowledge that the way in which England was governed began to change dramatically in this period. As late as 1836, Melbourne was still clinging to the belief that 'the duty of a Government is not to pass legislation but to rule', but by the 1840s central government was involved in the administration of the Poor Law, in working conditions in factories and mines, in education, in public health. It was, as Robert Owen had foreseen some years earlier, inevitable that industrialisation 'will produce the most lamentable and permanent evils, unless its tendency is counteracted by legislative interference and direction.' Driven by a series of investigations and recommendations in which disciples of Bentham such as Edwin Chadwick and Southwood Smith played important roles, government attempted to control and remedy the abuses inherent in an industrialising society. In political terms these men took as their starting point the recognition that only central government had the authority and resources to deal with many of the problems which were threatening to overwhelm local authorities and private agencies.

As Parliament became increasingly sensitive to public pressure, and in particular to revelations of what were regarded as insupportable evils – whether plantation slavery in the West Indies or women and children working underground in coal mines – the government accepted new responsibilities in areas which earlier had been left to private initiative. This extension of the sphere of government activity was subject to severe limitations: the reluctance to interfere with property or with what were regarded as the natural laws of economic behaviour; the dislike of bureaucracy and its expense; the stubbornness of vested interests. In practical terms there were political obstacles in the way of sweeping changes. What was left of the government's education proposals in 1839 scraped through the Commons by only two votes because of the religious implications involved. Ashley's Coal Mines Act of 1842 to control working conditions underground was mangled in the Lords, where coal owners held sway. The Railway Act of 1844 to control monopolistic pricing was emasculated by the railway lobby in the Commons, working on the uneasiness of many members about the spreading area of state intervention. The Public Health Act of 1848 which set up a Board of Health with officials empowered to inspect local authorities, was in the end a political compromise which represented a considerable dilution of Chadwick's original recommendations.

If the remedial legislation of this period was subject to competing pressures and special interests, its general movement was unmistakable, and was marked by signposts along the way – investigation and report, legislation and inspection. That the number of inspectors was always too small for the task in hand is self-evident. More constricting still were the limited areas subjected to even this cursory form of control, basically factories and mines. Omitted from scrutiny and protection were the vast numbers employed in agriculture, home industry, and domestic service. Nevertheless a pattern had been sketched, a beginning made to the complex task of improving living and working conditions for the masses. More inspectors were appointed, more areas of activity included in new legislation. There remained a discrepancy between formal statutes and the practical reality of their operation, but legislation was becoming more comprehensive and its enforcement more effective.

12 The politics of protest and protection, 1836–1852

Whatever the long-term implications of the Whig legislation of the 1830s, it seemed to do little for the working classes. The Factory Act was regarded as a disappointing dilution of the abortive Ten Hours Bill; the Municipal Corporations Act followed the Reform Act in benefiting those with property; and a priority of the new councils seemed to be the establishment of police forces based on the model – a suspect one as far as many workers were concerned – of the metropolitan police force. The severity of the judicial treatment handed out to the Swing rioters in 1831, the Tolpuddle 'martyrs' in 1834, and the striking Glasgow cotton-spinners in 1838, was resented and long remembered. Most hated of all was the New Poor Law. Once more, the main parties seemed to have nothing to offer working men and women. The excitement, the alliances and the promises of the Reform Bill agitation were seen to be a false dawn as the legislation of the Whig government unrolled. Edward Baines, editor of the *Leeds Mercury*, represented the voice of middle-class radicalism after the Reform Act as he outlined the future in a way which offered little to the working classes: 'Vast commercial and agricultural monopolies are to be abolished. The Church is to be reformed. Close corporations are to be thrown open. Retrenchment and economy are to be enforced.'

Even before the Reform Bill became law, there were those among the working classes who preferred to look to their own organisations, and their numbers swelled after 1832. Of the vitality of working-class movements in this period there can be no doubt. There were ambitious trade union ventures: in the textile areas John Doherty's Grand General Union of Operative Cotton Spinners in 1829, followed by his National Association for the Protection of Labour; and in London Robert Owen's Grand National Consolidated Trades Union in 1834. Owen, founder of the New Lanark model co-operative earlier in the century, was back from the United States to encourage workers to support his new enterprise. The membership numbers and achievements of these general unions never justified their heroic titles; but their weaknesses should not conceal the fact that political radicalism was driving deeper into the previously unorganised ranks of workers. Apart from the unions there was the National Union of the Working Classes of the Reform Bill years, Henry Hetherington writing in the *Poor Man's Guardian* and representing the best of the unstamped or pauper press of the period, Cobbett having his last fling – the voices of protest and agitation were loud, but discordant. Ambitions were greater than resources, so the grandiose and millenarian ventures of the period faltered and collapsed. There was little of that concentration on a single end, that concerted action, which had characterised the middle-class radicals whose energies had helped to propel the Reform Bill through its difficult passage. But if these were familiar weaknesses, the next manifestation was remarkably different from the disintegration and apathy that might have been expected; for despite its ultimate failure Chartism was the most impressive demonstration the country had seen of working-class determination and commitment. In scores of different areas, participation in Chartist meetings, ceremonies and propaganda offered a counter-culture to set against the exclusive forces of the local establishment. The movement was evidence of how little the government of the day, and the political structure, reformed or not, met the expectations and needs of much of the population.

Among the radical organisations which appeared at this time was the London Working Men's Association, another in the long line of London societies which stretched back to the days of Wilkes and Hardy. In 1836 the Association's secretary, William Lovett, published a tract, *The Rotten House of Commons*, in which Whigs and Tories alike were castigated as 'robber factions', and the House of Commons represented as the arena in which landed and moneyed interests struggled for supremacy regardless of any consideration for 'the sons of labour'. The next year the Association, with the help of parliamentary radicals such as Hume and Roebuck, the London veteran Place, and Attwood in Birmingham (where the Political Union was re-formed) drew up a petition to the House of Commons requesting a bill which should embody the celebrated Six Points. These were manhood suffrage, annual parliaments, secret ballot, equal electoral districts, abolition of property qualifications for MPs, and payment of MPs. This was the Charter, accepted amid great excitement in the summer of 1838 as the campaigning platform for a whole array of radical, trade union, and anti-Poor Law organisations. On the face of it there was little new about the objectives or tactics of the campaign. The Six Points, or something very like them, had been aired in radical circles since the time of Cartwright. Mass petitions and public meetings were time-honoured devices used by Thelwall, Hunt and others; while the calling of a general convention, the 'alternative Parliament', was a tactic blessed by Painite ideology and hallowed by memories of Peterloo.

What was different was the scale of the new movement, genuinely national in extent, with an appeal which brought together many strands of working-class attitude and activity. The rapidity with which the movement grew in the late 1830s was due to a number of circumstances, but linking them was the pent-up frustration and disappointment at the reformed Parliament, after 'five years of patient trial' as a Birmingham petition put it. Feargus O'Connor in the main Chartist newspaper, the *Northern Star*, listed the abuses from which the labouring classes, 'the real people' of the country, suffered – 'a corrupt system of patronage hanging around their necks like a host of locusts . . . the pressures of taxation . . . the operation of the Corn Laws which made rents high and bread dear . . . the horrors of the factory system . . . the abominations of the poor law.' All this amounted to what Attwood called the 'deep and unrewarded wrongs, injuries and sufferings' which moved men to action. The sense of betrayal was strong. As Bronterre O'Brien, the leading theoretician of Chartism, put it, the New Poor Law proved that the claim that the middle and labouring classes had much in common was a 'delusion . . . no working man will ever again expect justice, morals or mercy at the hands of a profit-mongering legislature'. In the Midlands and North especially, the New Poor Law was crucial in arousing the fears of the working classes, and protest against it became the touchstone which distinguished working-class from middle-class radicals.

The year 1837 was notable for much else besides the Six Points. It saw the beginning of the recession which lasted until 1843, was to be the deepest of the century, and had profound political as well as economic consequences. On the political scene the general election which followed the death of William IV in June saw a further erosion of the ministry's strength in the Commons which made the last years of Melbourne's government difficult and unrewarding. This was despite the political advantage which the Prime Minister gained from his close relationship with the young Queen Victoria, who was more Whiggish and more malleable than the irascible William IV had been in his later years. The disappointing election results of 1835 and 1837 confirmed Whig suspicions that a radical programme would be unacceptable to the electorate. When confronted with demands at the end of the year for secret ballot, extension of the franchise, and triennial Parliaments, Russell declared, in words which were to earn him the sobriquet of 'Finality Jack', that having 'only five years ago reformed the representation, having placed it on a new basis, it would be a most unwise and unsound experiment now to begin the process again.' The only one of the radicals' three demands put to the House was crushed by 509 to 20 votes. The several disillusionments of 1837 signalled the end of radical expectations that the Reform Act was the prelude to a rapid reshaping of the country's institutions. However contentious the legislation since 1828 it seemed to have left intact the foundations of aristocratic power. In the last years of the decade the emergence of Chartism on one side, and the Anti-Corn Law League on the other, were further signs that the non-aristocratic sections of society did not form a coherent whole, but that they were in turn subject to powerful forces of class consciousness and antagonism.

The paternalistic, pre-industrial society of 'orders', 'degrees', 'ranks' and 'sorts' had in most parts of the country disappeared into a haze of nostalgic remembrance. There were still ties of dependence and deference, but they were no longer based necessarily on ownership of the land. Speenhamland was one of the last spasms of the old protective role. The pressures of a rising population, increasing industrialisation and urbanisation, and sharpening political demands, were bending economic and social divisions towards the horizontal layers of a class system. Any attempt to force the infinite variety of income, occupation and attitude into the rigid strata of a three-class society falters before the complex realities of early nineteenth-century Britain. Even so, an emergence and intensification of a separate group consciousness allows for the first time use of the familiar class terminology without a collapse into anachronism. None of the conventional divisions – landed élite, middle class, working class – is applicable in terms of exclusive categories. In social ambition, for example, many leading manufacturers and merchants identified themselves with the landed class. To this extent, the campaigns in the last years of the Napoleonic Wars against the Orders in Council and the Corn Laws, had given a misleading impression of a battle to the death between a class representing the rising interests of trade and industry, and a traditional landed aristocracy. The middle class was characterised by the professional men, small entrepreneurs, managers, and lesser property owners, whose numbers grew with the economic developments of the period, and by infusions from above and below. It was a class which lacked nothing in assertive publicists; it contained, James Mill insisted, 'the greatest portion of the intelligence, industry and wealth of the state'. Philosophic radicalism was its cutting edge, and its strength was seen in much of the legislation of the 1830s – from one perspective a series of tactical concessions by a governing élite anxious for the support of this new organised force in the face of lower-class demands.

If the rise of the middle class in political terms can be followed through the writings of its self-confident leaders, the emergence of a working class is more difficult to chart. The depressed, the deprived, the exploited, had always existed; and common misery had not hitherto produced much in the way of effective organisation. Some historians have traded the development of class consciousness from the years of agitation and repression under Pitt to the 1830s, taking in the Luddites, Peterloo, the Reform Bill agitation, and Chartism on the way. One does not need to accept the unbroken continuity of this line to recognise that new groupings were emerging, force-fed in their learning process by disillusionment and oppression. As Cobbett proclaimed in 1825, 'here is one class of society united to oppose another class'. This unity was more limited and fleeting than Cobbett and others liked to think, and a year later another writer anticipated much modern scholarship by dividing the working classes into nine different layers, ranging from well-paid 'mechanics' down to paupers. The skilled craftsmen and artisans who were often prominent in political activity might feel little in common with the impoverished masses of handloom weavers, agricultural labourers and domestic servants.

The concentration of the work-force which came with industrial-isation clearly helped to nurture a sense of class distinctiveness, but as late as 1830 there were probably no more than 100,000 men (though many more women and children) working in factories. The urban manifestations of working-class activity can be deceptive. The Swing riots of the southern counties or the desperate resistance of Scottish crofters to eviction were as significant in their own ways as the Luddite outbreaks or the Plug Plot of 1842. To many, the great landowners or the increasing number of clergymen JPs were the enemy, rather than the factory owners. Nor did trade unions play as significant a political role as the publicity given to them in the 1830s might indicate. The general unions, with their inflated membership claims and short lives, had a balloon-like fragility. More effective were the smaller craft unions based on a single occupation, but these were rarely in the front line of political campaigning; for they were as concerned about the threat to their livelihood from unskilled workers as they were about exploitation by employers. And if, at one extreme, there were political activists, at the other there were the millions of workers who were unorganised, indifferent, or timorously deferential. It took Chartism to sweep some at least of these millions into bouts of political agitation, helped by the sharper sense of class consciousness which had emerged from political discrimination and economic deprivation.

The dramatic rise of Chartism carried with it the seeds of the movement's ultimate collapse. There were predictable difficulties of organisation and tactics, clashes of personality, misunderstandings and jealousies. 'Chartism' is a term which imposes a misleading sense of unity on a conglomerate of individuals, groups and regions – on supporters who ranged from dedicated radicals prepared to face imprisonment and deportation to the massed ranks at the torchlight meetings and processions, the depth of whose commitment and understanding of the issues involved is more difficult to ascertain. Some trends at least are clear. Despite the early importance of the London Working Men's Association the main centres of activity were outside the capital – in the North, the East Midlands, Scotland and South Wales. Support for Chartism was found in all save the deepest rural counties, but it was probably strongest in the areas of decline, where O'Connor boasted that he led those of 'unshorn chins, blistered hands, and fustian jackets'. Yet among the more active Chartists were many from the skilled trades, and as in earlier radicalism tailors, shoemakers and blacksmiths were all prominent. It was a movement which, especially in its first years, involved many women, in the demonstrations and processions, even though proposals that women's suffrage should be included in the Charter were rejected. The universal motive behind the upsurge of support was to improve the economic position and bargaining power of the working classes – the Charter was a political remedy for an intolerable economic situation. As O'Brien insisted, though the labouring classes were told that they were unrepresented because they had no property, 'I tell you on the contrary, it is because you are unrepresented that you have no property.' But there were narrower hopes and grievances as well. Many of the Irish who followed Feargus O'Connor assumed that gaining the Charter would mean the end of the Union. The nonconformists who supported Chartism, in Wales for example, hoped its success would eliminate that Anglican supremacy which the Whig government had eroded but failed to remove. Other radicals, some of whom were soon to join a different pressure group, wanted a more representative Parliament which would abolish the Corn Laws. Yet others saw the priority as teetotalism, or universal education, or a return to the land.

With hindsight it is easy to explain the failure of Chartism – a loose-knit movement with revolutionary objectives which it hoped, by and large, to carry out by persuasion. But the perspective of 1838 and 1839 was different. It was only a few years since Parliament had conceded the Reform Act because of outside pressures which at times seemed to assume revolutionary proportions. As O'Connor reminded questioners who demanded to know whether Chartism was based on 'moral force' or 'physical force', the Reform Bill had been carried against the backcloth of the destruction of the Bristol riots, the arming of the middle classes in Birmingham and elsewhere, threats of a run on the banks to bring national bankruptcy. When Chartists declared, 'We want to strike terror to the foe, and yet not touch a hair of their heads', they were echoing, consciously or not, the rhetoric of some politicians at the time of the Reform Bill struggle. In 1830 Wellington had refused to contemplate changes in the representative system, and had unleashed a storm which not only pushed through the Reform Bill but almost blew away the power of the House of Lords in the process. In 1837 Russell made a similar declaration and aroused similar antagonisms. The parallel is of course an inexact one; at no time did the Chartists have allies in Parliament comparable to the pro-Reform agitation of 1831–32. Nor, in the glow of self-confidence of the early months of the movement, did they make a particular effort to find them. In O'Connor's lexicon of abuse, the Radical-Whig group stood as 'non-descript animals', 'pocket politicians'. In a sense the failure of Chartism to achieve its objectives was a justification for those, like Grey, who had seen the Reform Act as a measure which would 'associate the middle with the higher orders of society in the love and support of the institutions and government of the country', a barrier against the unpropertied and unlettered masses.

The fate of the National Petition, rejected without discussion by the Commons in July 1839, was a familiar one, as was the subsequent disarray which overtook the Chartist leaders. A run on the banks, destruction of property, a general strike in the shape of a 'sacred month' or 'national holiday', were discussed with varying degrees of enthusiasm , but no clear lead was given. O'Connor, self-proclaimed successor to Hunt, was the one Chartist leader with a national reputation; but it was a mark of serious organisational weaknesses that his oratorical skills, displayed at meetings and through the columns of the *Northern Star*, formed the main binding force of a movement lacking formal structure, unified leadership and agreed tactics. However inflammatory his platform rhetoric, in his soberer moments O'Connor warned his followers not 'to unfold their breasts to an armed soldiery', an option which seemed to some the only one left in the dismal latter months of 1839. Faintly glimpsed through the swirling crowds, the platform oratory and the torchlight processions which made up the visible face of Chartism, were flickers of insurrectionary activity. There were several abortive risings in the north, and in November 1839 occurred the most serious and mysterious of them at Newport, where an attack by an armed Chartist force led to twenty or more deaths. But the lurid and rather public instruction which some Chartists expected to signal a general insurrection – the appearance of the *Northern Star* printed in red – was never given. Chartism in London, not yet touched by the worst of the depression or by the rigours of the New Poor Law, did not provide the mass support for the movement at the nation's nerve-centre which the provincial organisers had expected. The recurrent dilemma of radical agitation since the 1790s – what action to take if resolutions, petitions and memorials were ignored – gripped the Chartist groups and their leaders.

Disturbances, the use of troops, arrests and trials, followed each other in inexorable fashion to make the Chartist years the most turbulent of the century. The government for its part, while insisting that Chartist activities were essentially a law and order question, avoided the brutal excesses of force which those Chartist leaders casting around for a strategy after July 1839 had half-feared, half-hoped for. In General Sir Charles Napier, appointed in charge of the troops in the northern districts, the ministry found a commander at once conciliatory and firm. Lovett, O'Connor, O'Brien, at odds with each, at least shared the common experience of a prison sentence – together with five hundred other Chartists – but the relatively short terms served, and the commutation to transportation of the death sentences passed on the leaders of the Newport rising, offered few martyrs to the cause.

The depression which helped to galvanise Chartism produced growing financial difficulties for the government, which also came under pressure from a new group, the Anti-Corn Law League. Whereas Chartists were convinced that sweeping political reform was a prerequisite to dealing with the economic depression, free traders saw the repeal of the Corn Laws as a more realistic way of stimulating the economy and relieving distress. Food prices would drop, and the entry of foreign corn would lead to a reciprocal increase in the export of British manufactures. Although the consensus of political economists was in favour of the removal of protection, and the reformed Commons had supposedly been better disposed towards industry and commerce than its predecessors, the governments of Grey and Melbourne had left the Corn Laws in their 1828 form. Their importance was not to be measured solely in economic terms. To Tories generally, as well as to many Whigs, they were essential to the well-being and political influence of the landed interest. The developing pressure of the radical attacks on the Corn Laws increased the determination of the defenders, for both sides agreed that more was involved than an adjustment of tariffs. To free traders such as Cobden their retention symbolised the fact that 'we are a servile, aristocracy-loving, lord-ridden people'. For Tories, looking back at a series of retreats – Catholic emancipation, the Reform Bill, Municipal Corporations, Ireland – defence of the Corn Laws represented the last ditch. If the link between Toryism and the land was cut, one proclaimed, then the party would disappear.

The year 1839 was no more successful for the free traders than for the Chartists. As well as finding many of their meetings swamped by Chartist demonstrators, the League experienced the same difficulty as its rival in influencing Parliament. Lectures, petitions, pamphlets, set out the case for abolition of the Corn Laws, but political reality was the rejection by the Commons of a motion for an enquiry into the operation of the Corn Laws by 342 votes to 195. The size of the minority was encouraging enough to turn the local Manchester Anti-Corn Law Association into the Anti-Corn Law League, and this became one of the most effective of the 'agencies out of doors', as Gladstone was later to call the extra-parliamentary movements of this period. Within Parliament the matter gradually became an issue between and within the main parties, with Russell's plan to substitute a low, fixed duty on corn for the sliding scale of 1828 opposed by most county and Irish MPs of his own side as well as by the Conservative opposition.

The weakness of Melbourne's government was revealed when it resigned in May 1839 after radical M.P.s voted against its decision to suspend the constitution of Jamaica. It returned to office after the Queen's refusal to part with her Whiggish ladies of the bedchamber convinced Peel that he could not form an effective administration; but time was running out for a ministry which was plagued by difficulties on all fronts. The spread of government intervention into unfamiliar areas seemed simply to increase the chances of stumbling into morasses of unknown extent and depth. One such area was education, where the government in 1839 proposed to increase and equalise the modest building grants made since 1833 to the two denominational societies, the National (Anglican) and the British and Foreign (nonconformist). It also proposed to pay grants to other schools, including Catholic ones, to establish non-denominational schools for teacher training, and to place supervision of the growing state involvement in education under a committee of the Privy Council with no clerical representation. These steps in the direction of state-aided lay education ran into furious opposition from Anglicans in and out of Parliament, and with the government's majority dwindling to vanishing point most of the scheme was dropped. The increased grant survived, and so did the new committee, which slowly began to play a more active role on the grounds, as its secretary James Kay-Shuttleworth explained, that as far as workers' children were concerned the state must oversee 'the duty of rearing those children in religion and industry, and of imparting such an amount of secular information as may fit them to discharge the duties of their station.' Four years after the uproar of 1839, the strength of pressures coming from the other side of the religious divide was displayed when Peel's Home Secretary, James Graham, was forced to abandon a Factory Education Bill which included provision for compulsory schooling under Anglican auspices for child workers. In a campaign which produced 25,000 petitions and four million signatures, nonconformists and Catholics united in a protest against what one described as 'a sort of Church of England Junior'. The emergence of 'The Oxford Movement' within the Church of England, with its Anglo-Catholicism, had sharpened the fears of nonconformists in a period of neurotic rivalry both between denominations, and between religious and secular agencies. The controversies of 1839 and 1843 indicated not only the sensitivity of issues which involved children, education and religion, but also defined the narrow band of manoeuvre within which governments, regardless of political complexion, had to operate when religious feeling were aroused.

After three years of deficits, increasingly desperate attempts to balance the budget ended in 1841 when the ministry was defeated on one of its financial proposals by a single vote. The subsequent election was held in an atmosphere of disillusionment with the Melbourne government, and in one of expectation that Peel, whose stature had grown in opposition, would provide steadier leadership. In this comparison of individual leaders, Peel benefited from the anticipation that the Conservative party would prove a more reliable defender of the Church against nonconformists and Catholics, and of the landed interest and the Corn Laws against radicals and free traders. Peel's majority of about eighty seats was based on the counties and the smaller rural towns. In the larger towns and cities the £10 householders, often nonconformist, tended to vote Liberal, while in the Scottish burghs, and in Ireland outside Ulster, the Conservatives remained weak. The election showed that the gloomier Tory predictions of permanent Whig/Liberal rule after the Reform Act were unjustified. The steady increase in Tory seats in the 1835 and 1837 elections, the shift to Peel of former Whigs and Canningites, and the support of young, promising politicians such as Gladstone and Cardwell, were pointers to the victory of 1841, in which Peel captured the middle group of politics.

Peel's ministry was strong and well-balanced, with Aberdeen at the Foreign Office, Goulburn at the Exchequer, the former Whigs Graham and Stanley as Home Secretary and Colonial Secretary respectively, and with Wellington holding office without portfolio. The situation which faced the new administration was a daunting one: economic depression, government deficits, and agitation by Chartists, the Anti-Corn Law League, and O'Connell's Irish repealers. Britain, a pessimist might say, was fast becoming ungovernable. On the eve of taking office Peel showed that he had a more open mind on the Corn Laws than many of his supporters assumed. Although he doubted whether they were responsible for the distress of the period, if convinced that they were then he 'would earnestly advise a relaxation, an alteration, nay, if necessary, a repeal.' The more uncompromising side of Peel was shown when in one of his first speeches as Prime Minister he insisted that no party considerations would make him 'the instrument of carrying other men's opinions into effect'. Finance, the area of government which had brought down the Whigs, was the priority. The issue turned on whether the government would nerve itself to reintroduce income tax, with its baleful if distant memories of a wartime imposition. With Wellington's support, the decision was taken, and the level was set high enough at 7*d.* in the £ (about 3%) to produce a surplus which would make possible substantial modifications to the tariff system (left more or less intact since Robinson's changes in the 1820s), and in particular to reduce duties on consumer goods. Of the 750 different imports involved, timber was the most important. Inevitably, the process of tariff cuts brought to the forefront the Corn Laws, where despite the success of protection as an electoral slogan the government proposed cuts in duty of up to a half at various points along the 1828 sliding scale.

Against a background of renewed Chartist agitation and strenuous activity by the Anti-Corn Law League (several of whose leaders, including Richard Cobden, had been returned at the general election) the 1842 budget was passed, despite some uneasiness by the agricultural lobby at the weakening of protection for home-grown wheat. The budget was a bold stroke in that it aimed to secure financial stability, lower the cost of living, and encourage production. What Liverpool and Castlereagh, twenty years earlier, had said could not be done, Peel was determined to attempt – to use the legislative powers of the government to reverse the plunge into depression and crisis. These were not measures of reform in the sense that the Whig governments had understood, but a broad-sweep approach to the 'condition of England' issue. 'We must make this country a *cheap* country for living', Peel told a colleague. Inevitably, it took time for the 1842 budget to prove itself, and not until 1844 was its success clear as the government moved into surplus despite the lowering of tariffs. It did little for the destitute of 1842, and the deepening economic recession led to another surge of Chartist agitation. A new National Petition attracted three million signatures, twice as many as in 1839, and with its demands for the Six Points together with repeal of the New Poor Law and of the Union, it was escorted to Parliament by a huge procession. London was by now badly affected by the depression, and there were demonstrations against the troops marching through the streets of the capital on their way to Euston for special trains to take them north. There the industrial areas were being torn by the worst unrest in living memory as employers attempted to cut wages by up to a quarter. Although the strikes and riots were prompted by these wage cuts, together with unemployment and lock-outs, the areas most affected were those which had experienced a high level of Chartist activity. It was the year of the Plug Plot in Lancashire, so called from the strikers' removal of plugs from factory boilers as part of an attempted general strike. Though this fell far short of its objective, it drew support from up to half a million workers, and included among its aims the Ten Hours Bill, a restoration of wages, and acceptance of the Charter. The level of bitterness exceeded that of 1839, in some areas all work ceased, and the violence was more continuous and extensive than in the disturbances of 1831–32. Among the Chartist leaders there was little coherent response to these developments. The cautionary lessons of 1839 had cut deep, and just as among the rank-and-file there was never again the optimism and spontaneity of the first years of Chartism, so the leaders were divided and uncertain as news reached them of events in the north.

The reports from the industrial areas of depression, misery and violence made further tariff reductions a matter of urgency as far as Peel and Graham were concerned. To Peel the crisis in manufacturing and trade loomed large enough to mute the farmers' insistent cry for protection. He had often expressed, usually in private, disquiet that the agricultural interest claimed a special and privileged position. Now, struggling to contain the first great industrial depression in British history, he heard complaints from farmers of low food prices with more irritation than sympathy. This irritation also extended to the Anti-Corn Law League and its protest meetings, for intensifying the nervousness of the landed interest, and for increasing public disorder in so turbulent a period. 'We hate the pressure from without', Peel had once said, and now a Leaguer echoed Peel's fears when he said that if the League joined the Chartists 'it would end in a revolution'. By the end of the year Cobden was guiding the League in a different direction. He observed that since Peel was moving towards the position held by Russell, the latter in turn would be thrust by the dictates of party closer to the League's policy. 'It is merely a question of time', Cobden insisted and, he might have added, of organisation; for he and the League's chairman, George Wilson, had learnt much from the first years both of the League and of the Chartist movement. An efficient 'party' machine was now assembled: among its tasks was distribution of tracts through the new penny post, systematic exploitation of the registration procedure to garner sympathetic votes, intervention at by-elections, national speaking tours by rail of Cobden, Bright and the other leaders, and the establishment of regional offices to collect funds and to circulate policy directives from the League's central Council. It was a new and effective form of alternative politics, and as the noise of the Chartist agitation fell away after 1842, so the quieter but no less insistent voice of the League was heard throughout the remaining years of Peel's administration.

If the 1842 budget was a triumph for Peel, other issues brought less a sense of achievement than a foreboding of disaster. Ireland, predictably, was foremost among these. The pattern of the 1830s was continued, in that concessions made were not enough to quell agitation, but went too far for opinion in England. In Ireland the main thrust of agitation under O'Connell was once more directed towards repeal. In economic terms Union seemed to have done irreparable damage as Ireland found itself shackled to the most advanced industrial nation in Europe. Emigration of the young and able-bodied, lack of capital investment, and predatory or absentee landlords, combined to depress the lot of the 'residual population', which had itself almost doubled in fifty years and now stood at more than eight million. It is true that contemporary accounts which assumed that the whole population lived in a state of feckless poverty were exaggerated. There was a dual economy in which a system of efficient commercial agriculture, producing grain, livestock and dairy products for export, as well as a flourishing linen industry, existed alongside a subsistence economy based on the potato as the staple diet and peat as the only fuel. This was the economy of most of Ireland's inhabitants, for whom one effect of Union was the extension of Britain's new-model Poor Law to a country where previously relief had been left to private charity. Whatever the arguments in England for threatening consignment to the workhouse for those unwilling or unable to work, there were none for introducing the system to a land where investigations had estimated that because of underemployment 585,000 men and their families (2,385,000 persons in all) were in distress for much of the year. As O'Connell said, Ireland was too poor for a Poor Law – certainly for one which assumed the existence of wage-earning employment where there was none, and which ignored the problems of those Irish living hand-to-mouth on small plots of land which had been subject to a continuous process of subdivision.

By 1843 O'Connell's Repeal Association had gained support from all sections of Irish Catholic opinion, and not least from the Church. 'Every priest is a drill sergeant and every chapel is an orderly room', the Lord Lieutenant complained. Although the arrest and imprisonment of O'Connell and other leaders of the

Association brought a lull, new initiatives were clearly needed. The Devon Commission was set up to look at problems of land tenure, and reported that they were such as 'to paralyse all exertion and to place fatal impediments in the way of improvement.' At the same time, the government made moves to conciliate the Irish Catholic hierarchy, in part as an attempt to drive a wedge between it and O'Connell. The new approach had several aspects, the most contentious being the proposal to give more generous state assistance to the clerical seminary at Maynooth in the hope, in Peel's words, that the young priests produced by that impoverished institution might turn out to be something other than 'sour, malignant demagogues'. In 1845 a bill making a capital building grant to the college and increasing its annual grant came before Parliament. It provoked the resignation of Gladstone, at this time a promising junior minister at the Board of Trade, but more serious parliamentary storms lay ahead, in waters already made turbulent by squalls over two earlier measures.

Although the government had given some assistance to Ashley's Coal Mines Act of 1842 which prohibited the employment underground of women and girls, and of boys under ten, it refused to support his Ten Hours Bill of the following year. Instead, Graham at the Home Office introduced a bill incorporating various reforms – on safety, powers of the inspectorate, and the education of factory children, but all on condition that the twelve-hour factory working day for adults should remain. Peel insisted that any reduction of the working day, particularly in the cotton industry, would harm production and exports, and lead to job losses. The strain of Tory radicalism – evangelical, humanitarian, paternalist – which encompassed Oastler, Sadler and Ashley found little echo in the free market orthodoxy of Peel. He looked instead to the lifting of restrictions and the expansion of trade to improve living conditions; as Ashley said, 'Imports and exports; here is Peel's philosophy. There it begins and there it ends.' The issue led to great excitement and even greater confusion in the Commons. With humanitarian sentiments at odds with economic considerations, and opposition to government meddling set against gentry dislike of manufactures, 'Whigs, Tories and Radicals were jumbled together in inextricable disorder', as one newspaper saw it. Some sort of control was brought to the situation only when Peel threatened resignation unless government supporters voted with him against Ashley's Ten Hours amendment.

Resentment inside the party at this ultimatum increased with a similar difficulty over sugar imports, when the government's compromise measure of a staged reduction in the colonial preference was defeated by an eccentric alliance of free traders, who demanded a total removal of the preference, and protectionists, who wanted it left intact. Again, it took the toughest talking by Peel, followed by much application of soothing ointment by Stanley, to reverse the decision. Some of the trouble on the Tory benches could be attributed to the restlessness of MPs unhappy at their role as backbench cannon fodder, unaccustomed during their years in opposition to restrictions on speaking and voting at will. Only a few of the rebels at this time had any intention of bringing down the government – hence the effectiveness of Peel's resignation threats – but the episodes were symptomatic of the strains in the relationship between a prime minister who saw his party as the servant of the government, and rank-and-file MPs resentful at his evident lack of interest in their opinions and worries. Among these was a small but flamboyant group led by Benjamin Disraeli which took on the name of 'Young England' to give expression to an alternative set of ideals. These exercises in nostalgia, which one Tory thought attracted 'more of wonder than respect', could better be categorised as 'Old England'; but Disraeli was to prove a more formidable adversary than his posturings at this time indicated.

It was in an atmosphere soured by recrimination and suspicion that the Maynooth bill was launched, amid uneasiness by many Conservative MPs who had not forgotten the 'betrayal' of 1829. With 'No Popery' opinion in the country roused by a measure seemingly intended to increase the number and influence of Catholic priests, the Bill passed only with the aid of opposition votes. Passions had not run as high since the Reform Bill crisis. The year before the Lord Lieutenant of Ireland had warned, 'We are walking upon hot cinders, and we must take care lest in conciliating the Catholics we do not stir up a Protestant fire that will set Ireland in a blaze.' The Conservative party was split – 159 to 147 in favour on the second reading, 149 to 148 against on the third reading. As in 1829 opponents of the measure had to contend with the frustrating realisation that opinion seemed overwhelmingly on their side in the shape of ten thousand petitions received against the bill compared with a mere ninety in its favour. Once more, Peel declared that 'the interests of the country' were paramount. Following this line, over the factory bill and the sugar duty, and now Maynooth, he had antagonised half his party, and for some the alienation was permanent. As Peel complained, his discontented followers ignored the achievements of his ministry, particularly in economic and financial matters. The Bank Charter Act of 1844 restricted the issue of notes by the Bank of England to the amount of its gold reserves and to specific government securities, and effectively centralised the issuing of notes in the Bank. In the financial crisis of 1847 (and again in 1857 and 1866) the Bank was released from these restrictions; but for all its imperfections the Act, seen by Peel as the logical sequel to the Currency Act of 1819, was a major step in regulating the money market. This steadying measure was followed by the budgets of 1845 and 1846 which used surplus revenues to make sweeping reductions in duties, and so achieved what had seemed economically and politically impossible. The economy had revived, Chartist agitation had faded from view, and peace had been restored to Ireland – 'offences for which nothing can atone', Peel drily observed.

Existing tensions within the ranks of government supporters form part of a chain of events which led to the break-up of the ministry over the Corn Laws, an issue brought to the forefront by the outbreak in Ireland of potato disease in the autumn of 1845. The failure of the crop was unexpected. There had been poor years and local scarcities before, but observers contemplating the two million acres of potato fields reassured themselves that they were 'more certain in produce and less liable to injuries' than wheat. The fungus which ruined much of the potato crop of 1845 (and almost all of it in 1846) shattered this complacency; instead the awful vulnerability of a population dependent on the potato as its main crop was exposed. As the magnitude of the disaster became apparent, so agitation grew for the unrestricted entry of corn, and its supply by the state to those facing starvation in Ireland. To run this policy alongside the Corn Laws was regarded by Peel as impossible. As he put it in October, the only remedy for the situation was 'the total and absolute repeal for ever of all duties on all articles of subsistence'. Here the cabinet balked: temporary suspension of the Corn Laws combined with limited government assistance to Ireland was one thing, repeal of the Corn Laws another.

There can be little doubt that for Peel the retention of the Corn Laws was unjustified; the whole thrust of the government's economic policy since 1842 had left them precariously isolated. In that year he had told a colleague, 'You might on moral and social grounds prefer corn fields to cotton factories, an agricultural to a manufacturing population. But our lot is cast, and we cannot recede.' Inner conviction was one thing; conversion of the massed ranks of Tory MPs, many of them sitting for rural constituencies, quite another. To MPs elected in 1841 on a protectionist platform, Peel was guilty of a whole series of crimes: capitulation to the agitation of the Anti-Corn Law League, a sacrifice of the true interests of the landed classes, an obstinate determination to follow his personal convictions regardless of the feelings and unity of his party. Suspicion that Peel had long since given up the Corn Laws for lost, and that he was using events in Ireland as an excuse for repeal, were sharpened when Peel stated that he was proceeding 'on the assumption that protective duties, abstractedly and on principle, are open to objection.' Protectionists made much of the point that abolition of the Corn Laws would not save the Irish peasantry from starvation, for they had no money to buy grain. And Peel's view that the government could not at one and the same time effect a large relief operation and keep the Corn Laws intact seemed to them an exercise in sophistry – as did his refusal to consider a suspension of the Corn Laws for a limited period. Whatever difficulties lay in the path of these various solutions, they seemed preferable to driving the party over the edge of the cliff.

Peel's resignation at the end of 1845 to allow Lord John Russell to take office with the explicit task of passing a repeal measure failed in its objective after eleven days in the face of Russell's difficulties with leading colleagues, and it was after all left to Peel to abolish the Corn Laws. In this he was supported by the Anti-Corn Law League, whose Council announced in February 1846 that although Peel's intention to phase out the Corn Laws over a three-year period fell short of the League's target of complete and immediate abolition, it would not offer 'factious or fanatical opposition'. By May the job was done, with the help of Whig votes. Although in the end only Stanley left the cabinet, two-thirds of Peel's MPs opposed the bill, including all but a handful of those who had voted against him over Maynooth. Led by an unlikely combination of Bentinck, for eighteen years a tongue-tied backbencher, and the loquacious Disraeli, 231 Tories voted against the government on the second reading, only 112 for. On other issues some returned to the fold, but enough were prepared to join with the opposition on other measures to bring down the government. In June 74 Tory MPs voted with the opposition on the unpromising subject of an Irish coercion bill, with another 51 abstaining, to bring about Peel's resignation and the fall of the government.

Peel's sense of duty had come into irreconcilable conflict with the deepest convictions of many of his party. Unlike some free traders who saw repeal as the first step in a new reform programme, Peel viewed it as a realistic concession on the lines of 1829 to avert a crisis which would weaken the position of the landed aristocracy and the Tory party. Repeal would 'fortify the established institutions of the country, to inspire confidence in the equity and benevolence of the legislature.' But what to Peel was political realism (and economic good sense) was to many Tories the ultimate betrayal, and the Prime Minister had neither time nor inclination to engage in a process of education. His attitude was revealed in his brusque comment after he had resigned, 'As heads see and tails are blind, I think heads are the best judges as to the course to be taken.' In the months before repeal he had adopted the stance of a national rather than party leader, and his celebrated resignation speech showed how far he had moved from many of his followers: 'I shall leave a name execrated by every monopolist who . . . clamours for protection because it conduces to his own individual benefit; but it may be that I shall leave a name sometimes remembered with expressions of good will in the abodes of those whose lot it is to labour, and to earn their daily bread by the sweat of their brow.' This was better received outside than inside Parliament; it was, said one MP, 'language à la Hunt'. Within the Tory party the disputes over factory reform, the sugar duty and Maynooth had paved the way for this greater revolt; and no longer were the dissidents willing to continue under Peel's leadership once the immediate issue was settled. Enough of them repudiated Peel to make the split in the party over the Corn Laws a lasting one. 'Peelites' and 'Protectionists' now emerged as political terms representing the reality of Tory fragmentation, and it was almost thirty years before a reunited Conservative party won another general election.

Neither in terms of leadership nor of party strength were the Whigs able to take full advantage of Peel's resignation. The government of rather elderly Whigs which took office in June 1846 was never able to shake off Russell's defects as Prime Minister or the depressing feeling that it was a second-choice as well as a second-rate administration. With radical and Irish MPs forming uncertain allies, all too often the ministry had to rely on Peel's lofty goodwill and the support of his followers. Some important legislation was passed, notably the Ten Hours Act in 1847, and a Public Health Act the next year, but these measures were consequences of long-term pressures rather than of any reforming initiative by the government. Above all, its failure to deal adequately with the worsening situation in Ireland showed the weaknesses both of power and imagination which afflicted Russell and his associates.

Peel's relief measures after the partial failure of the potato crop in 1845, which included the purchase of Indian meal for shipment to Ireland, and the opening there of food depots, had helped with the worst of the distress; but this took on a new dimension with the catastrophic failure of the 1846 crop. The potato production figures for these years tell their own bleak story.

Table 12.1. Potato Production in Ireland

1844	14,862,000 tons (estimated)
1845	10,063,000 tons (estimated)
1846	2,999,000 tons (estimated)
1847	2,046,000 tons
1848	3,077,000 tons
1849	4,024,000 tons

[Cited in Mary E. Daly, *The Famine in Ireland* (Dublin Historical Association, Dundalk, 1986), p. 56]

Determined not to interfere with the operations of the food market, the Russell government decided on a programme of public works, partly financed by the Treasury, which would provide destitute Irish labourers with enough money to buy food. Although the unprecedented sum of £5 million was committed to the programme in the autumn and winter of 1846–47, the machinery of local administration could not cope with the scale of the disaster, and even where work was done and wages paid, the sums earned did not meet escalating food prices. In 1847 the government reluctantly accepted the necessity of outdoor relief and soup kitchens; but the gap of several months between the dropping of one policy and the implementation of another saw the first mass deaths. In all, the famine years resulted in about a million 'extra' deaths, some from starvation, most from typhus, dysentery and other diseases. Another million or more emigrated in the period up to 1852, and not only the poorest left, for many businesses and sizeable farms had collapsed during the famine.

Although the accusations of genocide sometimes levelled against the Russell government cannot be sustained, there is no doubt that the practical difficulties, and particularly the lack of transport and distribution facilities in Ireland, were exacerbated by an official reluctance to move beyond what were thought to be proper levels of government intervention. The failure was one of administrative competence and human comprehension – a fatal combination which was seen again in the Crimean War a few years later. In the long term, the disappearance of a quarter of Ireland's inhabitants, and a significant decline in the birth-rate, halved the country's population in the hundred years after the famine. In the changed conditions the Irish agricultural system shifted from labour-intensive potato and grain cultivation to livestock; landholdings were consolidated, and new landlords replaced those bankrupted by the events of the 1840s; both the small farmer and labourer classes declined. In political terms, the psychological scars of the famine were lasting. Some among the survivors were crushed rather than angered by the famine and its exposure of Ireland's economic vulnerability. For others, and not least among those who had emigrated, the dreadful death toll was laid at the door of a parsimonious British government, and emotions were kindled which before long led to the emergence of Fenianism.

If the very structure of society seemed to be collapsing in Ireland, the government could console itself that at home it had survived 1848 – that year of tension and revolution in Europe – despite a third and final Chartist petitioning campaign. The number of signatures collected was greater than ever, but troops, the metropolitan police, and special constables, formed an unbreakable barrier between Westminster and the Chartist meeting of 10 April on Kennington Common. There was to be no repetition of the great march on Parliament of 1842 as the government packed the Queen and court off to the Isle of Wight, put cannon at the Thames bridges, and turned London's public buildings into sand-bagged citadels defended by batteries of guns. The threat of revolution loomed larger in the minds of ministers and property-owners than it did among the Chartist leaders at Kennington, but the day was in its own way decisive – a 'Waterloo of peace and order', Palmerston claimed. Further Chartist assemblies in the capital were contained by the police, as were meetings in Manchester, Sheffield and other northern cities. As the misery of the depression years lessened, as parliamentary reform became a subject moderate politicians could again espouse, so working-class agitation became more sectionalised and less apocalyptic.

Experience at the head of government seemed to weaken rather than strengthen Russell's judgement as he stumbled from one self-induced crisis to another. His plans to remove the ebullient but prickly Palmerston from the Foreign Office collapsed after the Foreign Secretary's parliamentary triumph of June 1850 over the Don Pacifico affair. At the end of the year the Prime Minister became needlessly embroiled in a dispute with the Roman Catholic hierarchy in which he alienated not only Irish MPs but also many Peelites. Early in 1851 he resigned after a minor if humiliating defeat on a radical motion on parliamentary reform in a House less than a quarter full, and though he was soon back in office after Stanley's protectionists failed to form a ministry his days were numbered. Russell had his own plans for parliamentary reform, partly on the grounds that 'a Government ought not to be the only body of politicians in the country who proposed nothing', but the cabinet was unenthusiastic. Palmerston's dismissal at the end of the year after one indiscretion too many lost the administration its most popular minister, and it was on an amendment proposed by Palmerston in

February 1852 that the government was defeated, and resigned. It 'had become too weak for dignified existence', a minister admitted. A few months of minority government by Stanley (now Lord Derby) and another inconclusive general election did little to settle the disturbed political scene. At the end of 1852, after the ministry had been defeated on Disraeli's budget, a belated exercise in political realism brought into office a coalition of Peelites and Whigs under Aberdeen. It was a coming together, after six years of confusion, of the temporary allies of 1846, under one of Peel's old ministers. Peel himself had died in 1850 amid widespread public mourning, but as *The Times* noted in 1852 – a year in which Russell told Aberdeen that 'I shan't insist on being called a Whig rather than a Liberal', and in which Disraeli accepted free trade – 'In one sense we are all Peelites'.

13 Workshop of the world, 1815–1850s

In 1833 the colonial reformer and promoter, Edward Gibbon Wakefield, sketched a beguiling prospect for his fellow countrymen: 'The whole world is before you . . . let the English buy bread from every people that has bread to sell cheap. Make England, for all that is produced by steam, the workshop of the world.' In these sentences Wakefield touched on much that was central to both the political and economic developments of the forty or so years after Waterloo. These were years in which Britain's economic strength, naval power and far-flung empire gave her a global supremacy not approached before or since. The period was a unique one which appeared to the later Victorians as a golden age, one to which the term 'Pax Britannica' could be applied without undue extravagance. A longer retrospect would reveal weaknesses in Britain's position, but while it lasted the achievement was impressive and many-sided.

At the heart of this dominance lay Britain's industrial supremacy. The earliest industrialising nation in Europe kept its lead until the second half of the nineteenth century, and at times seemed to be increasing it. The growth of the British economy can be seen most clearly in the production figures for the three giant industries which formed the basis of Britain's economic miracle: coal, iron and textiles. Since coal was almost the sole source of energy for industry, its production figures form a yardstick for measuring industrial expansion. In the fifty years from 1815 production increased from 13,000,000 to 100,000,000 tons. By mid-century about half of the coal produced was going into the iron industry, which experienced a similar pattern of growth. During the Napoleonic Wars pig iron, the basic product from which cast and wrought iron were made, was being turned out at the rate of 400,000 tons a year. With the help of technical improvements such as the introduction of the steam-driven, hot-air blast (first developed to deal with the ironstone of Lanarkshire), annual production had increased to 3,000,000 tons by the 1850s as the demand grew for iron machinery, beams, locomotives and ships. If coal and iron formed the basis of Britain's heavy industry, the most spectacular growth area was in textiles, particularly cotton goods, where production expanded at the rate of 6 to 7 per cent a year in the quarter-century after 1815. The 1830s saw a technical breakthrough with the introduction of the powerloom which by mechanising weaving removed the main bottleneck in the production process (as well as destroying the livelihood of a quarter-million handloom weavers). In the woollen industry Cunliffe-Lister's machine for combing wool brought a similar improvement in production figures. By 1837, just before the onset of the depression, the textile industry absorbed 30 per cent of the industrial labour force, and accounted for 70 per cent of British exports (mostly cotton products). Raw cotton in turn made up a fifth of Britain's imports. The second phase of British industrialisation, after 1815, was the age of cotton, when the quality and cheapness of Britain's cotton goods found markets on a worldwide scale.

The increase in cotton exports highlights the growing importance of foreign trade in this period. The combined value of imports and exports rose from 19 per cent of the Gross National Product in 1800 to 27 per cent in 1850, by which time 93 per cent of British exports were manufactured goods, with textiles still dominant at 70 per cent or more. A significant rider needs to be added to this story of growth, for the terms of trade became progressively less favourable after 1815 as the prices of exports fell faster than the prices of imports. Between 1816 and 1830, although the volume of British exports increased by 64 per cent, their value fell by 8 per cent. Survey of a longer period shows a 100 per cent deterioration in the terms of trade index between 1800 and 1860, or, to put the situation in more workaday fashion, by the latter date Britain had to export twice as much in the way of manufactured goods to buy the same amount of imported raw materials and food. Despite this hurdle, by mid-century more than 40 per cent of the world's output of traded manufactured goods came from Britain. In all areas of technical development and commercial enterprise Britain was setting the pace. In this age dominated by iron and steam British engineers were involved in one innovation after another: in transportation the locomotive, screw-propeller and marine compound expansion engine; in manufacturing processes a whole range of machine tools; in the construction industry the steam pile-driver. To export the flood of cheap manufactures Britain built on an existing, already extensive base of shipping resources, financial and insurance expertise, and global possessions. Striking evidence of the increase in both British shipping and trading activity in general is shown by the steady rise in the tonnage figures of British ships entered and cleared at United Kingdom ports – from 3,218,000 tons in 1820 to

13,915,000 in 1860. As early as 1844, though the great surge of British steam shipping was still to come, the pasha of Alexander Kinglake's account of his visit to the East exclaimed that 'the ships of the English swarm like flies; their printed calicoes cover the whole earth, and by the side of their swords the blades of Damascus are blades of grass. All India is but an item in the ledger-books of the merchants, whose lumber rooms are filled with ancient thrones.'

In one way the worldwide expansion was a continuation of trends already evident before and during the French wars, in another it was a reflection of necessity. Hopes after 1815 that the European markets closed to British manufactures by Napoleon's policies would be thrown open were dashed by the imposition of high tariffs which seemed to British exporters the equivalent of another Continental System. The trade figures for the first half of the nineteenth century tell their own story of stagnation and decline (in relative terms) in the European markets, unpredictable fluctuations in North America, and expansion in Asia, Africa and South America. It was these latter regions, some within the formal empire, many not, which took the overspill of Britain's manufacturing industry in the first decades of peace. Their need to import manufactured goods, capital and immigrants, and to export their primary products, formed a mirror image of Britain's unrelenting quest for markets on the one hand and raw material on the other.

Table 13.1   Overseas trade markets

			Percentage of export values		
	Europe	*Africa*	*Asia*	*N. America*	*S. America*
1816–18	44.2	1.0	8.3	37.3	9.3
1836–38	44.1	3.6	11.3	21.2	20.7
1849–51	38.0	3.8	14.8	24.5	16.0

[W. Schlote, *British Overseas Trade 1700–1930s* (Oxford, 1952)]

The locking of Britain into a world economy had a whole range of side-effects: a cycle of boom and slump within Britain; pressures towards free trade which forced the agricultural interest onto the defensive; and a new orientation in British diplomacy. The first interruption to the climb out of the immediate post-war depression came in 1825 as over-optimistic investment, irresponsible banking practices, and the collapse of the South American market, triggered a slump. It was a reminder of the vulnerability of an economy becoming increasingly dependent on world markets, and was followed a dozen years later by the depression of 1837–43. This was not only the most severe of the century, but it was especially ominous in its implications since its root cause was overproduction in those industries – textiles, coal and iron – on which the nation's prosperity now seemed based.

The depth of the depression, and the misery it brought, have given a sharp edge to investigations into the reality and spread of the new prosperity. Although the lengthy adversarial debate among scholars on the impact of the industrial revolution on standards of living has by now taken on the appearance of a veteran boxer who has had one fight too many, the points it raises are substantial ones. On some fundamental matters there is general agreement. In the long term industrialisation created wealth and employment; its main achievement was to sustain (at least outside Ireland) a population which had doubled in size in the fifty years between the censuses of 1801 and 1851 without the horrors of famine. After mid-century a marked increase in the standard of living was clear in most sections of the population as the economy entered the era of 'the great Victorian boom'. At this point, differences begin to outnumber the areas of agreement, especially over the trends in the early period of industrialisation, from the 1780s to the 1840s. Discussion has been bedevilled by the difficulty of establishing real wage rates (that is, the relation between wages and prices, or, more pertinently, between *earnings* and prices). The lack of reliable, long-run statistics has made the establishment of national trends difficult, and in any case other factors intrude: complications of piece-work, casual labour, 'living-in' employment, and the problem of ascertaining rents which, alongside food prices, dominated workers' family budgets. Wage rates concerned only those in work, but in this period there were pronounced shifts in the pattern of employment. The widespread unemployment and underemployment, much of it seasonal, of the traditional economy, were being replaced by different, and often more acute and less predictable, forms. Cyclical unemployment related to periods of boom and slump became common after 1815; the tyranny of the trade cycle, it has been said, replaced the tyranny of the harvest. Technological unemployment, as machines replaced men, and structural unemployment, as the drift from the land quickened, also became permanent features of the economy. Then there was the question of more general environmental considerations, to which attention has turned as arguments about wage rates have run into the sands.

Measurement of the 'quality of life' is even more impressionistic than evaluating wage rates in a non-statistical age, though the main thrust of the argument is clear. Even if there was a marginal increase in real wages between 1815 and the 1840s – and this, it seems, is the most that can be conceded – such an increase did not compensate for the deteriorating conditions of life and work for those caught up in the industrialisation of the period. The question is as much one of perception as of reality. Certainly the temptation to contrast the documented squalor of the early nineteenth century with the fainter, sometimes roseate, images of pre-industrial society is to be resisted. Working conditions had been dismal in many traditional occupations. Well before the factory age women and children had worked long hours; miners, grinders and masons had choked to death on dust; those working with lead and mercury had been slowly poisoned; the squatting position and close work of tailors had made them cripples or brought blindness; manual labourers were disabled by strains and ruptures. But in the factories and mines the long hours, the neglect of safety, the exploitation of women and children, were at once more visible, and more shocking, to a society moved by religious revival and affected by humanitarian campaigning. As more than one radical pointed out, it would be ironic if the compassion felt for distant Negro slaves was not matched by a similar concern for factory operatives, agricultural labourers and domestic servants nearer home. Most intolerable was the knowledge that the factories and mines in which so many experienced hardship and degradation brought unprecedented wealth to their owners. Modern scholarship has pointed to the risks as well as profits of the early industrial revolution, the failures as well as the successes; but it was the latter which caught the contemporary eye. The old structure of paternalistic regulation of wages, conditions, and apprenticeship, where it had not rusted away, had been dismantled. The dictates of *laissez-faire*, strengthened by the conviction that nothing should interfere with economic growth, left the workers unprotected. The largest and most depressed group were the handloom weavers, totalling with their dependants 840,000 people on the estimate of a select committee in 1834–5. But three successive attempts by private member's bills to rescue them from their desperate plight by sanctioning wage-fixing by local boards were rejected by Parliament, with the government objecting that such intervention would distort the free operation of the labour market.

By the 1840s for the first time more people in England lived in an urban than in a rural environment. Around the areas of heavy industry spread the new cities, where the physical separation of the workers from owners and management was most evident, and the signs of class conflict were most marked. These conurbations were both vast and squalid, industrial barracks of back-to-back terraces which had grown untrammelled by government regulation. In those dense areas of low-quality housing, with inadequate or non-existent lighting, paving and sanitation, tens of thousands of the new work force lived and died. These were the killing-grounds of the new industrial age, swept by typhus and cholera, and with a population which expanded only because of the relentless waves of immigration, much of it from Ireland. Their inhabitants saw few of the benefits of the industrialisation of the period, for the main beneficiaries were the factory owners, investors, landlords and business classes generally. Their acquisition and ostentatious display of wealth helped to prod working-class discontent into political life, with Chartism encapsulating the main strands of distress and frustration.

As reformers' attention centred on the awful warrens depicted in the novels of Dickens and the sombre surveys of Engels, at another level of early Victorian society the lower middle classes increased in number and affluence as the economy emerged from the depression of 1837–43. *The Times* described the improvements in diet, clothing and furniture which could be seen in the home of 'a small tradesman, or a small clergyman, or a small clerk in a counting-house'; and it thought that the high import figures of 1845 showed that these improvements were spreading among the working classes. While not overlooking the effect of his own policies, there were, Peel said in the 1845 budget debates, 'many causes combining to increase the prosperity of the country' – among them the renewed railway boom, the availability of ready capital, and the demand factor stemming from the steadily rising population. The linking of steam locomotives and iron rails had been the most momentous technical development of the period. After the opening of the Liverpool and Manchester Railway in 1829 marked the beginning of modern commercial railway management, it was soon clear that the new transportation would attract passengers as well as freight, and the 1830s saw the building of trunk lines out of London before the first railway boom petered out with the collapse of some of the wilder projects and the onset of the depression. Even so, by 1844 some two thousand miles of trunk line were in operation, and a second and greater railway boom was gathering momentum. The figures give some idea of the scale. In the five years from 1844 to 1848 720 Acts of Parliament were passed authorising the building of 12,000 miles of line at a capital cost of £267m. (five times the annual national income). Although not all the planned construction took place, and not all the authorised capital was raised, by 1852 more than two hundred companies were operating 7,500 miles of trunk line.

The impact on the economy was both immediate and long-term. In the boom years of construction, the new system called for colossal amounts of capital, labour and materials. In the peak years 30 per cent of gross domestic investment was being swallowed up by the railways, and capital was being attracted from classes not previously involved in share-owning. The boom was a stimulus to a faltering economy, to the crucial iron and steel industry, to a depressed labour market, and to the construction sector. In the longer term the new rail network with its reliable, fast and cheap transportation of goods, removed one of the most frustrating bottlenecks from the developing industrial system of the country. It was followed by a similar revolution in marine transport as the iron steamship was developed, though its gradual overhauling of the traditional sailing vessel as the cheapest form of bulk transport lies outside this period. The British shipbuilding industry, now relocating on the Humber and Clydeside, became a world leader in scale, techniques and cost; and from the 1850s half of Britain's steam tonnage was being built for export. As the statistician John Glover said later, 'Other nations might produce wooden ships cheaper than we could, none could produce an iron steamer cheaper.'

Long after the heady years of domestic railway construction, foreign orders for British iron, British rolling stock, and British engineering skills, gave a long lease of life to the railway boom. Already by 1850 the Dowlais Iron Company had supplied sixteen foreign railway companies compared to twelve at home. In the five years after the ending of the domestic railway boom in 1852 British exports of iron and steel doubled. The cutting of delivery times and costs by the transport revolution helped both the exports and imports of British industry; while the income from shipping became an essential and increasing component of those 'invisible earnings' which helped to close the gap which still existed in Britain's trade balance. Between the ending of the depression in 1843 and the financial crash of 1857 British exports increased 130 per cent. Overseas, markets for British goods expanded and multiplied, while at home governments pursued policies designed to remove all hindrances to trade.

The logic of the new industrialism pointed conclusively towards free trade. The removal of tariffs, prohibitions and other barriers, it was asserted, could only help Britain's industry, whose overpowering competitive supremacy made any form of legal protection both superfluous and counter-productive. Cobden, Bright and their allies produced a whole range of supplementary arguments in support of this. Industrial costs were kept high by the tariffs on the import of raw materials. Such discrimination lessened the willingness and capacity of foreign countries to buy British goods. The removal of outdated protection for British agriculture would open up export markets, and bring down food prices and wage costs at home. Between the free traders and their goal lay an array of obstacles: the loss of government revenue which would follow the abolition of tariffs; the obstructive power of the agricultural lobby; the awkward fact that many of the discriminatory duties helped Britain's colonies. Within five years the Peel government had swept aside these obstacles. The re-introduction of income tax gave the government room for financial manoeuvre, and smoothed the way for the lowering and abolition of protective duties including, in 1846, the Corn Laws. Three years later the Navigation Acts, which for two hundred years had protected British shipping, and had earned even Adam Smith's approval, were repealed. By 1860 Russell and Gladstone between them had completed the work of making Britain a free trade nation, while the 'Cobden Treaty' removed or lowered the tariff barriers on Anglo-French commerce.

For all the political controversy at the time, the repeal of the Corn Laws did not deal the landed interest the deadly blow many had prophesied. For some time their importance had been as much psychological as fiscal. Since 1820, when for the first time agriculture was overtaken by industry both in terms of national product and size of labour force, the five-year averages of wheat prices had steadied between margins of 54s. and 62s. a quarter. Agriculture had put its own house in order. After the wartime inflation of prices and rents the area of arable land had been reduced, and by the 1830s even the southern grain counties experienced a return of modest prosperity. There was no sharp dip in wheat prices after repeal, and the feared flood of surplus grain from Eastern Europe at rock-bottom prices never materialised. Instead, the introduction of new crops, and the increased use of fertilisers (especially guano from Peru) kept British farming competitive across the middle decades of the century. Many landowners were moving away from total dependence on returns from agriculture. The steep rise in urban land values benefited some. Others profited from the sale of land for railways, or from the rents and royalties from the new mines and factories. As in the first era of industrialisation, agriculture, industry and trade were more complementary than the political postures struck by their advocates sometimes indicated.

The foundations of Britain's mid-century prosperity are clear enough in general outline. The boom in railways, machine-tools and other high-priced capital products in demand both in Europe and farther afield, added a new and reassuring dimension to an export economy which had become heavily dependent on textiles. What is more difficult to assess is the relation between these developments and the country's external relations, both in the conventional diplomatic sphere and in the more general area of overseas activity. Generally, British foreign policy in this period had a double role. On the continent it was to maintain the settlement of 1814–15, guard against aggressive, destabilising moves by any other power or combination of powers, and keep a watchful eye on sensitive areas such as the Low Countries and (increasingly) the Mediterranean. Along with this went an enhanced commitment to the country's worldwide interests, for as British trading activity expanded so did the potential area of official intervention. The settlement of 1814–15 had established that Britain's priorities lay in Europe, but less loudly advertised than her magnanimous return of overseas conquests in the Dutch East Indies and elsewhere was the retention of strategically-sited bases, which were to be added to as Singapore (1819), Aden (1839) and Hong Kong (1841) were among those acquired.

In turn Castlereagh, Canning, Palmerston and Aberdeen all played the difficult role of ensuring stability on the continent – which usually implied a mediating role – while paying due attention to British interests globally – which often involved a more aggressive stance. Castlereagh's main concerns after 1815 remained within Europe, when as the threat of Napoleonic restoration faded differences began to appear between the partners of the Quadruple Alliance (joined in 1818 by France). Head-on attempts by the Tsar to turn the Alliance into a crusade aimed at repressing nationalist and democratic movements, and at regaining lost possessions overseas, were adeptly side-stepped by Castlereagh. As he pointed out in the celebrated state paper of 1820, unlike the Tsar and (by inference) other continental rulers, a British Foreign Secretary had an alert and informed public opinion to consider: 'if embarked in a War, which the Voice of the Country does not support, the efforts of the strongest Administration would soon be unequal to the prosecution of the Contest.'

Canning's policies were even more pragmatic in substance, if more declamatory in tone, than Castlereagh's. He reluctantly recognised the limits of British power when he made no attempt to stop French intervention in Spain to restore the noxious Ferdinand VII in 1823; but he made it clear that the British navy would prevent any attempt to reimpose control from Spain over its former American empire. There, British trading interests had taken a firm grip during and after the wars of independence, and it was characteristic that the first formal recognition by Britain of the new republics emerging in South and Central America came in the form of commercial treaties. In the policy considerations of the European powers the threat of the British navy, rather than the high-sounding 'Monroe Doctrine' of the American government in 1824, was the decisive deterrent. It was this chain of events which led to Canning's most grandiose speech on foreign affairs when, in an attempt to draw attention to the triumph overseas and away from the setback in Europe, the Foreign Secretary told the Commons that he had 'resolved that if France had Spain, it should not be Spain "with the Indies". I called the New World into existence to redress the balance of the Old.' Where naval power was effective then it was used. A fleet was sent to Lisbon in support of the constitutional monarch of Portugal, John VI. In 1827 combined Anglo-French naval forces destroyed the Turkish fleet at Navarino, though this escalation from the threat of force to the use of force was not premeditated by Britain. Indeed, her growing anxiety about the stability of the eastern Mediterranean region, and preoccupation with the overland routes to Asia Minor and India, were pushing her towards the preservation of the Ottoman Empire. The Eastern Question, with its juxtaposition of Turkish weakness, Egyptian obduracy, Russian ambition, and Anglo-French rivalry, became one of the most intransigent issues in British diplomacy, and in the end led to the first major European war since 1815.

The recognition of the strengths and limitations of British power, the insistence on preserving the status quo in Europe, the readiness to acknowledge new interests on a global scale, were to be given even more prominence and publicity by Palmerston, who as Foreign Secretary or Prime Minister dominated British foreign policy for most of the period from 1830 to 1865. Much of his work lay in protecting what he once called Britain's 'eternal interests'. So, his main achievement during his first spell at the Foreign Office was the patient repair work he carried out after the crisis of 1830 in the Low Countries, and which resulted in the emergence of an independent Belgium with a great-power guarantee of its neutrality. In the last months of the Melbourne administration in 1841 he carried his Near East policy to a successful conclusion, against the inclinations of many of his own party. After coercing the pro-French ruler of Egypt, Mehemet Ali, with a naval bombardment of Acre, and coming close to war with France itself, Palmerston was able to calm fears of Russian domination of the crucial Straits area with the Straits Convention of July 1841. This prohibited the passage of all foreign warships (including Russian) through the Straits while the Ottoman Empire was at peace, and so cancelled out the advantage which Russia was felt to have gained at the earlier Treaty of Unkiar Skelessi.

For all these forays into traditional areas of British diplomacy, what was most striking about the Palmerstonian period, even during those intervals when Palmerston himself was not in office, was the spread outside Europe of British diplomatic and naval activity: the Opium Wars with China; repeated disputes with the United States over boundary demarcations, slavery, and maritime rights; a clash with France over Tahiti; an obsessive determination to suppress the international slave trade. Two declarations by Palmerston, almost a decade apart, seemed to typify the new thrust of British policy. In 1841 he explained that since British manufactures were still excluded from much of Europe 'we must unremittingly endeavour to find in other parts of the world new vents for the produce of our industry . . . it is the business of government to open and secure the roads for the merchant.' In 1850 Palmerston took the opportunity of the Don Pacifico affair to introduce a large commitment when he pledged, on behalf of 'a political, a commercial, and constitutional country', that any British subject 'in whatever land he may be, shall feel confident that the watchful eye and strong arm of England will protect him.'

Such episodes seem to confirm that the period was one in which a purposeful use of naval power supported national interests throughout the world – a Pax Britannica in which warships were the equivalent of the Roman legions of old. There can be no doubt that in the navy the government possessed a formidable instrument of intervention and pacification. From Algiers to the China Seas, from Lisbon to the coastline of British Columbia, it made its presence felt. With no continental power possessing either the great fleets or the commitment to acquire them until near mid-century. Britain's naval lead seemed as unassailable as her industrial lead. Yet the use of naval power was more fitful than might at first appear. Palmerston's boast that 'well-appointed three-deckers' were the best peacekeepers neglected the awkward fact that they could not travel overland; and the Crimean War was to show the limitations of naval force against a land power. Not all traders in remote parts could look to the navy for help, and belligerent *Civis Romanus Sum* speeches were matched by more cautious ministerial reminders that 'traffic with half-civilised peoples has risks of its own, which are generally compensated by more than ordinary profits.' And as memories of the age of Nelson were obscured by the smoke from steam-driven ironclads, so periodic 'naval scares' disturbed government and public alike. With its advanced industrial capacity, and bases abroad which now doubled as coaling stations, Britain was better equipped than ever to sustain the warfleets of the new technology; but this could only be done after scrapping that huge stock of wooden walls which had given the Royal Navy its commanding superiority.

The mid-century situation abounded in paradoxes which weaken any attempt to build an interlocking structure of British global activity in which pieces labelled 'industrial supremacy', 'free trade', 'seapower', 'colonies', 'diplomacy', fit neatly together. Some free traders were among the most vociferous critics of what a later generation would call gunboat diplomacy, or of the possession of colonies and bases abroad. Criticism of, or indifference towards, the empire seemed so widespread that for long the mid-Victorian period was seen as one of 'anti-imperialism'; yet the process of acquiring territory seemed to continue unabated right through the period generally seen as marking the triumph of free trade. Recent interpretations have looked more closely at the distinction between formal and informal empire, with much debate revolving around such concepts as 'the imperialism of free trade'. Such work has done much to resolve the older paradoxes of the period, though sometimes at the cost of substituting a new set of conundrums.

Formal empire in 1815 consisted of a miscellany of territories acquired in different ways and at different times, scattered across the world. There were relics left over from the earlier Atlantic empire. Oldest among these were the West Indian colonies, once the jewel in the crown, now an increasing embarrassment as the plantation-owners' resistance to the humanitarian impulses reaching them from England seemed to increase in proportion to their economic decline. On the mainland north of the United States were colonies large in area but scanty in resources: the maritimes along the Atlantic seaboard; the reluctant colony of Quebec, acquired in 1763, and given the new name and status of Lower Canada by Pitt in 1791; and Ontario, or Upper Canada, which took shape as a refuge for loyalists after the American Revolution, and was now attracting emigrants from Britain. Loss of the American colonies had been counterbalanced by expansion in the East, above all in India where at the 1815 peace settlement France had recognised the sovereignty of the East India Company over the vast area it controlled after Richard Wellesley's wartime acquisitions.

In 1813 the Company lost its commercial monopoly in India (though it retained that of the China trade for another twenty years), acknowledgement of the fact that it was no longer primarily a trading organisation. As Wellesley had put it, 'its duties of sovereignty must be deemed paramount to its mercantile interests, prejudices and profits.' Lancashire manufacturers now exported their machine-made cotton textiles to India; and in an ironic reversal one of the world's greatest exporters of cotton products in the eighteenth century became in the nineteenth the most important single market for British textiles. The value of cotton exports to India rose from £100,000 in 1815 to more than £5,000,000 by 1850, and though large sectors of the Indian handicraft textile industry survived, Marx's foreboding description of 'the British intruder who broke up the Indian hand-loom and destroyed the spinning wheel' still says much about the priorities of the Raj. Although the amount of land revenue extracted from India grew steadily during the first half of the century, the British were not simply predators. The new currents of utilitarianism and evangelical

Christianity were channelled towards India as the old respect for Hindu culture faded, and the non-interventionist attitude of the East India Company was replaced by more positive and aggressive policies. By the Governor-Generalship of Lord William Bentinck (1828–35) the shape of things to come was clear. Action was taken against the most obvious abuses such as *suttee* (widow-burning), *thuggee* (the almost routine murder of travellers by a hereditary sub-caste), and infanticide. In the first stages of a protracted effort at westernisation Thomas Macaulay arrived in 1834 to draft a new legal code, and to introduce English forms of education which would hopefully produce a class, 'Indian in blood and colour, but English in taste, in opinions, in morals, and in intellect.' The following decade was marked by war and annexation in response to the threat posed to India's North West Frontier by Russian expansion in central Asia. Even the usually pacific Melbourne insisted that 'Afghanistan must be ours or Russia's' – an attitude which led to the disastrous British incursion of the First Afghan War (1838–42), and indirectly to the annexation of the Indian border states of Sind and the Punjab.

Among the skein of bases and trading stations acquired during the war years, the Cape was becoming the focus for new English arrivals among the unwelcoming Afrikaner population. In the south Pacific the convict establishments around Sydney were fast changing character as more free migrants arrived, and settlement spread along the coasts and inland. Even so, 137,000 convicts were transported to Australia, mostly to New South Wales and Tasmania, before the ending of the system in 1867. With the ten-year census returns from 1801 onwards showing massive increases in Britain's population, emigration was favoured by the government and Poor Law authorities, while political economists saw a source of weakness at home being transformed into one of strength (and purchasing power) abroad. In the first years of peace official attempts at emigration were limited to sending settlers, often ex-soldiers, to plug strategic gaps in Britain's colonial frontiers – in one continent along the St Lawrence, facing the expansion of American settlement, and in another along the sensitive eastern Cape frontier. But by the time Wilmot-Horton became Under-Secretary for Colonies in 1821, such limited schemes seemed of little import in the face of the census figures of that year which showed that the population of England alone had increased from 9,476,700 to 11,198,604 in ten years, or in the face of the natural inclination of emigrants to take advantage of cheap passages to the United States. Although many of the emigrants on Wilmot-Horton's schemes for assisted passages came from the poorer parts of Ireland, and from Scotland where the Highland clearances were driving people off the land in favour of sheep, the outflow of population involved more than pauper migration. The long period of agricultural depression between 1815 and 1830 turned the thoughts of small farmers, retired army officers, some professional people, even a few of the gentry, to emigration. It was this type of potential settler who was attracted by the ambitious 'systematic colonisation' projects of the 1830s and 1840s which aimed to reproduce in the wide spaces of Canada, Australia and New Zealand something approaching the social hierarchy of England. It was in such attempts to establish planned and balanced communities abroad, with a proper mix of capital and labour, rather than in Wilmot-Horton's 'shovelling out of paupers' that the future lay according to Wakefield and his associates.

The tussle over ways and means between Wakefield and the Colonial Office obscured their combined achievement in building up the supply of labour, skill and capital for the colonies. Although in the sixty years between 1815 and 1875 about two-thirds of the seven million emigrants from the British Isles went to the United States, the remaining third put flesh and blood on the skeletal outlines of many British possessions abroad. In the first half of the century, large areas of Australia, New Zealand, South Africa and Canada began to take on the form of 'white settlement' colonies, and as they did so some of the political problems which such colonies experienced in the eighteenth century were resurrected. Predictably, it was Canada, with its mix of French and British inhabitants uneasily co-existing under a form of representative government which had been tried and found wanting in the old American colonies, where the trouble was most serious. Lower and Upper Canada were joined in the Union of 1840, a move followed by a gradual realisation by British governments of the 1840s that the concession of some form of internal self-government was necessary. The concession was eased by the adoption of free trade by the Peel administration, for with the economic side of the old mercantilist empire removed, the political supports became both less necessary and less logical. By the end of the decade Canada had achieved a form of responsible government which, for the time being, satisfied colonial demands for autonomy and Britain's concerns with external security; and other settlement colonies followed a similar path in the 1850s.

It was this 'retreat from empire', as it once seemed, together with some voluble criticism of colonies as expensive, dangerous and redundant, which gave rise to the assumption that the early Victorian period was anti-imperialist. Clearly, there is a fundamental difficulty in setting such a conclusion in the context of the continuing overseas expansion of this period. In terms of the area of territory acquired there was no difference at roughly five million square miles between the first and second half of the century. Advocates of the importance of informal empire have stressed that 'empire' has a wider connotation than simply those regions coloured red on the map. In this interpretation Cobden and Bright won the battle over free trade in the 1840s, but lost the war over the global implications of the new policy. To Cobden 1846 marked the beginning of a process of 'drawing men together, thrusting aside the antagonism of race, and creed, and language, and uniting us in the bonds of eternal peace.' But Cobden's idealism was never representative of the free traders in general, another one of whom boasted in the same year that Britain had made 'every corner of the globe tributary to her wants'. Yet another free trader summed up the thesis of informal empire when he explained how 'foreign nations would become valuable Colonies to us, without imposing on us the responsibility of governing them.' If such a process was blocked when a trading area collapsed into anarchy, or uncontrolled settlers clashed with the native inhabitants, or foreign rivals appeared – then other, more formal and forceful methods might be necessary. It was, as the advocates of this interpretation have put it, 'trade with informal control if possible; trade with rule when necessary' – an echo of Shelburne's declaration during the peace negotiations of 1782–83 that 'We prefer trade to dominion'. What was modestly seen as the dictates of necessity led to an imposing list of acquisitions in the decades after 1840: the Punjab, Sind, Oudh and Lower Burma in the Indian sub-continent; Labuan (off the Borneo coast) and Hong Kong and Kowloon farther east; New Zealand and western Canada; coastal areas in West Africa; Natal and (briefly) the Transvaal and the Orange Free State. It was an expansion both official and unofficial, formal and informal, in which traders, explorers, concession hunters, and missionaries were often as important as ministers in London. Settlement colonies acquired their own momentum of growth; so the discovery of gold in Australia in 1851 brought almost a trebling of the population within the decade, while in Canada notions of federation and nationhood accompanied the westward push of the railroad after mid-century.

In retrospect, there was an air of unreality, impermanence, almost of illusion, about much of this. Britain's new global position had emerged during what has been called 'a peculiar interlude' – a period of unbroken peace among the great powers of Europe for almost forty years. Only on sufferance could Pax Britannica flourish; nor would Britain's economic lead continue indefinitely since both across the Channel and across the Atlantic other nations were busy industrialising. But for the British governing and manufacturing classes of this period the omens seemed set fair. Their record was set out in Herman Merivale's confident proclamation in his *Lectures on Colonization and Colonies* in 1861: 'Masters of every sea, and colonists of every shore, there is scarcely a nook which our industry has not rendered accessible.'

14 'Tory democracy', 1840s to 1880s

To Liberals of the 1850s the association of Toryism with liberty, freedom or democracy seemed an inherent contradiction: a Liberal candidate early in the next century argued that Conservatives had throughout his lifetime been the party that 'resisted every liberty won by the people except, perhaps, the liberty to drink as much beer as they could carry without being locked up.' Many Liberals felt so, but the paradox remained that, as Britain made the transition towards democratic politics, the Tories survived and indeed flourished while many of their continental counterparts vanished. The reform acts of 1884 and 1918 which produced the biggest increases in the size of the electorate were each followed by long periods of Conservative government. Once working-class voters became a significant part of the political system in 1867, Conservatives recognised that they could succeed as a party only by securing a major share of those votes. In this survival and prospering of modern Conservatism, Benjamin Disraeli was a pivotal figure.

In part the paradox of 'Tory democracy', connecting all that was backward-looking, hierarchical, Anglican and rural with an increasingly urbanised, secular and democratic politics, rests on semantic confusion. The word 'democracy' did not have the same connotations in the early nineteenth century as in the twentieth, for it was Victorian scholars who rediscovered Aristotle and Plato and so reintroduced into British political thought ideals derived from classical Greece: British radicals of the 1790s, like Chartists of the 1840s, looked for *liberty* or *reform* or *freedom* (even from the state) rather than democracy, though their detailed plans added up to a democratic programme. As a noun, *democracy* was used often as a term of abuse – roughly equivalent to 'mob-rule' or anarchy – rather than as an ideal political condition, and in general parlance *the democracy* was synonymous with 'the people' (whatever their political condition). *Democracy* was more associated with the United States than with Britain, though receiving its classic definition from

Abraham Lincoln only in 1863; to many British politicians American politics was famous for corruption and jobbery, not an example to be followed. 'Tory Democracy' in the 1840s was more about a populace that identified with Toryism than about Toryism that was democratic; it was more about building support for an existing order than about making concessions to an emerging democracy, more about making government popular than about encouraging popular government. Electioneering played a more important role than political theory or principle, and policy often came second to both. It is not surprising that Disraeli, and his chief Tory Democrat successor in the next generation, Lord Randolph Churchill, were both widely regarded as unprincipled opportunists. The Liberal novelist Anthony Trollope created in the character of 'Mr. Daubeny' a sharp parody of Disraeli and his party, 'There's only one thing they care about at all now . . . It's very likely that if Daubeny were to ask them to vote for pulling down the throne and establishing a Republic they'd all follow him like sheep. They've been so knocked about by one treachery after another that they don't care for anything beyond their places.'

None the less, there was a solid core of principle and generosity in the roots of Tory Democracy – it was after all perfectly possible to be patriotic and Anglican while still maintaining a practical sympathy for the dispossessed; in its ideology Toryism laid great stress on the obligations that the leaders of society incurred alongside their privileges. It was that belief, and a horror of the consequences of unrestricted liberty, which had made John Wesley a Tory, and many Wesleyan Methodists continued to support the Conservative Party well into the 1840s. The growth of industrialisation gave a basis, if a fragile one, for an alliance between landowners and workers, each hostile to the owners of new industrial wealth, and it was on that ground that the Yorkshire politicians Michael Sadler and Richard Oastler sought to outflank Whiggism from the left by promoting in the 1840s a Tory Chartism. A more detached humanitarianism had also been a longstanding feature of Toryism, as in the factory reforms that Robert Peel's father had introduced, but its chief exponent in the 1840s was Lord Shaftesbury, crusader for factory laws which would reduce children's working hours – a reform resisted strongly by Peel as untimely and likely to damage the economy in hard times; since Shaftesbury sat in the Commons for Dorset where there were few factories, there is no doubting the genuineness of his convictions. Even Disraeli, in his novels of the 1840s, contributed with Charles Dickens, Elizabeth Gaskell and George Eliot to the bringing forward of the 'condition of England question' and the greater prominence given thereafter to social issues in political debate.

When Peel fell from both Prime Ministerial office and the leadership of the party that had emerged under his guidance, it was protectionism and Protestantism rather than reform which held the field in the party wreckage which he left behind. Most former Conservative ministers went like Gladstone, Cardwell and Aberdeen into a temporary purdah with Peel. Although Conservative candidates did reasonably well in the 1847 election and won almost half the parliamentary seats, some ninety Conservative MPs backed Peel while more than twice as many opposed him. Government could only be carried on by the Whigs with Peelite backing; the period of opposition between 1846 and 1852 therefore marked a time in which Peelite and Protectionist factions drifted apart forever – the 1846 split became permanent. The leadership of the protectionist majority of Conservatives therefore devolved on those who had overthrown Peel, especially on Derby whose authority and experience were unchallengeable; he remained leader for twenty years and was three times Prime Minister of brief, minority governments at times when the unstable Liberal–Peelite grouping could not cohere. Derby did much to keep Conservatism alive by offering a respectable lead, attracting steady support in the Lords and respect at the Palace, but he was neither an energetic leader nor the man to inspire a revival. In any case, key issues continued to focus on the Commons where the party had far more trouble in getting a leader – or even a presentable front bench. Derby's first minority government earned in 1852 the nickname the 'Who, who? Government' because of the reaction of the aged and deaf Wellington to the list of unknown ministers read out in the Lords.

The first leader in the Commons was inevitably Bentinck who had led the squires to their victory over Peel, but his erratic guidance was always a problem; once the excitement of the Corn Law debates was over he was reluctant to give .enough time to the job to be effective. He was also reluctant to take criticism and soon resigned rather than change his ways. Experiments with other equally unsuitable possibilities and a resort to teams of leaders only delayed the inevitable promotion of Disraeli; he finally took over the party leadership in the Commons in 1849 and kept it for nearly thirty years. Disraeli was a quixotic choice: Conservatives in their most rural, squirearchical, ultra-Anglican phase had turned to a man who was born into London literary society, who was by birth a Jew (albeit Anglicanised) and who did not ride a horse. The lack of correspondence between leader and followers could be only minimally offset by Disraeli being provided with a modest country seat in Buckinghamshire (through the generosity of the Bentincks). He was for years distrusted as much by his supporters as by his opponents, not least because of his Jewishness in a time of general unthinking anti-semitism; in the 1870s a Conservative MP could still describe him as 'that hellish Jew'. But Disraeli had one thing that made him indispensable to the Conservatives, sheer natural ability in a party that was woefully short of it. His tactical skills (and his cynical opportunism too) made him a superb leader of opposition, which was mainly what the Conservatives required between 1847 and 1868. The negative aspect of this was that he lacked the power to mould and lead opinion outside Parliament, a power which Palmerston and Gladstone each used to win and hold power.

The partnership of Derby and Disraeli had first to deal with unfinished business. In opposition before 1852 and then briefly in government, the party's main concern continued to be with protection, still entranced by the mirage of reversing 1846. Hopes remained of bringing back the Peelites and even Palmerston (like Derby a Canningite convert from Toryism in the 1820s, but one who then stayed with the Whigs); the leadership of Disraeli was in itself an obstacle to the healing of splits because of his own part in the fall of Peel and his regular rhetorical references even to the more distant splits of 1827–29. The fact that bad harvests and a trade depression encouraged the party to go on hoping for a restoration of the Corn Laws also contributed to keeping both Palmerston and the Peelites away. By-elections went well but proved highly misleading when the next general election was fought in 1852, in better economic conditions. This was a battle recognised by both sides as unusually important: it would settle whether or not there could be any going back on free trade, and as a result there were more contests than usual. Tory protectionists gained seats on balance but they were still about eighty seats short of a majority to restore protection. Although Derby found himself briefly in office until Whigs and Peelites could negotiate a new basis of co-operation, it was a tentative experiment by inexperienced ministers who dare not even try to bring back the Corn Laws. Thereafter, although wilder spirits on the back benches and in the agricultural shires continued to call for protection, it had passed from the realm of practical politics for the party leaders, who quietly resumed the name 'Conservative'. When a period of prosperous 'High Farming' followed in the countryside in the third quarter of the century, based on more intensive farming methods, even these wilder spirits were temporarily silenced. The reappearance of the name 'Conservative' symbolised not only the death of protection, but the recognition that the Peelites would not return. The party would have to restore its fortunes and its front bench without them.

The circumstances could hardly have been more unpromising

in the 1850s: Aberdeen's coalition government could rely on solid parliamentary backing; the country was beginning a period of prosperity in which industrial production surged ahead while food prices fell, hardly the basis for opposition optimism; the war policy against Russia in the Crimea was popular in the country and as the maladministration of the war effort dented that popularity it was Palmerston from within the government who reaped the benefit and not the opposition. The gradual coalescence of radicals, Whigs and Peelites into a single 'Liberal party' under Palmerston in and after 1859 made the task even more difficult. The Peelite–Liberal side of the Commons gained seats in 1857 and kept comfortable majorities in 1859 and 1865. Worse, these elections of mid-century were characterised by a general torpor, half the constituencies being uncontested each time, which demonstrated an even broader acquiescence in the status quo among the political nation. Palmerston's combination of popular policies abroad and a resistance to structural changes at home built a patriotic majority across the classes and generally retained the backing of his more advanced supporters without allowing scope to schemes which might antagonise the better off. It was a stance which could have been threatened only by a more radical strategy, and this the Conservatives were entirely unable to offer.

Nonetheless, the Conservatives retained throughout a strong second place and were always the leading force in rural England. They never fell below 250 MPs and had even at their lowest point the reliable support of most of the English and Welsh county members, and of a high proportion of members from the smaller boroughs in the south. Conservative as well as Liberal seats went uncontested in Palmerston's heyday, a tacit recognition that Conservatism was unassailable in its heartlands even if a minority nationally; the old Tory alliance of squire and parson had failed to retain control of Parliament in the 1840s, but still had sufficient authority and will power at the local level to keep their party alive and awaiting a change of circumstances in the 1850s. They also had in Disraeli a leader who, while forced to practise his considerable skills generally in opposition, never lost his ambition for office or his hope to place the Conservatives back in a dominant position. So although the Conservatives were overwhelmingly the rural party, they did not become the Country party with only an oppositional mentality. They retained a healthy appetite for power and its fruits; each of Derby's ministries produced an outpouring of patronage in the Conservative direction as nominations were tilted to their party's candidates. In 1868 Disraeli told Derby that 'you have done very well for your friends – 3 Garters, 4 Bishoprics, 8 Lord Lieutenancies, and almost the whole Bench in the three Kingdoms.' But it must be admitted that the Liberals were able to achieve similar results less provocatively because they occupied office for longer periods. Each ministry also demonstrated the growth of the front bench's capacity, both individually and collectively. Disraeli, as Chancellor of the Exchequer but no very learned political economist, was pitchforked in 1852 into areas where he could hardly shine in comparison with Gladstone or Peel and his speeches were derided as a result, but his later more experienced periods in office were less generally condemned – if still dominated more by politics than by policy. Since the party had only minority office, it was unable to carry important bills, but the opportunity to introduce government bills could be used for propaganda effect, and such uncontentious measures as the 1859 Act on trades unions, though passed with Liberal support, could be claimed as a legislative achievement. Younger men emerged too, untainted by the storms of 1828 or 1846, but gradually acquiring the knowledge necessary to make the front bench team a credible if still weaker alternative to the Liberals. This was specially important, for the possession of competent 'men of business', fit to be trusted with the administration of the country in a non-political context, had been one of the party's inheritances from Pitt and Liverpool, laboriously restored by Peel in the 1830s and lost with him in 1846. It was the more important from the 1850s as government itself became steadily more complex and as a sudden widening of informed political debate that followed a rapid increase in the circulations of newspapers made it even more important to show what a later age called 'fitness to govern.'

While Palmerston remained, the party could only fight to survive and plan for a future hope, but all this changed when Palmerston died in 1865. Firstly, it changed the balance of the Liberal government by removing the one man who could both hold it together and at the same time contain pressure for divisive reforms. He was succeeded as Prime Minister by Russell, now in the Lords, and by Gladstone leading the Commons. This opened a second opportunity, for Gladstone was to prove not only a Liberal leader who would provide issues on which conservative reaction could be mobilised against him – his disestablishment of the Irish Church even allowed the re-use of 'the Church in danger' approach last heard convincingly in the 1830s – but he was also deeply suspicious of Palmerstonian traditions in foreign policy, and he therefore left the field open for Disraeli to play the patriotic card. The time in which the new Liberal leader had to play himself into office was also a time in which industry and agriculture suffered their severest setbacks since the 1840s. Any political reaccommodation had to be accomplished against the backdrop of revived popular agitation for reform. Gladstone was in any case favourable to an extension of rights of political participation, especially if he were able to shape the course that it took; he believed that the 1832 franchise was not now sufficiently wide (though population growth and inflation had increased the electorate by more than 70 per cent since 1832, with no major legal changes). He believed that it would be both prudent to widen once again the base of political participation and morally just to extend the franchise to those in the skilled working class whose sober lifestyle and recent political quiescence had shown them to be 'worthy' of the vote, fit to be brought 'within the pale of the constitution' – a phrase from mediaeval Ireland that evoked images of the electorate as civilised settlers surrounded by savages without. Since Russell was no longer the 'Finality Jack' of 1837 but now also a supporter of franchise extension, Gladstone was able to proceed in 1866 to the major reform which Palmerston had blocked. He was aware that conservative Whigs like Robert Lowe were strongly opposed to such ideas, ready to see in the most moderate proposal the precursor of anarchistic democracy, but had hopes to limit a possible rebellion on his own side and to secure Conservative backing for a non-party bill. This was not implausible, for Conservatives like Liberals had talked much of the *idea* of franchise extension, and in minority office in 1859 Disraeli had himself introduced a bill, if more for the appearance than from any real intention of passing it; Conservatives had anyway little reason to fight to retain the system of 1832 under which they had enjoyed only one majority government in thirty-five years. Gladstone's principled conversion to reform therefore made him dependent on Conservative support and this at last provided Disraeli's opportunity.

Gladstone's franchise bill was opposed as too radical by Disraeli who saw in it a chance to split the Liberal government and party. As Conservatives rallied against the bill, Liberal opponents recognised that it could be defeated and united with Conservatives to throw it out. This not only denied Gladstone a triumph, but wrecked the Russell government so that Derby once more took minority office. However, popular opinion had been antagonised by the offer and then withdrawal of reform, and the rest of the crisis took place against constant public clamour for change, orchestrated by a powerful Reform League. Riots in Hyde Park were widely credited with pushing the Derby government into introducing reform, but this seems unlikely in itself; what such riots certainly did was to produce a general unease and lack of confidence in parliamentary circles, as in 1831–32, and to that extent may have helped to remove obstacles rather than create an impetus in the first place. The real problems for the new government were how to stay in office and how to answer the reasonable question of why Conservatives had opposed in 1866 what they had proposed in 1859. The solution to the first question was that only a Liberal split had created a Conservative government and it was therefore essential to the survival of Derby's government to keep open that split by prolonging debate on the issue that had caused it. The answer to the second question was to say that Conservatives were not against all reforms but only those detailed in 1866 – which prompted the next question as to what would they do themselves. It was therefore a tentative start: the government introduced resolutions instead of a bill, which gained them time and the appearance of action while keeping Liberals divided. But the response to the debate showed that most Conservatives would back reform if their own leaders introduced it, and the Cabinet therefore decided on what Derby called 'a leap in the dark', their own reform bill. Conservative MPs were in fact even more keen than the Cabinet on a bill, and a wide one at that, and Disraeli was only then converted to their view. He told Derby that 'the bold line is the safer one, and moreover . . . will be successful'. The bold line was to go for household suffrage – a vote for the head of all households of a set value in the boroughs (the mainly Liberal areas – changes in the Conservative counties were to be lesser), but with compensating 'fancy franchises' which would give additional voting power to property owners. This was more than Gladstone had offered, and was too much for three of the Cabinet who resigned, including Lord Cranborne (who as Salisbury was to be three times Conservative Prime Minister). Derby's authority was invaluable in getting replacements that included the Dukes of Marlborough and Richmond, two of the greatest Conservative grandees in the country, and the government had to surmount no more internal divisions.

Derby and Disraeli had nonetheless a problem not unlike Gladstone's – a divided party and therefore no control over the Commons. The difference was Disraeli's tactical skills, and the wish of his backbenchers to get *any* bill through rather than suffer further humiliation. Since conservative Liberals would not vote for the bill, Disraeli could pick up support only from radicals, who wanted the measure so badly as to accept it from anyone, and who could in any case amend it practically at will as the price of their support. The fancy franchises and other safeguards were therefore swept aside, and in the headlong pursuit of success the Conservatives swallowed it all, rejecting only proposals made from the Liberal leaders which might give back to Gladstone authority in the House. Derby's reputation and the positive influence of the Queen saw it through the Lords, and it became law. *The Economist's* Walter Bagehot wrote that while it might not be a good bill or a great bill, it was certainly Disraeli's bill: 'it was not a fraud itself which won, but fraud in a convenient place, and with singular ability.'

The change was quite considerable, for the electorate more than doubled to about two and a half million voters; somewhere around one third of adult men in Britain now had the vote, far less in Ireland, and there was a large working-class presence among potential voters for the first time. That in itself need not have frightened the Conservatives, for research into elections before the secret ballot came in in 1872 shows that they polled quite respectably among working-class voters. They had in any case determined the redistribution of parliamentary seats and the drawing up of new boundaries which shored up even further their rural strongholds and made life a little more difficult for the Liberals. Where expanding cities like Birmingham were given a third MP, the whole city was to remain a single constituency, but with each voter having only two votes – a hope that the Conservative minority would at the least take one seat in such places.

The necessity to stay in office until an electoral register had been compiled on the new basis gave the Conservatives more time to show what they could do, an opportunity that fell to Disraeli since Derby now retired; his recent triumph was enough to ensure Disraeli succeeded as Prime Minister. Minor and relatively non-contentious measures in public health, employment and factory laws were passed, but these could again be the basis of an electoral appeal, a better record of legislation than the party had within memory, and the Reform Act itself was a valuable asset in electioneering: the first annual report of the Metropolitan Conservative Working Men's Association observed in 1868 that the past year had been chiefly notable for 'the fact of a Conservative Government having given to the masses of the people what had been withheld from them by the Liberal party, namely, a voice in the legislation of this great empire.' The very fact of a working-men's organisation in London and its reference to 'this great empire' showed that Conservatives recognised in the non-parliamentary sphere the changed world which the death of Palmerston and the extension of the franchise had opened up. The imprisonment of missionaries in Ethiopia occasioned Disraeli's dispatch of a British expeditionary force to the interior of Africa; when the army accomplished its limited but expensive objectives, it returned home with flags waving and drums beating to a heroes' welcome in London – as extreme an example of Palmerstonianism as anything in the century. Disraeli himself went to Edinburgh to address a major political rally of supporters, an unusual carrying of the political battle outside London, but another harbinger of things to come: it was in Edinburgh of all places that Disraeli identified 'the Tory Party as the national Party of England'. Most significant of all was Disraeli's reaction to the Liberal majority elected at the

1868 general election: without even waiting to meet and be defeated by Parliament, Disraeli resigned and advised the Queen to send for Gladstone, so marking an important milestone. Sir Spencer Walpole called it 'the first open recognition in history that the House of Commons itself was of less importance than the electors who formed it.'

In a wider sense too 1867 marked the beginning of a new political world – not particularly because it was a Conservative success passed by Disraeli, for much of the wider impact would have been similar had Gladstone's 1866 bill become law. Firstly, the very fact of a *second* reform of the franchise dealt the death blow to any ideas of 'finality', for while 1832 could be plausibly defended as a once for all change, the second time could only be part of a series. As Lowe and Cranborne both argued, and as Ultra Tories had done in 1832, reform was now set on a path which would sooner or later introduce democratic government. Sometimes this objection was explicit: the reformer G. C. Brodrick argued sarcastically in the influential *Essays on Reform* (1867) that 'such a warning comes thirty years too late. It was the Reform Bill of 1832 that commenced the fatal descent towards democracy.' More conservative politicians, Whigs as well as Conservatives, would continue to resist further extensions of the franchise, but henceforth they knew that they could fight only a tactical battle of delay and not a genuine resistance. This in turn placed emphasis once again on the House of Lords and potentially on the monarchy too, as the only remaining curbs to 'democratic excess'.

The immediate impact was to intensify the battle for votes; the number of uncontested seats fell steadily at four successive elections after 1867, reaching the lowest point of the century in 1885 when only thirty-nine constituencies were not contested. This necessitated a drive to find suitable candidates, which had traditionally been run through the party whips and the Carlton and Reform Clubs, too unsystematic a method for the emerging era of mass politics. A Conservative Central Office was opened in 1870 to give a fully professional lead to the party organisation, previously in the hands of part-timers who were also lawyers, while the Liberals were moving in the same professionalising direction. Local supporters were encouraged to bring into being permanent political associations to raise money, enlist members and keep a close eye on the annual revision of electoral registers. This had begun in the 1830s under the similar impetus of the 1832 reform, but many of those local associations had not developed far beyond being rich men's dining clubs – except in such contentious times as 1846. They were now put on a standing basis, so as to socialise electors into partisanship between elections as well as during actual campaigns – what a Russian observer in the 1880s called 'social bribery'. Such methods were more successful in towns where traditional Conservatism was weak than in its county areas of strength; by 1874 there were associations in only half the English counties, and such strongholds as Dorset and Cambridgeshire were still resisting pressure to modernise their organisations. The secret ballot at elections introduced in 1872 made such methods even more vital, as did legal controls of election expenditure begun in 1883, only slightly effective at first but gradually driving corrupt and illegal practices to the margins of the electoral system. The parties therefore developed a new breed of professional political agent in the constituencies, an amalgam of lawyer, administrator, fund-raiser and propagandist, linked in a network of regional and national offices. Such developments of permanent organisation with paid staff gave encouragement to the arrival of party politics in local government too, though only in urban areas at first. The new local associations were federated so that members could feel a sense of involvement with what their national party was doing. Hence the National Union of Conservative Associations was formed in 1867 with strictly limited objectives, set up by the party's leaders as a supporters' club – or as a speaker at the inaugural conference called it 'rather . . . as a handmaid to the party than to usurp the functions of party leadership'. The assumption of permanent partisanship that professional standing organisations demonstrated in the 1880s was a world away from the quiet politics of twenty years earlier, more characteristic of the years around 1840 (albeit briefly) or of the reign of Queen Anne; it was in 1882 that W. S. Gilbert ironically suggested in *Iolanthe* that nature itself contrived that

> Every boy and every gal, that's born into the world alive,
> Is either a little Liberal, or else a little Conservative.

The enlistment of the nation into two political camps was also encouraged by means other than formal party organisation. The parties' head offices printed great quantities of election literature and posters for permanent political campaigning and assiduously courted the newspapers, both for the impact that such small circulation papers as *The Times* or the *Pall Mall Gazette* could have on informed opinion in Westminster, and such emerging giants as Lord Northcliffe's *Daily Mail* (first to top a million circulation, in the 1890s) for the range of their readership. 'Press barons', rewarded for services to party but conscious of their independent power were major figures requiring regular attention from ministers and would-be ministers by the end of the century; Lord Northcliffe believed that he had it in his power to tell the nation what to think, and though generally Conservative in support he was far from predictable on individual issues. The recognition that the increased readership of the newspapers expected a different sort of news-making from politicians was shown by the new readiness of both Gladstone and Disraeli to take politics out of Westminster to the provinces. Gladstone's provincial tours of 1862 and Disraeli's Edinburgh visit of 1868 were followed by a series of major Conservative rallies in opposition, notably at the Crystal Palace in London and in Manchester's Free Trade Hall. These used the large audiences that could be gathered by the newly extended party organisation to create a momentum for the party, but they were far more important for the millions who read about them than for the thousands who attended in person. Platform politics, previously the preserve of radical pressure groups, was becoming an integral part of politics for party leaders. Gladstone's meetings on the Bulgarian issue in 1876 and in his 'Midlothian Campaigns' of 1879–80 were similar in appealing *through* meetings of supporters to the wider reading public. Electoral politics in the 1870s was highly personalised around the figures of Gladstone and Disraeli; it had been common practice for candidates to seek letters of endorsement from well-known national figures, but this now went much further to local candidates seeking election to Parliament 'on the coat tails' of national leaders. Gladstone's Lord Chancellor thought the Midlothian meetings 'very remarkable, but it was a precedent tending in its results to the degradation of British politics, by bringing in a system of permanent canvass, and removing the political centre of gravity from Parliament to the platform'. *The Economist* noted in 1871 that 'the power of addressing twenty five thousand people for two hours and holding their attention' would now 'give a vast advantage in the political race to any statesman.' Politics came to be seen less and less as the practice of local partisanships in different constituencies and more and more as a single national battle for power; in 1880 many newspapers wrote of '*the* general election' rather than using the traditional phrase 'general elections', a semantic change of considerable import in the nationalisation of politics. The actual change was much slower than the mere choice of words might imply, with different localities polling on different days until 1918 and retaining a strongly localist affiliation well into the 1920s, but the trend was in a constant direction.

The growing primacy of national issues and an increasing use of national organisations to propagate them had a further constitutional implication, partly recognised by Disraeli's 1868 resignation. If there was to be a direct appeal to the people, and if governments could be brought down directly by election results, then it would be important to define the relationship between national leaders and electors. Politicians were thus forced to evolve the theory of the 'mandate' by which power had been given in return for specific pledges, a new concept among ministerial politicians in Britain though a familiar enough idea in the USA and to British radicals. The entire logic of leaving Westminster to appeal to the people implied that politicians would have something specific to say that related to electors' decisions about how votes were cast. The Conservative Lord Salisbury conceded in a public meeting in Liverpool in 1882 that such meetings 'can give an impulse to the public policy of the nation which is, in some degree, independent of the actions of its representatives at Westminster.' He went on to argue that the danger that this might allow the evolution of an elective dictatorship justified the continued power of an unelected House of Lords. Radicals in both parties could use the idea of mandates to promote 'programme politics' whereby specific promises would be described as a virtual contract with the voters, though ministers and likely ministers still saw such ideas as trenching on their freedom of manoeuvre in office. Victoria was keen to warn Gladstone in 1879 of 'the *extreme* danger of binding themselves by foolish, violent declarations about their policy beforehand . . . as change is so disagreeable and bad for the country.' The Queen, suspicious of Peel in 1839 had moved well to the right in the course of her reign, much more appreciative of Disraeli's attentions than of Gladstone's stiffness towards her. She retained a lively and detailed involvement in political events.

More immediately party whips could use the idea to enforce a unity in the parliamentary voting lobbies that was almost unknown in the mid-century 'golden age of the independent Member'. If votes were being won by a national appeal by party leaders then it was extremely difficult for MPs to claim such independence as Burke had claimed in the 1770s except on key issues of conscience. The trend towards party cohesion in the lobbies was also encouraged by the increasing complexity of government, the consequent need to pass more legislation and the necessity of doing that quickly if parliamentary sittings were not to occupy more than half the year. In the 1850s, whips (representing leaders' advice to their supporters on how to vote) were issued for only two-thirds of parliamentary votes, generally for issues treated by governments as of particular importance, while on the rest MPs were free to do as they liked; by the 1890s, whips were issued on almost every clause and every amendment. Not only did the whips' advice become more regular, so did their success in having their advice heeded. In 1860, in votes for which whips were issued, almost as many Liberal and Conservative MPs voted against their parties as for them; in the 1890s, nineteen out of twenty MPs of both parties were backing their leaders – an average figure which conceals a far greater degree of solidarity on issues of real importance. The freedom of MPs was further restricted in 1882 by the introduction of the first standing orders to limit debate. Obstruction of debate by Irish MPs was the ideal justification for this, but the need of governments to control the timetable of the Commons as well as the result of votes had been growing for some time. Thereafter government control grew steadily until by the turn of the century the timetable was effectively at the disposal of government whips, with the opposition reduced to choosing subjects for debate on a few specified days and with individual MPs having little room left to initiate or affect legislation except through their parties.

Such developments were well in the future when Disraeli returned to opposition in 1868. After the exhilaration of the 1867 triumph and the period in office his heavy election defeat was a grave disappointment, and doubts began to be expressed whether Disraeli had not been wrong to carry a franchise extension which might actually have further weakened the Conservative position. In fact the Conservatives were not yet ready to mount a serious bid for a parliamentary majority; their party organisation had scarcely begun to catch up with the recent changes – in 1868 a third of the constituencies still went uncontested; they had not yet put across effectively the Conservative identity to the mass electorate; most importantly, there had not yet been a lasting Liberal government since Palmerston's death which would give them anything much to oppose. Properly evaluated 1868 was probably as good a result as the party might have hoped for, and it contained a few straws which showed the way that the wind would blow: in working-class East London, Tower Hamlets, not even contested in 1865, elected a Conservative as one of its MPs; W. H. Smith, the wealthy wholesale newsagent who had been a Palmerstonian and had switched parties only in 1865, now gained for the Conservatives Westminster, the former stronghold of Fox, and Francis Place, a symbolic shift of loyalties which showed the impact both of social change and a growing Conservative strength in London as a whole. Smith was an Anglican and hence differentiated from many of his social background, but his move to the right was to be followed by many who in previous generations would have been radicals, men who now saw an increasingly democratic electoral system as a threat to their property. In opposition, Disraeli's strategy was to set forth his own position, use the expanding party organisation to make more voters aware of it, and await the harvest of support that would come from those alienated by Liberal reforms.

The claim that the mature Disraeli was also a social reformer rests on two major speeches of 1872 and on the legislation passed between 1874 and 1876, none of which gives strong support to the argument. His Crystal Palace speech in particular became a familiar definition of the principles on which popular Conservatism was based, much re-visited by Conservatives of later generations. As summarised in party literature, it enunciated a three-cornered policy of objectives: to maintain and preserve the institutions of the country, to uphold 'the empire of England', and to 'elevate' the condition of the people. This last social reforming passage of the speech occupied only a fraction of its overall length, was unspecific in promises and concentrated on comparing the irrelevance of Gladstone's secret ballot proposals with the vital need for public health improvements – 'a policy of sewage' – as if the two could not be combined. But the weight of the speech fell in any case on the first two objectives. A promise to uphold the institutions effectively claimed the monarchy, the House of Lords, the Church, army, law courts, landholding and other vested interests which Liberalism sought to attack as Conservative spheres of influence. The 'empire of England' did not imply territorial expansionism, merely a promise to don the mantle of Palmerston in defending British prestige. In this sense the Crystal Palace speech like the entire period of opposition was conceived more with an appeal to the disaffected and frightened middle class in mind than as an uninhibited bid for working-class votes, though the social reform and 'empire' issues both provided material that could be exploited for working-class votes too. Disraeli was walking a tightrope, for more affluent middle-class recruits would be easier to associate with the party's more traditional support than would working-class voters who might be increasingly important as time passed; in opposition the circle could be squared, but in government it would take all of Disraeli's 'one nation' ideas and all his tactical skills to bind together such conflicting objectives.

Even in opposition, it was often easier to take refuge in attacking the Gladstone government than in articulating alternatives. Sometimes Conservative MPs could use their voting strength to moderate measures which Liberal MPs found too tame, as in the 1870 Education Act, or in offering cross-party support on constitutional issues such as the Ballot in 1872; more often the tactic was to oppose. The benefits of such a negative stance were considerable, as the government lost by-elections steadily throughout its life, but the best case came with the Licensing Act of 1871, where Conservative opposition to a Liberal measure brought a substantial addition of support. Before this time the drink industry had been broadly split between Conservatives and Liberals with wide regional and local variations, though the Liberals had encompassed an increasing number of temperance reformers;

after 'the trade' was incensed by the Licensing Act, it became an overwhelmingly Conservative interest. Gladstone himself attributed his 1874 defeat to being 'borne down in a torrent of gin and beer', and while this was undoubtedly an exaggeration, there is no doubt that the considerable influence of the brewers was now against the Liberals; brewers appeared in increasing numbers on the Conservative benches in both Houses and the industry contributed heavily to party funds and has done so ever since – the heaviest and most consistent backing ever given by any industry to a British party. Equally the pubs – and especially the political clubs which the brewers supplied – provided a solid base for working-class Conservatism at the local level, an alternative political culture to the life of chapel, trades unions and mechanics' institutes around which much of working-class Liberalism revolved.

There was a considerable improvement in party organisation while in opposition, involving in particular a concentration of effort on the registration, a bonus which the electoral system allowed well-run and well-financed parties to claim until 1918. There were also more candidates for the 1874 election than in 1868 and a much better run campaign, but it was probably the voters' antagonism to Liberal measures that did most to generate the Conservative victory. Overall the Conservatives returned with a majority of about fifty, the first majority Conservative government elected since 1841. Disraeli reflected the broadening base of Conservative support in the composition of his government, making the middle-class Richard Cross Home Secretary responsible for most of the domestic legislation, and in due course adding W. H. Smith to the team as First Lord of the Admiralty – an appointment which, as Gilbert observed in *HMS Pinafore*, reflected less a specialist choice than a signal to those whom Smith represented. But the majority of the government team was from more traditional Conservative stock, and much would in any case depend on Disraeli's own initiatives, for the election victory had raised him to a pinnacle of party authority. Cross himself was surprised to find that, despite all his opposition speeches, Disraeli had no agenda of social proposals to introduce, and he was thus thrown back on his own ideas and those of his officials. Nonetheless, the first three sessions did produce a considerable quantity of domestic legislation. In 1874 there was a Factory Act which further restricted employment hours for women and children; in 1875 came the Public Health Act, providing for 'a policy of sewage', controls of food and drugs, a measure to control friendly societies, trades union reforms which clarified the law in allowing 'peaceful picketing', and – domestic centre-piece of the whole government – the Artisans' Dwellings Act which authorised the first slum clearance programmes. Cross's Cabinet paper describing the bill saw it as providing 'an easy and effective process' whereby waste land and property could be acquired and cleared to allow the building of 'a class of houses suited to the requirements and limited means of the labouring classes'. In 1876 came an act regulating co-operative societies, a Merchant Shipping Act to provide for better safety at sea, and an act extending educational entitlement.

There are difficulties in evaluating this programme: how generous were the measures themselves? Why did they stop in 1876 when the government ran on to 1880? How far did they contribute to Conservative support? The measures were often narrow in scope, originated from officials or back-benchers, and had limited application: factory acts and shipping acts could be effective only if they were adequately enforced; the statutes were generally 'permissive', allowing local councils to improve sewage or to clear slums, but making nothing compulsory and providing no cash to fund such schemes; other reforms codified or regulated existing structures but initiated little. Cross argued for the Artisans' Dwellings Act in Cabinet by reminding ministers that though local authorities would be obliged to receive medical reports on housing schemes, 'it does not also compel them to make a scheme if there be difficulty on financial grounds.' Disraeli neatly presented permissive legislation as 'the characteristic of a free people', for 'in a free country, and especially in England, you must trust to persuasion and example . . . if you wish to effect any considerable change in the manners and customs of the people.' The reason that reforms ran out in 1876 has been variously attributed to the obstruction practised by Irish MPs which made it increasingly difficult to get any legislation through and to the increasing concentration of the government on foreign and imperial measures. Disraeli himself had never shown a passionate personal commitment to reform, but his promotion to the Lords as Earl of Beaconsfield may also have contributed to the loss of impetus. A government run on such a loose rein was unlikely to maintain momentum when ministers and their officials ran out of ideas: Salisbury was convinced that the government lost its way through having 'at the head of affairs a statesman whose only political principle was that the Party must on no account be broken up'. But it is hard to find evidence that other plans were in existence and held up by these obstacles. In the later 1870s, when the onset of the 'great depression' actually increased the need for measures of social amelioration at least in the countryside, the Disraeli government had little to offer except the advice that the state of the economy made this a bad time to interfere in industry – Disraeli had become a Peelite from this viewpoint. Nonetheless, the catalogue of reforms and the chorus of approval that had greeted them could be listed in a Conservative leaflet of 1880 as *What the Conservatives have done for the British People*, a leaflet almost continuously in print thereafter (though with a less patronising title substituted after 1945). The TUC had passed a resolution of thanks to Cross in 1875, with one delegate describing his work as 'the greatest boon ever given to the sons of toil'; the radical Birmingham mayor Joseph Chamberlain had said of the Artisans' Dwellings Act that it had 'done more for the town of Birmingham than had been done in twenty preceding years of Liberal legislation', and a Lib–Lab MP argued in 1879 that 'Conservatives have done more for the working classes in five years than the Liberals have in fifty.' Such pamphlet tributes were certainly wrenched out of context and owed much to comparison with the Liberals' equally limited record, but they made all the same a good electioneering appeal. When repeated over successive elections they can hardly have failed to have an impact in persuading working class voters that the Conservatives were the true heirs of Sadler, Oastler and Shaftesbury; in this electioneering battle the Conservative record looked the more impressive because there was little more that could be attributed to Liberals. Whatever the reality there is no doubt that after the 1874 government Conservatives themselves believed that they were a party with a creditable reform record and approached working-class voters for support without inhibition, possibly Disraeli's greatest contribution to Conservatism in the long term.

There is in any case no reason to doubt that the events of the second half of the government on the international scene were equally valuable in building support. Disraeli's strong response to Russian expansionism yielded a diplomatic triumph at the Congress of Berlin in 1878. The great coup by which Disraeli bought for Britain a major shareholding in the Suez Canal in 1875 was soon built up as one of the romances of the British Empire. Disraeli himself had had a highly ambivalent personal attitude to colonial development, but now seemed to undergo something of a change of heart. Afghan and Zulu Wars were not begun by his government as such – like most such events they owed more to the men on the frontiers than to decisions in London – but they were pursued enthusiastically when once begun and celebrated after victory. The greatest coup of all came with the addition of 'Empress of India' to Victoria's royal titles, a gesture of little importance in India (except to the independent princes) but of the first importance as a fulfilment of Disraeli's first two Crystal Palace objectives. It certainly pleased the Queen herself who had pressed for the change, and may be the greatest of all examples of Disraeli's own maxim that monarchs must be flattered on a grand scale. The reality of British colonial and imperial policies was not advanced much by Disraeli's premiership, but the domestic rhetoric changed considerably; he has with justice been called 'the impresario of Empire'. The upholding and demonstration of British power was as valuable a vote-winner for Disraeli as for Palmerston, especially as he unlike Palmerston was faced by an opposition that criticised many of his more patriotic gestures and appeared also to act differently in office. When Disraeli and Salisbury returned in triumph from Berlin in 1878, a Liberal journalist sourly noted the political credit that they extracted from the event: 'at the Charing Cross railway station there was a great gathering . . . which was turned for a time into a flower garden, and the Plenipotentiaries stepped from the train in a shower of bouquets'; after Disraeli had reported 'peace with honour', and threw in 'renewed prosperity to the people' for good measure, Salisbury concluded with 'an appeal to the multitude always to support a government which supports the honour of England.'

By 1880, Disraeli was ageing fast and his government was running out of steam. The agricultural depression which had followed the international collapse of food prices hit Conservative support hard in the party's best areas, a threat to which the government had no answer. The Liberals were campaigning hard and unitedly behind Gladstone, with a fervour which denounced 'Beaconsfieldism' as morally corrupt. Misled by the successful result in a couple of by-elections, Disraeli called an election and lost it heavily. Disraeli himself died in the following year, still the hero of his party, for despite the 1880 defeat he had left it far stronger than in 1847. The party had surmounted the first surge of political change towards democracy and had evolved a twin programme of unapologetic patriotism and limited domestic reform that was to win strong support in the next generation. *The Times* noted in its obituary of Disraeli that he had perceived potential Conservative strength in the inchoate mass of the working class as a sculptor sees an angel imprisoned in a block of marble. Insofar as 'Tory Democracy' was about associating popular support with Toryism, he had achieved much. The limitations were though considerable. In the years after Disraeli's death, a more radical group of younger men led by Lord Randolph Churchill tried to use the party apparatus to enforce a genuinely radical policy on the leadership: though they were (briefly) able to take control of the machinery of the National Union, they succeeded only in demonstrating that the party outside Parliament had no effective power to enforce anything on the parliamentarians. The mass membership achieved by the party was without power, and seems not to have seriously expected any; the local parties recruited members as much through narrowly local and social means as for any overtly political purpose, most of them depending for their financial health on contributions from a few rich men. As for the membership, the greatest problem according to a senior agent at the end of the 1880s was 'to keep them amused'. Nonetheless this mass membership party of limited commitment and limited liability did succeed in involving very large numbers indeed. The Primrose League, founded shortly after Disraeli's death to promote Conservative support and named after his favourite colour and flower, was a feudal, hierarchical and institutionally snobbish organisation, the epitome of all that was backward-looking: it was able to claim (if with some exaggeration) over two million members in 1910 – a membership rather larger than that of all the trades unions in the TUC at that time. The Association of Conservative Clubs, most of whose affiliated members were working men's drinking clubs, claimed at the same time about a million members, though its affairs were entirely in the hands of a paid secretary working at Central Office and a committee nominated by such gentlemen's clubs as the Carlton. Toryism might still not be even remotely democratic but there was no denying the width and diversity of its popular base.

15 Victorian Liberalism, 1850s to 1886

For two decades after the Corn Law crisis of 1846 parliamentary politics were fragmented in a series of unstable governments at the mercy of unreliable majorities in the Commons and of independent action by the Lords. With hindsight and nostalgia this was seen as 'the golden age of the independent member', contrasting with the organised partisan battles of the 1830s. As early as 1846 Lord John Russell had drawn attention to the 'much greater agreement in opinion' and the 'much greater identity of conduct' between ministries and their supporting party in recent years than earlier: 'I do not think that it is an attempt likely to be successful again, or to be advantageous to the country.' In 1872 on the other hand Disraeli asserted that 'without party parliamentary government is impossible.' In the quarter century between these opposed views – each typical of the current of thought in their time, there were nine ministries. Russell headed two Liberal ministries and two were led by Palmerston, there was a coalition under the Peelite Aberdeen, three minority Conservative administrations, and from 1868 a Liberal government under Gladstone. By comparison the seventeen years between the 1867 and 1884 reform acts witnessed only three new ministries. But the change should not be exaggerated – Liberal governments in particular continued to be unstable, fractious groupings for the rest of the century. These middle years produced a continuous though unsteady drift back to a two-party alignment – and even that was true only of Great Britain, for Ireland moved almost entirely outside the mainstream of British party politics in the same period. The catalyst for change was the Conservative split of 1846 and the period that ensued before Peel's free trade followers were able to find a permanent political home in a reconstructed Liberalism.

At first the 'Peelites', a group defined more by their support for Peel than by their views on policy, continued to regard themselves as Conservatives and to anticipate an eventual return to their old party. This was prevented by Peel's own reluctance to heal recent wounds, but also by the refusal of the Conservatives' protectionist majority to accept that the corn law decision of 1846 was final. The longer that Peelites were accustomed to support Whigs in office, the less they were likely to feel that the Conservatives were the friends with whom they must eventually reunite. Peel's death in 1850 and the eulogies to his reputation that followed fixed his above-party identity in the popular mind, and so made it even more difficult for his disciples to revert to Conservatism; but this also freed Peelites to go elsewhere without his restraint.

The first important step came in the ministerial crisis of 1851–52. The inability of Whigs and radicals, generally now described together as 'Liberals', to remain united in office produced a short Conservative minority government. The refusal of the Peelites to join Derby in office marked an important step on the road to realignment. After ten months, Whigs and Peelites combined in coalition government under Aberdeen, their first experience of working together in cabinet. Aberdeen himself already anticipated that the two groups must eventually fuse into one party, favouring 'Liberal–Conservative' as a new name, but expected that it would be a long process. Others were more cautious, Russell counting the members of the proposed administration and finding that there were too many Peelites and not enough 'of the old Liberal party (I must not say Whig)'. These suspicions were in part deflected by including more Whigs and by the experience of actually working together; Gladstone maintained that the Aberdeen Cabinet did not work in a way that showed its 'dual origin', and the Duke of Argyll felt an immediate 'sense of comradeship'. The ministry was in fact riven by personal battles, but not between the factions which had come together to create it.

In policy too the Aberdeen government may be seen as a forerunner of Liberalism to come. Important legal reforms were passed, including the phasing out of the system of transportation to the colonies as a regular form of punishment. Education was to be a centre-piece of the government's policy: increased grants were planned in 1853 in a bill which would have done much that was eventually left until 1870; the bill fell foul of denominational cross-currents, another link with times past and a sign of things to come, but was eventually lost as a financial casualty of the Crimean War. More generally, as *The Times* predicted when war began, 'the duties of a War Ministry and a Reform Ministry are totally incompatible.' The Northcote–Trevelyan committee of investigation into the civil service was set up by Gladstone in 1853 and produced a scathing report on the country's administration; it was particularly critical of the system whereby appointments were made by patronage rather than on merit, an indictment accepted by *The Times* which wrote of the need to 'put an end to the barter of places for support, and to all that network of solicitation and intrigue'. Such views were soon reinforced by the mismanagement of the war, but the war itself had to have first call on the Cabinet's energies and reduced the impetus for domestic change. Although some of the Northcote–Trevelyan proposals were half-heartedly introduced in 1855, it was not until Gladstone was himself Prime Minister that a full system of entry to the home civil service by competitive examination was adopted in 1870.

Gladstone's role at the Exchequer was crucial to the government's strategy, with his 1853 budget widely compared to Peel's great budget of 1842. Much of his work was technical and administrative, but in at least two areas there were important policy initiatives: in taxation policy, he finally ended stamp duty and advertisement duty for newspapers, much resented as 'taxes on knowledge', and so encouraged a cheaper press with a wider readership. While continuing to profess like Peel the intention to abolish income tax, he widened its scope by lowering the level of income at which it was levied, and so made it bear on a wider cross-section of the people. Gladstone saw this widening of direct taxation, still paid only by the better off, as a guarantee to the poorer (who contributed a large share of the yield of indirect taxes) that their exclusion from the franchise would not disadvantage them; extending direct tax to a bigger proportion of those who had votes had the added advantage of building a political barrier against government extravagance. In these ways, the Aberdeen government seems a transitional phase between Peel's attempt to build on the legacy of Pitt and Liverpool in the 1840s, and the Gladstonian Liberalism of the 1870s. It proved a false start only because the government was broken up by the Crimean War and by the restlessness of Palmerston. Although Palmerston's main disagreements (and his very temporary resignation in 1854) were ostensibly over foreign and diplomatic policy, Aberdeen at least thought •that domestic issues were the greater concern: Peelites who had been Conservatives only a few years earlier were now pressing domestic reform at a faster rate than some Whigs were comfortable with.

The later part of the Crimean War, and particularly its successful outcome, made Palmerston's domestic position unassailable for a time, but the basis of his dominance was not one that commended itself to Peelites, who were therefore out of office again by the end of 1855. They now found themselves in mid-ocean; the Conservatives were no longer protectionist, and hence there was no great issue of policy to bar their return, but there was considerable distrust of the political morality of Disraeli. There was on the other hand the memory of office recently shared with Whigs, but many of these Whigs now served with Palmerston, while Peelites disliked and distrusted Palmerston almost as much as Disraeli. In the meantime, as Gladstone wrote, 'the interval between the two greater parties has, by the practical solution of so many congested questions, been very greatly narrowed'. The decision whether to go forward to Liberalism or back to the Conservatives was decided in 1858–59, mostly by attitudes to the actual holding of office.

Gladstone was by this time the senior figure among Peelites, and it was Aberdeen's advice that persuaded Gladstone against rejoining the Conservatives. One difficulty was the fact that Disraeli must be leader of the Commons in any new Conservative ministry, and Gladstone could not imagine being able to work harmoniously with him; but beyond matters of personality there was a common attitude to government itself which the Peelites now knew that they shared with Whigs but not with most Conservatives. They could agree with the Whigs on the need for an efficient, professional administration, for economy in the expenditure of public funds, for the treating of office as a public trust and the professing of an elevated political morality that contrasted sharply with Disraeli's undisguised cynicism. This fundamental seriousness of attitude to government was even a link with Palmerston, who appointed ministers mainly on merit, even promoting radicals whose policies he strongly disliked. The experience of office under Aberdeen and of exclusion from it after 1855 convinced the Peelites that they were natural men of government; Gladstone in 1857 'greatly felt being turned out of office. I saw great things to do. I longed to do them. I am losing the best years of my life out of my natural service.' He worked out some of these frustrations by designing a practical agenda of reforms that he would push through if he returned to the Treasury. Peelites doubtless also reflected on the fact that they were voluntarily denying themselves the considerable salaries paid to ministers – Gladstone earned £5,000 a year as Chancellor of the Exchequer.

Having refused to join the Conservatives when they again returned to minority office in 1858 after Palmerston's Whig cabinet fell apart, Peelites could now only join the Whigs or stay in permanent opposition. Although Palmerston's foreign policies remained an objection, there was hope that a stronger cabinet might be able to moderate them, and that Palmerston's great interest in diplomacy would leave determined ministers a freer hand in the domestic field. A foreign issue provided the basis on which co-operation could be agreed, the first of many from outside the mainstream of domestic politics that would be used to rally Liberalism. It became necessary to reach a view on the emerging unification of Italy, a question on which Palmerston took a more 'liberal' view than the Conservatives; a meeting of Whig, radical and Peelite MPs agreed that this was a basis on which to turn the Conservatives out of office and form a united government. It was this parliamentary, office-broking deal which brought about the final Palmerston government in which Peelites participated fully, Gladstone again taking the Exchequer. The press correctly saw this as the end of the period of re-alignment. It was in fact the six years of subsequent government until Palmerston's death which confirmed the fusion of separate groups into one parliamentary Liberal party.

The combination under Palmerston was sometimes a stormy one – Gladstone regularly threatening resignation – but was largely justified by the fact that an active domestic policy was carried on despite Palmerston, as it had not been before 1858. The linchpin was again Gladstone at the Exchequer, where he was able to carry through most of his private agenda of financial reforms. Some of these were again technical and procedural, though no less important for that: he consolidated the year's financial legislation into a single finance bill following the annual budget debate and introduced a Public Accounts Committee of the Commons so that MPs would have a better mechanism for overseeing government expenditure, a surer means of enforcing economy. Over time this and other reforms which aimed at improving 'treasury control' prolonged the situation whereby British government was cheap by international standards, if allowance is made for the costs of keeping up a world position: the proportion of gross national product taken for government expenditure fell from about 10 per cent in 1860 to 6½ per cent in 1875, then rose only slightly to the end of the century. But these trends may indicate at least as much about changing rates of economic growth as they do about government spending. Other reforms continued previous policies; duties on paper were abolished in 1861, so finally removing taxes which had kept newspapers artificially expensive.

The move towards free trade was accelerated by Gladstone and partly through the free trade treaty with France negotiated by Cobden in 1860; about four hundred tariff duties were abolished, leaving only fifteen. The few items still subject to duties were those like tea, sugar and beer which were widely consumed and which thus produced a significant revenue; consumption taxes therefore applied relatively evenly across the classes, while direct taxes were payable only by the well off. Over the series of reforming budgets introduced by Peel and Gladstone, the proportion of government revenue contributed by indirect taxpayers fell steadily, and continued to fall in later years; in the early 1840s indirect taxes provided about three-quarters of total revenue, but by 1870 it was under two-thirds, and by the end of the century only about half. These drives for reform – some of them carried against the opposition of much of the Cabinet and of the Lords – not only improved procedures but also created a strong momentum for the government; Gladstone argued that 'public opinion is disposed to view with great favour all active and efficient government'. They also made Gladstone himself the government's star performer, especially in relation to social and economic issues which were less remote from popular attention than were the diplomatic questions on which Palmerston and Russell concentrated. When Palmerston died in 1865, he was succeeded by the aged Russell, but Gladstone led for the government in the Commons and was now the real driving force; since he was 56 and Russell 73, he was clearly heading for leadership of the parliamentary Liberals and the premiership.

The period since 1846 had also witnessed a more fundamental political change on the progressive side of politics; it is appropriate to see the formation of the Liberal party in terms of parliamentary manoeuvrings, but that is only part of the story. The Victorian Liberal party also functioned outside parliament, and whereas the party structures of Disraelian Conservatism were largely artificial creations subservient to the parliamentarians, Liberalism in the country was self-generating and self-sustaining. 'The Liberal Party' was therefore the union of two independent worlds, a union always potentially explosive, always gaining supporters as well as always losing them, never in a state of normality or equilibrium. Popular Liberalism was essentially provincial – the party always had difficulties in establishing a firm base in London – and was the delayed outcome of industrial and religious changes earlier in the century.

The industrial revolution had transformed the nature of manu-facturing towns and of many of their inhabitants; by the middle of the century, each town had its wealthy manufacturers, secure enough from the proceeds of their predecessors' efforts to be able to spend time away from the family businesses and confident enough in their powers to have political ambitions that went beyond their native towns. Most such manufacturers were nonconformists who saw themselves as still suffering from civil disabilities (though most legal restrictions had been removed); their decision to enter politics was frequently motivated by sharp consciousness of relative status and a desire to advance themselves, their co-religionists and their class. This reforming impulse, however limited in practical matters ensured that there was common ground with the craftsmen and skilled workers of their towns, men they met in the chapel on Sundays and who also resented the legal barriers to their further progress. Neither group was as yet much worried by a political threat from unskilled workers.

While nonconformity provided much of the fuel for popular Liberalism, its association with parliamentary Liberals was facilitated by wider religious changes. Although Methodists and other dissenting groups had the field largely to themselves in spreading the gospel to new industrial towns in the 1780s, by the early nineteenth century, the Church of England was anxious to catch up. This was demonstrated by the 1818 Church Building Act, but it was also shown by the ferment of theology and belief that wracked Anglicanism in and after the 1830s. One aspect of this was the Tractarian controversy that originated from Oxford University and which led a number of prominent Victorians to convert to Catholicism and many more to go through spiritual torments before deciding not to do so. But what united all Anglicans, and particularly those who had been through the old universities since the ferment began, was a strength of Christian conviction that was a world away from the easy-going Anglicanism of the eighteenth century. There was a considerable religious revival right across Britain. The number of Catholic priests in England tripled between 1830 and 1863 (influenced in part by immigration from Ireland), while the number of convents and monasteries rose from 24 to 217; Baptist membership doubled over the same period, and rates of participation in other sects also showed spectacular increases. Bernard Shaw wrote of this period of his youth that 'religion was alive again, coming back upon men, even upon clergymen, with such power that not the Church of England itself could keep it out.' The change must not be exaggerated, for the religious census of 1851 demonstrated both the limits of the revival and the continuing relative vitality of the free churches: well under half the population attended a church on the day of the count, and the Church of England accounted for only about half of the total. Nevertheless, there is no doubt that a change both qualitative and quantitive had taken place in the country's religious life.

This began to have an impact on the House of Commons only after mid-century, as men who had converted to militant Christianity as young men reached the climax of their careers. Parliament therefore gradually caught up with the more religious tone of the country. It was claimed in 1861 that there were over three million abstainers in the country; one radical MP estimated that there was only one total abstainer from drink in the Commons in 1865, but that this had risen to over twenty by 1885. The combination of militant nonconformity and a more distinctively Christian country had important consequences for Liberalism. On the one hand nonconformists could recognise fellow believers in such Anglicans as Lord Selborne – who when Lord Chancellor also continued as a Sunday School teacher. The language of conviction and the vocabulary of the pulpit helped to cross sectarian divides and bind Liberalism together. The essential seriousness of religious men of all denominations also chimed in well with the elevated political morality which the Peelites had brought to parliamentary Liberalism.

The vehicles that brought popular Liberalism into being were good causes for which campaigning organisations emerged, and which to a greater or lesser extent sank their combined efforts in the party. The Liberation Society sought the freeing of nonconformists from their disabilities, and the disestablishment of the Anglican Church; the U.K. Alliance, led by Sir Wilfrid Lawson, pressed for controls on the sale of alcohol, even for prohibition; the agitation against the Contagious Diseases Acts mobilised moral pressure against the government for condoning prostitution in military towns; the National Education League argued for an extension of schooling taken outside Anglican control. These various groups often shared a common membership, but each had its central aim, its whole reason for existence, which made compromise in the pursuit of realistic policies difficult to achieve. As a temperance man argued in 1873, 'questions of right and wrong are involved, and therefore political-expediency doctrines . . . cannot . . . be taken into account.' Lawson himself argued that he wanted 'above everything to get a sober people, and if we get that, all these questions about county franchise, disestablishment &c we shall fight out much better . . . than if we refer them to the decision of an intoxicated people'; the disestablishment lobby replied that the resistance of the Church was such that *no* useful reforms would be carried until it was out of the way, and then 'all the other things will follow as a matter of course.' This conflict between Liberals for the priority of their pet causes was to remain an inhibiting factor almost as long as the Liberals were a major party, but it was only the conviction that these moral crusades inspired that made many men Liberals at all. It was such pressure groups for reform that provided the party with a local organisation which the parliamentarians could create in no other way.

The enthusiasm of provincial Liberals, pressing for good and mainly nonconformist causes, was also a matter of status within their own local communities. Many industrial towns had vicious internal battles for local control, battles that often involved non-electors as much as voters; shopkeepers might be systematically driven out of business by threats and by boycotts from supporters of the other party, struggles that had very little to do with parliamentary politics or national policy: a Huddersfield poem spoke darkly of the 'terrible might of working men's votes on a Saturday night.' Dickens ironically described such a divided town in *The Pickwick Papers*:

'every man in Eatanswill . . . felt himself bound to unite, heart and soul, with one of the two great parties that divided the town – the Blues and the Buffs. Now . . . whenever the Buffs and the Blues met together at Town Hall, fair or market, disputes and high words arose between them . . . Everything in Eatanswill was made a party question . . . There were Blue shops and Buff shops, Blue inns and Buff inns – there was a Blue aisle and a Buff aisle in the very church itself.' When Gladstone's son won the seaport constituency of Whitby for the Liberals, it was not just a battle between national parties but also a fight between local railway and fishing interests, each with their local client groups of employees, contractors and consumers. Victory in that sort of contest meant that social relationships in Whitby itself would never be the same again. The real mainstay of urban Liberalism were the skilled manual workers enfranchised in 1832 and especially in 1867, still both recognising the leadership of their town's industrial leaders and urging the removal of privileges which they associated with the Church and the land. For such men the fact of an election victory would be more important than anything that Parliament did as a result of it. The same fierce partisanship was not yet dividing communities in the support of organised sport, a development only from the 1880s; politics in the 1860s could still have many of the attractions that association football was to have from the 1880s, and in deeply divided cities like Liverpool or Glasgow, mass support for rival football clubs when it emerged actually aligned along pre-existing religious, social and racial divides.

Local Liberalism and its gradual identification with national causes owed much to a change in the nature of the press. In place of a small number of papers, massively dominated by *The Times*, emerged a competitive and open market. Gladstone's removal of financial barriers was one influence, but the demand for information from an increasingly articulate provincial readership was just as important. There were only 266 newspapers in 1824, but there were already 795 in 1856, nearly fifteen hundred in the 1870s and over two thousand at the end of the century. By the 1860s the structure of the press had evolved as it was to remain – only the size was to change: there was already a small group of serious papers aiming at a national readership, though no longer dominated by *The Times* (which had by then only the fourth highest circulation), and variable but much larger numbers of popular and local papers. The most important provincial papers like the *Yorkshire Post* (selling as many copies as *The Times* by the 1880s), *Manchester Guardian* and *Birmingham Post* were regional opinion-formers. In big cities there were newspapers openly associated with local party factions, and the ownership of such important moulders of opinion provided vital avenues both to local influence and to national politics. Such were the papers owned by Edward Baines in Leeds, Joseph Cowen in Newcastle and the Leader family in Sheffield.

Popular Liberalism therefore had its own local motivations, its campaigning organisations, its own media and leadership. What is on the face of it surprising is that this radical grouping should have associated itself in the 1860s with a parliamentary party that still had a very different social character and outlook. Liberals in Parliament had a significant presence in the Lords, often men whose association with Whiggism went back at least as far as Fox and Rockingham, and its representatives in the Commons were overwhelmingly made up of landowners, gentlemen of leisure and lawyers – many of them Anglicans and not very different in character from their Conservative counterparts. What made this seem a suitable vehicle for radical Liberalism? Firstly, there was not much alternative; the industrial towns remained under-represented until 1884 and most were Liberal anyway, so there was little leverage that they could exert except in association with MPs who sat for county seats and country towns. Secondly, even the most assertive businessmen were often unsure of themselves; their knowledge of trade might be great, but the business of government was still more to do with diplomacy than with economics and taxation, at least until Gladstone's politicisation of the Chancellor's role after 1859. Thirdly the conflict between radicals and social conservatives was often hidden by a common language and a common heritage. The new earnestness of Liberal ministers in office seemed to be evidence of sound common sense of which a nonconformist businessman could approve, and ministers' determination to keep down the cost of government was as popular to property owners in towns as in the countryside. Right across the Liberal party was a shared sense of history, rooted in the seventeenth century. The Duke of Argyll, socially conservative though he was as the owner of vast tracts of Scotland, regarded himself as a progressive because his ancestors had opposed the Stuarts and one had lost his life opposing James II. Whigs also had a belief in themselves as progressive reformers which sometimes amounted to an ideological motivation in its own right. Anthony Trollope's Duke of Omnium, whose very name suggests immense power, 'was heir . . . to one of the greatest fortunes in the country . . . and yet he devoted himself to work with the grinding energy of a young penniless barrister . . . and did so without any motive more selfish than that of being counted in the roll of the public servants of England' – as his ancestors had been. History counted lower down too: Cromwell and Milton remained great popular heroes in progressive circles, 1862 was widely celebrated as the bicentenary of exclusion of Dissenters from Anglican pulpits, and Bunyan's *Pilgrim's Progress* was required reading among radicals; men throughout the party were very conscious of which side their families had taken in the civil wars of the 1640s.

There was calculation in the alliance too. If the radicals needed the parliamentary Whigs to give them leverage in Parliament, then at least some of the Whigs were conscious that by allying with radicals they could contain rather than advance radicalism: Lord Spencer wrote in 1867, refusing to oppose Gladstone over electoral reform, that 'the more the moderate Liberals separate themselves from their party, the stronger will eventually be the radicals.' With such disparate motives, it is no wonder that Liberals could more cheerfully unite around Italian unification in 1859, against the brutality of British colonial methods in Jamaica in 1865–66 and South Africa in 1901, and over massacres in Bulgaria or Armenia, than they could on more divisive industrial or financial questions nearer home.

The final impetus to the formation of 'the Liberal party' in the 1860s was the emergence of Gladstone as a popular national figure. This was in part contrived: provincial tours to Lancashire and Tyneside in 1862 were the beginning of a systematic working of the Liberal provinces and Gladstone himself noted two years later that 'I am become for the first time a popular character'. He was though happy to facilitate the process, insisting to his secretary that his photograph should be available for no more than sixpence. In Manchester he was received by cheering crowds and he was similarly welcomed in Yorkshire and in Stoke. It even became something of an embarrassment – he had to turn down regular requests that he should himself stand for various industrial constituencies. He was also well aware of the new importance of the popular press which he had helped to create, being in close touch with the *Daily Telegraph*, not only the largest circulation paper in the 1860s but a strongly Liberal one too; a Liberal journalist claimed that it was the support of the *Telegraph* that made Gladstone 'the People's William'. Gladstone was also helped by getting ringing endorsements as the coming man from other Liberals with reputations of their own, from John Stuart Mill who described him as 'the greatest parliamentary leader the country had had in the present century, or, perhaps since the time of the Stuarts' (a telling choice of comparison), and also from John Bright who stumped the country to rally the party behind Gladstone.

But if the tricks of the politician's trade helped, there were deeper factors at work too. Gladstone almost alone could encompass within his multi-faceted personality the various strands that were coming together in Liberalism. He was a High Anglican, but his moral earnestness made him popular with nonconformists; he was conservative and in some matters even reactionary which gave comfort to Whig colleagues, but he spoke the crusading language of popular radicalism; he was, as a Whig told Walter Bagehot, 'Oxford on the surface but Liverpool below'. Each faction could see in him an ally, and all could trust his independence from other factions to give their case a fair hearing. As his successor Rosebery was to put it at the end of Gladstone's career, 'for the last thirty years our party has been more or less Mr. G.'

How much still needed to be done to pull a Liberal party together was demonstrated by its chaotic condition during the reform crisis of 1866–67; how far Gladstone was able to work the trick was clear only one year later. The strategy chosen, and one that was to remain Gladstone's favourite, was the concentration on a single idea which would have such high moral voltage as to unite his moralising followers behind it. In 1868 this issue was for the first time Ireland. Russell in retirement helped to pave the way with writings that argued the urgency of action to prevent increasing disaffection. Fenian outrages in Ireland and on the mainland had given Irish issues a greater prominence than at any time since the famines of the 1840s. Russell called for a radical attack on the Anglican Church in Ireland and Gladstone seized on this as an issue to reunite his party. Gladstone had reached these conclusions for himself and, with prophetic foreboding, wrote privately that 'The Irish question which has long been grave is growing *awful* . . . English policy should set its face two ways like a flint: to support public order, and to make the laws of Ireland such as they should be. This is what we should try, though I believe we shall have to go to martyrdom on it.' Resolutions passed by the Commons in 1868 while Disraeli was still Prime Minister showed that the Liberal majority of MPs had found a uniting moral cause to take to the anticipated general election and into a subsequent Liberal government. The 1868 elections, the first under the extended franchise, were a triumph both for Gladstone and his party, the first in which his 'hold over the country' (as Argyll put it) was fully at his party's service; Liberals won a majority increased to over a hundred. Although the redistribution of seats makes exact comparisons difficult, it is clear that Liberals gained ground in the urban areas and especially in Scotland and Wales which had been steadily moving closer to Liberalism over many years; in Scotland and Wales Liberals now took 74 of the 90 seats.

Gladstone interpreted his election victory as 'the moral union of the majority', but his colleagues recognised how far it was due to their chief's direct relationship with the electorate. He entered on government full of confidence, but without an agenda of reforms such as he had taken to the Treasury in 1859. The government of 1868–74 had an impressive record of legislation, but apart from Ireland little of it had been worked out in detail before taking office. One of the government's most determined objectives was in fact administrative rather than legislative, the holding down of expenditure and the improvement of efficiency – as for example in completing civil service reform. As government became more complex a more professional approach was essential: the number of civil servants, only fifty thousand in the 1870s, had more than doubled by 1900 and risen to 280,000 by 1914. A new Local Government Board set up in 1871 helped to tighten up local administration, sometimes imposing harsh limits to poor relief payments. Even the government's most radical minister was unsentimental about poverty: Bright had written of cotton workers in 1861 that 'their wages are such that the bulk of them could live moderately well on half their present incomes, and they and their employers might well learn something useful from a little suffering.' There was a positive side too, as in the formation in 1869 of the Charity Organisation Society to co-ordinate voluntary relief work, and to encourage in the working classes the values of independence and thrift. Liberals were great givers of private relief as well as great retrenchers of state funding.

Irish issues were in any case sufficiently pressing to dominate the legislative timetable of the first two years, and as a result unity held out fairly well too. Gladstone in 1870 believed Ireland to be 'the basis on which the late remarkable co-operation of the Liberal majority has been founded.' It was also a convenient way of keeping open the divide between Liberals and Conservatives, with government bills passed steadily through on Liberal votes. After 1870 that was less often the case, and the second half of the government's life was a time of gradual disintegration. The first real battles came over education in 1870–71, with the initiative in the hands of a very moderate minister, W. E. Forster. The need for extensions of educational provision was widely accepted among Liberals, not only by the nonconformist zealots of the National Education League, and was given a greater urgency by the Prussian success in the war with France: Gladstone noted that 'the conduct of the campaign, on the German side, has given a marked triumph to the cause of systematic popular education.' In 1869, about 30 per cent of children were at schools receiving government grants and inspected by government officers to ensure efficiency, about 23 per cent were at schools without grants or inspection, and the rest were not at school at all – mainly in the expanding cities. Most schools were run by voluntary bodies, mainly those associated with the Church of England. Forster's first proposal was to make elementary education compulsory but to graft state encouragement, inspection and financial support onto the existing system – a plan denounced by nonconformists as putting Church schools on the rates

– and this bill failed to pass. A compromise allowed for secularised 'board schools' that would be paid for by the state but these were to exist only where (partly-subsidised) Church schools did not exist. In 1870 Anglicans rejoiced and nonconformists were outraged by the government's desertion of its supporters; in the long run though it was the board schools that expanded most quickly, and by the end of the century they educated nearly half the nation's children. The new school boards also provided in themselves an education in methods of political action: in 1876 the Conservative education minister told his colleagues that they 'afford platforms and the notoriety specially needed by the political Dissenting Ministers (many of them to my mind the most active and effective revolutionary agents of the day) and also provide a ready machinery for lowering the legitimate and useful influence of the leading personages of the place.' Overall educational provision improved and illiteracy which had been a major problem now declined.

Table 15.1   Growth in Educational Provision

Year	Government Expenditure	Numbers in Inspected Schools
1870	£1.6 m.	1.7 m.
1880	£4.0 m.	3.6 m.
1890	£5.8 m.	4.7 m.
1900	£12.2 m.	5.7 m.

Other issues proved equally divisive. A proposal to modernise the High Court introduced a structure that was to last for a century, but in the process antagonised many lawyers who felt that their vested interests were at risk – much as controllers of patronage had disliked competitive examinations for the civil service. The most damaging antagonisms arose over army reform and licensing. The navy, generally regarded as the basis for national defence and hence taken rather more seriously, had practised promotion on merit for a long time, but in the army commissions for officers had to be purchased. This ancient practice was out of keeping with the government's assault on inherited privilege, and might be dangerously inefficient in the future European wars feared with the rise of Germany. An army officer published in 1871 *The Battle of Dorking*, a best-seller which inspired popular fear of a successful German invasion. The government's bill to abolish purchase of commissions was fought tooth and nail through the Commons although substantial compensation was offered – it was the implications of the proposal for the social character of the army and the precedent created that was resented, not only the financial issue. Eventually the bill could not be forced through and the government had to exercise the surviving royal authority in army affairs to achieve its aims – a method for which it had good enough reason, but which nonetheless stirred up further opposition to what was described as arbitrary use of power. A restrictive reform of liquor licensing also had much to recommend it, considering the nation's drinking habits; in England and Wales in 1871 there were on average licensed premises for each two hundred people, and 1876 was the all-time high for beer consumption per head. But the bill also succeeded in antagonising the vested interests of 'the trade' without satisfying temperance supporters on the Liberal benches. Active opposition in Commons and Lords also led annually to the abandonment of many popular Liberal reforms for lack of parliamentary time, and this inevitably increased the fractiousness of the party's constituent groups.

By 1873–74, even Irish issues were unable to hold the party together and a major bill on Irish universities was lost. The strain of office was such that Gladstone was looking for 'some perfectly honourable difference of opinion among ourselves' which would 'release us collectively from the responsibilities of office.' Like Peel he had contributed to the government's difficulties by forgetting in office some of the political arts that had helped to put him there: after 1868 he was rarely available for speaking engagements and paid little attention to the cultivation of the press. In 1873 he tried a tactical resignation but Disraeli refused minority office, sensing that by waiting he might do better, and the Liberals had the humiliation of resuming office after the confession of their weakness. Disraeli compared the government front bench to a row of 'exhausted volcanoes', a jibe made the more painful by its aptness. The last few months were worsened by what Gladstone called the 'scandals', irregularities in the administration of government contracts which necessitated the removal of Lowe from the Exchequer and which damaged the government's central claim to competence and probity. The final crisis came early in 1874 when Gladstone was striving to hold off a major escalation of military costs sought by ministers for colonial campaigns. His bold initiative was to propose the abolition of income tax and to dissolve parliament immediately to secure popular approval for the policy; this would at once concentrate attention on a policy likely to be popular on Gladstone's home ground of finance and, by reducing the scope of government income would also reduce the opportunities for unnecessary expenditure. Unfortunately, the policy failed to enliven the moral force of popular Liberalism, as Ireland had done in 1868, and had rather the reverse effect: the radical paper the *Bee Hive* argued that the removal of a tax paid only by the better off was socially unjust (though Gladstone himself would certainly have substituted other direct taxes), and Joseph Chamberlain, just emerging as a radical leader, denounced Gladstone's manifesto as 'the meanest public document that has ever . . . proceeded from a statesman of the first rank . . . simply an appeal to the selfishness of the middle classes.' Even more unfortunately, middle-class voters do not seem to have been sufficiently impressed by Gladstone's initiative to forget real and imagined threats that they had seen in earlier reforms, or to discount an increasing attraction to Disraelian Conservatism. The Liberals therefore lost heavily in the 1874 elections, with their greatest losses in the English boroughs. Since Disraeli had achieved a Conservative majority of over fifty, Gladstone immediately resigned office, so confirming Disraeli's 1868 view that the verdict of the electors was final.

In 1874 Gladstone was sixty-four and did not envisage heading another government. He was so depressed by what he called his 'emphatic dismissal' and the state of the party as to resign the leadership without delay: he noted that the party had 'no public *cause* upon which it is agreed' and that the practice whereby some Liberal MPs made their names by 'constant active opposition to the bulk of the party & its leaders has acquired a dangerous predominance.' He was prevailed upon to remain nominal leader for one more session, but only on condition that he need not be active in the role, and it was not long before he stepped down altogether, leaving the leadership in the Commons to the Whig Lord Hartington – whose leadership was distrusted by many radical Liberals. The first half of the 1874–80 parliament was therefore a period of Liberal inaction, a time in which the focus of activity swung away from parliamentary politics. This phase ended dramatically with an outburst of moral indignation over the massacre of Bulgarians by the Turks in 1876. The Conservative government sought to maintain friendly relations with Turkey as a barrier to Russian expansion, and in this case (unlike the Jamaica controversy of 1865–66) a few Liberals accepted that British interests might justify the overriding of moral considerations (a line of thought that led on to the later grouping known as 'Liberal Imperialists' in the 1890s) but the vast majority of Liberals saw no such dilemma and an absolute certainty that morality must come first. A great wave of demonstrations and petitions was launched, before Gladstone himself entered the fray with a pamphlet, *The Bulgarian Horrors and the Question of the East*, which put him at the head of the agitation. He was actually lukewarm about the most extreme propositions put forward by other agitators, but his association with the campaign put him back into the mainstream. For his part he saw the crisis as demonstrating that the people had recovered their moral sense, lost in 1874: 'the game was afoot and the question yet alive.' In Liberal politics he was again the dominant force. He capitalised on that position in 1879 and 1880 as a general election drew nearer with a highly-publicised campaign out in the country: he gave up his constituency at Greenwich to fight the marginal seat of Midlothian in Scotland. This 'Midlothian campaign' was a spectacular, barnstorming affair, with railway tours and torchlight processions borrowed from American practice; since his opponent was a Tory lord, it could be presented as a progressive fight against feudal forces (though the equally feudal Liberals of Midlothian were campaigning for Gladstone more traditionally, and with less publicity). Gladstone turned this local campaigning into a great moral effort, aimed through the press more at the country than at Midlothian. When he won the seat and his party won the elections of 1880 by a sweeping majority, he attributed it to 'the great hand of God, so evidently displayed'. There could be no doubt that he would be Prime Minister for a second time.

Events though had moved on significantly within the party during the years of opposition, and the result was that the 1880–85 government was to be even more difficult to control than that of 1868. The new Cabinet included men whose various objectives would be difficult to harmonise; agreement could not be reached on many issues, and as a result many Cabinet decisions were – most unusually – taken by votes rather than by consensus. Hartington as the Whig leader was determined to keep Gladstone in charge, not least because of fears that if Gladstone was finally freed to associate with the radical wing he might discover the energy and moral conviction for some sweeping changes. But the Whigs were determined to exact a high price for their backing: Lord Fitzwilliam, a major landowner in Yorkshire, wrote after the elections to claim personal credit for a share of the Liberal success and to make it clear that he expected the Cabinet to have a preponderance of Whigs.

Radicals were also confident that they had contributed to victory and expected their reward as a result. The spearhead here was Chamberlain, who had moved on from a much publicised mayoralty of Birmingham, widely regarded as an object lesson in Liberal municipal management, to become an MP in 1876, and had immediately claimed leadership of the parliamentary radicals. Chamberlain was a superbly effective self-publicist – far too often taken then and since at his own valuation – but he was a formidable debater who took quickly both to parliament and to the public meeting, and he was a man of limitless ambition. The new structure of political organisation developed in Birmingham after the 1867 Reform Act was popularly associated with him. An elaborate hierarchy of precinct and ward committees enabled opinion and instructions to flow between the city's leaders and the rank and file Liberals who ran campaigns on the streets. This complex 'caucus' system was offered as a model to Liberals of other towns, at least some of whom copied it. The caucus was defended by Chamberlain as an ideal form of democracy through which the views of party members could prevail (though derided by the Russian observer Ostrogorski as a 'hierarchy of wire-pullers'), and it became the basis of a National Liberal Federation formed in 1877 to unite Liberalism of the British regions in a similar structure; all of the NLF's first team of officers were associated with Birmingham. This was intended by Chamberlain as a means of uniting radicalism behind agreed policy priorities and enforcing them on the party leaders. He claimed after the 1880 elections that the caucus organisation had won at least seventy seats for the party. His appointment only to the Board of Trade in 1880, in a Cabinet that contained few of his radical allies, was not likely to satisfy him for long.

The worsening situation in Ireland was the main reason that the 1880 government failed to achieve much in domestic legislation, but this explanation did not continue to satisfy the Liberal rank and file as each year bills were introduced only to be shelved. Temperance reformers were furious that Ireland occupied so much parliamentary time: Lawson asked in 1881 how long attention would be concentrated on five million Irish when there were thirty-five million on the mainland. Chamberlain more quarrelsomely observed that 'thirty millions of people must go without much-needed legislation because three millions are disloyal.' Ireland was, in the much used phrase, 'blocking the rails', and preventing other legislative traffic from proceeding. There were of course other blockages too, and little overall control of the traffic by a Prime Minister who was often tired and ill, and who took little interest in the future since he still expected an early retirement; by 1885 he was seen by a senior civil servant as 'madly keen to get out', much as he had been in 1873. The will-power to press through the government's biggest legislative achievement came largely from outside. When the NLF insisted on a reform of the county franchise it became impossible to resist. The 1884 reform bill was an extensive measure, increasing the electorate of England and Wales by 67 per cent, Scotland by 77 per cent, and Ireland by 229 per cent; for the first time a majority of adult males were entitled to vote. The biggest changes came in the counties, which had been least affected by the 1867 reform, but the exact impact was difficult to predict because some plural votes remained in existence and the Lords had insisted on a large redistribution of seats as the price of their approval for franchise extension. From 1885 almost all constituencies were electing a single MP, often a slice of a town or a county arbitrarily carved out to equalise the size of the electorate; the ancient concept of MPs representing recognisable communities was now secondary to equality of numbers.

Radical Liberals saw the new franchise as opening their way to power. Determined not to allow himself to be frustrated in the next parliament as in that elected in 1880, Chamberlain published in 1885 his *Radical Programme*, more widely known as the 'Unauthorised Programme' since it did not have the official support of the party or its leader. This was a comprehensive programme of radical reform that offered something to almost all potential Liberal supporters, the exact opposite of Gladstone's traditional strategy of one thing at a time. The circumstances of the 1885 election when it came were heavily influenced by Ireland, first because the loss of Irish support prompted Gladstone's resignation, and then because the campaign that ensued developed more into a series of bids for the support of Irish electors living in Britain than a debate on radical policies. Nonetheless, the Liberals did well, winning a majority of the county seats for the first time since 1832 as the newly enfranchised agricultural labourers exercised their rights. On the other hand Conservatives also did unexpectedly well, especially in the city suburbs that now had separate constituencies, and took a majority of English borough seats for the first time since 1832. Liberals had 334 MPs to 250 Conservatives, but Irish Nationalists had 86 MPs and so could determine which of the other parties should govern. From being a blockage on the rails, Ireland had become the points that would determine which track British party politics would now take.

The 1885–86 crisis over Ireland must be seen in the context of the previous twenty years of policy towards Ireland. Irish MPs and radicals had long complained of the injustices suffered by Irishmen under the Protestant Ascendancy – a Church alien to most of the population and a rural economy dominated by absentee landlords. The climax of distress had come in the famine of the 1840s; from a peak of over 8 million in 1841, the combined effects of starvation and mass emigration had reduced Ireland's population to only 5½ million by 1871, 4½ million by 1901. Those who were left were increasingly embittered. A new factor was support for Irish agitation from Irishmen who had migrated to the United States, and the members of these 'Fenian' clubs attempted to mobilise an uprising in Ireland and committed bomb outrages in Britain too in the 1860s. Few in Ireland responded with positive support for the Fenians' revolutionary message, but it was clear that there was a strong underlying sympathy. The problems seemed threefold, religion, land and nationality, but British politicians were often unsure as to which was the most urgent at any one time and above all anxious that in remedying Irish grievances they should not set precedents that would be taken up elsewhere in the Empire. A humorist of the next generation wrote of the 'Irish Question' that whenever Gladstone discovered the answer the Irish changed the question.

There was not much imaginative reform in Ireland by the Whig and Conservative governments of 1846–68. Russell had struggled unavailingly to deal with the consequences of famine in the 1840s, but could not press structural reforms through a government which included many Irish landowners. Palmerston was not only strongly anti-Catholic but an Irish peer himself and the owner of land in County Sligo; he dismissed demands for land reform with the uncompromising view that 'tenants' right is landlords' wrong'. The 1868 election campaign and Liberal victory therefore marked a new departure, and for Gladstone Ireland was both a convenient means of uniting his party and a clear moral cause; on being summoned to the palace to be made Prime Minister he had remarked, with at least one eye on posterity, that 'My mission is to pacify Ireland'. His real motives were much the same as those which had driven Peel to support the Maynooth grant in 1845, a conservative purpose of strengthening Ireland's attachment to the Union: 'our purpose & duty is to endeavour to draw a line between the Fenians & the people of Ireland, & to make the people of Ireland indisposed to cross it.' The first year of his government was dominated by the bill to disestablish the Irish Church and the second by the Irish Land Bill. Success in disestablishing the Church was not enough for Gladstone: 'if we succeed with the Church and fail with the land, we shall have done less than half of our work.' But land reform proved more difficult because of Whig opposition. The final decision only to grant compensation to tenants evicted because they could not pay their rent was much less than the demands of Irish leaders, including the Catholic Church, now made a more formidable force by the disestablishment of Anglicanism in Ireland. Gladstone also had to struggle against the Whigs in his efforts to win Irish sympathy by releasing the least dangerous of Fenian political prisoners from gaol.

Irish MPs seemed to show little gratitude and it was their opposition that wrecked plans to reform Irish universities in 1873 and almost brought the government to an end. Gladstone believed that his first government had done well by Ireland, and argued that a separate parliament for Ireland could not have done better. Irish voters seem not to have agreed, for the general elections of 1874 and 1880 effectively destroyed Irish Liberalism and returned to Westminster instead sixty MPs backing Charles Stuart Parnell's call for Home Rule. The effect in 1874 was slight, for the Conservatives had a clear majority and could not be persuaded even by obstruction in parliament to take up Irish reform. In 1880 Disraeli even tried to capitalise on Irish intransigence by pointing out that Liberals were imperilling the Empire by their concessions to Ireland – a dim foreshadowing of Unionist electioneering to come; Gladstone was already replying that British intransigence was the swiftest way to wreck the Union with Ireland. Sixty Irish MPs who had pledged to work for Home Rule – effectively internal self-government – were re-elected.

Back in office in 1880, Gladstone had to meet a far graver danger than the Fenians, for the world slump in agricultural prices had dealt the feeble rural economy of Ireland another hard blow; as tenants fell into arrears evictions again became widespread and such outrages as shootings and rick-burnings again increased, co-ordinated by a Land League. Parnell was no man of violence but he was prepared to use this disorder as a political bargaining counter. After the numbers of evictions and the level of rural violence both soared, the government had little option but to imprison him, alleging that his speeches had provoked disorder. The disorder itself then reached new heights and a junior minister was actually murdered in Dublin. British authority in Ireland was further weakened when Parnell was later released, a pragmatic decision to lower the political temperature but one which when described as the 'Kilmainham Treaty' (after the gaol where Parnell was housed) seemed more like a bargain between rivals than an act of clemency. The extent of violence at least allowed Gladstone to force through the 1881 Land Act which granted much of what the Land League had campaigned for over the previous decade – fair rents, freedom of sale and fixity of tenure – the 'three Fs' of tenant rights. But by that time the focus of disaffection was already shifting away from land and religion to nationality. From his own observations in Italy, Greece, and Norway, Gladstone had a strong personal sympathy with the idea of small nations struggling to be free, though he had no illusions about the obstacles that Irish nationalism was likely to meet from Britain; he wrote in 1883 of the need to 'take the sting out' of Irish issues by dealing with them 'in correspondence with a popular and responsible *Irish* body – competent to act for its own portion of the country'; he also noted 'the utter impossibility of the English and Scotch majority assenting to the legislative separation of the two countries.'

The 1884 extension of the franchise, most extensive of all in Ireland where little had been changed in 1867, allowed Parnell's followers to sweep the board in Catholic Ireland and come back to Westminster with the balance of power. But it was a power that could be used only one way, once the Conservatives showed little interest in Irish reforms when the election was over. Given the very tight parliamentary arithmetic, Salisbury, insecure as Conservative leader, could not expect a lasting period in office even if Parnell's MPs backed him, while any flirting with Irish reform would threaten his party's unity and his own leadership. Parnell could turn only to the Liberals and put Gladstone back into office.

Gladstone had hoped that Salisbury would grasp the nettle and put forward a bipartisan measure of Home Rule, but now he could only take it on himself. His tactics were not good; like Peel in 1846 he almost deliberately rode for a fall and rejoiced in the political martyrdom that a 'smash' would bring him. Chamberlain, already incensed that the Irish issue had again blocked his agenda of radical reform, was not even given a senior Cabinet post. The news of Gladstone's conversion to supporting Home Rule was inexpertly leaked, probably an event engineered by Liberals anxious to widen the breach with Chamberlain. And when a major split was looming, there was little effort to persuade opponents in the party. Instead Gladstone saw Home Rule as disestablishment had been in 1868 – an over-arching moral cause that would unify the party if proclaimed with enough fervour, and one that could cleanse the party of compromise in the process.

Chamberlain and Hartington, leading factions of radicals and Whigs opposed to Home Rule, could not find in Gladstone any readiness to compromise or any means of avoiding a split, though each rejoiced in the fact that by leaving the party together they would not leave Gladstone as hostage to the other. The government's Home Rule bill was therefore defeated in the Commons in 1886, with ninety Liberals combining with Conservatives to vote it down. Gladstone resigned office and was replaced by Salisbury, governing with the backing of the 'Liberal Unionists' of Chamberlain and Hartington, who now formed their own party organisation in the country. A general election in which these new 'Unionist' allies collaborated resulted in a major Liberal defeat. The Unionists successfully stirred up latent anti-Irish and Protestant feeling in England and Scotland in their determination to save the Union and the unity of the Empire: Lord Randolph Churchill resolved to play 'the Orange card' and found that it was indeed a trump. These 1886 elections ushered in twenty years of Unionist dominance.

The Liberal split of 1886 can be explained as the outcome of the complex political manoeuvrings of ambitious politicians – a four-handed poker game between Gladstone, Salisbury, Chamberlain and Churchill which proved that Salisbury had the strongest nerves and the best judgement. But it was also an issue on which longer-term decisions were made. Owners of property had become increasingly concerned by the extent of Liberal reforms, and Ireland in 1886 forced them to decide whether they wished to remain on the radical or the conservative side of politics. Liberal Unionism proved to be a bridge over which many of the better off, businessmen like Chamberlain as well as landowners like Hartington, could cross to the Conservatives, many of them finally forgetting the legacy of Cromwell and James II. So many peers made that transition that the House of Lords became almost a private Unionist preserve, with important political consequences. Financial papers like *The Economist*, Liberal in the past, opposed Home Rule vehemently as threatening prosperity with an Anglo-Irish tariff war; the City of London constituency, which had been Russell's seat until 1861, now became a very safe Conservative preserve. Locally, the owners of property were so solidly on the Conservative side that it became difficult to get any real political balance on benches of magistrates. For the Liberals, Gladstone had succeeded in associating the party with a strong moral cause, but one that was hard to gain support for in the English, Welsh and Scottish constituencies which made up five-sixths of the House of Commons. Ireland would continue to 'block the rails' for Liberalism, without the Liberal party having the power to do much for Ireland. Gladstone's friend the historian Lord Acton had written as early as 1880 that 'taking party in the practical and popular sense, of an instrument for holding office, people are uneasily conscious that Mr. Gladstone will sacrifice it to loftier purpose.' Not for nothing had Gladstone seen himself since 1850 as the residuary legatee of Sir Robert Peel.

16 Britain at the summit, 1850s – 1900

The nineteenth century was the time in which both Britain's economic might and her political influence in the world reached their highest point. It was a period when the country was hardly ever fully engaged in war yet never entirely at peace; the Crimean War of 1854–55 was the only conflict between 1815 and 1899 in which anything like a national mobilisation took place, and there was no British military operation at all in Western Europe for a century after Waterloo. And yet the 'little wars' in which small forces of regular British soldiers defeated larger forces of half-armed and untrained natives in Asia and Africa were a feature of every decade. The paradox lies largely in the dominance of the Royal Navy, the formative years of which were first analysed in the American historian Alfred Mahan's *The Influence of Sea Power upon History* in 1890; Mahan wrote of the 'overbearing power' given to the country that commanded the sea, which 'by controlling the great common, closes the highways by which commerce moves.' No European power had a navy as powerful as Britain, and no power had an overland route to the Far East either. Such plans as Russia's Trans-Siberian railway and Germany's for a railway from Berlin to Baghdad were jealously watched by British strategists at the end of the century precisely because they threatened the monopoly of long distance communication that was both quick and secure. British naval dominance survived transitions to iron and then steel warships, steam propulsion, electric telegraphs and eventually radio signalling, though only at the price of an ever-increasing need for coaling and telegraph stations all across the world's oceans. Technological innovation in shipping also cut journey times and so increased the importance of sea power; sailing from London to Sydney took about four months at mid-century but steaming took only about a month by 1914. The extent to which Britain's world role depended on control of sea communications was well enough understood to be a major determinant of policy in its own right.

With this advantage the size of the economic and imperial

expansion was remarkable. About 10 per cent of the world's total land surface was added to the Empire in the half-century before 1914; combined with already large territory, this made the Empire of 1914 the largest in the history of the world, controlling the lives of a quarter of mankind. When the imperial poet Kipling spoke of 'dominion over palm and pine' or when popular journalists wrote of the 'Empire on which the sun never sets' they were not merely celebrating size (and not even predicting permanence), but drawing attention to an Empire that extended spatially to every continent and to every time zone. The growth of political authority was greater even than the size of the Empire would suggest, for many parts of the world that never came near to being colonised by Britain were under Britain's economic guidance and the political influence of the 'informal Empire'.

There was also a spread of the English language and of British attitudes mainly through an unprecedented emigration from the British Isles: of about 23 million people who left Europe in the second half of the century, as many as ten million seem to have been from Britain and Ireland. One result was the accumulation of new nations of predominantly British stock in such places as Australia and New Zealand, a major British contribution to the racial melting-pot of the USA – and through that to English becoming the main world language of the next century. It also led to such apparent eccentricities as Canadian soldiers who wore kilts and Argentinians who spoke Welsh a century after the great migration.

Such measurements of Britain's power and influence must be qualified with the perspective of hindsight. It was during the later nineteenth century that Britain actually lost the industrial and commercial lead over other developed countries which had been the real basis of her pre-eminence in the world. By the 1870s both economists and politicians were already seeking explanations for Britain's apparent decline, at least relative to her European neighbours and the USA. Nonetheless, in 1914 Britain was still responsible for a quarter of total world trade in manufactured goods and owned most of the world's shipping. If Britain had lost her 'unchallenged supremacy', then that is best regarded as a (natural) challenge by economies that had industrialised later and by countries only recently unified; the challenges were the new and worrying feature, but Britain remained the world's major economic power until the First World War.

The ability to do so depended on the performance of the domestic economy, which was 'unsuccessful' only by comparison with Britain's earlier performance or with that of her rivals at the time; the British people as a whole continued to enjoy rises in their standards of living throughout the 'Great Depression', and by any measurement were better off in 1900 than at any previous time in British history. The economy continued to grow rapidly until about 1873, though with customary peaks and troughs – such as the hiccough which helped to produce both distress and electoral reform in 1865–67. After this, the underlying growth rate slowed to about 1 per cent each year, slower than either Germany or the USA, whether measured in absolute terms or in output for each person employed.

A large influence on this relative decline may have been the very fact that other countries were now also industrialised. A contributory cause was the steady increase in food and raw material imports; Britain had been unable to produce enough food for her own needs since the 1820s, but by 1890 she could provide for only 40 per cent of wheat required for the nation's bread, and even this low proportion continued to fall. The cause was to be found both in demand and in supply; a continuing rise in population meant more mouths to fill, but domestic food production actually fell because of the collapse of world food prices from the 1870s when railways opened up the North American prairies and refrigeration ships facilitated an international trade in cheap meat. On the eve of the First World War, Britain imported four-fifths of its wheat and nearly half of its meat and dairy products; industry imported all its raw cotton and copper, and most of its wool, iron, tin and lead. The nation depended on trade to avoid starvation and industrial collapse, and the sense of vulnerability that this occasioned when naval dominance was threatened cannot be over-emphasised.

Fortunately in an age of steam shipping, resources of British coal were such as to allow for all the demands of shipping and the economy and for substantial exports too; the contemporary economist Jevons wrote of coal as 'not beside but above all other commodities' in its importance to the economy. The building of ships was another strength, for the British industry not only supplied Britain's enormous merchant fleet and the Royal Navy, but had additional capacity to supply ships for export. Other manufactured goods were less competitive and British exports rose less slowly than world trade in manufactures, partly because Britain had previously exported heavily to places like Germany that now had their own industries, partly because Germany was typical of such industrialising rivals in erecting tariff barriers around her new industries. Again the decline is only relative: Britain still supplied a third of the world's manufactured goods at the end of the century.

There was a regular deficit on the trade in goods throughout the century, a deficit covered by international earnings of service industries like finance, insurance and shipping, and by returns from foreign investments. There was a great and perhaps dangerous tendency to invest abroad rather than in British industry, understandable in view of the decelerating rate of British economic growth, but a factor which may itself have contributed to the slowing down of the economy. Britain's massive international investments were to be a crucial national asset in the First World War, but their virtual liquidation to pay for armaments removed the cushion which the late Victorian economy had enjoyed and which had helped to limit the impact of its structural weaknesses. There was a second weakness in the trading position, an increasing dependence on the countries of the Empire as trading partners. In 1870 India was Britain's third most important customer, but by 1913 she was the first; colonies and white dominions had more complex patterns of trade, but the neat equation whereby British manufactures were exchanged for colonial foods and raw materials could last only as long as the colonies were content to remain unindustrial. As soon as colonial self-government came, so did demands for tariffs to protect infant industries against *British* competition, and by 1900 Canada at least was well on the way to a trading relationship that had as much to do with rivalry as with partnership.

Britain's hour of 'high imperialism' was also a time of rapid economic and social change within Britain. Most obviously, population continued its rapid surge forward, with the total population of England and Wales rising from eighteen to over thirty-two million between 1851 and 1901. Scotland rising at a similar rate to four and a half million. From the 1880s this growth was slackening, and the continued increases owed most to a falling death rate, as the impact of scourges like tuberculosis, cholera and typhoid was reduced. Birth rates and family sizes fell, first among middle-class families and then more generally, an incidental effect of a population more urbanised, more conscious of possibilities of consumption in an era in which prices fell continuously and living standards rose – discontinuously but appreciably over time. Within the growing population totals there was a large rearrangement of occupational and regional patterns. Employment in agriculture halved to just 9 per cent of the workforce between 1861 and 1911, with a compensating increase in the service sector, up to a third of the workforce by 1911; manufacturing remained stable at 39 per cent of the total.

The last quarter of the century was for agriculture one of continuous decline and with few exceptions, the one sector of the economy for which the contemporary description of a 'Great Depression' was apt. During thirty years of falling food prices, the total value of crop production almost halved – the value of British wheat output fell by two-thirds even while demand steadily increased;

other sectors at best held their own, and only milk production, fruit-growing and market-gardening became more profitable, all marginal sectors of traditional agriculture that had found local markets in a more urbanised country. Employment fell absolutely as well as in proportion to national population, so that by 1914 there were a third fewer farm labourers than fifty years earlier, and 10 per cent fewer farmers. The contemporary novels of Thomas Hardy are a testament to a South West in which rural unemployment was endemic and hopelessness near universal, the steam-driven threshing machine as much the rural workers' enemy as ever the spinning machine was to the Luddites. His fellow novelist Rider Haggard, though unlike Hardy a man of the right rather than the moderate left, reminded readers of his *Rural England* (1902) that even after the worst had passed, 'resentment against past suffering . . . is deeper than gratitude for present benefits.'

Such misery was the cause of much of the century's migration, as the pattern of wages shows; in Lancashire and West Yorkshire (where booming factories, city lifestyles and emigration ports like Liverpool beckoned) farmers had to pay up to twice as much to hire labourers as in Hardy's counties of the South West. Between 1851 and 1911 some regions expanded at breakneck speed while others hardly shared in the national population boom at all; internal migration was overwhelmingly from country to town.

Table 16.1 Net population change by region 1851–1911 (millions)

Region	Overall Change	Net Migration
London/Home Counties	+5.39	+0.92
South West	+0.47	−1.05
Rural South East	+1.47	−0.90
Midlands	+2.55	−0.55
Lincs & E. Yorks	+0.61	−0.29
Lancs, Cheshire & W. Yorks	+4.94	+0.54
North	+1.44	−0.08
South Wales	+1.12	+0.22
Rural Wales	+0.06	−0.30
Central Scotland	+1.71	−0.07
North & South Scotland	+0.15	−0.79

The same phenomenon meant that over seventy years from 1841, the population of Greater London rose from 2.2 to 7.3 million, a third of the increase as a result of migration, and the total of the eight largest English cities outside London shows the same rate and pattern of growth. By 1851 for the first time a census showed that a majority of the population lived in towns, but the urbanised part of the population continued to grow faster than the rural part, and to concentrate more in the bigger cities. By the end of the century over a third of the British population lived in London or in the big cities. This sometimes involved very rapid rises indeed: Sheffield tripled in size in fifty years after 1851, and Middlesbrough quadrupled in forty. The need to create civic pride and social control in places of such mushroom growth was one reason for the rapid advance of local government.

In some places it remained possible to move up through the social scale with speed, particularly if as in the Sheffield and Birmingham metal trades the emphasis remained on small workshops and there was little physical separation between employers and employed, but as industry settled into its second century of industrialisation, the phenomenon of individuals moving from poverty to fabulous wealth in a single generation (never widespread though much discussed) became rarer, though social mobility between adjacent social groups was common, and many people moved in and out of classes according to age, income and employment. More industrial ownership was concentrated in limited companies, which were being formed at the rate of nearly five thousand a year by the end of the century, compared to the six hundred a year of the 1860s. By the 1890s such things were part of the satirists' range of targets: when W. S. Gilbert's King of Utopia imported British advisers to help him modernise his country in 1893, these 'flowers of progress' included a company promoter and a County Councillor as well as representatives of army, navy, parliament and the court. The result is the creation of *Utopia Limited*, 'registered under the Joint Stock Company Act of 1862'.

Wales and Scotland were more affected even than England by these movements of population. In 1914 a fifth of all Scotsmen lived in Glasgow and a tenth of Welshmen in Cardiff or Swansea. Welsh industrialisation came later than England's and was heavily concentrated into the two counties of Glamorgan and Monmouthshire, with the Rhondda valley achieving one of the most rapid rates of all in population growth. The result was a deeper rural–urban divide than in most of England, not least because the industrialising South Wales had drawn in many non Welsh-speaking English migrants. A similar divide had long existed in Scotland, but this was reinforced both by the acute distress and consequent depopulation of the Highlands, by the further rapid growth of towns in the central industrial belt, and by immigration of Irish Catholics who contributed a religious element to existing social divisions. Both Wales and Scotland provided a disproportionate share of those migrants who went overseas, as well as suffering net losses from migration within Britain.

Social and geographical mobility within Britain no doubt helped to create a single national economy, especially in the distributive trades, where the first branded goods selling to a popular market in all regions were now being popularised through the same posters and through newspaper advertisements in such vehicles as the *Daily Mail*, read throughout the country. Bovril, Lipton's Tea, Beecham's pills and Boots the Chemist were all trail-blazers for an emerging single national market. A factor which pointed in the same direction was the growth of the railways: expansion slackened after the 'mania' of the 1840s but the network continued to grow steadily and reached eighteen thousand miles at the end of the century, at which level it more or less remained until the 1960s. In 1892 a *national* system was finally in existence when the Great Western Railway changed its gauge to correspond with that common to the other companies, so that freight traffic could now travel across the land without the need for unloading. The last main line and the last London terminus were completed when the Great Central reached Marylebone in 1899. Speeds improved too so that by 1900, travel between British cities was as quick as it was to be until motorways, internal air services and high-speed trains began a different transport revolution after about 1960. All of these factors – and the availability of cheap internal postage – helped in creating the sense of a single nationality, certainly resisted by Welshmen and Scotsmen and perhaps helping to generate the first stirrings of a revived national separatism in both countries, but inexorably permeating the English regions.

This drift towards a single nationality may well have both reinforced and been reinforced by the idea of Empire. What is certain is that the connection between economic forces and the country's international position was generally recognised. Burke had lamented in 1790 that the age of romantic politics was over and had been succeeded by the age of the economist. Joseph Chamberlain, with characteristic exaggeration, argued in 1896 that all government was now about economics:

The Foreign Office and the Colonial Office are chiefly engaged in finding new markets and defending old ones. The War Office and Admiralty are mostly occupied in preparations for the defence of these markets and for the protection of our commerce. The Boards of Agriculture and Trade are entirely concerned with those two great branches of industry.

Since education was about educating the workforce and the Home Office concentrated on conditions in factories, he concluded that 'commerce is the greatest of all political interests.'

Such a view would have seemed odd to Palmerston and his contemporaries, who recognised trade as being among British interests but who defined 'interest' differently, much more a matter of status than of rates of return. Attitudes to British foreign policy of mid-century were heavily under Palmerston's influence, for he had been Foreign Secretary for fifteen years and was then Prime Minister with a personal interest in diplomatic matters for a further ten. His popular reputation – and much of his diplomacy was conducted with at least one eye on opinion in Britain – was of a man who would intervene strongly, even foolishly, when the interests of Britain or a British subject were at stake. His real long-term aim was to prevent any one country achieving a preponderance in Europe as great as that which Britain enjoyed at sea; it was, despite appearances of bluff and bravado, a more interventionist version of traditional 'balance of power' policies. In 1848–50 Palmerston was popularly celebrated as the defender of a Greek with some dubious claim to British citizenship, Don Pacifico, with the full might of the Royal Navy, as a public sympathiser with Hungarian rebels against the Austrian Emperor, and as being unconcerned about insults offered by British crowds to a visiting Austrian general.

Such 'Palmerstonian' activities caused consternation among his Cabinet colleagues and brought down the government when Russell sacked him; they also alarmed the Queen, who later described Palmerston and Russell as 'those two dreadful old men' on account of their adventurous foreign policies. In the Don Pacifico debates Palmerston claimed for all Britons anywhere in the world the same unlimited rights as a citizen of the Roman Empire and implied that the armed forces were in constant readiness to enforce such rights. Gladstone responded with calls for a policy which he called 'non-intervention', based more on morality and less on risk-taking bluff. The difference between the policies advocated by Gladstone and Cobden, and Palmerston's own private views (as well as his robust public defence of his policies) is striking; he argued privately that 'these half-civilised governments such as China, Portugal, Spanish America, all require a dressing every eight or ten years to keep them in order. Their minds are too shallow to receive an impression that will last longer . . . and warning is of little use. They care little for words and they must not only see the stick but actually feel it.' These apparently fundamental debates over principles can obscure the fact that during Palmerston's lengthy control of policy the country hardly fought a serious war. The major war of mid-century, with Russia in the Crimea, was one for which Palmerston could take no blame and which he himself fairly believed would have been avoided had he had charge of the Foreign Office in 1854.

The Crimean War was in many respects a classic example of 'balance of power' diplomacy, for Britain and France declared war on Russia precisely to prevent too great a shift in that balance towards Russia and against Turkey. The decision was influenced too by unwarranted diplomatic risks, Russian and French as well as British, which converted a crisis into a war. As public opinion seemed more than ready for war, an opinion probably by then inflamed by Palmerston himself as well as by expectations raised by years of Palmerstonianism, even Russian retreats did not deter an Anglo-French invasion of the Crimea, an arena chosen because it was open to attack and easily supplied from the sea. Expectations were of a long and serious war to settle the domination of Europe for a generation. The war's actual course was therefore a disappointment, for a series of indecisive skirmishes and a bloody siege showed only Britain's military and administrative unpreparedness, until the war itself petered out into a virtual draw at precisely the time when Palmerston's promotion to the premiership had again raised expectations. Spurred on by the reporting of *The Times'* war correspondent (whose editor was thought to be an 'enemy of his country' by the Foreign Secretary), the public was highly critical of the army and government and hardly mollified by the stoical endurance and heroism of ordinary soldiers or by the unprecedented contribution of Florence Nightingale's women nurses. Young men from one Oxfordshire village were said to have gone out seeing themselves as brave adventurers ready to face the country's enemies but found that the only foes they had to face were 'sand storms, mosquitoes, heat stroke or ague'. The war gave a severe jolt to uncritical believers in Britain's power and influence, and to admirers of her institutions (of whom there had been quite a number in the age of economic predominance celebrated by the Great Exhibition at the Crystal Palace, held only in 1851).

The immediate effects on foreign policy were not obvious while Palmerston retained his dominant position and his enterprising attitude to the press. But there was in reality a period of diplomatic disengagement, occasioned partly by the sobering lessons of the war, and partly by the fact that from 1859 Palmerston's colleagues in government included Gladstone, who still had a very different idea of foreign policy, and was himself influenced by Cobden whose economic diplomacy was carried on largely outside the Foreign Office. The dominant considerations were therefore economy in finance (which forced Palmerston to fight a long battle with Gladstone before securing funds for fortifications to secure the south coast against a feared French invasion), and free trade – which operated for Liberals in its own world of international morality.

Gladstone saw Cobden's 1860 economic treaty with France as having 'the great aim . . . of binding the two countries together by interest and affection.' The real value was not in trade but in 'the social good'. Cobden himself, more rhapsodically, saw free trade as acting 'on the moral world as the principle of gravitation in the universe – drawing men together, thrusting aside the antagonism of race and creed, and language, and uniting us in the bonds of eternal peace.' Palmerston though spoke of 'that dangerous lunatic Cobden' and saw Liberal resistance to armaments as meaning 'that we should cease to be an influential Power in the World.'

Whatever the debates within government, the reality was of disengagement, indicated clearly enough by the conduct of British relations with the USA in a series of difficult crises occasioned by the American Civil War of 1861–65. Several ministers including Gladstone favoured the Confederates' attempt to secede, and the impact of a Federal blockade of Confederate cotton exports had severe effects on the British textile industry. Disputes and legal actions which dragged on until 1871 several times threatened war with the USA but on each occasion prudence ruled. Gladstone later recalled that Palmerston had wanted the separation of the USA into two as 'the diminution of a dangerous Power, but prudently held his tongue'. Over Poland in 1863 and Denmark in 1864 Palmerston was less cautious, but the setbacks administered to British policy in each case by Bismarck's Germany only strengthened the feeling against Palmerstonian interventionism.

After Palmerston's death in 1865, the shift to a policy of non-intervention became official. The government let it be known when war threatened between Prussia and Austria that Britain's policy would be 'neutrality at all events and as long as possible'. Cobden spoke of 'a change amounting to a revolution . . . in our foreign policy . . . Henceforth we shall observe an absolute abstention from continental politics.' Bright felt 'the theory of the balance of power to be pretty nearly dead and buried.' The Conservative Foreign Secretary of 1867 argued that 'there never was a time when the English public was more thoroughly bent on incurring no fresh responsibilities for continental objects.' So often was this policy set forth that his Liberal predecessor complained that it was unnecessarily weakening Britain's diplomacy: 'the policy of not meddling is of course the right one, but it is not necessary that all mankind should be let into the secret twice a day.' The whole stance was given an official approval when as Prime Minister Derby promised that the country would not 'entangle itself with any single or monopolising alliance; above all to endeavour not to interfere needlessly or vexatiously with the internal affairs of any foreign country, nor to volunteer to them unasked advice.' All the same habit remained strong; in the same year Britain invaded Ethiopia for imprisoning British missionaries and sent the fleet to Cadiz to overawe Spain.

Within Britain's overseas possessions too there was something of a disengagement in the 1860s, influenced more by events in New Zealand, Jamaica and India than in Europe. By mid-century the maritime Empire was already beginning to move apart as settled colonies in North America and Australasia developed their own representative institutions and from there moved to autonomous economic and political futures. Canada had possessed a sort of federal government since 1840, struggling to unite Empire loyalists who had fled from the USA when it became independent and French-speakers around Quebec who were not enthusiastic about any sort of British rule. The American Civil War intensified these difficulties, but an initiative by the smaller colonies in 1864 led on to negotiations which in 1867 produced the Dominion of Canada. A difficult negotiation with the Hudson's Bay Company gave the new dominion control from Atlantic to Pacific by 1871, at which point British troops left. A similar but much lengthier process led to Australian federation only in 1901, but the separate colonies had achieved self-government much earlier, just as New Zealand had become a self-governing colony in 1854 and Cape Colony in 1872. In almost every case self-government led on quickly to the adoption of a tariff, so that Britain's major colonies adopted protection just as Britain herself was abandoning it. The process of granting locally responsible governments was largely one of yielding gracefully to colonial demand, no doubt with memories of America's war of independence in mind, but there was no obvious strategy for the future.

Local self-government by colonies of white settlers forced hard thinking about the nature of colonies, for it was not in the government's mind to concede similar rights either to colonies where there were few white settlers (as in the West Indies) or where the whites in residence had an unacceptable attitude to native populations, as had the Dutch in Southern Africa (though the Dutch 'Boers' had in any case moved further to the hinterland beyond Britain's reach for the time being). As a result of riots and extreme counter-measures taken to suppress them in Jamaica in 1865, the concept of a 'crown colony' was adopted for those possessions expected to remain under direct rule. Responsibility for these would remain with the British government.

The major exception in all consideration of the Empire was India, easily Britain's biggest possession. A little power was still uneasily vested in the East India Company, though working alongside governors who were crown appointees. The 1857 explosion of racial violence in parts of northern India which was known to Britain as the Indian Mutiny (technically correct since it began with the Company's Indian soldiers murdering their British officers) but more prophetically dubbed by Marx 'the first Indian War of Independence', was a terrible shock to Anglo-Indians. The fragility of British control and the fear of a recurrence of such mass murder as at Cawnpore in 1857 changed attitudes fundamentally. The Crown finally took over from the Company, the proportion of British to Indian troops was increased, and British viceroys sought co-operation from the Indian princes rather than a steady process of expansion into their lands. Without pressing the tactless policies of modernisation and westernisation that had helped to provoke the Mutiny, more was done in road-building and laying railways – both to help the Indian economy and to strengthen strategic control. At a deeper level 1857 changed attitudes to race within the Empire, but especially in India itself. This may be explained too by the increasing number of white women who now came to India, which led to the greater separation of the races, but the lasting distrust that 1857 itself occasioned may well be explanation enough of this ominous development.

The Mutiny had obvious defence implications, for like the Crimea it had shown how widely spread were Britain's garrison forces, how vulnerable were their lines of communication and how long it took to concentrate troops to put down a rebellion; the same was even more true of the Maori wars in New Zealand. After 1857 the 'route to India' was often to be a determining factor in foreign policy and in the acquisition of new territory. Palmerston, who had frequently argued that Britain's objective was 'trade not land', bluntly and typically responded to the expansionist implications of this argument when Egypt was presented as a vital staging post on the route to India:

We do not want Egypt any more than a rational man with an estate in the north of England and a residence in the south would have wished to possess the inns on the north road. All he could want would have been that the inns should be well kept, always accessible, and furnishing him when he came with mutton chops and post horses.

But it was the needs he enumerated that were the key to the question: substitute coal for chops and add highwaymen to the analogy, and it is not hard to see how the most anti-expansionist British statesmen found themselves occupying more and more territory to make secure the road to the East.

In the meantime the defence review of the 1860s concentrated on bringing British troops home, both to reduce the cost to the taxpayer and to improve their availability for the next conflict if it were in Europe. The review originated in a Commons debate of 1861, when MPs decided without even a vote that self-governing colonies ought also to defend themselves – except in emergencies on an 'imperial' scale. Little happened at first, until Gladstone and a determined military reformer, Cardwell, took office in threatening European circumstances in 1868, determined to halve the numbers in the colonial garrisons: even a small garrison like that in New Zealand had taken ten years to extricate. The symbolic importance of the policy was widely misunderstood to be a complete turning away from Empire by Gladstone's government, since it almost simultaneously pulled troops out of Australia, New Zealand, and Canada (where they left Quebec with bands playing 'Auld Lang Syne'); it was also intended to withdraw troops from South Africa. There was a storm of protest over this 'abandonment' of Empire, until the government made clear that this was only the application to self-governing colonies of the duties as well as the rights of their position, a policy which all parties at Westminster had supported.

The level of misunderstanding of what Gladstone was doing in 1871 says much about the character of the mid-Victorian debate on the Empire. On the one hand there were unashamed advocates of Empire like Disraeli, whose earlier and much-quoted references to the colonies as 'millstones round our necks' and 'colonial deadweights' were part of the universal view that the colonies should share the burden of their own defence, not a plea to get rid of them. A few real critics like the radical Goldwin Smith argued for dismembering the Empire altogether; but even non-interventionists in foreign policy set severe limits to any policy of retreat from Empire. Cobden argued that colonies should be held by affection and moral bonds, not by force, much as Gladstone later favoured Empire but not Imperialism, and Bright regarded dismemberment as impractical nonsense: 'Give up all the colonies & dependencies of the Empire? Can any statesman do this, or any country do this? I doubt it.' Liberals could indeed be more open than most to the argument that Britain's world power was a force for good: in 1855 Gladstone argued that

if it please Providence to create openings for us upon the broad fields of distant continents, we should avail ourselves in reason and moderation of those openings to reproduce the copy of those laws and institutions, those habits and national characteristics, which have made England so famous as she is.

If Liberal 'non-interventionists' talked more of moral causation and Conservative imperialists talked more about power and prestige, there remained a core of common ground in their actual policies.

And yet in these mid-Victorian decades of what has been called 'the imperialism of free trade', a period in which detachment and non-intervention were the professed policy of all governments, the actual extent of territory in the Empire continued to expand in a way which suggests an overriding continuity of activity almost independent of the rhetorical debate. To prevent an expansion of the parts of South Africa under Boer control, the Colonial Secretary Kimberley annexed in 1871 an area around the diamond city that was to bear his name; he also prepared the way for the uncontroversial annexation of Fiji, a process that was little more than the acceptance of responsibility for territories that British commercial enterprises had already opened up. Lands were acquired in this way by steady accretion, though without any great pomp or excitement, and with little of the intention of 'pegging out claims for the future' which characterised the more rapid expansionism of the 1880s and after.

A change of mood came in the 1870s because of a long-term shift in the balance of European power. The defeat of both France and Austria by Prussia removed two of the checks which Palmerston and his predecessors had used to maintain that balance. Germany and Italy, both of which completed their unification only in 1871, were hungry for status and recognition, and the old empires of Russia, Austria and Turkey seemed in constant danger of disintegration. Initially the rise of Prussia in the 1860s was welcomed by British statesmen as a reinforcement of modern and Protestant forces in Northern Europe, a country still committed to free trade, a natural check to French or Russian expansion, and one with which the British monarchy had family ties. In fact during the Franco-Prussian War of 1870, British ministers were above all anxious that *nobody* should violate the neutrality of Belgium since that might force Britain in honour to intervene. (There is a striking contrast with 1914, when British ministers almost longed for a German invasion of Belgium so that they might have a good reason for a war with Germany that they already felt to be unavoidable.) Immediate reactions to the military power that the new German Empire had demonstrated by 1871 were mixed. Gladstone saw France's defeat by Germany as the 'disabling by land and sea of the only country that has the power of being formidable to us.' Disraeli noted more presciently that 'the balance of power has been entirely destroyed, and the country which suffers most and feels the effect of this great change most, is England.' Invasion scares after 1871 were generally based on fear of the German rather than the French army, demands for fortifications generally for the east rather than the south coast. The vulnerability that this indicated was much enhanced by increased economic competition from Germany and the USA, by tariff barriers, and above all in the 1890s when both Germany and the USA began major naval building programmes.

After the change in the military balance, there was an end to non-intervention. Disraeli's government in 1878 took a hard line of policy to deter a Russian threat to Turkey, calling out the reserves, moving troops from India to the Mediterranean, and preparing the country both administratively and psychologically for war. Britain's aim in the crisis was to secure 'the waterway to India' – shorter but more vulnerable since the opening of the Suez Canal, and when the crisis subsided the Mediterranean sector of that route had been made more secure by the British acquisition of Cyprus. Salisbury, who took over the Foreign Office in the midst of the crisis, and who was to be the chief architect of Britain's international policy for the rest of the century, set out to ensure that such risky policies would not be needed again. In his view it was Britain's relative isolation from power-relationships in Europe that had forced her into so dangerous a course. Back as Prime Minister in 1886 he determined to re-enter the Palmerstonian world – not of rash adventures but of constant attention to the shifting relations between the European powers. Relations with France, Germany and Russia were all given constant attention, without any one of these becoming a partner in a long-term, binding alliance. Long-term alliances would in any case have proved difficult, since Britain had at some time in the 1880s colonial frontier disputes with almost all the European countries.

One line of policy was more continuous – the gradual har-monisation of relations with the USA. The British withdrawal from Canada removed one bone of contention, and there was a less-publicised but equally important withdrawal of Britain's military and naval presence from the rest of the Western Hemisphere too; without fuss and with no treaty, Britain quietly conceded that the Americas were a US sphere of influence and the USA with equal tact accepted Britain's limited territorial presence in the Caribbean. The great extent of British emigration to the USA, both directly and via Canada, no doubt helped too; over half of all European immigrants to the USA in the century before 1914 came from the British Isles. Bismarck for one regarded this Anglo-American racial connection as one of the vital facts of international political life, and later German governments might have done well to remember the fact. Individual issues could still raise hackles, as in a serious dispute over the frontier of British Guiana and Venezuela in 1896, but the interesting thing by then is how surprised British ministers were by the fierceness of American feelings: one wrote that 'We expect the French to hate us, and are quite prepared to reciprocate the compliment if necessary. But the Americans, No!' Expectations of a natural Anglo-American affinity were probably always greater in London than in Washington. This is illustrated by the fact that when confronted by rapid naval building programmes by both Germany and the USA at the end of the century, the Cabinet decided that it could quietly ignore the American navy as not threatening Britain in practice, but must build to keep ahead of Germany. It was already a vital distinction in the drift of Britain's international policy.

British accommodation with the United States, still very conscious of its own anti-colonial past (and regularly reminded of the fact at least by its *Irish* immigrants) is the more surprising given that this same period was one of further and more open colonial expansion. In part Britain shared in a common European desperation to seize colonial territory while there were still potential markets to grab, and there is a good case to say that the main factor of change was Bismarck's policies in 1883–85 when almost all the colonies that Germany ever possessed were suddenly acquired in a series of raids that set off the 'scramble for Africa'. Salisbury had no doubt that the turning point came between 1880 and 1885: he recalled that in 1880 'nobody thought about Africa' but that when he returned to office in 1885 the scramble for Africa was in full swing, 'a sudden revolution' which he could not explain or understand. One reason may well have been Britain's occupation of Egypt, triggering off adventures by France and then Germany. Competition with other countries as the supply of available territory dwindled was certainly one explanation (as was shown when the focus of interest shifted to China in the late 1890s), and this was the more important for Britain, unlike her European rivals still practising free trade, and thus more dependent on markets in her own colonies; if Britain did not occupy Kenya, somebody else would and there would then be a tariff wall around it against British goods. *The Times* still argued in 1884 the traditional view that 'we wish for more markets, not for more dominions', but this was no longer a meaningful distinction; Salisbury reluctantly conceded in 1893 that 'we feel that we cannot suffer . . . that the unoccupied parts of the world, where we must look for new markets for our goods, shall be shut from us by foreign legislation.' Britain therefore added large tracts of Africa and Asia to its colonial Empire in the last two decades of the century.

The process may have been helped along by the Liberal split of 1886 which brought the imperial wings of both parties together in a single grouping which dominated political life for twenty years. But it is unlikely that this made a great difference, for Gladstone's Liberal government of 1880–85 acquired more territory than any of Salisbury's. Gladstone's struggle to avoid a territorial commitment in Egypt indicates the problem. Despite Palmerston's earlier resistance to the idea, the Suez Canal now seemed to make Egypt crucial for the passage to India, and the Liberals were forced to take an increasing role, agreeing to a bombardment and eventually to a military occupation. This led on to concern for Sudan (since the Nile as the core of Egypt's economy flowed through the Sudan – much as in 1893 another Liberal government had to take over Uganda where the Nile began); Gladstone's refusal to advance permanently beyond Egypt was imperilled by his man on the spot, General Charles Gordon, whose death at the hands of Sudanese tribesmen in 1885 made him an imperial and a Christian hero; it also made the government which had first tried to withdraw him and then failed to reinforce him, very unpopular indeed.

Gladstone's problems with Gordon illustrates another regular feature of imperial expansion, the power of the man on 'the turbulent frontier' to influence events in a way that the government did not necessarily support. Disraeli's government had been pushed into Zulu and Afghan wars in exactly that way in the 1870s. Milner and Rhodes were architects of British policy in South Africa in the 1890s more than was any politician in London. Disraeli objected to these local initiatives only if they failed: 'when Viceroys and Commanders-in-Chief disobey orders they ought to be sure of success in their mutiny.' In public though he backed his local commanders and spoke of the need to secure defensible frontiers by the advances which he had not even intended. The fact was that the Colonial Office which had a total staff of only a hundred as late as the 1890s could exercise no real control even had it wished to do so. It was well understood that powerful individuals like Rhodes or Goldie and trading companies like the British East Africa Company must to an extent be a law unto themselves and were generally doing a good job for the country, and that the government had little choice but to rescue them when they got into trouble. The Empire was run on the cheap – the Colonial and Indian civil services added together had less than six thousand officials throughout the world – and the hands-off approach to expansion by trading companies had obvious benefits in keeping down taxation. Regular loss of control in detail was the price to be paid for this. Intervention by government in support of traders was also being pressed on ministers by commercial interests like Chambers of Commerce at home. Salisbury claimed in 1890 that the government would 'always decline to place the power of the country at the disposal of individual investors', but the permanent head of the Foreign Office accepted only a year earlier that 'an ambassador or minister's duty is to look after British interests, and our commercial interests are naturally the most important.' When the (British) Indian government sought to raise revenue by placing a tariff on cotton imports in the 1870s trade pressure from Britain secured its removal.

India after the mutiny presented a pattern of consolidation rather than territorial expansion. Having fought and defeated a nascent Indian national movement in 1857 many Anglo-Indians came to think of India as British by right of conquest, bought with the blood of the martyrs of Lucknow and Cawnpore. An increased emphasis was placed on Indian princes after Queen Victoria was proclaimed Empress of India, though it was under the auspices of British officials that the Indian National Congress was formed in 1885. At its second meeting, delegates were entertained by the Viceroy, who noted privately that

now that we have educated these people, the desire to take a larger part in the management of their own domestic affairs seems to be a legitimate and reasonable aspiration, and I think there should be enough statesmanship among us to contrive the means of permitting them to do this without unduly compromising our imperial supremacy.

Such confidence meant that concessions to Indian nationalist aspirations were made, but it was certainly not envisaged that India would follow the path of the white self-governing colonies, evolving towards what was from 1907 called 'dominion status'.

Victoria's Golden Jubilee of 1887 provided an occasion on which the leaders of the self-governing parts of the Empire could meet together for the first time to co-ordinate commonly agreed policy, as for example in the laying of oceanic cables, but it was significant that trade policy had to be kept off the agenda if harmony was to be achieved. Meetings became more regular and more formal, but never approached ideas of federating the Empire into a single family unit as romantics in Britain and the colonies occasionally dreamed from the 1880s.

The question remains: what really motivated Britain into this unprecedented burst of expansion? For Lenin and Hobson, writing shortly after the advance halted, there was no doubt that the motive was economic; imperialism represented a way of shifting the surplus capital of a country past its first wave of industrialisation into new and profitable fields. Unfortunately for this view, investment simply did not follow (or even lead) the flag. By the end of the century, under half of Britain's foreign investment went to the Empire (and mainly to old colonies like Canada, not to East and West Africa), and no one part of it received as much British capital as either the USA or Argentina. If capital went abroad in the search for profit, then it did not get directed to recent colonies. If there were ever profits from Empire, who made them? Marx wondered whether India 'does not threaten to cost quite as much as it can ever be expected to come to', and Disraeli in 1872 argued that it had been 'mathematically proved' that the colonies cost more than they yielded and that there 'never was a jewel in the Crown of England that was so costly as the possession of India.' Government and British taxpayer footed most of the bills because local representative governments refused to do so, and memories of the Boston Tea Party suggested the unwisdom of British insistence. This Empire 'subsidy' was paid from general taxation and hence paid mainly by the middle and working classes (especially the middle class) who paid a large share of all Victorian taxes; profits from commerce in the Empire seem on the other hand to have been disproportionately routed towards the rich and especially to those in London and the South of England. The Empire of the 1890s can indeed be seen as a giant mechanism for transferring wealth from the middle to the upper classes, some compensation for the opposite effect of urban prosperity and rural decay. More generally a large number of British workers, managers, seamen and domestic investors derived employment and income from Empire trade, and some industries – some towns – virtually depended on the links with colonies. Dundee's dependence on imported Indian jute is one such example, but the mass production of jam, chocolate, margarine and rubber products all depended on cheap imports of Empire raw materials. In that sense at least the benefits of Empire were shared by all the producers and consumers in the British Isles. For a working man it could be just as simple as that: 'what use is the British Empire to me? . . . All I want is my victuals', as one was reported as saying in 1897.

But there were also social reasons for developing colonies, as in the earlier age of 'shovelling out paupers' by mass emigration and so reducing poverty at home; in the 1890s that still appealed to Cecil Rhodes who saw the need for new lands to settle surplus population as the only way of saving Britain from a 'bloody civil war'. There were sound religious and civilising motivations too. Railways might benefit British tradesmen and investors but they were also a lasting legacy for the economic improvement of lands in which they were built. David Livingstone had done as much as any one man to awaken interest in Africa, and other missionaries had a similar impact in popularising Burma and the Pacific islands: Livingstone's impact was perhaps inseparable from that of H. M. Stanley, the American journalist who created his fame around the world, and sold a lot of newspapers in the process. In Britain the *Daily Mail* found that imperial issues were popular with its readers and stated that it was 'the embodiment and mouthpiece of the imperial idea'. Even biology could be a motive. Charles Darwin had grave reservations about the application of his evolutionary theories to man or to nations, but politicians regularly made such 'social darwinist' comparisons all the same. Chamberlain argued that 'the day of small nations has long passed away. The day of Empires has come.' In 1898 Salisbury divided the world into 'living' nations which were expanding and 'dying' nations which were falling back. 'For one reason or another – from the necessities of politics or under the pretence of philanthropy, the living nations will gradually encroach on the territory of the dying.'

Only a man as incurably pessimistic as Salisbury himself would have doubted in 1898 that the British Empire was to be counted among the 'living' nations with a positive future. The previous few years had witnessed the greatest of all outbursts of popular patriotism across the Empire, culminating in Victoria's Diamond Jubilee celebrations of 1897, when the power and might of the British Empire were on display, a naval review off the Isle of Wight displayed 'thirty miles of warships', and the *Mail* enthused over a London parade that contained troops of 'every colour, every continent, every race, every speech . . . a living gazetteer of the British Empire.' Even a few imperialist voices like Kipling's were raised in protest against such vainglorious flag-waving; in 'Recessional' he warned of the pride that comes before a fall and reminded readers that other empires had also celebrated with 'such boastings' before melting away, but these sober truths were drowned in the din of patriotism.

The patriotic mood encompassed the whole of Britain's international policy. When in 1896 a casual remark was made in the Canadian parliament to the effect that Britain's isolation from binding European entanglements was 'splendid', the idea was quickly turned into an article of popular faith. Salisbury was not in fact seeking isolation from Europe in any case, and the Queen was warning him that Britain's temporary actual isolation was 'dangerous', but the phrase 'splendid isolation' caught on nonetheless when it was picked up and given a wider currency by Chamberlain: he claimed that 'the great Mother Empire stood splendidly isolated', but that the isolation was only from Europe. As he was to put it in 1902, 'alone, yes, in a splendid isolation, surrounded and supported by our kinsfolk.' The extent to which this attitude was reciprocated in the colonies is demonstrated by a Canadian stamp issued in 1898 with the legend 'We hold a vaster empire than has been', and by the rapidity and enthusiasm with which colonial troops came to Britain's aid in the Boer War in 1900.

It is impossible to know how far down the social scale such sentiments permeated, though since every town had sent migrants to almost every part of the Empire by 1897 it is not difficult to believe that the idea of the Empire as a family of kinsfolk was easily accepted – at least superficially. There is little doubt that the few articulate anti-imperialists were shocked and appalled by the celebrations of 1897, as they were to be by the Khaki election of 1900; the socialist Beatrice Webb wrote of 1897 'imperialism in the air – all classes drunk with sightseeing and hysterical loyalty'. One minor consequence of the Jubilee was the commissioning for the 1898 Leeds Music Festival of *Caractacus*, a cantata by Elgar based on the story of an ancient British hero, to a libretto by a retired Indian Civil Servant. The final chorus achieved the remarkable feat of turning a historic British military and moral defeat into a hymn of praise to Queen Victoria, who accepted the work's dedication:

> For all the world shall learn it, though long the task shall be
> The text of Britain's teaching, the message of the free.
> And when at last they find it, the nations all shall stand
> And hymn the praise of Britain, like brothers, hand in hand.

Questioned by a German-born friend on the tactfulness of such sentiments, the composer replied in the uninhibited spirit of Jubilee, 'I knew you would laugh at my librettist's patriotism (and mine). Never mind, England for the English I say – hands off! There's nothing apologetic about me.'

17 The emergence of Labour, 1880s–1914

Between the gradual withering away of Chartism after 1848 and the development of the Labour party after 1900, Britain did not have a working-class political movement with mass support. None the less, even in this long period of relative quiescence, there continued to be elements of continuity in attitude (if not in organisation) which suggested the survival of an alternative political culture; seeds were sown for a much later harvest.

The single most important element of continuity for British labour's future was trades unionism, which was actually given a boost by Chartism's failure; the unions' recovery in the 1850s and after owed something to men whose energies had previously been devoted more to politics than to industrial organisation. Britain's prosperity in mid-century and the opportunities of individual advancement given by the mass emigration meant that there was no great surplus of skilled workers. These members of the 'labour aristocracy' – such craftsmen as carpenters, glaziers and engineers – therefore had ideal opportunities to establish viable unions. The 'new model unions' like the Amalgamated Society of Engineers exacted high subscriptions from their relatively prosperous members but were therefore able to build a strong financial base from a stable membership (which in its turn gave them greater power in industrial matters). However the ethos and character of their membership among 'respectable' working men dictated unions which generally acted more like benefit societies, supporting members in time of sickness and temporary unemployment, than as agents of industrial militancy and social change. That change should not be exaggerated though, for there remained forces for militancy within the unions, notably in coal and textiles. In Sheffield in 1865–66, militancy involved even the use of dynamite to secure union recognition from hard-line employers in a series of outrages locally called 'stirrings', which led the government to set up a public enquiry – but this was far from typical.

With sustained economic growth in the third quarter of the

century there was in any case plenty of room to advance their members' interests without threatening industrial profits. It was precisely such union members, many of them with savings in the post office, active in their local chapels and the mainstays of educational and charitable causes, to whom Gladstone was referring when he spoke in 1864 of men 'earning' the right to participate in democratic politics as electors. The social reformer Josephine Butler had the same point in mind when she noted that

the temperance men always lead in this matter – abstainers, steady men, and to a great extent members of churches and chapels, and many of them are men who have been engaged in the anti-slavery movement and the abolition of the corn law movement. They are the leaders in good social movements, men who have had the most to do with political reforms in times past . . . They are secretaries of trade councils, and presidents of working men's clubs.

The unions were closely involved with the Reform League which demanded extensions of the franchise in the 1860s; the change from 1848 was striking, for where Chartists had sought the overthrow of the political regime, the Reform Leaguers of 1866 (more like those of 1830–32) mainly wished to climb on board. Many union members were indeed offered the vote by Gladstone in 1866 and received it from Disraeli in 1867. This in itself helped to make the unions more acceptable to government: trades union law was more regularly discussed in parliament after 1867, union officials found themselves consulted by governments, sitting on local school boards and even appointed to membership of royal commissions. These new model unions for the first time created in Britain a recognised and permanent trades unionism on a secure base. Their leaders went further in establishing in 1868 the Trades Union Congress, to co-ordinate their activities nationally, and especially to co-ordinate representations to government. The second TUC, held in Birmingham in 1869, was attended by only forty delegates, but represented organisations with a quarter of a million members. By 1874 the TUC was reporting growth in union organisation across the board and claimed an affiliated membership of over a million, a figure not to be reached again until after 1890.

Despite their success, the unions of the 1860s were based on very limited objectives. Their leaders were for the most part committed Liberals who were on good terms with the party's leaders at least until disputes over trades union law emerged in the 1870s, in many cases even long after that. Henry Broadhust and George Howell, dominant figures in the politics of trades unionism, were themselves strongly Liberal and determined to avoid political interventions that would split the Liberal vote: Howell in 1869 was specifically opposed to 'the old Chartist principle' of 'opposing all parties except those pledged to Labour principles'. In 1867 he had written that 'as to working men representatives, as a rule our time has not yet come.' In any case the industrial strength of these unions depended on their keeping a monopoly of skills and preventing the dilution of that monopoly by the employment of unskilled men to do craftsmen's jobs. Their success was therefore based on the denial of class solidarity, and unions which tried to organise unskilled workers were generally cold-shouldered. Other types of union fared less well, as the doomed attempt to found an effective agricultural workers' union to combat the rural depression of the 1870s showed. Only in one industry did unionism cross the skill divide and base itself on something like class solidarity; this was in coal mining where there were special industrial circumstances: dangerous working conditions encouraged a unique sense of interdependence in whole communities (generally one-industry villages in any case) and the existence from an early date of state regulation of safety in mines encouraged miners to think of the inherent connection of unions and political activity. Even here unity was local or at best regional, for the miners had several generally county-based unions, and miners like other workers could divide on national lines where there were Irish immigrants in the industry. Since miners either existed in areas in large numbers or not at all, and were well enough paid for many to have votes under an electoral registration system that reflected property values, they could be a formidable voting force too. The Durham miners exercised a strong influence over county elections as early as the 1840s.

But the miners in counties like Durham were also steeped in nonconformist Liberalism and sent their own MPs to parliament as Liberals. Elsewhere some of the nonconformist sects, particularly Primitive Methodists and Baptists, fostered more radical ideas. The chapels often provided local centres of education and the arts, and were places where working men could gain experience of financial responsibility (as trustees), of public speaking (as lay preachers) and of committee work and other such political skills. Rather as the puritan sects of the seventeenth century had provided training in methods later practised by the Levellers and Fifth Monarchy Men, the chapels now provided a similar training for future socialist politicians. If the main emphasis continued to be on Liberalism, it was also a world imbued with a theological motivation and a crusading language, and as theological fashions changed in the later part of the century, stressing now the brotherhood of man rather than the fatherhood of God, nonconformists came to see a greater social imperative in their religious life. 'Labour churches' were a popular way of spreading the 'gospel' of socialism, especially in the North of England. So for example in 1897, the socialist orator Tom Mann addressed five thousand at a Sunday rally in Halifax, on 'some agitators of the Old and New Testament'. A week later in the same hall, Philip Snowden delivered one of his famous lectures, 'The Christ that is to be': he spoke of 'the promised new Jerusalem', which would be both a material and a spiritual revolution, 'an industrial order where every man for a fair day's work has a bountiful harvest and plentiful leisure.'

Alongside the chapels there were also other influences towards an alternative working–class political culture. The greatest was probably the friendly society movement which had in 1872 four times as many members as the trades unions and twelve times as many as the co-operative societies. These varied considerably, with some of the largest (like the Foresters or the Oddfellows) achieving more than half a million members each. They were generally mutual insurance societies, providing only funeral expenses in the cheapest societies but a wider range including sickness benefits in the more ambitious. They acted as agencies for class co-operation.

The widely read books of Dickens and other 'condition of England' novelists had an effect on generations in highlighting social problems, as *Nicholas Nickleby* had drawn attention to the worst of education in the 'Yorkshire Schools'. Later writers, like William Morris (in *News from Nowhere*, which established its own genre of utopian socialist writing) and John Ruskin, gave a wide currency to forms of intellectual socialism. Henry George's *Progress and Poverty* provided an economic rationale as well as a moral case for the removal of 'landlordism'. Robert Blatchford's *Merrie England* sold a million copies at a penny each in 1894–95 and helped to re-create the myth of a vanished democratic past – another inheritance from the English radical tradition; but it was a particularly effective appeal to action: 'My work is to teach Socialism, to get recruits for the Socialist army . . . The most useful thing you can do is to join the recruiting staff yourself, and to enlist as many volunteers as possible. Give us a Socialistic people, and Socialism will accomplish itself.' The classic of such literary propaganda came in 1908 with Robert Tressell's *The Ragged-Trousered Philanthropists*, far more intellectual in its appeal but more realistic in recognising the hard work and disillusion that socialist propagandising entailed.

The co-operative societies which had sprung up, first in Lancashire and then all across urban Britain, were another reminder to members on every shopping trip of the value of working–class collaboration, and an encouragement to savings and other virtues of self-improvement. It gradually developed into a separate network, with its own newspaper from 1871; the Co-operative Wholesale Society was established in 1863 and extended to Scotland in

1871, rapidly becoming one of the chief distributors and even manufacturers of groceries; from the 1880s the Co-operative Union had its own parliamentary and education committees; it did not join the infant Labour Party, but gave sympathetic support and eventually affiliated in the 1920s.

As the century wore on housing became more socially stratified; the most wealthy moved away from houses near the factories, and whole new suburbs (for example in South London) were developed for the growing army of lower middle-class clerical workers. This left the manufacturing working class more isolated in the industrial areas than before and as a result the social institutions of these areas – chapels themselves, pubs, clubs and institutes – came to have a single class character for the first time. The redistribution of parliamentary seats in 1884–85 gave an added edge to this by dividing boroughs generally into single-member constituencies. Henceforth there were recognisably working– and middle-class constituencies: at the end of the century, the county of London had twenty-four predominantly working-class constituencies, eighteen predominantly middle-class, and fifteen of mixed class. Even travel to work could become equally stratified; the parliamentary provision of cheap workmen's tickets on specified trains meant that early trains arrived at London stations from working-class suburbs before the white-collar workers followed later in the morning. Other cities saw a slower class separation, but the trend was all one way.

Despite the alternative culture which developed and the growing sense that there was a 'working class' and not a number of separate 'working classes' (in itself a very significant change in the use of language) the obstacles to working-class political activity remained enormous. Most obviously, Britain was in no serious sense of the word a democracy, for about a third of adult men (and all women) did not have the right to vote even after the third Reform Act of 1884; it is unclear exactly which sections of the community were excluded but the unfranchised certainly included some middle-class men like sons living with parents and lodgers in transient occupations, but there were also many working-class men excluded. This was partly because of a franchise based generally on the value of property occupied, which naturally most excluded the poorest, but also because the byzantine complexity of the registration system itself made it difficult and expensive for the uneducated to *claim* their rights; over time, this obstacle became less significant, and the class bias in the electorate was therefore not very great by the early 1900s. In 1896 the Fabian Society argued that 'England now possesses an elaborate democratic State machinery . . . elected under a franchise which enables the working class vote to overwhelm all others. The difficulty in England is not to secure more political power for the people, but to persuade them to make any sensible use of the power they already have.' That power was itself limited by the continuing existence of second votes mainly for the owners of property; these 'plural votes' provided further obstacles in particular constituencies where they were concentrated – the most extreme case being the nine MPs elected by graduates in special university constituencies.

Beyond legal obstacles was the cost of politics: bribery only began to be eradicated in 1883, and the 1880 general election was the most expensive in real terms of any ever fought in Britain. In 1900, general election candidates spent on average £776 each, at a time when a well-paid working man might be on about a pound a week; even if a working-class candidate was elected, he would then need to support himself as an MP, for there was no salary for MPs until 1911. The law, finance and the lack of class solidarity were all powerful barriers to labour's political advance.

It is not then surprising that the last third of the nineteenth century should have been littered with failed attempts to get working men into Parliament and to found effective groups for that purpose. By any normal standards by which political parties are judged (and by their own aims too) all these experiments failed, but in failing they helped to lay the foundations for later success. The 1867 extension of the franchise prompted the first attempts to elect working-class MPs, but a series of defeats showed that only the miners could yet achieve a breakthrough; but the miners' combination of a wealthy union and a geographical concentration of voters was a sign of what was to come. In 1881 came the formation of the Social Democratic Federation, the creation of a small group of Karl Marx's disciples determined to bring an explicitly socialist ideology to the fore. The four policy objectives adopted at its first meeting – manhood suffrage, triennial parliaments, equal electoral districts, and payment of MPs – showed it to owe as much to Chartism as to Marx. Its leader H. M. Hyndman hampered its prospects by his inability to see trades unions as anything but a diversion from the political struggle, and this at a time when the unions were the only working-class organisation with funds. Tom Mann felt that 'Hyndman's mentality made it impossible for him to estimate the worth of industrial organisation correctly. For many years he attached no importance whatever to the trade union movement, and his influence told disastrously on others.' The SDF converted individuals and promoted the idea of socialism, but made no wider impact; Hyndman remembered the early years at the SDF as a time 'when none of us were above doing anything. We distributed bills, took collections, bawled ourselves hoarse at street corners and sold *Justice* down Fleet Street and the Strand.' It was, as this suggests, a propagandist organisation, exciting to belong to but not very effective. Nor was its reputation much improved when it was shown that in 1885 it had put up two candidates paid for with 'Tory gold', candidates that had divided the Liberal vote and helped only the Conservatives.

In 1884 the SDF was joined in the field by the Fabian Society, as measured and gradualist as the SDF was impetuous and enthusiastic; the Fabians' aim was the 'permeation' of politics with socialist and collectivist ideas, though not necessarily through a separate political party. Fabians emphasised above all the role of the State in achieving social change, a motivation that was worlds away from the moral regenerationism of Philip Snowden, or the simple propagandism of the SDF. The real emphasis was on practicality: Webb argued in 1899 that

important, organic changes can only be (1) democratic, and thus acceptable to a majority of the people, and prepared for in the minds of all, (2) gradual, and thus causing no dislocation, however rapid may be the rate of progress, (3) not regarded as immoral by the mass of the people . . . and (4), in this country at any rate, constitutional and peaceful.

Since early Fabian leaders included the playwright George Bernard Shaw, the sociologist Graham Wallas, and the political scientists Sidney and Beatrice Webb – all people of outstanding talent – they were guaranteed an audience. The Fabians were an avowedly élitist group, like the SDF contemptuous of the calibre of trades union leaders, but they had a real interest in power. Their *Fabian Essays in Socialism* (1889) had a large sale and created its own popular audience for intellectual, moderate socialism. Fabians joined in the 1890s with radical Liberals to push for socialist causes at the local level. The London County Council set up in 1888 had a vocal socialist minority, and socialist members were prominent too in London boroughs, notably in West Ham and in St Pancras where Shaw was a councillor. To an extent, all these intellectual activities, whether moderate or revolutionary, were beside the real point, but they gave regular prominence to the basic idea. The Liberal leader Harcourt remarked ironically that 'We are all socialists now'. In 1890, the Conservative Prime Minister Salisbury had resisted the appointment of an Archbishop of York who had 'socialist tendencies' because it would be inopportune to appoint such a man 'when Socialism is so burning a question'. Salisbury's sensitivities had perhaps been aroused along with those of many of the nation's rulers by remarkable outbreaks of violence in the West End of London; in 1886 Victoria wrote of a riot which was 'a momentary triumph for socialism and a disgrace to the capital'. The culminating event was

'Bloody Sunday' in 1887, when a large but peaceful demonstration got seriously out of hand after excessive counter-measures: so concerned were the authorities that fifteen hundred police were called out, as were two hundred cavalry and the Grenadier Guards: an observer wrote of 'the river of steel and scarlet that moved slowly through the dusky swaying masses' in Whitehall itself. By then in any case a further, more serious prospect had been opened up by changes within the unions and in the overall industrial situation. In the last years of the century Britain was undergoing a 'second industrial revolution' as a result of increasing foreign competition. Industrialists and government enquiries had lamented the sluggish performance of British industry in comparison with other countries since the 1870s. By the 1880s, industrialists were having to build bigger and bigger factories in order to compete for exports, and small firms were being combined into larger units; major industrial agglomerations emerged for salt, chemicals, tobacco, sewing cotton and soap-making. One consequence of such concentrations was an accelerating separation of owners from earners, now divided from each other by the ranks of foremen, overseers and professional managers, and particularly in what had been family firms but which now became more impersonal limited companies. Harmonious and interdependent family firms like Sir Titus Salt's entire community at Saltaire, the Cadburys' at Bournville and the Rowntree works at York, always the exception, became steadily less common. Modernised companies proved to be tougher in labour relations, more determined in their drive for sales and to deliver profits for their shareholders. Industrial change therefore simultaneously distanced the classes in the workplace (while they were also being residentially distanced) while introducing provocative issues of industrial modernisation. Engels correctly predicted that these changes to the international and national economy must bring political change in their wake, though he was less farsighted in identifying just what it would be: he wrote in 1881 that 'it will break the last link which still binds the English working class to the English middle class . . . The British working class will be compelled to take in hand its own interests, its own salvation, and to make an end of the wages system.'

The response of the workforce was both psychological and organisational. The immediate impact was an outburst of militancy in a series of bitter strikes and lock-outs in which non-union labour was as regularly introduced by employers as union labour was withdrawn. One violent climax came with the 1889 dock strike. The more considered response was a revolution within the trades unions themselves to create 'new unionism'. This transformed the unions from narrow and relatively small craft combinations to groups which sought to be as large as possible, with low subscriptions to attract a mass membership and with no restrictions to keep out the unskilled. Between 1880 and 1900 the total membership of trades unions in the TUC rose from half a million to a million and a quarter. The London Trades Council, which had had eleven thousand members in the 1860s before going almost out of existence for a time, was re-formed in 1871 with eight thousand, but rose to sixty thousand in the 1890s. The Engineers were just one of the new model unions which revised not only their rule-book but their whole manner of operating to meet the new circumstances; not all members approved the change – one wrote of the change of 'our characters of peaceable defenders of our rights for that of industrial jingoes.' In effect the strategy changed from one of protecting crafts (which was class-divisive) to one of consolidating all workers to resist blackleg labour (which was class-uniting). A parallel movement came with the formation of a single national miners' federation in 1888, not only enhancing solidarity but demanding militant action to get a minimum wage and a cut in hours.

There were even attempts to revive the idea of 'general' unions without a single industrial base, 'utopian' when attempted in the 1830s but seen as necessary defensive measures half a century later. Many small, craft unions were able to continue in business on the old pattern, but the overall balance of unions affiliated to the TUC was now on the side of unskilled workers. The new solidarity that mass membership denoted was celebrated with the first major May Day demonstrations in Britain in 1890, with half a million people attending a rally in Hyde Park. Changed perspectives may also be seen in the views of two veterans of the working-class movement, both former Chartists: in 1885, Thomas Cooper wrote gloomily that 'if you could get a grant of life to the age of Methuselah, you would not see the programme of socialism . . . realised and established'; in 1889 on the other hand, flushed with the optimism that followed the London dock strike, George Harney felt that 'not since the high and palmy days of Chartism have I witnessed any movement corresponding in importance to the great strike of 1889. How poor and paltry in comparison appear the make-believe . . . "movements" of recent years . . . The strikers have felt their strength and made it felt.' The new generation of union leaders were seen to be of a different stamp too, as the Conservative journalist J. L. Garvin noted in describing a meeting addressed by Tom Mann in 1895: 'He called upon his audience to dare to be men; and "Now, young chaps," he trumpeted . . . "what are *you* going to live for?" The "young chaps" were electrified.' Garvin significantly entitled his article 'A party with a future'.

Such reading can only have confirmed employers in their fears, and in their determination to resist; one wrote in *The Times* in 1897 that 'a stand must be made for the common good against the common enemy. This stand is being made by the engineering employers.' With unemployment remaining high, it was not difficult for employers to find men to break strikes, and agencies developed for that specific purpose: the 'Free Labour Exchange' had in 1901 some 2,500 skilled railwaymen on its books and 'available for immediate mobilisation'. The changed industrial climate and the constant warfare between unions and the more militant employers in the 1890s helped to change class attitudes, but could also have a more directly political consequence. A battle with Liberal employers in Leeds in 1890, in which strike-breaking and the army were used, turned Arthur Shaw from an active Liberal into a socialist who headed the city's trades council and was later a Labour parliamentary candidate.

In addition to battles in the factories and the docks, the 'Employers' counter-offensive' against the unions extended to the law courts. This was the more serious because the basis of trades union law which had emerged in the 1870s was not a codification of unions' rights but a series of specific immunities – exemptions from legal action against them; if the employers could argue that industrial conditions had changed, they could also secure the weakening of these immunities. In a series of test cases, employers' organisations were successful in reducing the effective freedom of the unions to conduct industrial disputes without risking substantial damages. With no clear statutory protection, the unions were at the mercy of unsympathetic judges, and particularly of the politically reactionary and legal arch-conservative Lord Chancellor, Lord Halsbury, who regarded immunities as such to be an affront to the legal system. The judgement in *Lyons v. Wilkins* seriously hampered picketing activity, but the final decision in the *Taff Vale* case in 1901 virtually destroyed the freedom of unions to call strikes. While union leaders were resigned to having to fight it out with employers in industry, they could draw only one conclusion from their defeats in court; since the law did not allow them the rights which they thought they already had, and since Salisbury's government showed no inclination to reverse these damaging judgements by legislation, the unions would have to take action of their own to influence Parliament; for the unions political action now became a conservative strategy necessary if they were to stay in business. The Labour party that emerged described itself in 1903 as having originated in

the desire of the workers for a party that really understands and is prepared to deal with their grievances, and has grown to its present strength by the systematic attacks in the Press and the Law Courts upon combined Labour and its funds. It is the workers' reply to the aggressive action of Federated Masters and Trusts.

The first serious attempt to associate the unions with the socialist cause came with the creation of the Independent Labour Party in 1893, mainly on the initiative of Keir Hardie – a Scottish pioneer of working-class representation whose 1888 candidacy in Lanark and subsequent election for West Ham had shown the way. The ILP was in principle prepared to intervene with wrecking tactics to wrest the initiative from the 'Lib–Labs': in 1893 it put up a candidate against Broadhurst, a former secretary of the TUC, and claimed the credit for his defeat by a Conservative. But this still remained a policy only for by-elections, as Hardie himself argued: 'better split the party now, if there is to be a split, than at the general election; and if the labour party only make their power felt now, terms will not be wanting when the general election comes.' The failure of this strategy in the short term was almost total; in the 1895 general election the ILP ran twenty-eight candidates and all of them were beaten. Where the Fabians and the SDF had been London-based and directed at the political élite, the ILP was based in Bradford and strongest in Scotland and the North, aiming to build strength within the trades unions and in local councils. Partly as generations of leaders changed, partly as individuals despaired of achieving working-class MPs through the Liberal Party, key local leaders like the Yorkshire miners' leader Herbert Smith came over to the idea of labour's independent representation. In this the steady refusal of local Liberal parties to select working-class candidates was an important influence, one symbolic snub being given when a strong campaign failed to secure even a very moderate Lib–Lab candidate for a by-election in working-class Walthamstow in 1897. Liberals seemed indeed oblivious to their dangerous position: the NLF report for 1891 complacently noted that 'a Labour party independent of party considerations cannot assume any real magnitude.' As more trades union leaders were themselves converted to some form of socialism, the chance of combining socialism and trades unionism became more real but the union leaders could still move no faster than their largely Liberal membership. The ILP was unable to adopt a sufficiently pragmatic approach for this purpose, and although its candidates in some places polled well enough in the 1895 election it won no seats, and thereafter lost momentum. The initiative had to come from the trades unionists rather than the socialists, and this came with a resolution narrowly passed at the 1899 TUC Conference (following a similar one a few weeks earlier in Scotland) which led to the calling of a general conference in London of all organisations interested in labour representation.

As a result of this 1900 conference, a Labour Representation Committee was formed; its initial affiliated supporters included the Fabians, the SDF (which left shortly afterwards), the ILP and a small number of trades unions. The objective was a limited one, to work for the election of labour representatives, more in the expectation of making a parliamentary pressure group like the Irish Nationalists than in the hope of taking power. There was no explicit commitment to a socialist ideology (though this gradually evolved in the decisions of later conferences and was substantially in place by 1908) and the first objectives had in any case more to do with trades union rights. The 1900 election came too soon for the new organisation; only two Labour MPs were elected, and one of these later took the Liberal whip; the LRC might well have gone the way of earlier experiments had the *Taff Vale* case not come at just the right time, and so reminded the unions of just what was at stake: the LRC secretary, Ramsay MacDonald, was quick to remind them that 'trades unionism is being assailed, not by what the law says of it, but by what judges think the law ought to say of it . . . That being so it becomes necessary for the unions to place men in the House of Commons.' Union affiliations to the LRC, which had been slow to come in, now rose sharply and by 1903–4 trades unions had affiliated almost a million members to the party, compared to just fourteen thousand from other sources. The large numbers were important not only for the impression of strength which they conveyed, but because small affiliation fees paid by the unions for large numbers of members were to be the secret of financial strength. After *Taff Vale* the LRC's financial resources were so considerable as to give it a real chance of running large numbers of candidates at a general election. In the meantime Labour could flex its muscles by making interventions at by-elections, in which it took three seats, including the victory of a former Liberal agent Arthur Henderson at Barnard Castle in 1903. It also had time to build up its organisational strength, under the guidance of MacDonald.

Two of Labour's by-election gains were at the expense of the Liberals, who watched the new force to their left with considerable apprehension, and this now demonstrated the correctness of Keir Hardie's strategy of using by-elections as a means of extorting 'terms' for general elections. The Liberals, though a far stronger party than Labour had a recent electoral record that was disappointing, having won only one parliamentary majority in the twenty years since the 1884 Reform Act, and in many areas their own organisations were extremely short of cash. It made considerable sense to the Liberal Chief Whip Herbert Gladstone, the Prime Minister's son, to engineer an alliance with the LRC, both to save his own party's funds and to avoid a damaging split of the anti-Unionist vote. Henderson and

MacDonald could both see that it would be of equal benefit to Labour in its infancy. This 'MacDonald–Gladstone pact' of 1903 was therefore an event of the first importance for Labour, since it offered the LRC a free run against the Unionists in a small number of constituencies in return for generally backing the Liberals elsewhere; in Parliament the Liberals would be attentive to Labour's aims, particularly on trades union law, and Labour would give general support to a Liberal government. A much later Liberal leader was to refer to the pact as 'inviting the socialist cuckoo into the radical nest', and there is no doubt that it did give Labour a vital first shove into Parliament. Even at the time the Liberal organisers recognised that it was 'the recognition of a vital change in the organisation of parties', but felt that it merely recognised a change that was in fact 'clear to every individual politician.' Herbert Gladstone consoled himself by noting that there were 'no material points of difference' between the parties on policy, and that a strong Labour contingent in the Commons would not only benefit Labour but would increase progressive forces generally and the Liberal party as 'the best available instrument of progress'. In 1906, LRC candidates took twenty-nine seats, almost all in constituencies which did not have Liberal candidates. The Labour contingent formally constituted itself after the election as 'the Labour party', but took their seats alongside the Liberals in the Commons.

For the next eight years Labour co-existed uncomfortably with the Liberal government, but had no share of office. Many Liberal policies were welcome to Labour supporters, as for example the social reforms that provided meals for school children; the Trades Disputes Act which reversed the effect of *Taff Vale* was almost the first Act of the Campbell-Bannerman government. Labour's support in Parliament was important to the Liberals, especially after 1910 when they lost their own majority; Labour provided more reliable voting support than the more fractious (and often absent) Irish MPs. None the less, the 'Progressive Alliance' of Liberals and Labour was after 1910 an armed neutrality rather than an open-hearted friendship; this was hardly surprising, given that Labour saw itself after 1906 as a potential government of the future and hence a rival to the Liberals. The Liberals had no intention of giving way to their younger ally. The rapid reversal of *Taff Vale* was not therefore repeated when the unions suffered a further legal setback in the *Osborne* judgement of 1909. This effectively debarred the unions from contributing to political causes from their general funds and hamstrung Labour's finances. An interim assistance was given with the introduction of salaries for MPs in 1911, so relieving Labour of expenditure and incidentally allowing Labour MPs a greater degree of freedom from their party sponsors than in the past – a change that was later to provide a strong bulwark for moderation in the party. It was not until 1913 that the Trades Union Act dealt with the legal issue, and then only half-heartedly; from that time, unions had to keep separate funds for political activities, had to ballot their members before affiliating to any party (as a result of which affiliations to the Labour party fell away) and could raise political subscriptions only from the members who individually agreed. It could only be seen as a Liberal warning shot fired across Labour's bows.

Labour did use the Edwardian years to build stronger foundations, and this too worried the Liberals. Unions continued to affiliate until the decision of the miners to join in 1909 brought in the last of the major industrial unions; in 1912 total party membership was approaching two millions. In Parliament, Labour began to develop a more professional approach, particularly when MacDonald was leader between 1911 and 1914 – but the lead was lost when he fell out with the party line over the war in 1914. Locally, Labour organisations developed through greater co-operative efforts of unions and ILP branches, often in trades councils which were effectively constituency Labour parties. Progress was discontinuous and subject to considerable local variations, but the overall Labour presence in local government undoubtedly improved. Consciousness of greater strength at the roots could be a problem in itself since it encouraged Labour's active members to seek advances at a rate faster than the Liberals would tolerate. There were a few gains with Liberal approval, as in the Attercliffe by-election of 1909 (where Liberal and Labour candidates fought it out, but the Liberals accepted that it had become Labour territory after Labour won the seat). More often the Labour leaders were forced to call off local parties to avoid offending the Liberals, generally but not always successfully. The victory of an independent socialist candidate Victor Grayson at Colne Valley in 1907, combined with a Labour victory at Jarrow a week earlier (both seats taken from Liberals) was a serious embarrassment for the party leaders, for Grayson wanted a strategy of no alliances or compromises. He was not the only spokesman for the disaffected in the party: in 1908 Ben Tillett wrote grumpily that 'the Labour Movement must not tolerate the further betrayal of interests by agitations about the House of Lords or Welsh Disestablishment'. Liberal causes were now blocking the rails for Labour's plans, and Labour shared Liberal frustration when Ireland again headed the agenda after 1910. The *Osborne* case and the need to avoid a Liberal defeat over the House of Lords issue in 1910 effectively defused the problem for a time. In the 1910 elections Labour won forty seats, again almost all of them without having to beat Liberal opponents, but the apparent increase is explained by the gain of the miners' existing Lib–Lab MPs; as a partner in the 'party of progress', Labour shared in the overall loss of votes sustained by the Liberals since 1906, and there was a reduction in the overall number of the labour movement's MPs.

Things were even more difficult between 1910 and 1914, for the agitation for a more independent line from Labour's hotheads became more difficult to resist. So irritated did the more radical sections of the party become, that some split away in 1911 to form with Grayson a British Socialist Party based on the old SDF. Within the unions the influence of French anarchist ideas of syndicalism weakened the hold of some moderate leaders and had political influence in the party too; the ILP members for the most part stayed in the Labour party and remained committed to political rather than industrial action, but stayed to fight for more radical policies and tactics. In by-elections after 1910 there were many three-cornered contests in which official Liberal and Labour candidates fought it out to the advantage of Unionists; these contests demonstrated the extent to which Labour still needed partnership with the Liberals, for four Labour seats were lost to Unionists on a split vote, including two mining seats. There were considerable frustrations in Labour's ranks, particularly among such left wing MPs as George Lansbury whose resignation to campaign for more advanced causes actually caused one of Labour's defeats. Local party organisations, prompted both by general frustrations and by the wish to retaliate against the Liberals for these setbacks, were preparing to run many more candidates at the next general election – though they had made similar plans before 1910 and not carried them out in the event.

It was certainly becoming more difficult to reconcile Labour's growing ambitions with the constraints of an electoral alliance with Liberals who had no intention of regularly reviewing the pact to allow for a steadily-increasing number of Labour MPs. Between 1906 and 1914 Labour was in effect on a plateau; it could only move forward by risking a big defeat: in the three-cornered by-elections of 1910–14 Labour was always in third place, even in seats which it had previously held. Labour could force a general free for all which would deny many victories to the Liberals and put the Liberals out of office in the process, but this would probably destroy its own parliamentary bridgehead. If Labour *were* to develop into a fully independent party, it could only be by taking the risk of such defeats, but an unnecessary defeat too early might end the forward movement altogether. Labour approached the general election due in 1914–15 with trepidation, but had the Great War not prevented that election from taking place, it would most probably have been with a new Lib–Lab pact, less watertight perhaps than in 1906 and 1910 but partly effective none the less. Labour's strength was still too limited to allow a strike for independence. Beatrice Webb noted in 1914 that 'the Labour Movement rolls on – the trades unions are swelling in membership and funds, more candidates are being put forward; but the faith of the politically active members is becoming dim or confused whilst the rank and file become every day more restive.'

Labour was held back in policy terms as well as in organisation and support. Although most of the working class had the right to vote in 1914, Labour had not succeeded in detaching very large numbers of working-class voters from more traditional loyalties. Religion, economic interest and local identity could still be at least as powerful an influence on voting as class, and in some areas like Lancashire the Liberals had in any case established something like a working-class base for themselves. Where Labour did build strong local roots, it was often by association with these non-class motivations – as for example in deference to Catholic interests in areas with a big Irish vote. Nor does the party's slowness to develop a clear socialist identity seem to have been a handicap in building a strong electoral base; it may even have been that the radical socialist policies needed to keep active members happy were a handicap in appealing for votes. What is most misleading is to think of Labour as just another party to the left of the Liberals which had only to outbid the Liberals to pick up votes – though Labour's radicals were keen to press for such a strategy; with a monopoly of office, and hence a monopoly of the ability to actually *do* things, the Liberals were rather better at producing popular policies than Labour. In any case, Labour was aiming at former Conservative as well as former Liberal voters, and some elements of the Tory tradition, like the acceptance of state intervention, were closer to Labour's ideas than was classic Liberal individualism.

By 1914 Labour had still not developed an identity that could subsume the tactical problems which impinged on it differently in different places. The Great War provided an unanticipated benefit to Labour, since it enabled Labour to escape the dilemma posed by electoral alliance with the Liberals and allowed a strike for independence without the risk of annihilation. But it also demonstrated on a national scale the relevance of Labour's most distinctive ideas and so solved the party's identity problem too.

18 Unionists and Liberals, 1886–1914

For twenty years after the Irish Home Rule crisis of 1886 realigned the parties there was Liberal frustration and Unionist dominance. The four general elections of the period produced solid Unionist majorities in 1886, 1895 and 1900, and one indecisive result in 1892, three years of weak Liberal government and seventeen years of Unionism in majority office. But then the whole balance of politics tilted in the first years of the new century, so that the Liberals won one of their best ever majorities in 1906; the last eight years before the First World War were years of confident Liberal government, with Unionism divided and despondent.

The Unionist dominance after 1886 relied at least as much on the weakness of opponents as on internal strengths. Liberals were routed in 1886 even in parts of the country that had previously been Liberal strongholds, most notably in the West Midlands which faithfully followed Chamberlain into the Unionist camp. It was not easy to react to such a defeat, for the Party could hardly abandon the commitment to Home Rule so recently entered into; the departure of the Unionists made it even more vulnerable to the need for Irish votes and the backing of Irish MPs. There was in any case no going back on Home Rule while Gladstone remained at the helm, and though his retirement continued to be expected, it did not eventually occur until 1894. The muted struggle for the succession to Gladstone lasted for twenty years and helped to postpone the taking of important strategic decisions. The wait for Gladstone to go also complicated the question of future relations between the official Liberal Party – revealingly listed in parliamentary handbooks of the time as *Gladstonian* Liberals – and the Liberal Unionists. A round-table conference of 1887 sought to bring the warring factions back together; it could hardly succeed given the impossibility of bringing Gladstone and Chamberlain back into the same team but demonstrated that neither side believed at that stage that the breach need be final. The passage of time tended to make the breach final while continuing uncertainty made Liberal strategy more confused.

The Liberals' Irish allies were also in disarray. There was first an understandable outrage that the hopes raised in 1885–86 had been dashed by what was seen as the selfishness of British politicians. Parnell's tactics during the crisis came under attack and he was never again to exert full authority over the Irish Party. On the other hand the opponents of Home Rule continued to fear him as a dangerous man who might break up the Empire. In an attempt to discredit him, *The Times* published in 1887 letters said to have been written by Parnell in 1882 in support of political murder; with the backing of the Unionist government, the paper unwisely editorialised on the inevitable connection between 'Parnellism and crime', and both *The Times* and government were seriously embarrassed when Parnell successfully sued for libel and proved that the letters were forged. But in 1889 Parnell's enemies did succeed in destroying him when he was damagingly cited as co-respondent in the O'Shea divorce case (he had been living with Mrs O'Shea since 1881 and they had three children). The Catholic hierarchy in Ireland and nonconformists who voted Liberal in Britain were equally shocked, and Gladstone formally disowned any wish to co-operate politically with Parnell in the future. As a result Parnell resigned the leadership of the Irish MPs, dying in 1891; the Irish Party split into competing but ineffective factions in the 1890s, and could not even make much use of holding the balance of power in the Commons in 1892. They reunited under John Redmond early in the 1900s, but in the meantime Irish nationalism had moved into a phase in which democratic action was discredited, and the emphasis had shifted from the political to the cultural field with a revived interest in the Gaelic language and the arts. In politics, the most extreme nationalists expressed public doubts whether Home Rule would ever be conceded by British politicians as a result of Irish votes. The first stirrings of a revolutionary movement re-emerged.

The discomfiture of the Home Rule movement also owed something to government policy under Salisbury, for the Unionists had their own policy for Irish grievances as well as a determination to oppose constitutional change to the Union. Unionists believed that Irish discontent was essentially materialist, and that constitutional issues had arisen only because Parliament had not given adequate redress, more or less what Gladstone had argued before 1885: in 1898 Salisbury's nephew and successor Arthur Balfour, who had himself been Irish Secretary, argued that the failure to give responsible local government to Ireland would be a confession of Westminster's inability to legislate responsibly; but when instituted these new local authorities became platforms for the projection of Irish nationalism – which Unionists saw as disloyalty. The policy aim was to 'kill home rule with kindness', a combination of tough government to restrain disorder and a generous policy to ameliorate social and economic problems – a policy described as 'heavy policing and light railways'. Substantial sums were invested in economic infrastructures; while this lessened the level of economic misery, it could never right the basic imbalance of an economy that depended on the export of agricultural goods which were cheap on the world market. More successful was the attempt to deal with landownership grievances: large sums were granted from the Exchequer at low interest rates to enable Irish tenants to buy their farms. This successfully transferred a significant proportion of Irish rural land to its occupiers, and simultaneously enabled the landlords to extract themselves from unprofitable investments with compensation. Most of those who remained as tenants now had legally determined rents. The class of owner-farmers thus extended proved to be a conservative force in Irish affairs (though this was incidental to the main objective) and land had by the early twentieth century ceased to be a major impetus for Irish grievances. The tough policy of repression that went alongside this enlightened attitude to the land helped to stamp out agrarian outrages, and earned Balfour the nickname 'bloody Balfour'. In combination, these policies had effectively restored order in Ireland by about 1900, as Table 18.1 shows. It was possible for both Unionists and Nationalists to believe that they had 'solved' the Irish question by their policies; an Irish Catholic Archbishop lamented in 1895 that the country had become 'shamefully apathetic. There is no desire for Home Rule.' Unionists had indeed solved some of the agitation's most serious symptoms, but both the cultural and the underground revolutionary movements that succeeded Parnellite nationalism were to be fatal threats to the Union in the future.

If the divisions of opponents helped the Unionists to hold power, there were more enduring foundations of success too. The 1884 extension of the franchise did not harm the conservative forces

Table 18.1 *Political Crimes and Evictions in Ireland*

Decade	Homicides	All 'Outrages'	Evictions
1860–69	40	2,792	9,801
1870–79	67	4,173	6,654
1880–89	94	16,166	32,704
1890–99	24	3,300	7,945
1900–09	10	3,038	2,583

in society as much as was feared; in 1886 Salisbury anticipated that 'Property is marked out as the next object of radical attack when the Radical party resumes its activity and unity.' This was true enough for the long term, but an exaggerated fear in Salisbury's lifetime, for the newly enfranchised voters proved to be responsive to the Unionists' uninhibited electioneering, and were as open to the patriotic impulses mobilised by imperialism as they were supporters of the Irish Union itself. The continuation of plural voting was also a help in many places. The redistribution of 1885 was a positive bonus, for it kept in being many Unionist constituencies in agricultural, market and cathedral towns, while creating new seats in growing middle-class suburbs. These last were an important area of expansion, for the increasing affluence of middle-class voters made them more open to conservative appeals, so that 'villa Toryism' was not only a present strength but a portent for the future too. The growing London suburbs which housed an increasing army of clerks and office workers were Unionist seats most of the time.

Salisbury successfully combined an appeal to these new conservatives and to traditional working-class Tories with an air of aristocratic authority. Unlike Lord Randolph Churchill, a self-confessed Tory Democrat, who sneered at 'the Lords of suburban villas . . . the owners of vineries and pineries', Salisbury and his family group were quite prepared to collaborate with middle-class wealth. In private they shared Churchill's views: Balfour recommended a businessman to Salisbury as having 'great tact and judgement – middle-class tact and judgement I admit, but good of their kind . . . He is that *rara avis*, a successful manufacturer who is fit for something besides manufacturing.' The regime took its popular name from Salisbury's town house at the 'Hotel Cecil', a title recalling the milieu of an aristocratic grandee of a previous age. But in reality the Hotel Cecil was constantly absorbing new social forces as well as prolonging the old. This was in part accidental; the need for party funds ensured that the character of the House of Lords would be adapted to those whose wealth had not originated from land (with a preference for financiers rather than manufacturers admittedly), but the lifestyle expected of the newly-ennobled ensured that wealth would continue to be associated with country living and traditional pursuits. Entry to the hierarchy of political society was opened up to more than those who could afford a title or a seat in the Commons, and in this the West End clubs were important. In addition to the Carlton Club, there were by 1900 many other political clubs on the conservative side, each with its own age-group and distinctive social character, but collectively providing a geographical unifier as centres where the leaders of provincial Unionism were able to meet and stay when in London. In 1868 the five Conservative clubs in the West End had a total membership of nine thousand; by 1885 that had risen to nine clubs with over fifteen thousand members, and by 1904 to nearly thirty thousand. Another unifier was the financial world of the City of London, traditionally open to new sources of wealth, and a Unionist stronghold from 1886. Although the party organisation continued to produce occasional demands for more democratic attitudes, they rarely built up much head of steam. Conversely, the strongest part of the organisation at this time was the semi-official Primrose League. The League's members, like those of Conservative clubs and lodges and of local party associations, paid little and expected little influence in return for their limited commitment of membership.

The party's appeal to such a disparate coalition of interests was enhanced by the growth of a more distinct patriotism; after her long period of widowed seclusion, Victoria's re-emergence into the limelight made her widely popular and her Golden and Diamond Jubilees in 1887 and 1897 provided excellent opportunities for the 'invention of tradition' and of ceremonial by which the monarchy became a focus of popular nationalism. It was a nationalism that could take pride in such celebrations as Empire Day and from the maps in which the countries of the Empire were coloured in pink on the wall of the typical schoolroom. The domestic political value of such national self-congratulation was considerable when the very name of the 'Unionist' party was a constant reminder of its view of Britain's place in the world.

Salisbury was equally successful in maintaining authority within his governments, a far from obvious outcome in 1886. The most important open challenge came when in 1886 Lord Randolph Churchill resigned from the Exchequer over the army estimates; Churchill mistimed his challenge but in any case overestimated his support in the places that mattered in the party. Salisbury accepted the resignation and went on as before. Churchill never held office again, partly because of the failure of his health, but Salisbury was not again challenged in this way. It was significant that Churchill did not get the support of Joseph Chamberlain for his Tory radicalism and that it was a Liberal Unionist who replaced him in office. Liberal Unionists gave only outside support to the 1886–92 government, but over time the connection became closer. Separate social and political organisations continued until 1912, but the coming and going of another Liberal government in 1892–95 (during which the Liberal Unionists sat with Conservatives on the opposition side and again voted against Home Rule) marked a point of no return as social integration steadily proceeded. In 1895 Oscar Wilde's Lady Bracknell noted that the Liberal Unionists 'count as Tories. They dine with us. Or at any rate they come in the evening.' In that year, the Liberal Unionists formally joined Salisbury's government, with Chamberlain becoming Colonial Secretary and with others like Hartington also entering the Cabinet. From that time, Liberal Unionists continued to need careful handling on specific issues (above all on education on which their nonconformist supporters were suspicious still of Anglican Conservatism) but the divisions were henceforth to be within Unionism as a whole rather than between its two component parties.

The alliance with the Liberal Unionists may have been one important factor in encouraging Salisbury to keep open avenues to reform: Chamberlain, still a programme politician, was the first major politician to take up the case for old age pensions (in 1891) and urged Salisbury in 1894 to adopt a 'large and generous programme' which would be 'likely to appeal to the popular imagination.' Salisbury was by instinct deeply and pessimistically conservative, but he was pragmatic and tough-minded in his wish to retain office – and to deny it to Gladstone – and recognised that reforms would be needed to keep seats won in 1886. He also retained some directly humanitarian motivations: his Chancellor of the Exchequer Hicks-Beach believed that 'on the leading questions of home politics of the time . . . he was more Tory than his colleagues; but though certainly no "Tory Democrat", he was keen about the housing of the poor and sanitary improvement.' As Balfour pointed out in 1895, 'social legislation . . . is not merely to be distinguished from socialist legislation, but is its direct opposite and its most effective antidote.' Faced with a rising tide of socialism and working-class unrest, Unionists had not only Liberals in mind in framing their policies.

The centre-piece of the 1886 government was the creation of County Councils in 1888, extending to the countryside something like the pattern of elected local government which had existed in the towns since 1835. The actual reform was less sweeping than intended, as every vested interest lobbied for amendments; in the end far too many small towns were excluded from the new system as 'county boroughs' and far too much diversity of size was allowed between the populous counties of Lancashire and London, and the tiny counties of Rutland and Ely. The structural change was anyway generally greater than the practical one, for in such rural counties as Cheshire the new councillors were the same men who had governed as magistrates before the Act, but in the more industrial West Riding, county politics was transformed. It was left to the Liberals to add a second tier of local government in the counties in 1894. Initially County Councils had only a limited role, but their existence alongside city corporations provided machinery which future governments could use to implement more interventionist policies. In 1902 the Unionists themselves made the County Councils the controllers of education when they extended secondary schooling. Other measures were more departmental than political in origin, but they could be cited as a reasonable list of social measures: a Mines Regulation Act in 1887 was described by a miners' MP as 'the greatest measure of its type that had ever been passed', and similar codifying measures were passed on shop hours, smallholdings, allotments, factories, and on working-class housing.

The 1895 government was less active, probably because the Liberal threat and disorder in the London streets seemed to have diminished, but it could point to the 1897 Workmen's Compensation Act as a signal achievement. Nevertheless, any Unionist claim to be sympathetic to working-class interests was damaged by government support for employers in the industrial disputes of the 1890s, notably in making troops available to protect blackleg labour and in the refusal to initiate legislative reversal of the defeats suffered by trades unions in the courts. All this showed the increasing difficulty of holding together the coalition of conflicting interests which made up the 'Hotel Cecil'. But there seemed little reason to think that these difficulties would greatly affect the political balance; in 1900 the Unionists were comfortably re-elected with over four hundred MPs and a majority of 134. Significantly, in 1895 and 1900 almost a third of the constituencies were uncontested, a sign of the political torpor of the nation which recalled Palmerston's ascendancy. Salisbury remained Prime Minister until 1902 and was then uncontroversially succeeded by his nephew Balfour, whose government included not only three of his own relatives but also both Joseph Chamberlain and his son Austen. The 'great cousinhood' seemed to have absorbed the impact of the realignment of 1886.

The issue which shifted the direction of British politics was the Boer War of 1899–1902, a conflict that began like so many of the colonial wars of the nineteenth century with British defeats, but which developed into a national crisis of confidence. The country's morale survived the 'Black Week' in which three British armies were successively defeated by Boer irregulars, and recovered confidence when defeats were succeeded by victories in 1900, reaching a peak of jubilation with the relief of Mafeking. From then the war lasted for two more years, during which the organisation and leadership of the army, the tactics of pacification used to subdue the Boers, and British methods from education to public health all came under scrutiny. It was a severe shock to the nation that the power of the Empire, so recently celebrated at the 1897 Jubilee, could not conquer a small farming people without resort to what the Liberal leader called 'methods of barbarism'; the Boer War also brought to public attention the uglier aspects of modern war – khaki uniforms, sniping by unseen enemies, trenches and the internment of civilians in the first 'concentration camps'. Faced with a hard fight, the Empire had drawn deep on its resources, but had found that those of the homeland were inadequate. This had major implications for the way in which the Empire itself was seen and subsequently developed, but it also had a direct domestic impact. British men were not slow to offer themselves as volunteers for the war, but in some of the conurbations large numbers were rejected by the army; it was noted that in Manchester, eleven thousand men volunteered, but eight thousand of these were found unfit to carry a rifle and endure the fatigues of army life, and eventually only twelve hundred of the original volunteers 'attained the moderate standard of muscular power and chest measurement required by the military authorities.' For a generation brought up with the evolutionary ideas of Charles Darwin, this produced deep fears for the future of the race; had industrialisation weakened the fighting-stock of the people by producing pale, under-nourished children who were denied the invigorating access to fresh air and exercise enjoyed by their rural forbears? A British general wrote in 1903 of the 'strong presumption that neither the unskilled labourer who has been tempted into the towns, nor the hereditary townsman who, after two or three generations, has deteriorated in physical vigour, will be able to rear a healthy family.' The War opened up questions about national fitness, and at the same time occasioned a wider drive for reform by exposing national institutions to a searching test which many of them seemed to fail. The Edwardian period was therefore characterised by a new readiness to make changes, especially in the social sphere, by a drive for 'National Efficiency' which encompassed to varying extents all the parties. The comfortable quiescence of the 1890s in which only a few token changes could be offered by Salisbury's government abruptly vanished. The very fact of a new century had occasioned some national soul-searching, as did the death of Victoria in 1901, for although her son and successor Edward VII was already a popular figure, the loss of the reassuring presence of a Queen who had reigned for as long as almost any adult could remember was itself a disturbing factor.

Since the new mood affected imperialist conservatives within the Unionist parties at least as much as radicals, it was possible that the Balfour government in office when the Boer War ended might have put itself at the head of the drive for reform. In some fields it sought to do so: Balfour himself steered through the 1902 Education Act which sought to apply some lessons of the war in its attention to secondary and technical education; the country's slackening growth rate was a further motivation here, for it was noted that both Germany and the USA had a far larger investment in university and professional education than Britain. Balfour also introduced army reforms and changes in military provision. His government developed naval building along new lines with the revolutionary design of HMS *Dreadnought*, launched in 1906, and sought to find a cross-party view on the issue of national health by setting up in 1904 a Royal Commission on the Poor Law. It remains uncertain whether the Unionists would have had the tenacity to tackle the many vested interests involved in a social reform policy; for the Liberal Unionists, Joseph Chamberlain itched for an opportunity to do so, incorporating the idea of old age pensions as a part of his tariff proposals. But it was the tariff issue itself which wrecked Unionism and opened the way for a Liberal government.

There had been a continuing undercurrent of support for import duties among some rural Conservatives, especially when the 'Great Depression' led to a world-wide fall in agricultural prices. Disraeli had joked when visiting the Free Trade Hall in 1872 that it would sooner or later ring with calls for tariffs, and in 1887 the Conservative conference had actually carried a motion calling for the reintroduction of tariffs. Such ideas, signified by the name 'Fair Trade' to indicate that their intentions were defensive, had not permeated deeply into the party, resisted especially by those whose need for urban votes made them hostile to anything that would raise food prices. There was also a folk memory in the party that Conservatism had once before been wrecked when the interests of producers had clashed with those of the consumer: when the tariff crisis arose Balfour was determined not to be 'another Sir Robert Peel'. The real problem was that the economic interests of different sections of the economy, even of different agricultural areas, conflicted. When Chamberlain launched his tariff crusade in 1903 he sought to sweep up all these conflicts into a single sense of national urgency: 'Agriculture, the greatest of all trades and industries of this country, has been practically destroyed, sugar has gone, silk has gone, iron is threatened, wool is threatened, cotton will go! How long are you going to stand it?' His initiative of 1902 envisaged a scheme that was simple and straightforward, but which could be introduced only at the price of antagonising some of these conflicting interests. Financial circles in particular were very doubtful of the wisdom of risking a trade war that could damage London's invisible earnings, and many of the Unionist MPs who remained true to free trade seem to have had financial rather than manufacturing connections. The Cabinet could not agree to Chamberlain's scheme and his resignation to campaign for tariffs through the country led to a bitter struggle for control of Unionism. By 1905 Balfour had lost control of his party inside and outside parliament, but had successfully fought a rearguard action to deny Chamberlain official acceptance of his ideas. The sudden reappearance of the issue of free trade against tariffs was on the other hand exactly what was needed to revive Liberalism, which rallied to the defence of its most basic creed, and welcomed the few Unionist free traders like Winston Churchill (son of Lord Randolph) who switched parties rather than accept tariffs.

The 1886 split had weakened the Liberal party without resolving its internal divisions. Although Chamberlain had left, the NLF remained if now without the preponderating influence of Birmingham, and radicals continued to disrupt the party with their programme demands. Although Hartington had led most of the old Whigs to the Unionist side there remained a powerful conservative element. The Liberals remained strong, particularly in their northern and Celtic strongholds, but uncertainty about the party's identity and direction also remained. Gladstone, who had decided against retirement solely because of his commitment to Ireland, was determined to keep Home Rule at the top of the political agenda as long as he was leader, though even he was at times pessimistic about the outcome; he wrote in 1887 that 'when I recollect . . . that the *minor* battle of R.C. emancipation lasted for twenty-nine years . . . and that English obstinacy only yielded *then* to the fear of civil war, a darker view asserts itself.' Home Rule was bound to weaken the party's appeal in British constituencies. It was also a single-issue approach that was increasingly difficult to sustain as objections to the blocking of the rails continued to arise. In 1891 the NLF Conference at Newcastle approved (much against Gladstone's wishes) a comprehensive programme of radical proposals, to an extent derived from Chamberlain's 1885 Unauthorised Programme but now officially accepted by the party. The illusion that this solved the problem of the overall coherence of the party's strategy was demonstrated by the fact that the NLF again declined to place the list of proposals in an order of priority. The 1892 election campaign was actually fought on differing issues around the country, and it was the fact that the Gladstone government that took office after the election would depend entirely on Irish votes for its survival that determined that Ireland would again head the legislative programme. It was by this stage not even clear exactly what sort of home rule for Ireland Liberals wanted; Liberal imperialists felt that the total exclusion of Irish MPs from Westminster would seem to go too far towards breaking up the Empire, and the new bill was a compromise on this issue. The second Gladstonian Home Rule bill passed the Commons, but was thrown out by the Lords by a colossal majority. Gladstone finally retired when his ministers would not back an assault on the powers of the House of Lords – which would have been a brave undertaking for a minority government, and one which would have tied the government's plans even more closely to Ireland.

Succeeding Gladstone in 1894 was by no means easy, for no minister had his ability to transcend faction; Victoria chose Lord Rosebery as Prime Minister, when the Cabinet probably preferred the more radical Sir William Harcourt. Rosebery proved an erratic leader for the party, well adrift from its radical faction, although his government did produce through Harcourt such radical measures as redistributive taxes – death duties – which prefigured the 'New Liberalism' to come. His appetite for office was not enough to endure the buffets of a team beset by internal divisions; after two months in office, he complained to the Queen that as a peer he was

more unfortunately situated than any man who ever held that high office. He has inherited from his predecessor a policy, a Cabinet and a Parliament; besides a party of groups, one of which is aimed against himself . . . He himself is only able to guide this tumultuous party through a leader, bitterly hostile to himself, and ostentatiously indifferent to the fate of the Government.

As early as 1893 Harcourt's son noted that 'the sentiment of Ministers is rapidly growing like that of the government of 1885 at the end when their only desire was to get out of office in any way they could.' After fifteen months as Prime Minister, Rosebery seized on an unexpected defeat in the Commons to resign. In the 1895 election, the Liberals were heavily defeated and went into opposition for ten years heavy with mutual recriminations. Rosebery abandoned the leadership, but Harcourt proved even more erratic and lacking in judgement, and the task fell to the little-known Sir Henry Campbell-Bannerman, a moderately-radical Scot of limited ministerial experience. His first years were a time of constant splits, especially when the Boer War introduced a new source of division. The party's right wing, newly christened 'Liberal Imperialists', wanted to give full backing to the government and the war, while radicals – especially the rising star of Welsh Liberalism, David Lloyd George – opposed the war and were branded as 'pro-Boers'. The problems fell away when Campbell-Bannerman could rally the Liberals against the way in which the war was being fought in its last year, so overriding the divisive issue of the war itself. Liberal unity only fully recovered as free trade came under threat and as the Unionists' divisions presented the tempting prospect of a return to office; in three years after the Boer War, Liberals gained nineteen Unionist seats in by-elections.

The ten years after Gladstone's final retirement therefore witnessed the collapse and recovery of his party, but they also saw a good deal of policy work that had been long delayed. Building on the disappointing experience of the Gladstone–Rosebery government, and on the frustrating consequences of the Newcastle Programme, Liberal theorists tried to develop a more coherent philosophical basis for modern Liberalism. J. A. Hobson dissociated it from the concept of imperialism, which he saw as 'a constant menace to peace', and L. T. Hobhouse developed a more interventionist social programme. These writers built on the regular investigations into poverty in urbanised England by such men as Henry Mayhew, Charles Booth and Seebohm Rowntree; from his investigations in York, published in 1901, Rowntree concluded that 'the wages paid for unskilled labour . . . are insufficient to provide food, shelter, and clothing adequate to maintain a family of moderate size in a state of bare physical efficiency.' Rowntree found in York, much as Booth had found in London, that poverty was more widespread than had been generally admitted: 'We are faced with the startling probability that from 25 to 30 per cent of the town population of the United Kingdom are living in poverty.' Backed by such detailed research, the 'New Liberals' developed a rationale for a more advanced social policy which accorded well both with lessons that could be drawn from the Boer War and with the radicals' wishes.

None the less, although radical Liberals had an up-to-date and coherent rationale, social reform did not figure prominently in the Liberal campaign for the 1906 election, which was fought overwhelmingly in opposition to Unionist policy and in defence of free trade. One of the Liberal leaders wrote of 1906 that the party had fought with 'no constructive ideas, merely objections to other people's ideas.' The election had been prompted by the resignation of Balfour, who had hoped that even a brief experience of office would reopen Liberal splits. But Campbell-Bannerman used the patronage available to a Prime Minister to complete the party's reunification and called an election without delay. In defence of free trade, in opposition to a divided Unionism, and in alliance with the new Labour party, the Liberals took a large majority and could anyway generally rely on Irish and Labour support; Liberals and their allies had over three-quarters of the seats, and Unionist representation was more than halved; in an election where few seats were uncontested the Liberal–Labour lead over Unionists in votes was about 12 per cent, an unusually large margin. The character of the Liberal victory was also important, for they had achieved a major breakthrough in Lancashire, a key electoral battleground, and the House of Commons now contained more nonconformists than ever before.

The first period of Liberal government under Campbell-Bannerman was disappointing. The Cabinet included ministers who were either personally disinclined to press for action or simply out of their depth in office, and as a result the government did not come forward with very ambitious plans to match its majority. In any case many key measures passed the Commons with handsome majorities only to be amended beyond recognition in the Lords. In the wake of his defeat, Balfour had unguardedly argued that 'the great Unionist party' should still control, 'whether in power or whether in opposition the destinies of this great Empire'. In this he certainly had in mind the large Unionist majority in the Lords, which enjoyed legislative power theoretically equal to the Commons and which had become almost a one-party House since 1886. Balfour could not anyway hold back the more determined peers, but he made little attempt to do so, except for the tactical purpose of letting through such Labour-inspired measures as the Trades Disputes Act, while wrecking measures derived from old Liberal causes like licensing and educational reform. Like Gladstone in 1894, Campbell-Bannerman was infuriated by the Lords' rejection of the will of the elected House, but had little option but to bide his time. He spoke of 'filling the cup' of popular grievances against the Lords, and hinted darkly about the consequences for the Lords when that cup eventually overflowed.

The mood changed in 1908, partly because the retirement of 'CB' paved the way for a reconstruction of the government and the promotion of more determined, more radical men, partly too because the political circumstances demanded a more positive attempt to build legislative achievements. Herbert Asquith took over as Prime Minister, a cultured, intellectual politician, himself more an old-fashioned and moderate Liberal than a radical, but a man whose authority and political skills were an indispensable cover for more advanced colleagues. Lloyd George, who had made an impact at the Board of Trade, was succeeded by Winston Churchill when he himself took Asquith's place at the Exchequer. Further down too, the government team was tilted towards a more interventionist stance, but it was the combination of Lloyd George and Churchill, under Asquith's leadership, that provided the driving force. The need for a new initiative was shown both by Labour gains in by-elections and by losses to the Conservatives: the London County Council was taken by the Conservatives in a buccaneering campaign in 1907 (and held until 1933) and there were twelve Conservative by-election gains from the government during the parliament, including a humiliation in Churchill's Manchester constituency when his promotion required a new election. By that time the tide had turned. While Chancellor, Asquith had initiated plans for the introduction of old age pensions, though it fell to Lloyd George to implement the plans. The motivation for this major social policy owed much to local social research studies, which had shown not only that lack of savings involved serious poverty for the old, but that the need to support aged parents was a serious handicap to families who were at the same time bringing up children, resulting in malnutrition of wage-earning adults and their children. The reform was characteristic of the period in uniting both humanitarianism and 'national efficiency'. It also helped the government to recover the initiative both from the Unionists and from its Labour allies.

Whatever the motive, there is no doubt that old age pensions were immensely popular, not least because they were non-contributory benefits, paid for from general taxation: a post office worker who saw the effect of the first pension payments in an Oxfordshire village recalled recipients saying 'as they picked up their money, "God bless that Lord George!" (for they could not believe one so powerful and munificent to be a plain "Mr") and "God bless you, miss!" Their popularity proved in fact something of a problem, for the cost was much larger than had been anticipated (much as the new National Health Service was to be in the 1940s); it was doubly unfortunate that this coincided with a speeding up of the naval race with Germany and increased demands on the Exchequer for rearmament. Lloyd George therefore inherited as Chancellor a party appetite for further reforms, which would involve additional costs, and a shortage of funds. From the Unionist benches he was regularly told that the social policies he wanted could not be afforded without tariffs (which Chamberlain had partly justified by their ability to raise revenue for social policies). The 1909 budget, Lloyd George's first, was therefore seen on both sides as a make or break for free trade. It was conceived on a broad scale, intended to deal with the Liberals' political problem with the House of Lords as well as with the Government's fiscal difficulties. It included a whole range of new taxes and duties, including land taxes, a more steeply-graduated income tax, and additional charges for liquor licences; these all hit at interests which supported Unionism, but the Unionists were as angered by the budget's form as by its content. Lloyd George used his speech to declare a 'war on poverty' and to argue that this was a 'People's Budget': it was a deliberate attempt to pursue social policies by financial means and was described in provocative (to Unionists) and inspiring (to Liberals) language. From that moment a vicious phase of party warfare broke out; rival propaganda teams toured the country whipping up opinion for and against the budget, which had one of the longest ever Commons debates. Lloyd George himself joined in the national debate with a will, making especially challenging contributions in speeches at Newcastle and at Limehouse: at Newcastle he referred to the Lords as 'five hundred men, ordinary men chosen accidentally from among the unemployed' and threatened them with a revolution; his even less inhibited speech in East London coined the word 'Limehousing' to describe the new populist politics that had suddenly arrived. The Liberals had put Unionists in an impossible dilemma, for their MPs could only delay the proposals which the Liberal majority would anyway push through in the end, even if a few moderate Liberal MPs had doubts about it. When it reached the Lords, they must either pass it in recognition of the Commons' traditional right to determine financial matters, which would provide a great boost for the government, or reject it, which would incontrovertibly 'fill the cup' and provide the government with the perfect excuse to take on the Lords in a full-scale fight. Unionist leaders gave only fitful advice, but the tenor of the debate in the country probably ensured that the enraged peers would reject the budget, which they duly did.

Asquith and Lloyd George had neatly engineered a basis on which they could appeal to the country, repeating the recipe of 1831–32, by threatening the Lords with a 'swamping' creation of new peers if they did not respect the will of the people. But the need for a new election as the basis of that strategy also placed Liberals in difficulties. Tensions between Liberals and Labour had been temporarily set aside by the *Osborne* case, but different problems now arose with Redmond's Irish MPs. It was expected that the Liberals would lose some seats and Asquith therefore needed to know how Redmond would react if he held the balance of power; the answer was that he would get Irish MPs' support only if he acted to remove the veto power of the House of Lords – and so open the way for Home Rule. Asquith anyway needed the King's backing if the Lords were to be coerced, but Edward VII gave only guarded and private assurances. The general election of January 1910 was therefore a confused affair, but the violence of party antagonisms produced the highest turnout of registered electors of the century, 86.6 per cent. As results came in, it was clear that Liberal losses were heavier than expected, but that Unionists had won back only about half of what they had lost in 1906: Unionists had won more votes than the Liberals but slightly less than Liberals and Labour combined. The two main parties each had about 270 seats, and the control of the Commons would rest largely with Labour and especially with the Irish.

Frightened by the constitutional revolution that they had un-leashed, the Lords at once passed the 1909 budget, but it was now too late to stop there. Asquith, under pressure both from radicals and from Redmond, had to proceed to reform the House of Lords; he was still unclear how far he could rely on the Palace, when the situation was transformed in May by the King's death. The new King, George V, might have different views but he was in any case too inexperienced to be plunged straight into a constitutional battle. In an attempt to avoid further damaging battles, and to avoid being held to ransom by Labour and the Irish, Liberal and Unionist front-benchers convened in autumn 1910 a conference seeking to strike a bargain between the two major parties, even to bring them together in a coalition government. Neither Balfour nor Asquith expected these talks to do more than occupy time, during which the new King could be crowned, but the conference of 1910 later looked rather different when some of their participants actually worked together in coalitions from 1915–16. The party antagonisms of 1910 were however insuperable and the breakdown of the conference in November placed the problem back with the King; George V now demanded another general election fought specifically on the issue of the Lords, as that of January had mainly been on the budget. This second election in December 1910 precipitated a further round of party battles as Liberals exploited the issue of 'Peers v. People' and Unionists claimed that Liberals were embarking on a drive for an elective dictatorship. The result was the worst of all, for although many seats changed hands the overall balance remained the same. Asquith would have to continue to govern though a minority government, but was also contentiously committed to abolish the Lords' veto and (in order to stay in power) to carry Home Rule too.

The battle with the Lords was quick and deceptively easy. The Lords' offer of reforms to avoid the loss of their veto power was easily brushed aside, and the Commons majority pressed through Asquith's Parliament Bill, which reduced the power of the Lords to a two-year delay of ordinary bills and abolished it altogether for money bills, at the same time amending the Septennial Act of 1716 and so reducing the maximum period between elections from seven to five years. Unionist peers could not bring themselves either to vote for such a bill or to risk collectively opposing it and risking the creation of several hundred Liberal peers – so devaluing the peerage and destroying the Unionist power even to delay Home Rule. With little guidance from their leaders, Unionist peers split into three factions and voted for, against, and abstained in the crucial vote in August 1911, though with enough joining the Liberals and the bishops to see the Bill through. This constitutional battle completed the effective disintegration of the Unionist parties begun by tariff reform. The right wing 'diehards' bitterly resented the loss of their party's power and the way in which they had been outmanoeuvred; they began to disrupt the proceedings of the Commons with rowdy scenes and over the summer prepared to carry on an even more bitter campaign against both the Liberals and their own leaders when Parliament resumed in the autumn. Balfour concluded that his party had drifted beyond his control and resigned as leader in November. Further problems arose over the succession, for discreet soundings among Unionist MPs could not produce a clear majority for either Walter Long, representative of rural English Conservatism, or Austen Chamberlain, Joe's son and the representative of urban Unionism – dismissed contemptuously by Long as 'Birmingham and Co.' Since neither would clearly agree to support the other if elected, a new split could only be avoided by choosing a third and less popular man, Andrew Bonar Law.

Bonar Law was a taciturn, unpolished and unfashionable Scot of Canadian and Ulster stock, a tough fighter who would mount an effective opposition, but a man who had never been in Cabinet; his election was testament to the extreme nature of the party crisis. Nevertheless, as Lloyd George noted in saying that 'the fools have stumbled on the right man by accident', Law was a shrewd choice. Having no real authority and experience of his own to offer, he was forced to rely on a team approach, but his close connections with back-benchers and the provincial roots of the party gave him a clear grasp of the wishes of the rank and file: 'I am their leader, I must follow them.' Law was therefore a uniting leader who set his sights lower than Balfour had done but who gave his troops a fighting lead and at least indicated by his own presence at the top the openness of Unionism to men of talent. The party had in fact already begun to put its organisational house in order after December 1910 gave it a third successive defeat. An internal enquiry produced a major reorganisation of Central Office and in the constituencies and the creation of the new, pivotal post of Party Chairman, occupied from 1911 to 1917 by the energetic Arthur Steel-Maitland; Balfour had been difficult to interest in such matters, but Bonar Law could not afford to ignore them, and as a result the reorganisation now began to bear fruit in better press relations, stronger organisation and healthier finances. Morale recovered with the sense that the party had a new direction, and recent splits were healed: diehard organisations withered away when the party got a strong lead from the top, and the Conservatives and Liberal Unionists at last formally merged in 1912. The fragility of this unity was shown though when Law tried to settle disputes over tariffs; the resulting outcry from the party's remaining free traders forced Law to renew in 1913 Balfour's 1910 pledge that there would be no tariffs until there had been a further specific appeal to the people for a mandate. The steady gain of by-election seats was though a boost to a party already level with the Liberals in 1910. By 1914 the Unionists could reasonably expect to win the election due within a year, though all predictions were made more difficult by speculation about the role that Ireland would play in the election.

Unionist recovery and Liberal loss of momentum between 1911 and 1914 both owed much to the resurgence of Home Rule. With the Lords' veto gone by 1911, Asquith had now to introduce a bill which would carry Home Rule, and preferably in time to be implemented before another general election. As a result the parliamentary sessions of 1912, 1913 and 1914 were each dominated by interminable, bitter and highly repetitive debates on the same issue, which had to be passed three times in order to deal with the power of delay which the 1911 Parliament Act had left with the Lords when taking away their veto. This wasted much of the Liberals' energies on an issue in which many of their supporters had no great interest. The three-year timescale also presented a greater problem since Irish Protestants, mainly in Ulster, were certain to oppose the bill. At the outset Lloyd George tried to persuade the Cabinet to exclude Ulster from the bill's provisions, at least for a time, but the Cabinet would not compromise the issue of Ireland's integrity (or did not believe that Redmond would agree to do so, at least until the strength of Ulster's resistance had been shown). As a result, the government met organised and effective opposition, not only from Protestant extremists in Ulster but also from the leaders of the community, police, administrators, army officers and judges, and all with the backing of Unionists in Parliament who counted Ulster's Unionists as an integrated section of their party.

The debates did not much affect the bill's content, but the time-scale allowed Ulster's leaders to whip up opinion to white-hot intensity, signified by a Covenant signed by hundreds of thousands of Ulstermen (some even signing in blood), and by preparations to set up their own government in Belfast if the bill ever passed. In support of these treasonable plans, Ulster volunteers secretly imported stocks of weapons: the inability of the Irish constabulary to prevent such occurrences only increased suspicion that Unionism had powerful friends in high places. That suspicion was underlined by rioting and bloodshed caused when the police tried to take tough action against similar military preparations amongst Irish nationalists, increasingly critical of Redmond's moderate lead. The climax of this phase came with the 'Mutiny at the Curragh' in 1914, when fifty-eight cavalry officers up to the rank of Brigadier offered their resignations rather than take part in what they saw as coercive manoeuvres in Ulster, an incident badly mishandled by the government but one which showed that it could not rely on the army to enforce Home Rule against absolutely certain loyalist resistance. Some English diehards were also preparing: Lord Willoughby de Broke, the diehards' hero of resistance to the Parliament Act, now offered to come to Ulster with his Warwickshire tenants, all of whom would be mounted and armed. By 1914 some form of Irish civil war over Home Rule seemed certain. Bonar Law casually told Asquith that he expected to win the coming election, but especially if there were a bloodbath in Ireland. Privately he believed that Asquith 'is in a funk about the resistance of Ulster, and I am convinced he will not face it when it comes to the point.'

By 1914 the government had indeed taken fright at the situation in Ireland. At the King's suggestion, talks were held at Buckingham Palace in the hope of finding a compromise; passions were so inflamed on both sides that common ground could not be found even when Asquith offered to exclude the four most Protestant counties of Ulster for several years, something very close to the settlement finally reached in 1920–21 after actual civil war. Having failed to get agreement, Asquith decided to amend the Bill on his own responsibility, but it was unclear whether such a fundamental amendment could be made within the Parliament Act procedure without starting the two-year process all over again – and so failing to carry any bill before an election; it was also far from clear that Irish MPs on whom the government depended for a majority would be able to bring themselves actually to vote *for* Ulster's exclusion. These imponderables remained when the outbreak of war intervened in 1914.

Despite the primacy of Irish issues, Asquith's government had a creditable record of domestic reform, as for example in the introduction of labour exchanges and of both meals and medical inspections for schoolchildren. The most ambitious reform and the most important for the long term was the introduction of National Insurance in 1911. This was the brainchild of Lloyd George who was influenced by German experience both in general and in detail; since Bismarck's time, Germany had built an impressive array of social benefits which both improved the health of her workforce (and her conscripts), and helped non-socialist politicians to resist the growth of support for socialism: Churchill was not alone in the government in wishing to 'add a thick slice of Bismarckianism to the underbelly of British society.' The scheme envisaged a partnership between employers, employees and the state, with each contributing to an insurance fund from which insured workers could draw in times of sickness or unemployment. It was this 'insurance principle' which commended it to employers and to moderate Liberals, compared to the *non*-contributory pensions, but it was also this that caused some resistance among workers, for many of whom it constituted the state's first direct raid on the pay packet, replacing an existing voluntary right to insure with a compulsory system. In the first instance it covered only a narrow range of the more organised trades, and the government was slow to respond to radical demands that it should be extended into more contentious and more administratively difficult areas like tailoring, fragmented into thousands of small workshops. None the less, it was an important precedent both of state intervention and of social provision on which future governments could build, as were limited interventions by the government in the field of fixing minimum wages.

Although social policy under Asquith demonstrated a steady growth in intervention and a steadily rising social budget, it would be a mistake to overstate the case: the combined effect of the Boer War, the naval race with Germany and the Liberals' welfare reforms, had driven up the basic rate of income tax, which had been 3.3 per cent in 1900, only to 5.8 per cent at the outbreak of the First World War. In 1914, a wealthy bachelor with an income of £10,000 still kept £9,242 after tax (£9,677 in 1900). The fact that he would be able to retain only £5,813 by 1919 shows how much greater an impact was made on private wealth by the Great War than by Lloyd George's 'war on poverty'.

A radical cause that was prominent in the last years before 1914 but which achieved no prominence in the government's programme was the issue of votes for women. Women's rights had been an increasingly prominent issue for more than half a century, though until the birth-rate and infant mortality fell the momentum for change was blunted by the fact that most women's place *was* still necessarily in the home: as late as 1900 a quarter of the country's married women were in childbirth every year. Nevertheless legal changes had been made, as for example in the provision of educational opportunities for women in the universities opening careers to educated women, and in the Married Woman's Property Act which had allowed married women a separate legal status. In the Edwardian period the focus was on the demand for the vote, mobilised by vocal pressure groups chiefly under the lead of Mrs Emmeline Pankhurst and her daughters Sybil and Christabel. The Liberal government treated the issue as one for individual MPs rather than for a government measure, and back-bench proposals were regularly debated and defeated, with Lloyd George a supporter, Asquith an opponent and Churchill a supporter but reluctant to give way to coercion. It is possible that a less strident campaign than that of street incidents, window-breaking and hunger strikes might have achieved the vote earlier, but the strength of the suffragettes' feelings did not allow such a strategy. By 1914 despite opposition that their campaigning had generated among MPs the argument had been largely won. It seems certain that even before the Great War reinforced the argument, votes for women would have come soon.

There remained in the government a radical impetus for reform, most especially concerned with rural Liberalism. The 1909 budget's attack on the position of landowners did not blunt the radicals' wish to reduce the influence of owners of unearned wealth. Lloyd George was closely associated with this Land Campaign of 1913 which had many characteristics of a religious crusade (including the anthem 'God gave the land to the people'). In 1913 Lloyd George compared landlords' malign influence unfavourably even with the threat of foreign invasion: 'he can do more than a foreign enemy . . . Landlordism can by legal process not merely ordain a wilderness, it can maintain a wilderness.' Such attacks certainly rattled the Unionists, who held the majority of rural seats and who began to dabble unconvincingly in such ideas as tribunals to fix wages of agricultural workers to head off the Liberal campaign. The political strategy behind these efforts was intended to come to a head with a 1914 budget which would be as important for retaining office in 1915 as the People's Budget had been in 1910. Unfortunately the 1914 budget was far less effective in uniting Liberalism together against a common foe, and a number of its proposals had to be withdrawn because based on inadequate preparation.

By that time in any case, too much of the attention of politicians concerned was tied up with Ireland for a repeat of the 1909 formula. None the less the Asquith government could look forward to a 1914–15 election as one which it might narrowly lose, and which might produce a damaging battle with its Labour allies, but which would still be sure to leave the Liberals as a strong party, securely rooted in populous regions of the country and with a record and a philosophy that were demonstrably still relevant to a great proportion of the British electorate. They could point to victory over the Lords and the imminent carrying of Home Rule and Welsh Disestablishment as the successful settlement of several of the most important Liberal causes of the past half-century. In 1914, Liberals were most concerned not about the survival of their party or by the danger of European war, but about Ireland. As Europe stumbled into a war which was to have a catastrophic impact on British Liberalism, the attention of Asquith's Liberal government was still riveted on parish boundaries in Ulster, on what Churchill later recalled as 'the dreary steeples of Fermanagh and Tyrone.'

19 Britain in and out of Europe, c. 1900–1939

Within a few years of Victoria's Diamond Jubilee in 1897 Britain was adopting a new outlook on the world, and especially on Europe. The last major colonial military victory came in 1898 when Kitchener's defeat of the Sudanese at Omdurman provided a delayed retribution for the death of Gordon. The last major frontier dispute between Britain and France also took place in 1898 in the depths of Central Africa at Fashoda; thereafter Britain moved steadily if not painlessly towards an understanding with France, formally reached in the *Entente* of 1904. Over the same few years the last serious suggestions of an alignment of Britain with Imperial Germany were fading, lost in a rising tide of anti-Germanism. As Britain's diplomatic weight had been thrown in with France rather than Germany, it was logical to extend the association by a closer understanding with France's ally Russia, reached in 1907 and again facilitated by the cooling down of colonial disputes. Through this diplomatic realignment Britain was shifted from being merely a detached oceanic power to a direct involvement in growing European antagonisms between two rival blocks of great powers. The commitments to France and Russia were limited and defensive, intended merely as a diplomatic counter-stroke to tilt the balance of power away from Germany's rising strength, and in that sense represented a continuation of traditional diplomatic policy. But the shift was in the longer term to begin Britain's direct and continuing military association with Europe after almost a century of relative detachment. The reasons for this unforeseen outcome lie in the gradual accumulation of moral commitments that went far beyond treaty obligations, the growing influences of sentiment and emotional commitment in an age which could no longer detach diplomacy from popular politics, and a widespread fear within Britain that isolation from Europe was now a luxury bought at too high a risk.

The treaty obligations to France and Russia did not in themselves tie Britain down to any great extent, but they did (and were intended to) send a signal to military men on both sides of the European alliance system. As the European powers stumbled through a series of international crises between 1907 and 1914, the generals and admirals made their plans on the obvious assumption that any likely war would be on the basis of Britain, France and Russia against Germany and Austria. The British and French armies foresaw the increasing probability of their military collaboration in what might be an urgent struggle as all the powers rushed to entrain their armies for the frontiers. With the approval of Asquith and of the Foreign Secretary Grey, the army began detailed staff talks with France, as did their naval counterparts. As a result, when the final war crisis broke in July 1914, the British government had in being detailed plans for a military and naval co-operation with France, but also had far less room for manoeuvre than it had expected. If Britain did not go to war alongside France, then France's northern coastline would be open to attack by Germany's powerful fleet (since joint planning assumed that the Royal Navy would look after the Channel while France concentrated on the Mediterranean) and the French army's strategic battle plan would need rapid revision to plug the gap created by Britain's non-appearance on its left flank. Any British decision not to fight in 1914 would thus have been not a decision for neutrality but consciously to allow France and Belgium to be defeated by Germany, an abandonment of the balance of power policy pursued since Elizabeth I had spoken of the Low Countries as 'the counter-scarp of England'. Asquith and his colleagues agonised over this until Germany's invasion of Belgium allowed them to declare war on Germany in strict adherence to a much older treaty; in reality they had already known that Britain must fight to protect her own interests.

The rush of volunteers when the Great War came in August 1914 shows how far much of public sentiment backed the government, but public opinion had itself contributed to the growing Anglo-German antagonism. The German government's undisguised pleasure at Britain's discomfiture in the Boer War, combined with genuine fears of the intentions behind Germany's naval building programme – the first such threat uniting naval and military power since Napoleon – built up a wave of fearful hysteria. This was lashed to a fury of anti-German feeling by the *Daily Mail* and other popular newspapers, and by a constant spate of books, articles and plays harping on the fear of espionage and invasion. The best of these was *The Riddle of the Sands* which in 1903 so influenced political opinion as to force a change of naval policy, reinforcing demands for modernisation being made by Admiral Fisher, the professional head of the service. But the most typical and most widely influential was William Le

Queux's *The Invasion of 1910*. Le Queux was helped in writing his book by Field Marshal Lord Roberts, Britain's best known soldier of the time, who himself led a campaign to put Britain militarily alongside the European powers by the creation of a large conscript army. Roberts' National Service League had vocal press support and the polemical backing of Britain's most widely read poet, Kipling, who bitterly attacked the 'flannelled fools at the wicket and the muddied oafs in the goals' who put sport ahead of national defence. The League had strong popular backing, but was never able to bring its one aim of conscription near to implementation. Even politicians who supported conscription as an idea were reluctant to become too committed to such a potentially unpopular policy; the pressure did though encourage the Liberal government in modernising the structure and training of the army and probably helped to prepare the nation psychologically for compulsory military service when it did come in 1915–16.

The invasion and spy scares also forced the government towards a more rapid rearmament of the traditional forces; the Navy League had much wider support than the NSL when it demanded a massive naval building programme. It pressurised the government through by-elections, campaigned for battleships in 1908 with the slogan 'We want eight and we won't wait' and largely won the fight. But the Navy's rearmament, unlike the demand for conscription, was based on an accepted, traditional policy and did not threaten to reintroduce a large garrison army – a concept distrusted since Cromwell and James II and hardly more popular with Liberals in the age of the 'Mutiny at the Curragh'. Above all an increased Navy would be manned by volunteers rather than by compulsion.

The anti-Germanism that led to some absurd charges of espionage against harmless tourists and German waiters was also underpinned by a growth in more uncomplicated patriotic attitudes among the young. Here the new Boy Scout movement, founded by a Boer War hero Baden-Powell, took the lead, but its imitators included the Boys' Brigade, Church Lads' Brigade, Jewish Lads' Brigade and many more. Hundreds of thousands of boys, brought up to regard uniformed organisation and marching with flags and drums as a normal pastime and a patriotic duty, provided unthinking recruits in 1914. At the same time, the nation's social leaders were trained more directly for a future military role in a mass army in new Officer Training Corps located mainly in the public schools. All these organisations reinforced the imperial message of children's fiction and of magazines like *Boy's Own*: Britain's world power had been won by an innate superiority but also through struggle and sacrifice, the Germans were natural (in the Darwinian sense) rivals for Britain's world position who threatened Britain with subjugation, and *dulce et decorum est pro patria mori*. It was in 1902, after the humiliations of the Boer War that the words 'Land of hope and glory . . . Wider still and wider, shall thy bounds be set' were added to the tune of one of Elgar's marches, creating a second and more vainglorious national anthem.

The increasingly strident proclamation of Britain's power and greatness concealed profound doubts about the reality. The invasion scares had touched a chord of insecurity about Britain's role which seems a world away from the confident rhetoric about splendid isolation and the white man's burden of only ten years earlier, though that rhetoric had always affected a confidence not universally felt. The gradual loss of Britain's economic lead over Germany and the United States was an affront to the generation born in the age of 'the workshop of the world'. The inscription *Made in Germany* (to which attention was drawn by a popular book of that name in 1896) came to symbolise both the affront itself and its cause: it could be carried to extraordinary lengths: 'you drop off to sleep only to dream that St Peter (with a duly stamped halo round his head and a bunch of keys from the Rhineland) has refused you admission to Paradise because you bear not the mark of the beast on your forehead, and are not of German make.' Since social darwinism, which asserted that for nations as well as for animals struggle was endemic and survival only for the fittest, was a dominant contemporary philosophy, economic failure and the actual physical unfitness of so many who volunteered for service in Africa came as unwelcome confirmation of the darkest fears. Kipling's view that Britain had had 'no end of a lesson' in the Boer War, but that 'it may make us an Empire yet' contained a threat as well as a moral: what if the lesson were not learned? Already, in the Edwardian period Britain was seeking friends in Europe to offset insecurity felt about the imperial future.

There were still those who continued to see a different way forward. One who quite consciously sought to learn the lessons of the Boer War for Britain's imperial future was Joseph Chamberlain. As Colonial Secretary he had spoken of a great crusade of imperial economic development; in office his practice was the more prosaic encouragement of such co-operative ventures as Australian federation which came about in 1901. The Boer War had in itself originated in an increasing feeling that the British and Afrikaners were struggling for supremacy and that the struggle for the future of the colony would sooner or later have to be settled by force, as well as in specific disputes and in mismanagement – including Chamberlain's own. The course of the war and Britain's inability to bring it to a satisfactorily triumphant conclusion only succeeded in demonstrating the relative weakness of Britain in European terms. But it also showed how far she could call on reinforcements for colonial warfare from other white dominions; Kipling's 'men who could ride and shoot' from Australia and New Zealand had been a significant factor in the final subjugation of the Boers. After the war ended, Chamberlain's visit to South Africa turned him into something of a romantic imperialist, but with his dreams still rooted in economics. He foresaw the danger that the dominions would drift steadily away from the mother country, towards entirely separate development or into other economic spheres of influence (as for example through Canada's links with the USA). Drawing on his admiration of Germany he devised a plan which would increasingly tie the Empire together as a giant trading block, much as Bismarck's *Zollverein* had laid the foundations for unifying the German Empire in a customs union; something similar had been floated at the imperial conference of 1897, but it was hoped that the co-operation and the shock produced by the Boer War would make it more practicable.

Chamberlain argued that Britain should follow Germany's example in erecting tariff barriers to protect her industries from European competition, while giving free entry to Empire produce and enjoying similar rights for British goods to enter the markets of the Empire. It promised to tie together in bonds of economic interdependence the mainly agricultural economies of the Empire and Britain's industrial economy. These grandiose plans foundered on the domestic political problem of selling a policy which would only work by increasing the prices of basic necessities like bread and on the reluctance of the dominions to accept a subordinated economic role. The debate on tariffs at Edwardian elections generally focused on the small change of prices and jobs and the tariff reformers were gradually argued to a standstill, but their real motivation was to be found in bigger worries about Britain's identity as a nation, even fears for the future of the race. One of Chamberlain's greatest supporters, the *Observer*'s editor J. L. Garvin, felt that the battle over tariffs was 'as much a sequel of Darwinism as of Cobden'; Chamberlain's victory would mean that 'an age of feminism in British policy will close.' The fears of imperialists were only strengthened when the Liberals gave self-government to South Africa under Boer leadership only eight years after the Boers were defeated, and when a Liberal government in Canada negotiated a trade treaty with the USA which gave America priority in the Canadian market. The Canadian Liberals were defeated in an election which engendered unusual interest in Britain and the policy was for a time reversed, but these signs of imperial disintegration – an inexorable process without a tariff system which neither the British electorate nor the dominions would accept – were foreboding signs of the future.

The Great War of 1914–18 provided at first a cathartic release from such pent-up emotions. The rush to the colours combined an opportunity to live up to the patriotic lessons of the past decade with a dash of adventure and glamour in a war expected to be over by Christmas. Britain's first military involvement on the continent since the 1850s, her first compulsory military service since the press gangs of Nelson's Navy, proved very different from initial expectations. Over four years, over nine and a half million men joined the armed forces from Britain and the Empire, a tenth of whom were killed; hundreds of thousands were missing in action and never seen again, an even larger number mutilated or otherwise wounded. Economic historians have calculated the additional loss of hundreds of thousands of births from the next twenty years as a permanent demographic legacy from the trenches. After these grim statistics, and the horrors of trench warfare which produced them, the British people could never again go to war with a light heart as in 1914.

General support for the war did not flag in Britain while it continued; indeed the high level of casualties in itself ensured that neither public nor government could waver on the need to win the war, for to do so would suggest that the dead had died in vain; those few who opposed the war or called for peace by compromise were often reviled and hated. The fact that Britain ended on the winning side, and that the war aim of unconditional German surrender (which had seemed inconceivable only half a year earlier) was actually achieved in November 1918 tended to fix these wartime attitudes for years ahead. The presence of large numbers of wounded soldiers and thousands of war memorials – in offices, factories, banks and colleges, as well as in churches and on village greens – was a constant reminder of the sacrifices made; with so many bereaved and mutilated, it was difficult even to ask serious questions about the war until immediate memories faded.

Britain attended the peace conference of 1919 as one of the main victors, and as one of the 'big three' that determined the shape of the postwar world her great power status seemed secure. Britain also shared in the spoils of war, not only through the destruction of German naval strength which had threatened British security, but also in the acquisition of colonial territories across the world from the defeated powers. The gaining of Tanganyika from Germany completed a continuous line of pink territory from north to south on the standard maps of Africa and made possible the building of the 'Cape to Cairo railway', a great imperial dream of the previous generation. The collapse of the Turkish Empire, however, involved Britain in an enlarged and expensive role in the Middle East and the rise of Japan provided a new threat of rivalry to come in the Far East. Most importantly, participation in the peace settlement which was eventually imposed on Germany committed Britain to share for years to come in the burden of enforcing that settlement if it were to be challenged.

There was wide popular support in Britain for the new League of Nations, an American initiative regarded initially with some suspicion in government circles. Across the political spectrum from moderate Conservatives to the left, the League was seen as a means of harmonising the conflicts of nations, a sign that the war's suffering had been to some lasting purpose as 'the war to end wars', and a sign that mankind could learn from its mistakes. It was an optimistic answer to social darwinism's gloomy assumption of the inevitability of conflict. The League of Nations Union, a popular domestic pressure group which had strong links with the churches, was a serious restraint on government after 1919, but the force of 'internationalism' which the League and the LNU symbolised was an even more powerful factor in shaping public opinion. It was clear from the start that articulate opinion would not stomach any policy that risked a further war. Attempts to get Britain involved in bringing down the new Soviet regime in Russia were halted by the resistance of trades unions, which owed much to fellow-feeling on the left, but also something to resistance to any war; Britain parted company diplomatically with France when the French army entered Germany to enforce payment of war damages; in 1922, the government's belligerent attitude to Turkey was a factor in bringing Lloyd George down, Bonar Law speaking for many in asserting that 'we cannot alone act as the policeman of the world.' The League of Nations was though an ineffective institution with little power at its disposal to enforce its decisions; if Britain were not careful, she would as the only naval power in membership be the only effective maritime policeman for the League's collective decisions.

As the immediate passions of wartime died away, British diplomats sought to rationalise this imbalance between the hopes for the League and its ability to deliver. First and unsuccessfully in 1924 it was hoped to persuade all members to surrender to the League a right of arbitration in international disputes; second, and successfully for a time, the main European powers stepped outside the League framework to right the imbalance by more traditional methods. By the Treaty of Locarno in 1925, Britain, Germany and France each promised to aid the others if attacked, so providing an automatic two-to-one guarantee against aggression. This effectively ended the association of Britain and France that had emerged in 1904, but it also ushered in a remarkable period of relaxation in European affairs in the later 1920s, vital for the re-establishment of international trade and prosperity. More ominously it ushered in too a period of misplaced optimism: in Britain Locarno was seen as a much bigger success than it was, and the welcomes given by British politicians to the many subsequent declarations of international goodwill were called by one wit 'Locarney-blarney'.

Behind this façade of peace and normality in Europe, imperial affairs also gave cause for greater concern. The extended Empire was often viewed as a source of extended commitments rather than of strength by politicians between the wars, and decisive steps were taken without much dissent which would lead on to its dismantling as a unified institution. War was declared by the British government in 1914 on behalf of the Empire as a whole, but in 1919 the white dominions were successfully demanding their own separate representation at the peace conference, a recognition that Britain's interests might henceforth differ from theirs. During the 1920s these tendencies accelerated, and the 1931 Statute of Westminster provided a new legal framework that recognised a 'Commonwealth' of self-governing nations in place of the older concept of a united Empire. When a political crisis threatened the abdication of the king in 1936, Baldwin as Prime Minister was careful to consult the dominion Prime Ministers before each step that he took; in 1939 Britain declared war only for herself and the colonies, leaving the dominions to make their own decisions – the fact that they mostly joined in without delay and participated to the full indicates the triumph of sentiment over political change for another generation, though Ireland remained neutral and South African participation was a close thing. But when Australia was threatened by Japanese victories in 1942 the Australian government unhesitatingly cut its links with the past by publicly recognising its future dependence would be on the USA rather than Britain. When facing Hitler in the 1930s, British governments could not know in advance whether the dominions would be with them in a future war but the collective dominion advice was always against any strong action that might lead to war. The speed of this change was rapid: in the Boer War, Britain had fought long and hard to maintain imperial control, and in 1911 British politicians had agonised over Canada's decision to extend its economic connections with the USA as a sign of imperial disintegration. By 1931 they could only put a brave face on things and welcome the arrival of a Commonwealth of independent nations as a sign of maturing imperial democracy; in reality it marked a decisive retreat from world power, made with scarcely an argument in the aftermath of 1914–18.

In India, British rule was now dependent on timely concession and the increasingly desperate exercise of a shrinking authority. The reforms introduced by Lord Chelmsford in 1919 promised eventual 'responsible' government, in effect a transition in due course of time to the status of Australia or New Zealand. From this point, and as Gandhi's resistance campaign gathered momentum, Indian nationalism grew in confidence and the British response became more hesitant; when British troops fired and caused many deaths during riots at Amritsar in 1919, their commander was sacked in humiliation, and only a few on the extreme right complained that this would undermine Britain's position further. By 1930, the Viceroy, himself a former and future Conservative minister, had all-party support for a quickening of the pace of change towards self-government, though bitterly opposed by such Conservative imperialists as Churchill. The 1935 Government of India Act provided a constitutional framework which would have led to internal self-government and a far more rapid Indianisation of the administration, had not the Second World War first halted progress and then brought full independence at the gallop. Here too, there was resistance only from the extreme right, many of them men who like Churchill had themselves known combat on the north-western frontier in their youth, in fiction if not in fact. But for most in Britain, a bloody colonial war to retain British power in India was an unacceptable alternative to timely retreat, so far had the will been sapped by the Great War.

The war had also produced more obvious strategic implications. When in 1921 Britain's longstanding alliance with Japan came up for renewal it was allowed to lapse, because the increasing rivalry between Japan and the USA in the Pacific made it impossible for Britain to remain close friends with both; she could not align against the Americans who had in 1917–18 financed Britain's war effort when Britain's own resources ran out. Japan was now a probable future enemy with a powerful navy, while the USA was for the time only a hoped-for future ally. Faced with the danger of a Far Eastern and a European war to fight at the same time, Britain which had confidently set out to outbuild all comers in the naval race before 1914 now called for treaties to limit naval building. The consciousness of economic and strategic weakness went along with the sapping of the will.

Despite the increasing separation between the units of the Empire, it was still to the Empire that Britain turned in time of economic need in 1931. Under the impact of the 1930s world slump, Britain finally turned to Joseph Chamberlain's solution, tariffs with imperial preference. An emergency tariff was introduced at the end of 1931 pending Commonwealth agreement which was reached only after some hard bargaining (by Canada in particular) at an Imperial

Economic Conference held at Ottawa in 1932; sentiment still dictated that Canada's Prime Minister should describe the treaty as indicating that for years to come it would be 'a proud boast' to be 'a British subject'. Neville Chamberlain was able as Chancellor of the Exchequer to introduce the bill to implement his father's greatest dream. But the context was now entirely different. Joseph Chamberlain had envisaged an imperial preference system binding together a disintegrating empire, a new *Zollverein* to 'make us an Empire yet', but the next generation turned to tariffs only as a last resort for a battered British economy and to the Empire only as a market. Even here the components of success were no longer present: the dominions were now even more determined to develop industrialised economies, and not to be imprisoned in a colonial trading system which would market only their raw materials. By 1935 Neville Chamberlain was already asking himself why tariffs had failed.

It is one of the ironies of the time-lag between reality and fiction that the 1930s produced alongside the silent retreat from imperialism the classic statement of Britain's imperial role for millions in cinema audiences, in such films as *Sanders of the River*, produced by Sir Alexander Korda (who was knighted for services to the British Empire, but who described his own motives as 'patriotism with profit'). Such films generally used story-lines from books of one or two generations earlier. It is equally notable that Korda was a Hungarian émigré celebrating the British Empire with all the enthusiasm of the convert, and that his film *The Drum* (which demonstrated British power in India) could not actually be shown in British India because the Viceroy's government feared that it would provoke nationalist riots.

A sense of Britain's weakness spread widely through society between the wars; lower down as well as at the top it was often rationalised into a belief that the abandonment of pretensions to military power might anyway be morally preferable. This became a major influence on policy towards armaments. In the immediate aftermath of 1918, the Great War's reputation as a necessary sacrifice was not widely challenged: the annual celebrations of Armistice Day were genuinely popular events and the new British Legion had a huge membership of war veterans. Then about ten years after the end of the war, the public mood began subtly to change: the war as a topic actually became more popular through an outpouring of novels, plays and autobiographies which were to fix the First World War's image enduringly in the popular mind. The image now was not of heroic sacrifice but of wasteful and senseless destruction; the moral to be learned was *Goodbye to all that* (as Robert Graves' autobiography was entitled). After 1930 the mood changed again, from a backward-looking refighting of the war in the trenches, 'lest we forget', to the fear of an even worse war in the future. There was an avalanche of cheap fiction and press stories about the threat of chemical and gas warfare, all inflicted on civilians by the deadly force of air power against which there was no possible defence. As Stanley Baldwin himself said, 'the bomber will always get through', a realistic enough projection in 1932, but one that was never revised in the public's mind when radar, monoplane fighters and other technological advances changed the tactical balance.

Newspapers and film newsreels continued to shriek such horror stories as the bombing of the Spanish town of Guernica in 1937 as a sign of things to come. The government's own preparations were based on the assumption that mass bombing would produce vast civilian casualties within days. The Home Office laid in stocks of cardboard coffins and designated London parks as mass burial grounds, preparing to use the army to maintain order and prevent looting in the anticipated wartime breakdown of public morale. As they learned something of these plans and suspected much more in the light of popular fiction, it is not surprising that many of the public began to panic. The wave of 'pacifism' that arose from 1933 owed far more to fear than to moral conviction, though politicians and churchmen of impeccable credentials were on hand to guide fears into the effectively organised channels of the LNU and the Peace Pledge Union. In 1933, the upper-class undergraduates of Oxford, a group whose predecessors had been more than decimated as subalterns in the trenches, passed a resolution vowing not to fight 'for King and Country' (a direct rejection of the recruiting slogan of 1914), and the middle- and working-class voters of Fulham deserted the Government in droves 'in a wild flood of pacifism', as Baldwin put it. The mood reached its climax in 1935 when a 'Peace Ballot' was held, an unofficial referendum in which over eleven million people took part, overwhelmingly voting for economic rather than military measures to preserve peace and security in Europe.

This mood in public opinion would have been a restraint on any government's policy in the mid-1930s, but its impact was reinforced by the politicians' own inclinations to share aspects of the public mood and by their consciousness of the country's strategic, economic and diplomatic weakness since 1918. Britain's political leaders between 1918 and 1939 were mainly men who had been too old to fight in the Great War, but they were still affected by the national loss: Neville Chamberlain suffered the loss of a cousin to whom he had been close; the Labour leader Henderson had lost a son, as had both Asquith and Bonar Law. It was understandable that this generation of political leaders, should feel both a continuing sense of responsibility for the losses of 1914–18, and a determination to prevent its recurrence, in the case of Chamberlain a deep loathing of war altogether. With the relaxed international relations of the post-Locarno period came a readiness to run down even further the level of armaments from the demobilised level achieved in 1919–21. This was consistent with the widespread psychological repugnance of war, but also reflected both the prevailing belief that an arms race had directly contributed to the crisis of 1914, and the more prosaic wish to spend more of the proceeds of taxation on ploughshares than on swords in difficult economic times.

With barely a dissentient the British armed forces were steadily run down: the 1920 figure of six hundred thousand men under arms fell by a quarter over the next ten years; over the same period military spending fell by four-fifths as little in the way of new snips, aircraft or equipment were ordered; by 1930 expenditure was in real terms far lower than in 1910. With this drift to lower spending came a hiatus in planning: in 1928 the Cabinet resolved that the armed forces should plan on the assumption that there would be no war within the next ten years, and thereafter this 'ten year rule' was regularly renewed until 1933. It reflected both the government's optimistic view of international relations and the public mood, shared across Europe as the labours of the League of Nations Disarmament Conference at Geneva demonstrated until 1933. It was, however, a mood and a policy easier to adopt and continue than to change when circumstances altered.

Circumstances changed with international aggression and the rise of expansionist dictators, which had been feared ever since Mussolini's appearance as Italian Duce in 1923, but came to actuality only with the Japanese invasion of Manchuria in 1931 and the arrival of Hitler as German Chancellor in 1933. In the Far East, in Abyssinia and in the Rhineland, the League of Nations proved unable either to accommodate the dictators' ambitions or to mobilise sufficient strength to prevent their aggression from succeeding between 1931 and 1936. In this Britain was at least as culpable as other League members, reluctant to surrender her freedom of action to an international body and thus helping to deprive it of effectiveness. By 1935 there was a widespread recognition of the need for action, but equally widespread disagreement as to what form that action should take. The idealistic belief that the League would achieve reconciliation of disputes by the moral force of public opinion or by painless and riskless economic sanctions had had many adherents in Britain, but that position was hard to sustain after 1935–36. By then the Labour Party had abandoned its earlier support for anti-war policies and was moving gradually over to a conviction that the spread of international fascism necessitated at least a readiness for military action. In this the Spanish Civil War of 1936–39 was crucial, a fight in which quite a number of British left-wingers participated personally but which many more regarded as *the* great moral cause of the decade.

Ministers seized on this tilt of opinion to accelerate the programme of rearmament, first published in 1934 and then steadily geared up as the international situation deteriorated, but approached it over-cautiously in the hope of taking no steps that would imperil Britain's fragile economy. Within months of being branded as war-mongers by pacifists, ministers were being denounced for rearming too little and too late, above all by Churchill – the Chancellor when Britain adopted the ten-year rule but the most articulate spokesman for quicker rearmament by 1936. British rearmament lagged a long way behind that of Germany and Italy and in 1936 Baldwin told the Commons that Britain was now well behind Germany in the vital field of air striking power. From that point British policy was dictated not by public opinion but by the country's military weakness; for the next two years, the professional advice to the government from its Chiefs of Staff was that Britain could not contemplate war against Nazi Germany without facing the near certainty of defeat. These predictions (possibly over-gloomy) were based like Churchill's criticisms on the exaggerated figures of German armaments published by Hitler himself, but it would have required a bold government to take the least risk of war against such advice.

The defence situation therefore combined with the psychological readiness of ministers, with economic factors and the cautious advice of both European and Commonwealth allies to determine a policy of 'appeasement'. This was in itself a policy both morally defensible and one that continued to attract strong public support at least until 1938, but which when pursued from a position of weakness was a policy all too likely to send the wrong signals to military dictators. The Foreign Secretary Anthony Eden commented that in 1914 the policy had been to keep Germany guessing about Britain's decisions (in the hope that Germany dare not risk war without being sure of Britain's intentions) but that Germany had guessed wrong; in the 1930s the policy was entirely different, to leave Germany in no doubt of Britain's views, but this was done so inexpertly that Germany once again guessed wrong all the same. The result was possibly the worst of all outcomes, a period of feeble diplomacy – much of it conducted without advice from, or behind the back of, the professional diplomats – a reluctance to rearm as fast as possible lest it should provoke both Hitler and pacifist opinion at home, and a determination to fight in the end which Hitler did not actually believe in 1939. After Britain threatened war over Czechoslovakia in 1938, but had not in the end made a fight, it was impossible to convince Hitler that Britain meant to fight over Poland in 1939.

British policy therefore failed to prevent Germany rearming to a level that threatened British security, the reoccupation of the Rhineland in 1936 which gave Germany once again a defensible Western border, and the German incorporation of Austria and parts of Czechoslovakia in 1938. The parliamentary debates over the Czech crisis of 1938 demonstrated the emergence of a wider group of 'anti-appeasers' than Churchill's immediate cronies, all now arguing the need for a stronger policy towards Germany. These included Eden (who resigned in general disgust over government foreign policy and because he could not get on with Chamberlain), and Duff Cooper (who resigned specifically over Czechoslovakia). They now argued that a war was the only way to halt Nazi expansionist plans, and that it would be tactically better to fight earlier than later. Chamberlain survived such criticisms in 1938, but could not resist them when Germany occupied the rest of Czechoslovakia in March 1939. Britain now reverted in a rush to the traditional policy of balancing European powers and the fastest possible rearmament: the first ever peacetime conscription was introduced and guarantees were given to several of Germany's eastern neighbours.

This stronger policy was still pursued without enthusiasm by ministers sickened at the very thought of another war. The chance of bringing in Russia as an ally to deter Hitler was bungled in 1939 through delays and hesitations by a government not happy to invite a Communist army to march to the West in any case. Britain's attempt to be resolute was anyway interpreted in Berlin as a bluff, but the pledges given could not but be honoured when Germany invaded Poland in September. Chamberlain had spoken of how 'fantastic' it was to be even contemplating war in 1938 over Czechoslovakia, 'a faraway country of which we know nothing', and had spoken of Danzig (ironically echoing Bismarck) as not worth the bones of a single British soldier. But when confronted by a House of Commons on the warpath he had no choice but to send an ultimatum when it was too late to be an effective deterrent. In 1939 then Britain went to war over Poland with no real chance of helping the Poles resist Nazi Germany, but because *British* interests once again demanded an unlimited European commitment.

Britain entered a Second World War in 1939 with Treasury advice that she was insufficiently rearmed to win a short war and too economically weak to endure a long one; the one secure ally, France, was known to be chronically weak and internally divided, Russia was neutral at best and probably hostile, while American policy continued to be determinedly detached from European commitments. She went to war with the accumulated international uncertainties of the past twenty years barely put behind her, and with a level of military preparedness that suggested the probability of defeat. Within a year, driven out of Europe and with no allies except the Commonwealth that possibility of defeat seemed to have become a near certainty.

20 Political realignments, 1914–1922

Until the middle of July 1914, when the chances of avoiding war were already ebbing away, the British Cabinet did not even discuss the growing European crisis, so enmeshed was it in domestic problems. In the last few days of the month ministers could find no way of avoiding the war which they had not foreseen. The Cabinet and the Liberal benches in parliament contained few men who would oppose all wars in all circumstances, but many who would look very critically at the circumstance that had led a *Liberal* government to embark on war. For these the German invasion of Belgium came almost as a relief, since it allowed them to support the war on a good moral principle – treaty obligations honoured and the support of a small country attacked by an aggressive neighbour. When the Great War came, only two Cabinet ministers resigned, though it was significant that one of these was John Morley, Gladstone's biographer and the self-appointed guardian of the Gladstonian tradition. In the short term, all the political parties and the mass of opinion rallied behind the government in a way that would have seemed impossible a few weeks earlier. Grey as Foreign Secretary and Churchill at the Admiralty both enhanced their standing by the way in which they handled the transition to war conditions, and the government was further raised in public esteem by the appointment to the War Office of Lord Kitchener, a distinguished professional soldier. This initial political rallying to the government lasted for half a year and survived even unexpected early defeats: but the long retreat from Mons was followed by Allied victory on the Marne, the naval defeat at Coronel by the victory at the Falklands. Even when the winter of 1914–15 produced the more continuous disappointment of a deadlocked trench war all along the Western Front, support remained strong.

The first days of the war did produce legislative and administrative change which indicated political problems to come. The Defence of the Realm Act (cosily abbreviated to DORA) passed through an excited parliament at breakneck speed and gave to the government unprecedented powers to censor press and post, power to ban meetings, powers to deport and intern, which consorted badly with the Liberal ideal of freedom. In due course the propaganda which DORA allowed – lurid stories of the raping of French nuns by German soldiers and the butchering of Belgian babies at the point of the bayonet – helped to sustain the war hysteria and hence support for such sanctions as DORA permitted. In the same mood, there was strong public pressure for the internment of aliens from enemy countries, a rage that was vented in attacks on shops with owners who had *any* foreign name. The same public intolerance drove from office Lord Haldane, who as War minister had done more than anyone to prepare the army for war but who was now suspect as an admirer of German culture, and Prince Louis of Battenburg, whose name alone was sufficient to ensure his removal from the post of First Sea Lord (to which the redoubtable Admiral Fisher returned from retirement). The royal family, in deference to such hysteria, changed its official family name from Saxe-Coburg to Windsor.

Less visibly, the government took other steps which broke with tradition. Under pressure of the war emergency, the Treasury suspended the sacred Gladstonian principle of 'Treasury Control', the doctrine that had ensured that no department could incur expenditure without prior Treasury approval: henceforth the service ministries could order war materials without limit and the Treasury undertook to find the finance. This casual change of procedure established like all the others in the expectation of a short war, put government expenditure entirely beyond civilian control for four years, and this in turn unleashed big increases in taxation, a dangerous level of inflation, and a massively increased national debt which made Britain internationally bankrupt by 1917. By 1915 the war was already costing more than three million pounds a day, and on one day in 1917 the artillery in France alone fired off shells worth nearly four million; by comparison, total government revenue in 1913 had been under two hundred million pounds.

Other aspects of traditional economic policy were also war casualties. Lloyd George as Chancellor since 1908 had always been ready to meet trades union leaders, but the importance of such contacts now assumed a far greater significance. In 1915 he signed with the unions what was virtually a treaty between equal partners: these 'Treasury Agreements' conceded to the unions a share in the implementation of industrial policy and symbolically demonstrated the centrality of organised labour to the war effort. Lloyd George's successor as Chancellor in 1915, Reginald McKenna, introduced tariffs on a range of luxury goods, partly to raise revenue and discourage unnecessary consumption, but also to protect such strategically important industries as motor vehicles, cameras and optics. Whatever the reason, it was a symbolic gesture for a Liberal Chancellor to suspend free trade for the duration, and these 'McKenna duties' survived to symbolise the ebb of Liberalism well into the 1920s. Frustration with the slowness of industrial mobilisation, especially after the 'shell scandal' of May 1915 when the log-jams of armament production produced a shortage of ammunition for the army, led Liberals along the path of even more direct intervention. Occupying the new post of Minister of Munitions Lloyd George set up national factories and provided direct financial inducements to existing firms to get them to expand production, well outside the tradition of sealed, competitive tendering for government supply which went back to the 1780s. All these changes, subordinating orthodox policy to the inexhaustible demands of the war, caused alarm to traditional Liberal minds.

One issue encapsulated Liberals' ambivalence towards the relationship of Liberalism and the war effort, the problem of finding men for the forces. Kitchener was one of the few who already foresaw in 1914 that the war would be a long one, but the first rush of volunteers was more than the army could train or the munitions industry could equip. The heavy rate of 'wastage' even at quiet times in the trenches, and the enormous casualty rates during big battles like Loos or the Somme changed all that. Asquith could retain the support of Conservatives and the military only by taking whatever steps were needed to provide a steady flow of men to the army, but the achievement of this by compulsion would alienate at least some Liberals. There was therefore a phased move towards conscription, first by increased exhortation and encouragement, then through the legal compulsion of first unmarried and finally of married men. These hesitant steps meant that Asquith satisfied nobody: the Conservatives and the most hawkish Liberals saw it as a policy adopted too late, while radical and pacifist Liberals could not forgive the sacrifice of principles of freedom. By the time that full conscription was eventually in force in the summer of 1916, these ideological debates had wrecked the foundations of Asquith's political standing.

The disappointing course of the war also weakened the personal authority of the Prime Minister and his closest lieutenants. His own reputation for procrastination and caution – epitomised in his much-quoted parliamentary catch-phrase 'Wait and see' – did not fit well with the wartime need to take decisions. Bonar Law was much irritated by an occasion when to consult the Prime Minister on an urgent matter he had to motor out to Oxfordshire and was then kept waiting while Asquith finished a game of bridge. And this reputation for casualness and indecision was widespread: the

Wipers Times, an unofficial soldiers' paper made Asquith its 'man of the week' in May 1916, 'for finally making up his mind'. Grey's hour of glory at the war's outset was also shortlived: increasingly he was attacked as a man whose diplomacy might have prevented war altogether, and the entry of Turkey into the war on Germany's side was a diplomatic setback from which his reputation never recovered. Churchill's appetite for war was unquestioned, but his judgement was another matter; he was blamed for the heavy losses of the Royal Marines at Antwerp and (unfairly) for defeat by Turkey at Gallipoli. Kitchener's failings as a minister – his lack of administrative grasp and his refusal to take civilian ministers into his confidence – were not generally known, but they paralysed the whole central direction of the war, for which Asquith had to answer. The good names of the men who had surrounded Asquith in office since 1908 were therefore seriously damaged by the war. When a double crisis broke in May 1915 over the shell shortage and the frustrated resignation of Admiral Fisher, Asquith had to seek outside help to shore up his government. For the first time, a Labour MP held government office when Arthur Henderson joined the Cabinet, an appointment fraught with future difficulties for the Liberals; far worse, loyal Liberals like Churchill were edged aside to make room for Conservatives, and though Asquith kept most key departments for Liberals, he had to admit even diehards like Carson to his team as the price of Conservative support. With a team that included men who had been actively seeking his destruction only a few months earlier, Asquith was no longer master in his own house.

The one great exception to the steady eclipse of Liberal reputations was Lloyd George. His flirting with the anti-war wing of Liberalism during the Boer War and his radical demagoguery from 1909 had done nothing to prepare either Liberals or Conservatives for his transformation into a patriotic war hero. As the first wartime Chancellor he found unprecedented resources for the war effort; as a senior minister he was unwavering in his backing of the war and of any means needed to wage it more successfully; at the Ministry of Munitions, he became the one minister ready to abandon all preconceptions, to invent where tried methods did not exist, to harness industrial and trades union potential, and above all to get the job done – earning the reputation as a 'man of push and go'. Nor was he slow to use his press contacts to make sure that the public knew what was being done and who deserved the credit. The loss of Kitchener at sea in July 1916 paved the way for Lloyd George's move to the War Office and for the restoration of civilian control. He had become the government's trouble-shooter, moved to plug any gap as it was detected. Lloyd George's rise coincided with a decline in

Asquith's standing, a coincidence which contributed both to the older man's sense of vulnerability and to LG's increasing frustration with Asquith's hesitations. The poor progress of the war itself only encouraged this growing rivalry between the two men whose collaboration had been at the heart of pre-war Liberal successes. War thus weakened not only Liberal philosophy but the party's collective leadership, and this opened the way for a split as well as a decline.

Since the Liberals' fortunes in the previous generation had been inherently tied up with Ireland, it is not surprising that this problem had its Irish dimension too. The most immediate impact of European war on Ireland was to defer the civil war which threatened in 1914. Redmond for the Irish Nationalists and Carson and Craig for the Unionists all pledged full support for the war effort, and many thousands of Irishmen from north and south joined the army. The first weeks of the war none the less spilled over from conflicts of the past, for a decision had to be made about Home Rule, due to come into force in the autumn. Asquith's decision to allow the Act to pass and then to suspend its operation for the duration upset both Nationalists who resented the delay *and* Unionists who saw the carrying of the Bill into law as an act of party advantage in a national crisis. But both views still anticipated only a short postponement for a short war and so for a time the critics were silenced by the din of recruiting; when the war dragged on into 1915–16 the political stalemate in Ireland developed into a dangerous tension.

Imperceptibly at first but with growing force, Nationalist opinion shifted from Redmond with his commitment to support parliamentary methods and Asquith's government to a growing revolutionary movement, *Sinn Fein*. This subterranean current, hardly noticed by Westminster politicians whose attention was fixed on the Western Front, was accelerated by perceived insults to Irish national pride. Although Redmond assured Asquith that Ireland would police itself, the government did not rely on such promises and continued to station large numbers of troops in Ireland even when desperately short of men. When links between Germany and Irish extremists could be found, as when Sir Roger Casement was arrested in 1916 on arrival from Germany to start an insurrection, the government was haunted by the memories of the 1790s and the traditional view that England's emergency would be Ireland's opportunity. To Nationalists it seemed that Ireland was still treated as a colony and not as a partner. Discrimination between Southern Ireland and Ulster increased resentment. Regiments enlisted in Ulster, many of them entire units of officers and men who had been preparing to fight the British army a few weeks earlier, were brigaded into an

Ulster Division, a great source of pride as the province's badge of the red hand became a divisional flag, symbolising the reconciliation of 'loyalism' and loyalty. This was a serious provocation elsewhere, for separate army units were not organised for other Irish provinces, whose recruits were placed in any convenient battalion and whose Irish battalions (when they existed at all) were generally brigaded with English or Scottish troops in case of need to overawe them. These signs that the army did not trust the Catholic Irish as it trusted the Protestants of the north were hardly surprising given the strong Anglo-Irish complexion that the officer class had had at least since Wellington's day, but they were insults to Irish identity all the same.

Worst of all was the passage of time. It was one thing to forgo Home Rule at the very hour of its achievement in 1914 when the interim seemed likely to be a short one, but as the war dragged on through 1915 Irish impatience grew apace. With the formation of a coalition government in May 1915, the political arithmetic also changed: no Home Rule measures had ever been introduced except when Nationalist MPs held the balance of power in Parliament. After May 1915, Redmond no longer had the influence of a balancing force which had been so potent since 1910, for he now led the only party outside the wartime coalition. By that time there was no likelihood of ever seeing Home Rule put into practice before a general election in which British voters might reject it as in 1886. The fact of Carson in the Cabinet and Redmond not even on the government side of the House was as great a provocation to non-Unionist Ireland as Asquith could have achieved. Under these pressures, the most militant nationalists decided to chance their arm with an insurrection, motivated as much by a chance to show the weight of Irish feeling and the difficulty of holding down Ireland without consent as by any serious thought of gaining and retaining power. On Easter Sunday 1916, about twelve hundred republicans seized public buildings in the centre of Dublin and proclaimed an Irish republic, a gesture which met with an indifferent response from most Dubliners but with a swift reply from the military. The army crushed the revolt in six days, proceeding to trial by courts-martial, and to the execution of fifteen leading republicans and the imprisonment of hundreds. These reprisals succeeded where the rising itself had failed, for a bush-fire of resentment was ignited in support of the republicans. A nation which had long found its romantic heroes in political martyrs found them anew in Arthur Griffith and his republican comrades, and again when Casement was executed for treason by the more leisurely process of criminal trial – and without any of the excuses of urgency which could exonerate the army in Dublin.

If ministers had underestimated the threat before the Easter Rising they did not do so afterwards. Augustine Birrell, the Liberal minister who had occupied the Irish Office since 1908, was another casualty, removed after a decent interval and replaced by a Conservative, while Lloyd George was given a wide brief by the Cabinet to seek a compromise solution. As in 1913–14, even extreme necessity could not produce a readiness to compromise; resignations and threats by Conservative ministers removed the option of immediate Home Rule, the only thing Nationalists wanted, but by the time that the mission failed another event had hardened opinion. In July the army's Ulster division was almost annihilated at the battle of the Somme; July would now be commemorated by Unionists for the Somme as well as the Boyne, and Easter Sunday by Nationalists – days on which political loyalties had been re-sealed in blood.

The rest of the war saw a drawn-out search for compromise that never came near to success. A Convention sat through 1917 and much of 1918, and the fate of the Irish National Party hung in the balance of its debates: each period of optimism produced a strengthening of the party as a possible provider of Home Rule without civil war, each setback produced by-election defeats for its candidates and recruits for republicanism. The final acceptance of the Convention's failure and the death of Redmond both paved the way for the final polarisation at the war's end. In the general election of 1918, only seven Nationalists held their seats (compared to eighty-four in 1910, and one of the survivors was sitting for a Liverpool constituency, not an Irish one) while Sinn Fein had seventy-three winners all pledged not to take seats at Westminster. In contrast, Ulster was if anything even more strongly Unionist. The Sinn Fein MPs formally constituted themselves as a *Dail Eirann* or Irish Parliament, and 1919 witnessed a battle for administrative control of Ireland as town councils, police, magistrates and other officials had to choose sides. In September the *Dail* was formally banned and escalating guerrilla warfare followed, with martial law proclaimed in the south-west of Ireland. Government resort to counter-terrorism through an organisation of para-military irregulars (called 'Black and Tans' after their improvised uniforms) failed either to halt the growing power of the Irish Republican Army or to reduce their civilian support. Counter-terrorism did though lead to heavy criticism of the British government in parliament and the press, and to the enlisting of considerable Irish-American support for the republicans.

Lloyd George had adopted counter-terrorism to bring the warring parties back to the negotiating table. His first postwar attempt at compromise was the Government of Ireland Act of 1920 which established separate parliaments in Belfast and Dublin; Unionists seized on this as giving them a legitimated self-governing Ulster, now excluded from Home Rule without time limit, but republicans rejected both Westminster's authority and the division of Ireland. The government returned to the military option until in 1921 George V's call for a 'truce of God' provided another chance to work for compromise. Several months of hard bargaining, threats, bluff and counter-bluff produced a draft treaty between the *Dail* and the British government whereby Ireland would enjoy dominion status like Canada – more than Home Rule – but with Ulster excluded for as long as its Parliament should choose. The Irish republicans accepted these proposals without enthusiasm, since such hated symbols of loyalty as the oath to the king would remain, but in the expectation that the boundary between Ireland and Ulster would be redrawn in such a way as to make an Ulster that opted out of a united Ireland economically and politically unviable. Their reluctance was underlined by the civil war which broke out between the pro-treaty and anti-treaty forces, producing a victory for the compromise deal only after much more blood had been shed. It was almost as difficult to get support for the treaty from British Conservatives, for feeling ran strongly against it in such Protestant bastions as Liverpool. In fact the Unionists had done well, for Ulster had achieved as much as it had fought for in 1912–14: the 1918 parliament with its Unionist majority therefore voted through the provisions that finally ended full Irish Union and created an Irish Free State. The final stage came in 1925 when the new border was finalised; this left Ulster more economically viable than the republicans had hoped, and hence able to remain in existence as a separate unit, but with a perilously long land border to defend when violence reasserted itself in the 1960s. The year 1925 marked the end of the sequence begun in 1885; the loose federation of Conservatives and Liberal Unionists which came together to oppose Gladstone's Home Rule plans in 1886 and merged into a single 'Unionist' Party in 1912 now officially reverted to the name 'Conservative'. Despite economic disputes between Britain and Ireland in the 1930s, an armed neutrality in the Second World War, and Ireland becoming a republic, Irish affairs never again held centre-stage at Westminster until the 1960s. It is not surprising that a half century of relative quiescence should have deluded British politicians into thinking that the Irish Question had finally been answered, or into counting it amongst Lloyd George's greatest achievements.

But Lloyd George's reputation does not so much rest on Ireland as on the Great War and its aftermath, for Ireland was not the only place where the Asquith government lost its grip on the run of events during 1916. Hopes of a quick end to the war were long gone and defeat at Gallipoli demonstrated the futility of hoping for a quick victory on another front. The first battle fought predominantly by Kitchener's new citizen army, the Somme, was a costly failure which generated half a million casualties. Meanwhile the Indian army was humiliated by the Turks in Mesopotamia and the Navy failed to win at the battle of Jutland. Full conscription had been achieved, but the war by attrition threatened steadily mounting losses and although the economy was now fully mobilised it too was showing signs of serious labour shortages. Of Britain's allies, Russia was fast crumbling, France harder hit even than Britain, and Italy had entered the war as an ally only to be so quickly battered as to be a liability rather than an asset. The USA clung resolutely to neutrality, which was particularly serious as Britain's cash reserves abroad ran out and as submarine warfare threatened the country's food supplies. It is therefore scarcely surprising that in the later part of 1916 a conviction grew that the country would be defeated unless changes were made. Liberals who wished to wage the war more determinedly turned increasingly to Lloyd George at a time when there were no safe options, and a Liberal War Committee of MPs emerged to press for the promotion at least of his ideas; the editor of the Liberal *Manchester Guardian* concluded that 'Lloyd George will be kill or cure . . . The point is that he will take decisions.'

More surprising is that Lloyd George was supported by Conservatives; they had after all regarded him before 1914 with an especial loathing, through a real distaste for his 'Limehousing' and a healthy fear of its effectiveness. But once in office with him from 1915, some Conservatives began to admire his way of doing things; in 1916 they were far from trusting him, but they saw the need to make greater use of him in the national interest. Their discussions were more about machinery than men, with Lloyd George and Bonar Law drawing up a plan for a small committee to get on with the war without constant need to get Cabinet or parliamentary backing. As the planning developed, it became clear that acceptance of the proposal and of Lloyd George as committee chairman would effectively make LG the first man in the government – irrespective of who was called Prime Minister. That at least is how Asquith saw it when he eventually rejected the plans, so provoking the resignations of Lloyd George and of all the Conservative ministers. After a very complex week in early December 1916, Lloyd George proved to be the only man able to put together a government with a parliamentary majority, backed by around half of the Liberal MPs and by the Conservatives. Asquith, baffled and feeling himself betrayed by a colleague who had sold him out to their old enemy, moved with his supporters to the opposition side of the Commons, though he hardly mounted an opposition while the war lasted. Over the next two years there were regular attempts to heal the Liberal breach, even to bring Asquith back into Cabinet, but none came near to success as feelings on both sides became more embittered. So without a formal division, the two wings of the Liberal Party drifted into separate factions defined only by support for Asquith or Lloyd George, though Asquith remained party leader in control of the organisation, except in Wales. There was nothing irrevocable about the split of 1916 and many individual Liberal MPs who were to end up as 'Asquithians' still supported LG until 1918, while others did not choose sides at all. But time in which to nurse grievances gradually widened misunderstandings and resentments until personal rivalries, a secondary issue in 1916, became the dominant factor.

The Lloyd George government certainly lived up to expectations concerning the machinery of government. A War Cabinet of five was set up with executive powers; for the first time an effective cabinet secretariat co-ordinated the execution of policy. New ministries sprang up as necessary to provide driving force for such policy areas as blockade, food, propaganda and national service, with many of their senior staff drawn not from the traditional Civil Service but from industry and the trades unions. The War Cabinet contained Henderson for Labour and Bonar Law for the Conservatives, but its other members with LG were Milner and Curzon, both men with experience of the wielding of vast proconsular authority (in South Africa and India respectively) – the war effort was to be run and Britain governed like a colony until victory had been gained. The government was in fact a coalition of men, albeit chosen after some traditional party horse-trading, rather than the coalition of party professionals which Asquith had run. It was the hope derived from this new start that carried Britain through 1917, the gloomiest year of the war, a year of further debilitating losses (including so much British shipping lost to submarine attacks as to make it necessary to impose a convoy system to ensure food supplies); there were also French mutinies, Russian surrender and Italian near-eclipse. With America now in the war but Americans not yet present in strength on the allied side, 1918 began even worse, with the British army's worst defeat of the war in March leading to fears that France could be knocked out of the war before the Americans arrived. The government's calm nerve in the crisis and the soldiers' endurance under immense pressure ensured that the army remained intact to play its part in the summer campaign that brought victory.

At the start of 1918 the best hope was of victory in 1920–21; in the middle of the year, the best hope was simply not to lose in 1918; by November Germany had surrendered unconditionally. The suddenness of these events meant that even those in Britain who had never lost faith in ultimate victory were stunned, exhilarated and relieved by what had occurred. One result was that much was done in a rush as the war speeded to its end that would no doubt have been better planned in a steadier transition to peace. Demobilisation plans were badly received, criticised as too slow and provoking mutinous riots in the army; Churchill was drafted to the War Office with a 'first in, first out' plan which headed off the disturbances and got millions of men back to their families in a few months. The flooding of the labour market in 1919 contributed heavily to the problems of the economy for years to come. Similarly, the government's reconstruction plans, drawn up in uninhibited wartime circumstances but never completed, never went through the stage of patient exposition to politicians and public which could have given them a solid basis for implementation later. Hopes were therefore raised of 'a land fit for heroes to live in', but neither the implications nor the costs of the policies had any very secure foundation. It was a recipe for massive disillusion.

Political decisions taken in a rush at the war's end had similarly lasting consequences. In the final war crisis of May 1918, Asquith was stirred into action with an attempt to mobilise an active opposition for the first time since 1916; he had a good case for attacking the government, which had itself contributed to the army's defeat by keeping it starved of troops (so that the generals would not waste manpower in offensives) and then given the Commons false information about army numbers after the defeat. Whatever the merits of the case the debate resolved itself into a choice between Lloyd George who might well be a liar but who ran things with energy and Asquith whose greater faults were well remembered. Conservative MPs rallied to Lloyd George and to his Conservative ministers, and Liberals for the first time divided openly between their party's two leaders. Although it won comfortably the government was given a real fright by the debate and began preparations for a wartime election in which support for the government would be the issue. The LG Liberals and Conservatives thus began in the summer to plan for a joint onslaught on Labour and the Asquith Liberals through an electoral pact, before they were overtaken by events. It was however easier to get into such a pact than to get out of it, and there was all to gain for its framers when it could be implemented in the very hour of victory. The coalition's members were publicly committed to continued co-operation to carry out reconstruction plans, but in private they were motivated at least equally by the desire to stand together against a rising tide of labour militancy. Lloyd George for one foresaw a period of intense economic difficulty when the war ended and wanted to get a new majority quickly so as to have five more years in which to 'stand the ramp'. The electoral pact designed to get a war majority was therefore used instead for peacetime politics, with little concern for the effect it would have on Asquith's Liberals – though after Asquith rejected another invitation to rejoin the government, Lloyd George had little alternative but to proceed as planned. Lloyd George and Bonar Law thus named the candidate who represented the war-winning government in most constituencies, their letters of support being called 'coupons' after the universal stationery of wartime rationing: a call to electors to vote *for* the couponed candidates was equally a call to reject Labour and Asquithians.

The 'Coupon Election' of 1918 was a rumbustious affair. Lloyd George was widely hailed by supporters as 'the man who won the war': government candidates canvassed in khaki and denounced as unpatriotic all who had opposed any part of the war, called for a punitive peace and the hanging of the German Kaiser as a war criminal. There was a strong public appetite for such views in the moment of victory, and opponents of the war fared very badly. The government won a spectacular victory, with couponed candidates taking 478 of the 550 seats where coupons were issued; but the mass of winning candidates were Conservatives, several of whom won either without or against a coupon, for the unbridled jingoism of the election suited Conservative electioneering well. The losers were Labour (which had won more seats but not done as well as hoped) and the Asquithians who held only twenty-eight seats and had no leader, Asquith himself having lost his seat. The less obvious loser was Lloyd George himself who had to continue a coalition through a parliament which had a one-party Conservative majority: this was an unstable basis for any government, but especially for one with ambitious reform plans.

Initial difficulties were hidden by the demands of the peace conference, on which Lloyd George concentrated for the first half of 1919; subsequently the government's life was dominated by industrial militancy at home and revolutionary threats in Europe. With the peace treaty complete, Lloyd George had to dismantle the War Cabinet system and restore parliamentary procedures, a clear sign that he was henceforth to be closely watched by his allies. New wartime ministries were unceremoniously wound up and attempts to set up new structures and reform policies met with stiff Conservative resistance. A new Ministry of Transport was shorn of interventionist powers before it even came into existence and the new Ministry of Health could make little headway while it was starved of cash. The financial implications of reconstruction reforms were indeed the Conservatives' greatest worry. Taxation had risen massively to pay for the war – income tax at the standard rate rising from 6% to 30% in four years – and while the increase was seen as a necessary wartime sacrifice, its continuation in peacetime was much resented. The financial impact of the war did not end with the coming of peace though; its cost was something over nine billion pounds more than normal defence expenditure, and although Britain paid a higher proportion of the costs of the war from taxation revenue than any other major combatant, the overall national debt rose from well under a billion pounds in 1913 to almost eight billion in 1920. Since these war debts would have to be paid back for generations to come, taxes could not be much reduced, but this only redoubled resistance to new spending plans in other fields. By-elections went badly as Labour made gains on the claim that the government was not fulfilling pledges, and independents of the right took seats in middle-class areas as a result of high taxes and of a campaign for 'economy' whipped up by the popular press. By 1921 the government had effectively abandoned its reforming plans; the minister most associated with reconstruction, Christopher Addison, was forced out, and instead there was a much publicised use of the 'Geddes Axe' to reduce expenditure (named after the minister who drew up the economy plans). With this turn of events, much of the positive case for coalition government had gone.

The negative case for coalition lasted longer. The years 1919 and 1920 did produce the expected industrial militancy, and Lloyd George's political skills were tested in dealing with it. Initially, tough action was taken against opponents who seemed to threaten the state, as in the police strike of 1919, but other unions gained major concessions on pay and conditions, though not on such structural changes as the miners' demand for public ownership of their industry. By 1921 the postwar boom had burst and the onset of high unemployment weakened the trade unions: the government's victory over the miners on 'Black Friday' 1921 was a turning-point. Fear of Labour was now concentrated not on unions but on the Labour party itself. Lloyd George's prewar reputation for radicalism had been valuable in this context but was a declining asset as the years passed. Rapid changes of government policy over industry, agriculture, Russia, Ireland and the Near East all combined to damage Lloyd George's standing in the country. After a Labour by-election win at Spen Valley in December 1919 Conservative and Liberal ministers tried to merge their parties into one to make a better anti-socialist campaigning organisation, but the plan did not get support among the back-benchers of either Conservative or Coalition Liberal parties and had to be dropped. This failure of 'fusion' in 1920 removed the one way forward; in the afterglow of success that followed the Irish Treaty Lloyd George tried again and was again thwarted. By this time Conservatives on the right were becoming increasingly frustrated by a position in which their party had a majority in both Houses but only a share of ministerial office under a Liberal Prime Minister, and in a government which refused to use its majority to carry such favourite Conservative policies as the reduction of trades union powers or the restoration of powers that the Lords had lost in 1911. As memories of the war faded, gratitude to LG faded too, and as the tide of industrial militancy ebbed after 1921 MPs were less likely to feel the *need* for Lloyd George either. Thinking Conservatives like Stanley Baldwin (just promoted to the Cabinet) came to similar conclusions by a different route: if all non-socialists were together in government under an increasingly discredited Prime Minister, would not there be a greater danger of a Labour government being elected?

The question of Lloyd George's reputation was sharpened by an honours scandal; there was nothing new in recommending honours for men who had contributed to party funds, but the lack of discrimination with which the trade was carried on by LG's agents was both new and to some rather offensive. On all these fronts a gap emerged between most Conservatives in parliament and the country and their leaders in the government. The division gradually widened to the point where Austen Chamberlain, Conservative leader from 1921, had to overcome his opponents, give way to them or fall. He called his MPs together at the Carlton Club in October 1922 to demand their backing, only to see his advice brusquely rejected by a parliamentary party that was by then far more worried about their party's future than about the government's. As had happened in 1846 (and was to happen in 1975) the real decision was made by the back-benchers against the collective advice of the front bench, but in 1922 it was facilitated by the return to active politics of a much-respected former leader, Bonar Law, who had withdrawn only through ill health eighteen months earlier. Lloyd George resigned office as soon as the decision at the Carlton Club was known and Law formed a Conservative government, despite the refusal of Chamberlain and most outgoing Conservative ministers to join it. Party government was restored after seven years of coalition.

The certainty that the party politics restored in 1922 were to be very different from the prewar pattern was to be found in the changed position of Labour, for by 1922 Labour had moved from the minor party status determined by its pact with Edwardian Liberalism to replace the Liberals as the second party in the state. The Labour Party's structures had developed alongside increased union membership before 1914, but there was no way of becoming a major party without cutting adrift from the pact, and so risking a big setback to gain an advance. The war provided Labour with the opportunity to make that transition without risk, a time in which competition with the divided Liberals could be safely risked. In 1918 Labour won on its own a greater representation than it had enjoyed (only in combination with the Liberals) in 1910, and by 1920 Labour had a secure base in organisation and in local government to demonstrate its independence and its major party status.

The first effect of the war on Labour was negative. Most Labour MPs and trades unions backed the war effort, despite earlier belief that socialist internationalism had rendered war impossible, but a minority of MPs took a more pacifist line; as one of these MacDonald had to resign the leadership which fell to Arthur Henderson, but resignations were not followed by expulsions and the disagreements did not take on a personal tone as among Liberals. Even when divided on the issue of the war, Labour MPs were not divided on their loyalty to their movement. Mobilisation of the war economy provided many opportunities to extend union influence: membership had risen sharply since 1911 and now doubled between 1914 and 1921, with workers seeing the importance of combination in times of rising prices and industrial change. Labour's importance was demonstrated both by its inclusion in the Asquith and Lloyd George governments, and by the recruitment of trades union leaders like J. R. Clynes of the shopworkers to posts in the war economy. The outburst of industrial militancy during the war in such places as 'Red Clydeside' was occasioned as much by traditional union fears of the dilution of skills, rising prices and housing problems as by revolutionary fervour but this only confirmed the importance of the Labour movement's moderate leadership to the war effort.

The parties had arranged a political truce for the duration of the war, which was generally observed in the constituencies, and no local elections were held that would have demonstrated changes in political support. Nevertheless, there was a general belief within the Labour Party and among its opponents that Labour's strength had greatly increased by 1918. Apart from the general raising of class consciousness that the war encouraged and the impact that it had on the perceived importance of the movement's national leaders, this was to be explained through two new factors of 1917–18, the revolutions in Russia and the new franchise introduced in Britain. Although Russia was a British ally the fall of the Russian monarchy was greeted with great enthusiasm by the British left which had long disliked being allied to what it saw as a backward, Asiatic dictatorship – in Ramsay MacDonald's phrase 'the most corrupt of all the governments of Europe'. Between February and October 1917 there were hopes that even this most backward country in Europe was set on a path towards democracy and socialism under Kerensky; even when the Bolsheviks seized power they tended to be regarded as just another variety of socialist – more violent than Britain's perhaps but responding to more violent opponents – and therefore still worthy of support. The effect of the Russian revolution was therefore to give a psychological boost to socialism in Britain as elsewhere in Europe, and in due course to bring into existence a powerful socialist government in what had been seen as the most unpromising country of all for the left. If it were possible in Russia, then why not in Britain?

Such raised expectations were encouraged too by the fourth reform act, the Representation of the People Act of 1918, which for the first time brought Britain close to democracy. The need for changes in the franchise had been debated actively in the last years of peacetime, but had never reached a high enough place in the Liberals' legislative programme to go through the resistance of the Lords. The case for change was made irresistible by the war: when the country called up men to fight for the freedom of Belgium, it could hardly deny them a say in the future of their own land, and even the most dedicated opponents of votes for women had to reconsider their position when women did so much to keep the war economy going in the absence of conscripted men. An all-party committee sitting in secret reached a compromise deal in 1916, which was in most important aspects the scheme carried into law in 1918: henceforth all men would have the vote when aged twenty-one (and would have no great obstacles put in their way when claiming that right), elections would be organised and paid for by the state, and most women would be able to vote at the age of thirty. The exact implications of the change are difficult to assess, for it is now clear that the changes made less difference to the class composition of the electorate than was once generally thought. The Act may have tilted the electorate only slightly in Labour's direction by enfranchising more poor people who saw Labour as their natural choice, but what is absolutely clear is that Labour believed that the Act gave a real opportunity, and that the actual *number* of new voters itself opened up avenues for political change. The 1918 election was fought with the electorate three times as large as that of 1910 (four times as large by 1928 when women were like men enfranchised at twenty-one); when the change in the law was combined with passage of time, it meant that something like 80 per cent of the post-war electorate had never cast a vote before 1914. This was a huge reservoir of uncommitted voters, or at least of voters who were not inured by long habit to the support of any one party. That was the opportunity for a Labour Party which needed to break the mould of prewar politics.

Confident that the war, the events in Russia and the franchise extensions had given it a great chance, Labour set out to modernise its organisation and its message in 1917–18. In this the party had a further bonus when Lloyd George insultingly sacked Henderson from the government because of disagreements about Russia. Out of office he remained a key figure as Labour Party Secretary and with Sidney Webb he drew up a new party constitution intended both to sharpen Labour's image and to improve its electioneering. After a difficult negotiation with the trades unions, some of whose leaders felt that the party of their creation was getting out of control, conference approved the new constitution. This provided for membership to be available through constituency parties as well as through such affiliated bodies as the unions, though with the unions still having the predominant voice in both the Conference through block votes and in the new National Executive. The commitment to socialism was made more explicit than ever before in the aims and objectives specified in the 1918 constitution, but policy work towards the end of the war also evolved distinctive Labour policies for a socialised economy (through nationalisation), for finance (through a wealth tax, a 'capital levy' especially on war profits) and in international affairs (where Labour like the Liberals called for an end to secret diplomacy and a new moral order).

The degree to which the war and Russia had changed political perspectives emerges from a joint trades union and Labour Party conference at Leeds in June 1917 which vigorously prepared for taking power and passed almost unanimously motions urging the creation in every corner of Britain of soldiers' and workers' soviets on the Russian model. Such dramatic gestures as this, and the very name 'Red Clydeside' to describe militant activity there, rang alarm bells elsewhere: George V anxiously asked a Labour MP whether the blood-curdling resolutions of republicanism and revolution passed at Leeds really meant what they said to the thousand and more delegates present, and was reassured to be told that 'there will never be a physical violent revolution in this country. But there will have to be many political and industrial changes.' Some at least of Labour's leaders were conscious that the sabre-rattling of class warfare had an immediate value in raising their bargaining power.

Compared to such high hopes, the 1918 result was a disappointment. Labour was at a severe disadvantage in the electioneering mood of 1918 and especially since many of its front-benchers had like MacDonald and Snowden opposed the war and now lost their seats as a result; even Henderson was defeated. Labour did take sixty-three seats against these heavy odds, nearly all of them won this time without a deal with any other party; independent existence as a serious party had been gained even if power still seemed far away. Fortuitously, with such a huge coalition majority and Asquith's defeat, Labour became the second party in Parliament and the official Opposition. In that role Labour did not shine, not least because its best men had all lost their seats and the new MPs had little parliamentary experience and in many cases little talent too. The main work of the movement continued outside parliament. In elections Labour continued to advance, winning by-elections when they occurred but more importantly building what was to be a permanent base in such local government areas as East London where Labour won control of several boroughs in 1919. With high levels of industrial militancy until 1921 the running was made mainly by the unions, but after Black Friday the pendulum swung back to political action.

The moderate leaders of the railwaymen and transport workers had their own political reasons for not backing the miners on Black Friday, for in 1920 had begun a battle for future control of the entire Labour movement. The revolutionaries and syndicalists had derived new hope from Clydeside and from Russia; in 1920 with guidance from Moscow they re-formed themselves into the Communist Party of Great Britain to unite these various revolutionary strands and to provide a British wing of the emerging Communist International. This new CP was regarded more as a rival rather than an ally by Labour's leaders, men who strongly identified with Soviet Russia but who none the less intended to retain control of their own party and their own unions. The CP was therefore refused the right to affiliate to Labour, and a schism steadily developed: it gradually became impossible for CP members to be Labour candidates, and eventually even to be members of both parties. Frustrated by 1924–25 in its attempt to influence Labour from within, the CP bid instead for influence in the unions, forming a 'Minority Movement' within the TUC and battling for control of several unions. There was therefore a bitter fight throughout the 1920s, a battle that the anti-communists won all along the line in the end but which nevertheless absorbed much of their time and left lasting wounds. By the end of the 1920s the CP was entirely outside the Labour Party and reduced to relative insignificance in the unions.

Labour's moderates were not just fighting off the Communists to protect their own position. They were also reacting to an electoral opportunity and to a growing belief that they could win power by parliamentary means, a chance which association with Communists could only harm. Events in 1918 had shown how widespread was support for Russia but the election had also shown how Russia could be turned against Labour by emphasis on such matters as the execution of the Tsar's family. In effect Labour's opponents discovered the value of red-scare tactics and were not to be slow to repeat the exercise as later opportunities arose. If Labour were to win the votes of former

Liberals and middle-class voters in general – as would be necessary to take power unless they could generate massive working-class solidarity in their support, which seemed an even harder task – it would only be by showing how far it was dissociated from Communism. It suited Labour's leaders to make the break in any case: Clynes told the Labour conference in 1920 that Labour should give up such subversive ideas as direct action which weakened the state, for Labour would shortly take office itself and would need all the state's authority to get its plans through: if Labour gave its opponents lessons in the thwarting of parliamentary majorities then how could Labour expect obedience from those opponents when it had a majority itself? The fact that such a case could be put, and with increasing chance of success as postwar militancy fell away, shows how far Labour had moved since 1917–18. The shift was confirmed at the election of 1922 when moderate policies seemed to be justified by Labour's advance to 142 seats and when the electoral casualties of 1918 returned; Labour's vote at over four million was nearly double its tally of 1918 and ten times its score in elections before the war. The significance of the party's move back to moderate politics was disguised by the first act of the new parliamentary party, which was to replace Clynes as leader by MacDonald. The change was much influenced by the support of Labour's new intake of left-inclined MPs from Scotland, but in backing MacDonald they had restored to the leadership a man who had good leftist credentials on the recent issues of war and peace, but whose deeper sympathies in domestic politics were entirely with the parliamentary course upon which Labour was now firmly re-established.

21 Politics between the wars, 1922–1939

Although party government returned when Lloyd George fell in 1922 and continued until 1931, for the first two years the idea of cross-party co-operation maintained its challenge to party as an alternative mainspring of politics. This confused period of 1922–24 with three general elections in under two years showed the three parties testing their strengths in the new electoral system of 1918. The wider franchise demanded from each party a more active and united campaign in the national competition for votes, for no party could rest secure on loyal voters inherited from the past; so for example, the Liberals crashed to their worst defeat in 1924 even when polling more votes than in their landslide victory of 1906, because the non-Liberal vote had quadrupled over the same period. It was thus doubly damaging that Liberals could not effectively reunite or overcome personal rivalries in this formative period.

During the postwar coalition, there had been an institutional separation between the followers of Asquith and Lloyd George. The NLF and most of the official organisation followed Asquith as the legitimate heir of traditional Liberalism and Lloyd George formed his own supporters' club as the National Liberal Party. Separation continued until 1922 when Liberals again fought the election as two parties, the Lloyd George supporters still in loose local alliances with the Conservatives where they could get them. Lloyd George took sixty-two and Asquith fifty-four seats, the first group extremely vulnerable to any future Conservative attack. With the two factions together in opposition during 1923, formal schism ended, but there was no smooth path towards open-hearted reunion. Asquith as leader made Lloyd George's followers suspicious and resentful, while Lloyd George's readiness to use his financial resources (the 'Lloyd George Fund' built up largely from selling honours) as a bargaining counter did not impress the Asquithians. A further election came in 1923 and earlier than expected but enabled them to fight on a free-trade platform: united for the campaign, Liberals took 159 seats and scored

30 per cent of the vote, but crucially were still only the third party in parliament. Another year in opposition, this time to a Labour government, was another wasted opportunity since organisational recovery was delayed and little work done on policy. The 1924 election was fought mainly on Labour's record in office, on which Liberals had little to say that differed from the Conservatives' criticisms. Three elections in twenty-four months so drained Liberal funds that they could not afford even to run candidates in many more than half the seats; unlike the Conservatives or Labour, the Liberals did not have industrial or trades union funds to fall back on, but neither did they have a large individual membership after a decade of bickering and disillusion. A party which could fight only half the seats was not a possible government and could easily be written off by opponents as an irrelevant obstruction to serious politics, an influence only for instability: the Conservative *English Review* told its readers that 'to get rid of the Liberal Party' was now the major priority, and even the Liberal *Nation* admitted that the wish to end 'this annual plague of general elections' was uppermost in the voters' minds. Therefore 1924 marked the Liberal point of no return: they were reduced to forty-two seats (exactly Labour's number in 1910), under 20 per cent of the national vote, and were not again to mount a credible bid for power. Asquith again lost his seat in 1924, finally relinquished the Party to Lloyd George in 1926 and died in 1928. With the party at last under his control, LG launched a well financed and well thought-out drive to restore the party's fortunes. But even when policy debates in the 1929 election campaign largely revolved around the Liberals' ideas, the party could not induce enough electors to vote for what was now seen to be a minor party: over five million votes – twice the Liberal total of 1906 – produced only fifty-nine MPs, for the British electoral system allows few rewards to parties that come third, as Liberals were to find for the rest of the century. This disappointment brought further recriminations, new splits and further decline in the 1930s.

By comparison with the downward spiral of the Liberals, the Conservatives emerged from the Great War and the coalition with renewed strength. Participation in a war-winning government and the removal of the Irish issue from Westminster enabled them to recover their self-esteem as the patriotic party of respectable government. That was enhanced by determination to restore what were seen as fallen standards of political morality under Lloyd George. The very fact of Labour's rise was a further benefit to Conservatives as the party of resistance; in effect a strong party of the left encouraged property-owners to rally to the best defender of their interests, giving the Conservatives not only votes but subscribing members – the mirror image of Liberal decline. A less obvious source of Conservative strength lay in the 1918 electoral system, for Conservatives had won important concessions during its framing and passing into law. Second votes for business occupiers and graduates remained a help to Conservatives until 1945, and the redistribution of seats provided a large bonus after a third of a century of population change in which housing areas had become even more based on class. These changes provided a net gain of about thirty seats, and created impregnable suburban seats to add to the bedrock of rural Conservatism. To this should be added the electoral effects of Irish independence: the departure of southern Irish MPs removed about eighty seats the Conservatives had never won in living memory, while Ulster's Unionists remained and functioned as Conservative MPs until 1972. The net effect of these changes was to add about thirty Conservatives and remove over a hundred non-Conservatives from the parliamentary balance. Conservatives became the dominant party which usually won elections; between the World Wars no other party won a parliamentary majority.

For all the underlying strength, it was a shaky Conservative team which Bonar Law formed in 1922. Law's health was uncertain, and he died only a few months later; the refusal of former ministers to join allowed the promotion of talented younger men who would find their feet only after a delay; above all, the decision to end the coalition was a negative act of party self-preservation, not a decision for a different Conservative policy. In the 1922 election Law promised 'tranquillity' after an exciting decade, a popular enough election strategy but a poor basis for government. His most telling achievement was the scaling down to normal of the office of Prime Minister: the cabinet secretariat was retained, but LG's other institutional changes were dropped and ministers were left with a more traditional freedom to run their departments. Law allowed himself to be overruled by his Cabinet on a major policy issue, the rate at which wartime debts should be repaid. Such a self-effacing lead went down well with the party but was less effective with the press or with former ministers watching for their successors' mistakes. Law's short ministry did have the lasting effect of bringing into prominence Stanley Baldwin as Chancellor of the Exchequer. Baldwin had been an unimpressive back-bencher since 1908 and had reached Cabinet only in 1921; he had made a vital speech in the overthrow of Lloyd George and the refusal of office by senior (and more talented) men provided his chance. When Law had to retire in May 1923 Baldwin and Lord Curzon were the only possible successors in Cabinet. The party rallied strongly to Baldwin, but George V decided in any case that the Prime Minister must be in the Commons where he could respond to opposition questions – a major constitutional change in twenty years since Salisbury's day, largely due to the advance of Labour. Baldwin thus became 'the unexpected Prime Minister' at about the time that Asquith was describing Law at his funeral as 'the unknown Prime Minister'; although he was also almost entirely unknown when he succeeded to office, he rapidly became the most familiar of all political leaders.

It is not easy to pin down Baldwin's appeal. He was not much of a political thinker and no great influencer of legislation. In Government he was a sore trial to more energetic colleagues like Neville Chamberlain; Curzon saw him as 'a man of the utmost insignificance', Balfour once described him as 'obviously an idiot', and when playing chess Churchill referred to the pawns as 'Baldwins'; yet he overcame these cleverer men when he wished to and he largely framed the context in which their more brilliant contributions were made. His real skills lay in the ephemeral arts of judgement, timing and communication, above all in the gift of interpreting public opinion – which may be defined in this case as what articulate people who voted Conservative would stand for. Neville Chamberlain saw Baldwin's contribution as 'retaining the floating vote', and noted that he had 'an instinctive sense of how the ordinary man's mind works'. Baldwin was an accomplished speaker with a resonant voice and an ability to sound sincerely non-partisan even when making a party speech. He was much in demand for such purposes as radio talks, opening fêtes and unveiling statues, and he was also a big draw at political rallies: when in 1927 he spoke to seventy thousand people at Welbeck Abbey, the party launched an enquiry to find out why so *few* had attended. His six volumes of published speeches achieved a circulation matched this century only by Churchill's war speeches. Such large outdoor rallies were possible only because electric amplification now made it possible for huge crowds to hear a single speaker, but Baldwin proved adept at other technological developments too. He was a skilled practitioner of the radio 'fireside chat' ten years before it was exploited by the American President Roosevelt; he was well-known too from silent news film, his ubiquitous pipe and familiar gestures giving him a recognisable image. When these talents were united in sound newsfilm from 1930, he was a formidable influence, able to speak regularly and directly to millions in the cinemas as no political leader before him had done, and with a style which none of his contemporaries could match, the first British Prime Minister whose voice and manner were actually familiar to the public. From such a position, he was able to shape the agenda of politics not by imposing his will, but by articulating much of what his followers wanted to hear. The most characteristic quality that he wanted to put across was honesty, in direct contrast to LG's public image. Baldwin himself pointed out that Bonar Law's honesty and simplicity were what the public had liked about him; Churchill's sourer verdict on Baldwin was that 'it is a fine thing to be honest, but it is also very important to be right'. A poster of 1929 called Baldwin 'the man you can trust', and in a film broadcast of 1935 he asked for voters' support, 'and I think you can trust me by now'; when the election was over and won, *Gaumont British News* re-showed this request and followed it with the caption 'AND YOU DO!'

Baldwin's first term scarcely hinted at these strengths to come. In the desperate search for a policy which would counter unemployment, he announced to the party conference his personal view that tariffs were the only answer. This launched in September 1923 a fierce controversy as it had done before 1914, propelling the government into an election for which it had not prepared and on a policy on which many Conservatives had doubts. Even in such unpromising circumstances and after a catastrophic campaign, the Conservatives remained the largest parliamentary party – but without a majority. In opposition in 1924, Conservatives healed the split of 1922 when ex-coalitionist ministers rejoined the front bench, and the party undertook its first major review of policy since the war began – a process that made the political name of Austen Chamberlain's half-brother, Neville. Baldwin gave voice to the policy review in a series of thoughtful speeches which the press called 'the New Conservatism', but which was mainly an updated presentation of Disraelian 'one-nation' ideas of moderate, progressive Conservatism. This 'New Conservatism' fitted well with Neville Chamberlain's plans for social reform, less well with the views of the party's right wing. The continuing disarray of the Liberals and the solid but unexciting performance of the 1924 Labour government enabled the Conservatives to mount a strong drive for power. United behind Baldwin, with both a positive policy of their own and an easy target for red-scare tactics in Labour's Russian policy, the Conservatives won the votes of many former Liberals in 1924 and swept back to power with a larger lead in votes over Labour than at any election since 1910 and with two-thirds of the seats in the Commons.

Baldwin's 1924–29 government began well. Party unity was cemented by the distribution of posts, with Austen Chamberlain going to the Foreign Office and Churchill to the Exchequer, so settling the split of 1903 as well as that of 1922. Policy too began positively with a long list of social policies presented to Cabinet by Neville Chamberlain and with Baldwin keeping the right firmly in check. There was to be no provocative gesture like the restoration of powers to the Lords, and he intervened purposefully to stop a back-bench measure to curtail the political activities of trades unions. In August 1925 he persuaded the Cabinet to continue for nine months longer a subsidy to the coal industry even though the concession was made under the threat of a general strike. The left celebrated this as a 'Red Friday' to blot out memories of 1921 and the miners' leader claimed to have beaten 'the most powerful government of modern times'. Although Baldwin had vowed that 'we shall not fire the first shot', he also said later 'we were not ready'. The government used its breathing space to prepare administratively and to organise middle-class volunteer groups so as to be ready for a battle if it should come, and was entirely united in its determination not to lose if a fight did occur.

In May 1926 the coal subsidy ran out, while the commission appointed to find a compromise had failed to find one that either owners or miners would agree to, and the TUC was backing the miners with the threat of a general strike. The climax came with a lock-out of the miners when the coal-owners imposed unilateral wage cuts to restore competitiveness and re-build exports (on which the industry's prosperity had depended, but which were now priced out of a world market in which there was a glut of coal). A wider strike began with printers at the *Daily Mail*, though the government may have seized on this as a pretext for a contest now seen to be unavoidable. Government preparations both through regional commissioners (a system devised by Lloyd George in 1920) and in the volunteers in the Organisation for the Maintenance of Supplies enabled basic life to continue for a time, but working-class support for the strike was very strong. Continuation of the strike for more than a few days would have faced the government with an unpalatable choice between surrender and the widespread and provocative use of troops. Baldwin steered a resolute but non-provocative course: the Guards moved to Victoria Park to overawe the East End, but a military convoy was used only once to move food from the docks; Churchill was made editor of the *British Gazette*, a government news-sheet intended to replace strike-bound newspapers, a post in which he could do little harm. But Baldwin was equally determined not even to negotiate until the strike was called off, regarding the very existence of a general strike as a political act of extreme constitutional significance; so simple an issue did it seem that he refused to allow the Archbishop of Canterbury to broadcast an appeal to both sides, lest it appear that both sides had equal moral responsibility for the crisis. Baldwin recognised, as many Conservatives did not, that union leaders were moderate men, many like J. H. Thomas of the railwaymen being MPs as well as union leaders. He knew well that they had slipped into the General Strike without the slightest idea of provoking constitutional revolution, but that it would nevertheless revolutionise the constitution if they won. It was in effect a bluff by the union leaders, a bluff which the government could call by determined resistance. After nine days the government won a complete victory when the TUC gave up the strike without winning any of its objectives. The government promised to stop victimisation of returning strikers, but was not always successful. No further positive action was taken: the miners stayed out for six months until starvation forced them back to work on the owners' terms. The General Strike was the peak of Baldwin's success in the 1924 government, but it was also the point at which he lost control of events.

Baldwin's moderation strengthened his national appeal and made him a politician who was admired by opponents, but it exasperated supporters. With the unions beaten and with Baldwin's nervous energy depleted by the strain of the events in May, the party's right wing reasserted itself. They were impressed less by the government's victory than by the fact that the strike had happened at all and had attracted such solid support; they were determined that it should never happen again (so were the TUC, but could hardly say so). Demands mounted for a punitive trades union bill and Baldwin could not stall these demands in 1927 as he had done in 1925. The Trades Disputes Act of 1927 therefore looked like a vindictive measure by a government which had promised to be unprovocative. Henceforth, general and sympathetic strikes would be illegal, and it would be more difficult than since 1913 for trades unions to support the Labour party financially. The right demonstrated its new confidence too by insisting that Britain break off relations with Soviet Russia, thinly disguised as a move against espionage, but they were stood off by Baldwin in an attempt to turn the clock back even further by restoring veto powers to the House of Lords. Within the Cabinet renewed arguments over tariffs surfaced as unemployment remained obstinately high, and the attempt to help industry by reducing its rates burden produced a clash between Churchill and Neville Chamberlain. In all these ways the Baldwin government was by 1928 devoting too much of its energies to internal disagreement.

The election campaign of 1929 was fought mainly on Labour and Liberal plans to combat unemployment, with Conservatives trying to rubbish their ideas as impractical while having little to offer themselves but a policy of 'Safety First'. With the electors not particularly frightened of Labour by 1929 there was little chance of red-scaring them into Conservatism. By-elections of 1927–29 had indicated the political trend which the general election only confirmed; votes were lost to Liberal candidates but it was Labour that mainly gained seats as a result. Labour for the first time became the largest party in the Commons, though without a majority, and this unstable parliamentary position generated two years of disorder within the Conservative Party too. Baldwin lost control of his party several times and almost lost the leadership; he would probably have done so if his opponents had found a single alternative candidate prepared to fight for it. He came under great pressure from Lord Beaverbrook's *Daily Express* and Lord Rothermere's *Daily Mail*, both more interested in the wielding of political power through their papers' circulations than in any detail of policy, and from MPs who wanted a stronger attack on the Labour government than Baldwin was prepared to sanction, especially over India. Gradually the deepening of the international slump allowed Conservative policy to consolidate again on tariffs as the weapon against unemployment, and Baldwin's moderate leadership was eventually reaffirmed by a victory on Indian policy; the cost of these two outcomes was the loss of the imperialist, free trader Churchill from the front bench. By the spring of 1931 as the international crisis of credit brought a change of government nearer, the Conservatives again had a fragile unity and were anxious to return to office, not least for a final chance to carry through their tariff policy.

Events in 1931 were affected more by Labour's experiences since 1924. Despite Labour's steady rise through the war and postwar years, and despite the confident titles of such books as Thomas's *When Labour Rules* (1920), the first Labour government when it came in 1924 was a considerable surprise to the party and the country. Baldwin's failure to win the 1923 Tariff election made it impossible to have a continued Conservative government and since Labour was the largest opposition party it had to be given a chance to take office – a prospect that caused a panic in London's financial markets and desperate but doomed attempts to cobble together new coalitions at Westminster. It was Baldwin and Asquith who put Labour into office: Baldwin's reasoning was that if Labour was to be fixed on the parliamentary course, then its leaders must be able to show that it could have a share in government; more negatively, Asquith noted that 'this experiment of a Labour Government' was not really very dangerous since the Conservative and Liberal majority of MPs could always vote it out of office if it got out of hand. Labour's opportunity was therefore a strictly limited one and received with mixed feelings; when the party's leaders met, it was noted that all had 'cold feet' at the prospect of office except Henderson, the only one with Cabinet experience. When considering the talent at his disposal MacDonald noted privately that they were 'a lot of duds' and chose to employ several non-Labour members in specialist posts for which he could find no suitable Labour candidate, such as the Admiralty. These somewhat defeatist initial steps were consistent with MacDonald's conviction that Labour's limited opportunity must be used politically – to show Labour's competence and fitness for future office rather than to achieve immediate legislative change. Labour would need to show that it governed in the national interest, not just as the representatives of a section of the people. Judged by these limited aims, the forty weeks of Labour government in 1924 has to be accounted a success.

As Chancellor of the Exchequer, Philip Snowden followed an austerely traditional line, mixing sound finance with a commitment to free trade which outdid even recent Liberal Chancellors. Snowden's budget permitted a 'free breakfast table' (free of import duties), allowed the McKenna duties to lapse and abandoned Lloyd George's experiment with defensive 'safeguarding' tariffs. MacDonald ensured that the government should appear just as orthodox: most ministers proudly paraded at the Palace in court dress to receive the seals of office, understandably impressed with what their generation of Labour leaders had done to bring the movement so far. When faced with industrial disputes, the government took a detached view, refusing to back the trade union side; behind the scenes the emergency anti-strike machinery was kept in force and handed on intact for use against the General Strike. The exceptions to this moderate stance were few, not least because ministers took all their time in office to get to grips with their departments and the Cabinet hardly functioned at all as a collective maker of policy. As Foreign Secretary as well as Prime Minister, MacDonald was overburdened, though he had diplomatic successes – foreign policy was the one major area of government that did not need daily affirmative votes from Parliament as did domestic legislation. The one clear domestic success was a Housing Act piloted through by the Cabinet's only left-winger, John Wheatley, which provided state subsidies for building council houses. In general though any chance of carrying more ambitious schemes was undermined by the government's weakness in Parliament – not even the largest party in the Commons and barely represented in the Lords; bill after bill was wrecked as opposition MPs obstructed almost at will.

By the summer of 1924 the other parties had wearied of MacDonald's government and were seeking a chance to force an election, finding suitable issues in Labour's policy towards Russia and towards the Communist Party. Labour tried to promote trade with Russia by officially recognising the Soviet government and negotiating a treaty to settle outstanding disputes, but the feeble state of the Soviet economy meant that trade could only be revived if credit was first made available from abroad and the treaties provided for this. Such a policy would be difficult to explain to a generation that remembered the Bolshevik repudiation of all foreign loans made to Tsarist Russia, only a few years earlier. Equally, the mishandling by the government of decisions first to prosecute for sedition, and then not to prosecute, a British Communist J. R. Campbell (who had written an inflammatory article in the *Workers' Weekly*) allowed allegations that ministers had interfered politically in a judicial matter. MacDonald was defeated on a parliamentary vote on the Campbell case, but would certainly have lost the vote on the Russian treaties had it come first; as a result, the general election that followed was dominated by the issues of Russia and Communism that were far from characteristic of the government's life. The final straw came with the publication in the *Daily Mail* of the 'Zinoviev Letter', just a few days before the election; this purported to be evidence of seditious instructions from Moscow to the British CP and cast a lurid light on both the Campbell case and the Russian treaties. The 'Red Letter' magnified the scale of what was already a red-baiting election but probably only increased the scale of Labour's defeat rather than causing it. In the event Labour actually increased its vote by a million at the 1924 election (partly by having far more candidates), despite red scares, and the eclipse of Liberalism at that election confirmed Labour as the major anti-Conservative force for the future. Since MacDonald had singled out the Liberals as the main target, by this criterion too his first government had achieved its objectives.

Loss of office led to an inquest within the party, though the general verdict that defeat had been due to the 'red letter' was unfortunate, for such an alibi prevented Labour from looking carefully for lessons that might have been learned from the first period in office to help prepare for next time. There was in 1925 a debate as to whether Labour should again accept minority office, with Conference taking the view that a serious political party could not refuse office when available, even in the most unpromising circumstances. The years in opposition between 1924 and 1929 were therefore a time in which more work was done to refine Labour's policy objectives, but little to prepare future ministers themselves for holding office or to think through the tactics of minority government. The entire movement's attention was in any case focused from 1925 to 1927 on the coal dispute and its consequences. To a large extent, the story of Labour after 1918 is of violent swings back and forth between industrial and political objectives: after the high hopes of 1918 had been dashed came the militancy of 1919–20; after Black Friday came a move back to parliamentary action; after 1924 came a further concentration on trades unionism; but after the failure of the General Strike, and after the 1927 Trades Disputes Act repeated for the unions the lesson of *Taff Vale* – that the law could only be changed in Parliament – the impetus moved lastingly back to seeking parliamentary power. The movement was thus united behind a drive to oust a Baldwin government now faltering into reaction in 1928; a wide-ranging policy review published as *Labour and the Nation* did not mark a new philosophy so much as a more explicit definition of Labour's existing aims.

The 1929 election came near to producing a Labour majority, for Labour took 288 of the 615 seats and was for the first time the largest party. This time office was taken without hesitation, largely with the same senior ministers but now with no non-Labour men in the team and fewer from the left. The balance of parties promised Labour a longer run in office and a stronger parliamentary position: there was no formal deal with the Liberals, but informal understandings were enhanced by the discussion of electoral reform – now the Liberals' prime objective as a weak, third party. The Labour government was therefore in office for over two years, if not always securely.

The government's life was dominated more by economics than politics, for the Wall Street Crash and the international slump which followed were both under way within weeks of Labour taking office. Having had less of a 1920s boom than other developed countries, Britain was less immediately affected by the world slump, but the British economy was further run down by falling trade and the level of unemployment rose steadily as a result. Unemployment had been continuously high at over a million since 1921 and that had helped Labour's campaign for power. That number rose to well over two million in 1930 and continued to rise to touch three million in 1932. This was not only a signal defeat for Labour's central economic aim, and a severe setback for many Labour voters. Since the benefits payable to the unemployed ('dole' payments) were a cost to the Exchequer these rapidly rising numbers were also a severe budgetary problem. In 1930 the Unemployment Insurance Fund was in serious deficit, threatening the central principle of insurance on which it was supposed to rest, for deficits could only be covered by the government from taxes. Even if the government had wished seriously to compromise the insurance principle (which it did not except in a marginal way), the mounting size of Exchequer contributions threatened to overwhelm the balancing of the government's own budget, an even more sacred principle in the eyes of the Treasury and of Snowden. Labour's political objective of seeming safe and orthodox when in office was now in direct conflict with its more general aim of improving – or at least not worsening – conditions for the least well-off.

Faced with this economic blizzard, Labour ministers' inexperience and lack of preparation for office showed through. A Cabinet committee charged with finding a solution to the problem made little impact, and a bolder scheme hatched by Sir Oswald Mosley to deal with it by a crash programme of public works was rejected first by the Cabinet (as too risky for Britain's international credit-worthiness) and, after he had resigned, by the party conference (rallying to support party unity). Mosley had left the Conservatives to join Labour and now left the Labour Party too; frustrated by what he saw as inaction by unimaginative old men on both sides, he formed a New Party in 1931 but failed to make much electoral impression, and lost most of his early recruits as he himself drifted towards fascism in the search for strong leadership.

The government was looking to more traditional solutions, though they did appoint a Committee on Finance and Industry. When this reported in May 1931 its objectives had already been overtaken by the rush of events, though it provided valuable advice to future governments and a platform from which the economist J. M. Keynes could mount a challenge to classical economic theories on which Snowden continued to rely. The committee accepted that Britain's prosperity had been built on 'natural causes' and a policy of limited intervention in the economy, but concluded that 'we may well have reached the stage when an era of conscious and deliberate management must succeed the era of undirected natural evolution.' Keynes, who was only developing his revolutionary ideas in the midst of these economic storms, and did not publish them in full until 1936, argued for an interventionist policy by which government spending would counter the 'natural' effects of boom and slump and so 'manage' a more smoothly operating economy. He had few adherents even among economists in 1931 and the Treasury held unshakeably to the view that, 'the supply of capital in this country being limited', government expenditure could only be at the expense of investment – exactly what Keynes was arguing against.

Labour ministers even came to see merit in tariffs as protection against 'dumping' of cheap goods by countries which could shelter behind their own tariff walls; just as by 1931 almost all the Conservatives finally backed protection, so MacDonald (but not Snowden) and even a minority of Liberals were ready to look again at tariffs. By 1931 though the real economic urgency had moved from trade to public finance as tax revenues fell in the depression and the cost of unemployment to the government rose. As the budget deficit widened, opposition politicians scented both a real danger to the economy and a political chance for themselves. Crisis was staved off in March 1931 when the government agreed to a small committee under the banker Sir George May, appointed to investigate the deficit and propose urgent remedies. Snowden welcomed this as a means of getting cross-party backing for tougher policies which Labour MPs might not vote for, but it was actually the Cabinet that was painting itself into a corner.

When the May committee reported in July, things had already got much worse, especially with the feared and actual collapse of several European banks; the committee reported a deficit of £120 million (and rising) by comparison with total government revenue of £850 million (and falling), and recommended cuts in expenditure of about a hundred million pounds, mainly by reducing salaries and dole payments. The background to this was that prices had fallen steadily since 1920 and the purchasing power of the pound was now fifty per cent higher than ten years earlier. Nevertheless, the recommendations caused an uproar in Cabinet and the summer recess was occupied with meetings which vainly sought a way of holding the government together. The majority of ministers, including MacDonald and Snowden, argued for the acceptance of May's proposals to retain foreign confidence in the pound sterling (vital to protect London's international earnings from finance) and British confidence in Labour's ability to govern; a large minority, led by Henderson but backed by the TUC, had no real alternative to propose, but would not accept that a Labour government could ever be justified in imposing hardship on the unemployed. MacDonald decided that the government must resign since it could agree no policy in a national crisis; he was already in touch with Conservative and Liberal leaders, not to plan a betrayal of his colleagues but because even an agreed Labour plan would need outside votes to get through Parliament. These discussions took on a quite different flavour when George V persuaded MacDonald that party differences should be sunk in a National government, and that MacDonald himself was its natural leader. It was the King who prompted the turn of events and who saw to it that the other parties backed the idea, though hard party bargaining followed on the details. MacDonald therefore resigned office on behalf of his Labour colleagues but was re-appointed to lead an all-party government. This National government was seen by its members as a temporary measure after which party politics would be resumed, and its special character was demonstrated by its having a Cabinet of just ten members – four Labour, four Conservatives and two Liberals (about half the usual size and reminiscent of Lloyd George's War Cabinet during a different crisis). By 25 August 1931 the National government was in being.

The fact that the National government rapidly developed into a very different body from the one its creators envisaged can be attributed to both political and economic causes. Politically, MacDonald's actions were immediately seen as a betrayal by his recent Labour colleagues: few even of the Labour ministers who shared MacDonald's views on the economy were invited to join the new government (though few probably wished to do so anyway), and the overwhelming majority of Labour MPs opposed the government from the first. MacDonald, Snowden, Thomas and others who had stayed in office were reviled as class traitors and expelled from the party which they had done so much to create and which they had largely led for three decades. Henderson again became Labour leader. This removed any hope of the government carrying its plans with all-party support before its members returned to their respective parties, for MacDonald and Snowden now had nowhere to go back to. Economically, the very fact of a National government did a little to restore confidence, but did not in itself make any difference to the country's economic position.

Fear remained a powerful factor, one on which ministers themselves traded: in speeches in the autumn, Baldwin compared Britain's position to Germany during the hyper-inflation of 1923 and MacDonald toured the country with a wad of worthless German banknotes as a visual aid. As pressure on the pound continued and forced further crisis measures during September, ministers had a strong sense that more than expenditure cuts would be needed to restore the pound's position; many drew the conclusion that the solution lay in tariffs, so that what had begun as a government above parties was within a few weeks considering the most contentious of all party issues. The first step was Conservative demands for an election in which the National government would appeal for public support and so get a more secure parliamentary base. Liberals opposed this, but after his own isolation from Labour, MacDonald had no real alternative, and anyway welcomed the chance to put to the country his own case against his late colleagues. Rather than haggle over a detailed programme, the Cabinet agreed to seek a 'doctor's mandate' to do whatever was necessary for the country's economic health: this allowed Conservatives who were as in 1918 the majority of government candidates the chance to campaign openly for tariffs – and, just as importantly, to oppose free trade Liberal candidates but not those who would vote for tariffs. The lack of an agreed government policy also ensured that the campaign would in effect be a debate on Labour's record in office and on the cause of the economic crisis.

Accusations that Labour had taken the country to the brink of catastrophe and then run away were particularly potent when voiced by MacDonald himself, while Snowden described Labour's policy as 'Bolshevism run mad'. Labour could not survive such an onslaught, and it was equally inevitable that with only a weak Liberal presence and a small National Labour group the main beneficiaries of Labour's defeat would be Conservatives. The civil servant Thomas Jones, a life-long Fabian socialist, and the philosopher Gilbert Murray, a prominent Liberal, both voted Conservative for the first time in their lives, Jones concluding that Labour could not for the present be trusted with office. Labour's vote fell sharply in all areas except the coalfields, while the anti-Labour vote was generally consolidated behind one candidate: Labour saved only fifty-two seats (scarcely any of their surviving MPs being former ministers) while the government took two-thirds of the votes and 554 seats, 473 of them Conservative. The 1931 crisis seemed to have put Labour back to where it had been ten or twenty years earlier.

Britain did not again have a one-party government until 1945, a succession of 'national' governments dependent on the support of Conservative majorities continuing until the end of the Second World War. The source of this lies in the crisis and election of 1931, and in the intentions of MacDonald and Baldwin. Both men had wanted something wider than party government for some time: Baldwin had called his 1924 victory a 'national' one and MacDonald had invited all parties to share in the responsibility of government in the 1929 Parliament; both were by 1931 centrist politicians who had chafed under party constraints, and both were impressed by the breadth of support for the National government in 1931. At the top a lead in making sacrifices in the national crisis was given by the King's decisions to cancel entertainments as an economy measure and to instruct royal staff to vote for the government; the same mood was demonstrated lower down not only by the support for the government in 1931 (the largest share of the vote ever won), but also by the millions of taxpayers who queued up at revenue offices in January 1932 when the Chancellor of the Exchequer appealed for early payment of tax to accelerate government revenue. The mood of the moment was caught by Noel Coward's play *Cavalcade*, which traced British history since 1899 and was staged amid scenes of patriotic fervour. The task of translating this patriotic mood into action fell to the partnership of Baldwin and MacDonald, well-suited for the task but backed by a Parliament with a huge one-party majority. The government did not reflect the balance of the Commons, for Liberals and National Labour MPs remained an important component among ministers at least until MacDonald's retirement in 1935, and were not a negligible factor even after that.

None the less, the greatest legislative priority for the National government after the 1931 election was a party one, the introduction of tariffs, from 1932 a permanent feature of policy. This resulted in the departure of Snowden and the free trade Liberals, though their places were mainly taken by other Liberals. In other ways, the government's economic and financial policies remained very traditional, with budgets balanced and expenditure held down. In due course the even greater demands of national defence allowed both more policy experiments and a greater economic recovery facilitated by rearmament from about 1937. In the meantime the government intervened in the economy only cautiously, and often indirectly, as in the rationalisation of the steel industry carried through by the Bank of England. Government policy, however, did facilitate the recovery of some sectors of the economy, such as housing and the newer industries, if only through the accidental effects of a 'cheap money' policy of low interest rates.

Domestic policy was therefore dominated by the symptoms of mass unemployment, rather than by tackling its causes. The reduced dole payments of 1931 did not solve the problems of the Insurance Fund, not least because of the wide variation in benefit given in various parts of the country. The creation of a new Unemployment Assistance Board in 1934 was intended to standardise payments, but the effect was of reductions in many places, an outburst of public opposition and postponement of the scheme; it was in due course introduced more carefully. There were also many efforts to deal with the physical effects of unemployment, for example in studies of the causes and pattern of malnutrition, though many of these were unofficial and treated with at best a guarded neutrality by a government convinced that only a balanced budget would stimulate economic recovery. Overriding concentration on the real hardship caused by long-term unemployment may in fact have been misleading as the 1930s wore on. Britain gradually developed two parallel economies: that of the North, Scotland and Wales still suffered the appalling consequences of long-term decline of traditional industries like coal, textiles and shipbuilding, but the south-eastern half of England enjoyed a boom based on house-building, and on electrics, cars and other consumer goods. By the end of the 1930s the car industry employed over half a million people and taxes related to motoring brought in 9 per cent of total government revenue. Where there had been well under a million electricity consumers in 1920, three-quarters of homes were connected by 1938, with an enormously increased demand for electrical goods as a result.

The regional pattern of unemployment shows how far this division went: in 1937, unemployment in London and the South-East was 6.4 per cent, and almost equally low in the Midlands and the South-West, but was more than twice as high in Scotland and the North, and 22.3 per cent in Wales. Within smaller areas the disparity was even greater: in 1934 the level of unemployment in car-making towns like Oxford or Coventry was already down to only 5 per cent, but in Jarrow on Tyneside (shipbuilding) it was 67.8 per cent and in Merthyr in South Wales (coal and iron) it was 61.9 per cent. The universality of unemployment in these black spots was a blight on the entire local economy as even shops and places of entertainment found it impossible to survive, their place taken by such free activities as choirs of the unemployed – a whole counter-culture in itself.

This bleak pattern across half the country seemed to provide fertile ground for the parties of extreme left and extreme right which were making such headway in Europe. But the comparison was a false one. Britain had emerged from the Great War as a victor, with a corresponding reinforcement of the prestige of her institutions, and the successful resolution of the 1931 economic crisis was claimed as further proof of that strength, in what Baldwin called 'the acid test of democracy'. Because the economy was in boom as well as slump, there was no unrelieved reservoir of gloom within which Communists or Fascists could fish for converts. All the same, the hunger marchers were natural targets for the left, and on the right Mosley had a considerable personal following. By 1932 Mosley's followers had adopted a black shirt uniform on the continental fascist model, and by 1934 the name 'fascist' was openly used; by that time too a full fascist ideology had developed, including a strong flavour of anti-Semitism. A big rally at Olympia in 1934 produced press stories of the systematic beating-up of hecklers by Mosley's stewards and a reaction against him in which most of his more respectable followers withdrew. As wealthier backers abandoned the cause, the fascists were driven into more extreme measures, a campaign in the Jewish East End of London coming to a climax with the 'Battle of Cable Street' in October 1936. By now the government were convinced that this type of street disorder had to be stopped, and a Public Order Act which was rushed through parliament banned all political uniforms and gave the police powers to stop or re-route any demonstration likely to cause disorder. With their source of romantic appeal and their ability to provoke both stemmed by the Act, the significance of the fascists declined rapidly, not least as they came increasingly to be seen as sympathisers with foreign dictators with whom Britain might soon be at war.

The lack of a serious threat from the extreme left lay in Labour's recovery from the events of 1931. Mass unemployment certainly did allow the CP to by-pass the official channels of the Labour movement from which it had been frozen out in the 1920s, and it was able to establish strongholds in areas of declining industry like the 'little Moscows' of South Wales. A National Unemployed Workers' Movement attracted mass support for a Communist leadership, but its strength lay in its ability to focus attention on the problem of unemployment through hunger marches, not in enforcing a change of policy. In any case, if unemployment gave the CP a chance, it came too late for a group that was already seen by 1930 as a Russian-run and Russian-financed front which had tried to break the unity of the left. Until the international Communist line changed, the CP labelled Labour's leaders as 'social fascists' and betrayers of the workers' interests, a 'class against class' doctrine that was well outside the British political tradition. The change of CP policy in 1934 to a call for co-operation on the left did not remove the distrust felt for Communists in the Labour movement, for example by Ernest Bevin who led the powerful transport workers' union. Those Labour politicians like Cripps who merely argued in favour of co-operation were for a time expelled from the party. Locally, there were some more collaborative moves: Spain provided a policy area where Labour activists could agree with Communists and the Left Book Club became a popular propagandising organisation that crossed party limits.

But if the CP remained at the political margin, Labour's success in keeping it there was positive as well as negative. The events of 1931 were a traumatic shock to Labour for they swept away a whole generation of leaders: the burden fell on younger men who had held only junior office under MacDonald – Attlee, Dalton, Morrison and Greenwood, with Attlee becoming leader in 1935. These were not men to whom the achievement of office was in itself what it had seemed to the party's founding fathers, and they were men who had learned about the government machine before they were called upon to run it. They now pushed on with the reconstruction (begun in the 1920s) of Labour's thrust to power from the bottom up, in the constituencies, in the trades unions, and above all in local government. Labour lost many council seats in the immediate aftermath of 1931, but they were quickly regained and further advances made: in 1934 Labour took control of the London County Council (retained until it was wound up in 1965), and Labour's strength in other industrial cities was also demonstrated. As the incumbent local party, Labour could be seen to mitigate the direct effects of the depression, a stance for which the Rotherham Council for example found itself in direct conflict with the government; there were other local initiatives like the improved health provision pioneered by Labour in Bermondsey.

The 1935 election consolidated Labour's recovery back to major-party status, with nearly 40 per cent of the vote and 154 MPs. Events after 1935 showed a similar pattern – by-election and local election successes which never quite added up to the prospect of Labour winning an early parliamentary majority. By 1939, Labour had put

1931 firmly behind it, but Labour's leaders did not expect to win the election that was pending when the Second World War intervened.

The limit to Labour's advance was set by the strength of support for the government and the level of prosperity in areas that predominantly voted for it. The economic basis of the growth areas was the relative affluence of the majority who were still in employment. Salaries were difficult to reduce and wages could not be driven down as far as prices – which went on falling until 1935. As a result, the standard of living of people in work rose by about a sixth between 1931 and 1939. More disposable income meant more opportunity to invest in available luxuries like home-ownership, cars, radio sets and other electrical goods. National daily newspaper circulation rose by over two million copies in the 1930s, for the first time reaching the majority of adults; there was a large and increasing audience for cinemas now moving into the plusher 'Age of the Dream Palaces', and the majority of homes had radios by the end of the decade; increasing affluence thereby allowed a media penetration which completed the creation of a single national market and a greater sense of national identity. With cheap unskilled labour, cheap credit, and land easily available during a world food glut, all the conditions existed for a house-building boom: over three hundred thousand houses were completed each year between 1934 and 1938, with the total housing stock rising by nearly two million in the decade; the majority of the new dwellings were built for purchase, new suburbs in every town in the land and great expanses of new building across outer London, but in the later-1930s the local authorities were also embarking on the first big slum-clearance programmes in the big cities. Britain in the 1930s was predominantly a country of big cities: half of the population lived in cities of over a quarter of a million people, most of them in seven large conurbations. Overall between the World Wars two-thirds of houses built in England and Wales were erected by private firms, while in Scotland (where Labour was stronger) two-thirds were built by local authorities, but even in England and Wales over a million homes were built by local councils.

It was this prosperous Britain living alongside the depressed areas that heightened the sense of a social divide in the politics of the 1930s, but it is also the explanation for the National government's continuing electoral popularity; the brute fact is that even in the 'devil's decade' (as a left-wing journalist called the 1930s) the majority who were government supporters were doing well. By-elections which were fought on defence and diplomatic issues could show big swings of opinion to the left, but the underlying strength of the government was clear when it needed it. Many ex-Liberal voters who had flocked to the National government's Conservative candidates in 1931 were unreliable supporters in by-elections, but rallied back when the government as a whole sought re-election in 1935. By that time Baldwin had replaced MacDonald as Prime Minister and the key issues related to foreign affairs. The government retained two-thirds of the seats and well over half the vote; no further general election took place until 1945, by which time the electoral battleground had been transformed.

The government's underlying strength can also be seen in the way in which the major issue of an abdication was dealt with. The death of George V in 1936 removed a politically-active King of great experience who had latterly enjoyed popularity almost in spite of himself. Edward VIII was less respectful of convention, duty or conventional morality, wishing to marry an American divorcee although the Anglican Church (of which the king was still the head) could not recognise such a marriage. Baldwin patiently gathered support while seeking to dissuade the King from the marriage, and with the press remaining obediently silent. Edward's final departure in December, after less than a year as king and without a coronation, was so smoothly stage-managed as to make what might have been a major constitutional crisis appear an easy transition. His brother became George VI and proved a more conventional monarch who rapidly gathered popular support after his coronation in May 1937. With the new King safely on the throne, Baldwin who was now seventy chose to retire, handing over party and government to the sixty-eight year old Neville Chamberlain.

By this time the deteriorating international situation dictated that the main events of Chamberlain's premiership would be in foreign affairs and war, but the son of Joseph Chamberlain and the foremost social policy administrator of his time could never be satisfied with such a limited role. The last two years of peace before 1939 therefore saw further advances in social policy – an advance in slum clearance, a major Factory Act, and a penal reform bill that was eventually held up by the war. The progress of the economy allowed similar benefits, with a growing trend towards holidays with pay encouraged by government into a general provision from 1938. In the 1930s the number of telephones doubled and the number of cars on the road soared: by-passes, belisha beacons and traffic jams on main roads at holiday times made their first appearance. The 1930s can be seen more justly as the precursor of the affluent 1950s than of the years of austerity that were to intervene.

22 War and reconstruction, 1939–1948

Despite the air-raid sirens that quickly followed Chamberlain's broadcast announcing the outbreak of war on 3 September 1939, and despite government measures to close theatres and cinemas in the expectation of mass bombing, the first months of the Second World War were an anti-climax. Since Hitler had not expected Britain to fight, there was no German plan to attack Britain, and since Anglo-French military planning had been defensive, the allies did not have either the equipment or the will-power to begin a shooting war themselves. The German conquest of Poland therefore proceeded unhindered by British actions, until Poland surrendered after a month and was partitioned between Germany and Russia. There followed a winter in which the only real fighting for Britain was at sea, with the RAF largely restricted to dropping leaflets rather than bombs. This 'phoney war' (or for the historically-minded the 'bore war') was a let-down to a government and people who had been led to expect poison gas and a war of extermination such as H. G. Wells had described in 1935 in *The Shape of Things to Come*, and who had therefore prepared themselves psychologically for a titanic struggle. Peace feelers put out by Germany were considered by ministers but rejected: it would after all have been a massive loss of face for a government (due to face an early general election) to make peace without achieving any of the war's objectives and without really fighting at all. The year's interval did at least allow Britain to be rather more ready for war in 1940 than she had been in 1939, a crucial extra year of rearmament before a real battle of survival began.

During that year though the government lost ground politically in its misjudgement of the national mood. Chamberlain created a War Cabinet to oversee the war effort, but only Churchill joined with an independent reputation the inner team that had supervised the policy of appeasement. Churchill at the Admiralty was anyway the only minister able to make much of a show in the first months, as in the battle of the River Plate and other operations to hunt down

German surface warships across the world: he was also politically astute enough to reserve such good news for personal announcement, ensuring that his star rose as those of Chamberlain and the old guard waned. The greatest misjudgement came in the work of the new Ministry of Information, planned by a nervous government to influence public morale in the expectation that mass slaughter would engender panic. The first propaganda efforts were earnest exhortations to do things that in a phoney war seemed unnecessary, delivered in a patronising tone that was much resented. This all helped to foster the image of a government suspicious of the people, failing to understand how deep was popular support for the war now that it had come.

Such a divergence would hardly have mattered if the war itself had promoted national solidarity behind the government, or had there been successes to celebrate. Instead the phoney war dragged on for eight months punctuated by such humiliations as the torpedoing of the battleship *Royal Oak* in the Royal Navy's main fleet anchorage. When real fighting came in April 1940 it was more characterised by defeats than by successes. In a series of brilliantly-executed surprise attacks, Hitler overwhelmed Denmark and Norway, while a much vaunted British counter-attack in Norway proved an expensive fiasco. Germany's defeat of Poland had been remote from the British Isles and was over almost before Britain had mobilised, but the conquest of Scandinavia was both nearer (and hence more threatening) and also a direct affront to the maritime strength on which Britain's historic security rested. The political effect of the Norway campaign was to destroy the Chamberlain government, much as the battles of Jutland and the Somme had brought down Asquith in 1916. An attack was mounted in the Commons, led by Labour politicians and by Lloyd George, but with strong support from senior backbench Conservatives. Chamberlain's appeal to his 'friends' to rally to the party fell on deaf ears for younger MPs who had learned at first hand the reality of the country's lack of military preparedness, deficiencies which Chamberlain still denied. The government won the vote in the Norway debate, but so many Conservative MPs voted against Chamberlain or abstained as to make his victory equivalent to a defeat. No government could wage total war against such cross-party opposition, as Chamberlain had to acknowledge. He tried to widen support by bringing Labour into government, but Labour would not serve under Chamberlain – a decision that had something to do with long pent-up dislike of a man who had always despised them (and acknowledged as much) as with the needs of the war. As in 1931 the King had to intervene to find a ministerial solution in a national crisis. Lord Halifax, Foreign Secretary, was preferred by most Conservatives, but Churchill was Labour's choice and was not backward in advancing his own claims. The appropriateness of Churchill as war leader had been widely speculated on in advance, and as early as 1935 Baldwin had noted that by excluding Churchill from government he was keeping Churchill's reputation in reserve for a future war. With a strong sense of history, Churchill took office feeling that he was 'walking with destiny' and that like Pitt in 1757 he alone could save the country.

A Churchill government was therefore formed with Labour fully participating and remaining partners with the Conservatives until Hitler had been overthrown. In his first months as Prime Minister Churchill continued to rely heavily on Chamberlain, who remained in the War Cabinet and deputised when Churchill was away on war business. The first months of Churchill's premiership were as eventful as the previous year had been quiet. German advances continued with an occupation of Belgium, Holland and France in May and June, inflicting on the British army a major defeat from which it only escaped through a near miracle of improvisation and good fortune at Dunkirk. When further German peace feelers had been brushed aside – though not until they had been given serious consideration in Cabinet – Germany moved on to plan an invasion of Britain, prevented only by the last gasp victory of the RAF in the Battle of Britain (August and September). After this the German bombers turned their attention to the cities, especially London, a nightly blitz that lasted without let-up through to the spring of 1941. Churchill's reputation soared in these months in which the country battled for survival; he dominated the war effort personally and with great relish for the fight, and his regular radio broadcasts both inspired and informed the British people in what he himself called their 'finest hour'.

By the time that the threat to Britain's survival as an independent nation was ebbing at the end of 1940, the political landscape was undergoing a dramatic change. After Dunkirk a press witch hunt began to seek scapegoats for the national defeat, mainly among pre-war ministers. From the right, the Beaverbrook newspapers joined in just as enthusiastically as did the *Daily Mirror* from the left; it was Michael Foot and other journalists working for Beaverbrook who encapsulated this campaign in a pamphlet cleverly entitled *Guilty Men*. Initially Churchill tried to protect his Conservative colleagues from such attacks, but not for long; the critics were after all saying little more than Churchill had himself said over and again before 1939. When Chamberlain died in October 1940 the attack on the 'appeasers' gathered momentum, and by that time Churchill's own standing was such that he no longer needed their support. He effectively dismantled

Chamberlain's team by removing all its key members from positions of power: Simon had been shunted off to be Lord Chancellor outside the Cabinet, Hoare became ambassador to Spain and Halifax to the United States, while former Conservative critics like Amery, Eden, Duff Cooper and Beaverbrook all came into office. By the end of 1940, the Churchill government was not only a long way from the National government which had gone to war in 1939, it was almost as far from the Churchill government formed eight months earlier. It was now an alliance of Labour and of Conservatives who owed their allegiance to Churchill rather than to party orthodoxy, an alliance of opposites which rested on the war effort and had little coherence except in that fact. For the most part, Labour held domestic spending departments while Conservatives continued to be responsible for military affairs, but with the control of the war lying firmly in Churchill's own hands as Minister of Defence as well as Prime Minister.

The Churchill government remained in being throughout the European war, its survival seriously threatened only once in its five year life, when the war itself went particularly badly in 1942. The end of the blitz, victories in North Africa and the Mediterranean, and the acquisition of new, powerful allies in the USA and Russia (all in 1941) seemed to promise that the worst was past. The first half of 1942 therefore came as a cruel disappointment: Russia seemed on the verge of defeat, the desert war turned for the worse as troops were withdrawn to face Japanese attacks, and in the Far East historic British possessions like Hong Kong, Malaya and Singapore fell like ninepins to the Japanese. Under the impact of these setbacks MPs and newspapers began to question Churchill's capability to wield undivided authority: a potentially serious Commons attack was defused as critics mishandled their case, but by-elections began to go badly and opinion surveys detected widespread dissatisfaction with Churchill's leadership. This largely explains his determination to achieve a military success without delay and hence his summary removal of generals who seemed to him to be unduly slow. In the summer Churchill was near to being forced to reconstruct his government to give more influence to his critics, particularly to Cripps whose reputation had suddenly soared. The new commanders in the Middle East proved to be what both Churchill and the British public needed, men who recognised the value of communication and morale as well as tactics and military logistics. A big victory at the second battle of Alamein in October–November 1942 therefore produced not only a real personality as the new war hero, Montgomery, but a truly *British* victory over crack German troops, celebrated in the Oscar-winning documentary *Desert Victory*, first of a series of such films that sought to explain the war to civilians – a long way from the first, fumbling propaganda efforts of 1939. Alamein coincided in time with the Russian victory at Stalingrad, with the first American advances in the Pacific, and with the dogged defence of the Indian border against Japan; the same period saw the Royal Navy beginning to gain ground against German submarines in the all-important battle of the Atlantic, so that the tide of the war turned in all the important theatres at about the same time. Churchill's position was not threatened again while the war lasted.

From early 1943, both Russia and America were firmly allied to Britain and going onto the offensive, and the allied economies were industrially mobilised for total war. The big battalions of population and industrial power which really determined who would win the war were now on Britain's side, and there was no real chance that Britain would not end the war on the winning side. Thereafter, although the path to victory was never an unbroken procession, the arguments were about *when* the war would be won and what the shape of the postwar world would be, not *whether* Britain would win at all. Italy was invaded and knocked out of the war in 1943, France re-invaded and liberated in 1944; for a time in the summer of 1944 the quick march to victory seemed almost unstoppable.

These expectations of victory explain the impatient demands in 1943 for a 'second front now' to relieve pressure on Russia, a campaign that produced a surprising alliance of the Beaverbrook press and the Communist Party, but much middle-of-the-road support too; hence also the frustration when a sudden German counter-attack in the battle of the Bulge delayed the end of the war for several months in 1944–45. But these were only stumbles in a steady forward movement and they never threatened to dent general support for the government and its waging of the war. More cause for concern came from inter-allied conferences as the war neared its end, with fears that the allies would fall out in the moment of victory, that on the worst reading a new war between Russia and America might not be far away. Such gloomy forebodings could be read into the Yalta conference of February 1945 and into the onward march of the Russian army into Central Europe; it was a moment of great relief for Britain when the advancing Russian and American troops met and fraternised as allies in April. These events remained an important influence on the British people at the end of the war and central to their concerns about the future.

The British people that emerged from the Second World War was very different from that which had gone to war in 1939. Almost six million Britons served in the armed forces, a quarter of a million of whom were killed. Although both the numbers in the forces and the casualty figures were rather lower than in 1914–18, there was in fact a higher level of overall participation in the Second World War. Bombing of British cities did not produce the high casualty figures predicted, but it did place the mass of the civilian population in the front line for the first time; thirty-five civilians lost their homes for every one killed, and over three million homes were damaged or destroyed. War also added a huge quasi-military uniformed force of fire-watchers and auxiliary firemen, air-raid wardens, special constables and voluntary relief workers to the military and the newly created Home Guard of part-time soldiers. The whole country was within bombing range and the whole country was mobilised in response; younger women were conscripted to munitions factories as their brothers and boyfriends joined the forces.

Beyond this, wartime measures like the blackout and the sirens affected the physical sight and sound of Britain for five years, while rationing, taxation and other controls took precedence even over the normal priorities of family life. Through such privations, people remained remarkably united on the central issue of the war. Despite the millions who had supported anti-war movements in the 1930s and voted for peace in the Peace Ballot of 1935, only sixty thousand conscripts refused to fight when war came. By comparison, Eden's broadcast in 1940 calling for volunteers for home defence produced so many volunteers that the police could not cope with the rush; a quarter of a million on the first day and a million within a month tried to join the Home Guard. Since this was over and above conscription, it may be fairly said to dwarf even the rush to the colours of 1914, though the determination to defend home and family in 1940 was grimmer by far than the light-hearted volunteering of 1914.

The British public, whatever they had felt about the policy of appeasing Hitler, did not now doubt that Nazi Germany was entirely responsible for the war and all that it entailed. The events of 1940, Dunkirk, the battle of Britain and the blitz all strengthened the view that Britain had achieved both greatness and unity in adversity. This was a theme constantly harped on by Churchill in his radio speeches, but it was underlined too by other popular broadcasters – the writers J. B. Priestley and George Orwell, Archbishop Temple, and American reporters Ed Murrow and Quentin Reynolds. That sense of living through a historic era in the life of the nation did much to maintain morale through a long period of strain and sacrifice.

Unity was fostered too by experience. The evacuation of children from bomb-threatened cities was an eye-opener. Slum children were often billeted on rural families who were shocked by what they saw; *The Economist* argued that evacuation was 'the most important subject in the social history of the war, because it revealed to the whole people the black spots in its social life'. Those left behind in the cities found a similarly enhanced sense of community and interdependence as they sheltered from bombing together in London's underground stations or in the basements of big department stores. Learning from the experience of profiteering in the First World War, the government devised a sensible rationing system which worked reasonably well to create a sense of fairness and sharing. Taxes rose to their highest ever levels, with an income tax at the basic rate of 50 per cent, but the public added to the tax-yield with voluntary fund-raising which ranged all the way from savings certificates to the collection of domestic saucepans for re-cycling into aeroplane parts. The social harmonisation that this denoted was both demonstrated and encouraged by a series of British films in which for the first time characters approximating to ordinary people played leading roles, watched by a population attending cinemas in record numbers in the search for escape from the strains of the time. *Millions Like Us* showed the life of women in the munitions factories; *The Gentle Sex* celebrated women's role in the army itself; *The Way Ahead* showed how the army welded men of all social origins into a united fighting force, and its title suggested that in total war a citizen army was itself a symbol of society's future; *The Life and Death of Colonel Blimp* urged that there must be no going back to old ways. It was fitting that films should both portray and help to shape the national mood, for the British cinema achieved for the first time its own distinctive style during the war. In much the same way the BBC, which had often seemed to be a remote and even patronising medium before 1939, now had a mass audience; it was the instant purveyor of war news and of light entertainment, but also the popular provider of such serious discussion programmes as *The Brains' Trust*.

It was indeed a characteristic of the way in which the war affected attitudes that it encouraged interest in serious issues. The arts flourished as never before in Britain and the state made its first hesitant steps into general sponsorship through the Committee for the Encouragement of Music and the Arts, direct ancestor of the later Arts Council. It was reflected too in the enormous appeal of Laurence Olivier's *Henry V*, a rare popular success for so serious a topic, though one that fitted well enough with the war mood – even if it was necessary to recruit the (neutral) Irish army to play both sides when filming the battle of Agincourt.

As in 1914–18, the government devoted much energy to the development of plans for postwar reconstruction, so as to be ready for the demands made on the economy and society when the war ended. There was an undeniable need for physical reconstruction to deal with the effects of bomb damage and homelessness, but there was public interest in wider issues of postwar policy, far wider than in

1918 – perhaps because in the Second World War unlike the First there was such a lengthy period during which victory could reasonably be assumed and attention concentrated on what the postwar world should be like.

The very fact of national unity in sacrifice and adversity encouraged a determination that the postwar world would be a better place at home as well as a safer place abroad. The actual post of Minister of Reconstruction was created only in 1943, but by then the detailed planning was well under way through a Cabinet committee chaired by Labour's Arthur Greenwood. To a certain extent the running was made by Labour ministers who headed relevant departments but the most important inputs were not made by politicians at all. The main agenda of change was set by the war itself and by those outside the mainstream of party politics who saw in the war a means of exerting an unusual influence. The war demonstrated inescapably just what could be achieved by state intervention and control, and how far the public would accept such initiatives in pursuit of a just cause. There was every reason to believe in 1944 that the creation of a fairer society would be perceived as such a cause. The economic ideas of John Maynard Keynes, which had been vigorously resisted by prewar governments were now quietly adopted and rapidly achieved the status of a predominating orthodoxy. His prescriptions published as *How to pay for the War* (1940) were too much for a Treasury trained to regard him as economic heretic, but his earlier ideas had been percolating into acceptance in official circles. The first Keynesian budget was that of 1941, introduced by the Conservative Sir Kingsley Wood.

Physical planning of resources through state control was also adopted without resistance for the better prosecution of the war; manpower was one such scarce resource, and as a result unemployment effectively ceased to exist. When the government issued its proposals for future policy in 1944, all parties committed themselves to maintain 'full employment' when the war ended. The commitment was hedged around by hesitations and doubts, at least in the private thoughts of the politicians, and the detailed provisions of the White Paper indicated that 'full employment' was actually taken to mean an acceptably low level of unemployment, but postwar governments of the next quarter century were actually more successful in holding down unemployment than the framers of the 1944 policy expected. They were to be less successful in allaying the Treasury's 1944 fears that, armed both with these new Keynesian methods for the management of the economy and the full employment pledge, politicians would seek short-term benefits rather than the necessary long-term investment. In 1944, the commitment to maintain 'full employment' was widely popular in the aftermath of the 1930s, but it was a commitment that accorded oddly with the assurances given by all prewar Chancellors of the Exchequer that such things were beyond government control.

The popularity of the Employment White Paper was itself dwarfed by the appeal of the *Beveridge Report* of 1942. Sir William Beveridge, its author, was an experienced civil servant who had specialised in social policy, and the government expected from him a technical report which would examine the options for welfare policy after the war. What they got instead was almost a charter of human rights whereby the government would insure the people against poverty through a social security system that was not to be means-tested, and using flat-rate contributions in the cause of equality; there would also be a nationalised health service and family allowances, to provide a comprehensive welfare package 'from the cradle to the grave'. Though couched for the most part in dry, academic language, the report was an immediate best-seller (selling a quarter of a million copies, and even more in a second abridged edition) and surveys of opinion demonstrated overwhelming public support for its recommendations. Beveridge himself became a national hero, a new 'People's William'. The report was accepted with enthusiasm by Labour and the Liberals, more guardedly by Conservative ministers who did not wish to arouse enthusiasms for schemes they could not expect to fulfil; in 1942–43 Churchill expected the war to take absolute priority for scarce resources for many years ahead and warned against 'raising false hopes, as was done last time by speeches about "homes for heroes" etc.'. Moderate Conservatives like Quintin Hogg of the Tory Reform Group lamented their party's grudging acceptance of Beveridge, but the impression was widely given of a Labour Party committed to social reconstruction and a Conservative Party that was at best unsure.

Others followed Keynes and Beveridge through the gap created by the curtailment of normal politics and the apparently wide popularity of reform by state intervention. Professional architects were largely responsible for promoting proposals that were to revolutionise town planning; the *Greater London Plan* of 1944 was the most influential example. The teaching unions and the churches were instrumental in bringing forward educational reform; in this case, legislation was passed even while the war continued, with R. A. Butler a rare Conservative hero in the reconstruction field as Minister of Education. So wide ranging was this policy-making exercise that 1944–45 became a 'White paper chase' as government proposals queued for publication. The assumptions throughout were of a postwar world that would be – *must* be – a different and better place, and that the state would have a central role in making it so.

Labour MPs fretted at the indecision of the wartime coalition and the truce which suspended normal party politics for the war's duration. When the war in Europe came to an end in May 1945, there was a strong opinion in the party against any continuation of coalition arrangements. Despite their own misgivings, Labour's leaders recognised this strength of opinion and gave Churchill notice of their immediate resignations. The National government therefore came to an end a fortnight after Germany's surrender, and the war against Japan, which continued until August, was continued at first by a caretaker team of Conservative and non-party ministers, pending the holding of the general election long delayed by the war. Polling would take place on 5 July but the announcement of the result would be postponed for three weeks so that votes cast by British troops around the world could be collected and counted.

Churchill's caretaker government demonstrated the effect that the war had had on the Conservative Party: apart from Churchill and Eden, there was scarcely a minister who had held major office before the war, and that despite the fact that the party had been almost continuously in office for thirty years. More prominent than the few orthodox party men (Butler, Stanley, and Hudson) were Churchill's personal friends (Bracken, Cranborne and Beaverbrook), former rebels (Macmillan) and non-party men being rewarded for war service (Anderson and Woolton). It was a team entirely subordinated to the will of Churchill the warlord, and it was not a very convincing team for an election campaign which would look more forward to peace than back to wartime, and which when it did go over the past would examine the record of prewar Conservative ministers which most of Churchill's team had denounced. The leadership team that had emerged from the events of 1922–24 under the lead of Baldwin and Chamberlain had vanished and – apart from their association with Churchill – the new team's identity was based on a war which was now over. Further down it was much the same. The Conservative organisational machine was in ruins: few constituency parties had kept going, few agents were still employed and Central Office was reduced to a handful of staff in a couple of rooms. Agents and candidates were rapidly demobilised from the forces to organise a campaign without preparations, but in most places no more than the most token of campaigns was fought. What had been a consistent Conservative advantage at all elections since 1918 simply failed to register in 1945.

Despite this weakness, Churchill and most of his team were confident that they would be re-elected, perhaps with a smaller majority; many Labour politicians shared that view, and most of the press continued to write of the inevitability of a Churchill victory even between polling day and the declaration of the results. Perceptions were heavily influenced by memories of Lloyd George's triumph after victory in 1918 and by the hero's welcome given to Churchill's motorcade as it processed around the country. Churchill was satisfied that like Lloyd George he could fight a brisk campaign on war issues and that national gratitude would see him home and dry; it is hardly surprising that he was reinforced in that view when he was cheered to the echo even in such places as Walthamstow, which was represented in Parliament by Attlee and which had remained faithful to Labour even in the catastrophe of 1931. What Churchill seems not to have appreciated either before or during the campaign is that the public could be sincere in their gratitude for the past without intending to give him their support for the future, but surveys showed that many intended exactly that.

There was in fact ample evidence that the public mood had shifted against the Conservatives long before the 1945 campaign began. Despite the party truce of wartime, Conservative candidates had been extremely vulnerable at by-elections to left-wing independent candidates since 1942, and a string of safe Conservative seats had been lost in rural Derbyshire, Cheshire, and Essex; eight were lost overall and many others were held only with embarrassingly thin majorities. It was easy to write off these results as meaningless, because it was not official Labour candidates who were successful, but they clearly showed the set of the electoral tide. It was equally possible to ignore opinion polls, taken in Britain only since 1938 and widely distrusted because of well-publicised failures to predict American elections. But from 1943 onwards Labour was comfortably ahead in every poll and in February 1945 Labour led the Conservatives by 18 per cent. Labour's victory was then easily foreseeable by the usual means by which later elections were to be analysed, but few recognised these omens at the time.

It is surely more than coincidental that measures of opinion tilted to Labour in 1942–43, at exactly the time when the outcome of the war was assured. This was the same period in which government reconstruction plans stirred up so much public interest. What is less obvious is why reconstruction planning in which all parties shared should have tilted opinion to Labour. By 1945 the plans jointly evolved in wartime were the common heritage of all the parties; most of the reconstruction plans appeared in one form or another in all the 1945 manifestoes. This was a regular theme of press comment on the parties' proposals, with *The Times* going so far as to argue that the electorate was fortunate in having so agreed a programme set before them, which allowed them to judge which team would be best fitted to carry it out. That choice was perhaps less open than the paper recognised, for the electorate had different perceptions of the parties' degree of commitment to that agreed programme. Churchill's lukewarm response to the Beveridge Report and the Conservative split in a debate on Catering Wages were just two examples that indicated a party unsure of itself on reconstruction. These doubts fitted too with the parties' instincts and with memory. Plans for increased interventionism, higher social spending and greater equality fitted well enough with what Labour had argued, at least rhetorically, in the past. Conservatives, on the other hand, could not convincingly argue for a whole range of policies which Conservative ministers had specifically rejected as unrealistic during the years of the slump; the problem for the Conservatives was that they could not very well defend both their record in office before 1939 *and* their commitment to the agreed programme for the postwar world. In trying to marry these opposites, Conservatives failed to make either point convincingly. The public mood was of a resolute determination to retain those things that had already changed for the better since 1939, and to see through the other changes now proposed; as the prewar governing party, Conservatives were irrevocably connected in the national mind with all that the war had changed.

The tide that had moved to the left since 1942 probably made the return of a Labour government irresistible, but the events of the campaign only increased that likelihood. Labour fought a skilful campaign, going hard on domestic issues and campaigning on the public's fear of deteriorating relations with Russia. Here too Labour could claim to be more consistent in seeking good relations with the Soviet Union than Conservatives like Churchill whose robust anti-communism had helped to isolate Russia ever since 1917. He had certainly spoken in favour of Russia while Soviet soldiers were bearing the brunt of the war, but as he had said privately, 'if Hitler had invaded Hell, I would make at least a favourable reference to the Devil in the House of Commons.' Labour's slogan 'Left can speak to Left' struck a deep chord, and few can have realised how inaccurate a prediction it would prove to be. Labour could also implicitly blame Conservatives (but not Churchill) for failings in prewar foreign policy, in neither avoiding nor adequately preparing for war. Quintin Hogg for the Conservatives tried to answer this charge by exhuming Labour's own voting record on defence issues in the 1930s in *The Left were never Right*, only to be countered by a Liberal MP's assertion that *We were not all wrong*; such pamphleteering only drew attention to an issue which Conservatives would have been better to avoid, for they could make no headway in exonerating Chamberlain's diplomatic record while Churchill headed their party. (After 1945, it was Churchill who gave Labour's account of 1930s diplomacy his stamp of approval in his *War Memoirs*, finally paying back his scores against Baldwin and Chamberlain in justifying his own record.) Above all, Labour's campaign boiled down to the slogan 'Ask your Dad': in 1918 a war-winning government had promised a land fit for heroes and peace, but delivered only a slump and another war, so how could they be believed again? In the words of Aneurin Bevan of the Labour left, 'Never trust the Tories'.

Where Labour's campaign was skilful, Churchill's was badly misjudged. He ignored such professional party advice as was available and relied instead on his own instincts and on the advice of such friends as Beaverbrook. The result was a roistering personality campaign out of tune with the sober public mood. The key moment came in a broadcast speech in which he argued that socialism inevitably implied totalitarianism and that Labour would be driven to the introduction of a *Gestapo* (pronounced in the inimitable tone that he reserved for sinister, foreign menaces) to enforce its interfering policies. The calm, slightly mocking response of Attlee hit just the right note: it barely made sense to attack as threats to democracy men who until a few days earlier had been Churchill's ministerial colleagues. The incident failed to alarm the electorate about Labour, but may well have confirmed doubts about Churchill's judgement. By comparison, Attlee kept the Labour left firmly under control, and quickly silenced Harold Laski when he seemed to claim that as chairman of Labour's National Executive he would have a right to be consulted by a Labour Prime Minister. Attlee's team looked an impressive one by comparison with Churchill's for Attlee himself, Herbert Morrison, Ernest Bevin, and Sir Stafford Cripps had all become instantly recognisable national figures through their part in the wartime government. For the first time ever, Labour could face the electorate with the better known team of experienced Cabinet ministers; as Morrison told George VI, they had learned from sharing government with the Conservatives how to run government departments. The votes cast in 1945 ensured that they were now to run the country too.

The results announced on 26 July caused a sensation. Labour took 393 of the 640 seats and swept to a huge overall majority, while the Conservatives lost over half their seats and several former ministers; Labour's lead over the Conservatives in votes was less impressive at 8 per cent, but also much less noticed. Such unlikely places as Dover, Wimbledon and Winchester elected Labour MPs; contemporary commentators, impressed by such seats won on the crest of the wave asked whether Labour had now made serious inroads into the middle-class vote. The truth was though that in 1945, for the first time, the majority of the working class voted for Labour candidates, a far more important shift, for Labour continued to enjoy the predominant share of working-class votes continuously for the next quarter century. Under Attlee, Labour now had the title to represent all sections of the national community which Ramsay MacDonald had sought but never quite achieved. For a party whose Fabian ideology had taught it to believe in the 'inevitability of gradualness' this shift to majority status after two generations of struggle seemed more than just an election victory. When Parliament reassembled, the government benches could not accommodate Labour's numbers. Labour MPs celebrated their millenarian triumph by singing *The Red Flag* in the House of Commons, and a Labour law officer hardly noted for being a radical demagogue announced in 1946 that 'We are the Masters at the moment, and not only for the moment but for a very long time to come.' In subsequent years, the second half of that claim tended to be forgotten, but in 1945–46 few on either side of British politics doubted it.

By any measurement, the Labour government of 1945 was an unusually talented team. Bevin of the transport workers was an authoritative presence at the Foreign Office; Morrison as the workhorse of the administration steered an enormous volume of legislation through Parliament; Bevan was a dynamic and flamboyant Minister of Health charged with some of the government's key tasks; and there was an economic team of outstanding ability in Dalton, Cripps, Gaitskell, Wilson and Jay. It was on the face of it surprising that a team of such outsize personalities should have been held in check by so unassuming a Prime Minister as Attlee. In fact, despite his upper-class and public school origin, Attlee's socialist conviction and political apprenticeship had both been formed in London's East End, where he had been Mayor of Stepney. He had a remarkable and innovative grasp of the machinery of Cabinet government and on occasion demonstrated an iron determination which easily dealt with the rare threats to his authority. He had led Labour for ten years and been Deputy Prime Minister for five when he succeeded Churchill, an invaluable period of acclimatisation to leadership; despite the talents of his team, it was undeniably Attlee's government.

As Labour's first majority administration, the Attlee government had a few scores from the past to settle. The Trades Disputes Act of 1927, passed after the General Strike and resented by Labour as a vindictive piece of anti-union legislation, was repealed. The Bank of England, celebrated in Labour's mythology as the centre of the 'bankers' ramp' of 1931 was nationalised to bring it firmly under government control; but memories of 1931 continued and when the parity of sterling was threatened by an outflow of capital in 1949, Attlee saw it as '1931 all over again'. The Representation of the People Act of 1948 effectively completed the transition to democracy as a fifth Reform Act, university constituencies and second votes for business owners were both abolished and Britain for the first time had a system of one vote for each adult. The Parliament Act of 1949 carried on from Asquith's Act of 1911 by reducing to one year the power of the upper House to delay legislation passed by the Commons: the Lords opposed this measure and delayed it for two years as the last exercise of the powers retained in 1911.

The centre-piece of the government's domestic legislation also had a constitutional significance, but an economic and political motivation, the creation of a large publicly owned sector in the economy which would give the government the 'commanding heights of economic power'. Labour set about nationalising the energy and transport industries as first priorities, industries whose influence as producers would spread through the entire economy. Coal was nationalised in January 1947, a symbol of the first magnitude for the Labour movement with its memories of Black Friday and the General Strike. Bills to nationalise Electricity and Gas went through in 1947 and 1948; railways, canals and road haulage were nationalised in 1947 and civil aviation reorganised under state control in 1946. The constitutional mechanism chosen to administer state control after nationalisation, often called 'the Morrisonian Public Corporation' since it was Morrison who piloted so many into existence, owed as much to prewar experience as to Labour's ideas. The precedents followed were those of the Port of London Authority set up under Asquith, the BBC and the Central Electricity Generating Board set up under Baldwin, and the London Passenger Transport Board – also a National government creation but one of which Morrison had direct experience as a London local politician.

Public corporations were to be semi-independent, responsible to Parliament through the relevant minister only for strategic matters, and to the Treasury for their capital investment, but retaining in theory flexibility and independence to manage their own internal affairs. What was strikingly absent from these plans was any provision for workers' participation or control, or even for increased trades union participation; some sign of a change might be detected in the new National Coal Board, where a former miner rose to be Chairman in 1956, but it was an isolated example. In some cases, nationalisation was a disappointment, for it could be seen from the left as the buying up on generous compensation terms of industries that were in a poor financial condition anyway, only for the former owners and managers to reappear after nationalisation to run the public corporation. To an extent this was inevitable, for Labour had no detailed blueprints for the running of industries after nationalisation and had therefore to take guidance from those who had been running the industries all their lives. The Minister of Fuel and Power, himself a former miner, told the House of Commons in a debate on Coal Nationalisation that many on his side of the House had been talking about nationalisation all their lives, but that he for one had never really understood what it involved until he became the responsible minister; his plan was largely derived from one worked out by the coal owners, and a similar process can be traced in the case of electricity. In these areas nationalisation was carried by tacit consent of the industries and the details could be worked out by co-operation.

The one clear exception to this in the first phase of nationalisation measures was road haulage, where an industry fragmented into many small, independent firms fought a bitter but unavailing campaign to resist nationalisation; in Parliament the Conservatives took up the case (as they had scarcely done over other nationalisation plans) and promised to denationalise the industry when the chance arose. This was in industrial policy the first clear breach of the wartime consensus. Significantly for later debates, the desire to retain a consensus and keep the temperature low may have encouraged Labour ministers (who were usually happy with the collectivist rhetoric of planning) to over-stress pragmatic grounds for their industrial policy rather than ideological ones – to argue that the railways needed state ownership to generate adequate investment rather than that railways were a vital national resource which must be under popular control. Leaders of industry and Conservatives could accept pragmatic arguments, with whatever reservations of detail in particular cases, but without having to concede the government's right to nationalise anything and everything, and so weaken the ideological case for free enterprise. In this context, it is no coincidence that road haulage which was both competitive and profitable provoked a fight where coal did not. In another way too, industry was not entirely discontented by the first phase of nationalisation measures: energy and transport were after all mainly service industries whose biggest customers were other industries, so that, as public ownership involved a state commitment to underwrite their losses, their nationalisation was really a subsidy to the rest of private industry as well as to private consumers. The balance of this entire argument would change if and when nationalisation moved on to deal with profitable manufacturing industries.

Alongside the onrush of state ownership measures came the steady implementation of Beveridge's plans of social welfare, given a very distinctive stamp by Bevan. In 1945 family allowances were paid on a non-contributory basis to families with more than one child, a direct response to the range of social investigations which had shown how far the cycle of family poverty related to the years in which children had to be supported. The National Insurance Act of 1946 introduced a compulsory and unified insurance system for all adults, covering benefits for health and unemployment as well as for old age and widows' pensions. But the crown of Bevan's work was the National Health Service, unifying the patchwork of local authority, charitable and voluntary hospitals into a national scheme and providing for free medical service throughout the country. Bevan had a stiff fight with the doctors, many of whom saw this as a threat both to their livelihood and their professional independence, but after their leaders had won the concession that private practice could continue within the new NHS, almost all doctors joined the scheme.

Bevan was less successful in Labour's other main social aim, that of housing, though for reasons largely beyond his control. The immediate aim of temporarily but securely re-housing the victims of war damage was quickly achieved, but the longer-term aim of building up the permanent housing stock ran into serious difficulties. The state of the economy did not permit sufficient imports of vital raw materials such as softwoods for a big programme of house-building, for domestic housing had to compete for the same shipping space as industry whose regeneration had a higher priority. Overall, in five years only about two-thirds of a million new homes were built, mostly by public authorities, for rent rather than for sale. In this, government policy fell far short of a public demand that greatly outstripped supply; they might have taken note of a survey published during the 1945 election which showed that housing was easily the most urgent issue in the mind of the people, ahead even of employment.

Bevan's housing policies were only one of the government's domestic policies that eventually fell victim to the needs of the economy. As in 1918, the greatest economic effects of the war began when the fighting stopped. To pay for war goods during the war the government sold off over a billion pounds of foreign assets, often at knock-down prices; gold and foreign currency reserves had almost ceased to exist, and a debt of some three billion pounds had been run up in the USA. During the war the whole of British industry had been geared up to the production of war goods (of which there was now a massive world over-supply) with scarcely a chance to think of the need for future exports. The British economy had been insulated from the international economy by the suspension of the pound's convertibility on the foreign currency exchanges and by the massive American financial assistance. With the return of peace the American government insisted on an early repayment of loans and the restoration of sterling's convertibility in quick time. Such moves would again subject the British economy to the vagaries of international exchange rates at its time of maximum weakness, but the American Congress did not intend to continue unquestioning aid to a country which had just elected a socialist government of which they were at first suspicious and which intended a social welfare programme such as many American states did not have themselves.

The immediate problem of the transition to peace was overcome by the negotiation of Keynes of a new American loan, but Attlee's government had then to fight its way through this 'convertibility crisis' and was forcibly reminded of Britain's economic vulnerability. The country's economic dependence on the USA remained a constant factor throughout the government's life. These were therefore another series of grim years for the British people in which the watchword was 'Austerity'; priority had to be given to re-establishing industry's export potential and the wishes of consumers were a much lower priority. The first years of peace actually saw a tightening of restrictions beyond the privations of wartime. In 1946, bread rationing was introduced – a policy described by a former Minister of Food as 'the last resort of a starving nation'; in 1947 potatoes were added to the list of rationed foods; by that time the ration levels of such basic foods as butter, bacon, eggs and meat were at their lowest ever; for a time petrol entitlements were suspended altogether.

Headlines continued to trumpet the weakness of the economy throughout 1946 and 1947, with a savagely cold winter adding fuel shortages to the list of troubles to be endured in 1947. As Chancellor of the Exchequer, Dalton sought to steer Britain through all this with a policy based on the continuation of the direct physical controls of the economy inherited from war experience, but a budget leak forced him out of the government at the end of 1947. The new Chancellor, Cripps, seemed to embody austerity in his very personality and appearance, and for a time economic policy was even harsher in the pursuit of industrial regeneration. But Cripps was actually more open-minded about methods of economic management than his reputation suggested. In 1948 Britain was one of the main beneficiaries of America's Marshall Plan, a major package of economic aid intended to shore up non–communist European regimes. At the same time, a shift in thinking about economic policy itself opened up a new era. Under Cripps Britain moved out of the phase of reconstruction in which everything was overshadowed by the experience of war.

23 The age of Keynesianism, 1948–1961

During the second half of Attlee's government the mood of both party and people clearly changed. This was perhaps clearest in relation to nationalisation. Once the energy and transport industries had been transferred to state ownership, by 1948–49, the government had to decide as no Labour leaders had ever had to decide before, how far and how fast they intended to move towards a fully socialist economy. The party constitution of 1918 committed Labour to the unlimited extension of public ownership, but that commitment had been hypothetical, and had in any case remained silent on the question of timing. It had been and remained hypothetical because no Labour government before 1945 had had a majority to allow the nationalisation of *anything* and there was little point in having a potentially divisive party row over subsequent stages of Labour's programme before the first had come near to achievement. But by about 1948, Attlee's ministers had carried through that first stage and hence moved into more difficult areas. Within the government opinion differed between those like Bevan who wished to press ahead with what was to be called a further 'shopping list' of industries for nationalisation; with capitalism on the run, it was vital that the momentum should not slacken. Conversely those on the right of the party like Morrison saw the successful achievement of the programme as a chance to consolidate, to evaluate what was already carried through before going further.

The difference of strategy was highlighted by some contentious test cases. Firstly, the government considered the nationalisation of the sugar-refining industry, but was on this case met with strong resistance from an industry never slow to mobilise politically. Like road haulage, sugar was a competitive and profitable industry, but unlike road haulage it was not fragmented and difficult to mobilise for a fight. Tate and Lyle's led the campaign, with the cartoon figure of 'Mr. Cube' warning the public from hoardings across the land about the government threat to a popular brand name. After a strong public reaction, the government decided that in this case the fight would not be worth undertaking and abandoned their plans. Consideration of public ownership for the insurance companies led to a similar conclusion, as the government shirked a contest with such big battalions as the Prudential.

There was a real fight when iron and steel, an industry far more central to the economy, came under consideration. Steel-making had been rationalised and reorganised in the 1930s, had not fared badly in the war economy and was central to such future profit-leaders as the car industry. It was on the other hand an industry that served other industries (like energy and transport) rather than the public (like sugar) and was vital to control of the economy. It was also too big a political issue to back away from easily and so the government pressed ahead; the steel debates ate up two years of parliamentary time as every clause of a complex bill was fought to the last comma in both Commons and Lords, with an opposition briefed by the industry itself. This also prompted industrial fund-raising for political campaigning on an unprecedented scale: large sums went directly to the Conservatives but money was also channelled through pressure groups formed to mobilise resistance to nationalisation. In the case of steel, the Act finally passed in 1949, but with the government forced to legislate in the teeth of an industry's non co-operation, it proved impossible to make much of a change in the industry's structure. More generally the steel debates strengthened the hands of the Cabinet's consolidationists, who were conscious of the dangerous division between government and industry that had now emerged, so different from the co-operative mood of 1945. Party manifestoes in 1950 and 1951 continued to list future target industries but Labour's leaders were at the least sceptical. The party's certainty about its own industrial policy was not to be re-established.

A similar loss of momentum can be seen in welfare policy. There was no doubting the real popularity of the National Health Service which Labour ranked as high as any of its achievements in office, but here success became a problem in itself. When treatment became free on demand, the public requirement for medical treatment, medicines, and such artefacts as false teeth and spectacles far exceeded both the predictions and financial provision. Financial pressures from the health programme came at an especially difficult time. The international climate had worsened at the onset of the 'Cold War' between Russia and the USA, and deteriorated further into actual fighting in the Korean War of 1950. In place of the steady reduction in military expenditure which had been anticipated, there was now a need both to rearm and to stockpile raw materials. The government had also taken the decision to build Britain's own nuclear weapons, a decision taken on strategic grounds, but involving a further commitment to uncontrollable expenditure. Ministers from other spending departments were reluctant to see their own budgets trimmed to provide for an open-ended commitment to health care; conversely most did not question the level of military spending, and hardly any ministers even knew much about the importance and cost of the nuclear weapons programme. The problem came to a head with a Treasury proposal to impose token charges for NHS false teeth and spectacles, intended both to raise additional resources and to discourage unnecessary demands on the service. This challenged the basic principle of free provision which had been central to Labour's original intentions; if that principle was surrendered, it might well lead to charges for a wider range of services, at least under different governments in future. As responsible minister, and as the politician most associated with the form that the NHS had taken, Bevan was unwilling to accept such a compromise of what he saw as a founding principle; when the Chancellor Hugh Gaitskell persisted and was backed by Attlee and the Cabinet, Bevan resigned in January 1951, taking Wilson with him. As a result, open division in public was added to the fundamental policy divide, a split with major consequences for Labour's image over the next decade. Like most who resign, Bevan departed over a single issue but actually felt a far wider dissatisfaction. There is little doubt that his ambitions had been thwarted by the promotion of Gaitskell to the Exchequer four months earlier: Gaitskell was a younger man with less ministerial experience, representing as clearly and articulately the consolidationist wing of the Cabinet as Bevan represented the left. Bevan was at least equally dissatisfied by the drift of government foreign and defence policy on which he was to concentrate after he left the government, and by the more general shift reflected in economic policy.

The darkening international situation was as bad an omen for the economy as for government expenditure. Rising world demand for raw materials which Britain needed to import raised their prices, at the cost of falling prices for goods that the country was now ready to export; this suggested a difficult future for the country's trade. Cripps as Chancellor forced through a statutory wage freeze in 1948 in a desperate attempt to improve competitiveness, but even so the large credits negotiated in 1948 under Marshall Aid, and intended to sustain the British economy for three years, were almost gone by the summer of 1949. The government had to resist a continuous economic battering occasioned by lack of overseas assets – the 'dollar gap' – but was none the less forced into a damaging devaluation of the pound in September.

In response to these economic pressures, first Cripps and then Gaitskell experimented with more informal methods of managing the economy, relying less on physical controls imposed by law and more on such indirect influences on the economy as interest rates. This trend culminated in the 'bonfire of controls' initiated by Wilson at the Board of Trade before his resignation. It accorded well enough with the consolidationist approach to industrial policy, for it implied the continuation of a private sector to be influenced informally rather than a steadily increasing public sector to be controlled. In part the change reflected the arrival of a younger generation than Dalton and Cripps, men trained under newer economic orthodoxies by Keynes and his followers. With increasing confidence in what informal economic management could achieve (and a greater scepticism as to whether direct control in a command economy was efficient) this new generation provided a line of economic reasoning in support of a shift which had an equally strong political motivation. From the left, the shift was seen more as a loss of confidence in what was distinctive in socialism, even as the betrayal of Labour's best-ever opportunity to sustain the momentum of institutional change. To hard-pressed ministers it offered a chance to avoid such damaging confrontations with industry and trades unions as the steel debates and the pay freeze had threatened. A shift to a policy based more on administration than on statute promised a chance to return to the broad agreement of 1945 rather than to the battles of 1948.

In part too the shift of emphasis may be attributed to the extent to which Attlee's team was running out of steam. When Labour faced re-election in 1950, its ministers had had a gruelling ten years in office, a period of continuous crisis management through total war and economic crisis. It was hardly surprising if its leaders were inclined to rest on their laurels. Attlee himself was sixty-seven in 1950 and beginning to slow down, Bevin sixty-nine (he died in 1951), and Cripps prematurely aged by the pressures of office (he died in 1950); Dalton was lost through resignation, as were Bevan and Wilson shortly afterwards. The team of men who had inherited the party from Ramsay MacDonald's generation in 1931 was past its prime, and with Bevan's departure most of the younger men were either well to the right of the party or of a much lesser stature than the Cabinet of 1945. None the less Labour had an impressive record to defend and there was no reason to expect defeat. Despite its large parliamentary majority, the Attlee government had not lost a single by-election seat in five years and opinion polls had not suggested any profound or lasting dissatisfaction with its performance. The public mood had certainly shifted towards greater demands for individual choice by 1950, symbolised by popular support for housewives' campaigns for less rationing. To that extent Labour was now to campaign on less comfortable ground, much as the Conservatives had been discomfited by the public's overriding concern with fairness and equality in 1945, but Labour had moved with the public mood with some success.

The 1950 election was regarded by Labour and Conservatives as a vital contest; Labour's clear re-election after years of austerity would confirm the belief that 1945 had ushered in a new age in which Labour would be the masters, and only a clear Conservative victory could remove such a belief. The result did neither, for Labour was returned to office but with an overall majority of only five.

Such a close result could hardly have been worse for a team of tired men nearing the end of their political careers and facing an increasingly difficult international situation – the election was in February, the Korean War broke out in June and Chinese military involvement was confirmed in November. In Parliament, the government faced a revived opposition full of young back-benchers seeking to make their names. The wilder Conservative spirits vowed to keep the government up all night in the Commons and to harass it to death; although more normal parliamentary practice was shortly resumed, the government was defeated from time to time in 'ambush' votes. It introduced a shorter programme of bills than in previous years and arranged shorter parliamentary sessions. The expectation on all sides was that the close parliamentary balance would not last, and that there must be a second general election soon. Attlee himself seems to have accepted that view without question, though subsequent governments were to see out longer terms with equally vulnerable parliamentary bases. Specifically, he was not happy that the country should be embarking on what might be a protracted war at the far side of the world without a government of unquestioned authority which might expect a normal term of office. His decision to call an election in October 1951, when the omens for his party were not very favourable and when the impact of Bevan's departure was still recent, provides a clear example of the placing of the national interest ahead of that of his party. The 1951 election was inevitably a hard fought campaign after the close result the year before, and largely resolved into a fight for the remnants of the old Liberal vote; in 1950, 475 Liberal candidates had accumulated 2.6 million votes, while in 1951 there were only 109 Liberal candidates as a result of the party's shortage of funds, and consequently there was a pool of Liberal voters with no Liberal to vote for. Both Labour and Conservatives increased their vote, and Labour actually polled the largest share of the vote, but the vagaries of the electoral system (and the last ever unopposed returns to parliament) produced an overall Conservative win by seventeen seats. With a confident statement that a majority of one was enough, Churchill took office.

Why did Labour lose office in 1951 after such a strong record of achievement and the millenarial hopes of 1945? Certainly not because its policies antagonised its natural constituency of supporters. Labour polled more votes in 1950 than in 1945 and more again in 1951, when it received almost fourteen million votes, more than *any* party has ever scored before or since. The result cannot lie to any large extent in Labour's record in office, except insofar as it necessarily did *not* do as much as voters wanted to limit austerity. Here the failure of its pledges on housing and the (short-term) impact of the Korean War were probably the most damaging. But a major reason for the change of government in 1951 must be sought in the ability of the Conservatives to re-build the alliance with Liberal (and liberal) middle opinion which had sustained it in power in the 1930s. For that explanation must be sought in the Conservative party itself.

The defeat of 1945 had been a severe shock to a Conservative party which had dominated parliament for thirty years. In the Commons, a rump of two hundred MPs without most of their former leaders were scarcely able to mount more than a token opposition to the ambitious reforming plans of the Attlee government. Churchill was so disappointed at his rejection by the electorate in the hour of victory that he withdrew into himself and the writing of his *War Memoirs*, finding a source both of income and of consolation but offering his party only a fitful lead. Party morale in the country reached rock bottom; it was only ten years later, long after both Churchill and his party had returned to office, that Conservatives truly recovered confidence in their own strength and ability to govern. While in opposition, the failure to make headway provoked waves of resentment and discontent: the narrow failure to take control of the London County Council in 1949 or to win by-elections at Bexley in 1947 and Hammersmith in 1949 each led to bouts of introspection. The disappointment of these failures was caused partly by the fact that the party had by then recovered its internal health and equilibrium. A basic level of organisation had been re-established by the summer of 1946 and by that time too the parliamentary party had revived effectively under the guidance of Anthony Eden.

In the country at large the years of opposition after 1945 were a time in which the Conservative Party applied the spirit of postwar reconstruction to its own affairs, through the collective leadership of Lord Woolton, David Maxwell-Fyfe and R. A. Butler. Woolton had come into wartime government as a non-party minister; his skills in administration and communication were now turned to party purposes, when he joined the Conservatives immediately *after* their 1945 defeat and became Party Chairman in 1946. His outgoing personality, which earned him the name 'Uncle Fred', was a major resource in the drive to improve morale. Bolton Conservatives' slogan 'Winston to lead us and Woolton to feed us' had more than symbolic aptness. Woolton's strategy was simple: party members would be inspired only by being given a sense that they were working to achieve things. He therefore set the party high targets for increased funds and membership and committed even larger sums in his own expenditure plans. The result was a recovery of momentum for the Conservatives that rapidly became self-sustaining. Membership advanced with impressive speed, so that by 1950 there were over three million individual subscribers, more than any British political party before or since. The new members sustained the party with their money but they were also the organisers and the customers at coffee mornings, fêtes and bazaars which further swelled both the funds and the sense of movement. More importantly, a party that was in regular touch with three million electors could mobilise large numbers for election work and could arrange a two-way flow of ideas that helped to keep the parliamentary leaders in touch with what the Conservative-inclined public wanted. (At the same time the Labour Party's membership peaked, at about a million individual subscribers in the early 1950s, but with over five million affiliated through trades unions.)

New members also provided new demands on the Conservative Party and new opportunities of development, much of which revolved around the Committee on the Party Organisation, chaired by Maxwell-Fyfe, which reported in 1949. This recommended structural changes and important financial reforms; henceforth no MP or parliamentary candidate could subscribe more than a token amount to his constituency party, so ending the practice whereby rich men had effectively purchased their way into Parliament. All of this accorded well with the spirit of a modernised party.

Alongside the gearing up of the Conservative Party as a social and organisational force were changes in policy and policy-making machinery. The Conservative Research Department had been formed in 1929–30 and functioned largely under Neville Chamberlain's personal control; it had gone out of existence in the war, but was now re-formed under the chairmanship of 'Rab' Butler, recently distinguished for his Education Act but also the product of a Cambridge academic family. Butler made it an important influence on policy; its small, mainly graduate, staff could be used as an effective way of bringing on young men of talent for future parliamentary use, and in this way Iain Macleod, Enoch Powell and Reginald Maudling all found their political footing in careers that were to lead to Cabinet.

In the short term the CRD was the hub of an official review of policy, the first the party had undertaken since 1924. In this Butler had to tread warily, for Churchill remained unassailably the leader and wished above all to avoid commitments that would restrict the freedom of a Churchill government when returned to office.

The way was cleared by demands from the 1946 party conference for a statement of policy; a committee was set up, which produced the *Industrial Charter* of 1947. This accepted the need for intervention by the state while arguing too for a revived private sector, balancing these conflicting objectives with a third commitment to co-partnership; it was suffused with the atmosphere of wartime reconstruction planning and is better seen as the last of the wartime reconstruction documents than as a precursor of the subsequent period of Conservative government. It differed little in content from the manifesto on which the Conservatives had fought the 1945 election, but differed enormously in the atmosphere in which it was produced and the response that it generated. In 1945, Conservative policy pledges were lost in Churchill's campaign, and in doubts as to whether the pledges were likely to be carried out. In 1947, the proposals were formally approved at a party conference with scarcely a dissentient and became the focus of a national publicity drive. At the first meeting of the Industrial Policy Committee, Butler had read to the assembled members Peel's Tamworth Manifesto of 1834, and urged them to think in equally fundamental terms. The parallel was apt, for in 1947 as in 1834 the party was really only committing itself not to reverse a change that had already happened; the *Industrial Charter* showed that the Conservatives were truly committed to a mixed economy and enhanced welfare provision, as they had been committed in theory in 1945. Beyond these general principles, the *Charter* was studiously vague.

More detailed policy work was undertaken after the publicity success of the *Industrial Charter*, work that looked more forward than back to the war, and which as a result marked a certain change of emphasis. Detailed policy documents were published in 1949 and as election manifestoes in 1950 and 1951. These marked a steady shift back to a less interventionist stance, culminating in the slogan 'Set the people free' in the 1951 general election, but the shift needs to be seen in a wider context. There is no real doubt that the popular mood changed after 1947 as memories of the shared experience and sacrifice of wartime faded. Rationing which had been necessary for the defeat of Hitler could still be justified as needed in the country's parlous economic condition in 1945, but as years passed the public became more vocal in demanding a restoration of traditional freedoms. Woolton was quick to catch on to this in calling for more 'red meat' for the public, a demand that had all the more significance when made by the country's most famous former Minister of Food. As the Labour government promised the scrapping of controls the terms of the political debate shifted onto natural Conservative ground. A further move towards individualism came when the party conference of 1950 extracted a pledge from Woolton that a Conservative government would build 300,000 houses a year – a clear placing of the concerns of individuals ahead of the need for industrial investment. It was also a shrewd position to take up electorally, for even in 1945 housing had been at the top of the electorate's own agenda of political issues, and a postwar boom in marriages and births had created an even greater demand for homes.

The Conservatives therefore completed their six years out of office and returned to power in 1951 with a potentially contradictory period of opposition behind them. The party remained jittery and only the successful re-election of the Conservative government in 1955 finally laid the ghost of 1945. Conservatives again enjoyed an organisational lead over other parties which was absent in 1945 but which they were not to lose again. In policy, there was contradiction between the *Industrial Charter*, overtaken by events but never disowned, and the words and policies which were emphasised to achieve victory in 1951. In that 1951 campaign, Labour had questioned as in 1945 the extent to which Conservatives meant what they said. In 1945 this had been a powerful argument to take to the electorate, less so in 1951 because of the Conservatives' successful demonstration of their commitment to the postwar consensus. Many Conservatives had, like R. A. Butler, entirely meant what they said in 1945, but by 1951 they had aligned the rest of their party with them. It was therefore a fact of considerable significance when Churchill as Prime Minister made Butler Chancellor of the Exchequer, a visible sign that the consensus would be respected.

The association of the idea of 'consensus' with the 1940s was an interpretation of later commentators and historians; although the quality press had pointed out the similarity of party programmes in 1945, this was not so in 1951, and neither Labour nor Conservative politicians were themselves conscious of a convergence of their policies. The 1951 campaign was indeed seen by Conservatives as a vital struggle to halt the onward march of socialism and by Labour as equally vital to prevent the undoing of the industrial and welfare policies of the past ten years. The pattern changed though in the 1950s, with the language of election campaigns continuing to reflect a deep partisan divide between left and right, but with commentators increasingly pointing to the lack of real difference. The concept that most fashionably reflected this growing sense of a similarity between the parties was the term 'Butskellism', coined by *The Economist* in 1954. By conflating the names of the Conservative Chancellor Butler and his Labour predecessor Gaitskell, it was suggested that in economic management at least the change of government had not been marked by a discontinuity of policy. To a large extent this congruence of policy reflected growing confidence in the Keynesian tools of economic management, often likened to the driving of a car, since it was a touch on the brakes (lower public spending or high taxes and/or interest rates) or a touch on the accelerator (higher spending, lower taxes, easier credit) that would be needed to keep the economic juggernaut moving along at a steady speed.

The commitment to full employment was unquestioned by any party – no party dared to question it after Labour had managed to achieve it for six years after 1945 – and the chief component in delivering full employment was therefore held to be steady economic growth, achieved not by structural change but by flexible management of the economy. The economic consensus was therefore mainly about methods of management, but within an over-riding common commitment to full employment. In view of the common ground of method in a central policy area, it is not surprising that the political temperature of the 1950s was rather low. The Liberals had almost ceased to exist as a separate party by 1951, reduced to a mere six seats (two of which were owed to local deals with Conservatives) and no other minor party mounted a serious challenge to the Labour–Conservative dominance. The two major parties shared over 95 per cent of the total vote throughout the 1950s, were fairly evenly matched over the decade, and only a small part of the electorate were inclined to change their votes. There was then, despite the apparent convergence of policy, a high degree of voter-loyalty to the major parties and consistently high turnouts at elections. The 1950s were at the time a heyday of political partisanship in the electorate and of political convergence between front-benchers.

The sense of convergence was encouraged by the way in which Churchill's Conservative party behaved when returned to office. The new MPs did not suggest that the Maxwell-Fyfe reforms had unleashed a democratic revolution on the Conservative benches, but they did indicate the opening up of wider opportunities to men of talent: many of the more able new recruits set up a 'One Nation' group in honour of the Disraelian tradition of moderation which they intended to work for. Higher up, the pursuit of a non-partisan policy suited both Churchill's own sense of his centrist political identity and a continuing insecurity about the party's position after the narrow victory of 1951. In opposition, the Conservatives had finally united with the National Liberals in 1947, and attempts had been made to form an anti-socialist alliance with the rest of the Liberals. When returned to office, Churchill offered a government post to the Liberal leader, Clement Davies, doubtless from an awareness of Conservative dependence on Liberal votes, and from a wish to absorb Davies' followers as those of Joseph Chamberlain, Lloyd George and John Simon had been absorbed in previous generations. It was Davies' refusal of office that kept a Liberal Party alive. But while denied a formal alliance, Conservatives continued to be aware of their dependence on Liberal votes. Churchill's government adopted a consciously low key approach to the trades unions, and in other ways sought to minimise any opportunity for Labour to claim that such popular new creations as the welfare state were in danger. Harold Macmillan noted in his diary that Labour had fought in 1951 on fear of what a Conservative government would do, fears that only the experience of such a government could dispel. It was equally true that if the Conservatives *did* dispel such fears, they would deal Labour a hard blow for the future.

While the Conservatives had campaigned with a call to 'Set the people free' Churchill's private strategy in the 1951 campaign was 'housing, red meat, and not getting scuppered'. His government's record in office reflected both approaches. After the pledge of 1950, housing had to have a high priority, and much detailed work had been done before the return to office in preparing what might well be a make or break policy. As Minister of Housing, his first ministerial office in the public eye, Macmillan proved a wise choice, not only for the drive that he put into the building programme, but for the flair and salesmanship with which such a high profile objective was pursued. He was much assisted by the running-down of the Korean War, which released resources for domestic consumption, and by the general improvement of the economy which allowed for sufficient imports of key materials. The annual number of dwellings built rose steadily, and passed the 300,000 pledge in 1954, with Macmillan on hand to present the keys to the lucky family whose house marked the exceeding of the target. That target figure was not to be exceeded again until 1964, but a high level of annual building did continue and the total national housing stock rose by over two million dwellings in the decade after 1951. It was an irony that three-quarters of the houses completed during the Churchill government were built by local authorities for rent.

None the less, it was an important policy success and one that was compared (with somewhat unfair advantage) to Labour's record. The promise of red meat was also delivered as a result of the beneficial economic and international position. Controls were in fact systematically wound down, though the greatest restoration of freedom did not come until a defence review of 1957 allowed the end of conscription. In 1952 the wartime requirement that civilians carry an identity card was withdrawn. Rationing was also removed, in stages which allowed for regular items of such good news as the ending of sugar rationing, celebrated as a 'red letter day' by children's television and radio; the final stage was the ending of rationing of meat and butter in 1956, but announced before the Conservatives faced re-election in 1955.

There was one aspect of the Churchill government's domestic policy which was a sharp and deliberate contrast to Labour's, an area in which freedom seemed a more direct objective. The Conservatives had before 1951 given few specific commitments to reverse Labour policies, and some of these like Churchill's unwise pledge to re-create university constituencies were scarcely thought of again, but there had been clear promises to reverse the nationalisation of iron and steel, and of road haulage. Both of these were implemented by 1953, but there was no attempt to reduce further the size of the public sector. There was contentious debate about the introduction of competition into broadcasting at the dawn of the television age, and the government pushed through the creation of an independent television sector to allow some choice, but there was no attempt to denationalise the BBC or to change the position of radio – still the predominant sector and still a public monopoly. Similarly, the selling off to private ownership of public houses in New Towns was not carried to any lengths of logical consistency: the New Town corporations remained powerfully interventionist public bodies, and the government did not even disturb public ownership of the Carlisle pubs which Lloyd George had taken over in 1916. The steel industry and these lesser symbols of a commitment to private enterprise were good talking points, yardsticks to differentiate Conservative and Labour, but the heat that the debates generated rather obscured the fact that the Conservatives had no more ambitious programme to upset the mixed economy of co-existing public and private sectors which Attlee had bequeathed to them, or even to study closely the public corporations that Labour had set up. In the shadow-boxing nationalisation debates of the 1950s it actually suited the Conservatives well that regular deficits reported by the National Coal Board and British Railways should contribute to their case against further nationalisation.

The case for continued Conservative government in 1955 rested less on these totems of party difference than on actual differences in the record of the economy and on the different appearances of the two leadership teams. After a sticky start in which Butler was forced by the economic situation to continue much of the content of Gaitskell's policy as well as its outward forms, there was a steady relaxation. With the end of the Korean War came a bonus to the country in the improvement of trade, and a bonus to the government both in reduced expenditure and an increased tax yield. After beginning cautiously – income tax was increased in 1952 – Butler was able to make two reductions in 1953 and 1955. In 1955, with an election in the offing, Churchill pressed for a reduction of a shilling, but Butler's more cautious reduction of sixpence (2½ per cent) was agreed by the Cabinet; with the benefit of hindsight even this reduction was to seem a dangerous addition of spending power in a booming economy – even as a stunt for the election – but at the time it had full Treasury support as a safe measure. Only the experience of repeated economic setbacks was to demonstrate that 'steering the economy' with Keynesian tools was more difficult than it looked. At the time of the election in May 1955 the Conservatives could point to steady progress in redeeming their pledges, and to the restoration of a level of industrial production, trading conditions and general prosperity that made Crippsian austerity seem to belong to a world happily gone for ever.

By that time too, the Conservatives had acquired a new leader in Anthony Eden and a leadership team that could stand comparison with Labour's. Churchill's second premiership had not been a great success: returning to Downing Street at the age of seventy-seven he had experimented unsuccessfully in the machinery of government in the hope of re-creating the 'action this day' mood of the wartime administration; neither the innovations nor some of the men were suited to the task, and Churchill himself was visibly weakening. When he had a stroke in 1953 the event was kept secret, but it became increasingly clear that he would not be up to the job for much longer. Churchill himself, still enjoying foreign affairs in particular and relishing his time in office as balm to the wound caused by his rejection in 1945, was difficult to convince that he should retire. Eventually, with an election coming he reluctantly made way for Eden in April 1955, a succession undisturbed by any thought of a contest, for Eden had been Churchill's designated successor since 1940 – had indeed been waiting his chance for too long. To capitalise on the promising political and economic climate, Eden called an immediate election and after an uneventful campaign (the press were on strike and the broadcasters were still not allowed to cover elections until they were over) he was comfortably returned to office with a majority increased to sixty. The fear that 1945 marked an irreversible shift to the left seemed finally to have been disproved.

Despite its rapid descent into calamity at home and abroad, Eden's government seemed at first marked out for a favourable reputation. Eden himself had earned a high standing as a diplomatic specialist, notably through his resignation over appeasement in 1938, but he had also acted as an effective spokesman on domestic affairs for the party's front-bench team after 1945. As a personality he was widely popular, a charmer with the public as well as with colleagues, and he perhaps *looked* the part of Conservative leader more than any other this century. After the re-shuffle of the team that followed Churchill's retirement, the front bench was rid of the friends and cronies of the great man who had been a mixed blessing to the Conservative Party since 1940; younger men had now come on and the rising star Macmillan had taken Eden's place at the Foreign Office. With a booming economy and an election victory, all seemed set fair.

The outcome was disappointment in every field. As Prime Minister Eden was nervy and irritable, intervening in colleagues' departmental work and seeming not to trust them to get on with their jobs, but creating at the same time a sense that the government did not know its own mind. Worse, the economic boom which had been such a political asset in the spring was out of control by the autumn. A second budget in October adopted deflationary measures to stave off a balance of payments crisis which April's budget had not foreseen. Not only did this seem a damagingly sudden change of direction, but it also allowed Labour to argue that the election had been fought on a false promise of economic strength. After the reversal of policy and a serious illness, Butler was moved from the Exchequer and replaced by Macmillan in December; a few weeks later Butler called for support for Eden as 'the best Prime Minister we've got', a characteristic gaffe which suggested that all was not well in the Cabinet. With the government in disarray, and the economy in trouble, unpopularity was quick to follow. Opinion polls showed Labour in the lead in 1956 and a safe Conservative seat was only just held at Tonbridge in June. The sense of crisis was compounded by a well-meant intervention by the Conservative *Daily Telegraph*, which called for 'the smack of firm government' – an especially wounding remark since it parodied one of Eden's favourite gestures when speaking in public.

It is hardly surprising that Eden, already unnerved by the constant habit of commentators and press to compare him unfavourably with Churchill, should have become even more harassed by the accumulation of these failures. It was just a month after the Tonbridge by-election that Egypt nationalised the Suez Canal and initiated a six-month crisis which was to produce Britain's biggest military operation since the Second World War, a unique and bitter division within British society, and finally a unique national humiliation at the hands of the USA and the United Nations – a humiliation that was clearly self-imposed. The strain of an international crisis after a year of domestic setbacks proved too much for Eden's health and after an attempt to recover with a holiday and rest failed to restore him, he resigned in January 1957. There is no reason to believe that Eden resigned for any reason other than his health, but equally there is no reason to think that his resignation when it came was unwelcome to his party or the government.

The succession lay between Butler and Macmillan, both associated with the party's postwar ethos, but different in personality as the politics of the Suez Crisis had shown. In an event widely compared to appeasement in the 1930s, Macmillan (who had been an anti-appeaser) had argued for a strong line, while Butler (who had served in the Foreign Office under Chamberlain) had been doubtful. Memories of appeasement ensured that Butler would not be chosen – in any case his health and consequently his resolution were suspect to Conservative MPs after 1955. Macmillan became Prime Minister, inheriting a prospective catastrophe much as Eden had seemed to inherit all the components of a triumph. In 1956–57 the increase in industrial production halted, interest rates reached their highest level since 1921, and for the first time the Conservative government had to line up international credits to support sterling after Suez damaged international confidence. Labour was well ahead in Gallup polls and scored significant successes in by-elections and in local elections. After five years of disappointment Labour looked forward confidently to a return to office; how this failed to materialise must be explained partly in the internal politics of the Labour Party, partly too in the underlying strength of the economy and in the extraordinary political skills of the new Prime Minister.

Labour's first response to the loss of power in 1951 had been bewilderment, but tempered with a conviction that the Conservatives were bound to revert to a policy of reaction, a dismantling of the public sector and the welfare state which would sweep Labour back to office. They were therefore badly placed to react when none of this happened and even worse placed when the unexpected upturn in the economy in 1953–55 put them on the defensive. Even before then the divisions that had emerged late in the life of the Attlee government had taken on a more dangerous hue. While Labour remained in office and an election was due, Bevan had done little after his resignation to rock the boat. In opposition the split widened and Bevan's small band of parliamentary supporters on the left began to organise as almost a party within the party, but defined essentially by their support for Bevan himself as 'Bevanites'. In opposition their differences with the leadership spread more into foreign and defence policy than domestic matters, with a sharp disagreement when Britain (and Labour) agreed to the rearmament of the new West German republic as a contributor to Western defence. The divisions widened with a dawning recognition of the horrors of potential nuclear war, horrors that generated the formation of the Campaign for Nuclear Disarmament in 1958; CND was in principle an all-party grouping, stronger among intellectuals than any other group and called by one of its founders a movement of 'egg-heads for egg-heads', but it had none the less a large impact on Labour politics. Bevan himself was equivocal on the issue of unilateral disarmament, but strongly supportive of the emotions that fuelled CND, and the Campaign's wider impact was to strengthen the hands of the left in Labour's internal politics. So for example, the Transport Workers Union, since Bevin's arrival as its leader in 1921 a powerful prop to the party's right wing parliamentary leadership swung to the left and elected a radical, unilateralist leader; it was not again to use its control of the largest block vote in support of the right. The group of powerful right-wing unions, whose support had allowed Attlee to take little notice of the activists of the left, was broken up by the end of the 1950s. By that time, Labour had a new leader and a more articulate right wing too.

Attlee continued to lead Labour through the 1951 parliament, but was seventy-two by the time of the 1955 defeat and ready to retire after twenty years as the party's most successful leader. Gaitskell defeated Bevan for the leadership in a contest that accentuated the left–right divide and demonstrated that the right were still in control of the parliamentary party. Gaitskell was a middle-class intellectual, no further from Labour's roots than Attlee had been but less able to bridge the gulf ; as a professional economist he was determined to show that Labour could have relevant policies for a time of economic growth as well as for austerity, but as a personality he seemed to demonstrate a coldness which could alienate even party supporters. Under his lead the drift to consolidationism which had emerged under Attlee as fact rather than principle became a search for a new rationale for a forward-looking Labour Party: consolidationism became 'revisionism'. The intellectual roots can be traced back at least to *The Politics of Democratic Socialism* published by Gaitskell's friend Evan Durbin just before his early death in 1947. The struggle of the next generation was to be for what the right called 'social democracy' rather than 'socialism' as such, but it was a change of terminology and of thinking bitterly resisted on the left. The key work in publicising revisionist thinking was not Durbin's academic text, but Anthony Crosland's *The Future of Socialism* (1956). Crosland produced a witty and coherent analysis of contemporary society and argued that a Labour position decided in 1918 no longer reflected economic reality; the problem of the future would not be who owned industry but how it was run, for the days of the great entrepreneurs had passed in both public and private sectors, and the day of the manager was at hand. A Labour government must move with these trends, adopt the full battery of Keynesian management methods and forget stale old battles about public *ownership*. This built both on academic foundations and on widespread admiration for European experiments on the moderate left, as well as carrying forward from where Gaitskell had left off as Chancellor in 1951. It also infuriated the left who saw it as an unashamed betrayal of all that socialism stood for; Richard Crossman wrote off both Crosland and his book as 'a mixture of Bohemian flippancy and economic punditry'.

Public disagreements with the Bevanites over international policy and the growing ferment over revisionism at home inevitably damaged Labour's standing with the public; surveys of opinion showed that the voters were conscious of Labour's divisions and less ready to trust the party as a result. These breaches were temporarily healed in the aftermath of Suez, partly because it was an issue around which Labour could wholeheartedly unite, and partly because it promised an early return to power which bickering must not be allowed to compromise. When Labour not only failed to win the next election in 1959 but actually had its worst result since the war, the uproar returned worse than ever. For the right Labour's defeat was attributable to the extent to which it had failed to modernise its image to match a changing society; unless Labour lost the image of the cloth-capped 1930s, it might never govern again. To the left, failure was due to the compromise of socialist fundamentals and to the leadership's inability to inspire loyalty from working-class voters. The explosion came in Gaitskell's attempt to meet the issue head on, with a proposal in 1960 for the revision of the party constitution, so that Clause IV, which committed Labour to unlimited public ownership, could be modified. There was very widespread resistance to this move, a resistance that included many who had no wish to see Clause IV interpreted literally but who none the less would not vote for its removal: Wilson described the attack on socialist fundamentals as equivalent to deleting the Book of Genesis from the Bible. The party conference rejected Gaitskell's proposal.

Worse for the leadership, the 1960 conference also committed Labour to unilateral disarmament against Gaitskell's express wishes. Over the next year an implied compromise emerged as Gaitskell's supporters fought to regain control of the party in the country; in 1961 the next conference effectively dropped the disarmament commitment but no further attempt was made from the right to challenge on public ownership. By that point in the autumn of 1961 Labour's standing was extremely low after two years of continuous disagreement and a revived Liberal Party was for a time able to make more running than Labour in challenging the Conservative government.

The economic and social change which had helped to prompt Labour's crisis of confidence had also underpinned Conservative recovery. After the setback of 1955–56, the economy grew strongly from 1957 until 1961; industrial production was by 1961 a third higher than ten years earlier. Interest rates were despite periodic fluctuations generally lower than in 1956, the balance of payments was in surplus throughout the late-1950s, and the relative value of UK exports compared to import costs continued to improve until 1960. As a consequence of a growing economy, government revenue rose by nearly a fifth between 1956 and 1961. The government could as a result increase expenditure in sensitive areas like education and social services while at the same time reducing taxes; income tax was cut by nearly 4 per cent in 1959 and such excise duties as that on beer were also substantially reduced. In this sense, government policy was closely related in the public mind with increasing affluence, but the growth of the economy had produced more direct consequences too in widening affluence.

The 1950s in general and the later 1950s in particular were the period in which the ownership of modern luxury goods spread in all classes of society. Macmillan's government naturally continued the house-building programme that had made his political name, but tilted the balance after 1955 more towards private building for purchase; home ownership was now a normal aspiration for middle-class families and beginning to come within the reach of the more prosperous working-class families too. Families were also far more likely to own expensive luxury items: the number of cars on the road rose from 3 million to 7.4 million between 1950 and 1960, and over the same period the number of telephones rose from 5.1 million to 7.8 million, the number of licensed televisions from a third of a million to over ten millions. Since the same tale was to be told in the case of labour-saving household devices like washing machines, refrigerators and vacuum cleaners, affluence was improving the quality of life as well as the availability of recreation. The increased demand for consumer goods could in itself provide a further boost for the growth of modern industries (and also for such traditional heavy producers as steel) and the regions which benefited most from the consumer boom were those in the Midlands and South where newer industries continued to be heavily concentrated. It is not surprising that widespread prosperity should have helped to sustain the government's popularity; more surprisingly the affluence itself opened up a debate. When Macmillan noted in an offhand remark in 1957 that 'some of our people have never had it so good' he was saying no more than was obvious fact, but he was roundly rebuked from the left and the churches for preaching a gospel of materialism; this was the era in the arts of the 'angry young men' and the time in which stirrings in the universities were producing the birth-pangs of a new satire and irreverence which was to change attitudes to authority for all time. But in 1959–60, there is little doubt that the mass of the people recognised the truth of Macmillan's remark and welcomed the truth that it demonstrated.

It is characteristic that 'Never had it so good' should have become a successful slogan on the rebound, popularised only when it was attacked, for that characterised an aspect of Macmillan's political skills. Much the same happened when the cartoonist Vicky drew Macmillan as Supermac, the mythically superhuman politician who could do no wrong; the name and the image stuck, not as criticism but as tribute. The Conservatives certainly made the right choice in making Macmillan leader in 1957. After an unimpressive parliamentary career before 1939, he had matured politically as a wartime minister and moved through the posts of Housing, Defence, Foreign Secretary and Chancellor since 1951. In 1957 he was a confident political leader at the height of his powers and exuding an air of calm. Broadcasting in the aftermath of Suez he ridiculed the idea that the recent crisis had demonstrated that Britain was now a minor nation: 'This is still a great country'. Similar confidence allowed him to shrug off the resignation of Lord Salisbury, widely thought of as a Conservative *éminence grise* in 1957, and to describe the resignation of the Chancellor and his entire Treasury team (over the level of government expenditure) as 'a little local difficulty' in 1958. The Conservative press described him admiringly as 'unflappable' and noted that his office contained the Gilbertian inscription that 'quiet, calm deliberation disentangles every knot.' Public knowledge of such matters was in itself a characteristic concession to the new media world of politics that was beginning. Macmillan affected a manner of dress and of public speaking, languid and dishevelled like his ragged moustache, which seemed to proclaim him as a survivor from Edwardian times, an image to which he played up for all he was worth. Beneath that exterior though was a formidable mind and an iron determination. It was a combination of image and reality not unlike Arthur Balfour's, but with the crucial added ingredient of sound tactical judgement. Despite appearances, Macmillan was much in tune with the politics of his time, and was certainly up with party policy, had indeed been ahead of it in his younger days only to see the party shift to his position. His advocacy of

Keynesianism in his book *The Middle Way* had been too advanced for Neville Chamberlain in the 1930s but it accurately reflected changes in policy since.

With Macmillan in command, the government's confidence recovered with surprising speed from the Suez disaster, and with returning prosperity the government's popularity recovered at the same time. What had not been anticipated was how far Macmillan was to be a master too of the vital art of mass communication, now and for the future essentially the art of television. Conscious of how far television 'performance' demeaned the holder of Gladstone's office, he none the less showed himself to be the first great master of political television, just as Baldwin had mastered radio and films. By comparison the rather dry television manner of Gaitskell was less effective. Gaitskell was also outmanoeuvred by Macmillan in the tactics of the 1959 general election, provoked throughout the campaign into making specific pledges which had financial implications, and then failing to explain how they were to be financed except by (electorally unpopular) tax increases. Macmillan made expert use of the visit of the American President Eisenhower, whom he had known well during the war in North Africa; Macmillan and Eisenhower appeared together on peak-time television, discussing the state of the world as if equals and friends – a major reinforcement of Macmillan's claim to be the world statesman at the very outset of the election campaign. But it is doubtful if such tactical niceties did much to affect the outcome of the 1959 general election, for a public enjoying such a period of economic well-being, which they clearly associated with the Conservatives, were never likely to turn to the divided Labour opposition. In October 1959 the Conservatives increased their majority to a hundred seats (though were less than 6 per cent ahead in votes), the only occasion in modern times that a party has improved its vote at four successive elections.

The 1959 election was not the crest of the wave. The strength of the economy continued unabated in 1960, though it began to show warning signs of troubles to come. The Conservatives embarked on a third term in office with a skilfully conceived strategy: several royal commissions were appointed to provide recommendations in the later part of the Parliament which would feed into the next manifesto and keep the government open to fresh ideas. In opinion polls, in local elections and in by-elections, the Conservatives were doing even better than at the 1959 general election. Faced with a Labour party seemingly splitting apart, many of its members openly asking with Crosland *Can Labour Win?*, Conservatives and Labour alike were tempted to believe that Keynesian management of the economy, and opinion polls that indicated good dates to hold elections, would together allow an uninterrupted period of both economic growth and Conservative government.

24 Britain back in Europe, from 1939

Britain's international position was irreversibly changed by the course and outcome of the Second World War, though it was almost a generation later before there was full public perception of the fact. By the summer of 1939, Britain was committed to a continental role once more, through her guarantee to Poland and through plans for a full-scale military effort if required to shore up France. By the spring of 1940 when real fighting began in the West, Britain had an army in the field that was still much smaller than that of the Great War, but far larger than any level of army planning since. It was only the defeat of that army in France in 1940 which placed the emphasis of the Second World War on sea and air power and on army operations outside Europe for the next two years. From the fall of France in June 1940, Britain's ability to survive as an independent power would depend on air and sea power, but any chance of defeating Germany must now depend on the acquisition of new allies. Indeed, from an economic point of view even survival would depend on gaining support from the USA, for Britain's international credit for the purchase of war materials would last only for a few months. The decision to continue the war after France fell was a highly irrational one, based more on pride and obstinacy than on calculation. British ministers were convinced that the USA must sooner or later come to Britain's aid, and that the German economy was even weaker than Britain's and so even more vulnerable to war pressures. Both assumptions were incorrect, though the first was given some credence when the 'Lend-Lease' agreement was reached, whereby Britain leased to the USA bases on the American side of the Atlantic in return for the loan of a large number of old destroyers to assist with convoy protection; from the American viewpoint this deal had as much to do with protecting the strategic position of the United States if Britain should be defeated as it had to do with helping Britain not to lose, and for the next eighteen months even the sympathy of President Roosevelt could not break down the strong neutralism of the US Congress. But for

Hitler's invasion of Russia in June 1941, which immediately absorbed a high proportion of Germany's military capability, and the Japanese attack on Pearl Harbour in December, which forced America into the World War, Britain would have had to fight on alone through 1941–42 under increasing pressure and with shrinking resources; it was Britain's enemies who rescued her from that disastrous situation.

The acquisition of Russian and American allies transformed the position. Churchill welcomed Stalin's Russia as an ally against Hitler; the British people were encouraged by the Ministry of Information to identify with the real sacrifices of 'our socialist ally', and the Royal Navy suffered heavy losses to keep open a dangerous route to supply Russia through Arctic convoys. The uncritical support for Soviet Russia owed at least something to the efficient Soviet system of press censorship: British editors continued to print dispatches from correspondents in Russia in the belief that they were independent, but in order to get dispatches out at all, the correspondents could only repeat official news. By 1942–43, there was such strong support for Russia as to provide backing for the 'Second Front Now' campaign which sought to relieve pressure on Russia by a re-invasion of France, long before Britain and America were ready. But Churchill had persuaded Roosevelt to move as fast as possible towards that objective, and America's war planning clearly identified the defeat of Germany rather than Japan as the priority, a decision that was far from popular in the western USA – and no more so in Australia.

Large numbers of American soldiers and airmen therefore moved to Britain in 1942–43 to conduct bombing raids on Germany and to prepare for the re-invasion of Europe. The British people, who could admire Russia's heroism from afar, had a more mixed reaction to the presence of large numbers of American troops 'over-paid, over-sexed and over here'. There was a generally supportive response to American troops, but there was also some resentment occasioned by American habits, wealth and manners (previously known only through the distortions of the cinema screen) and criticism of the fact that vulnerable Atlantic convoys were risking British lives to provide GIs with such home comforts as American beer.

There would doubtless have been more resentment had the British people understood that military planning for the invasion of Europe had steadily reduced Britain to the position of junior partner in the Anglo-American alliance, that the British would be – as the GIs' joke had it – 'under-paid, under-sized and under Eisenhower'. The same was true to an even greater extent in the Far East where American suspicions of the British Empire also intruded. In view of the disparity in the two countries' manpower and economic resources, their contributions could hardly have been kept on an equal basis, but American officers definitely (if quietly) asserted their right to the major voice in the allocation of those resources. The supreme commander in the European theatre had to be an American officer, though potential conflict was reduced both by the appointment of British personnel to key posts at the second level and by the choice of Eisenhower as supreme commander, a man who had already got on well with British officers in the North African campaign.

The joint action and shared sacrifice over the last year of fighting which followed the D-Day invasion of June 1944 did much to remove public suspicions. Trouble continued behind the scenes, not only with such rivalries as that between the British general Montgomery and the Americans Bradley and Patton, but through the emergence of different strategic thinking. With the backing of Churchill, Montgomery wanted to push through into Germany even at some risk, so that Anglo-American troops would get there before the Russian army occupied most of Germany. Eisenhower, suspicious that politics was determining British attitudes to military strategy, preferred the more cautious 'broad front' advance, and his view inevitably prevailed once it was backed in Washington. This was strongly reinforced by the Anglo-American defeat at Arnhem on the only occasion that Montgomery's 'quick thrust' strategy was given a try. In public there was in general amity between Churchill and Roosevelt, and Stalin too, though real differences in their plans for postwar Europe did emerge (and were seen to) at the last wartime summit conference at Yalta in February 1945; even then, Britain seemed to be the honest broker seeking to draw the two Allied super powers together, and to the public at least Churchill was an equal partner in the tripartite direction of the war.

At the war's end, Britain could therefore enjoy the psychological and moral boost of participation in victory over the evil forces of Nazism and Japanese aggression. The British position in the world seemed to have been reinforced by the war: the colonies, dominions and India had once again contributed heavily to Britain's war effort, and Britain's possessions remained as before. Britain was a leading spirit in the foundation of the new United Nations organisation, and her great power status was confirmed by permanent British membership of the Security Council and the endowment of the power of veto on any decisions of the Council, a power enjoyed along with Russia and America. British troops occupied Germany and Austria alongside Russians and Americans (and French troops too in due course) and had their own occupied zone on an equal basis with the other Western powers. Even in the Far East, where British defeats in 1942 had been a particularly acute humiliation at the hands of an Asian people, British possessions were restored intact when Japan surrendered; whereas Dutch possessions in the Far East were never effectively reinstated and French possessions never brought back under control, the British Empire in the Far East was back in being and could boast in Malaya in the 1950s the most successful of all the colonial wars fought by Europeans after 1945.

The development of the Empire seemed set to continue where it had left off in 1939: a federation of Central African colonies which had been mooted in 1938–39 was brought into being in 1953, and similar federations were established in the West Indies and Malaysia, with the watchword being consolidation rather than retreat. The one apparent flaw in this optimistic imperial world picture was India; the damage to British prestige inflicted by Japan was irreparable in a sub-continent which already had a strong nationalist party and an educated class with aspirations to self-government. After a short hesitation, India was divided from the new Muslim state of Pakistan and made independent in an unseemly rush in 1947: Ceylon and Burma followed in 1948, as did Israel (governed as the Palestine Mandate since 1922 but subjected to serious terrorism against continued British rule in 1947). The decisions not to hold on to India, Pakistan, Burma and Palestine were a conscious cutting of losses, the surrender of territories which needed a large military presence that might not be worth the cost entailed. It did not signal any intention immediately to dismantle the rest of the Empire, either by Attlee's Labour government or by Churchill and Eden when they returned to office.

The less apparent flaws were economic rather than military. British weakness in the international economy had been vastly increased between 1939 and 1945 and American policy after 1945 only confirmed that vulnerability. Britain had henceforth a greater weight of international debt to carry – and repay – and a much-weakened export position with which to support it. The Empire itself could be an asset of sorts for this purpose, as an export market favourable to British goods for reasons both of language and of sentiment, and the 'sterling area' allowed Britain to count on other Commonwealth holders of British currency to assist in the support of the pound sterling, but there was no real consideration as to whether the economic benefits of keeping up a world role were justified by the costs. It was perhaps too much to ask that a people who had endured so much since 1939 and still ended as a winner in the war should give up so much of what the war seemed to have been fought for; how could the colonies in the Far East be tamely surrendered after British troops and civilians had suffered so much for them at the hands of the Japanese so recently? The real truth was perhaps concealed by more traditional means as well as by self-deception: when the British cinema made films about the Second World War, it was to tell a story of heroism and success, not to question the outcome: *The Dam Busters* and *The Wooden Horse* – both best–selling books as well as films – celebrated British ingenuity and inventiveness as well as courage, and as a result they had an apparent message for peace as well as a war story to tell. In this the cinema did little that was not equally reflected in the press, in popular fiction and biography, and in the speeches of politicians.

The vulnerability of Britain's world position was in fact made much greater by the need in 1945, for longer than in 1919, to maintain an expensive European presence at the same time. The nature of Nazism (and the very fact of a German war for the second time in the century) suggested the need for prolonged military occupation this time: there was an elaborate programme for the re-education of Germany to democracy, backed by Allied bayonets. Although the speed with which the restoration of German democracy was accomplished came as a surprise, the need for a substantial British military presence in Germany continued for another reason. The increasing coolness between Russia and the United States led on inexorably to the armed hostility of the Cold War as the later-1940s progressed, notably with Communist subversion of Czechoslovakia and the Russian blockade of Berlin in 1948. By 1950, even before the Korean War demonstrated international Communism to be a direct military threat, the British army remained in Germany not to subdue Germans but to protect both them and Britain from a perceived Russian Communist danger. Traditional balance of power assumptions dictated that Britain's weight should be thrown in the scale against Russian preponderance, and the international conflict of ideology was a supporting reason for the same policy. As Britain lined up self-consciously with the United States against a Russian threat – a threat apparently kept alive by Russian espionage within Britain – the suspicion of Americans and lack of scepticism about the Soviet Union which had characterised the war years were suddenly and sharply reversed. Instead of popular anti-Americanism came a belief in 'the Special Relationship' whereby Britain's linguistic, almost *family*, ties, consecrated by common sacrifice between 1941 and 1945, made Britain not just an ally for the USA, but a natural ally that was thought to be regarded with a unique warmness in Washington. For politicians like Churchill or Macmillan who had American mothers, had regularly visited the United States and who had made new friendships with Americans during the war years, such thoughts came naturally; but the same idea permeated British broadcasting in the persons of pro-British Americans like Ed Murrow and pro-American Britons like Alistair Cooke. In 1940 Churchill (from that year a powerful influence on British thinking about the world) had said in a broadcast that

the British Empire and the United States will have to be somewhat mixed up together in some of their affairs for mutual and general advantage . . . I do not view the process with any misgivings. I could not stop it if I wished; no one can stop it. Like the Mississippi, it just keeps rolling along. Let it roll. Let it roll on in full flood, inexorable, irresistible, benignant.

Britain's official view of her international position in the early 1950s was that of a country which had deservedly enjoyed victory in the recent war, had been weakened economically in the process but only until 'reconstruction' had been achieved, had committed herself again to a world role in a reduced but still widely dispersed and formidable Commonwealth, had committed herself militarily to the defence of Europe against Soviet Communism, and had a 'Special Relationship' with the West's greatest power that somehow shed a glow of greatness on Britain too. The diplomatic language which reconciled these conflicting ideas was the concept of the 'three circles' of British policy: Britain seemed central on this concept to the unity of the non-Communist world, for she alone combined a presence in Europe, a natural relationship with the USA and a similar family relationship with English speakers in the British Commonwealth. It was this conviction which prevented British policy becoming too closely committed to the emerging forces of European integration, but it was an illusion of power that was rudely shattered when put to the test by independent British action in Egypt in 1956.

When the Egyptian leader Nasser nationalised the Suez Canal in July 1956, the decision seemed to threaten both the historic and contemporary bases of British power. Historically, the canal had been the main link of the Empire, astride the route to India, Singapore and Australia, and British and Commonwealth troops had won their biggest recent victory in 1942 precisely to deny Suez to the Germans: it would be a humiliation to allow Nasser to succeed where Hitler had failed. It also seemed vital to demonstrate the viability of deterrence as the strategic basis of policy, to show that the mistakes of the 1930s were not to be repeated: in Britain in 1956 Nasser was widely compared to Hitler as an aggressive nationalist dictator – in the words of Gaitskell, 'We have seen it all before'. With Eden as a Prime Minister who was both a foreign policy specialist (an anti-appeaser even in the 1930s) and under severe political pressure at home, Britain prepared strong counter-action and confidently expected support from her three circles of influence. The American government was anxious not to upset a forthcoming presidential election or to take action which might make Egypt pro-Russian;

of the European countries, only France wanted to take any action, largely because of her parallel problems with Arab nationalists in Algeria; the dominions were reluctant to act except as mediators. Britain's allies did not support any effective action through the United Nations (which only strengthened perceived lessons from the 1930s) and the government therefore pressed ahead with a full invasion plan in collaboration with France and in secret (and much-denied) collusion with Israel. So high did feelings run among ministers that Macmillan, who strongly supported armed intervention and who assured the Cabinet that his contacts in Washington were sure that the United States would back Britain once fighting began, saw it as the vital test of Britain's power and status in the world. For Eden, as his health and judgement wavered, it became a personal battle with Nasser: 'It's him or me'.

Anglo-French forces landed in Egypt in November from a larger fleet than that used to invade France in 1944 and after preliminary bombing; within a few days they had almost reached their objective and taken control of the Canal, but then the campaign was called off. Despite Britain's confidence, the American government reacted with great hostility to the invasion, so putting great pressure on the plummeting pound, the Commonwealth was mainly hostile, and Europe apart from France was indifferent (or concentrating on a simultaneous crisis in Hungary). Worse, opinion at home was deeply divided about the morality of the invasion of an under-developed country by two industrial powers, and especially by the collusion with Israel. Great demonstrations took place in Trafalgar Square to protest against the war; Labour which had initially opposed Nasser now called only for action through the UN; only junior ministers resigned, but divisions within the government were significant all the same. Economic weakness was the determinant of the outcome, for the Chancellor Macmillan was forced to advise the Cabinet that only an immediate cease-fire would save sterling from collapse. Macmillan (who was said to be 'first in and first out over Suez') was soon afterwards the Prime Minister charged with learning the lessons.

Internal dissension was the easiest problem to deal with, for time healed the scars remarkably quickly, and although 'Suez' remained a favourite heckling cry against Conservative speakers for some years, it seems to have made little impact on the public after 1957. More serious was the lesson about the reality of the 'three circles': without the active co-operation of the USA, Britain's postwar economy could not stand the pressure of international hostility, and nor was there much actual strategic benefit to be derived in time of need from the Commonwealth either. The shock to national pride was too severe to encourage a frank public debate and Macmillan had to use all his considerable political skills to proclaim a stance of no change while rearranging all the priorities of defence, diplomatic and international economic policy behind the scenes. Diplomatically, Macmillan was able to restore good relations with the USA and to establish close working relationships with Presidents Eisenhower and Kennedy, but it was on a personal rather than a national basis, and it was on the unspoken assumption of Britain accepting the role of junior partner: Macmillan found a comforting historical parallel in the analogy of Greeks (Britain, cultured but now lacking economic and military preponderance) continuing to exercise great influence over the less-cultured and less-imaginative Roman Empire (the USA) even after the golden age of Greece had passed. Britain was therefore able to retain a seat among the big three powers at the Summit Conference of 1960 long after the independent status to sustain that role had been seen to have vanished.

If Britain were unable to use her conscript army independently, then it made little sense to tie up such a large economic resource at a time of labour shortage; the Defence White Paper of 1957 began to shift British policy from manpower to firepower, from a large army to a heavy reliance on nuclear weapons. The nuclear role was tied up with the defence of Europe and the UK, and had relevance to any dispute Britain might be involved in outside Europe only insofar as membership of the exclusive club of nations with nuclear weapons in itself conferred status and prestige. Conscription, which had still required two years' service from most young men from 1950, was now phased out, with the last conscripts leaving the army in 1962. Planning for an increased nuclear role, and the removal of the alternative of a large conventional army, led to a problem in itself on each subsequent occasion that the nuclear weapons required major investment for updating. The abrupt cancellation in 1962 of America's Skybolt missile which was intended to be the bedrock of British security in the 1970s, occasioned a serious crisis; Macmillan managed to secure from President Kennedy the alternative offer of submarine-based Polaris missiles to carry Britain's nuclear warheads, a sign both of the political and economic liabilities involved in an independent nuclear role, and of the extent to which nuclear independence still required at least American acquiescence. In the meantime the professional armed forces continued to be based mainly in Germany, though with significant numbers still scattered around the world where Britain had possessions.

The reorientation of colonial policy was quicker and so clear as to make its disguise easily penetrable. In the few years after the Suez crisis, Britain had in any case to face an increasing nationalist pressure in most of the African and Asian colonies, and with a much reduced power or will to resist. The Gold Coast received independence as Ghana in 1957, but other colonies which had been far behind on the path to independence were now accelerated towards the goal. The clear public recognition of the need for quicker decolonisation came with Macmillan's address to the South African parliament in 1960, in which he told a very hostile audience that 'the wind of change is blowing through this continent, and whether we like it or not, this growth of national consciousness is a political fact'. The reluctance of white South Africans to take such advice invited strong criticism of their government's policies from other members of the Commonwealth (and from many Britons), as a result of which South Africa became a republic and left the Commonwealth in 1961 – a sign too of the extent to which the Commonwealth itself was no longer under Britain's control. During the 1960s, the whole of Britain's West African and East African colonies were given independence, as were most of the British West Indies, Cyprus and Malta, Malaya and Singapore; by 1970, the only British colonies left were oceanic islands and such places as Gibraltar or the Falkland Islands which had no effective separatist movement and a powerful, predatory neighbour to encourage the popularity of continuing association with Britain. Britain was decolonising no quicker than France or Belgium in this period, but had more colonies to free.

The one great obstacle in this 'scramble to get out of Africa' was the Central African Federation, only recently created to integrate the developed economy of Southern Rhodesia with the more backward ones of Northern Rhodesia and Nyasaland. The problem was faintly reminiscent of French problems in Algeria, for the number of white settlers had allowed the emergence of a full political system there and an entrenched opposition to democratic independence. By the early 1960s, opinion on both sides had hardened: Rhodesian whites pointed to the chaotic state of the nearby Congo, plunged into bloody civil war after independence from Belgium, and to the one-party regimes in other newly independent African states, while liberal opinion in Britain had moved increasingly against the *apartheid* practised by the white government in neighbouring South Africa. The problem was more localised after Britain broke up the Central African Federation in 1963, allowing Northern Rhodesia and Nyasaland to become independent as Zambia and Malawi in 1964, but this only exacerbated the problem in (Southern) Rhodesia where the embattled white settlers became more extreme. In 1965 the white Rhodesian government declared independence without British parliamentary approval, and Wilson's government imposed economic sanctions though continuing to seek a compromise solution. All-party agreement was maintained at Westminster for these sanctions, though sometimes with a few Conservative dissentients, and it fell to Edward Heath's Conservative government to deal with the long-running problem.

The compromise reached over Rhodesia in 1972 could not be implemented because Heath like Wilson had become committed to approve no settlement without majority rule – effectively to impose nothing on the black Rhodesian people, who firmly rejected the 1972 proposals. A further delay led to a further deterioration of the local economy and the beginnings of a violent campaign for independence, until a more limited compromise was finally implemented in 1980. This compromise provided a breathing space for transition to full majority rule and so removed Britain's last major tract of colonial territory. With possessions liquidated, garrisons, dockyards and fleet bases were no longer needed; in the stress of the economic troubles of 1967, Wilson's government withdrew permanent forces from 'east of Suez' – the use of a phrase drawn from Kipling giving the policy a particularly final ring. Henceforth Britain was to maintain mobile forces and a Navy and RAF organised for trade protection rather than for the garrisoning of places around the globe. The number of men in the armed forces, two-thirds of a million men under conscription in the 1950s, was still almost half a million in the volunteer forces of 1966, but was down to under a third of a million by 1980.

The reorientation of trade policy after Suez was equally fundamental and also had major political implications. While Britain had pursued the illusion of the three circles of world status, Western Europe was transforming itself; the countries defeated and occupied in the Second World War – and nearer to the Red Army since 1945 – had begun important moves towards the economic and political integration of Europe. When the European Coal and Steel Community began to mesh together the European economies, Britain could not join because of her Commonwealth and American links, and it was largely Britain's reluctance that killed the plan for a single European Defence Force. When the six nations of the original Common Market (France, Germany, Italy and the Benelux) came together to sign the Treaty of Rome, Britain was not present, greatly underestimating the seriousness of their intentions. The British reaction was to organise an 'outer seven' to rival the six in the new EEC, through a European Free Trade Area. EFTA was a purely trading organisation without any aim of future political collaboration, and hence could include neutral Austria and Switzerland, but it contained no other industrialised market as big as Britain's own and largely co-ordinated those who were already Britain's best European customers; it did co-exist well enough with the Commonwealth and therefore allowed Britain to avoid for a time the awkward choice between a European future and the wider ties of older sentiments.

By 1960 the successful development of the EEC could no longer be ignored, and by that time the recognition was growing that Britain's economy – despite affluence – was significantly under-performing by comparison with Western Europe. As markets grew in the EEC, it was increasingly dangerous for Britain to be unable to compete there on equal terms, or to rely instead on a Commonwealth moving rapidly to a lesser dependence on Britain. The public recognition came with Macmillan's decision in 1961 to apply for Britain to join the EEC, but this was a national turning point that had to be handled with extreme sensitivity. For Labour, Gaitskell denounced the move as the abandonment of the Commonwealth and the turning away from 'a thousand years of history', and many Conservatives were even more suspicious. As a result, the application was hesitant and conditional: it was not actually an application to join at all, but a request to know what the terms of admission would be *if* Britain *did* apply. The ministerial team was re-shuffled to ensure that pro-Europeans held the key portfolios, especially Edward Heath who undertook the actual negotiations. These negotiations went well enough, and it seemed likely that Britain would get an acceptable transitional deal on such things as New Zealand lamb and butter (without which Macmillan could not have got his party's support). What was never clarified was the political stance: since Macmillan had to appear hesitant to offset doubts at home, his negotiators could never convince France in particular that Britain meant to be a whole-hearted member if she joined. France's President De Gaulle still nursed wartime grievances about his treatment in exile in London, and many Frenchmen remembered that it was sterling's international weakness that had defeated Anglo-French action at Suez; Britain's begging for Polaris missiles from the USA therefore seemed a further example of a reliance on America, a wish to keep open non-European avenues to world influence.

De Gaulle eventually vetoed Britain's entry, but by this time the idea had begun to generate a greater commitment among British political leaders. Gaitskell's more pragmatic successor Wilson was open to the same economic arguments that had convinced Macmillan, and conducted a second unsuccessful application in 1967 and was beginning a third when he lost office in 1970. The passage of time merely strengthened the economic case, as Western Europe took an increasing share of Britain's trade even despite tariff barriers, and the Commonwealth took steadily less: whereas in 1964 Canada, Australia and New Zealand were all in the top half dozen suppliers of British imports, by 1972 only Canada remained a major trading partner, and had fallen from second to fourth place; conversely, the Common Market countries and the USA took more British exports than any country of the Commonwealth by 1972. The arrival of Heath in office in 1970 indicated for the first time a Prime Minister who was convinced of the political case for European integration as well as the economic need for Britain to join the EEC: he could therefore articulate that conviction in a way that sounded genuine to Europeans. Because of this (and also because De Gaulle had departed) the third negotiation proved successful, and Britain joined the EEC in January 1972, bringing in Ireland and Denmark of the EFTA countries at the same time.·

There remained a problem for the Labour Party, whose commitment to entry had never been more than front-bench deep under Wilson, and which moved steadily away from a pro-European position during the 1970s resurgence of the left. The problem was solved in a neat Wilsonian compromise, whereby the party would try to improve Britain's terms of entry through re-negotiations and then submit the terms to a national referendum. In that referendum in 1976, in which membership of the EEC was supported by the party leaders of all the major parties against only back-bench critics and minor parties, the decision to stay in the Common Market was backed by two-thirds of those who voted. Britain was thus committed to a European future, but the delay had had serious consequences: by joining a going concern instead of getting in at the start, Britain had lost the opportunity to influence much that was to happen, at least until she had been a member for several years.

By the mid-1970s Britain was therefore firmly set on a European path and British politicians were forced to discuss such future prospects as a greater harmonisation of European economies and moves towards political integration. All British Prime Ministers after 1972 found that their domestic political circumstances made them reluctant converts to such ideas. From 1980 British electors rather half-heartedly sent MPs to a European parliament in Strasbourg, though a parliament still with very limited powers and in which only half the countries even of Western Europe were involved. Summit meetings of the EEC Prime Ministers became an increasing part of the British Prime Minister's workload, and equivalent meetings for agriculture, finance and industry ministers were always in the programme. Increasingly, as the implications of the Treaty of Accession were felt, British law was affected by European ordinances and British politics were 'Europeanised'. Over much the same period, the Commonwealth came to have a lower priority in ministerial timetables (and as ties of sentiment relaxed, in the public mind too) though relations with the USA remained both economically and strategically crucial.

It seemed that Britain's defence forces were unlikely to act independently again, though their running down in the postwar period had finally been matched to a reduced level of international commitments. British governments did though continue to maintain a strong and occasionally even a military involvement where colonial conditions remained: Spanish pressure against Gibraltar was resisted and hostility from Irish Americans over Britain's continuing involvement in Ulster was endured. British police were sent to Anguilla to restore order after a threatened revolution and British forces helped to support the independence of the former colony of Belize against pressure from Guatemala. Most significantly, when faced with Argentinian threats to the most remote of all colonies, the Falkland Isles in the South Atlantic, Britain exerted a strong and eventually a massive counter-pressure. James Callaghan's Labour government in 1977 responded to Argentinian threats with strong warnings and the dispatch of a few warships, though without giving the incident the publicity that could have led to its escalation. Over the next few years, a Foreign Office wish to tidy up this outstanding dispute sent misleading signals to the Argentinian military government, which in April 1982 invaded and occupied the islands.

The Falklands invasion brought the Thatcher government to a point of crisis and provoked both a widespread sense of national outrage, a quite unexpected resurgence of patriotism, and some especially violent manifestations of this in the popular press. A large naval and air task force was mobilised to land troops and marines on the Falklands and so restore British rule. After a short campaign in which heavy casualties were inflicted on both sides and the Royal Navy had six ships sunk, the outcome was a complete British tactical victory and a considerable boost to national pride, a cathartic release of feelings pent up through a quarter century of colonial retreat since Suez. The victory left Britain even more committed to maintaining an expensive and difficult presence in the South Atlantic.

The Falklands campaign of 1982 was in one sense a success directly comparable to the failure at Suez, since it involved a single-handed war against a significant country outside Europe, but it was actually the differences that mattered most: in 1982 Britain was relatively united at home (in part because Argentina had a right-wing military dictatorship which few Britons could admire) and enjoyed steady support both from her EEC partners and from the USA (largely because of Thatcher's personal friendship with President Reagan), so that unlike 1956 she did not need to worry about being isolated at the United Nations or about an international loss of confidence in sterling. Most importantly, the Falklands were remote from the Argentinian mainland and had no indigenous population wanting anything but the existing loose association with Britain; it is hard to see that there could have been any effective British response if the Argentinians had taken over a neighbouring British territory on the South American mainland. In that sense the Falklands campaign was not an answer to Suez or a reaction against decolonisation. It really showed how both resources and commitments had been more closely matched in the later stages of retreat from Empire, and how far integration into the politics of Western Europe could give Britain a still useful *share* of the great power status that she had believed she still merited on her own until 1956 – provided always that it could be combined with the close association with the USA on which Britain's world role has really depended throughout the century.

25 Going for growth, 1961–1974

The mood that followed the 1959 general election, the zenith of 'Supermac', proved to be an illusion, though a widely shared one. When Labour lost its third successive election, the party embarked not only on a further period of division, but on an analysis of its prospects that was pessimistic in the extreme: it seemed that the growing prosperity of the 'affluent' working class voter was turning many of Labour's natural supporters into Conservative home-owners, especially in the Midlands and in South-Eastern boom towns like Luton. It was possible for serious political scientists to speculate plausibly on whether effective democracy would be possible as Britain became a one-party state under perpetual Conservative government. Some Labour front-benchers grew weary of constant opposition and sought alternative careers: Alfred Robens left Parliament to head the Coal Board. The divisions which hit Labour in 1960–61 could only increase such fears for the party's future. In the longer term, these fears about the way in which social change would affect the political balance were shrewdly accurate, but far ahead of the event. In the short term, the entire analysis depended on continued 'affluence' for its confirmation; the analysis therefore seemed wide of the mark when the economy entered a recession in 1961.

The boom of 1958–60 was always insecurely based, with the economy over-heating badly in 1960 and precipitating both labour shortages and pressure on the balance of payments. The rapid growth of industrial production slackened in 1961–63 and in key sectors of the economy like steel and textiles production fell sharply. Credit was again tightened, with the cost of borrowing returning to the high levels imposed just after Suez. Inevitably unemployment rose alongside the economic downturn and almost reached a million for the first time since the war in the winter of 1962–63. A 'pay pause' was introduced in 1961 to improve the competitiveness of exports, but more workers were involved in industrial disputes in 1962 than in any year since the General Strike of 1926, another sign of the conflict occasioned by the economic downturn. Public opinion reacted more sharply against the 1961 recession than that of 1955 for a number of reasons: first, it was far from easy to persuade the public for a second time that an economic recession after an election-year boom was coincidental; in the meantime public expectations had in any case been raised by the rhetoric of affluence as well as the reality. There was also an increased awareness of how badly Britain was doing economically when compared to the most successful industrial economies – ironically the 'defeated' powers of 1945, Germany and Japan.

Table 25.1 Industrial Growth Rates, 1950–64 (per cent annually)

	1950–55	1955–60	1960–64
UK	2.9	2.5	3.4
France	4.4	4.8	6.0
West Germany	9.1	6.4	5.1
USA	4.2	2.4	4.4
Japan	7.1	9.0	11.7

With the Labour party in a state of chaos, it was the Liberals who first reaped the harvest of government unpopularity, most of all in traditionally safe Conservative areas where the slowing of prosperity was most resented. A spectacular Liberal victory in the London suburban seat of Orpington was only one of many Liberal successes in 1962, and for a brief moment the Liberals headed both Labour and Conservatives in the opinion polls.

Under both economic and political pressure, the government experimented with ideas drawn from France – much as Labour's social democrats were seeking to emulate West Germany. France's relative economic success since 1945 was attributed to 'indicative planning', and to a consensus about the economy which had survived many changes of government. Macmillan saw this as a way of extending government influence without having to meet the accusation of interference, and of associating both sides of industry with the broad thrust of national policy. The pay pause was therefore accompanied by an important new departure in economic management: a National Economic Development Council was set up with the Chancellor of the Exchequer as its chairman and with high level representatives from both industrialists and the trades unions. Changes in earnings similarly were to be supervised by a National Incomes Commission, though that got off to a bad start since its responsibility for statutory pay controls greatly antagonised the unions. Thus began a period in which governments sought to bring both sides of industry together in a 'corporate' effort to promote growth from which all could benefit: the NEDC generated sub-committees responsible for individual industries and for regions, some of them very influential in the allocation of government industrial investment. The NEDC and its offshoots developed a life of their own, though all its participants continued to operate independently in their own spheres at the same time; those who joined this 'corporatist' structure made only strictly limited commitments.

The country's economic problems provided an opportunity through which wider changes of attitude could take place. Intellectual and artistic life had been in a ferment since the time of Suez, and much that had been hidden now came to the surface. The most visible symbols of popular culture in a country which had within a few years become almost universally exposed to television were no longer those of the social and political establishment. The aggressive promotion of provincial lifestyles, through such diverse avenues as Granada TV's *Coronation Street* or the beat music of Merseyside, conquered much of popular taste even in 'swinging London'. Much of the new popular culture was classless, disrespectful of the establishment, and characterised above all with idealising youth. Its most pointed form came from Oxford and Cambridge Universities with a sudden boom in social and political satire – *Beyond the Fringe*, the BBC's *That Was The Week That Was*, the new magazine *Private Eye* and a night club ironically called 'The Establishment'. The new culture made the reputations not only of The Beatles and other musicians, but of entertainers who were to be more serious influences over the next generation – Jonathan Miller, David Frost, Lindsay Anderson, Alan Bennett and Bernard Levin. Wide and disparate as these influences were, they combined to undermine the unthinking acceptance of authority which had been at the heart of the mass media's political impact since its arrival as a cheap and universal form of entertainment in the 1890s.

A more directly political impact was to be seen in a tireless questioning of all that was traditional in the search for scapegoats for national economic and political decline. There was an increasing readership for investigative reports of institutional failure, particularly in the serious Sunday press, and a ready market for a series of Penguin books on the 'What's wrong with Britain?' theme. Serious writers like Hugh Thomas found the answer to that question in the outmoded attitudes of *The Establishment*, or like Anthony Sampson found that the *Anatomy of Britain* was a suitable case for treatment. Not only was there a reported need for change: there was also a growing confidence that such change could not be resisted, for what Michael

Young called *The Rise of the Meritocracy* would sweep away all that was inefficient and backward-looking.

In the event the establishment proved to have far more staying power and adaptability than such theories allowed for. In the short term though the sea-change of attitudes removed the foundations of Macmillan's political position: his success before 1959 had been achieved by adopting a consciously antiquated style to reassure people at a time of rapid change, while pursuing change without inhibition himself. He was more ready to adapt to the changed mood than his critics expected – as when he made use of The Beatles for a joke in a political broadcast – but his own age set limits on his ability to adapt. This was especially so when the new and young American President Kennedy became an international hero for the cult of youth after his assassination in 1963. By that time Macmillan had taken drastic action to remodel his government to keep up with popular attitudes: in July 1962, under the impact of serious by-election reverses, he sacked a third of the Cabinet in a purge which the press called 'the night of the long knives'. Instead of a surgical operation to keep his government up to date, it looked like an act of butchery – 'to lay down his friends for his life' (as a Liberal critic put it). None the less, the new team did mark a significant new departure both in reducing the overall age of the government and in bringing into high office Reginald Maudling (Chancellor), Enoch Powell (Health) and Edward Boyle (Education), all men much associated with the postwar ethos. The Macmillan strategy depended on his own survival as the presiding director of this blend of youth and experience.

But Macmillan's position was now threatened from his own side. The root cause lay in part in old antagonisms and recent sackings, but was the more dangerous because of a series of spy scandals which cast doubt on ministerial competence in an area for which he had personal responsibility. Much of this was merely bad luck: as he himself later noted, no government is ever credited with catching spies, only blamed for not catching them earlier. Much also resulted from poor judgement, especially when a Navy minister was forced from office on unjustified suspicions; worse, a judicial investigation into the allegations ended by imprisoning journalists who refused to name their sources, so unleashing a storm of press hostility about the government's ears just before the worst of the scandals broke. This involved an affair between the War minister, John Profumo, and a girl who was also well known to the Russian military attaché in London; no actual risk was ever shown, but the potential danger to security was immense, and Profumo in any case made both the risk and the subsequent scandal far worse by denying to the Commons that the stories were true. There was a period of months when the press hinted what they dare not print, until in June 1963 Profumo admitted everything and resigned.

The government almost fell in the storm of outrage that followed, with the most extravagant stories circulating about immorality in high places: the report of the judge appointed to investigate the affair was so eagerly awaited by a press and public avid for more salacious gossip about the great and the good that Her Majesty's Stationery Office had to open in the middle of the night to deal with queues of purchasers. For the opposition, Harold Wilson sought to avoid the moral issue (which the popular press was exploiting for him in any case) and concentrate on exposing the security lapses, but *The Times* angrily editorialised that 'it *is* a moral issue', and linked it (to the government's disadvantage) with the materialist basis of affluence: in place of 'You've never had it so good', *Private Eye* concluded that the government's motto ought now to be 'You've never had it so often'.

The affair showed a seamier side of the ruling class just as the opposition was making capital out of unscrupulous property owners whose opportunities for profit-making had been increased by the 1958 Rent Act; it also showed a Prime Minister who seemed to have been too hesitant in asking crucial questions and demanding satisfactory answers. One Conservative MP urged Macmillan to go, for the best of his rule had passed into shame – there would 'never [be] glad confident morning again'. But Macmillan was more resilient than his critics imagined and had resolved to soldier on with his new team to the next election, only to be forced into resignation by illness in October. The timing was especially unfortunate, for his resignation was announced to the Cabinet only days before ministers entrained for Blackpool for the annual party conference. The result was a conference overlaid by an open fight for the leadership, and although the actual decision was not taken until the following week in London, the passions aroused in Blackpool prevented a quiet, clean leadership decision such as the Conservatives had usually practised. Neither of the two front runners, Butler and Hogg, could command general support and each was strongly opposed by some in the party; from his sickbed, Macmillan superintended the negotiations which ensured that the Earl of Home succeeded him. Home's claims were strong, for he had been in government since 1951, in Cabinet since 1955 and Foreign Secretary since 1960. He was on the other hand in the Lords (and effectively eligible only because recent legislation allowed him to give up his peerage) and he seemed archetypally representative of the old Conservative party of the Scottish shires, of an 'establishment' now under strong attack. A last minute attempt to prevent Home becoming leader foundered on Butler's refusal to make a fight and risk party unity, but Home was unable to persuade either Macleod or Powell – symbols of modern Toryism – to join the new government and as a result took office only with a divided party and with a year at most to go before an election.

This situation was the more dangerous because of the extent to which Labour had recovered from its travails. The unspoken truce between Gaitskell and the left in 1961 had been accompanied by a reassertion of his leadership in a contest with Wilson. From the Blackpool conference of 1961 the right again assumed a dominant role; organising behind Gaitskell, the Campaign for Democratic Socialism sought to influence trades unions and local parties – especially when selecting parliamentary candidates in which the CDS was astonishingly successful. With the government again unpopular for economic reasons as well as through spy scandals, Labour regained its momentum and drive for power, taking three by-election seats from Conservatives in the second half of 1962; the Liberals were again relegated firmly to third place and every monthly Gallup poll in 1963 showed Labour well ahead of the government. Gaitskell's determined leadership contributed to this, but he did not see its outcome, for he himself suddenly died early in 1963.

Because Labour's moderates had rallied behind Gaitskell they were not ready for a succession contest; Wilson from the left fought a clever campaign against a divided right and defeated George Brown and James Callaghan to become leader. Wilson, like Thatcher was to be in 1975, was a leader elected by the votes of back-benchers over the heads of more moderate front-benchers and had to surround himself in shadow cabinet, subsequently in Cabinet, with those who had not wanted him: in his own later, somewhat overstated account, 'I was a bolshevik in a cabinet of tsarists'. His claim to be a man of the left derived from his 1951 resignation with Bevan and from his defensive campaign for socialist fundamentals in 1960–61, rather than from radical intentions for the future. He was quoted in 1957 as admiring the skill with which Macmillan rallied the Conservatives over Suez, holding it up as a banner but marching his troops the other way: 'That's what I'd like to do with the Labour Party and nationalisation.' His disagreement with Gaitskell had been more about style than content, and this provided a basis for future leadership which would be long on the rhetoric of the left while actively pursuing the policies of the right, exactly the formula of MacDonald's successful leadership in the 1920s.

Wilson proved to be a superb leader of opposition, perhaps the best since Disraeli, and with the advantages which the Profumo affair gave him he soon had the Conservatives reeling. He was only forty-seven when elected leader and hailed in the press as 'Britain's

Kennedy' – the epitome of the coming meritocratic age, highly photogenic, more attentive to the needs of television even than Macmillan, and far more effective a communicator than Home. He also had an instinctive sense of the memorable phrase, not always his own but put across to great effect: the whole period of Conservative government since 1951 was summed up as 'thirteen wasted years'; Home was always 'the fourteenth Earl of Home'; the discontinuity of boom and slump since 1951 were castigated as 'stop-go'; Labour's more dynamic plans were modern and technological, and would unleash 'the white heat' of 'the scientific revolution', all excellent headlines and quotable clips for television news bulletins. Labour discovered for the first time since 1945 the exhilaration of a contest in which they were making the running and confidently expected to return to power.

Home's one-year premiership was in fact far more successful than anticipated: his team could not match Macmillan's blend of age and experience, but it had in the promotion of Edward Heath to senior office a man of Wilson's age and of equal determination. Heath's major initiative, the abolition of price-fixing by manufacturers, proved a costly victory, for it was only carried through after major revolts by Conservative MPs and antagonised many Conservative voters because of the threat it posed to small shops. The real basis of Conservative strength was again economic prosperity: as Chancellor Maudling unleashed a roaring boom with interest rate and tax cuts, so that unemployment fell away in 1963 and both production and consumption surged ahead. The balance of payments, safely in surplus in 1962 and 1963 as a result of the 1961 measures, moved dangerously into deficit in 1964; it was no accident that the Chancellor was among the ministers who wanted an early election in spring 1964, so that policy adjustments could then be made. Unfortunately the economic cycle was out of synch with the electoral cycle: polls showed Labour still well ahead in the spring, and the election was therefore put off to autumn as the economy got further out of control. Over the summer, Conservative popularity continued to grow with the increased earnings which the boom allowed, and October produced a hard-fought and close election which Labour just won by five seats. Home had done well to get so near a fourth successive Conservative victory, but he and his party now had to face the consequences of defeat. Wilson took office with enthusiasm and – taking his cue now from Roosevelt rather than Kennedy – promised the country 'a hundred days of dynamic action'.

The first period of Wilson's government proved to be a carry-over from opposition: the defeated Conservatives offered little resistance and the small majority brought Wilson's tactical skills to the fore. He

was constantly on television explaining the government's intentions
to the people, so much so that the broadcasters eventually decided
that he was exceeding his right to ministerial broadcasts without
opposition replies, the beginning of what was to become a bitter
antagonism between the Prime Minister and his recent media allies.
The government moved quickly to demonstrate its capacity for
action. Tough import controls were imposed to stem the flow of
imports and fairly blamed on the balance of payments crisis left by
the previous regime; but a chance to devalue the pound and blame that
too on the Conservatives was lost in a rush decision made immediately
after the election, an error which was to have disastrous consequences
for the government.

Labour had fought the election on two main strategies; the first
was a claim that more expenditure was needed in key social policy
areas like education and health, and the second was a belief that these
increased provisions could be made without generally raising taxes
by getting a more sustained level of economic growth than the
Conservatives had managed. The first aim would show Labour's
caring concern, and the second Labour's greater competence. The first
was easier to initiate than the second, not least because of the economic
conditions that the government inherited and which dictated a policy
of deflation rather than growth. Pensions were increased, plans were
made for a higher school-leaving age, a great increase in provision for
universities and an 'Open' university teaching through television: the
symbolic issue of 1951 was faced with the abolition of prescription
charges to demonstrate Labour's commitment to a free health service.
All of this would depend on the availability of finance through either
increased taxation rates or higher taxation revenue resulting from
economic growth.

Labour planned both structural change and a greater corporatist
commitment to joint planning to encourage that steady growth; it
was indeed under the auspices of the Labour government that British
industry's various representative bodies finally came together as the
Confederation of British Industry – a central body to parallel the
TUC in the government's corporatist set-up. A new Department
of Economic Affairs was created under Brown as Deputy Prime
Minister, following the unsuccessful experiment of 1947, in the hope
that it would create a 'pressure group for economic growth' within
Whitehall, where the Treasury was more traditionally concerned
with finance and the international parity of the pound. The DEA
was supposed to work in 'creative tension' with the Treasury (headed
by Brown's old rival Callaghan), but in practice things were more
tense than creative. On each occasion on which the two departments
collided, the Treasury emerged victorious: by the time of the

economic crisis in the summer of 1966, it was clear that the Treasury's concerns with sterling continued to predominate, and the DEA was first downgraded and then closed down altogether. By that time too, the corporatist idea had taken a severe knock. Brown was able to bring together both sides of industry in a joint undertaking to work for growth, and a full scale National Plan which went far beyond Macmillan's aims was produced in 1965, but without the government taking many new powers to enforce the Plan's objectives. NEDC's role expanded and generated a whole generation of 'little neddies' which the newly self-appointed champion of economic liberalism, Powell, dubbed Trojan horses of state interference. But the Plan's internal contradictions were far more serious than its outside critics. Agreement had been reached because the government had promised a level of economic growth from which all could benefit, but which was higher than had ever been achieved over an extended period this century. When economic crisis forced the government unwillingly into a deflation in July 1966, all the growth assumptions on which the National Plan had been based became irrelevant.

By that time the government's political position had been secured by a second general election victory in March 1966. The government's life before that time had been difficult, for a by-election had reduced its majority to three and a couple of backbenchers were able to hold up the key proposal to renationalise steel by withholding their votes. Wilson had been able to achieve little that was lasting as a result, but had used the eighteen month period to bring on younger and more able ministers than had been available in 1964 after thirteen years in opposition: Barbara Castle, Roy Jenkins, Anthony Crosland and Tony Benn were all promoted to the Cabinet. By March 1966, with a temporary respite from economic pressures which could be claimed as Labour's achievement (but with memories of the recent Conservative government still recent enough to allow the re-use of the successful rhetoric of 1964), Labour could treat this election as the second round of the earlier contest, asking for confirmation of a decision already reached: echoing Churchill in wartime, Labour's posters asked for the tools (a majority) to finish the job. Against a lacklustre Tory campaign under the new leader Heath, unable to avoid defending the previous Conservative record though really wanting to strike out in fresh directions, Labour had an easy ride and its second best result ever: Wilson retained office with a majority of a hundred and moved on to a full term – now without alibis from the past to sustain him.

Once securely in office for a second term, Wilson devoted more of his time to foreign affairs and less to the economy and to the domestic political scene, as bad a mistake for him as it had been for Macmillan after 1959. The decision not to devalue in 1964 had ensured that his government would have to carry the burden of an over-valued currency, and increases in government expenditure without economic growth involved continuing inflationary risks. The fragility of the situation was exposed within three months of the 1966 election, when economic crisis broke as a result of a seamen's strike: expenditure cuts and tax increases were rushed through to restore foreign confidence, at the price of delays in cherished programmes and Brown's resignation from the DEA. This was the third round of deflation since 1964 and production in heavy industry had fallen as a result, but the balance of payments remained in deficit. Worse, the July measures also included the legal control of prices and incomes such as the Conservatives had introduced (and both Labour and the trades unions had denounced) in 1961; 1967–68 were therefore years bedevilled by constant bickering between the government, unions and industry which wrecked the harmonious atmosphere of partnership in which the National Plan had been adopted. Worse yet, the July measures still did not deal with the central question of sterling's parity: Wilson was determined that his government should not devalue as Attlee's had done (and as MacDonald's had done too – though after Labour's ministers left) and the Treasury was forbidden even to discuss the question lest word should leak out and bring on a further crisis. Privately the Treasury planned for an event which many of its professionals believed to be in the end unavoidable, and as a result was ready when the unavoidable could be postponed no longer in November 1967. The pound was devalued from $2.80 to $2.40 and interest rates were raised simultaneously to the highest level since the Great War; in his first budget, the new Chancellor Jenkins promoted in 1968 a strategy which would intentionally cut purchasing power further, and government expenditure was again reined in. This last round of deflation finally did the trick, producing a return to trading surpluses and confidence in the economy in 1968–69 as the government's term ended.

The government's economic problems naturally provided a golden opportunity for the Conservatives to recover from the shock of the 1964 and 1966 defeats. As in 1955, the opposition was able to claim after 1966 that the election had been won on a false claim of economic strength. The government could scarcely hold a by-election seat in 1967–68 and Labour was almost wiped out in local government: the Conservatives took control of London in 1967 for the first time since 1933 and in 1968 won almost every London borough – including some where they had previously had no councillors at all. It is hardly surprising that Wilson should have turned his attention not only to his own party's weaknesses, but to what might be the

Conservatives' policy strengths in order to re-establish his position. Once out of office, the Conservatives made big organisational and policy changes. Home had always found it personally offensive that the way in which he had become leader allowed critics to cry foul, and he therefore prompted the review which led in 1965 to the setting up of an open system of election for the Conservative leader, a system not unlike that which Labour then used. Home's talents had in any case been essentially governmental and after a recent career spent mainly in the Lords he was less comfortable in the rough and tumble of opposition; in 1965 repeated calls arose for his resignation, and he waited only for the new electoral system to be in place before stepping down.

The contest for the leadership between Heath and Maudling was notable more for the extent to which they were both more meritocratic than was traditional (and both agreed on the need to modernise policy) than for any real policy disagreement between them: Powell's candidature offered the party a different, more free-market approach, but only a handful of MPs backed him. Heath won because he offered to present a more abrasive response to Wilson, and his early brushes with the Prime Minister in Parliament were notable for their bad temper on both sides, but Heath rarely got the better of Wilson. Heath was also helped in becoming leader by his reputation for energy and his association with the policy review which the party began after the 1964 election. Conservatives had felt acutely uncomfortable in 1964 about the way in which Wilson had accused them of incompetence in managing the country and associated their incompetence with outdatedness. They went into opposition with a strong sense that the party's 'grouse-moor image' had to be changed – hence the generation change between the 1964 Cabinet and Heath's shadow cabinet of 1965, with the retirement of Butler and others more associated with the period after 1945. But modernisation would mean a fundamental review of policy too: one aspect was the decision to commit the Conservatives more definitely to Europe, a policy that went well with Heath's leadership and proved less and less painful to the right as colonies were shed in the 1960s. At home the focus was on providing means to get faster growth, not least because of the need to toughen up the economic performance of the country for the time when Britain was in the EEC. The goal of growth could not be pursued by the same means as the recent Conservative government had used, both because some shadow ministers were now highly sceptical about incomes policies and other such corporatist ideas, and because Conservatives were in public deriding both Labour's National Plan and the incomes policy which succeeded it.

If neither the pursuit of partnership nor legislative control of incomes seemed a viable way to improve productivity and competitiveness, then the only way forward would be to take a tougher governmental line with both unions and industry. Politically, this would satisfy the many Conservative activists who had been pressing for years for strong action to control trades unions, it would show that the party was offering something both new and different from Labour's policy, and it would allow the Conservatives to claim a degree of toughness in their general approach which could be contrasted with Labour's more pragmatic record (and by implication with previous Conservative governments too). The announcement of this approach was rather lost in 1965, but as the policy was systematically propagated in 1966–68 it evoked a positive public response. After many years in which the press had increasingly picked on the unions as the scapegoats for national economic decline, highlighting every 'wildcat strike' and each demarcation dispute as a national liability, a diagnosis echoed in Peter Sellers' film portrayal of a destructive shop steward in *I'm Alright Jack* and by the BBC's *The Rag Trade*, it is hardly surprising that there was strong support for an intention to take action: the issue was unintentionally highlighted by Labour's problems with the unions while in office, as when Wilson blamed the seamen's strike on 'a tightly-knit group of politically-motivated men'. When the Conservatives published detailed proposals as *A Fair Deal at Work*, opinion polls showed overwhelming public support, even among trades unionists.

Looking at the Conservative policies, Wilson was undoubtedly attracted to some of them both by the logic that lay behind them and by their apparent popularity. It was recognised that statutory pay controls could only be temporary in any case, but since they had soured relations with the unions they could not therefore be easily followed by a return to partnership. When Labour applied to join the EEC in 1967 the government's need to improve industry's competitiveness and avoid a wages explosion after pay controls expired took the government along the same logical path that the Conservatives had already followed. Wilson bent all his political skills to an effort to steal the Conservatives' most distinctive policy by carrying through a reform of trades unions before the coming election; in Cabinet the strongest supporter was the Chancellor Jenkins, well aware of the economic background to the issue, but Wilson tried to defuse the issue in advance by putting the government's plans in the hands of Castle, its most obviously left-wing minister. But the policy was too serious an error of political judgement to be rescued by tactics, not least because it created an additional crisis at the time in 1968–69 when the economy was at last coming right and money was available for the expansion of popular programmes.

The TUC reacted in outrage to *In Place of Strife*, the announcement of the government's intention to introduce a major reform of trades union law, not only because it seemed almost fratricidal for the political wing of the Labour movement to attack the industrial wing, but because there was little tradition of statutory regulation of unions against which to measure Castle's plans. The British tradition since the 1870s had been of laws which freed trades unions from restraints in law, allowing them to regulate themselves and to exert their influence by industrial muscle rather than by legal rights: the 1968 proposals like the Conservative plans were intended to bring the unions into an overall framework of legal control, and were therefore a bigger symbolic issue even than their detailed provisions suggested. The TUC rejected both the need for reform and the way in which the government intended to act, and made the most threatening of noises both in public session and in private meetings with ministers – prompting Wilson to tell the engineers' leader to 'Get your tanks off my lawn, Hughie'. The Unions had such extensive influence within the parliamentary Labour party that the government's proposals could not be carried – too many Labour MPs simply would not vote for them. A compromise in 1969 whereby the TUC's *Programme for Action* committed it to produce a scheme of self-regulation to meet the government's objectives saved ministers' faces without ever looking very convincing. The government, having argued in favour of legal change but failed to carry it through, could not convincingly attack the Conservatives on the same front, and was now a sitting target for Conservative attack in a policy area which it had itself helped to highlight: the *Daily Telegraph*, conflating the titles of the government and TUC proposals, concluded that there was now 'a programme for strife – in place of action'. The theft of Conservative policy had rebounded on the government, and the problem was redoubled when Labour's attempt to join the EEC also ended in failure.

The government's trades union reform plans soured what was otherwise a very successful last eighteen months. As unemployment fell away again from the levels reached after the 1966–67 deflation and as the country's healthier trading position allowed the government room to relax taxation levels and to increase spending in 1969–70, Labour regained popularity. The speed of the recovery in the opinion polls was spectacular and after trailing far behind the Conservatives for three years the government got back into close contention in the winter of 1969–70 and then edged ahead in the following spring. By that time an election was due within a year, but the government's confidence was restored and Wilson was satisfied that he could find a suitable time to get re-elected. When he dissolved Parliament for a June polling day, few politicians doubted that he had done that, and the course of a campaign in which Labour led continuously in the polls only confirmed the belief in Labour's inevitable victory. Conservative popularity seemed to have peaked too soon in 1967–68 and their tough plans seemed to have alarmed rather than attracted the public; Labour now had all the advantages of an incumbent party in a time of relative contentment. The campaign did bring to the fore doubts about the solidity of the country's economic strength. Conservatives reminded electors that the 1966 election had been followed by the July crisis, and bad trade figures published in the last few days of the 1970 campaign reinforced their claims. The campaign also brought to the fore a relatively new economic issue, certainly one which reached predominant status for the first time in 1970 – inflation. Prices had been rising gently since the war, and Macmillan for one had believed that a little inflation was not harmful and was in any event preferable to deflation and unemployment. In 1969–70 for the first time inflation reached levels that began seriously to worry those on fixed incomes, but unemployment was simultaneously higher than in most of the years since 1945. The Conservatives found a ready response to their pledges to reduce the rate at which prices were rising and their election broadcasts concentrated increasingly on the issue of prices as the campaign went on; this may have helped to turn out the Conservative vote, as may the expectations of a strong Labour showing, but the overall expectation remained that Labour would win.

The outcome was therefore hard to explain when Heath won an overall majority of thirty on a larger swing of opinion between the parties than at any election since 1945 – the only time since 1945 in which a comfortable parliamentary majority for one party was turned into a similar majority for another party at a single election. The unexpectedness of the result had in itself a number of consequences. Labour's factions could each find in the unexplainable result reasons to make opposite changes to the party's position and policy. Heath, whose position in his party had remained vulnerable since becoming leader, acquired a new authority not only because as Prime Minister he now had the formidable power of patronage, but also because almost alone among Conservative leaders he had continued to believe in victory. Since Conservatives like Labour could not be sure of the reason for the result, they could only press ahead with their programme, confident that it had somehow returned them to office. Two less promising omens existed for Heath's new government. Although they had carried out a more thorough policy preparation in opposition than any British party before or since, internal divisions had prevented them from seriously discussing their attitude to incomes policies in general and public sector incomes in particular (where the government could not avoid having a detailed policy). And in opposition Powell had left the front bench over immigration; he became an influential figure on that issue, so that Conservative candidates did exceptionally well in 1970 in the West Midlands where his influence on the party's behalf was greatest, an influence quite outside Heath's control.

The life of the Heath government fell naturally into two halves – before and after the 'U-turn' of 1972. In its first two years the government moved confidently to carry out its pre-election plans, though in this it suffered an early setback when the Chancellor Macleod died unexpectedly only a few weeks after taking office; his replacement, Anthony Barber, had not had years of preparation and the re-shuffle that Macleod's death necessitated also brought unexpectedly into Cabinet John Davies, previously leader of the Confederation of British Industry but only just elected as an MP. Barber proved a brave Chancellor, determined to 'dash for growth' even in most discouraging economic circumstances but was perhaps lacking in judgement. To Davies fell the sensitive task of running down the machinery for intervention in industry, a policy intended to give a freer rein to market forces and to allow 'lame-duck' industries to go to the wall. The rhetoric with which he proclaimed this uncompromising intention to leave industry 'to stand on its own feet' left little room for future reconsideration. In these key domestic posts ministers were short on political experience and flexibility.

But it was the entry to the EEC and the reform of trades unions which were the centre-pieces of government strategy. The trades union policy had been so carefully prepared in detail that it was put onto the statute book almost intact in 1971, though such rapid action had drawbacks; firstly, the implementation of pre-arranged policy allowed no room for consultation with the trades unions or advice from civil servants; and secondly, the carrying out of plans effectively completed in 1967–68 made no allowance for the fact that Wilson and Castle had tried and failed to reform trades unions in the meantime. Having seen off the Labour government, the TUC were in no mood to give way meekly to plans imposed on them without consultation by Conservatives. The Industrial Relations Act of 1971 therefore came into force, with its new Industrial Relations Court, its system of registration and of controls, but with a clear determination by the trades unions to kill it. In opposition, Conservatives had been privately assured by trades union leaders that the TUC would have to oppose such a change for the sake of appearances, but would obey the law once it was enacted. By 1971 union attitudes had hardened so far that this outcome became impossible; the TUC instead devised a neat strategy whereby the unions would simply carry on as if the Act had not been passed. The TUC ensured that no affiliated union even registered under the Act, despite considerable benefits that registration could bring, and unions that did not register remained largely outside the scope of the Act's other provisions. When the government or employers sought to bring the Industrial Relations Court into play they were met with a wall of industrial solidarity; the imprisonment of a group of London dockers for contempt of court led to a retreat by the government and to their early release, and the imposition of strike ballots was generally followed by majorities for strikes as union members rallied to their leaders and to the defence of union rights. By early 1972 the Industrial Relations Act was effectively inoperative, though it remained the law until 1974–75.

The failure of its central policy to improve industry's international competitiveness was a serious blow, not least because Britain had succeeded in entering the EEC and would therefore have to face the full shock of European competition. It was also the more serious because by the start of 1972 the combination of international circumstances and the government's industrial policy had produced a recession and a rise in unemployment to over a million for the first time since the war. At the same time in the winter of 1971–72 the Heath government suffered a humiliating defeat at the hands of the miners in a strike which resulted in very large wage increases. Deprived of the weapon on which they had planned to rely – trades union law – and sincerely horrified by the rise in unemployment, ministers rapidly changed course. The 1972 budget launched a spending boom, and an Industry Act introduced at the same time gave to ministers unprecedented powers of intervention through financial incentives to direct industry to depressed areas. At the political level the government sought to move back from imposed methods of improving industry to seeking a partnership with industry and the unions through the NEDC and a voluntary restraint of prices and incomes. The CBI was prepared to offer restraint of prices, conditional on the unions doing the same for earnings, but union hostility to the government over recent events was too great for this to be possible. When talks broke down in summer 1972, the government introduced statutory wage and price controls.

As in 1966 it proved far easier to get into statutory controls than to get out of them, and the Heath government struggled unavailingly to find new ways of associating the unions with its policies as they moved through successive phases; at the end of 1973 it was offering the TUC a great share in the determination of policy in the search for partnership, but was still unable to strike a deal. The position had deteriorated further in 1973 as the domestic economy moved into a boom which reduced unemployment back to 1970 levels but generated much higher levels of inflation in the process. At the same time, a Middle-Eastern war prompted Arab oil producers to combine to enforce massive price rises, an event far beyond the government's control but especially damaging for them since it gave even greater bargaining power to the miners who controlled Britain's only major domestic source of fuel.

The National Union of Mineworkers, which had patiently accepted a continuous run-down of their industry through the 1960s, in which the number of miners in the union fell from about two thirds of a million in 1958 to only a quarter of a million by 1973, had now moved into a more militant phase; equally, Conservative MPs who had smarted at their government's defeat by the miners two years earlier were not willing to accept anything but a victory this second time. The end of 1973 therefore saw a position in which Heath's ministers were on the one hand offering the TUC partnership on a more extended basis than ever before and on the other hand preparing for a major fight with the miners in the immediate aftermath of the international oil crisis. The issue gradually became more political than economic, as the question of the government's domestic authority (already in the balance since the destruction of the Industrial Relations Act) and its right to govern became paramount questions. Under these pressures, the government in December 1973 first planned for a long battle of attrition with the miners, putting industry onto a three-day working week and imposing other draconian energy savings, and then, when faced with mass picketing which the police could not control (notably at the Saltley coal depot in Birmingham where almost all of the local unions rallied to back Arthur Scargill's Yorkshire miners' pickets), the government found defeat staring it in the face. It could only go for a political solution to what was now a political problem: ministers who heard the Scottish miners' leader tell them that the NUM's objective was now the government's destruction could hardly reach any other conclusion.

There were two political ways forward. One was to seek a compromise, even at the risk of losing face in a miners' pay settlement as in 1972; the other was to escalate the conflict on the 'Who Governs?' issue by putting the question to the electorate. During January 1974 the government considered the alternatives, with the Prime Minister one of the last to be convinced that an election was the best course. It did after all carry enormous risks: what would be the position of British democracy if the government were re-elected but the miners were still to continue (and probably win) their strike? It was a question not posed since Baldwin had put it during the General Strike of 1926. The election campaign called in February was the shortest allowed in law, though the fact that a dissolution had been known to be under discussion for weeks rather reduced the impact of a snap election. It began stridently with the government trying to keep the campaign to the single issue on which it had been called, though giving only hesitant answers to the question of what they would do about the strike if they won. Labour argued that the confrontation was characteristic of the government's whole life and was entirely unnecessary; they also argued against a one-issue approach to the election by pointing out that a Conservative victory would mean five more years of *all* the Conservatives' policies. In any case the insatiable appetite of the press and the broadcasters for different news stories ensured that the debate would gradually widen onto the familiar questions of jobs, houses and prices, on none of which had the Conservatives expected to fight. As the two major parties conducted an unusually bitter campaign, it seems clear that more and more of the electors turned away from both of them and from the stark choice that the 'Who governs?' question posed. The Liberal share of the vote in opinion polls rose steadily through the campaign and the Liberals eventually scored six million votes, their highest total ever and their biggest share of the vote since 1929.

Between the major parties the campaign of confrontation produced no clear outcome: the Conservatives just scored the higher vote but Labour got five more seats, with neither getting a majority. And even that was due to an accidental factor, for it was only the defection of Ulster Unionists from the Conservative side (angry about the Heath Government's Irish policy) that deprived the Conservatives of a lead in seats as well as in votes. In the two days after the result was announced, Heath sought vainly to arrange a coalition with the Liberal Party to retain a share of power – or at least to deny it to Labour. But with even the total of Liberals and Conservatives not adding up to a majority, and with Heath unable to offer electoral reform which was the price of Liberal co-operation, the basis of a deal never really existed and he eventually had to give way to a minority Labour government under Wilson. It was rather like the hung Parliament of 1923–24, for once again it was the Conservatives who had sought a specific mandate but not achieved it and Labour who came unexpectedly to office as a result.

The period from Macmillan's pay freeze of 1961 to Heath's defeat by the miners embraces several continuing features. There was the assumption common to all governments and almost all party leaders that Britain could and should have a higher level of economic growth, which would allow more concentration on shared benefits than on the redistribution of wealth. Governments sought to put their own houses in order by regular rearrangements of government departments to improve their managerial performance, a process begun with Macmillan's restructuring of the Treasury. In pursuit of the goal of growth all governments were driven back and forth between the pursuit of a tripartite partnership between government, unions and industry and the imposition of their own legislative solutions by ministers who had to be responsible to the electorate. The period saw a steady rise in the extent to which political issues centred around industrial relations and a steady increase in the muscle of the larger trades unions. Despite a high level of political antagonism between Labour and Conservative leaderships, it was a time in which a Liberal poster could show the faces of Heath and Wilson and ask 'Which twin is the Tory?'. One influential writer called the choice 'a bogus dilemma' and in 1974 many electors clearly felt the same. Many of these themes continued, but after the watershed of 1974–75 they operated in a very different political world.

26 The end of the post-war consensus? 1974–1988

From the 1970s, the Labour and Conservative parties had to face challenges to their joint political dominance, challenges within each party to the way in which they had traditionally conducted themselves, and challenges to the rule of law which prompted from a senior broadcaster in the mid-1970s the question 'is Britain governable?' In part, what happened in Britain was part of a more widespread challenge to the fabric of the unitary industrialised state across the Western world; the resurgence of political nationalisms in Scotland and Wales had its counterpart in Brittany and Quebec, while Britain's terrorist problem in Ulster was matched in Germany, Italy and Spain.

The greater assertiveness of national minorities in a time of decolonisation, when applied to Ulster and to its Protestant community's readiness to feel under siege, undoubtedly contributed to the reappearance of an 'Irish Question' in 1968–69. Northern Ireland's Catholics had kept alive ultimate hopes of Irish reunion during the half century since the partition of Ireland, their hopes fed on real grievances about discrimination against them for jobs and housing – though Catholic families from the Irish Republic continued to migrate to join that deprived community. Since 1920, Northern Ireland had been ruled by a devolved Unionist government at Stormont but the Province had never developed an effective opposition along British lines: the Northern Ireland Labour Party and the Liberals were always feeble groups with only shallow roots in the Catholic community and always challenged at least by the shadow of Sinn Fein, while the Protestant majority overwhelmingly voted for Unionists. Very little inter-communal social or political activity developed. Under the pressure of increased assertiveness from the Catholic community and a renewed interest in Ulster from some British politicians, Unionists were suspicious and slow to respond as the Wilson government constantly prodded them to further action to redress Catholic grievances.

As a result Stormont lost much of its authority and credibility without taking the urgency from the problem, and Ulster's own politics became polarised between a more militant Unionism (which now derived more from the streets of East Belfast than from county families of Fermanagh) and a nationalism which bordered on support for terrorists. The decision to introduce the British army was made to protect the Catholic community from perceived ill treatment allowed by Stormont's own police and auxiliary forces, a major snub to the Unionist government. This raised expectations which the British government could not itself meet and led on to clashes between the army and Catholic nationalist rioters, most notably when thirteen fatal casualties were inflicted in Londonderry on 'Bloody Sunday' in 1971.

The last years of the Wilson government were therefore marked by the downward spiral to terrorism and counter-terrorism like that of 1919–20, and the issue became one of the Home Secretary's greatest concerns. The number of violent deaths in Ulster, thirteen in all in 1969, had risen to 467 in 1972 – with over ten thousand shooting incidents in that year. It was easier to destroy the authority of the Unionist government which had at least produced a sort of peace and security over its lifetime, than to find any way to fill the vacuum so created. Neither the Wilson nor the Heath governments had the slightest intention of carrying through Irish union without the consent of the Northern Irish Unionists (which would not be forthcoming, as all tests of opinion showed), but they were determined to see civil rights guaranteed in Ulster as on the mainland and they conscientiously sought a means of associating the minority as well as the majority with government in the Province. To Unionists brought up on the myths of 1688, 1886 and 1914 this was a betrayal of 'loyalism' and of the rights of a democratic majority too. When all-party talks chaired by Heath failed to produce a compromise, the British government abolished the Stormont parliament in what was intended to be just a clearing exercise prior to other reforms; there was again an Irish Secretary in the Cabinet from 1972. This caused even greater antagonism in loyalist circles and ended the historic alliance of Unionists and the Conservative party.

For a time in 1973 it seemed that Heath's effort to establish a 'power-sharing' administration in which Unionists would work with the other parties might establish itself, but its support was always stronger in London than in Belfast. A demonstration of Unionist voting strength in the February 1974 general election and a Protestant workers' strike which followed brought down the power-sharing executive and destroyed the reputations of moderate politicians who had joined it. The referendum held in 1973 demonstrated conclusively the strength of feeling among Protestants against any all-Ireland union, and attempts to associate the Irish Republic with the security problems inherent in a long, rural border only exacerbated loyalist fears of a sell-out to come. Thereafter the story was of progressively more desperate attempts by British governments to hold the security line, a policy of variable success, while their efforts were derided or disowned by both Ulster communities.

The savage experience of political murder in Northern Ireland affected the way in which politicians reacted to the resurgence of Scottish and Welsh nationalism. There had always been some connection: Irish Home Rule in its land aspect in the 1880s had been mirrored in a Welsh Tithe War and a crofters' agitation in the Highlands. In the 1960s, Scotland and Wales both felt a sense of deprivation as prosperity had moved steadily towards South East England, and the regional policies adopted by successive governments had proved ineffective except in the very short term. Both countries had been Labour strongholds and were unlikely to turn to Conservatism (often still synonymous with Englishness in parts of Scotland and Wales) when disillusioned by the record in office of Wilson's 1964 government. The take-off came with a strong Scottish National Party showing in a Glasgow by-election in 1967, after which it won the very safe Labour seat of Hamilton in 1968 – the Welsh chipping in too by giving a fright to Labour candidates in two South Welsh mining seats. Although the SNP also took a large number of local government seats and the temporary control of Glasgow, this proved a false dawn: by 1970 normal attitudes had returned and in the general election neither nationalist party achieved much. But their second wave then came more strongly. By 1972 the SNP in particular was riding high, drawing extra credibility from the first exploitation of North Sea oil resources and the slogan 'It's Scotland's Oil'. In the February election of 1974 the SNP took nearly a quarter of the Scottish vote and seven seats: in October this rose to almost a third of the vote (more than the Conservatives and not much less than Labour) and a tally of eleven seats – which almost matched the Liberal Party in the whole of the UK. Welsh Nationalists also made an electoral impact in 1974, though on a lesser scale.

This mushroom growth of nationalism came nearer to producing a break-up of the Union than at any time since 1707. Leaders of the Scottish media, industry and society began to recognise the viability of some form of home rule for Scotland in its own Edinburgh parliament; joining the EEC had brought Britain into close contact with smaller democracies than an independent Scotland would be. Conservatives and Labour (but especially Labour which had more than forty Scottish MPs to defend) felt the need to offer something to head off what might otherwise become an unstoppable separatist movement. The real problem for the Labour government from 1974 was that they had to steer a difficult constitutional bill through Parliament without much of a majority and in the teeth of opposition from many Labour MPs; some MPs from Scotland and Wales were sceptical about devolution, believing that it could eventually reduce Labour's control over events, while Labour MPs from some English regions saw it as likely to re-direct regional aid away from their own areas.

The first devolution bill was talked out after the waste of much parliamentary time and later bills which gave only a very limited devolution to Wales and a reduced form to Scotland eventually passed only in 1978 and then only when much amended. By that time, Scottish expectations had been raised, with much publicised work being done to prepare a new Edinburgh parliament house. The amendment which most damaged the cause of devolution was the deceptively simple requirement that devolution would be implemented only if 40 per cent of Welsh or Scottish electors voted for it in a referendum. These referenda were held in March 1979 at a time of great unpopularity for the Labour government – which scarcely helped to mobilise support for what was widely seen as a Labour policy – and the proposals were by then opposed by a Conservative Party which had reverted to traditional Unionism. The Nationalists themselves hardly knew whether to support devolution as a step in the right direction or to oppose it as a half measure. In Wales a majority voted against the proposals, while in Scotland the majority in favour did not reach the required level, and so both schemes fell through. Nationalist MPs threatened dire reprisals but it was their own parties which appeared to suffer most: their vote fell in 1979 and again in 1983 as their parties suffered from internal splits occasioned by acute disappointment. In the 1980s Scotland and Wales responded initially to continuous Conservative government by returning to strong support for the Labour Party, an outcome that indicates the extent to which the rise and fall of nationalism was influenced by a desire to protest as well as by a considered wish to change the constitution.

In England as well as in the Celtic fringe the major parties came under challenge. Growing tensions in declining industrial areas which had also become homes for immigrant communities provided the basis for a flowering of political extremism. From its brief appearance in the 1964 general election, racial politics became a permanent feature of elections at the street level in British cities, though not in Parliament. There was support that cut across political loyalties for such politicians as Powell who articulated fears about the effects of coloured immigration and called for restrictions that popular reaction forced governments to impose. On the right the National Front briefly flourished in 1977–78 when it scored higher votes in the north and east of London than Mosley's fascists had ever done, only to fade away again in internal dissension after a Conservative government was elected and imposed both tighter immigration controls and new nationality laws. The main impact of fascists of the 1970s, like those of the 1930s, was to arouse a militant anti-fascism among the burgeoning groups of the far left, and to provoke street fights between anti-fascists and the police. With this myriad of parties on the left and right to add to the fragmented politics of Ulster and to the nationalist parties, it seemed that the dominance of the major parties was at an end: in 1974 Labour and Conservative candidates took only 70 per cent of the national vote (compared to 95 per cent in the 1950s) and the other parties had between them forty seats in the Commons – well above any level since the war, and a centre force large enough to make it difficult for any one party to win a majority on its own. 'Multi-party Britain' might be here to stay.

The biggest contributor to (and beneficiary of) this loosening of political loyalties was the Liberal Party. Threatened with extinction in the 1950s, and often disappointed by unrequited hopes since, the Liberals had steadily widened their base, mostly in times of Conservative government. While Labour voters disappointed by Labour ministries tended to abstain or switch straight to the Conservatives, disillusioned Conservatives were more likely to vote for a centrist alternative, and these protests gradually consolidated into a larger base Liberal vote. But Liberals could not overcome the handicap imposed by the electoral system: six million votes in 1974 won only fourteen seats because Liberal votes were so evenly spread across the constituencies. Briefly, after their 1974 defeat, it seemed that Conservatives might also support a change of the electoral system, but not for long, and the Liberals' own attempt to force a change through popular pressure did not keep up momentum. All the same the Liberals came close to government in the 1970s for the only time since 1945: in 1974 they negotiated with Heath about a share of office and in 1977–78 they agreed a parliamentary pact with Labour which gave them advance notice of government policies and an opportunity to influence them – both situations occasioned by their holding of the balance of power in the Commons. An attempt to use that control to enforce proportional representation for the new European parliament elections proved just how fragile was the control of the balance of power: Labour MPs could not be persuaded to vote for anything but a traditional British voting system.

Throughout the period, the Liberals' strategy for the breaking of the restraints imposed by the electoral system was to work for a general realignment of parties in which they would be reinforced in the centre by Labour moderates and so replace Labour as the main anti-Conservative party (much as Labour had replaced the Liberals in the 1920s). This much anticipated opportunity finally came about in 1981 with the secession from Labour of Roy Jenkins, three front-benchers and two dozen MPs to form a new Social Democratic Party. This brought to the political centre a group of former ministers such as David Owen and Shirley Williams who could make a formidable force when allied to the Liberals' existing organisation and to the formerly uncommitted voters that the SDP now managed to mobilise. The SDP and its 'Alliance' with the Liberals began with strong press support, though perhaps more for the novelty of a strong third force than as sincere backing, and won some spectacular by-elections. But like so many earlier Liberal revivals, this one was unable to put what opinion polls showed to be its full potential into effect in general elections. With the assistance of a Labour campaign that was both feeble and well to the left, the Alliance almost outvoted Labour in 1983, but was as far as ever from making a parliamentary breakthrough: its 7.8 million votes elected twenty-three MPs, while for 8.5 million votes Labour got 209 seats. This was manifestly unfair, but only MPs who had been elected under that unfair system could change it. In 1987 the Alliance again fell away but retained a position equivalent to Labour in 1914: it was a powerful third force with a strong base in local government, but with a vote more evenly spread than Labour's had always been, a party for whom a national breakthrough still seemed out of reach.

Labour and the Conservatives proved more resilient than the prophets of multi-party politics had foreseen. The 1970 defeat was a bad blow to Labour for although in 1968 all had expected a Labour defeat, few still foresaw it by election day. With hindsight morals could be drawn: Wilson's years in office had accelerated a dramatic decline in the party's individual membership, a clash with its union allies, and bitter disillusion among those who had had high hopes encouraged by Wilson's confident rhetoric of 1963–64. In 1964 Labour support was unusually fashionable in middle-class and industrial circles and Labour's policies were welcomed even by *The Times* (which moved on to urge Labour's moderates to form a new party by 1972 and had reverted to its traditional support for Conservatism by 1976). The years of opposition from 1970 to 1974 were therefore difficult ones for Labour and saw a prolonged inquest on the recent government in which its record was as critically reviewed by the Fabian Society on the right as by Tribunites on the left. Organisationally, the swing to the left within the party machine which had been occurring since the later 1950s was consolidated behind Tony Benn's championing of the left's cause; Benn's own ministerial record within Wilson's government had been unexceptional but he rapidly emerged as a key figure in opposition, when as chairman of the party's Home Affairs committee he exerted a powerful influence over policy-making; under his guidance the party evolved a more radical strategy in *Labour's Programme, 1973* than any since 1945. The left's view was that power had been lost because the Wilson government had been insufficiently radical, had not paid enough attention to the needs of its supporters, and that Labour could take and hold power only by consolidating working-class support – hence the need for radicalism (though this was far from the way in which Labour had actually succeeded in winning majorities in 1945 and in 1964–66).

The same diagnosis led Labour to drop its traditional resistance to infiltration from the far left in the search for new allies to build working-class support; this allowed membership to political activists who had been banned earlier in their own careers. This led on to the activities of the Militant tendency as an organisation within the party, genuinely dangerous to constituency parties which now had only small memberships, but in any case a wonderful propaganda opportunity for Labour's opponents. This was the more dangerous as the overall balance of the national press swung against Labour: in the 1950s, when the Labour-supporting *Daily Mirror* had the biggest circulation, Labour-inclined papers had made up about 40 per cent of total national newspaper sales; the weakening of the *Mirror*'s hold on the popular market, the rise of new populist papers of the right, and above all the loss of the Labour/TUC-owned *Daily Herald* to become the strongly anti-Labour *Sun* from 1969 changed all that: by the 1980s, Labour was 'outvoted' by the Conservatives in newspaper circulations by about three to one. To an extent, the greater imbalance of Fleet Street was offset by the public's increasing reliance on television for its news and opinions – and television was legally obliged to balance its output politically – but it is no coincidence that the historic period of Labour strength between the 1940s and the 1960s was also the period of the *Daily Mirror*'s dominance in Fleet Street. After 1969 the *Sun* was an extremely hostile market leader just as Labour support declined.

The Labour right's traditional response to such attacks from the left had been to rely on the relative moderation of Labour MPs (who alone elected the leader) and on union block votes at party conferences, but both were now more difficult to mobilise. Some MPs were under pressure from their constituency supporters, especially those who had supported Heath's bill to take Britain into the Common Market, and the unions were too likely to remember 1968–69 with resentment to fall into line easily with Wilson's team. This began to come right just in time for Labour with a gradual reaccommodation of the industrial and political wings of the Labour movement, greatly encouraged by Callaghan and by Jack Jones of the transport workers. Callaghan was the most senior minister to oppose the 1969 trades union proposals and so had kept open his own good relations with the unions, while Jones led the largest union, still aligned to the left but very conscious of the benefits his union could receive from the existence of a Labour government.

The result of their joint efforts was the 'Social Contract' of 1973, in which the Labour Party promised specific reforms which the unions wanted, including the repeal of Heath's Industrial Relations Act, increases in pensions for which Jones had campaigned, and the nationalisation of the docks which appealed directly to the transport workers; in return the unions promised to forget past antagonisms and to co-operate with Labour in running the economy responsibly. This was quite accidentally timed to coincide with Heath's final battle with the miners: it made an excellent opportunity to contrast Labour's partnership with the unions with Conservative confrontation, and after Labour returned to office the contrast was underlined in the settlement of the coal dispute and a period of industrial harmony achieved with substantial pay settlements. The opposition period did though leave some legacies for the 1974–79 Labour government: the industrial crisis was a convenient reason for campaigning with a manifesto based more on the Social Contract than on *Labour's Programme 1973*, which caused suspicions on the left; the party's disagreements about the EEC had been covered over by the compromise suggestion of a referendum, but this had led to Jenkins' resignation from the deputy leadership of the party and deep divisions remained here too; the leadership's reluctance to accept party conference decisions created suspicion on the left that was to last long into the future.

Minority government in 1974 like the narrow majority of 1964 brought out the best of Wilson's talents. A skilful use of each week's opportunities kept the focus on the government while time was gained to build a real majority in a second election. The two keys to this were the avoidance of divisive issues while ministers encouraged the prosperity that would allow its re-election, and the disarray of the opposition parties. As Chancellor of the Exchequer, Denis Healey had only to continue the policies he inherited for the 'Barber boom' was already greatly increasing purchasing power, for which the government reaped a benefit in short-term popularity and a terrible longer-term harvest as inflation then rocketed. The opposition largely wrecked its own chances: Liberals simply did not know what to do after polling so many votes and winning so few seats in February, while Conservatives were divided about their own party's leadership after Heath's second electoral defeat in three contests, and were in any case fatally compromised by their attempt to do a deal with the Liberals in March. The October election therefore provided like 1966 the second round of a single contest with all the cards in the Wilson government's hands. In these circumstances, the result was surprisingly close. Very few seats changed hands, and Labour gained an overall majority of only three – an insecure position considering that the previous Labour government had lost fifteen seats at by-elections. Wilson proved once again adept at such situations. Most of Labour's controversial bills, like the nationalisation of docks and ship-repairing, a bill to extend employment protection, the renegotiation of terms with the EEC and the subsequent successful referendum on the issue, were all pressed through while Labour's majority remained; the only setback for this strategy was the enforced postponement of legislation on devolution into the second half of the government's life.

Labour's political divisions arising from the opposition period were dealt with equally neatly: Benn's ability to disrupt the government's plans was reduced when, after his relative isolation on the European issue, he was re-shuffled from the Department of Industry to become only Energy minister: his counterpart as leader of the right, Jenkins, later left altogether to become a European Commissioner and returned only to found the SDP rather than to rejoin Labour. When Wilson unexpectedly retired as Prime Minister in 1976 the first phase of the Labour government was over and his political standing was high, though his personal credit took something of a knock when his resignation honours recommendations caused the first serious honours scandal since the days of Lloyd George. Perhaps the parallel was an appropriate one, for Wilson like Lloyd George had a great relish for the contests of political life and a remarkable tactical skill, as well as a genuine commitment to social betterment: like Lloyd George too, his early support for radical causes palled somewhat once installed in Number Ten.

The new Prime Minister Callaghan was highly experienced, for he had been Chancellor of the Exchequer, Home Secretary and Foreign Secretary as well as a junior minister under Attlee: no previous Labour Prime Minister had held even one of these high offices of state. None the less, he inherited a government with a losing hand to play: the loss of three by-election seats deprived the government of its majority by the end of 1976 and four later losses further reduced room for manoeuvre. The major outstanding legislative commitment was the poisoned chalice of devolution on which Labour was divided. Above all, the state of the economy which had hamstrung the 1964–70 Labour government was now again the pivot of political life. Immediately after the October 1974 election, the government had begun to rein back expenditure, but the effects of decisions made in 1973–74 were a brief period in which inflation was entirely out of control: in 1974 prices rose by 19 per cent – briefly touching a post-war peak of 27 per cent in 1975 – and wage rates by 29 per cent.

Many of the old benchmarks of economic policy seemed to be fading from sight as inflation and unemployment were simultaneously high, so that any policy adopted to curb one was likely to lead to an increase in the other, a situation popularly believed to be almost impossible under Keynesian economic theory, and one that therefore encouraged the search for new economic ideas; great increases in oil prices had ushered in (until Britain's own oil began to flow) a period of 'stagflation' in which the economy could flounder along at a low rate of growth while the rate of inflation remained so high as to make exports uncompetitive. Since 1971, the pound had no longer been tied to fixed international exchange rates, which provided the government with greater flexibility, but also made for violent fluctuations in difficult times. By 1976 the pound was at its lowest ever level against the dollar, but supporting the pound had – as ten years earlier – exhausted Britain's currency reserves. An application for international credits from the International Monetary Fund was damaging to the government's prestige and further weakened its domestic position when it appeared that the IMF were dictating changes to Britain's economic policies as the price of support; in fact, the changes made were recognised as necessary by almost all except the Labour left in any case, but the IMF proved a useful outside ally for the policy which most ministers wished to pursue, much as international bankers had been in 1931. It was at this time that Callaghan, clear that Labour's unpopularity would prevent him from turning his government's minority position into a new majority at an election, turned to a pact with the Liberals to buy another year in office.

Callaghan's deep knowledge of the Labour movement and background in the unions made him successful in holding his team together over three difficult years, and he was for a time equally successful in persuading the trades unions at least to acquiesce in incomes restraint, though that tolerance was wearing thin in 1978. By summer 1978, as the one year Lib–Lab parliamentary pact came to an end, the decisions taken with IMF approval had effected a measure of economic recovery and an equivalent increase in the government's popularity. The intractable problem remained the level of unemployment, at a postwar high of about one and a half millions in 1978. Nevertheless Labour was matching the Conservatives in opinion polls and by-elections were again going well. It was generally anticipated that, now that the government would not have Liberal support, it would call an election to resolve the parliamentary deadlock. The 1978 TUC conference was carefully orchestrated by Callaghan's allies so that divisive debates were kept to a minimum; he himself addressed the TUC in a speech expected to provide a launching pad for his election campaign but only joked about the decision still to be made and shortly afterwards let it be known that no autumn election would be called. His caution was probably due to the gloomy advice of Labour's private pollsters (though, ironically the Conservatives' private polls showed a stronger position for Labour!) and by memories of 1970 when Wilson had gambled on an early election and lost. The trades union leaders were furious, believing not only that they had been taken for a ride at their conference, but that he had underestimated the potentially explosive situation created by government control of incomes. As a result the 1978 Labour conference voted against further statutory pay restraint and shortly afterwards it was Labour MPs whose rebellion in Parliament wrecked the government's plans to tighten the control of wage increases paid by private firms. The Callaghan government fell foul of the same problem of trying to return from pay restraint to free collective bargaining without a pay explosion which had wrecked the Wilson and Heath governments' industrial relations policies in 1969 and 1973. The final ingredient was increasing disillusion on the Labour left over the government's economic policies: when Callaghan personally telephoned a local union leader to point out the damage which strikes were doing to Labour in 1979 and to ask for loyalty to the party they both belonged to, the reply was 'Jim, we're not even on the same planet.'

In 1979 the stakes were higher for both the parties and the unions, for this time there was a Conservative opposition with a very different approach to future policy and a public far less tolerant of trades union power. The only weapon left to the government in influencing pay settlements was control of the pay of public employees, and this unleashed a series of bitter battles with the public sector unions over a 'winter of discontent' in 1978–79. In a few weeks these disputes destroyed all the patient efforts made since 1970 to demonstrate that Labour could co-exist with trades unions where the Conservatives could not; faced with regular television pictures of rubbish piled in the streets, of picket lines turning ambulances away from hospitals and even hearses from graveyards, many of the public drew the conclusion that what was needed was not co-existence but control. To a great extent these events reversed the balance of the argument of 1974 and convinced at least some electors that when asked the question 'Who governs?' they had given the wrong answer. Labour's stock plummeted and at the depth of this slough of national despair some ill-judged comments by Callaghan seemed to show that he was out of touch with the public's anger. Added urgency was given when the referendum defeat of the government's devolution plans infuriated the SNP, who had tacitly kept the government in office since the end of the Lib–Lab pact but who now vowed to take their revenge by forcing an early election. Callaghan was correct when he joked that the SNP wish for an election was 'like turkeys voting for an early Christmas', but his own goose was to be cooked in the same oven. In April 1979 the Callaghan government became the first to be overthrown by a Commons vote of no confidence since MacDonald in 1924. Labour was dragged to an election which it had not wanted and which all indicators showed it to be bound to lose.

The 1979 general election was substantially a referendum on Labour's term of office, perhaps unavoidably in view of recent events, but a carefully co-ordinated Conservative public relations campaign carried this issue through from the winter disputes to the spring election in any case. The keynote had been the traditional gambit of 'time for a change', but carried much further than usual; the first Conservative broadcast of the campaign encapsulated its objects with the repeated idea that 'Britain's going backwards', and culminated with Michael Heseltine announcing 'Backwards or forwards, because we *can't* go on as we are'. This campaigning stance allowed the Conservatives to avoid too great a scrutiny of their own programme or of their new leader, Margaret Thatcher, whose inexperience was the one unknown factor in the election. The change of leadership had become inevitable when Conservatives lost both the 1974 elections, but Heath's replacement by Thatcher was none the less a contentious change, not because it seemed to mark any great policy change at the time, but because it was achieved by ordinary MPs organised against the wishes of most of the front bench. Thatcher was certainly inexperienced, having been only Education minister (traditionally a woman's post), and was the first woman to lead any British party. It was a move like that of 1911, across a frontier of determination rather than a deliberate change of policy. It is doubtful if even her keenest supporters understood the magnitude of the change that they were making.

The years of Thatcher's opposition leadership were difficult ones just as they had been for Heath before 1970, and she had the added problem of knowing that he was still there and a focus of discontent (as Home had not been after 1965). Thatcher like Heath was slow to discover an effective television manner, but quicker to take and act on professional advice; unlike Heath she rapidly developed a gift for inspiring her party activists even if in 1979 she had still to make much of a wider impact. But by 1978 she already worried some colleagues by the strident tone in which policies were presented and by her willingness to strike out in unexpected directions, as in 1978 over immigration. Labour confidently expected a campaign 'gaffe' from her which would contrast damagingly with Callaghan's calm, avuncular experience.

Callaghan fought in 1979 a cautious campaign, pointing out Labour's responsible record over its whole five years as an answer to recent memories, but he personally felt that there was an unstoppable tide running against Labour; sometimes he seemed to be going through the motions of a campaign that he knew he could not win – which was probably true enough but bad for morale none the less. Thatcher was efficiently shepherded through the campaign by advisers and did not make a gaffe that could turn the election. The result was that the Conservatives led in opinion polls throughout the campaign, although fighting it in a very low key, and returned to power with an overall majority of forty-three; the strong showing of third and minor parties meant that the Conservatives won their majority with a share of the vote which would have defeated any party in the two-party regime of the 1950s, a pattern continued throughout the 1980s. Conservative success under Thatcher relied heavily on the fragmentation of opposition and minor party under-representation in parliament as a result of the electoral system.

Labour's share of the vote in 1979 was its lowest since 1935; this confirmed that the 1970s had witnessed a significant decline in its reliable working-class voting base, a decline previously hidden by the even worse Conservative performance in the 1974 elections. The loss of office led to a long-awaited party crisis, the fourth round of those unleashed by the results of 1951, 1959 and 1970, but deeper than those earlier contests between left and right. This time the parliamentary leaders were unable to control the demands for constitutional change within the party, partly because of the further drift to the left in some large unions and in the constituency parties, partly because their own authority in the party was weakened by Callaghan's record in office. This problem was worsened by the actual experience of the Thatcher government's first years, for it seemed to demonstrate a depth of conviction – in pursuing policies which Labour loathed more than those of any earlier Tory government – which contrasted damagingly with Labour's own more pragmatic record in office since 1964.

Under these pressures the left's drive for constitutional change became irresistible: the system for electing the leader and deputy leader was changed to introduce a majority participation for unions and local parties. A system of regular re-selection of MPs which greatly increased the theoretical control of local parties over Labour in parliament was also introduced, as was a direct control given to the party machine in writing election manifestoes. These changes were complete by 1981 and occasioned the Labour split which produced the new SDP. In the short term this split only damaged the chances of any party on the left beating the Thatcher government, and the departure of some leaders of the right consolidated the left's hold over Labour. Policy moved the same way, with the adoption of a more left-wing programme than Labour had had before: there would now be a defence policy based on unilateral nuclear disarmament (a policy appealing more widely to Labour activists than only the left), an industrial policy based on extensions of state control, and a reversal of such Conservative policies as curbs on trades unions and the sale of council houses (which all evidence showed to be attractive even to many Labour supporters).

The logical extension of this shift to the left came with the election of a man of impeccable though dated left-wing credentials, Michael Foot, as the leader when Callaghan retired in 1980. Foot had been a key figure in the 1974–79 government, keeping lines open to the unions and the left even when backing policies that they most disliked. As leader he threw his weight entirely behind the policy changes, especially on defence policy on which he had been a crusading supporter of unilateralism since his Bevanite days in the 1950s. As leader he proved something of an incubus, since he had traditionally been seen as an extremist but was now also widely perceived as too old and not especially competent. The Labour election campaign in 1983 was a disaster for the party both in its manner and in its content. Labour's vote fell to a level lower than it had managed in the 1920s and the party was almost pushed into the third place from which it could have been squeezed into oblivion. From that point recovery began.

The 1983 election had in fact given a highly misleading impression of Labour's strength and intentions. In local government Labour was the dominant party throughout the 1980s, despite some Alliance advances, and it continued to enjoy an overwhelming support in Scotland, Wales and the North of England (though unfortunately a half of the country with a falling population and collapsing industrial base). Although all opinion surveys showed Labour's voting strength and the support for some of Labour's traditional policies to be reducing, both remained ahead of support for any third party. Equally the loss of MPs to the SDP had weakened but not destroyed the Labour right, and the 1983 defeat proved to be exactly what was required to enable it to argue convincingly that party policy should move at least partially with the views of its supporters. Amendments were introduced to limit the effects of the constitutional changes of 1980-81, adjustments of policy were made to enable Labour to appeal more directly to working–class voters, and Foot was replaced by Neil Kinnock, who like many of the younger generation 'soft' left had recognised that an element of pragmatism must be embraced if Labour was ever to win power, pursue its other policies and look after its supporters. Kinnock was able to unite these pragmatic approaches with a language of conviction that did much to restore the leadership's authority in the party.

A third consecutive defeat in 1987 only confirmed this diagnosis, though the party's reluctance to abandon a unilateralist defence policy of which Kinnock like Foot was a keen supporter continued to threaten the loss of votes. At the end of the 1980s, Labour had not yet re-built the wide voting coalition that had sustained the 1945 and 1966 victories, had not in fact made a lasting recovery of the votes lost in and after 1970; it remained a party most of all associated with the shrinking social groups of council tenants, trades union members and public sector workers, the secure foundation of a major party but not in itself a sufficient basis for majority government.

Labour's uncomfortable 1980s were largely the mirror-image of Conservative strength. In terms of rhetoric or policy, the objectives of the Thatcher government in 1979 were not very different from those of Heath in 1970; to curb trades union power, to cut taxes by holding down public expenditure, and to foster an economy more reliant on free enterprise than on the state. What was certainly different was the underlying economic rationale, at least of Thatcher and her closest supporters. Since 1945, challenges to the economic philosophy of Keynes had gathered strength even on the left. This was especially true among younger Conservatives, now more likely to see the free market philosophy propounded by Friedrich Hayek as the best defence of liberty against socialism, and to see an economic policy of 'monetarism' (the control of public expenditure as a bulwark against destructive national inflation) as propounded by the American economist Milton Friedman as the way forward.

Enoch Powell had been the first leading politician to articulate such ideas, but was now outside the mainstream of politics as an Ulster Unionist MP. The main influences in the 1980s were Sir Keith Joseph, a politician unusual in formally recanting the policies he had himself practised in government up to 1974, and such younger men as Sir Geoffrey Howe. Joseph now became the minister with greatest personal influence over the Prime Minister and Howe the Chancellor. The economic policy of the first years of the Thatcher government was therefore uncompromising in its determination to root out inflation at any cost. Where the Heath government had begun with some of the same objectives, but had turned aside rather than accept the human cost of those policies in recession and unemployment, the Thatcher team saw persistence as necessary to save the economic strength of the country in the long term. They also came to see determination as a political virtue in its own right. As a result, productivity certainly increased and inflation fell dramatically in the mid-1980s so that exports became more competitive, but at the cost of unemployment rising to over three millions and the de-industrialisation of much of Britain. The Prime Minister's often repeated assertion that 'there is no alternative' to such a policy specifically rejected any suggestion of compromise, though it took a ruthless use of the power of patronage to keep the less convinced Cabinet ministers in line.

The large rise in unemployment and its consequent cost to the Exchequer in benefits made a major impact on the government's budget, sustainable only because the same years were those in which the North Sea oil industry got into full swing, and so both cushioned the balance of payments from the effects of the recession and made large tax contributions to government revenue. As a result, the government's gradual establishment of tight control over its own expenditure was not widely recognised until it allowed substantial tax reductions when unemployment and its cost did fall steadily in the later 1980s.

Government revenues were also assisted by a policy adopted both for political and revenue motives, the privatisation of Britain's public sector. The first halting measures seemed likely to go no further than the token changes that had been made in the early 1970s (when the Thomas Cook travel agency and the Carlisle pubs had been privatised), but an unexpected public demand for shares in such first experiments as the privatised British Telecom led on to bolder measures. By the end of the 1980s, the Thatcher government had privatised or was planning to privatise almost all the industries that Attlee had nationalised (and some much older parts of the public sector); the size of the public sector in industry had been approximately halved and the number of people who owned shares had more than tripled to about a quarter of the adult population.

A related policy, in which finance definitely took second place to politics was the sale of council houses to their tenants: Conservative local councils had been doing this for more than ten years, but the government's introduction of the 'right to buy' enforced the same policy on all councils and offered large discounts to tenants who purchased. About three million families became home owners by this route during the 1980s, and the overall proportion living in homes they owned (a steady trend upwards throughout the century) accelerated sharply: where only 10 per cent of families had owned their own homes in 1914, this had risen to 25 per cent by 1939, 50 per cent in 1970, and to nearly 70 per cent by the end of the 1980s. Encouraging housing for ownership had always been a political objective of twentieth-century Conservative governments, but this exercise achieved a similar extension to that of the 1930s and 1950s while actually bringing in revenue rather than costing money to the taxpayer. The idea of the 'property-owning democracy', which radical Conservatives like Macmillan had put forward in the 1920s and to which Eden had given the official stamp of approval in the 1940s was now a reality in the 1980s. Macmillan himself, a celebrated exponent of home-ownership in the 1950s but also a lifelong supporter of intervention in industry, was a critical elder statesman in the 1980s, describing privatisation of industry as selling-off 'the family silver'. It is not clear how far home- and share-ownership were taken up only because of the cash discounts offered, but the fact that ownership was far more widely dispersed than ever before was undeniable. On the other hand, the government's steady encroachment on local government's powers and its increasing centralisation of authority in ministers raised doubts about its commitment to democracy even while property-owning was increased.

Extended ownership was also a contribution to Conservative electoral strength throughout the 1980s; as during the slump of the 1930s, the sections of society which backed the government were doing rather well in all except the leanest years, and the heartland of Conservatism in the South East of England did very well indeed when the recession gave way to an accelerating economic boom from about 1985. The cut of income tax by a quarter (at the standard rate) benefited those in work and most benefited high earners, while the less well off were most affected by the holding down of government expenditure and the increasing of charges for public services. Throughout its life the government had been prepared to accept a high social price of homelessness and poverty in the midst of comparative affluence – and a depressed public service – as the cost of achieving its economic objectives. In the third term which began in 1987, the determination to end the 'dependency culture' of widespread state support became in itself a government priority, a contribution in the government's mind to the country's economic health.

The 1980s were therefore a decade in which the gaps between north and south and between richest and poorest in all regions widened considerably, until the government itself was driven into a more interventionist response to deal with the social problems that inner cities now faced. Here too it turned to the ideology of the 'enterprise culture' rather than to traditional public sector methods; the boom unleashed in London's docklands after decades of decline was fairly attributed to the drive of the government's own innovative development corporation (which had powers to override the local councils) and this became a model for later initiatives. A similar intolerance of traditional democratic forms motivated the steady erosion of the independence of local government, though here the government was equally motivated by the wish to deny a platform to the Labour left where it was most strongly entrenched.

There was in all a most *unconservative* readiness to innovate and then to abandon such innovations without regret; by 1988 the government had wound up the Greater London Council (created by Conservatives in 1963) and Metropolitan Councils (created by Conservatives in 1972), and it had considered a review of County Councils (reorganised by Conservatives in 1972) and of the structure of the National Health Service (re-structured by Conservatives in the 1970s and again in the 1980s). Although Thatcher's government pursued many policies espoused by Conservatives in the past, and certainly looked after the interests of Conservative voters, how far it was in any sense *conservative* was more doubtful. In a deliberate reversal of roles, the government even adopted the word 'radical' as a positive description of its philosophy and to contrast with its portrayal of Labour and the Alliance as standing for past worlds which had been banished for ever by changes in public attitudes and by technological change.

However, in the context of postwar politics, the government's most important policy success came with the dismantling of trades union power. In 1979 the prospects were not propitious, for the unions had effectively destroyed the authority of the last three governments. The success was owed to reasons part political and part economic. Unlike 1971 or 1968 the Thatcher government did not introduce one all-embracing trades union bill which the unions could smash in a single fight. Rather they chipped away at trades union immunities by a series of annual acts, each of which included an extension of members' rights as well as reductions in the unions' institutional independence. There was popular support for these moves and little chance for the unions effectively to mobilise even their own members against them, though they continued to seek repeal or amendment through the Labour Party and so contributed to Labour's difficulty in getting elected. In detail the legislation drew on what had gone wrong in 1971; there was this time no need for voluntary participation by the unions, so the Acts could not be ignored, and penalties tended to be financial ones imposed on the unions as organisations by ordinary courts. This allowed for no martyrs and made trades union leaders reluctant to risk in unwinnable fights the assets built up over decades, especially after both the printers and the miners made the attempt and were financially crippled in the process.

But what was equally important was the effect of recession on the unions; as the economy fell into slump the unions lost members at an alarming rate, so placing them in great financial difficulties even without incurring legal fines, and making them more ready to seek deals to save their members' jobs than to take militant action to improve earnings. The key example which demonstrated how much power the unions had lost came with a year long miners' strike in 1984–85, a contest which the government may even have welcomed (or at least not sought to avoid) since it enabled them to teach an old enemy a lesson in the changed conditions, and to keep Labour party politics in a ferment too. The miners ended up split into two unions and the overall number of miners in employment fell even faster than before the strike. Over the decade the trades unions as a whole lost several million members; equally seriously they lost any recognised right to consultation or partnership with government and were left with only industry rather than politics in which to operate constructively. When the southern half of the economy moved back into growth in the second half of the 1980s the unions found themselves competing with each other for members in the newer industries and so were even more divided than before.

The defeat of trades union power where so many predecessors had failed, like victory in the Falklands War, provided an extra boost to both the government's and the Prime Minister's authority: the miners' leader Scargill like General Galtieri of Argentina provided an opportunity for the 'iron lady' (as the Russians had dubbed Thatcher) to show her mettle. While these two conflicts left some in Britain feeling that the government was dogmatic, inflexible and confrontationist, they created for others a message of determination, leadership and unusual political stature. In that sense too, Britain was divided. By any political standards though, Thatcher's achievements were exceptional. She led her party to three successive election victories (albeit helped by divisions on the left) and built an international reputation which only British war leaders had previously enjoyed. By 1988 she had been in office for longer than any twentieth-century Prime Minister and uninterruptedly in office for longer than any since Lord Liverpool in the 1820s. She remained a figure hated as well as admired, a politician about whom few Britons did not have a strong opinion.

The prominence of Thatcher's personality during her years as Prime Minister can mislead in encouraging the assumption that the 'conviction politics' of what came to be embodied in 'Thatcherism' was a personally inspired break with the past, a turning away entirely from consensus and compromise to confrontation and the single-minded pursuit of ideology. It suited both her admirers and her critics to assert that there *was* such a change (though they described it in very different language) but that too may obscure the truth.

There remained far more common ground between the front benches of all the British parties than rhetoric suggested: the first moves to haul back inflation by limiting the money supply (and causing an upsurge in unemployment) had after all come when Callaghan was Prime Minister, as had the beginnings of financial restraints on local government when Crosland announced that 'the party's over' in 1975; the beginnings of educational reform in pursuit of higher standards for entrants to industry (through greater state intervention if necessary) can be traced back to a speech by Callaghan himself; some elements of the privatisation initiative also go back before 1979 to Callaghan's government. And while a battle with the trades unions was won by Thatcher, the need to curb the unions had been accepted by every government since 1968. All governments had encouraged home-ownership, and all had expressed doubts about the structure of the public sector at least since *The Future of Socialism* opened that debate on the left.

After 1983 the Thatcher government experimented with variations in monetary policy which did not in any case suggest a single set of ideological imperatives, or even a set of policies with which Labour would necessarily entirely disagree. There remained then a great deal of common ground, and Britain's 'radical right' was anyway practising policies that had their counterparts in other countries such as Australia and France (which did not have right-wing governments at all), as well as both influencing and being influenced by Ronald Reagan's Republican regime in America.

To a considerable extent, the *idea* of a consensus had become associated in the British political debate with a particular package of policies that Labour had helped to devise during the Second World War and which Conservatives had not fundamentally dismantled in the 1950s. This was always a package which accorded better with socialist thinking than with the uneasy combination of conservatism and liberalism which the postwar Conservative Party represented. In the 1960s, the country's disappointing economic performance encouraged Macmillan, Wilson and Heath all to experiment more freely within that common package of ideas and economic methods in the search for faster growth which would itself narrow social divides. Expectations changed again in the 1970s and after, a shift to which the

Thatcher Conservatives contributed substantially but from which they also benefited, and this moved the mid-point of the political agenda once again nearer to the Conservatives' home ground. But while the terms of the debate constantly shifted, any party wishing to bid for power within Britain's curious electoral system in which all prizes go to the single winner, and in the British political culture that remained remarkably homogeneous even in times of social division, could not afford to distance itself too far from that moving political centre. It was in that sense that a new consensus emerged in the 1980s: we were (almost) all Thatcherites then.

In 1988, Britain marked the three-hundredth anniversary of the Glorious Revolution with parliamentary and media celebrations which hailed 1688 as the foundation stone of democratic progress over the next three centuries. At the end of 1988, Margaret Thatcher approached ten years of continuous occupancy of Downing Street, a record unequalled since Lord Liverpool in the 1820s. As the Thatcher Cabinet accelerated into a more radical third term in office, opponents saw it as a threat to democracy itself, supporters as a real driving force for the extension of individual freedom. The 'Thatcherite' revolution, which had materially shifted the centre of gravity of British politics since 1974, was poised between these different perspectives as Britain moved towards the twenty-first century.

Bibliography

This bibliography is a selective guide to further reading, and an acknowledgment by the authors of the debt they owe to the work of other scholars. It is mainly limited to recent publications, and as far as possible is organised to follow the general arrangement of the text. Place of publication is London unless otherwise stated. The following abbreviations have been used for periodicals: *BIHR* – *Bulletin of the Institute of Historical Research*; *EEH* – *Explorations in Economic History*; *EHR* – *English Historical Review*; *HJ* – *Historical Journal*; *JBS* – *Journal of British Studies*; *JMH* – *Journal of Modern History*; *P&P* – *Past and Present*; *TRHS* – *Transactions of the Royal Historical Society*.

GENERAL

Surveys of modern British history include R. K. Webb, *Modern England from the eighteenth century to the present* (2nd edn., 1980), and the shorter, more interpretative Geoffrey Alderman, *Modern Britain 1700–1783: A Domestic History* (1986); and, on economic and social aspects, two recent books for non-specialist readers, Trevor May, *An Economic and Social History of Britain 1760–1970* (1987) and Charles More, *The Industrial Age: Economy and Society in Britain 1750–1985* (1989). D. L. Keir, *The Constitutional History of Modern Britain since 1485* (9th edn., 1969) is a clear exposition of a subject full of technical difficulties, while the best general book on the development of party is Alan Beattie, *English Party Politics 1660–1970* (2 vols., 1970). On the British overseas T. O. Lloyd, *The British Empire 1558–1983* (Oxford, 1984) is a dispassionate guide. Naval and military matters are covered in Paul M. Kennedy, *The Rise and Fall of British Naval Mastery* (rev. edn., 1973) and Correlli Barnett, *Britain and her Army 1509–1970* (Harmondsworth, 1970). Good introductions to Scottish history are Rosalind Mitchison, *A History of Scotland* (2nd edn., 1982) and W. Ferguson, *Scotland: 1689 to the Present Day* (1968). On modern Irish history J. C. Beckett, *The Making of Modern*

Ireland 1603–1923 (1966) has long been the standard account; to it can now be added the fuller and more astringent R. F. Foster, *Modern Ireland 1600–1972* (1988). E. N. Williams, ed., *The Eighteenth Century Constitution 1689–1815* (Cambridge, 1960), H. J. Hanham, ed., *The Nineteenth Century Constitution 1815–1914* (Cambridge, 1969), and G. H. Le May, ed., *British Government 1914–1963* (1964) are clearly-arranged collections of documents with accompanying commentaries. Bulkier collections which go well beyond political developments are the volumes in the *English Historical Documents* series: A. Browning, ed., Vol. VIII, *1660–1714* (1953); D. B. Horn and M. Ransome, eds., Vol. X, *1714–1783* (1957); A. Aspinall and E. A. Smith, eds., Vol. XI, *1783–1832* (1959); G. M. Young and W. D. Handcock, eds., Vol. XII(i), *1833–1874* (1956); W. D. Handcock, ed., Vol. XII(ii), *1874–1914* (1977).

1688–1763 (CHAPTERS 1 TO 5)

Recent text-books include J. R. Jones, *Country and Court: England 1658–1714* (1978), W. A. Speck, *Stability and Strife 1714–1760* (1977), and Dorothy Marshall, *Eighteenth Century England* [1714–1784] (2nd edn., 1974). The events leading to the 1688 Revolution are examined by J. R. Western, *The English State in the 1680s* (1972), while their European dimension is brought out in John Carswell, *The Descent on England* (1969). The tercentenary of the Revolution afforded the opportunity for reappraisals by W. A. Speck, *Reluctant Revolutionaries: Englishmen and the Revolution of 1688* (1988), John Miller, *The Seeds of Liberty: 1688 and the Shaping of Modern Britain* (1988), and John Childs, '1688', *History*, 73 (1988), 398–424. Lois G. Schwoerer, *The Declaration of Rights, 1689* (Baltimore, 1981) stresses the activities of the 'radical' Whigs, a theme also pursued in Richard Ashcraft, *Revolutionary Principles and Locke's 'Two Treatises of Government'* (Princeton, 1986). The edition of the *Two Treatises of Government* (1960) by Peter Laslett has an important introduction. Post-Revolution developments are covered in the essays in Geoffrey Holmes, ed., *Britain after the Glorious Revolution 1689–1714* (1969). Stephen Baxter, *William III* (1966) remains the best biography of the monarch. Some of the financial implications of the Revolution settlement are considered in Clayton Roberts, 'The Constitutional Significance of the Financial Settlement of 1690', *HJ*, XX (1977), 59–76; Colin Brooks, 'Public Finance and Political Stability; the Administration of the Land Tax, 1688–1720', *HJ*, XVII (1974), 281–300; J. V. Beckett, 'Land Tax or Excise; the levying of taxation in seventeenth- and eighteenth-century England', *EHR*, C (1985), 285–308. Over a longer period P. G. M. Dickson, *The Financial Revolution in England: A Study in the Development of Public Credit 1688–1756* (1967) remains indispensable, as does in a narrower sphere Henry Roseveare, *The Treasury* (1969). The Whig/Tory struggle is described at one level in Henry Horwitz, *Parliament, policy and politics in the reign of William III* (Manchester, 1973), at another in G. S. De Kreay, *A Fractured Society: the Politics of London in the First Age of Party 1688–1715* (Oxford, 1985). J. A. Downie, 'The Commission of Public Accounts and the formation of the Country Party', *EHR*, XCI (1976), 33–57 and David Hayton, 'The "Country" interest and the party system, 1689–c.1720', in Clyve Jones, ed., *Party and Management in Parliament, 1660–1784* (Leicester, 1984) are clear discussions of a tortuous subject. Sections on diplomacy and war in this period will be found in the general surveys by Paul Langford, *Great Britain, 1688–1815* (1976), J. R. Jones, *Britain and the World 1649–1815* (1980). On foreign trade between 1660 and 1774 see the articles by Ralph Davis reprinted, with a useful introduction, in W. E. Minchinton, ed., *The Growth of English Overseas Trade in the Seventeenth and Eighteenth Centuries* (1969).

In an influential general interpretation J. H. Plumb, *The Growth of Political Stability in England 1675–1725* (Harmondsworth, 1969) argues that the violence of party antagonisms lessened over the period. J. P. Kenyon, *Revolution Principles: The Politics of Party 1689–1720* (1977) stresses the interaction of political ideology and party behaviour, as does, over a longer time-span, H. T. Dickinson, *Liberty and Property: Political Ideology in Eighteenth Century Britain* (1977). Geoffrey Holmes returns to the Plumb argument in 'The Achievement of Stability: The Social Context of Politics from the 1680s to the Age of Walpole', in John Cannon, ed., *The Whig Ascendancy* (1980), and analyses King's 1695–96 tables in 'Gregory King and the Social Structure of Pre-Industrial England', in *TRHS*, 5th Series, 27 (1977), 41–68. A collection of essays by Holmes, *Augustan England: Professions, State and Society 1680–1730* (1982) does something to compensate for the lack of a general survey of the professions for this period. Edward Gregg, *Queen Anne* (1980) shows the last Stuart monarch to have been a more significant political figure than often thought. The most important book on her reign remains Geoffrey Holmes, *British Politics in the Reign of Anne* (rev. ed., 1987), supplemented by a collection of his articles in Holmes's *Politics, Religion and Society in England, 1679–1742* (1986). Studies which focus on the electorate and its size are W. A. Speck, *Tory and Whig: the Struggle in the Constituencies, 1701–1715* (1970), Geoffrey Holmes, *The Electorate and the National Will in the First Age of Party* (Lancaster, 1976), and Clyve Jones, ed., *Britain in the First Age of Party: Essays presented to Geoffrey Holmes* (1987). The tangle of High Tory, Church, and Jacobite politics is scrutinised by G. V. Bennett, *The Tory Crisis in Church and State: the Career of Francis Atterbury, Bishop of Rochester* (Oxford, 1975), Geoffrey Holmes, *The Trial of Dr Sacheverell* (1973) and Daniel Szechi, *Jacobitism and Tory Politics 1710–14* (Edinburgh, 1984). P. W. J. Riley casts a cold eye on the politicians involved in *The Union of England and Scotland: A Study in*

Anglo-Scottish Politics of the 18th century (1979). For a brief joint study as lively as its title see Daniel Szechi and David Hayton, 'John Bull's Other Kingdoms: the English Government of Scotland and Ireland', in Jones, *First Age of Party*. The role of the press in politics is outlined in J. A. Downie, *Robert Harley and the Press: Popularity and Public Opinion in the Age of Swift and Defoe* (1979) and W. A. Speck, 'Political Propaganda in Augustan England', *TRHS*, 5th Series, 22 (1972), 17–32. G. A. Cranfield, *The Development of the Provincial Press 1700–1760* (Oxford, 1962) remains the standard work. J. A. Downie has examined the political dimensions of Swift's activities in *Jonathan Swift, Political Writer* (1984). H. T. Dickinson, *Bolingbroke* (1970) is a splendid biography; the most recent study of the enigmatic Harley is Brian Hill, *Robert Harley: Speaker, Secretary of State and Premier Minister* (1988).

For the early Hanoverian period Ragnhild Hatton, *George I Elector and King* (1978), stronger on European than domestic affairs, attempts a rehabilitation of one of Britain's less attractive monarchs. The search for the Tory party after 1714 looms large in Brian Hill, *The Growth of Political Parties, 1689–1742* (1976) and in Linda Colley's stimulating *In Defiance of Oligarchy: The Tory Party 1714–60* (1982). The standard, though incomplete, biography of the Tories' arch-opponent is J. H. Plumb, *Sir Robert Walpole: The Making of a Statesman* (1956) and *Sir Robert Walpole: The King's Minister* (1960). Shorter and cooler is H. T. Dickinson, *Walpole and the Whig Supremacy* (1973), while Jeremy Black, ed., *Britain in the Age of Walpole* (1985) is a first-class collection of essays, including one by the editor on Walpole's foreign policy. Some indication of Walpole's predominance in public life is given in Paul Langford, ed., *Walpole and the Robinocracy* (1985), a collection of prints and caricatures. Langford has also examined the mid-point crisis of Walpole's tenure of office in *The Excise Crisis: Society and Politics in the Age of Walpole* (1975). Walpole's relations with the City are examined in Nicholas Rogers, 'Resistance to Oligarchy: the City Opposition to Walpole and his Successors, 1725–47', in John Stevenson, *London in the Age of Reform* (Oxford, 1977). The City more generally is the subject of several of Lucy Sutherland's essays in Aubrey Newman, ed., *Politics and Finance in the Eighteenth Century* (1984). There is no worthwhile biography of George II, though John Owen has an interesting sketch, 'George II Reconsidered' in Anne Whiteman *et al.*, *Statesmen, Scholars and Students* (1973).

Scotland and Jacobitism are almost synonymous in most of the studies of this period, among the best of which are Bruce Lenman, 'A Client Society: Scotland between the '15 and the '45', in Black, *Britain in Age of Walpole*, and his unsentimental account, *The Jacobite Risings in Britain 1689–1745* (1980). Frank McLynn, *The Jacobites* (1985) is a popular account written by a specialist. G. V. Bennett, 'Jacobitism and the Rise of Walpole' in Neil McKendrick, ed., *Historical Perspectives* (1974) shows the use Walpole made of the Jacobite threat. The impact of Jacobitism on the Tories is examined by Eveline Cruickshanks, *Political Untouchables: The Tories and the '45* (1979), whose conclusions on the strength of their continuing Jacobite attachment differ significantly from those of Colley, *Defiance of Oligarchy*. The neglected area of 'Walpole and Ireland' is dealt with by David Hayton in Black, *Britain in Age of Walpole*. Several scholars have tried to define and locate radicalism in this period, among them H. T. Dickinson, 'The Precursors of Political Radicalism in Augustan Britain', in Jones, *First Age of Party*; J. G. A. Pocock, 'Radical Critics of the Whig Order in the Age between Revolutions', in Margaret and James Jacob, eds., *The Origins of Anglo-American Radicalism* (1984); Linda Colley, 'Eighteenth-Century English Radicalism before Wilkes', *TRHS*, 5th Series, 31 (1981), 1–19. Attempts to relate the criminal law of the Hanoverian period to its political and social history are made by Douglas Hay *et al.*, eds., *Albion's Fatal Tree: crime and society in eighteenth century England* (1975) and E. P. Thompson, *Whigs and Hunters: the origin of the Black Act* (1975). A different view is contained in John Styles, 'Criminal Records', *HJ*, XX (1977), 977–81 and John H. Langbein, 'Albion's Fatal Flaws', *P&P*, No. 98 (1983), 96–120.

Several works with a long time-span have particular relevance to the oligarchical dominance of the mid-eighteenth century: G. E. Mingay, *English Landed Society in the Eighteenth Century* (1956) and *The Gentry: the Rise and Fall of a Ruling Class* (1976); John Cannon, *Aristocratic Century: the peerage of eighteenth-century England* (1984); J. V. Beckett, *The Aristocracy in England 1660–1914* (Oxford, 1986). J. B. Owen, *The Rise of the Pelhams* (1957) makes sense of the confused political scene after Walpole's fall. Brian Hill, *British Political Parties 1742–1832: from the Fall of Walpole to the First Reform Act* (1985) is a steady guide along a twisting road. J. C. D. Clark, *The Dynamics of Change: the Crisis of the 1750s and the English party system* (1982) argues at length that the years 1754 to 1757 saw the disappearance of the old Whig and Tory parties; a short cut will be found in his 'The decline of party, 1740–1760', *EHR*, XCIII (1978), 499–527. T. W. Perry's grandly-titled *Public Opinion, Propaganda and Politics in 18th-Century England* (Cambridge, Mass., 1962) is in fact a study of the 'Jew Bill' of 1753. Tony Hayter, *The Army and the Crowd in mid-Georgian England* (1978) explains the problems inherent in the use of the military as a police force. Reed Browning, *The Duke of Newcastle* (1975) is particularly good on the Duke's financing of the Seven Years War. Stanley Ayling, *The Elder Pitt: Earl of Chatham* (1976) deals better than most with the complexities of his subject's character. Different strands of Pitt's wartime tenure of office are teased out by Marie Peters, *Pitt and Popularity: The Patriot Minister and London Opinion during the Seven Years War* (Oxford, 1980), and Richard Middleton, *The Bells of Victory: the Pitt–Newcastle Ministry and the Conduct of the Seven Years War 1757–1762* (1985).

1763–1815 (CHAPTERS 6 TO 9)

Recent text-books include I. R. Christie, *Wars and Revolutions: Britain 1760–1815* (1982) and Eric J. Evans, *The Forging of the Modern State: Early Industrial Britain 1783–1870* (1983). Older books which have worn well and whose early chapters cover this period are Asa Briggs, *The Age of Improvement* (London, 1959) and Harold Perkin, *The Origins of Modern English Society 1780–1880* (1969). Any serious reading on the politics of the period begins with L. B. Namier, *The Structure of Politics at the Accession of George III* (2nd edn., 1957), and *England in the Age of the American Revolution* (2nd edn., 1961). The different approach of Richard Pares, *George III and the Politicians* (1953) provoked a debate which has recently been reassessed by I. R. Christie, 'George III and the historians – thirty years on', *History*, 71 (1986), 205–21. A series of important articles by Christie on politics from the 1760s to the 1790s has been collected together in his *Myth and Reality in late 18th-century British Politics* (1970). Frank O'Gorman, *The Emergence of the British Two-Party System 1760–1832* (1982) is a compact synthesis of this elusive subject. John Brooke, *King George III* (1972) is particularly strong on the early years of the reign. K. W. Schweizer, ed., *Lord Bute: Essays in Re-interpretation* (Leicester, 1988) attempts to rescue Bute's historical reputation from its normal lowly position. John Brewer, *Party Ideology and Popular Politics at the Accession of George III* (1976) breaks new ground with his examination of Wilkes in the context of popular political culture and propaganda, a theme illustrated over a longer period in his edition of *The Common People and Politics 1750–1790s: The English Satirical Print 1600–1832* (Cambridge, 1986). George Rudé, *Wilkes and Liberty* (1962) pays particular attention to the identity of Wilkes's supporters; see also the essays in his *Paris and London: Studies in Popular Protest* (London, 1952). I. R. Christie, *Wilkes, Wyvill and Reform: the Parliamentary Reform Movement in British Politics, 1760–1785* (1962) and Edward Royle and James Walvin, *English Radicals and Reformers 1760–1848* (Brighton, 1982) are particularly useful in that they deal with the reform movements across long periods of time.

On religious life Norman Sykes, *Church and State in England in the Eighteenth Century* (Cambridge, 1934) remains indispensable; some of its themes are continued in E. R. Norman, *Church and Society in England, 1770–1970* (Oxford, 1976). A. D. Gilbert, *Religion and Society in Industrial England: Church, Chapel and Social Change 1740–1914* (1976) makes a valiant attempt to quantify some of the religious shifts over a long period. Bernard Semmel, *The Methodist Revolution* (1973) stresses the paradoxes of Methodism under Wesley, while David Hempton, *Methodism and Politics in British Society 1750–1850* (1984) is especially good on the 1790s, the starting point of a general study by W. R. Ward, *Religion and Society in England 1790–1850* (1972).

A good short introduction to the American Revolution in its British political setting is I. R. Christie, *Crisis of Empire* (2nd edn., 1974); some of the problems it touches on are examined at more length in P. J. Marshall and G. Williams, eds., *The British Atlantic Empire before the American Revolution* (1980). Bernard Bailyn, *The Ideological Origins of the American Revolution* (Cambridge, Mass., 1967) uses pamphlet evidence to show colonial fears of British 'tyranny'. An unusual collaborative exercise is I. R. Christie and B. W. Labaree, *Empire or Independence 1760–1776: A British-American Dialogue on the Coming of the American Revolution* (New York, 1976). Paul Langford, *The First Rockingham Administration 1765–1766* (1973) and P. D. G. Thomas, *British Politics and the Stamp Act Crisis* (Oxford, 1975) offer detailed analyses of the government's American policies in the mid-1760s, while the latter's 'George III and the American Revolution', *History*, 70 (1985), 16–31 is a guide to recent work. P. D. G. Thomas, *Lord North* (1976) and John Sainsbury, *Disaffected Patriots: London Supporters of Revolutionary America 1769–1782* (Gloucester, 1987) illustrate contrasting reactions to the crises of the 1770s. The best study of the War of American Independence from the British point of view remains Piers Mackesy, *The War for America, 1775–1783* (1964). The war's impact on domestic politics is covered in I. R. Christie, *The End of North's Ministry 1780–1782* (1958). Detailed accounts of Irish affairs in this period are R. B. McDowell, *Ireland in the Age of Imperialism and Revolution 1760–1801* (Oxford, 1979), Gerard O'Brien, *Anglo-Irish Politics in the Age of Grattan and Pitt* (Dublin, 1987), and Thomas Bartlett, 'The Townshend Viceroyalty, 1767–72', in Bartlett and D. W. Hayton, eds., *Penal Era and Golden Age* (Belfast, 1979). The Indian issues which loomed so large in the 1770s and 1780s are covered in several books by P. J. Marshall, *The Impeachment of Warren Hastings* (Oxford, 1965), *Problems of Empire: Britain and India, 1757–1813* (1968), and *Bengal: The British Bridgehead – Eastern India 1740–1828* (Cambridge, 1987). The political turmoil which followed the American war is examined in John Cannon, *The Fox–North Coalition: Crisis of the Constitution 1782–4* (1969), in the first volume of what, when complete, will be the standard biography of Pitt by John Ehrman, *The Younger Pitt: the Years of Acclaim* (1969), and in J. W. Derry, *Charles James Fox* (1972).

The period of economic history loosely associated with the industrial revolution abounds in good general studies such as Phyllis Deane, *The First Industrial Revolution* (2nd edn., Cambridge, 1979) and Peter Mathias, *The First Industrial Nation: An Economic History of Britain 1700–1914* (2nd edn., 1983). Some of the themes of the latter are further explored by Mathias in *The Transformation of England: Essays on the Economic and Social History of England in the 18th Century* (1979). A useful collection is R. M. Hartwell, ed., *The Causes of the Industrial Revolution in England* (1967). The text-book by Maxine Berg, *The Age of Manufactures 1700–1820* (1985) shows a refreshing emphasis on the fortunes of the traditional economy of domestic and artisan manufacture. Much of the 'new economic history' of the period first appeared in accessible form in Roderick Floud and Donald McCloskey, eds., *The Economic History of Britain since 1700: Vol I 1700–1860* (Cambridge, 1981); another recent interpretation is N. F. R. Crafts, *British Economic Growth during the Industrial Revolution* (Oxford, 1985). On individual areas within the general framework of economic developments, population trends have been studied in the authoritative work by E. A. Wrigley and R. S. Schofield, *The Population History of England, 1541–1871: A Reconstruction* (Cambridge, 1981). Those who want a 'taster' of the new demographic history rather than a full-scale meal should try Wrigley, 'The Growth of Population in 18th-Century England: A Conundrum Resolved', *P&P*, 98 (1983), 121–50. Developments in transport, including canals, are dealt with in H. T. Dyos and D. H. Aldcroft, *British Transport: An economic survey from the seventeenth century to the twentieth* (Leicester, 1969). Some of the most influential work on agriculture is to be found in J. D. Chambers and G. E. Mingay, *The Agricultural Revolution 1650–1880* (1966), and in the two volumes of essays edited by E. L. Jones, *Agriculture and Economic Growth in England 1650–1815* (1967) and *Agriculture and the Industrial Revolution* (Oxford, 1974). The case for foreign trade as a lead factor in the economic expansion of this period is put by François Crouzet, 'Toward an Export Economy: British Exports during the Industrial Revolution', *EEH*, XVII (1980), 48–93.

Examples of the revisionist approach to the working of the electoral system in the late eighteenth century and early nineteenth century are John A. Phillips, 'The Structure of Electoral Politics in Unreformed England', *JBS*, XIX (1979), 76–100, and *Electoral Behaviour in Unreformed England: Plumpers, Splitters and Straights* (Princeton, 1982); and Frank O'Gorman, 'Electoral Deference in "Unreformed England": 1760–1832', *JMH*, 56 (1974), 391–429. The declining fortunes of the Whig party after 1784 are set out in J. W. Derry, *The Regency Crisis and the Whigs 1788–9* (Cambridge, 1963), Frank O'Gorman, *The Whig Party and the French Revolution* (1967), and L. G. Mitchell, *Charles James Fox and the Disintegration of the Whig Party, 1782–1794* (1971). Good introductions to radicalism in the period of the French Revolution are the full-length study by Albert Goodwin, *The Friends of Liberty: the English Democratic Movement in the age of the French Revolution* (1979), and the much briefer H. T. Dickinson, *British Radicalism and the French Revolution 1789–1815* (Oxford, 1985). Although some of the emphases and conclusions of E. P. Thompson, *The Making of the English Working Class* (rev. edn., Harmondsworth, 1968) have been challenged since the book's first appearance it remains essential reading. A counterthrust to the radical positions of Thompson and others has emerged in recent work which emphasises the social cohesion and political stability of the period: I. R. Christie, *Stress and Stability in Late*

Eighteenth Century Britain: Reflections on the British Avoidance of Revolution (1984), John Cannon, *Aristocratic Century: the peerage of eighteenth-century England* (1984), J. C. D. Clark, *English Society 1688–1832: Ideology, social structure and political practice during the ancien régime* (Cambridge, 1985). Contrasting views of the extent of Jacobinism in England come from Roger Wells, *Insurrection: the British Experience 1795–1803* (Gloucester, 1983) and Robert R. Dozier, *For King, Constitution and Country: the English Loyalists and the French Revolution* (Lexington, 1983). Handy editions of the works of Burke and Paine at this time are those by Conor Cruise O'Brien, *Reflections on the Revolution in France* (Harmondsworth, 1968) and by Henry Collins, *The Rights of Man* (Harmondsworth, 1969). John Ehrman, *The Younger Pitt: the reluctant transition* (1983) is a subtle, intricate study of the Pitt ministry between 1790 and 1796, and of the machinery of government in the late eighteenth century. For the wartime period generally Clive Emsley, *British Society and the French Wars 1793–1815* (1979) is a most useful survey, while his 'Repression, "terror" and the rule of law in England during the decade of the French Revolution', *EHR*, C (1985), 801–25, brings together much recent scholarship. The standard account of the Union with Ireland is G. C. Bolton, *The Passing of the Irish Act of Union* (Oxford, 1966). Thomas Pakenham, *The Year of Liberty: 1798* (1968) is a chilling account of the Irish rebellion and its suppression.

The political background to the Napoleonic war years is sketched in A. D. Harvey, *Britain in the Early Nineteenth Century* (1978). Richard Glover, *Peninsular Preparation: the Reform of the British Army 1795–1809* (Cambridge, 1963) and *Britain at Bay: Defence against Napoleon 1803–14* (1973) have much spirited passing of judgement on men and measures, but also clear explanations of the administrative structure of the British war machine from recruitment to grand strategy. G. J. Marcus, *A Naval History of England: Vol II The Age of Nelson* (1971) has some good material on commerce protection as well as on the set-piece battles. Michael Duffy, *Soldiers, Sugar and Seapower: the British Expeditions to the West Indies in the War against Revolutionary France* (Oxford, 1987) makes the best of a sorry story. Two closely-argued books by Piers Mackesy on the British war effort between 1798 and the Treaty of Amiens are splendid examples of the historian's art, *Statesmen at War: the Strategy of Overthrow, 1798–1799* (Oxford, 1974) and *War without Victory: the Downfall of Pitt, 1799–1802* (Oxford, 1984). Edward Ingram, *Commitment to Empire: Prophecies of the Great Game in Asia 1797–1800* (Oxford, 1981) is an iconoclastic book which has more to do with Britain and the war of the second coalition than the title implies. Important theatres of operation are dealt with in A. N. Ryan, 'The defence of British trade with the Baltic, 1807–1813', *EHR*, LXXIV (1959), 443–66, and Piers Mackesy, *The War in the Mediterranean 1803–1810* (1957). John M. Sherwig, *Guineas and Gunpowder: British Foreign Aid in the Wars with France 1793–1815* (Cambridge, Mass, 1969) sheds much light on Britain's subsidy arrangements. Much of the military detail of the campaigns of the period is brought together in Elizabeth Longford, *Wellington. The Years of the Sword* (1969). For some discordant notes struck at home in the last years of the war see Dean Rapp, 'The Left-Wing Whigs: Whitbread, the Mountain and Reform, 1809–1815', *JBS*, XXI (1982), 35–66; Naomi C. Miller, 'John Cartwright and radical parliamentary reform, 1808–1819', *EHR*, LXXXIII (1968); and Malcolm Thomis, *The Luddites* (Newton Abbot, 1970). The influence of war on the economy is examined in Phyllis Deane, 'War and Industrialisation' in J. M. Winter, ed., *War and Economic Development* (Cambridge, 1975), and Glenn Hueckel, 'War and the British Economy 1793–1815', *EEH*, X (1973), 365–96. In the serried ranks of modern scholarship on the slave trade and its abolition Roger Anstey, *The Atlantic Slave Trade and British Abolition 1760–1810* (1975) stands out. The fullest account of the peace negotiations remains C. K. Webster, *The Foreign Policy of Castlereagh, 1812–1815. Britain and the Reconstruction of Europe* (1931).

1815–1850s (CHAPTERS 10 TO 13)

Recent text-books include Norman Gash, *Aristocracy and People: Britain 1815–1865* (1979) and, bent more towards the people than the aristocracy, J. F. C. Harrison, *Early Victorian Britain 1832–51* (1971); those by Evans, Briggs and Perkin listed in the previous section cover this period also. Norman Gash, *Lord Liverpool 1770–1828* (1984) is the first serious biography, though much has appeared on various aspects of Liverpool's government: J. E. Cookson, *Lord Liverpool's Administration: the Crucial Years 1815–1822* (Edinburgh, 1975); Boyd Hilton, *Corn, Cash and Commerce: the Economic Policies of the Tory Governments 1815–1830* (Oxford, 1977) and 'Lord Liverpool: the art of politics and the practice of government', *TRHS*, 38, (1988). The rather misleading title of Neville Thompson, *Wellington after Waterloo* (1986) conceals a thorough study of Wellington's political role until his death, while popular biographies by Wendy Hinde cover the careers and diplomatic policies of *George Canning* (1973) and *Castlereagh* (1981). On the Whig side Austin Mitchell, *The Whigs in Opposition 1815–1830* (Oxford, 1967) remains the standard account, though it can now be supplemented by Robert Stewart's biography of the charismatic *Henry Brougham 1778–1868* (1986) and by Peter Jupp's study of the distinctly less charismatic *Lord Grenville 1759–1834* (Oxford, 1985). E. A. Wassoon, 'The Great Whigs and Parliamentary Reform, 1809–1830', *JBS* (1985), 434–64, finds more interest in the subject among the landed Whigs than often supposed. The fashionable economic dogmas of the day are examined in their political context in a pair of useful if unexciting books: Barry Gordon, *Political Economy in Parliament 1819–1823* (1976) and *Economic Doctrine and Tory Liberalism 1824–1830* (1979), and in Norman

Gash, *Mr Secretary Peel* (1961). Elie Halévy, *The Growth of Philosophic Radicalism* (1928) remains a fine exposition of the doctrine of Bentham and his followers; William Thomas, *The Philosophic Radicals: Nine Studies in Theory and Practice 1817–1841* (Oxford, 1979) stresses divergences rather than unity among Bentham's successors. John Stevenson analyses 'The Queen Caroline Affair' in his *London in the Age of Reform* (Oxford, 1977), while W. D. Rubinstein takes an overview in 'The End of "Old Corruption" in Britain 1780–1860', *P&P*, No. 101 (1983), 55–86. John Belchem, *'Orator' Hunt: Henry Hunt and English Working-Class Radicalism* (Oxford, 1985) is a sustained but not uncritical attempt at rehabilitation. J. R. Dinwiddy, *From Luddism to the First Reform Bill* (Oxford, 1986) is a lucid summary of recent research, including his own. The events leading to Catholic emancipation are viewed from different sides of the Irish Sea in G. I. T. Machin, *The Catholic Question in English Politics 1820 to 1830* (Oxford, 1964) and Feargus Ferrall, *Catholic Emancipation: Daniel O'Connell and the Birth of Irish Democracy 1820–1830* (Dublin, 1985).

Geoffrey Finlayson, *England in the Eighteen Thirties: Decade of Reform* (1969) combines succinct narrative and analysis. Eric Hobsbawm and George Rudé, *Captain Swing* (rev. edn., Harmondsworth, 1973) is radical historiography at its best. Michael Brock, *The Great Reform Act* (1973) should be read with the final chapters of John Cannon, *Parliamentary Reform 1640–1832* (Cambridge, 1972). Reform movements in the provincial cities are brought to light in several articles by Asa Briggs reprinted in *The Collected Essays of Asa Briggs*, I (Brighton, 1985); that in Birmingham is scrutinised with a critical eye in Carlos Flick, *The Birmingham Political Union and the Movements for Reform in Britain 1830–1839* (Hamden, Conn., 1978). D. C. Moore, *The Politics of Deference* (Hassocks, 1976) argues for the conservative nature of the Reform Act. Joseph Hamburger, *Intellectuals in Politics: John Stuart Mill and the Philosophic Radicals* (1965) deals with their unsuccessful attempts to establish a new political party in the period covered in Ian Newbould, 'Whiggery and the Dilemma of Reform: Liberals, Radicals and the Melbourne Administration, 1835–9', *BIHR*, LII (1980), 229–41. Angus Macintyre, *The Liberator: Daniel O'Connell and the Irish Party 1830–1847* (1965) is a study of the first Irish nationalist party in the House of Commons rather than a conventional biography; see also A. D. Kriegel, 'The Irish policy of Lord Grey's government', *EHR*, LXXXVI (1971), 22–45. A. J. Taylor, *Laissez-faire and State Intervention in Nineteenth-Century Britain* (1972) and Oliver MacDonagh, *Early Victorian Government 1830–1870* (1977) are level-headed guides to a contentious subject; at a general level the argument has been carried forward in Harold Perkin, 'Individualism versus Collectivism in Nineteenth-Century Britain: A False Antithesis', *JBS*, XVII (1977), 105–18, and P. W. J. Bartrip, 'State Intervention in Mid-Nineteenth Century Britain: Fact or Fiction?', *JBS*, XXIII (1983), 63–83.

A considerable literature has accumulated on class divisions in this period. Some of it is surveyed in R. J. Morris, *Class and Class Consciousness in the Industrial Revolution 1780–1850* (1979), while the work of a prolific writer on the subject is collected in R. S. Neale, *Class in English History 1680–1850* (Oxford, 1981). On the Poor Law see Anthony Brundage, *The Making of the New Poor Law 1832–9* (1978), Derek Fraser, ed., *The New Poor Law in the Nineteenth Century* (1976), and Peter Dunkley, 'Whigs and Paupers: the Reform of the English Poor Laws, 1830–1834', *JBS*, XX (1981), 124–49. For Chartism J. T. Ward, *Chartism* (1973) is a good, straightforward account. The provincial and other studies in Asa Briggs, ed., *Chartist Studies* (1959) showed the way for much later work, including James Epstein and Dorothy Thompson, eds., *The Chartist Experience: Studies in Working-Class Radicalism and Culture 1830–1860* (1982) and Dorothy Thompson, *The Chartists: Popular Politics in the Industrial Revolution* (1984). James Epstein, *The Lion of Freedom: Fergus O'Connor and the Chartist Movement 1832–1842* (1982) puts the case for O'Connor as something more than a demagogue, while David Goodway, *London Chartism 1838–1848* (Cambridge, 1982) examines why support for Chartism in the capital was so spasmodic. The essays in J. T. Ward, ed., *Popular Movements c.1830–1850* (1970) and Patricia Hollis, ed., *Pressure from Without in Early Victorian England* (1974) cover campaigns ranging from anti-slavery to factory reform. On the latter, two books by Ward, *The Factory Movement 1830–1855* (1962) and *Sir James Graham* (1967) serve as an introduction for more recent work such as A. P. Donajgrodski, 'Sir James Graham at the Home Office', *HJ* (1977), 97–120; Alan Heesom, 'The Coal Mines Act of 1842, Social Reform and Social Control', *HJ*, XXIV (1981), 69–88; P. W. J. Bartrip, 'British Government Inspection, 1832–1875: Some Observations', *HJ*, XXV (1982), 605–26.

For the period of Peel's dominance Norman Gash, *Sir Robert Peel* (rev. edn., 1986), *Politics in the Age of Peel* (rev. edn., 1977) and *Reaction and Reconstruction in British Politics 1832–52* (Oxford, 1965) make an imposing phalanx of scholarly work which shows Peelite Conservatism in its best light, and Donald Read's study of Peel's reputation in *Peel and the Victorians* (Oxford, 1987) follows the same tradition. More critical studies have come from Robert Stewart, *The Foundation of the Conservative Party* (1978), Boyd Hilton, 'Peel: A Reappraisal', *HJ*, XXII (1979), 585–614, and Ian Newbould, 'Sir Robert Peel and the Conservative Party, 1832–1841: A Study in Failure', *EHR*, XCVIII (1983), 529–57. Peel's Irish policy is dealt with in Donal A. Kerr, *Peel, Priests and Politics* (Oxford, 1982), while G. I. T. Machin, *Politics and the Churches in Great Britain 1832 to 1868* (Oxford, 1977) examines the links between religion and politics generally. Opposing sides on the Corn Law issue are studied in Norman McCord, *The Anti-Corn Law League 1838–1846* (2nd edn., 1968) and Travis L. Crosby, *English Farmers and the Politics of Protection 1815–1852*

(Hassocks, 1977), while Nicholas C. Edsall, *Richard Cobden Independent Radical* (Cambridge, Mass., 1986) has much information on Cobden's role in this period. Cecil Woodham-Smith, *The Great Hunger: Ireland 1845–9* (1962) is a moving account; Joel Mokyr, *Why Ireland Starved: A Qualitative and Analytical History of the Irish Economy 1800–1850* (1983) and Mary E. Daly, *The Famine in Ireland* (Dundalk, 1986) reveal the complexities which modern scholarship has brought to the subject. J. B. Conacher, *The Peelites and the Party System 1846–52* (Newton Abbot, 1972), and John Prest, *Lord John Russell* (1972), cover the confused years after the fall of Peel.

Economic developments in this period are examined in several of the general works listed in the previous section. To them should be added S. G. Checkland, *The Rise of Industrial Society in England 1815–1885* (1964), Roy Church, *The Great Victorian Boom* (1975) and François Crouzet, *The Victorian Economy* (1982). On agriculture and the landed interest F. M. L. Thompson, *English Landed Society in the Nineteenth Century* (1963) and E. L. Jones, *The Development of English Agriculture 1815–1873* (1968) still have much of value. Articles by leading proponents in the standard of living debate are collected in A. J. Taylor, ed., *The Standard of Living in Britain in the Industrial Revolution* (1975), but for a survey which puts the subject in a longer perspective see John Rule, *The Labouring Classes in Early Industrial England 1750–1850* (1986). The links between finance, free trade and empire are examined in A. H. Imlah, *Economic Elements in the 'Pax Britannica'* (Cambridge, Mass., 1958), Bernard Semmel, *The Rise of Free Trade Imperialism 1750–1850* (Cambridge, 1970) and P. J. Cain, *Economic Foundations of British Overseas Expansion 1815–1914* (1980). Kenneth Bourne, *The Foreign Policy of Victorian England 1830–1902* (Oxford, 1970) brings together documents and commentary in model fashion, while his *Palmerston. The Early Years 1784–1841* (1982) is a detailed and painstaking first volume of what will become the standard biography. The role of the navy in the era of Pax Britannica is examined in G. S. Graham, *The Politics of Naval Supremacy* (Cambridge, 1965) and in C. J. Bartlett, *Great Britain and Sea Power 1815–1853* (Oxford, 1963). There is good material on emigration, and particularly on Wakefield's, projects, in Peter Burroughs, *Britain and Australia 1831–1855* (Oxford, 1967). For the sad background to much Scottish emigration see Eric Richards, *A History of the Highland Clearances* (1982). Different aspects of British rule in India are tackled in Eric Stokes, *The English Utilitarians and India* (Oxford, 1959) and Neil Charlesworth, *British Rule and the Indian Economy 1800–1914* (1982). A. G. L. Shaw, ed., *Great Britain and the Colonies 1815–1865* (1970) includes the important article by John Gallagher and Ronald Robinson, 'The Imperialism of Free Trade', as well as a riposte by Oliver MacDonagh, 'The Anti-Imperialism of Free Trade'.

1850–1900 (CHAPTERS 14 TO 18)

Recent text-books include Richard Shannon, *The Crisis of Imperialism* (1974). Donald Read, *England 1868–1914* (1979) is fuller and more approachable, Keith Robbins, *Britain, the Eclipse of a Great Power, 1870–1945* (1983) is shorter and sometimes idiosyncratic. T. R. Gourvish and A. O'Day (eds.), *Later Victorian Britain 1867–1900* (1988) is an exceptionally valuable collection of essays. Peter Stansky (ed.) *The Victorian Revolution: Government and Society in Victoria's Britain* (New York, 1973) usefully collects together journal articles on political themes. Karl Marx, *Surveys from Exile* (1973) has interesting, though not always well-informed, insights. Norman St John Stevas (ed.), *Walter Bagehot's Historical Essays* (1971) also contains much of value from a shrewd observer. Chris Cook and Brendan Keith, *British Historical Facts 1830–1900* (1974) is a convenient handbook of ministries, election results, and other statistics.

The political system cannot be explored without reference to H. J. Hanham, *Elections and Party Management: Politics in the time of Gladstone and Disraeli* (new edn., Hassocks, 1978), and the changes in underlying structures over time are examined in Martin Pugh, *The Making of Modern British Politics, 1867–1939* (Oxford, 1982). Derek Fraser, *Urban Politics in Victorian England* (Leicester, 1978) contains a wealth of material on local politics, and T. J. Nossiter, *Influence, Opinion and Political Idioms in Reformed England 1832–74: Studies from the North-East* (Hassocks, 1975) has both local and national value, as does John Vincent, *Poll-books: how Victorians voted* (Cambridge, 1967). The most straightforward account of the struggle for reform in 1867 is F. B. Smith, *The Making of the Second Reform Bill* (Cambridge, 1966), but this should be read in conjunction with the more challenging Maurice Cowling, *1867: Disraeli, Gladstone and Revolution* (Cambridge, 1967). Cornelius O'Leary, *The Elimination of Corrupt Practices from British Elections 1868–1911* (Oxford, 1962) and W. B. Gwyn, *Democracy and the Cost of Politics* (1962) remain standard works. Trevor Lloyd, *The General Election of 1880* (1968) is the best detailed survey of a late-Victorian election from a national perspective. Andrew Jones, *The Politics of Reform 1884* (Cambridge, 1978) concentrates on the party manoeuvrings over parliamentary reform. Henry Pelling, *The Social Geography of British Elections 1885–1910* (1967) is an inexhaustible mine of information on politics at constituency level.

The most influential work on Liberalism remains John Vincent, *The Formation of the British Liberal Party 1857–68* (1972), though Donald Southgate *The Passing of the Whigs 1832–86* still retains its value for this period. The nature of the Liberal Party is illuminated by D. A. Hamer, *The Politics of Electoral Pressure: a study in the history of Victorian Reform Agitations* (Hassocks, 1977) while Brian Harrison, *Drink and the Victorians:*

the Temperance Question in England 1815–72 (1971) examines in detail one such agitation. Alan Lee, *The Origins of the Popular Press 1855–1914* (1976) outlines one of the major forces behind Liberalism. Much of the politics of mid-century is best found in biographies: John Prest's, *Lord John Russell*, Muriel Chamberlain, *Lord Aberdeen* (1982) and Jasper Ridley, *Lord Palmerston* (1970) are all useful. The collaboration of their subjects can be seen in J. B. Conacher, *The Aberdeen Coalition 1852–55* (1968) and in Olive Anderson, *A Liberal State at War* (1967) which considers the impact of the Crimean War on Britain. The nearest equivalent to Vincent for the later period is D. A. Hamer, *Liberal Politics in the Age of Gladstone and Rosebery* (Oxford, 1972). Gladstone is being brought alive in his own words by the complete publication of his diaries, edited in numerous volumes by M. R. D. Foot and Colin Matthew; biographies of his early life drawing on these are Colin Matthew, *Gladstone 1809–74* (Oxford, 1986) and Richard Shannon, *Gladstone 1809–65* (1980). The later Gladstone is not yet so well covered, but Michael Barker, *Gladstone and Radicalism* (Hassocks, 1975) can be recommended. Also of value are John Vincent's *Gladstone and Ireland* (1977), and A. J. B. Hilton's essay on Gladstone in M. Bentley and J. Stevenson (eds.), *High and Low Politics in Modern Britain* (1983). A key moment in his career is dealt with in Richard Shannon, *Gladstone and the Bulgarian Atrocities Agitation* (1963). Gladstone's chief radical opponent was memorialised in J. L. Garvin and J. E. Amery, *The Life of Joseph Chamberlain*, 6 vols. (1933–69), and more summarily in Peter Fraser, *Joseph Chamberlain, Radicalism and Empire* (1966). An essential corrective to all previous accounts is Roland Quinault's reassessment of Chamberlain in Gourvish and Day, *Later Victorian Britain*. Liberal divisions in 1886 are entertainingly described in John Vincent and A. B. Cooke, *The Governing Passion* (Hassocks, 1974). The party at the end of the century can be considered through Peter Stansky, *Ambitions and Strategies: the struggle for the Liberal Leadership in the 1890s* (Oxford, 1964) and in David Brooks (ed.), *The Destruction of Lord Rosebery: from the diary of Sir Edward Hamilton* (1986).

Robert Blake, *The Conservative Party from Peel to Thatcher* (new edn., 1985) is a brief but lucid guide to the subject, as is the more variable Donald Southgate (ed.), *The Conservative Leadership 1832–1932* (1974). Bruce Coleman, *Conservatism and the Conservative Party in Nineteenth Century Britain* (1988) is unusual in stressing the successful resistance to change rather than the party's adaptability. Robert Stewart, *The Foundation of the Conservative Party*, continues up to the 1867 Reform Act and is the only detailed modern account of the party at its lowest point. Conservatism after 1867 has attracted more attention; Paul Smith, *Disraelian Conservatism and Social Reform* (1967) is the irreplaceable analysis of policy, while E. J. Feuchtwanger, *Disraeli, Democracy and the Tory Party* (1968) concentrates on organisation. Articles of value on the Disraelian period include Freda

Harcourt, 'Disraeli's Imperialism 1866–68; a question of timing', in *HJ*, XXIII (1980), 87–109; Peter Ghosh, 'Disraelian Conservatism, a financial approach' in *EHR* XCIX (1984) 268–293; Colin Matthew, 'Disraeli, Gladstone and the politics of mid-Victorian budgets', *HJ*, XXII (1979) 615–643. Martin Pugh, *The Tories and the People* (Oxford, 1985) gets to the roots of popular Toryism and demonstrates the astonishing appeal of the Primrose League; it can be usefully read alongside Patrick Joyce, *Work, Society and Politics: the Culture of the Factory in late Victorian England* (Hassocks, 1980). The lack of anything approaching democracy in the party emerges from Roland Quinault, 'Lord Randolph Churchill and Tory Democracy, 1880–85', *HJ*, XXII (1979) 141–165. Robert Blake, *Disraeli* (1966) is one of the foremost biographies of the century; others recommended are Roy Foster, *Lord Randolph Churchill* (Oxford, 1981) and Viscount Chilston, *W. H. Smith* (1965). Salisbury is not well covered in the literature though Robert Taylor, *Salisbury* (1975) is a useful short life, and Robert Blake and Hugh Cecil (eds.), *Salisbury the man and his policies* (1987) contains interesting essays. Peter Marsh, *The Discipline of Popular Government: Lord Salisbury's Domestic Statecraft* (Hassocks, 1978) is the only lengthy study of domestic policy in Salisbury's heyday, though the biography of his chief party organiser by Viscount Chilston, *Chief Whip, the political life and times of Aretas Akers-Douglas* (1961) is informative. The use of the monarchy as a focus for national unity and patriotism is brought out by David Cannadine's essay in E. J. Hobsbawm and T. O. Ranger (eds.), *The Invention of Tradition* (Cambridge 1983), and similar ideas are explored in R. Colls and P. Dodd (eds.), *Englishness, politics and culture, 1880–1920* (1986). A related and very influential work is Martin Wiener, *English Culture and the Decline of the Industrial Spirit* (Cambridge, 1981).

A good recent introduction to Labour history is Keith Laybourn (ed.), *The Labour Party 1881–1951: a reader in history* (Gloucester, 1988). Many aspects of the Labour movement are illuminated by E. J. Hobsbawm, *Labouring Man* (1964) and by Henry Pelling, *Popular Politics and Society in Late Victorian Britain*, (1968). R. Gray, *The Aristocracy of Labour in Nineteenth Century Britain c.1850–1914* (1981) shows divisions within the working class, and F. M. Leventhal, *Respectable Radical: George Howell and Victorian Working Class Politics* (1971) describes the role of a moderate trades union leader. Ross McKibbin, 'Why was there no marxism in Great Britain?', *EHR*, XCIX (1984) 297–331, provides a convincing answer to the question. The change in Labour politics from the 1880s is dealt with by Henry Pelling, *The Origins of the Labour Party* (2nd edn., Oxford, 1965), in E. J. Hobsbawm, *Labour's Turning Point 1880–1900* (2nd edn., Hassocks, 1974), and in H. A. Clegg, A. Fox and A. F. Thompson, *A History of British Trades Unions, 1889–1911* (Oxford, 1964). The Fabian Society is considered in A. M. McBriar, *Fabian Socialism and English Politics, 1884–1914* (Cambridge 1962), in an essay in Hobsbawm's *Labouring Men*, and from a literary perspective in Michael Holroyd, *Bernard Shaw*, Vol. 1, (1988). The key role of Keir Hardie in the ILP is brought out by Kenneth Morgan, *Keir Hardie* (1984). Labour's formative years after 1900 are covered in detail in Frank Bealey and Henry Pelling, *Labour and Politics 1900–1906* (1958), and in Roy Gregory, *The Miners and British Politics 1906–1914* (Oxford, 1968). Labour's growing strength is demonstrated by Ross McKibbin, *The Evolution of the Labour Party* (Oxford, 1974), and in the biography of another key figure, David Marquand, *Ramsay MacDonald* (1977). The view that Labour was not in fact advancing is to be found in Roy Douglas, 'Labour in Decline, 1910–14' in K. D. Brown (ed.), *Essays in Anti-Labour History* (1974). The view that Labour had only to await the extension of the franchise for an inevitable advance is demolished in Duncan Tanner, 'The parliamentary electoral system, the fourth reform act and the rise of Labour', *BIHR*, 56 (1983), 205–219. The development of an important policy area is analysed in K. D. Brown (ed.), *Labour and Unemployment, 1900–14* (1971) and the threat from the left is recounted, perhaps with some exaggeration, in Bob Holton, *British Syndicalism 1900–14* (1976).

British society is described by Geoffrey Best, *Mid-Victorian Britain 1851–75* (1971). An essential work of social history is H. J. Dyos (ed.), *The Victorian City*, 2 vols. (1973), now to be read in conjunction with P. J. Waller, *Town, City and Nation: England 1850–1914* (Oxford, 1983). F. M. L. Thompson's *English Landed Society* and J. V. Beckett's *The Aristocracy of England* are of particular value for this time, but it is characteristic of the period that Geoffrey Crossick, *The Lower Middle Class in Britain* (1977) must also be recommended, as is T. R. Gourvish's essay on the rise of the professional class in Gourvish and O'Day, *Later Victorian Britain*. Problems lower down are highlighted in J. P. D. Dunbabin, *Rural Discontent in Nineteenth Century Britain* (1974), and the development of policy in M. E. Rose, *The Relief of Poverty 1834–1914* (1972), and in E. J. Evans, *Social Policy 1832–1914* (1978). The social investigators of poverty are anthologised in Peter Keating (ed.), *Into Unknown England* (1976). On the British economy, Peter Mathias, *The First Industrial Nation* remains valuable for this period, and there is useful material in the second volume of Floud and McCluskey, *An Economic History of Britain*, notably Floud's own general survey of the economy and Pat Thane's essay on 'British social history 1860–1914'. R. S. B. Saul, *The Myth of the Great Depression 1873–96* (1969) deals effectively with a complex economic issue.

The standard source for British foreign policy is Kenneth Bourne, *The Foreign Policy of Victorian Britain 1830–1902* (Oxford 1970). C. J. Bartlett (ed.), *Britain Pre-Eminent: Studies in British World Influence in the Nineteenth Century* (1969) contains several useful essays, particularly those by D. F. Macdonald on emigration and Kenneth Fielden on the diplomacy associated with free trade. D. C. M. Platt, *Finance, Trade and Politics: British Foreign Policy 1815–1914* (Oxford, 1968) demonstrates the connections of economic motivations and diplomacy, while L. E. Davis and R. A. Huttenback, *Mammon and the Pursuit of Empire: the economics of British Imperialism* (abridged edn., Cambridge, 1988) applies econometric methods to imperial history. J. C. Wood, *British Economists and the Empire* (1983) shows how far contemporary economists were aware of the same connections. On the Empire itself, Trevor Lloyd, *The British Empire*, Bernard Porter, *The Lion's Share* (2nd edn., 1984) and R. Robinson, J. Gallagher and A. Denny, *Africa and the Victorians* (2nd edn., 1981) are particularly useful for this period. C. C. Eldridge, *Victorian Imperialism* (1978) is a concise guide to the congested debate, and C. C. Eldridge (ed.) *British Imperialism in the Nineteenth Century*, (1984) contains several useful contributions. An often neglected area is covered by R. A. Cage (ed.), *The Scots Abroad: Labour, Capital, Enterprise, 1750–1914* (1985), though in this case 'abroad' includes England.

1900–1939 (CHAPTERS 18 TO 21)

A. J. P. Taylor's *English History 1914–45* (1966) was always a highly personal account and is now rather dated, but remains a good read. Max Beloff, *Wars and Welfare 1914–45* (1984) and Trevor Lloyd, *Empire to Welfare State* (3rd edn., Oxford, 1986) are the most recommendable general books. The study of Welsh history has been much enhanced by K. O. Morgan, *Wales, Re-birth of a Nation 1880–1980* (Oxford, 1981), and Scotland can be studied in Christopher Harvie, *No Gods and Precious Few Heroes, Scotland 1914–80* (1981).

On the Labour Party, David Marquand's *Ramsay MacDonald* and Ross McKibbin's *Evolution of the Labour Party* continue to be essential reading. The impact of the Great War on Labour is considered by Peter Stansky, *The Left and War* (1969) by J. M. Winter, *Socialism and the Challenge of War* (1974), and from a particular angle in H. A. Clegg, *A History of British Trades Unions 1911–33* (Oxford, 1985). The ferment on the left after 1918 can be examined through R. Challinor, *The Origins of British Bolshevism* (1977), in Noreen Branson, *Popularism, 1919–25* (1979), in an official *History of the Communist Party of Great Britain* between 1920 and 1927, by J. R. Klugmann (2 vols., 1969), and in R. Martin, *Communism and the British Trades Unions* (Oxford, 1969). The fiftieth anniversary brought a spate of books about the 1926 General Strike, of which the best were Margaret Morris, *The General Strike* (Harmondsworth, 1976) and G. A. Phillips, *The General Strike* (1976). The first Labour government still awaits a full-scale modern study, so that R. W. Lyman, *The First Labour Government* (1957) remains on its own, though the political background is extensively covered by Chris Cook, *The Age of Alignment: Electoral Politics in Britain 1922–29* (1975). The second Labour government has fared better. Robert Skidelsky, *Politicians and the Slump* (1967), and David Carlton, *MacDonald versus Henderson, the Foreign Policy of the Second Labour Government* (1970) were both written with the benefit of official papers. More detailed aspects are investigated by Ross McKibbin, 'The economic policy of the second Labour government', *P&P*, 68 (1975) 95–123, and by J. D. Fair, 'The second Labour government and electoral reform', *Albion*, 13 (1981) 276–301. There are adequate biographies of two of MacDonald's closest colleagues, Colin Cross, *Philip Snowden* (1966) and Gregory Blaxland, *J. H. Thomas, a life for Unity* (1964).

Labour's opposition period in the 1930s has also fared well in the literature. Roger Eatwell and A. W. Wright, 'Labour and the lessons of 1931', *History*, 63 (1978) 38–53, is a good starting point. Ben Pimlott, *Labour and the Left in the Nineteen Thirties* (Cambridge, 1977) corrects the perspective of earlier writers, but the autobiographical account of Wal Hannington, *Unemployed Struggles* (new edn., 1977) demonstrates a different contemporary view. Good biographies abound, but for this period the best are: Kenneth Harris, *Attlee* (1982), Ben Pimlott, *Hugh Dalton* (1985) and Alan Bullock, *The Life and Times of Ernest Bevin*, Vol. 1 (1960). Labour's problems over international affairs, and Spain in particular, can be followed up in J. F. Naylor, *Labour's International Policy* (1969), K. W. Watkins, *Britain Divided* (1963), and John Lewis, *The Left Book Club, an historical record* (1970). The party's feebleness in a key propaganda area comes out in Stephen Jones, *The British Labour Movement and Film, 1918–39*, (1988).

The eclipse of the Liberal Party is a lively topic of debate, represented by the two perspectives of Roy Douglas, *The History of the Liberal Party 1900–75* (1978) and Trevor Wilson, *The Downfall of the Liberal Party 1914–35* (1966). Edwardian Liberal governments have generated a huge literature. A. J. A. Morris (ed.), *Edwardian Radicalism* (1974) is unusual in its breadth of approach, Stephen Koss, *Nonconformity in Modern British Politics* (1975) is important background and Peter Clarke, *Lancashire and the New Liberalism* (Cambridge 1971) is the most influential regional study. The 1906 election is covered by A. K. Russell, *Liberal Landslide* (Newton Abbot, 1973) and the elections of 1910 in Neal Blewett, *The Peers, the Parties and the People* (1972). Peter Rowland, *The Last Liberal Governments* 2 vols. (1968–71) is a reliable narrative. The greatest Liberal initiative of the period is outlined in Bruce Murray, *The People's Budget 1909–10* (Oxford, 1980) and a lesser one in Henry Pelling, 'The Politics of the Osborne Judgement', *HJ* XXV (1982) 889–909. Lloyd George's land campaign is enthusiastically described in Roy Douglas, *Land, People and Politics: a history of the land question in the UK 1878–1952* (1976), and relations with the suffragettes in D. Morgan, *Suffragists and Liberals* (Oxford, 1975), and Constance Rover, *Women's Suffrage and Party Politics* (1967). The vital question of what motivated Liberals towards social reforms is analysed by J. R. Hay, *The Origins of the Liberal Welfare Reforms 1906–14* (1975), and these changes are dealt with in detail in B. B. Gilbert, *The Evolution of National Insurance* (1966) and in W. J. Mommsen (ed.), *The Emergence of the Welfare State in Britain and Germany* (1981). The internal politics of the Liberal government can be grasped in Edward David (ed.), *Inside Asquith's Cabinet: the diary of Charles Hobhouse* (1977) and in Cameron Haselhurst, 'Asquith as Prime Minister', *EHR* LXXXV (1970) 502–531. The theory of inevitable Liberal failure before 1914 is seductively set out by George Dangerfield, *The Strange Death of Liberal England* (new edn., 1966). Biographical material is strong. Roy Jenkins, *Asquith* (1964) is stylish, Stephen Koss, *Asquith* (1976) more scholarly but less readable. John Wilson, *CB: the Life of Sir Henry Campbell-Bannerman* (1973) is unlikely to be surpassed. John Grigg's multi-volume life of Lloyd George has so far reached only 1916 but is already the standard work for the years covered: in the meantime, for the later period or for those wanting a shorter account, B. B. Gilbert, *David Lloyd George, a political life* (1987) is recommended. For sheer stimulation, A. J. P. Taylor's 'Lloyd George, rise and fall' in his *Essays in English History* (1976) and K. O. Morgan, *David Lloyd George, Welsh radical as world statesman* (Cardiff, 1964) should be added. R. S. Churchill and Martin Gilbert, *Winston S. Churchill* (7 vols, 1966–86) only really comes alive from 1914, but has the great advantage of additional companion volumes in which Churchill's incomparable letters are reprinted. The problems of Liberalism in wartime are outlined in Cameron Haselhurst, *Politicians at War* (1971), in John Turner's own essay on British politics during the war in John Turner (ed.), *Britain and the First World War* (1988) and in Peter Fraser, 'British War Policy and the Crisis of Liberalism', *JMH*, 54 (1982) 1–26. M. and E. Brock (eds.) *H. H. Asquith letters to Venetia Stanley* (Oxford, 1980) gives the Prime Minister's inside view of the early months of the war. Cameron Haselhurst, 'Lloyd George: the conspiracy theory' in Martin Gilbert (ed.) *Lloyd George* (New Jersey, 1968) disposes of the idea of a secret plot against Asquith; Edward David, 'The Liberal Party divided', *HJ*, XIII (1970) 509–532, shows how damaging to the party was a continued split after 1916.

Ireland in the final years before partition can be approached through Roy Foster's *Modern Ireland*, F. S. L. Lyons, *Ireland since the Famine* (1971), and Nicholas Mansergh, *The Irish Question, 1840–1921* (1965). Ulster's resistance to Home Rule emerges from Ian Budge and Cornelius O'Leary, *Belfast, approach to crisis* (1973) and in Patrick Buckland, *Irish Unionism*, 2 vols. (1973). The Liberal policy on Home Rule is dealt with by Leon O'Broin, *The Chief Secretary, Augustine Birrell in Ireland* (1969) and in Patricia Jalland, *The Liberals and Ireland: the Ulster Question in British Politics to 1914* (Hassocks, 1980). The final crisis in 1914 is described in detail in A. T. Q. Stewart, *The Ulster Crisis* (1967). The Easter Rising and British reactions can be traced in Thomas Coffey, *Agony at Easter, the 1916 Irish uprising* (1970). Lloyd George's postwar Irish policy and its critics are covered respectively by Charles Townshend, *The British Campaign in Ireland 1919–1921* (Oxford 1975) and D. G. Boyce, *Englishmen and Irish Troubles* (1972). The negotiations that led to partition were described by Lord Longford, *Peace by Ordeal* (new edn., 1972), and can be traced from the government's viewpoint in Keith Middlemas (ed.), *Thomas Jones: Whitehall Diary 1916–25*, Vol. 3, (1971).

The Great War has generated an outpouring of books since the 1964 anniversary. In addition to John Turner's *Britain and the First World War*, the best recent examples are J. M. Winter, *The Great War and the British People* (1985) and Trevor Wilson, *The Myriad Faces of War: Britain and the Great War* (Cambridge, 1986). A broader approach to the whole war experience is taken by J. M. Winter, *The Experience of World War I* (Oxford, 1988). There are excellent accounts of individual campaigns, one of the best being Martin Middlebrook's *The First Day on the Somme* (1971). The naval war is effectively dealt with by Richard Hough, *The Great War at Sea* (Oxford, 1983). The life of ordinary soldiers is evocatively portrayed by Denis Winter, *Death's Men* (1978) and the iron discipline that the army exerted is demonstrated in Anthony Babington, *For the Sake of Example, Capital Courts Martial, 1914–18* (1983). The enlistment of writers to the war effort is the subject of P. Buitenhuis, *The Great War of Words* (1989), and a lasting cultural effect of the war through its literary legacy is claimed in Paul Fussell, *The Great War and Modern Memory* (New York, 1975). One effect was a growth of pacifism during and after the war, described by Keith Robbins, *The Abolition of War: the 'Peace Movement' in Britain 1914–18* (Cardiff, 1976) and Martin Ceadel, *Pacifism in Britain 1914–45* (Oxford, 1980). The lasting impact of such attitudes to war even in the 1930s can be found in D. S. Birn, *The League of Nations Union 1918–45* (Oxford, 1981) Uri Bialer, *The Shadow of the Bomber, the fear of air attack in British politics, 1932–39* (1980), and Martin Ceadel, 'The first British referendum: the Peace Ballot 1934–35', *EHR*, XCV (1986) 810–839. The more immediate effect on British society was classically demonstrated by Arthur Marwick, *The Deluge: British Society and the Great War* (1965). The war's effect on the nature of British government is described by Kathleen Burk (ed.), *War and the State: the transformation of British government 1914–19* (1982) and by John Turner, *Lloyd George's Secretariat* (Cambridge, 1980). The changed franchise that emerged from the war in 1918 is explained by Martin Pugh, *Electoral Reform in War and Peace, 1906–1918* (1978). Postwar planning in wartime is rehearsed at length in P. B. Johnson, *A Land fit for Heroes* (1968), and the reasons for its not materialising are discussed in M. Abrams, 'The failure of social reform, 1918–20', *P&P* 24 (1963). The Lloyd George government's postwar record is best charted by Kenneth Morgan, *Consensus and Disunity; the Lloyd George coalition government, 1918–22* (Oxford, 1979). Keith Middlemas, *Politics in Industrial Society* (1979) and John Turner (ed.), *Businessmen in Politics* (1984) both have a good deal to say about the coalition period of 1916–22. The causes of Lloyd George's fall are complicatedly presented by Maurice Cowling, *The Impact of Labour 1920–24* (Cambridge 1971) and episodically by Michael Kinnear, *The Fall of Lloyd George: the political crisis of 1922*, (1973).

The Conservative Party has now generated considerable coverage after a period of relative neglect. John Ramsden, *The Age of Balfour and Baldwin: a History of the Conservative Party 1902–1940* (1978) is the fullest. Reference should also be made to Blake's *The Conservative Party* and Southgate's *The Conservative Leadership*. For the Edwardian period, R. F. Mackay, *Balfour* (1985) is a sympathetic study, Robert Blake, *The Unknown Prime Minister, the life and times of Andrew Bonar Law* (1955) still essential reading. The battles in the party over tariffs can be seen in Alan Sykes, *Tariff Reform in British Politics 1903–13* (Oxford, 1979), in R. Rempel, *Unionists Divided* (Newton Abbot, 1972) and, from the viewpoint of Darwinism, in G. R. Searle, *The Quest for National Efficiency 1899–1914* (Oxford, 1971). The attitudes of the right wing are analysed by Gregory Phillips, *The Diehards* (Cambridge, Mass., 1979) and demonstrated in documentary form by D. G. Boyce, *The Crisis of British Unionism: the domestic political papers of the second Earl of Selborne, 1885–1922* (1987). The papers of many Conservative politicians of this era are now easily available, some useful recent examples being John Vincent (ed.), *The Crawford Papers, 1892–1940* (Manchester, 1984), John Ramsden (ed.), *Real Old Tory Politics, the political diaries of Sir Robert Sanders, Lord Bayford, 1910–35* (1984), and Philip Williamson, *The Modernisation of Conservative Politics: the diaries and letters of William Bridgeman, 1904–35* (1988). The Conservative Party between the wars has produced much biographical material, a good example being David Dutton, *Austen Chamberlain, Gentleman in Politics* (Bolton, 1985). Keith Middlemas and John Barnes, *Baldwin, a biography* (1969) is the most exhaustive, though H. M. Hyde, *Baldwin, the unexpected Prime Minister* (1973) also has useful things to say. Stuart Ball, *Baldwin and the Conservative Party, the Crisis of 1929–31* (1988) has revised the accepted view of Baldwin's worst dispute with his party. The press opposition to Baldwin has been presented, in a somewhat favourable light, by A. J. P. Taylor, *Beaverbrook* (1972). Baldwin's relationship with his party is also illustrated by R. Rhodes James, *Memoirs of a Conservative: J. C. C. Davidson's Letters and Papers, 1910–37* (1969), and the party's effectiveness in public relations is outlined in T. J. Hollins, 'The Conservative Party and Film Propaganda between the Wars', *EHR*, XCVI (1981) 359–369, and in John Ramsden, 'Baldwin and Film Propaganda' in N. Pronay and D. W. Spring, *Film, Politics and Propaganda* (1982), Jeffrey Richards, *The Age of the Dream Palaces* (1984) shows how important such things were by this time. There is also much added to the understanding of Conservative politics between the wars by Martin Gilbert, *Winston S. Churchill*, Vol. 5, covering 1922–39, (1976) and by David Dilks, *Neville Chamberlain*, Vol. 1,

(Cambridge 1984). Since the latter takes its subject only up to 1929, the later part of Chamberlain's career must still be followed in Keith Feiling, *The Life of Neville Chamberlain* (1946). The way in which Conservatives benefited from the 1931 crisis is shown by J. D. Fair, 'The Conservative basis for the formation of the National Government of 1931', *JBS*, XIX (1980) 142–64. The fluctuating support for the National government is considered in several chapters of Chris Cook and John Ramsden (eds.), *By-Elections in British Politics* (1974), and the government's underlying strength in Tom Stannage, *Baldwin Thwarts the Opposition: the general election of 1935* (1980). Baldwin's triumph over the king is best described by Brian Inglis, *Abdication* (1966). The standard biographies of monarchs who survived to play longer and more significant political roles are Harold Nicolson, *King George V* (1953) and John Wheeler-Bennett, *George VI* (1958).

Arthur Marwick, *Britain in a Century of Total War* (1968) and John Stevenson, *British Society 1914–45* (1984) are good introductions to the social history of the period. Social policy is described by G. C. Peden, *British Economic and Social Policy from Lloyd George to Thatcher* (1985) and by B. B. Gilbert, *British Social Policy 1914–39* (1970). Economic ups and downs are charted in Floud and McCluskey, *Economic History of Britain*, Vol. 2, and in Sidney Pollard, *The Development of the British Economy, 1914–1980* (1981). The inter-war years are described in more detail in N. Branson, *Britain in the Nineteen Twenties* (1975) and N. Branson and M. Heinemann, *Britain in the 1930s* (1971). A similarly gloomy picture emerges from N. Gray (ed.), *The Worst of Times: an oral history of the Great Depression in Britain*, (New Jersey, 1985). More balanced viewpoints can be found in John Stevenson and Chris Cook, *The Slump* (1977), B. W. E. Alford, *Depression and Recovery? British economic growth 1918–39* (1973), and Stephen Constantine, *Unemployment in Britain between the Wars* (1980). The extremists of the right may be studied in K. Lunn and J. A. Thurlow, *British Fascism* (1980), R. A. Thurlow, *British Fascism, a History 1918–45* (Oxford, 1987), G. C. Lebzelter, *Political Anti-Semitism in England, 1918–39* (1978), and in Robert Skidelsky, *Oswald Mosley* (1975).

For students of Britain's international policy in this period, the fundamental works are C. J. Lowe, *The Mirage of Power*, 2 vols. (1972) and David Dilks (ed.), *Retreat from Power* 2 vols. (1981). For the period before 1914, F. H. Hinsley (ed.), *The Foreign Policy of Sir Edward Grey* (Cambridge, 1977) is massively authoritative, though it can be supplemented at the personal level by Keith Robbins, *Sir Edward Grey* (1971). The main theme of the period is impressively recounted by Paul Kennedy, *The Rise of the Anglo-German Antagonism* (1980), to which can be added A. J. A. Morris, *The Scaremongers: the advocacy of war and rearmament, 1898–1914* (1984) which concentrates on domestic influences, and Zara Steiner, *Britain and the origins of the First World War* (1977). The effect that the Great War had on Britain's international bargaining power is clear from Kathleen Burk, *Britain, America and the Sinews of War 1914–18* (1985). The British reaction to events in Russia can be gleaned from Stephen White, *Britain and the Bolshevik Revolution* (1979) and the gradual British disengagement from alliances at the end of the war is the theme of M. L. Dockrill and J. D. Goold, *Peace without Promise, Britain and the Peace Conferences 1918–1922* (1981). The effect of this on Britain's position outside Europe is considered in Max Beloff, *Britain's Liberal Empire, 1897–1921* (1969), though Lloyd's *The British Empire* and Porter's *The Lion's Share* are also useful for this period. The weakness of diplomacy and will that followed from 1918 are the subject of Martin Gilbert, *The Roots of Appeasement* (1966), and Correlli Barnett, *The Collapse of British Power* (new edn., Gloucester, 1984), both somewhat polemical in tone. The realities of strategic weakness emerge from Michael Howard, *The Continental Commitment* (1972), Brian Bond, *British Military Policy between the two World Wars* (Oxford, 1980), and H. M. Hyde, *British Air Policy between the Wars* (1976). The financial and economic obstacles placed in the way of rearmament in the 1930s are brought out by R. P. Shay, *British Rearmament in the 1930s, politics and profits* (Princeton, 1977), and G. C. Peden, *British Rearmament and the Treasury* (Edinburgh, 1979). The feebleness of policy in individual incidents is demonstrated by Christopher Thorne, *The Limits of Foreign Policy* (1972) and by Jill Edwards, *The British Government and the Spanish Civil War 1936–39* (1979). W. K. Wark, *The Ultimate Enemy: British Intelligence and Nazi Germany 1936–39* (1986) indicates how much the British government was able to find out, and Richard Cockett, *Twilight of Truth: Chamberlain, Appeasement and the manipulation of the press* (1989) shows how little they were prepared to tell.

SINCE 1939 (CHAPTERS 22 to 26)

General books on the history of contemporary Britain include Alan Sked and Chris Cook, *Post-War Britain* (1979), C. J. Bartlett, *A History of Post-War Britain* (1977), and Arthur Marwick, *British Society since 1945* (Harmondsworth, 1982). Alan Thompson, *The Day before Yesterday* (1971) recounts the period from 1945 to 1964 using extensive interviews with participants. Anthony Seldon (ed.) *Ruling Performance: British governments from Attlee to Thatcher* (1987) includes an essay on each government. Study of the period since 1945 is much enhanced by coverage in *Contemporary Record*. The standard source for election results and other statistical data is David and Gareth Butler, *British Political Facts 1900–1985* (6th edn., 1986).

The best account of Britain at war between 1939 and 1945 is Angus Calder, *The People's War* (1969), though the experience of the home front is also interestingly illustrated in Susan Briggs, *Keep Smiling Through* (1975). The worst of civilian warfare is recovered from contemporary interviews in Tom Harrisson, *Living Through the Blitz* (1976). The role of the RAF has been recently celebrated in John Terraine, *The Right of the Line: the RAF 1939–45* (1985), and the social life of conscripts recorded in Charles Whiting, *Poor Bloody Infantry* (1987). The politics of the war effort is summarised in J. M. Lee, *The Churchill Coalition, 1940–45* (1980), and considered at extreme length along with strategic considerations in Martin Gilbert, *Winston S. Churchill*, Vols. 6 and 7, (1983 & 1986). Pimlott's *Hugh Dalton*, Harris's *Attlee*, Taylor's *Beaverbrook*, and Bullock's *Ernest Bevin* (Vol. 2) are all useful for wartime politics. T. D. Burridge, *British Labour and Hitler's War* (1976) and Kevin Jeffreys (ed.), *Labour and the Wartime Coalition, from the Diaries of James Chuter Ede* (1987) explore the Labour party's contribution. Paul Addison, *The Road to 1945: British Politics and the Second World War* (1975) is a hugely influential book; its argument that reconstruction helped to swing opinion to the left is supported by Jose Harris, *William Beveridge, a biography* (Oxford, 1977). The belief that this era of reconstruction planning was a crucial factor in postwar economic decline is claimed in Correlli Barnett, *The Audit of War* (1986). The role of cinema both in maintaining morale and in radicalising opinion is dealt with in A. Aldgate and J. Richards, *Britain can take it* (1986). R. Hewison, *Under Siege, literary life in wartime London* considers the effect of the war on the arts, and Asa Briggs, *The War of Words* (1965) outlines the contribution of the BBC. Britain's difficult alliance with the USA is investigated in Christopher Thorne, *Allies of a Kind* (1979), in A. P. Dobson, *US Wartime Aid to Britain* (1986), and more provocatively in David Irving, *The War between the Generals* (1987).

The transition from wartime to postwar reconstruction is the theme of Paul Addison, *Now the War is over* (1985). The 1945 election is unexcitingly expounded in R. B. McCallum and A. Readman, *The British General Election of 1945* (1947), more critically in Henry Pelling, 'The 1945 election revisited', *HJ* XXIII (1980) 399–414, and with great verve in Anthony Howard, 'We are the masters now', in Michael Sissons and Philip French, *The Age of Austerity 1945–51* (1963). The best history of the Attlee government is Kenneth Morgan, *Labour in Power 1945–51* (1984), though Roger Eatwell, *The 1945–51 Labour Government* and T. E. B. Howarth, *Prospect and Reality: Great Britain 1945–55* (1985) are also useful. The government's economic policy is impressively analysed in Alec Cairncross, *Years of Recovery, British Economic Policy 1945–51* (1985), while the nationalisation programme is massively documented in D. N. Chester, *The Nationalisation of British Industry 1945–51* (1975). In addition to the biographies mentioned above, the 1945 government and the subsequent opposition require reference to G. W. Jones and Bernard Donoughue, *Herbert Morrison, portrait of a politician* (1973),

Philip Williams, *Hugh Gaitskell* (1979), Michael Foot, *Aneurin Bevan* Vol. 2 (1973), and Susan Crosland, *Anthony Crosland* (1983). Labour's splits in opposition after 1951 are dealt with from opposite sides by Stephen Haseler, *The Gaitskellites, Revisionism in the British Labour Party 1951–64* (1969) and Mark Jenkins, *Bevanism, Labour's high tide* (1979).

The Conservative recovery from the 1945 defeat is described in J. D. Hoffman, *The Conservative Party in Opposition 1945–51* (1964), but further material is in R. A. Butler, *The Art of the Possible* (1971) and other memoirs, and the role of the Research Department is discussed in John Ramsden, *The Making of Conservative Party Policy, the Conservative Research Department since 1929* (1980). The period of Conservative government after 1951 is considered in V. Bogdanor and R. Skidelsky (eds.) *The Age of Affluence 1951–64* (1968), with particularly useful essays by Siedentop on Macmillan, and by Pinto-Duschinsky on Conservative domestic policy. Churchill's last premiership is covered by Anthony Seldon, *Churchill's Indian Summer, the Conservative government 1951–55* (1981), and its most partisan act is unravelled in Kathleen Burk, *The First Privatisation, the politicians, the City and the denationalisation of steel* (1988). The government's inner workings are illustrated by John Colville, *The Fringes of Power, Downing Street Diaries 1939–55* (1985), and there is a wealth of material in the final volume of Martin Gilbert's *Churchill*. Robert Rhodes James, *Anthony Eden* (1986) and David Carlton, *Anthony Eden* (1986) are complementary biographies each of considerable weight; Anthony Howard, *Rab, the life of R. A. Butler* (1987) is less successful. Alastair Horne, *Macmillan* Vol. 1, (1988) gets its subject to the threshold of power, but for Macmillan as Prime Minister the best source is his own memoirs (6 vols. 1966–74). George Hutchinson, *The Last Edwardian at Number Ten* (1980) is a useful if slight portrait, and Harold Evans, *Downing Street Diary 1957–63* (1981) does for Macmillan what Colville does for Churchill. Macmillan's triumph is analysed in David Butler and Richard Rose, *The British General Election of 1959* (1960). The seeds of subsequent Conservative unpopularity may be found in the change of mood denoted by Christopher Booker, *The Neophiliacs* (1970) and Richard Ingrams, *The Life and Times of Private Eye* (1971). The worst of the Conservatives' later difficulties can be usefully examined only in contemporary sources until official papers are released, C. Irving, *Scandal '63* (1963) and Randolph Churchill, *The Fight for the Tory Leadership* (1964). Other recommended biographies are Kenneth Young, *Sir Alec Douglas-Home* (1970), Reginald Maudling, *Memoirs* (1978) and Nigel Fisher, *Iain Macleod* (1973). Andrew Roth, *Enoch Powell, Tory Tribune* (1970) contains much of interest, but the best source on Powell is his volumes of published speeches, beginning with John Wood (ed.), *A Nation not Afraid* (1965).

Harold Wilson's first government is best described by Clive

Ponting, *The 1964–70 Labour Government* (1989), Brian Lapping, *The Labour Government 1964–70* (Harmondsworth, 1970), and Robert Rhodes James, *Ambitions and Realities, British Politics 1964–70* (1972). Economic problems are weighed up in Wilfrid Beckerman, *The Labour Government's Economic Record 1964–70* (1972). The Prime Minister's media skills and his battles with the television companies are described in Michael Cockerill, *Live from Number Ten* (1988). For very different inside views see Harold Wilson, *The Labour Government, a personal record* (1971) Richard Crossman, *Diaries of a Cabinet Minister* (3 vols. 1975–77), and Tony Benn, *Out of the Wilderness, Diaries 1963–67* (1987). A hostile view from the left is given in Paul Foot, *The Politics of Harold Wilson* (Harmondsworth, 1968) and a sceptical view of the battle with the trades unions in Peter Jenkins, *The Battle of Downing Street* (1970). The deteriorating conditions in Ulster can be seen in Patrick Buckland, *A History of Northern Ireland* (1981), and the national movements of Wales and Scotland in Alan Butt Philip, *The Welsh Question* (Cardiff, 1975) and Keith Webb, *The Growth of Nationalism in Scotland* (new edn., 1978). The furore in the Labour Party after the 1970 defeat is covered by Michael Hatfield, *The House the Left Built* (1978) and John Campbell, *Roy Jenkins* (1983). Politics in the 1970s were extensively recorded from television interviews for Philip Whitehead, *The Writing on the Wall* (1985). The 1974–79 Labour government is critically described by David Coates, *Labour in Power 1974–79?* (1980), less so by its participants; Harold Wilson, *Final Term* (1979), James Callaghan, *Time and Chance* (1987), and Barbara Castle, *The Castle Diaries 1974–76* (1980). Some insiders do offer an uncomplimentary picture in Joel Barnett, *Inside the Treasury* (1982) and Bernard Donoughue, *Prime Minister* (1987). Relations with the Liberals are described in A. Michie and S. Hoggart, *The Pact, the inside story of the Liberal–Labour government 1977–78* (1978), and a 1987 issue of *Contemporary Record* recorded from participants' recollections of the 1979 'Winter of discontent'. Labour's opposition period after 1979 is less well covered, but a few books can be recommended: Patrick Seyd, *The Rise and Fall of the Labour Left* (1987), Austin Mitchell, *Four Years in the death of the Labour Party* (1984), and G. F. Drower, *Neil Kinnock, the path to the leadership* (1984). The origins of the SDP are recounted in Hugh Stephenson, *Claret and Chips* (1982).

Conservatism since 1970 has been extensively (but not often illuminatingly) written about. David Butler and Michael Pinto-Duschinsky, *The British General Election of 1970* (1971) explains Heath's unexpected victory. Margaret Laing, *Edward Heath, Prime Minister* (1972) describes only the successful early months in government, but Andrew Roth, *Heath and the Heathmen* (1972) suggests a social as well as a political change under his leadership. The government as a whole is described in Martin Holmes, *Political Pressure and Economic Policy, 1970–74* (1982) and from the inside by Douglas Hurd, *An End to Promises* (1979). The state of disarray on the Conservative benches is charted in Philip Norton, *Conservative Dissidents, 1970–74* (1978). The end of the Heath government is the subject of a *Contemporary Record* 'witness seminar' (1988), of the *Sunday Times* 'Insight' book, *The Fall of Heath* (1974), and of David Butler and Denis Kavanagh, *The British General Election of February 1974* (1974). Martin Holmes, *The First Thatcher Government* (1985) and Peter Riddell, *The Thatcher Government* (1985) are both serious investigations of Margaret Thatcher's first years in office. The *Sunday Times* 'Insight' book, *Strike* (1985) gives a detailed account of the defeat of the 1984–85 miners' strike, and several issues of *Contemporary Record* in 1987–88 dealt with the debate on what exactly was 'the Falklands factor' in British domestic politics in 1982–83. The best overall account is Denis Kavanagh, *Thatcherism and British Politics* (Oxford, 1987), though much is to be learned of Thatcher's own political skills and her use of talented advisers from Michael Cockerill's *Live from Number Ten*.

Britain's international policies since 1945 can be found in F. S. Northedge, *Descent from Power, British Foreign Policy 1945–73* (1974). Defence policy changes have been described by W. P. Snyder, *The Politics of British Defence Policy 1945–62* (Ohio, 1964), C. J. Bartlett, *The Long Retreat, British defence policy 1945–70* (1971), and Philip Darby, *British Defence Policy East of Suez 1947–68* (Oxford, 1973). The adoption of atomic power is analysed in Margaret Gowing, *Independence and Deterrence* (1974) and the shift of colonial policy in D. M. Goldsworthy, *Colonial Issues in British Politics* (Oxford 1971). The Suez fiasco can be traced in Hugh Thomas, *The Suez Affair* (1967) and in David Carlton, *Britain and the Suez Crisis* (1988). The reorientation of policy that followed Suez was demonstrated in Pierre Uri, *From Commonwealth to Common Market* (Harmondsworth, 1968). Britain's tortuous path towards the EEC is shown in Uwe Kitzinger, *The Challenge of the Common Market* (1962), his *The Second Try: Labour and the EEC* (1968) and his *Democracy and Persuasion, how Britain joined the EEC* (1973). How Britain chose to stay in is recounted in David Butler and Uwe Kitzinger, *The 1975 Referendum*. Finally, the Falklands War of 1982 is described from a military viewpoint in Martin Middlebrook, *Operation Corporate* (1985) and in David Brown, *The Royal Navy and the Falklands War* (1987). The overall background to the war is analysed in the *Sunday Times* book, *The Falklands War* (1982), and with a longer perspective by Laurence Freedman, *Britain and the Falklands War* (1988). The inglorious story of the British media at war is told in R. Harris, *Gotcha! The media, the government and the Falklands Crisis* (1983).

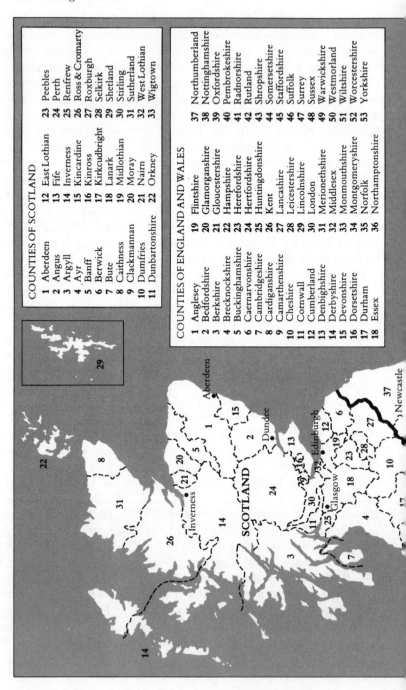

COUNTIES OF SCOTLAND

1	Aberdeen	12	East Lothian	23	Peebles
2	Angus	13	Fife	24	Perth
3	Argyll	14	Inverness	25	Renfrew
4	Ayr	15	Kincardine	26	Ross & Cromarty
5	Banff	16	Kinross	27	Roxburgh
6	Berwick	17	Kirkcudbright	28	Selkirk
7	Bute	18	Lanark	29	Shetland
8	Caithness	19	Midlothian	30	Stirling
9	Clackmannan	20	Moray	31	Sutherland
10	Dumfries	21	Nairn	32	West Lothian
11	Dunbartonshire	22	Orkney	33	Wigtown

COUNTIES OF ENGLAND AND WALES

1	Anglesey	19	Flintshire	37	Northumberland
2	Bedfordshire	20	Glamorganshire	38	Nottinghamshire
3	Berkshire	21	Gloucestershire	39	Oxfordshire
4	Brecknockshire	22	Hampshire	40	Pembrokeshire
5	Buckinghamshire	23	Herefordshire	41	Radnorshire
6	Caernarvonshire	24	Hertfordshire	42	Rutland
7	Cambridgeshire	25	Huntingdonshire	43	Shropshire
8	Cardiganshire	26	Kent	44	Somersetshire
9	Carmarthenshire	27	Lancashire	45	Staffordshire
10	Cheshire	28	Leicestershire	46	Suffolk
11	Cornwall	29	Lincolnshire	47	Surrey
12	Cumberland	30	London	48	Sussex
13	Denbighshire	31	Merionethshire	49	Warwickshire
14	Derbyshire	32	Middlesex	50	Westmorland
15	Devonshire	33	Monmouthshire	51	Wiltshire
16	Dorsetshire	34	Montgomeryshire	52	Worcestershire
17	Durham	35	Norfolk	53	Yorkshire
18	Essex	36	Northamptonshire		

Map 1: Great Britain: county boundaries before 1974

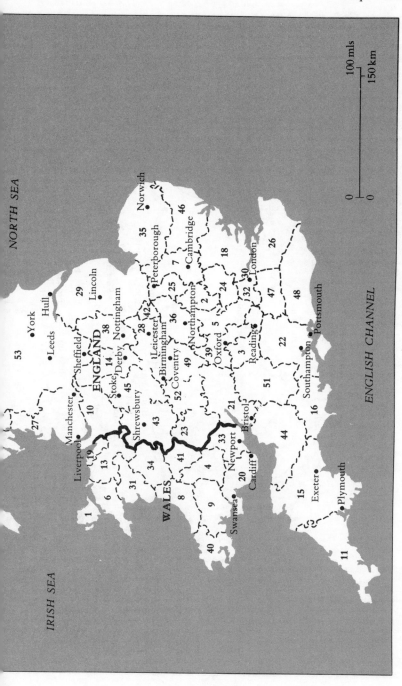

NORTH SEA

IRISH SEA

ENGLISH CHANNEL

Liverpool
Manchester
York
Leeds
Hull
Sheffield
ENGLAND
Lincoln
Stoke
Derby
Nottingham
Shrewsbury
Birmingham
Leicester
Coventry
Peterborough
Norwich
Cambridge
Northampton
Oxford
Reading
London
Southampton
Portsmouth
Bristol
Newport
Cardiff
Swansea
WALES
Exeter
Plymouth

53
27
29
14
38
28
42
36
25
7
35
46
10
45
52
49
39
2
24
18
30
32
47
48
26
19
13
43
23
21
3
5
51
22
16
44
31
34
41
33
20
15
6
8
4
9
40
11
1

100 mls

0

150 km

0

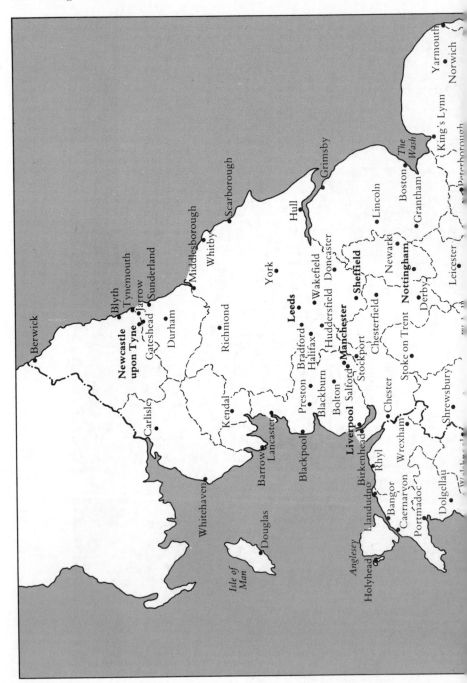

Map 2: England and Wales

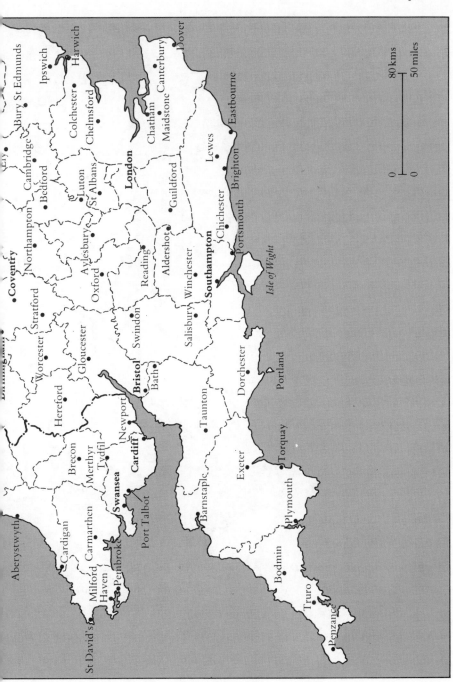

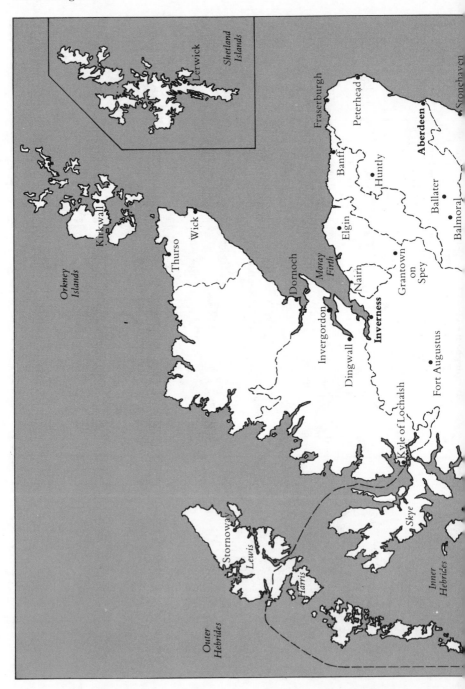

Map 3: Scotland

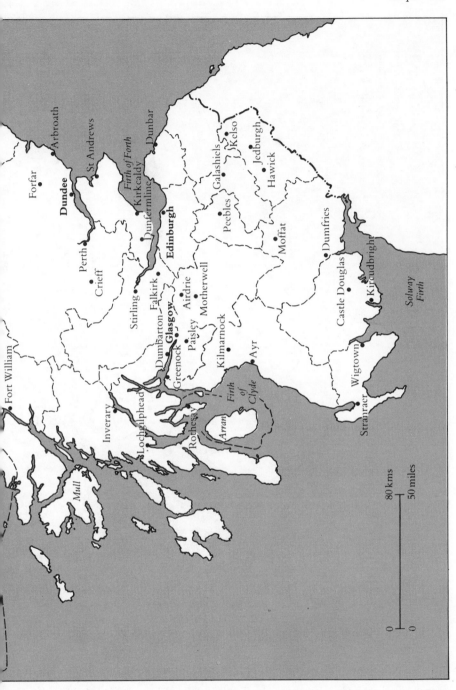

Forfar

Arbroath

Dundee

St Andrews

Perth

Crieff

Fort William

Firth of Forth

Kirkcaldy

Dunfermline

Dunbar

Edinburgh

Stirling

Falkirk

Airdrie

Glasgow

Motherwell

Paisley

Greenock

Dumbarton

Kilmarnock

Inverary

Lochgilphead

Rothesay

Arran

Firth of Clyde

Ayr

Mull

Galashiels

Kelso

Jedburgh

Hawick

Peebles

Moffat

Dumfries

Castle Douglas

Kirkcudbright

Solway Firth

Wigtown

Stranraer

80 kms

50 miles

0

0

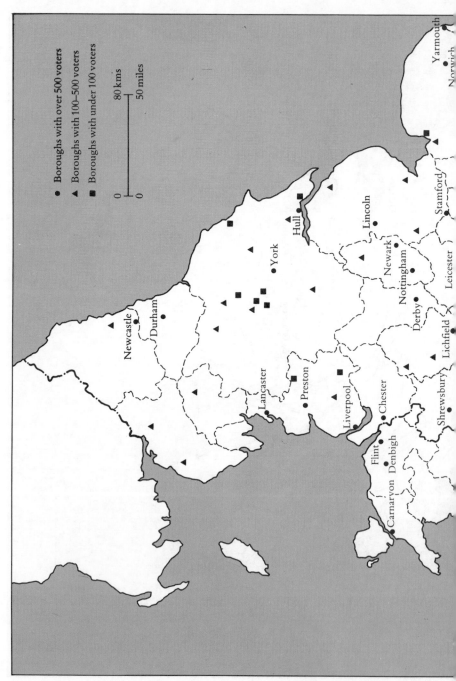

Map 4: Parliamentary boroughs in England and Wales before 1832 (from W. A. Speck, *Stability and Strife: England 1714–60*, Edward Arnold, 1977)

Map 5: Ireland

Index